# JOHN WESLEY

*Edited by*

ALBERT C. OUTLER

*New York*

OXFORD UNIVERSITY PRESS

OXFORD UNIVERSITY PRESS

Oxford   London   Glasgow

New York   Toronto   Melbourne   Wellington

Nairobi   Dar es Salaam   Cape Town

Kuala Lumpur   Singapore   Jakarta   Hong Kong   Tokyo

Delhi   Bombay   Calcutta   Madras   Karachi

FIRST PUBLISHED BY OXFORD UNIVERSITY PRESS, NEW YORK, 1964
FIRST ISSUED AS AN OXFORD UNIVERSITY PRESS PAPERBACK, 1980

LIBRARY OF CONGRESS CATALOGUE CARD NUMBER: 64-15525

ISBN 0 19 502810-4

printing, last digit: 20 19 18 17

PRINTED IN THE UNITED STATES OF AMERICA

# Preface

John Wesley's eminence is secure—as evangelist, reformer, practical genius. Few men in the eighteenth century have left a mark so clear and ineffaceable. Even his dispraisers, like Bishop Warburton, allow that "he was formed of the best stuff Nature ever put into a fanatic to make him the successful head and leader of a sect." There is, however, no such consensus in respect of his place in the history of Protestant thought. His earliest biographers (John Whitehead, Henry Moore, Luke Tyerman) combined to shape a common image which still persists: the sometime Oxford don turned pietist whose most significant achievement was the founding and forming of yet another denomination in Protestantism. The quite different estimate of Alexander Knox — that he was a major theologian who managed to fuse the best of St. Augustine and St. Chrysostom! — has passed almost unnoticed and with slight credit. His most widely read writings — the only ones available in current editions — are the records of the evangelist-reformer. His theological essays have, for the most part, gone unread by the generality of "the people called Methodists," who are more inclined to honor Wesley as their founder than as their mentor. Others have had small incentive to exceed the Methodists in their interest in Wesley as theologian.

For Wesley, however, evangelizing and theologizing were two functions of his single chief endeavor: the effectual communication of the gospel. He was never the typical pietist. He was, indeed, opposed to obscurantism in almost all its forms. His "appeal" was addressed "to men of reason and religion" as well as to the lowly and disowned. It is true — and this is the truth in the conventional Methodist stereotypes of him — that he was not a theologian's theologian. His chief intellectual interest, and achievement, was in what one could call a folk theology: the Christian message in its fullness and integrity, in "plain words for plain people." The substance of this message, as Wesley understood it, had been gathering in his mind before the Revival began. But it took its characteristic form and finish under the heat and pressures of the Revival and its needs.

iii

Theology, for Wesley, was always to be vindicated in its service to the Christian life.

He was not a contemplative man. The marks of incessant haste and urgency are everywhere in what he wrote and did. But this constant activity was everywhere informed and ordered by a clear and conscious understanding of the Christian truth, related always to the exigencies of his life and work. From the beginning of his long career to its end he was in one controversy after another — but his zeal in such battles came chiefly from his sense of responsibility for the theological health and vigor of his people. The sort of theology he approved was one in which practical consequences were appraised in the light of sound doctrine; doctrinal opinions were to be valued for their service to vital faith.

Viewed from one side of his profile, Wesley appears as a downright commonplace man. His tastes and his prejudices — even his superstitions — were thoroughly typical of his time, place and culture. This was at least one reason why the common people heard him gladly and responded to him as one of their own. The other side of the same profile, however, poses a very different picture — anything but commonplace. From this angle he appears as a major figure in a major religious movement — one who had glimpsed the underlying unity of Christian truth in both the Catholic and Protestant traditions and who had turned this recognition to the services of a great popular religious reform and renewal. In the name of a Christianity both Biblical and patristic, he managed to transcend the stark doctrinal disjunctions which had spilled so much ink and blood since Augsburg and Trent. In their stead, he proceeded to develop a theological fusion of faith and good works, Scripture and tradition, revelation and reason, God's sovereignty and human freedom, universal redemption and conditional election, Christian liberty and an ordered polity, the assurance of pardon and the risks of "falling from grace," original sin and Christian perfection. In each of these conjunctions, as he insisted almost tediously, the initiative is with God, the response with man.

One might apply a faintly fuzzy label to this distinctive doctrinal perspective: *evangelical catholicism*. Its most important immediate source in Wesley's thought was the Anglican theological literature in which he had steeped himself at Oxford and in Georgia. Its deeper wellspring was the Bible and its interpretation by the ancient Fathers of the Church. From his great mentors in piety (Jeremy Taylor, Thomas a Kempis, William Law, Henry Scougal) he learned that faith is either in dead earnest or just dead. From the great scholars of the seventeenth-century revival of patristic studies (William Beveridge, Robert Nelson) he learned the intimate correlation of Christian doctrine and Christian spirituality. From the "latitudinarians" (Edward Stillingfleet, Gilbert Burnet) he learned that the church's polity is more validly measured by its efficacy than its rigid, dogmatic "purity." To all these shaping forces he added the decisive influence of his own sustained immersion in the piety and wisdom of the early Christian fathers: Ignatius, Clement, Macarius, Ephraem Syrus, and others. His theological reading and reflection scarcely slowed over the span of six decades — but it was constantly controlled and guided by his practical concerns. He was always striving to clarify his message and to communicate it to the people of his day and age. The result is a distinctive theological perspective that merits serious consideration, even in another age and atmosphere.

This volume in A Library of Protestant Thought is designed to exhibit Wesley as theologian by providing a representative collection of his writings, together with what are intended as useful introductions and notes for a general reader's guidance. The principles of selection for such an anthology are difficult to defend against knowledgeable critics with biases of their own. The editor is prepared to sympathize with every protest against almost any significant omission. He hopes, however, that what is presented here will serve as a valid sampling of Wesley's *main* ideas in their scope and depth, without serious omission or imbalance.

It belongs to the Methodist stereotype of Wesley that he has never had a complete and scholarly edition of his writings. The only "collected edition" in his own lifetime (32 volumes printed by William Pine in Bristol in 1771–74) was naturally incomplete and also sadly marred by careless printing. The second edition, with Joseph Benson as editor (17 volumes printed in London, 1809–13), was more complete but no more critical. The Benson edition was then republished in Philadelphia and New York (10 volumes) in 1826–27, and advertised as the "First American Edition." A "third edition" was published by Thomas Jackson (14 volumes, London, 1829–31), and this has remained ever since as the basic edition of Wesley's "collected works." It has often been reprinted but never revised; its lack of a critical apparatus never repaired. A photo-offset reproduction of the 1872 reprint of the Jackson edition was recently published (1958–59), and advertised as "the first complete unabridged edition in nearly 100 years!" Modern editions of *The Journal* (Nehemiah Curnock, ed.), the so-called *Standard Sermons* (E. H. Sugden, ed.) and *Letters*

(John Telford, ed.) represent major advances over the "Jackson" edition. However, they comprise only a small fraction of Wesley's authorship and, even so, are far from adequate. But because they are generally accessible, our anthology has followed the principle of choosing other items from the Wesley corpus in cases of arguable choice.

Beyond the irreducible uncertainties of a satisfactory table of contents looms the baffling problem of a definitive text for the items selected. The casual reader will scarcely believe how difficult this has turned out to be. Wesley's printers were notoriously careless, and Wesley himself, much too busy for rigorous proofreading. Besides, the general styles of orthography, punctuation and emphasis were undergoing a major mutation during Wesley's lifetime, and this transition shows up in the successive editions of Wesley's pamphlets and books. To cap it all, Wesley felt naturally entitled to amend earlier texts to suit later circumstances — but not always improving the basic argument thereby. An editor who sets no store by eighteenth-century archaisms — supposing that Wesley did not, either — is still sore beset when, in accordance with the general format of A Library of Protestant Thought, he undertakes to referee these variations and to "modernize" the orthography and punctuation of the originals. It was Wesley's habit to punctuate his texts chiefly for the benefit of those who would read them aloud. Thus, he used commas and other stops far more freely than modern manuals recommend. In this volume the principle of minimal punctuation has been adopted, along with a device not used by Wesley's printers, the dash, to indicate those breaks in thought which would constitute "asides" in a spoken version. For the texts themselves, the general rule has been to start with the latest edition known to have been authorized by Wesley himself, and to collate this with earlier editions — and with Jackson. Significant variant readings have been noted, but the attempt to show all *varia lecta* was soon abandoned as hopelessly pedantic. Save for the letters, the only item in the volume for which a holograph control could be found is the treatise *On Baptism* (below, p. 317 ff.). Where they applied, Wesley's handwritten errata and marginal notations in his own set of the Pine edition (1771–74), now in the Library of Richmond Theological College, have been utilized. Generally speaking, the footnotes have been restricted to the business of identifications, cross-references and bibliographical suggestions. And, for a generation unaccustomed to Wesley's habitual interlarding of Scripture passages in all that he writes (quotations, composite texts, paraphrases, etc.), citations for these are supplied parenthetically within the text itself. Even here, however, precision is hard to come by, for Wesley was so fully steeped in the Biblical vocabulary and rhetoric that the line between an obvious echo of Scripture and a definite quotation is often blurred. Moreover, he thought nothing of citing various translations (including his own), and he regularly quoted the Psalms from the Psalter in the Book of Common Prayer.

Wesley was a prolific author, editor and publisher. But in his literary work, as in all else, it was the requirements of the Revival that dictated what he wrote and what he published. He regarded himself — and was so regarded — as the chief theological tutor of the Methodist people. In this role he undertook to supply them with an abundance of edifying literature which was cheap enough to buy, concise enough to read. This accounts for his predilection for pamphlets and short treatises. It also explains the fact that he felt quite free, in so good a cause, to produce something of his own or to borrow freely from others (with or without acknowledgment!) as the circumstances warranted. Only a small portion of the vast bulk of the material he published was his very own, but every piece of it bears his personal cachet. Although not a meticulous man, he had a remarkable gift for "extracting" the gist of another's writing without essential distortion. In this way he was able to increase the scope and force of his impact on the minds and hearts of his people. A very important sample of this artful "extracting" is included below (p. 123 ff.).

The contents of this volume have been chosen so as to indicate the various levels of Wesley's work as a theologian: leader of the Revival, theological teacher in the Church of England, disputant in major doctrinal controversies. Most of what he wrote was a conscious projection of his pastoral office — his printed words in place of his personal presence. Thus, in PART ONE below, we get brief glimpses of the theologian in formation and of the Revival as he understood its peculiar genius. PART TWO sets out the major motifs of the Wesleyan theology in a variety of literary forms: treatises, "minutes of conference," sermons, letters. PART THREE presents the polemical theologian in conflict with those particular parties and opinions which seemed to him to threaten the truth and efficacy of the gospel in the circumstances of the Revival.

In the notes more attention is paid to Wesley's "sources" and contemporaries than to his disciples. This follows from the conviction that he is more fruitfully understood in terms of his own background and context than in the light of the evolution of the Methodist movement after his death. That evolution constitutes a significant chapter in the history of Protestantism — but it cannot be said to have followed straitly the course Wesley plotted for it. In the contemporary theological situation, therefore, Wesley may be more readily appreciated as an "ecumenical theologian" than as the eponymous hero of a particular denomination. It is in some such perspective as this that he is presented here — fully and fairly enough (it is hoped) to demonstrate that he shares and contributes to the common concerns of A Library of Protestant Thought.

A volume like this is naturally the work of many hands. It has had the unusual advantage of expert supervision by a committee of editorial consultants, appointed by the Editorial Committee of A Library of Protestant Thought — in this case, Professors Frank Baker (Duke University), Raymond P. Morris (Yale University) and Claude Welch (University of Pennsylvania). Professor Baker, himself an eminent Wesley specialist, went the "second mile" and gave the manuscript two very painstaking reviews. It is a far better book for all the criticisms and suggestions of these men. None of its remaining blemishes, however, can be charged to their account. In addition, a goodly company of librarians, in America and England, were wonderfully generous with their skills and zeal in the endless bibliographical problems that turned up along the way. The whole list would be cumbrous, but I must record an especial indebtedness to Dr. Frank Cumbers (The Epworth Press, London), Professor Norman Goldhawk (Richmond Theological College), Mr. G. R. C. Davis (the British Museum) and, most of all, to Mrs. John Warnick (Curator of the Methodist Historical Collection, Southern Methodist University), who made the project her own.

At a more personal level, I have good reason to be deeply grateful for the generous interest in and support of this enterprise by three dear friends, Dr. Merrimon Cuninggim, Mrs. Thomas A. Beckett and Bishop William C. Martin. Finally, for her patience and help in what has been a rather tedious *ménage à trois* (with John Wesley and me), my wife is due much more by way of thanks than an acknowledgment in a preface.

ALBERT C. OUTLER

# Abbreviations

| | |
|---|---|
| *ACW* | *Ancient Christian Writers*, Johannes and Joseph C. Plumpe, eds. (Westminster, Md., 1946– ) |
| *ANF* | *Ante-Nicene Fathers* (Buffalo–New York, 1885–97) |
| A.V. | Authorized Version, or King James Bible (1611) |
| B.C.P. | Book of Common Prayer |
| *CSEL* | *Corpus Scriptorum Ecclesiasticorum Latinorum* (Vienna, 1866– ) |
| *FC* | *Fathers of the Church* (New York, 1947– ) |
| Green, *Bibliography* | Green, Richard, ed., *The Works of John and Charles Wesley. A Bibliography* (1896) |
| *Journal* | *Journal of the Rev. John Wesley, A.M.*, Nehemiah Curnock, ed. (1909–16) |
| *LCC* | Library of Christian Classics (Philadelphia, 1953– ) |
| *Letters* | *Letters of the Rev. John Wesley*, John Telford, ed. (1931) |
| Moore, *Life* | Moore, Henry, *Life of the Rev. J. Wesley* (1826) |
| *NPNF* [1] | *Nicene and Post-Nicene Fathers of the Christian Church*, 1st ser., Philip Schaff, ed. (New York, 1886–90) |
| *NPNF* [2] | *Nicene and Post-Nicene Fathers of the Christian Church*, 2d ser., Philip Schaff and Henry Wace, eds. (New York, 1890–1900) |
| *PG* | *Patrologiae Cursus Completus: Series Graeca*, J. P. Migne, ed. (Paris, 1857–66) |
| *PL* | *Patrologiae Cursus Completus: Series Latina*, J. P. Migne, ed. (Paris, 1878–90) |
| *RGG* | *Religion in Geschichte und Gegenwart*, 3d ed. (Tübingen, 1957) |
| R.S.V. | Revised Standard Version of the Holy Bible |
| *Sermons* (Sugden) | John Wesley, *Standard Sermons*, Edward H. Sugden, ed., 4th ed. (1955–56) |
| Tyerman, *Life* | Tyerman, Luke, *Life and Times of Rev. John Wesley, M.A.* (1870) |

Whitehead, *Life*        Whitehead, John, *Life of the Rev. John Wesley, M.A.*
                         (1793–96)

*Works*                  *Works of the Rev. John Wesley, A.M.*, Thomas Jack-
                         son, ed., 3d ed. (1829–31)

*Works* (Pine)           *Works of the Rev. John Wesley, M.A.* (printed by
                         William Pine, Bristol, 1771–74)


Place of publication has been specified only when it is not London.

# Table of Contents

✥

# JOHN WESLEY

✥

# Introduction

ONE measure of a man's concern is what he is willing to add to a schedule already busy and overborne. It is typical of John Wesley that, from September 1745 to March 1748 — a time when his affairs were in especial turmoil — he took the time to engage in an extended and serious theological debate with an eminent but anonymous churchman who signed himself "John Smith." [1] It turned out to be a searching review of Wesley's theological methods and motifs. It was notable for its high level of competence and courtesy. In theological terms, the principal issue came finally to focus upon Wesley's theory of religious knowledge — which "Smith" labels a doctrine of "perceptible inspiration." Besides holding a mirror to his mind, these letters are a notable study in psychological character, in their double reflection of Wesley's reactions to Smith's appraisals of him. From the outset it is clear that Smith is convinced that Wesley's doctrines and temperament are reciprocals:

> I dare say you mean no harm; yet suffer me to say frankly, I think
> you unwittingly do a great deal. . . . Cartwright and the old Puri-
> tans, I believe, meant no harm; yet what a scene of disorder did their
> lectures produce! Strict order once broken, confusion rushes in like
> a torrent at a trifling breach. You find yourself every day going far-
> ther and farther from the orderly paths; you are now come to ap-

1. In the form of twelve long letters, six from "Smith" to Wesley and six from Wesley in reply. A manuscript of the correspondence, a hundred and fourteen pages in Wesley's hand, is in the Library of Drew University; it is printed in Moore, *Life*, II, 277–322. Wesley's letters are reprinted in *Letters*, II, 42, 57, 68, 87, 97, 133. It is not possible with the available data to establish a positive identification of "John Smith." Moore (who hints that he had the story from Wesley) reports that "Smith" was an "archbishop" (*cf. Life*, II, 61). If so, there would be two possibilities: Thomas Secker (Bishop of Oxford, 1747–50, and Archbishop of Canterbury, 1758–68) and Thomas Herring (Archbishop of York, 1743–48, and of Canterbury, 1748–57). Herring's dates fit the puzzle better than Secker's, but not his theological interests. Secker's theological stature and outlook would match those of the man who wrote these letters, but other internal details leave the question open. What can be said for certain is that John Smith was comparatively well informed about Wesley and the Methodists, that he was a responsible churchman and a good theologian — and that Wesley took him seriously!

3

# INTRODUCTION

prove of lay preachers.[2] "Well, if they preach the Gospel of peace, where is the harm?" But what if, order once broke, unsent persons take upon them to preach all sorts of error, discord and confusion? . . .

It was past [the devil's] skill to make Tertullian a *profligate*, but he found the means to make him a *Montanist*. The son of a Wesley and an Annesley is in no danger of *lukewarmness*, but ought to take great care on the side of *impetuosity* and *zeal*. The tempter will never make you a *saunterer* or a *sluggard*, but if you are not upon your guard, may, possibly before you are aware, make you a *Quaker*. Nay, "perceptible inspiration" admitted, you ought to be such; for I will be bold to say that, allowing that one false principle, Mr. Barclay's[3] is a very consistent and coherent system.[4]

In reply, Wesley professes not to recognize himself in Smith's characterization:

I sincerely thank you for endeavoring to assist me herein, to guard me from running into excess. I am always in danger of this and yet I daily experience a far greater danger of the other extreme. To this day, I have abundantly more temptation to lukewarmness than to impetuosity; to be a saunterer *inter sylvas academicas*[5] — a philosophical sluggard — than an itinerant preacher.[6]

This forced Smith to restate his point in slightly altered form:

I had warned you against an impetuous zeal, but it seems that this is not your weak side; your chief danger is from lukewarmness. The overdone humility in the first paragraph of your last letter may serve to convince you of the contrary, if compared with paragraphs 93 and 94 of the *Earnest Appeal*.[7] The comparison, I am persuaded, will show you that whatever side of the question is for the present uppermost in your mind, *that* you are apt to push with such impetuosity and excess as unavoidably occasions the appearance of great variety (not to say inconsistency) of sentiment.[8]

In his concluding letter, Wesley thanks his critic for his admonitions but declines to slacken his zeal for fear of any prospective trouble:

2. This had actually begun as far back as 1740, with Thomas Maxfield; by the time of this letter, Wesley had already organized his preachers into an annual conference; see below, pp. 134–35.
3. Cf. Robert Barclay, *Apology for the True Christian Religion as the Same Is Set Forth and Preached by the People Called in Scorn "Quakers"* (1678).
4. Moore, *Life*, II, 297–98.
5. "Within the academic grove"; cf. Horace, *Epistles*, Bk. II, Epistle ii, l. 45.
6. Moore, *Life*, II, 298.    7. See below, pp. 421–22.    8. Moore, *Life*, II, 303.

I am not careful for what may be a hundred years hence. He who governed the world before I was born shall take care of it likewise when I am dead. My part is to improve the present moment. And whatever may be the fruits of lay-preaching when you and I are gone to our long home, every serious man has cause to bless God for those he may now see with his eyes, for the saving so many souls from death, and hiding a multitude of sins.[9]

Taken all together, these letters make plain that the salient traits of John Wesley's psychological character were well known. Even a stranger like John Smith recognized the fact that Wesley's strong-mindedness was something of a family trait; that caution and faintheartedness had been bred out of him; that he was constitutionally incapable of doing anything by half. Both Smith and Wesley agree in their testimony as to the latter's psychological pattern: hard-driving, yet also sensitive; intense, yet also patient; detached, yet also charming; self-disciplined, yet also intensely emotional; opinionated, yet also curious; open to counsel, yet impervious to pressure; brusque with bad faith, yet also tolerant of contrary opinions. This "character," once identified, is discernible in every aspect and context of his entire career.

That career had begun in the rough fen country of Lincolnshire, June 17 (O.S.), 1703, at Epworth, where his father, the Reverend Samuel Wesley, was the learned and rather eccentric rector. Samuel was a devout and faithful High-churchman, so ardent in his advocacy of Church and Crown that he was once jailed in Lincoln Castle, ostensibly for debt but actually because of the offense which he had given by his violent attacks upon the Dissenters.[10] In prison (June 27, 1705) the sturdy royalist bears witness to his crusading spirit in a letter to a friend in London:

9. *Ibid.*, 309.

10. Cf. *A Letter from a Country Divine to His Friend in London, Concerning the Education of the Dissenters in Their Private Academies in Several Parts of This Nation; Humbly Offered to the Consideration of the Grand Committee of Parliament for Religion, Now Sitting* (1703). A prominent Dissenter, Samuel Palmer, fired back an angry *Defence of the Dissenters' Education* ... (1703). To this Wesley replied with *A Defence of a Letter Concerning the Education of Dissenters* ... *Being an Answer to the Defence of the Dissenters' Education* (1704). Palmer's return volley was an outraged *Vindication of the Learning, Loyalty, Morals, and Most Christian Behavior of the Dissenters Toward the Church of England. In Answer to Mr. Wesley's Defence of His Letter Concerning the Dissenters' Education in their Private Academies. And to Mr. Sacheverel's Injurious Reflections Upon Them* (1705). It was this last that the Reverend Mr. Wesley was "answering" while in prison: *A Reply to Mr. Palmer's Vindication* ... (1707).

Thanks be to God, for my confinement is very easy and comfortable to me, since I need not have suffered it if I would have deserted the cause of the University and the Church of England. I am now answering the Dissenters' last book against me, having but too much leisure; and will never drop the controversy unless I lay my bones here. God preserve the Church, whatever becomes of your most humble servant. . . .[11]

John's mother, born Susanna Annesley, was the daughter of a prominent Nonconformist minister in London.[12] She was both matriarch and saint, who presided with equal grace and firmness over the affairs of a large, impoverished family — mother, teacher, lodestar. She was capable of defying her husband in matters ecclesiastical and of debating with her sons on questions theological. In 1709 young "Jackie" was dramatically rescued from the burning Epworth rectory. This deliverance was taken thereafter, both by mother and son, as a sign of special providence for him.[13]

In 1714 he went up to the Charterhouse in London on a scholarship provided by the Duke of Buckingham. Six years later he was matriculated as a Charterhouse Scholar in Christ Church, Oxford, in the twilight of one of its most glorious epochs under a famous trio of deans: John Fell, Henry Aldrich and Francis Atterbury. Despite the fact that Oxford was in the doldrums during Wesley's time there, it was still a splendid repository of books and learning where he could and did lay claim to a great cultural heritage.[14] With good tutors and a compulsive disposition, the young Mr. Wesley actually acquired an excellent education which continued to serve him well for his whole life long.

Up to the year 1725 his religious interests were typically immature. Then came a sudden focusing of faith and personal commitment. One of his several reports of this Oxford "conversion" is given in *A Plain Account of Christian Perfection:*

11. From an unpublished manuscript in the Methodist Archives, Epworth House, London. For Samuel Wesley's alliance with Henry Sacheverell, *cf.* John Wesley, *A Concise History of England* (1776), IV, 72–76.

12. Dr. Samuel Annesley (1620?–1696). *Cf.* his sermons in *The Morning Exercise at Cripple Gate; or, Several Cases of Conscience Practically Resolved by Sundry Ministers* (1664), and his biographical notice in Edmund Calamy, *The Nonconformists' Memorial* . . . , 2 ed. (1802–03), I, 124–28.

13. *Cf.* the somewhat premature epitaph which Wesley composed for himself in 1753: "Here lieth the body of John Wesley, a brand plucked out of the burning: who died of a consumption in the fifty-first year of his age . . ." (*Journal*, IV, 90).

14. *Cf.* A. D. Godley, *Oxford in the Eighteenth Century* (1908).

In the year 1725, being in the twenty-third year of my age, I met with Bishop Taylor's *Rules and Exercises of Holy Living and Dying*. In reading several parts of this book I was exceedingly affected, by that part in particular which related to "purity of intention." Instantly I resolved to dedicate *all my life* to God, *all* my thoughts and words and actions, being thoroughly convinced there was no medium, but that *every* part of my life (not *some* only) must either be a sacrifice to God, or to myself; that is, in effect, to the devil. . . .

In the year 1726 I met with Kempis's *Christian's Pattern*. The nature and extent of *inward religion*, the religion of the heart, now appeared to me in a stronger light than ever it had done before. I saw that giving even *all my life* to God (supposing it possible to do this and go no further) would profit me nothing unless I gave my *heart*, yea, *all my heart* to him.

I saw that "simplicity of intention and purity of affection," *one design* in *all* we speak or do and *one desire* ruling all our tempers, are, indeed, "the wings of the soul," without which she can never ascend to the mount of God.

A year or two after, Mr. Law's *Christian Perfection* and *Serious Call* were put into my hands. These convinced me more than ever of the absolute impossibility of being *half a Christian*, and I determined, through his grace (the absolute necessity of which I was deeply sensible of) to be *all-devoted* to God: to give him *all* my soul, my body and my substance.[15]

Into this radical change — a conversion if ever there was one — there had come many converging lines of significant influence: the rich nurture of a remarkable home and family, an emerging personal maturity in a university setting, the guidance of a "religious friend," [16] and the radical demand for utter seriousness in religion as this had been presented to him by Taylor, a Kempis, and Law. For all their diversity, these three had actually taught him the same thing: that the Christian life is *devotio*, the consecration of the whole man in love to God and neighbor in the full round of life and death.

After his conversion and his consequent decision to prepare for ordination, Wesley's education altered form but did not slacken its pace. Classics now gave over first place to Bible and theology. It was Wesley's way to read more widely than exactly, but it is worth noting how much

15. *Works*, XI, 366–67. For another version of the same experience, see below, pp. 61–62.

16. *Cf. Journal*, I, 467. Miss Sarah Kirkham, sister of Robert Kirkham, later a fellow member of the Holy Club. *Cf.* G. Elsie Harrison, *Son to Susanna* (Nashville, Tenn., 1938), 72–73.

of what he read he could thereafter recall and put to various uses, as preacher and author.[17]

In 1726 he was elected fellow of Lincoln College. This established his academic status in the university and assured him of financial security so long as he remained celibate.[18] This exemption from economic stringency was a very important factor in his being free to develop as he did, especially in the early days of the Revival. At Lincoln, he was moderator of the classes (the formal disputations arranged for the training of the students in logic), Greek lecturer, and claviger.[19]

He was ordained deacon by Bishop Potter of Oxford on Sunday, September 19, 1725, and priested by the same bishop three years later (September 22, 1728). He served as his father's assistant at Epworth and Wroot on two separate occasions, in 1726 and 1729.[20] On his return to Oxford he found that a small semimonastic group had been gathered by his brother Charles for systematic Bible study, mutual discipline in devotion and frequent Communion.[21] This group had developed a keen interest in the ancient liturgies [22] and the monastic piety of the fourth-century "desert fathers." It must have seemed natural to everyone involved when John assumed leadership of the group. Its strenuous piety was soon notorious among the lax undergraduates, and tempted them to coin what must have seemed clever and devastating nicknames: The Holy Club, The Reforming Club, Bible Moths, Methodists, Supererogation Men, Enthusiasts. *Methodist* was the label that stuck fastest. Wesley disliked it,[23] but with characteristic aplomb, he accepted it as a badge of honor and proceeded to define "the character of a Methodist" [24] as one who really believes and lives "the common principles of Christianity." On this

17. For an extensive list of books read by John Wesley in the period 1725–34, see Appendix I in V. H. H. Green, *The Young Mr. Wesley* (1961), 305–19.

18. In February 1751 Wesley married, and on June 1 he submitted his resignation to the rector and fellows of Lincoln; *cf.* the text in *Journal*, III, 513–16 and note; 527 and note. For a perceptive account of the unhappy marriage, see also Harrison, *Son to Susanna*, chap. XXXII.

19. *Cf.* Green, *Young Wesley*, chap. VI.

20. The entry in the Epworth parish register for 1726 seems to be that for the office of parish clerk; that for 1729 is "Johannes Wesley, Cure de Epwth."

21. *Cf. Works*, XIII, 303 ff. See also *Journal*, I, 89 f., 467 f., and J. Simon, *John Wesley and the Religious Societies* (1921), 87 ff.

22. One of their guides was Robert Nelson, the learned Nonjuror whose *Companion for the Festivals and Fasts of the Church of England* (1704) and *Great Duty of Frequenting the Christian Sacrifice* (1734) were mines of patristic learning.

23. And gave various accounts of its original referent; *cf. Works*, VIII, 334–48, 506.

24. *Cf. Works*, VIII, 346–47.

premise, he was able to invite his detractors to join "the Methodists"!

With the help of one of his fellow "Methodists," John Clayton, who was a competent patristics scholar, Wesley began the study of ancient Christian literature, newly available in editions produced in the patristics renaissance of the last half of the seventeenth century. In the thought and piety of the early Church he discovered what he thereafter regarded as the normative pattern of catholic Christianity.[25] He was particularly interested in "Macarius the Egyptian" [26] and Ephraem Syrus. What fasci-

25. Cf. his Address to the Clergy (1756), Works, X, 484: ". . . Can any who spend several years in those seats of learning [the universities] be excused if they do not add to that of the languages and sciences, the knowledge of the fathers — the most authentic commentators on Scripture, as being both nearest the fountain and eminently endued with that Spirit by whom "all Scripture was given." [cf. 2 Tim. 3:16] . . . I speak chiefly of those who wrote before the Council of Nicea. But who would not likewise desire to have some acquaintance with those that followed them — with St. Chrysostom, Basil, Jerome, Austin, and, above all, the man of a broken heart, Ephraim Syrus?"

26. Cf. Moore, Life, I, 292. See also Wesley's estimate of Macarius's piety in A Christian Library (Bristol, 1749-55), I, 72 (in the preface to his Extract from the Homilies of Macarius): ". . . such a victorious faith as overcomes the world and, working by love, is ever fulfilling the whole law of God." See also Letters, II, 387, and below p. 275 f. In Wesley's day it was generally agreed that the corpus Macarianum was the work of "Macarius the Egyptian," despite the fact that Gennadius, Rufinus and Palladius had all agreed in crediting the Egyptian Macarius with only a single writing (the so-called Epistula Magna, "To the Monks"). Recent scholarship has revolutionized the state of knowledge in this area and has opened up a hitherto unnoticed but highly significant linkage between the writings of "Macarius" and those of Gregory of Nyssa! In Two Rediscovered Works of Ancient Christian Literature: Gregory of Nyssa and Macarius (Leiden, 1954), Werner Jaeger has reviewed the recent studies of the historical and literary problems involved and has exhibited the evidence which demonstrates that the author of the so-called Macarian Homilies (PG, XXXIV, 446-822) was not a fourth-century Egyptian "desert father," but rather a fifth-century Syrian monk, whose conception of Christian spirituality was derived almost exclusively from Gregory. The first part of the Macarian Epistula Magna is in fact an abridgment of Homily XL (cf. PG, XXXIV, 762-67, and Jaeger, Two Rediscovered Works, 208-30); the second part is an expanded metaphrase of Gregory's De Instituto Christiano (cf. ibid., 174 ff.). The rest of the Macarian Homilies are similarly indebted to Gregory, as is also the striking little treatise Περὶ Τελειότητος ἐν Πνεύματι (PG, XXXIV, 842-52). Herman Dörries's assumed identification of Macarius as a Messalian (see RGG, IV, 619) is gratuitous. What matters most in connection with Wesley is that in the writings of what he thought was "Macarius the Egyptian," he was actually in touch with Gregory of Nyssa, the greatest of all the Eastern Christian teachers of the quest for perfection. Thus, in his early days, he drank deep of this Byzantine tradition of spirituality at its source and assimilated its conception of devotion as the way and perfection as the goal of the Christian life. Once this somewhat curious and roundabout linkage with the theological fountainhead of Orthodox monasticism is recognized, it is illuminating to read Wesley and

nated him in these men was their description of "perfection" (τελείωσις) as the goal (σκόπος) of the Christian in this life. Their concept of perfection as a process rather than a state gave Wesley a spiritual vision quite different from the static perfectionism envisaged in Roman spiritual theology of the period and the equally static quietism of those Protestants and Catholics whom he deplored as "the mystic writers." [27] The "Christian Gnostic" of Clement of Alexandria became Wesley's model of the ideal Christian.[28] Thus it was that the ancient and Eastern tradition of holiness as *disciplined* love became fused in Wesley's mind with his own Anglican tradition of holiness as *aspiring* love, and thereafter was developed in what he regarded to the end as his own most distinctive doctrinal contribution.[29]

Nevertheless, at this stage of his spiritual development Wesley found that the quest for perfection at Oxford was a dedicated chore. He did not weary in well-doing, but neither was life joyous or serene. He once considered the possibility of removing the Holy Club from Oxford to a more desolate environment where its members might be less distracted and overborne.[30] In 1734 his family began to importune him to seek the Epworth living as successor to his aging, ailing father. This, plainly, would have been a very convenient arrangement for all concerned — save for John himself. It seemed to him all too likely that the life of a parish priest would inhibit his ascetic discipline and would deprive him of the communal support of the Holy Club, on which he was still heavily dependent. After a grim soul-searching, he rejected his father's proposal, arguing that his prime duty was to maintain himself in a corporate religious rule.[31]

His father died April 25, 1735. Three months later Dr. John Burton, Trustee of the Georgia Colony and patron of the Society for the Propa-

---

Gregory in dialogue with each other. This possibility has now been greatly enhanced by the publication of the first critical edition of Gregory's work (*cf.* Werner Jaeger, *Gregorii Nysseni Opera Ascetica* in *Gregorii Nysseni Opera*, VIII [Leiden, 1952]). The ~~echoes~~ and resonances are striking in both directions. For a helpful summary of Gregory's theology of perfection in aid of a comparison of Wesley and Gregory, see Jaeger, *Two Rediscovered Works*, 26-29, 70-114.

27. See below, p. 46 f.        28. *Letters*, V, 43.

29. In September 1790 he wrote (to Robert Carr Brackenbury): "This doctrine is the grand depositum which God has lodged with the people called Methodists, and for the sake of propagating this chiefly he appears to have raised us up" (*Letters*, VIII, 238).

30. *Cf.* Whitehead, *Life*, I, 410-11; *Letters*, VI, 128.

31. *Letters*, I, 166-78. *Cf. Journal*, I, 109; but see also *ibid.*, VII, 457-58.

gation of the Gospel (S.P.G.), invited John Wesley to transfer the Holy Club to Georgia, as missioners to the Indians and the colonists.[32] Here was a call "to the desert," indeed! [33] In September the invitation was accepted and formally approved by "the Georgia Society." [34] The following January Wesley was formally appointed as an S.P.G. missioner.[35] It proved impossible, however, to muster the entire Holy Club for the Georgia venture. Actually, only three members were aboard the *Simmonds* when she sailed from Gravesend, October 21, 1735: John, his brother Charles, and Benjamin Ingham.[36] A new recruit, Charles Delamotte, made a fourth. George Whitefield, still at Oxford and not yet ordained, promised to join them later.

The Methodist mission to Georgia was a fiasco. Charles proved a maladroit secretary to General Oglethorpe; John, a tactless pastor, Ingham and Delamotte, ineffectual assistants. Their general frustration was further complicated by John Wesley's falling in love with Sophie Hopkey, the eighteen-year-old niece of the bailiff of Savannah. It was a preposterous and pitiful affair in which Wesley was torn between his long-standing inhibitions and his new-found affections. It was resolved by Sophie herself, who finally eloped with a rival suitor. Her jilted lover then barred her from Holy Communion, and was in turn sued for defamation of character by her new husband.[37] The result was a furious turmoil, cli-

32. *Cf. Journal*, I, 30; *Letters*, I, 187. See also Sir John Perceval, *The Diary of the First Earl of Egmont* (1920–23), II, 194, 196, 200, 203, *et seq.*

33. *Cf.* Moore, *Life*, I, 144.          34. *Cf.* Perceval, *Diary*, 195–96.

35. *Cf. Two Hundred Years of the S.P.G. . . . Based on a Digest of the Society's Records*, C. F. Pascoe, ed. (1901), 26, 27.

36. *Cf.* the following entries in E. Merton Coulter and Albert B. Saye, eds., *A List of the Early Settlers of Georgia* (Athens, Ga., 1949), 56–57, 13, 25:

1608. WESLEY, Cha., A.B. — Embark'd 14 Oct. 1735; arrived Feb. 1735–6. Mr. Cha. Wesley took the oath of Secy. for the Indian trade 19 Feb. 1735–6 but quitted the Colony & ret. to England, July 1736. Quitted July 1736.

1609. ———, Jn, A.M. — Brother of Cha.; Minister at Savannah; embark'd 14 Oct. 1735; arrived Feb. 1735–6; run away 3 Dec. 1737.

336. DELAMOT, Cha. — Schoolmaster; embark'd 14 Oct. 1735; arrived Feb. 1735–6; ret. to Engl. 2 June 1738.

724. INGHAM, Ben. — A.M., Missioner to the Indians; embark'd 14 Oct. 1735; arrived Feb. 1735–6. He return'd to England to bring over more missioners, but never went back. A Methodist. Quitted 26 Feb. 1736/7.

See also *Journal*, I, 112 and 160 ff.

37. There is a holograph manuscript in the Methodist Archives, Epworth House, London, in which Wesley rehearses the whole story of his relations with Sophie

maxed by a formal grand jury indictment of Wesley on twelve separate counts. The trial was dragged out, and after six months of harassment, Wesley fled the tragic farce in disgust and high dudgeon.[38]

Despite this sad reversal of his hopes and expectations, the Georgia mission had its positive value in Wesley's personal and theological development. It saw all but the final form of his doctrinal ideas hammered into their basic shape. From "Dr. Bray's Associates" [39] Wesley had a generous subsidy for books, which he spent to gather a remarkable theological library for himself and his company. It numbered slightly more than sixty titles, the bulk of them by Anglican authors of the seventeenth and eighteenth century, a few by Nonconformists, and still fewer by Continental Protestants.[40] The most impressive single item in the library was the massive two-volume folio of William Beveridge's *Pandectae*,[41] a vast array of ancient Eastern liturgical texts. It makes a picture — John Wesley and his Georgia Methodists, poring over Beveridge by lamplight at Savannah and Frederica! An interesting by-product of this study of early Christian worship was that Wesley was prompted to try his hand at liturgical experimentation.[42] These innovations, as they were bound to be regarded by his parishioners, made for bewilderment and protest. The magistrate of Frederica (Mr. Horton) complained to him: "The people

---

Hopkey. A postscript reads: "Transcribed, March 12, 1738." There is, however, internal evidence that it was first written in Georgia and not long after Sophie's elopement and marriage. It is an uncommonly candid account of the commonplaces of the romance; one might guess that it was written for the eyes of his mother and sisters. It has never been published in its entirety.

38. *Journal*, I, 376–400.

39. Cf. *Journal*, I, 137, 319, 322. See also Thomas Bray, *Bibliotheca Parochialis* . . . (1707).

40. Of these last, one was already a classic of Lutheran pietism: A. H. Francke, *Pietas Hallensis*; or, *An Abstract of the Marvellous Footsteps of Divine Providence*; [Part I with a preface written by Josiah Woodward . . .] *To which is added a Short History of Pietism* (1707).

41. Συνόδικον, *sive Pandectae Canonum SS. Apostolorum et Conciliorum ab Ecclesiae Graecae Receptorum . . . Totum Opus in duos Tomos Divisum* (1672).

42. Cf. *Journal*, I, 175, where he reports spending three hours "revising" the B.C.P.! At Wesley's house in City Road, London, there is a small octavo manuscript in Wesley's hand, commenting upon the *Apostolic Canons* and his own views of liturgy. It has been published in R. Denny Urlin, *John Wesley's Place in Church History* (Edinburgh, 1870), 68–71; and in John C. Bowmer, *The Sacrament of the Lord's Supper in Early Methodism* (1951), 233–37. Urlin dates the manuscript around 1741, but without convincing evidence; Bowmer thinks an earlier date is possible, but leaves it as "an open question." Judging by context, however, the Savannah episode

. . . say *they* are Protestants. But as for *you*, they cannot tell what religion you are of. They never heard of such religion before. They do not know what to make of it." [43] Eight of the grand jury charges against Wesley relate to these liturgical or ecclesiastical affairs.[44] They could hardly have understood the sources and influences guiding Wesley in this aspect of his work.

A third positive development for Wesley in his Georgia experience was the acquaintance he formed with the Moravians — who taught him, by example and precept, that faith should be fearless and that piety can be buoyant.[45] It was no accident that when he returned to England, he made immediate contact with the Moravians there, having already formed a plan to visit the Moravian communities in Germany as soon as possible.

He landed back in England, February 1, 1738, sadly discredited and painfully uncertain of his faith and his future. For a dozen years he had been toiling up the path to perfection, striving by the best models he knew to attain true blessedness. The Georgia mission, which had earlier seemed fantastic to some of his friends, now seemed so to him. He and his brother resolved "to retire out of the world at once . . ." But, as he recalls it later, "We were dragged out again . . . and so carried on . . . without any design except the *general* one of saving souls." [46] The

---

(*Journal*, I, 274-76) is a far more plausible circumstance for such a memorandum than any we know after Wesley's return to England. The text of the memorandum is as follows: "I believe [myself] it is a duty to observe, so far as I can [without breaking communion with my own Church]: 1. To baptize by immersion; 2. To use Water, Oblation of the Elements, Invocation, Alms, a Prothesis in the Eucharist; 3. To pray for the faithful departed; 4. To pray standing on Sunday in Pentecost; 5. To observe Saturday and Sunday Pentecost as festival; 6. To abstain from blood, things strangled. I think it prudent [our own Church not considered]: 1. To observe the Stations; 2. Lent, especially the Holy Week; 3. To turn to the East at the Creed." The words in brackets have a line drawn through them in the manuscript — but one cannot be sure that Wesley did this himself.

43. *Journal*, I, 234. Wesley was always picking up nicknames which reflect the bafflement of critics misled by the familiar stereotypes of Protestant polemics. He was, for example, dubbed "a papist," "a Jesuit," "a Jacobite," and, once, a "Presbyterian-papist" (*Journal*, III, 110)!

44. Cf. *Journal*, I, 385–86. Number 12 reads: "By calling himself 'Ordinary' and thereby claiming a jurisdiction which we believe is not due to him and whereby we should be precluded from access to redress by any superior jurisdiction." Wesley evidently understood "ordinary" as meaning pastor-in-charge (πρωεστόs, "abbot"); his critics took it to mean "bishop." Cf. *The Prayer Book Dictionary*, George Hanford and Morley Stevenson, eds. (n.d.), 510.

45. Cf. *Journal*, I, 142 f., 151 f., 168 f.       46. *Works*, VIII, 227.

marks of the great evangelist and practical genius had not yet appeared in Wesley's career.

Within two years, however, this paradoxical man, with his strange talent for stirring an emotional swirl around him while himself remaining calm, had become the acknowledged leader of a tremendous revival that was to grow and spread under his hand for half a century. The unique mixture of theological notions thus far accumulated was now to be smelted and forged into an integral and dynamic theology in which Eastern notions of *synelthesis* (dynamic interaction between God's will and man's) were fused with the classical Protestant *sola fide* and *sola Scriptura*, and with the Moravian stress upon "inner feeling."

Wesley's own account of how all this happened is given in his dramatic story of "the Aldersgate experience." [47] This has come to be the most familiar event in Wesley's life. It often goes unnoticed, however, that it actually stands within a series of significant spiritual experiences, and is neither first nor last nor most climactic. There is ample evidence that fixes the year 1738 as the decisive period in Wesley's change from a faith in faith to faith itself, from aspiration to assurance. But the fact remains that the Aldersgate story as such drops abruptly out of sight after its publication in the second *Extract of the Rev. Mr. John Wesley's Journal* (1740). Nor could it be reconstructed or even confirmed from other references in his writings. Moreover, the Aldersgate experience was followed by a long series of spiritual upheavals and frustration which lasted well into the spring of 1739. [48]

In the summer of 1738 Wesley visited the Moravians in their homeland at Herrnhut and Marienborn. It was, in effect, an attempt to test, at the source, the reality and power of the piety he had encountered in Spangenberg and Peter Böhler. His impressions of the German Moravians were mixed. On the one hand, he met many quite remarkable people; among

47. See below, pp. 51–69.
48. Cf. *A Plain Account of Christian Perfection*, par. 7–8 (*Works*, XI, 369–70), where Wesley, in a rehearsal of his early spiritual development, passes directly from Georgia to Germany with no mention of Aldersgate as intervening. See also *Journal*, I, 414, where Wesley defines "uneasiness' as prima facie evidence of "unbelief." Yet his own reports of disturbances recur frequently after his heartwarming (*Journal*, I, 481, 483; II, 125), and continue intermittently for ten months. On his visit to Germany, the Herrnhuters barred him from Holy Communion because they adjudged him *homo perturbatus* (cf. Daniel Benham, ed., *Memoirs of James Hutton* [1856], 40). In the period from October 1738 through March 1739 there are dozens of references to severe fluctuations of mood and temper (cf. especially *Journal*, II, 89 ff., 103, 125, and *Sermons* [Sugden], II, 244).

them, one Arvid Gradin, who both defined and exemplified "the full assurance of Christian faith." [49] On the other hand, he was also quick to spot the signs of self-righteousness among them, and to be repelled by the cult of personality which had grown up around their leader, Count Ludwig von Zinzendorf.[50]

He returned from Germany in September, rejoined his friends in the Fetter Lane Society [51] and resumed his preaching in the churches. His zeal was unabated, and yet the results of his efforts were no more satisfying than before. The inner reality and outward force of the gospel, believed and preached never so faithfully, still were lacking. Then, almost by chance, while "walking from London to Oxford" (October 9, 1738), he began "to read the truly surprising narrative of the conversions lately wrought in and about the town of North Hampton in New England." [52] It is an arresting and moving account, and it struck Wesley with terrific force.[53] The crisis which followed ranks with Aldersgate in importance if not in drama. It is significant that, thereafter, Wesley adopted Edwards's analysis of "the distinguishing marks of a work of the Spirit of God," and published an abridgment of it, along with a substantial "ex-

49. Πληροφορία πίστεως (Heb. 10:22); cf. Journal, II, 49. See also Arvid Gradin's definition of sanctification as quoted in A Plain Account of Christian Perfection (Works, XI, 369–70): "Repose in the blood of Christ; a firm confidence in God and a persuasion of his favor; the highest tranquility, serenity and peace of mind, with a deliverance from every fleshly desire and a cessation of all, even inward sins." This, said Wesley, "was the first account I ever heard from any living man of what I had before learned myself from the oracles of God. . . ." See also Journal, II, 49.

50. See below, pp. 372–76.

51. For an account of the origin of the prototypes of the Aldersgate and Fetter Lane societies, see Josiah Woodward, An Account of the Rise and Progress of the Religious Societies in the City of London, . . . and of their Endeavours for the Reformation of Manners, 3 ed. (1712).

52. Journal, II, 83, 84. Cf. Jonathan Edwards, A Faithful Narrative of the Surprising Work of God in the Conversion of Many Hundred Souls in Northampton . . . in New England. In a letter to the Rev. Dr. Benjamin Colman of Boston . . . (1737).

53. Journal, II, 88–91: "An extract from this I wrote to a friend concerning the state of those who are 'weak in the faith' [Rom. 14:1]. His answer, which I received at [Oxford] on Saturday the 14th, threw me into great perplexity." Wesley adds a very revealing self-analysis as to the validity of his faith, which concludes: "Yet, upon the whole, although I have not yet that joy in the Holy Ghost, nor the full assurance of faith, much less am I, in the full sense of the word, 'in Christ a new creature' [2 Cor. 5:17], I nevertheless trust that I have a measure of faith and am 'accepted in the beloved' [Eph. 1:6]; I trust that 'the handwriting that was against me is blotted out' [cf. Col. 2:14] and that I am reconciled to God through his Son" (p. 91).

tract" of *A Treatise Concerning the Religious Affections* — all of them
with Edwards's high Calvinism carefully filtered out.[54] It is not too much
to say that one of the effectual causes of the Wesleyan Revival in England was the Great Awakening in New England.

Meanwhile, developments in the Fetter Lane Society had faced Wesley
more sharply than ever before with the conflict between Moravian quietism and Anglican synergism. How, for instance, can the same theologian
consistently support the notions of justification by faith alone and still
insist on good works as appropriate to repentance at one and the same
time? Many of the members at Fetter Lane had come to agree with the
Moravian position which, in Wesley's view, amounted to a fatal antinomianism. Pressed for an adequate alternative, he began, in mid-November, "more narrowly to inquire what the doctrine of the Church of England is concerning the much controverted point of justification by faith;
and the sum of what I found in The Homilies I extracted and printed for
the use of others." [55] It is very important to notice this conscious self-
identification with the English reformers. It marked the final stage of
Wesley's maturation as a theologian and it continued to serve as the basic
datum-plane for all subsequent developments in his thought. His prag-
matic temper was prepared, of course, for contextual modifications of
various sorts for new situations. But now at last — with his "Moravian"
conversion at Aldersgate, followed by his disenchantments with Moravianism in Germany and Fetter Lane, his encounter with Edwards and
his vital reappropriation of his Anglican heritage — the frame of Wesley's
theology was finally set, and would so remain thereafter.

In the four months following his review of The Homilies, we have a
detailed record of Wesley's unremitting diligence, his intermittent anxieties and only occasional moments of joy and high-heartedness.[56] On No-

54. Wesley extracted, published and distributed to his people the following works
of Edwards: *A Faithful Narrative* . . . (n.d. [1742?]); *The Distinguishing Marks of
a Work of God* (1744); *Thoughts Concerning the Present Revival in Religion in
New England* (1745); *An Extract of the Life of the Rev. Mr. David Brainerd, Missionary to the Indians* (Bristol, 1768; reprinted in *Works* [Pine], XII); *An Extract
from a Treatise Concerning Religious Affections* (Bristol, 1773); rev. ed. of the
*Narrative, The Distinguishing Marks*, and *Thoughts* (1773); a sermon of Edwards's
entitled "God Is Love," in *The Arminian Magazine* for 1785. In his own *Thoughts
Upon Necessity* (see below, pp. 472–91) Wesley argues against Edwards's *Freedom
of the Will*. It is plain from all this that Edwards — always minus his "Calvinism" —
was a major source of Wesley's evangelical theology.

55. See below, pp. 123–33.          56. Cf. *Journal*, II, 131; III, 440–41.

vember 30, George Whitefield returned from his first American tour, flushed with success and eager to duplicate it in England. Wesley was impressed by this — yet he was also dismayed when Whitefield sought to conscript him as leader of a revival he had started in Bristol and was now about to leave.[57] Wesley's account of this episode is quite remarkable: [58] his own negative reactions, his pleas to his colleagues in Fetter Lane for support in declining Whitefield's invitation, the opposition of his brother Charles, their final recourse to a pious sortilege and, finally, John's reluctant decision to go to Bristol as to a martyr's death.

It turned out, of course, that he had come at long last to the threshold of his true vocation. "At four in the afternoon [April 2nd] I submitted to be more vile, and proclaimed in the [Bristol] highways the glad tidings of salvation, speaking from a little eminence in a ground adjoining to the city, to about three thousand people." [59] The next day he preached in the fields at Baptist Mills (a Bristol suburb), and on the following Sunday on Hannam Mount, to the desperate miners in the King's Wood. The reaction of the people was amazing, and to no one more than to Wesley himself. Here were great crowds of eager listeners, who apparently were hearing the gospel in his preaching, whose behavior was visibly affected, whose lives were being "revived." Conversions were taking place fully as impressive and real as he had read about in Edwards's "narrative." The Revival had begun. Moreover, these experiences served to signalize the full maturing of the revivalist as well.

It is most impressive to observe the marked effect this success at Bristol had on Wesley's spiritual equilibrium. Up to this point the story is full of anxiety, insecurity, futility. Hereafter, the instances of spiritual disturbances drop off sharply and rarely recur, even in the full records of a very candid man. Peter Böhler had exhorted him to "preach faith till you have it and then because you have it, you will preach faith." [60] At Aldersgate he had passed from virtual to real faith, from hoping to having. Edwards and Whitefield had shown him that the Word rightly preached bears visible fruit. And now, before his eyes, was a harvest of such fruit. What had happened was that he had preached faith until *others* had it, and now his own was confirmed by theirs! For the next half-century, in failure and triumph, tumult and peace, obloquy and fame, the picture rarely varies: a man with an overmastering mission,

57. Cf. *Ibid.*, II, 115 ff.
58. *Ibid.*, 156–67.
59. *Ibid.*, II, 172–73; *Works*, VIII, 113.
60. *Journal*, I, 442.

acutely self-aware but rarely ruffled, often in stress but always secure on a rock-steady foundation.

It is useful to notice the main phases of Wesley's career as leader of the Methodist Revival, even if only in the broadest outline.[61] The first decade (1739–49) was the most decisive. In it we can see the flowering of that practical genius thus far invisible but henceforth in constant evidence. It began with the formation of the United Societies and continued in the development of a distinctive pattern of order and discipline for "the people called Methodists." [62] With their organization of societies, classes and bands, the brothers Wesley [63] provided their converts with a unique program of association and involvement, which included Christian nurture, discipline and pastoral care. This effectual stress upon organization and the use of lay preachers as associates in the Revival mark off the principal difference between the long-term, cumulative results of the Wesleyan movement and the rather more episodic successes of other popular evangelists in the same epoch (e.g. Whitefield, John Berridge, and others).

61. He has not lacked for dutiful biographers. The first ones (John Whitehead, Thomas Coke, Henry Moore and Luke Tyerman) set the stereotype of "the founder of *Methodism*," and this has dominated subsequent studies. Of these, the ablest and most complete is John Simon's five volumes of biography and history (1921–34). Robert Southey's *Life* (1820) is easily the most distinguished literary monument to Wesley; Lecky's section on "The Religious Revival," in his *History of England in the 18th Century*, III (1878), is still its most perceptive historical survey. But neither poet nor historian could comprehend the theologian. Of recent biographical studies, the most interesting are V. H. H. Green, *The Young Mr. Wesley* (1961) and Martin Schmidt, *John Wesley* (1953; the English version, trans. by Norman Goldhawk, 1962). They are, however, confined to the early years. Green focuses mainly on Wesley the Oxonian, whereas Schmidt makes him out virtually a Moravian. An adequate study of Wesley's life and thought is still greatly needed.

62. Cf. Wesley's account of this in *The Nature, Design and General Rules of the United Societies* (1743), and *Works*, VIII, 269–71, and *A Plain Account of the People Called Methodists* (1748) and *Works*, VIII, 248–68.

63. From the days of the Holy Club, Charles Wesley had been an almost constant companion to his brother, and his contributions to the Methodist revival — in his remarkably effective preaching but chiefly in his incomparable facility as a hymnwriter — were very substantial indeed. One may speak realistically of the theology of John in the hymns of Charles Wesley. Between 1737 and 1742 they had published six separate volumes — the first, in Charleston, S.C., the rest, in London: *Psalms and Hymns*, 1737 and 1738; *Hymns and Sacred Poems*, 1739, 1740 and 1742; *Psalms and Hymns*, 1741. In 1742 Charles published a sermon on Eph. 4:14 ("Awake, Thou That Sleepest"), which John chose to print with his own *Sermons on Several Occasions* (1744) and made normative for Methodist doctrine. For Charles's role in the Georgia mission and in the early stages of the Revival, see his own *Journal, 1736–39*, John Telford, ed. (1909). See also Frank Baker, *Charles Wesley* (1948).

This first decade also saw the guidelines of the Wesleyan theology delineated and spelled out circumstantially.[64] Inevitably, this made for new tensions — with the Moravians over the question of faith and good works; with the Church of England hierarchy in respect of the irregularities of the Methodists and their "enthusiasm"; [65] with the Calvinists on the question of "the decrees [of predestination]." [66]

The bishops and clergy came to have a common image of the Methodists as a rabble of fanatical preachers and hysterical converts. This disapproving judgment was exacerbated by Wesley's decision to "employ" laymen as preachers and personal assistants. The bishops were unimpressed by the fact that Wesley carefully avoided calling his lay preachers "ministers" and steadily refused them any authority whatsoever to administer the sacraments. These men, he said, were his personal "helpers," directly responsible to him in their work, as he was responsible for them to the Church. With a few ordained colleagues and still fewer of his lay preachers, Wesley initiated an annual conference in 1744,[67] which came to be a unique instrumentality in shaping policy and doctrine in the Methodist movement.

By mid-century, and as it entered its second decade (1749–59), Methodism was a going concern, established as an evangelistic "order" within the Church of England, feeling and exercising a vigorous freedom to criticize and alter certain Anglican proprieties but deeply attached to the Church and determined to carry forward her true mission to the people. Wesley conceived his own ministerial office as that of "a special messenger" — an evangelist raised up by the Holy Spirit to supply the defects of the crippled and ineffectual ministry then being rendered by the conventional clergy (*ministerium ordinarium*). Convinced of the essential integrity of his mission within the Church of England, he steadfastly repudiated every charge of separatism and every push toward separation within the ranks of the Methodists.[68] In the darkest days of the anti-Methodist disorders (in the 1740's) he allowed the trustees of his "preaching houses" to register them under the Act of Toleration, but this was

64. See below, p. 134 ff.                    65. See below, p. 389 ff.
66. *Cf. Free Grace: a sermon preached at Bristol* (1739); reprinted in *Works*, VII, 373–86.
67. See below, p. 134 ff. After 1745 Wesley's lay assistants began to outnumber his clerical associates.
68. Broached before, the issue of "separation" became an open quarrel at the Twelfth Annual Conference of 1755, when Charles Perronet and others made a determined bid to lead the Methodists out of the Church of England into dissent.

a technical move to gain legal protection from the mobs which had plagued the Methodists during their first decade.[69]

Not even its stoutest advocates have argued that the eighteenth-century Church of England was either zealous or free.[70] It had a minimum quota of saints and sages, but these were sadly thwarted in their efforts to lift the life of the Church to the challenge of the times. In polity, it was an Erastian establishment in a demoralized environment. The so-called Restoration Settlement had settled very little. Walpole and the Whigs had furthered the ruin of the Cavalier tradition, domesticating the Church within the web of a cynical secular policy and going so far as to suspend its convocations, thus depriving it of its machinery for progress and reform. Ironically enough, this disintegration had actually been re-enforced by the Act of Toleration — the solution preferred by an alliance of High-churchmen and Dissenters over any scheme of "comprehension" of the various parties within the Church of England. Over all there hung a stifling miasma of apathy and stale devotion.

In his attack upon such a situation, Wesley deployed his "assistants" as a sort of militia, moving them frequently from one assignment to another but insisting on their common task: evangelism and Christian nurture. "We look upon ourselves, not as the authors or ringleaders of a particular sect or party — it is the farthest thing from our thoughts — but as messengers of God, to those who are Christians in name but heathens in heart and life, to call them back to that from which they are fallen, to real, genuine Christianity." [71] He was prepared to ignore various

Cf. Tyerman, *Life*, II, 198–212, for a circumstantial account of the controversy, avowedly in sympathy with the separatists. From Wesley's laconic note on that conference in the *Journal* (IV, 115), one could hardly guess how grave a crisis he had met and mastered. In the year following, Edward Perronet (author of the familiar hymn, "All Hail the Power of Jesus' Name") published an intemperate denunciation of the Church of England in a long poem, *The Mitre* (1756). Wesley was sufficiently outraged so that he undertook to suppress the entire edition, with considerable success. Extant copies are extremely rare.

69. Cf. Max Beloff, *Public Order and Popular Disturbances, 1660–1714* (1938), for an illuminating study of the general disorder of English life in this period. The Methodist histories give the impression that only the Methodists were victims of English mob violence at this time.

70. Cf. G. M. Trevelyan, *History of England*, 3d ed. (New York, 1945), II, 309–10; III, 27–34; Basil Williams, *The Whig Supremacy, 1714–60* (*Oxford History of England*, IX) (Oxford, 1952), chap. iv; Norman Sykes, *From Sheldon to Secker* (Cambridge, 1959), VI; C. J. Abbey, *The English Church and Its Bishops, 1700–1800* (1887), I, chap. iii.

71. *A Preservative Against Unsettled Notions in Religion*, (1758) 241; cf. the

clerical protests that this involved the invasion of other men's parishes —
since he was convinced that his own collegiate ordination had given him
an extraparochial license which he was justified, in the actual circumstances, in extending to his lay preachers — but for preaching and teaching only, not for the administration of the sacraments. It was in this sense
of *minister extraordinarius* that he came to look upon the *world* as his
parish.[72]

Just as he felt called to preach to any and all who would hear, so also
he welcomed them into his audiences, including Dissenters and Roman
Catholics. He even accepted several Dissenters in the ranks of his lay
assistants. At the same time, he deliberately constricted the liturgical form
of Methodist preaching services so that the people would still need the
normal ministrations of the Church for the full liturgy and the sacraments.[73] As might have been expected, however, the Anglican hierarchy
rejected the notion of this evangelistic order within the Church, and
many Methodists became increasingly ill-at-ease in what they felt was an
anomalous connection with a corrupt establishment. John Wesley recognized the complexity of the issue, but he stood equally unmoved by the
pressures of the Dissenters from the one side or, from the other, the pained

---

whole of sec. III, 240-46, for an uncommonly clear statement of Wesley's under-
standing of his own ministry and of Methodism as an evangelical order within the
Church of England. See also below, pp. 73-76; 104-16. Cf. *Letters*, I, 322-23; *Journal*,
II, 217-18; *Works*, VIII, 309.

72. See below, p. 72. Wesley seems to have held the view that his Oxford ordination conferred on him the *ius ubique praedicandi*, the right of preaching everywhere. Hastings Rashdall, *The Universities of Europe in the Middle Ages*, Frederick
Maurice Powicke and Alfred Brotherston Emden, eds. (Oxford, 1936), III, 136, notes
that the Chancellor of Oxford had by tradition the right to "license preachers to
preach in every diocese in England." This was evidently in Wesley's mind in his
rejoinder to Bishop Butler's advice "to go hence" from Bristol in August 1739: "Being
ordained as Fellow of a College, I was not limited to any particular cure, but have
an indeterminate commission to preach the Word of God in any part of the Church
of England. I do not therefore conceive that, in preaching here by this commission,
I break any human law" (Moore, *Life*, I, 270; cf. *Journal*, II, 257). In later controversy
he was even more specific: "I was not appointed to any congregation at all; but was
ordained as a member of that 'College of Divines' (so our statutes [of Lincoln Col-
lege] express it) 'founded to overturn all heresies and defend the Catholic faith'"
(*Works*, VIII, 117; cf. *Letters*, II, 236). Cf. F. Makower, *The Constitutional History
and Constitution of the Church of England* (1895), 491: Canon 33 of "The Canons of
1604." Wesley also seems to have felt some sort of private assurance of King George's
unofficial support of his itinerant preaching; cf. *Journal*, III, 494, and below, p. 113.

73. Cf. *Works*, VIII, 321-22.

outrage of his brother Charles and other ordained clergymen. But the pressures did not relax and, finally, Charles began to tire of the struggle and to fear its outcome. It was his aversion to schism, more than any other factor, which influenced his gradual and quiet withdrawal from the Methodist movement.[74] John stoutly denied that he intended to separate, or would allow it. His maxim, coined for the crucial Conference of 1755, was "that, whether it was *lawful* or not, it was no ways *expedient*" to separate from the Church.[75] Three years later he repeated the formula in the opening paragraph of his *Reasons Against a Separation from the Church of England*.[76] But his chief concern in the whole matter was that the ecclesiological tumult over separation not be allowed to enfeeble the Revival or to distract the Methodists from their distinctive mission and witness.

The Revival's third decade (1759–69) saw its general spread and consolidation, along with new signs of acceptance and respectability. But this made for new strains in the patterns of group association and new dissensions amongst Wesley's lay assistants as to their status and prerogatives.[77] Even more significant, however, from the standpoint of Wesley's theological development, was the increasing number of professions of "entire sanctification" by members of the societies, especially in the Midlands.[78] "Holiness of heart and life" had been one of Wesley's cherished mottoes from the beginning. Now, as if somewhat belatedly, many people came forward to profess the gift of perfection which Wesley had explicitly taught them to expect. Himself no "professor," he was quite prepared to investigate the claims of others — and concluded that many of them were authentic. As a consequence, he began to stress more than ever before the vital urgency of "the fullness of faith" as a promise implied in God's gift of faith itself.

---

74. His last extended preaching tour was in 1756. He and his family were settled in Bristol until 1771, when they moved to London, to a house near St. Marylebone's Church. He died there on March 29, 1788, and was buried in the churchyard, expressly refusing his brother's wish that they both be buried in the cemetery behind the City Road Chapel. For evidence of the protracted tension between the brothers on the issue of separation, see *Letters*, III, 129–36.

75. *Journal*, IV, 115.

76. *Works*, XIII, 225. See also *Journal*, IV, 186; V, 180; VII, 112, 192, 217, 232.

77. Cf. *Journal*, IV, 535–42; 178–79.

78. Cf. *The Arminian Magazine*, III, vi, where Wesley recalls "the year 1758, and a few of the following years, . . . that unusual outpouring of the Spirit with which both London and many parts of England and Ireland were favoured during that happy period." See also Tyerman, *Life*, II, 416, 426.

To safeguard against "enthusiasm," however, he published a stiff warning against spiritual pride and self-righteousness, entitled *Cautions and Directions Given to the Greatest Professors in the Methodist Societies.*[79] In addition, he wrote three new sermons intended to reject any notion of perfection as static or "sinless": *Wandering Thoughts* (1760), *On Sin in Believers* (1763) and *The Repentance of Believers* (1768). In 1766 he published a review and digest of his thoughts and writings on the subject in *A Plain Account of Christian Perfection as Believed and Taught by the Rev. Mr. John Wesley from the Year 1725 to the Year 1765.*[80]

Our scheme of decades fails to provide a neat outline for the final score of Wesley's years. It was filled with turmoils, disasters and triumphs. In 1770 a controversy broke out between Wesley and his disciples on the one side and the Calvinist chaplains of the Countess of Huntingdon on the other.[81] The Calvinists took huge offense at a carelessly drafted minute from the Conference of 1770.[82] They renewed their attack upon what they labeled "Arminianism" — even though Arminius himself had never been one of Wesley's really decisive "sources." However, as he had done before with the nickname Methodist, he turned this epithet into a badge and boldly christened his new house organ *The Arminian Magazine* (1778 et seq.). Against the Calvinists' doctrines of predestination and perseverance, he opposed his own conception of "conditional salvation within the universal redemption wrought by Christ." In the preface to the first volume he explains that

> . . . each number will therefore consist of four parts: first, a defense of that grand Christian doctrine, 'God willeth all men to be saved and to come to the knowledge of the truth'; secondly, an extract from the life of some holy man, whether Lutheran, Church of England man, Calvinist or Arminian; thirdly, accounts and letters, containing the experience of pious persons, the greatest part of whom are still alive; and fourthly, verses explaining or confirming the capital doctrines we have in view.

79. See below, pp. 298–305.

80. *Cf.* Green, *Bibliography*, #238: "This tract underwent several revisions and enlargements, one of which appears in Volume XXIV of the collected *Works*, 1773. In each successive edition the date of the most recent revision was specified. The last revision appears to have been made in the year 1777; and since that period, this date has been generally continued on the title page of the several editions."

81. *Cf.* John Stoughton, *The Church in the Georgian Era* (*A History of Religion in England,* VI) (1881), chap. xi–xii. See also John Hunt, *Religious Thought in England* (1873), III, 292–300; J. Simon, *John Wesley, the Master Builder* (1927), 276–300; Tyerman, *Life*, III, 71, 108.

82. *Minutes of the Methodist Conferences* (1862), I, 95–96.

While this furor was raging, Britain's conflict with her American colonies was ripening into war. Royalist and Tory that he was, Wesley's social conscience moved him to support the early pleas of the colonists for liberty and justice.[83] But when the American demand for "liberty" became the cry for "independence," Wesley's inbred loyalty to the Crown and his doctrine of nonresistance turned him violently against the rebels. In the six years of the Revolution he published no fewer than thirteen royalist tracts and open letters.[84] In them the American rebels appear as avatars of those seventeenth-century anarchists who had murdered Charles I and brought England to the brink of ruin. In 1775 Wesley finally withdrew his trade from his printer, William Pine of Bristol — not for incompetence (as well he might),[85] but for his espousal of the colonies' cause. Such views naturally complicated Wesley's relations with the American Methodists. They had either to bear the stigma of "Tory" or else disassociate themselves as far as possible from their leader.[86] The consequences of this dilemma had far-reaching effects in the subsequent development of American Methodism. American independence weakened Wesley's control over the American Methodists and at the same time strengthened the hand of the separatists in the Methodist societies in Britain (many of whom had been sympathizers with the American cause). Wesley's "ordinations" for America in 1784 are better understood in *this* light than in terms of his general doctrine of the ministry. For one

83. *Cf.* his letters to the Earl of Dartmouth (Secretary of State for the Colonies) and to Lord North (First Lord of the Treasury), *Letters*, VI, 155–64.

84. *A Calm Address to Our American Colonies* (Bristol, 1775); *A Sermon Preached at St. Matthew's Bethnal-Green, on Sunday, November 12, 1775 . . . for the Benefit of the Widows and Orphans of the Soldiers Who Lately Fell Near Boston in New England* (1775); *Some Observations on Liberty* (Edinburgh, 1776); *A Seasonable Address to the More Serious Part of the Inhabitants of Great Britain, Respecting the Unhappy Contest Between Us and Our American Brethren . . .* (Bristol, 1776); *A Calm Address to the Inhabitants of England* (1777); *A Serious Address to the People of England with Regard to the State of the Nation* (1778); *An Account of the Conduct of the War in the Middle Colonies* (1780); *Reflections on the Rise and Progress of the American Rebellion* (1780); two letters on Lord Howe's inept conduct of the war ([1781]; *cf. Letters*, VI, 155–64; VII, 47–48); and three collections of hymns relating to the war ([1782]; *cf.* Green, *Bibliography,* #366, #367, #368).

85. For example, Pine had published Wesley's collected *Works* from uncorrected galley proofs. For Wesley's reference to his political views as "barefaced treason," see *Letters*, VI, 170.

86. *Cf.* Francis Asbury, *Journal and Letters*, Elmer T. Clark, ed. (1958), III, 62: "There is not a man in the world so obnoxious to the American politicians as our dear old Daddy; but no matter, we must treat him with all the respect we can and that is due him."

thing, the American Methodists — never well cared for by the colonial clergy — now had no church home in which they might receive the sacraments. The Church of England was moving very slowly in its arrangements for American bishops, and was altogether averse to Wesley's proposal that some of *his* preachers be ordained for ministerial service in the new nation. In this situation, therefore, there was an urgent need for Wesley to restore his authority in America, as far as this was possible. His concern is made plain in his letters to "Our Brethren in America" and to Freeborn Garrettson.[87]

In circumstances too obscure to reconstruct fully and much too complicated to explain simply, Wesley decided to "appoint" two of his lay preachers, Richard Whatcoat and Thomas Vasey, for a full ministry in America, and to commission his own closest associate, Dr. Thomas Coke (himself a fellow presbyter of the Church of England), as "superintendent" of the American Methodists. It was his apparent design that Coke was to convey this commission to Francis Asbury, whom Wesley had sent to the colonies before the Revolution and who had emerged as the postwar leader of the American Methodists. Together, Coke and Asbury were to serve as Wesley's deputies, and to provide the Methodists with a necessary ministry. This plan was only partially successful. Asbury refused to accept Coke's transmissal of Wesley's commission until after they had both been elected "superintendents" by the free suffrages of the American preachers (at the "Christmas Conference," Baltimore, 1784).[88] He and Coke then proceeded to supervise the organization of a new and autonomous denomination, the Methodist Episcopal Church. Asbury assumed the title "bishop," and blandly ignored Wesley's indignant rebuke for this pretension.[89]

The Methodists in America were willing to reckon Wesley as their father in God but no longer as their actual leader.[90] In 1786 they quietly

87. See below, p. 84.

88. *Cf.* Asbury, *Journal and Letters,* I, 471: ". . . I was shocked when first informed of [Coke's] intention. . . . My answer . . . was, if the preachers unanimously choose me, I shall not act in the capacity I have hitherto done by Mr. Wesley's appointment." See also Asbury's protest against the proposal of "our old Daddy . . . to appoint a joint superintendent with me . . ." (*Journal and Letters,* III, 63).

89. *Cf. Letters,* VIII, 91: "How can you, how dare you, suffer yourself to be called 'bishop': I shudder, I start at the very thought! Men may call me a knave or a fool, a rascal, a scoundrel and I am content. But they shall never by my consent call me 'bishop.' For my sake, for God's sake, for Christ's sake, put a full end to this!"

90. *Journal,* VII, 295; *Letters,* VII, 294, 387; VIII, 73, 91; see also Asbury, *Journal and Letters,* I, 547 and note.

dropped his name from the *Minutes* of the annual conferences, and in 1787 they ignored his explicit directive that Richard Whatcoat be elected "superintendent." [91] When Wesley's name reappeared in the *Minutes* of 1789, a clear distinction was drawn between his spiritual pre-eminence and his practical authority.

His closing years were scarcely less intent or fruitful than the very first decade of the Revival. The reader of his *Journal* may rightly marvel, even as he himself did, at his continuing vigor and competence. He was often ill but rarely incapacitated. The visible signs of old age were scarcely noticeable until very near the end.[92] He was planning yet another tour, just the month before his death — in London, March 2, 1791.

From the organization of the first society until the day of his death, Wesley maintained his role as the sole leader of the Methodists, people and preachers. Thereafter, his *persona* was perpetuated in a legal corporation of a hundred men chosen by Wesley to constitute "The Conference of the People Called Methodists." [93] This Conference was designed to govern and guide the societies as Wesley had done, and to continue them within the Church of England, faithful to the doctrinal standards established earlier in the *Model Deed*.[94] For all this, however, the drift into schism was strong, and finally prevailed. Reverence for Wesley obscured the fact that when he died, he was the staunchly conformist leader of a nonconformist movement.[95]

It is instructive, in trying to comprehend Wesley's way of working as a theologian, to notice the reiterative pattern in his doctrinal formulations. Basic themes appear repeatedly, yet always freshly modulated to fit some new occasion or context. Wesley was a born debater. His training at Oxford had settled him in the habit of pitching on to the vulnerable links

91. For the Whatcoat affair and the dropping of Wesley's name from the *Minutes*, cf. Asbury, *Journal and Letters*, III, 49–53, 75, 94; see also David Sherman, *History of the Revisions of the Discipline of the Methodist Episcopal Church* (New York, 1874), 68–69. For Wesley's own bitter comment on the breach, cf. *Letters*, VIII, 183. There is also a curious comment on this affair in the Coke and Asbury preface to Volume I of their *American* edition of *The Arminian Magazine* (Philadelphia, 1789), v: ". . . he [Wesley] is not, as some have falsely advanced, in his second childhood; . . . his exercising the episcopal office for the forming of our church in America was not the fruit of infancy in him or in us."

92. Cf. for example, his annual tour of the societies in the spring and summer of 1788 in *Journal*, VII, 357–435.

93. Cf. *The Deed of Declaration* in *Journal*, VIII, 335–41; see also J. S. Simon, *John Wesley; The Last Phase* (1934), chap. xv.

94. *Works*, VIII, 329–31.                    95. Cf. *Letters*, VIII, 58, 59, 66, 71.

in an opponent's argument and trying to smash them, one by one. His polemical writings are not always fair and constructive; nowadays, at least, they make rather tedious reading. But they served their purpose in their time — which was more to lift the morale of his own people under the poundings of disapproval and the seductions of error than to silence or convert their enemies.

He seems never to have felt the impulse to produce anything resembling a comprehensive exposition of his theological ideas — and this may have been just as well. Short doctrinal summaries are scattered throughout his writings,[96] and these give ample evidence that his thought was consciously organized around a stable core of basic coordinated motifs. But there is no extended development of his system, and for the simple reason that there never seemed to be a *practical* need for such a thing. His single, sufficient motive in theologizing was to reinforce the spiritual and ethical concerns of his societies in particular and the Church in general. Theology, in this context, was a dialectical affair: [97] faith seeking self-awareness and self-expression. This neglect of a developed systematic statement, however, has encouraged all too many of his followers to misperceive the organic unity of Wesley's thought, or to ignore the pivotal place or rational understanding in his mind and method. Wesley himself cannot be invoked on behalf of an anti-intellectual attitude toward Christian truth.

It was of set purpose that he held the Revival to his own compounded premise of "salvation, faith *and* good works." This put him into tension with other viewpoints in which, as it seemed to him, the essential integrity between evangelical faith and Christian ethics was split, one way or the other. Against all such disjunctions, he asserted the reciprocal unity of belief and behavior. In the same mood and to the same effect, he strove constantly to enforce the distinction between faith itself and all conceptualizations of faith. What he meant by his phrase, "a catholic spirit" (and his favorite text on this theme, "if thy heart be as my heart, give me thy hand"),[98] was the disposition to make and keep the vital reality of faith forever regnant over any and all of its verbalizations.[99] Many have supposed that this was meant to minimize the role of theology in the Christian life. Any such interpretation is as wide of Wesley's mark

96. Cf. *Journal*, III, 320, 534; IV, 419. See also *Letters*, IV, 146, 149, 159, 235–239; VI, 28; and *Works*, VIII, 46, 56, 67, 472; IX, 174.

97. *Letters*, IV, 181–82.     98. See below, p. 91 ff.

99. Cf. *The Character of a Methodist, Works*, VIII, 340 ff.

as its antithesis would be — that "pure doctrine" and authentic faith are *identical*. In Wesley's mind, the data of faith provide the theologian with the problems he ponders; the results of his pondering are significant and valid only insofar as they further support the life of faith. Reason generates neither its data nor its presuppositions; faith does not provide its own self-evident conclusions. It is worth noticing in this connection that the familiar Wesleyan dictum — "we think and let think" — refers, in *his* usage, solely to those "opinions" "which do not reach to the marrow of Christian truth." [100] That Wesley should have become the patron saint of theological indifferentism is mildly outrageous.

The great Protestant watchwords of *sola fide* and *sola Scriptura* were also fundamentals in Wesley's doctrine of authority. But early and late, he interpreted *solus* to mean "primarily" rather than "solely" or "exclusively." [101] Faith is the primary reality in Christian experience but not its totality. It is, Wesley urged, a *means* — a necessary means — to a still higher end: "Faith . . . is only the handmaid of love. . . ." [102] The goal of the Christian life is holiness, "the *fullness* of faith." This means the consecration of the whole self to God and to the neighbor in love. This, in turn, involves a process of corporate discipline and effort, guided by the motives of "devotion," by which he meant the delivering up of one's *whole life* to God. The outcome to be expected in this endeavor is the renewal of the *imago Dei*, mutilated by sin and ruined by waywardness. But our aspiration to holiness is as truly a function of faith as justification itself is. The faith that justifies bears its fruits in the faith that works by love.

Wesley never doubted that the rightful expectation of the Christian life is love, joy and peace in the Holy Spirit. But, certainly as a young man, strong feelings had normally been for him far more disturbing and demoralizing than creative. The program of Christian discipline as he had first practiced it was, therefore, an experiment in suppression. This rigid

---

100. *Journal*, VII, 389; *Letters*, IV, 297; *Works*, VIII, 340.

101. *Letters*, IV, 175: "We are justified by faith alone, and yet by such a faith as is not alone." Cf. *Works*, VIII, 46–70; see also *An Earnest Appeal*, below, pp. 386–88; and *Works*, XI, 373: ". . . the year 1730, when I began to be *homo unius libri*, regarding none, comparatively, but the Bible" (why *comparatively* if *unius* meant "exclusively"?). See also "The Large Minutes" (*Works*, VIII, 315: ". . . 'but I read only the Bible.' . . . This is rank enthusiasm. If you need no book but the Bible, you are got above St. Paul. He wanted others, too. 'Bring the books,' says he, 'but especially the parchments,' those wrote on parchment. 'But I have no taste for reading.' Contract a taste for it by use, or return to your trade."

102. See below, p. 226.

self-control, however, had taken its toll in the "deadness" and the "lack of joy or peace" of which he complained so often — *before* the Revival had got under way. It was not mere rhetorical flourish, therefore, when he said that, in the Aldersgate experience, his heart was *"strangely warmed."* In the later Wesley there is a remarkable balance between expression and restraint — and this marks a genuine transformation from what had earlier been his hunger for and fear of vivid emotion. There is impressive testimony to the fact that he came finally to understand that Christian maturity is chiefly faith's freedom to respond to God's grace without fear of rejection or pride of possession. This was the positive and dynamic view of sanctification that explains, in part at least, Wesley's own unwearied and unanxious diligence, his stress upon the serene strenuousness of the Christian life.

The essence of faith, whether at the threshold or in its fullness, has always to do with man's immediate and indubitable assurance of God's living and loving presence in his heart. Wesley followed Locke in the denial of "innate ideas" and appears never to have taken seriously the traditional "arguments" for the existence of God. In their place, he put an alternate notion of the self-evidence of God's reality as strictly implied in the faithful man's awareness of God's gracious disposition toward *him*. This awareness of God's gracious "presence" is what Wesley meant by "experience," and it was, for him, as real and unmistakable a perception as any sensory awareness might be. This doctrine has often been construed as a subjective theory of experience in general. In Wesley's view, however, it is a theory of religious knowledge, a corollary of his view of revelation.

John Smith had been right, after all, about the fact that Wesley had a doctrine of "perceptible inspiration." But its reference is always confined to the experience of faith — that is, to that inner persuasion that God in Christ is graciously disposed and reconciling. This persuasion is wrought inwardly by the Holy Spirit ("the witness of the Spirit"), and it is as indubitable a perception as sight, sound or self-consciousness.[103]

The most delicate of all the balances which Wesley tried to maintain

---

103. Wesley's standard definition of faith is taken from Heb. 11:1 — πραγμάτων ἔλεγχος οὐ βλεπομένων — which he interprets as tangible evidence of the intangible reality of God's Spirit. *Cf.* "The Witness of the Spirit," *Sermons* (Sugden), I, 202–18; "The Law Established Through Faith," *ibid.*, II, 74–75; "The Wilderness State," *ibid.*, 244–63; "The Witness of the Spirit" (Discourse II), *ibid.*, 341–59; and "On the Discoveries of Faith," in *Works*, VII, 232 ff. As for the analogy between faith and sight, *cf. Letters*, I, 255, 330; II, 24, 48, 50, 64; IV, 116 f., 126, 176; *Works*, VIII, 48, 408.

in his conjunctive theology was the correlation between justification and sanctification. The striking of this balance was what had made 1738 his *annus mirabilis*. It was then that he finally came to know, once and for all, that faith alone is the sole ground of pardon and reconciliation; that no merit of any sort whatever can be linked to man's ultimate concern. Here, said he, "I think on justification just as I have done any time these seven-and-twenty years and just as Mr. Calvin does. In *this* respect, I do not differ from him an hair's breadth." [104]

At the same time, he was equally insistent that the righteousness of faith is designed by God to promote actual righteousness in Christian living. He would therefore never allow the primacy of faith to weaken his stress on human responsibility or his concern for the self-understanding of the Christian as ethical agent. When George Whitefield and the Calvinists began to "preach up the decrees" (*i.e.* the doctrine of predestination) Wesley entered the lists against them, with small quarter asked or given.[105] Similarly, when the Moravians protested his synergistic coupling of faith and discipline, Wesley denounced them as perverters of the whole gospel, and broke with them. When his doctrines of assurance and experience were labeled "enthusiasm," he carefully distinguished between "enthusiasm proper" [106] and that true earnestness based upon the Spirit's witness in our hearts. In these terms, he could insist, against all formalists, that until faith is deeply personal, it is not yet authentic.

The chief interest and significance of Wesley as a theologian lie in the integrity and vitality of his doctrine as a whole. Within that whole, the most distinctive single element was the notion of "Christian perfection." [107] In this he has been consistently misunderstood by all who would understand the English word "perfect" as a translation of the Latin *perfectio*. In medieval Latin *perfectus* meant "faultless" [108] — unimprovable! That any human state can be perfect in *this* sense had rightly been denied

---

104. See below, p. 78.                          105. See below, pp. 425–91.

106. See below, pp. 300–01, *cf. Journal*, III, 26, 202. Compare and contrast the sermons on "The Witness of the Spirit," Discourse II (*Sermons* [Sugden], II, 343–59), and "The Nature of Enthusiasm" (*ibid.*, 84–103). In the latter, after a review of various sorts of enthusiasm, Wesley comes down finally upon the worst "enthusiasm" of them all: "fancying you are a Christian when you are not."

107. See below, pp. 251–305.

108. *Cf.* J. F. Niermeyer, *Mediae Latinitis Lexicon Minus* (Leiden, 1954–62), fascicle 9, 788.

by Aquinas,[109] and had been reserved by the Westminster Divines "for the state of glory only." [110]

The Calvinists promptly decided that Wesley's stress on "perfection" was tantamount to a reintroduction of "works-righteousness" into the doctrine of sanctification. This is part of the implication of heterodoxy that went with the label "Arminian." They pointed to Wesley's insistence upon a time span separating the experience of saving faith and sanctifying faith as a necessary interval for Christian growth and discipline. The Calvinists, however, were not the only ones to misconstrue this doctrine according to their own particular prejudices. The Methodists in America, especially in the nineteenth century, contributed to a very considerable confusion by interpreting "perfection" in terms of "the second blessing" or "entire sanctification as a state of grace distinct from justification, attainable instantaneously by faith." [111]

Wesley, however, had learned about the goal of the Christian life from a different tradition — the τελείωσις of "Macarius," Gregory and Ephraem, the "holiness" of Jewel, Hall and Taylor. "Perfect love," as Wesley understood it, is the conscious certainty, *in a present moment*, of the fullness of one's love for God and neighbor, as this love has been initiated and fulfilled by God's gifts of faith, hope and love. This is not a state but a dynamic process: saving faith is its beginning; sanctification is its proper climax.[112] As faith is in order to love, so love is in order to goodness — and so also goodness is in order to blessedness. This complex pattern of means and ends is designed to unfold in the life process itself, and thus requires some sort of temporal interval for its fulfillment. It is almost as if Wesley had read ἀγάπη in the place of the Clementine γνῶσις, and then had turned the Eastern notion of a vertical scale of perfection into a genetic scale of development within historical existence.[113]

It seemed so obvious to Wesley that no human state is absolute that he was constantly baffled by those who misconstrued his teachings to this effect. All human experience, being temporal and processive, is also pro-

---

109. In his *Summa Contra Gentiles*, Bk. III, 47–48.

110. "*Non nisi in statu gloriae*"; cf. the Westminster Confession, IX, v; cf. XIII, ii.

111. For a review of this development, cf. J. L. Peters, *Christian Perfection and American Methodism* (New York, 1956), 129; see also 127, 169 f., 177–78.

112. *Letters*, IV, 173, 177; see also "Christian Perfection," in *Sermons* (Sugden), II, 150–77.

113. Cf. the hesychastic theme of "the ladder of the soul" (κλίμαξ θείας ἀνοξοῦ), in St. John Climacus, *The Ladder of Divine Ascent*, trans. by Lazarus Moore (1959).

visional. Men may lapse from perfection as tragically as they fall from
grace at any other stage or point. There is no level of spiritual achievement from which pride or self-will may not topple us. So long as we are
"in the body," as Wesley puts it, we are fair prey to Satan's wiles. "Perfection" is the fulfillment of faith's desire to love God above all else and
all else in God, *so far as conscious will and deliberate action* are concerned.[114] To deny this as at least a possibility seemed to Wesley to
imply that deliberate sin is inevitable and unavoidable — which would be
to say that man was made to sin and that his sinful disposition is invincible. But this effectively impugns God's sovereignty as well as his goodness. The assumption that our "wandering thoughts" have power superior
to grace entails the consequence that sin inheres in man's created essence,
and from this it follows that sin is a part of God's design and purpose!

In the normal course of Christian life, Wesley believed, the gift of
perfect love is deferred until the "moment of death" (*articulus mortis*).
In the face of death a man is forced into a mood of "seriousness," if he is
ever likely to be. It was, therefore, neither accidental nor morbid that
Wesley should be so deeply interested in the *ars moriendi*, with so avid
an interest in reports of "triumphant deaths" of all sorts.[115] However,
there is no good reason why a man may not come to be utterly earnest
while still alive. Thus, the gift of perfection is to be sought and expected
— but never scheduled or advertised!

Nevertheless, what is given may also be cast away. A man may come
to enjoy a pure intention to love God and his neighbor with all his wit-
ting powers. Still, in the actual course of implementing such an intention
he will inevitably be led to further discoveries of hitherto unwitting
faults, unrecognized and indeliberate reservations of his love. These
moments of self-awareness precipitate recurrent crises in the course of
Christian living. In the face of such self-discovery the man of faith repents
— or else he cancels his avowed intent and lapses from "perfection." Thus
repentance belongs to the fullness of faith quite as truly as it does to
faith at every other level.

114. *Letters*, IV, 155 f., 191, 208. See also Homily II ("On the Misery of Man")
for a similar distinction between deliberate and indeliberate action, conscious and
secret sins.
115. *Cf. Journal*, II, 536; III, 197–99, 527; IV, 33–34, 204–10, 246, 306, 425; V, 357,
389; VI, 43, 311; *Letters*, III, 111; IV, 222; V, 96; VI, 43–45, 264; *Works*, VII, 320 ff. See
also Elizabeth Richey's account of Wesley's own death, in *Journal*, VIII, 131–44, as a
sample of this concern, shared by all the dramatis personae (including Wesley!)
that a triumphant end should rightly crown a faithful life.

The Christian life, in Wesley's view, is empowered by the energy of grace: prevenient, saving, sanctifying, sacramental. Grace is always interpreted as something more than mere forensic pardon. Rather, it is experienced as actual influence — God's love, immanent and active in human life. Its prior initiative makes every human action a re-action; hence, it is "pre-venting." It is a function of God's mercy that is over all his works; hence, it is universal. It can be "resisted"; hence it is co-operant rather than irresistible. And since it is always mediated in and through various outward and visible signs, grace is typically sacramental. But since it is always God's grace, it is never at man's disposal. Thus, it cannot be sequestered by any sacerdotal authority; it can neither be dispensed nor withheld, appropriately, by any recourse to magic or priestly rites.

Wesley's doctrine of the means of grace [116] illustrates the fact that both the most and least original elements in his theology belong together. His doctrine of grace as preventing, co-operant and sanctifying is hardly to be found, in the form he developed it, anywhere else in the body of Anglican divinity. It is worth remarking, however, that in this area he was never drawn into controversy, and consequently was never moved to write anything of his own in exposition or defense of his sacramental theology. He was, therefore, able and content to rely on suitable texts from others for the instruction of his people in the meaning of baptism and the proper uses of the Eucharist.[117]

No summary review of Wesley's life and work can convey an adequate sense of constant vitality and cumulative force that comes with a sufficiently broad and sustained reading of Wesley himself. More than most theologians, he needs to be analyzed in terms of his historical context and the pressures that shaped his thought. His life and work make up a complex integer of action and reflection within the confusions and mutations of Georgian England. The following pages, one may hope, provide an opportunity for exploring his mind at firsthand, yet also in its unique setting and circumstances. What is here is only a sample — but such a sample as may make evident something of his total achievement and the import of the Christian traditions which converged in him.

116. Cf. his sermon, "The Means of Grace," Works, V, 185–201; Sermons (Sugden), I, 237–60.
117. See below, p. 317 ff.

PART ONE

❖

*The Theologian Self-Interpreted*

# Introduction to Part One

THROUGHOUT a compulsively busy life, Wesley kept a cool, clear eye on the passing scene and on himself as an actor in it. His *Journal* is a wide-angled mirror of his own life and of the eighteenth-century Britain in which he lived. It was a by-product of his habit of autobiography which had begun with his conversion in 1725: [1]

> It was in pursuance of an advice given by Bishop Taylor in his *Rules for Holy Living and Dying*, that about fifteen years ago I began to take a more exact account than I had done before of the manner wherein I spent my time, writing down how I had employed every hour. This I continued to do wherever I was, till the time of my leaving England. The variety of scenes which I then passed through induced me to transcribe from time to time the more material parts of my diary, adding here and there such little reflections as occurred to my mind. Of this journal thus occasionally compiled, the following is a short extract, it not being my design to relate all those particulars which I wrote for my own use only and which would answer no valuable end to others, however important they were to me.

For the span of two full generations he continued to keep a narrative record of the meaningful events of his life.[2] Besides his diaries, he usually carried about with him folded folio sheets on which he reported his doings and impressions. Along with this was his copious correspondence, which is also highly autobiographical. From the unpublished journal and these other sources he would from time to time produce and publish the so-called "Extracts of the Journal," such as the ones from which the following samples are taken. There were twenty-one of the "extracts"; together they constitute the published *Journal*. Thus it turns out that we have more autobiographical data from John Wesley than from any other figure in church history.

1. Preface to *An Extract of the Rev. Mr. John Wesley's Journal from His Embarking for Georgia to His Return to London* (Bristol, 1739). Cf. also *Journal*, I, 82–84.

2. Cf. *ibid.*, 3–77. See also V. H. H. Green, *The Young Mr. Wesley* (1961), v–vi *et passim*.

In point of fact, however, Wesley was far less introspective than the typical diarist; he was certainly no exhibitionist. What was "extracted" for the published *Journal* was chosen by the same selective principles that guided him in the rest of his writing and publishing: the practical needs of his people and the furtherance of the Revival. As the central figure in the movement, he appears in all its accounts as a matter of course. Nevertheless, it is very difficult to frame an authentic image of Wesley's psychological character. He was a candid and forthright man, yet also curiously reticent about his own personal feelings — as if his vital interest lay rather with events than with his own inner states. Generally speaking, therefore, the *Journal* is not an intimate document, as one may readily see by comparing it with Rousseau's *Confessions* or Pepys's *Diary*. Rather, it is the carefully constructed narrative of Wesley's involvement in what he regarded as an unparalleled renewal of essential Christianity.[3]

This knack of semidetached, participant observation makes it possible for his readers to see Wesley's ways of working at close range. In this Part One, then, we have selected samples of his self-understanding as a theologian, using the man himself as witness and interpreter. The selections are limited, but they are typical of the whole. Besides, the *Journal* is generally available to interested readers. Both of the following passages were written in the crucial year 1738. The first is a memorandum in which he rehearses the formation of his theological perspective from the beginning of his career to the end of his Georgia mission. The second is a reconstruction, after the fact, of the drama of "Aldersgate." His subsequent life story may be read in the remainder of the *Journal* and in the various summary accounts of the Revival and its progress which he prepared from time to time.[4]

With the excerpts from the *Journal* are also included a small but quite typical group of autobiographical letters. Each of them reveals Wesley as he saw himself in one or another of the significant phases of his work. They have all been published in the Telford edition.

---

3. Cf. *A Farther Appeal to Men of Reason and Religion*, Pt. III, *Works*, VIII, 205. See also below, pp. 41–69.

4. *The Nature, Design and General Rules of the United Societies* (1743); *A Farther Appeal to Men of Reason and Religion*, Pt. III (1745); *A Plain Account of the People Called Methodists* (1749); *A Short History of Methodism* (1765); the sermon "On Laying the Foundation of the New Chapel Near the City Road," London (1777) (*Works*, VII, 419–30); *A Brief Narrative of the Revival of Religion in Virginia* (1778); "A Short History of the People Called Methodists," published as an appendix to *A Concise Ecclesiastical History* (1781).

From his hundred and fifty-one sermons, it seemed sufficient to present, in this particular part, the preface which Wesley wrote for the whole collection of *Sermons on Several Occasions* (1746) — which is a brief explanation of his theological method in general — plus two self-interpreting sermons: "A Catholic Spirit," which characterizes his theological temper and aspiration; and "On God's Vineyard," his retrospective appraisal of the Revival after fifty years.

These pieces are intended to serve as a personal introduction of Wesley to the reader. As such, they form a sort of minimal background for the analysis and appraisal of the remainder of his essays in theological construction.

# AN EARLY SELF-ANALYSIS [1]

*Sun. 8* January 1738: — In the fullness of my heart, I wrote the following words: [2]

By the most infallible of proofs, inward feeling, I am convinced:

1. Of unbelief — having no such faith in Christ as will prevent my heart from being troubled, which it could not be if I believed in God and rightly believed also in [Christ];

1. *Cf. Journal*, I, 418–24. This passage is a conflation of a portion of the published *Journal* with a memorandum from the unpublished journal, first printed in Whitehead, *Life*, II, 53–57, and reprinted in Moore, *Life*, I, 198–202. The copy text used is Curnock's, corrected by that in the fifth edition (1775).

2. This entry is the comment of a frustrated man on his way home to report the failure of a mission. What makes it peculiarly significant is the theological memorandum in the middle, in which Wesley reviews his early theological development. This sketch goes with what else we know of his education at Oxford, and it outlines the rough shape of his basic theological perspective, both then and thereafter. In later years he was fond of insisting that the basic shape of his theology had been cast before the Revival began — although its accents and emphases had often changed under the heat and pressures of the Revival. For a careful survey of his reading at Oxford and in Georgia, *cf.* V. H. H. Green, *The Young Mr. Wesley* (1961), 305–19; Appendix I, "Wesley's Reading, 1725–34." Also, the diary entries in the *Journal* (I, 110–314), compared with his subsequent theological writing, strongly suggest that, whatever may be said of his "heart," Wesley's mind-set was already firmly settled before "Aldersgate" — centered in Scripture, guarded by The Homilies and Articles, interpreted by a wide array of patristic and "modern" authors, mostly Anglican (see below, p. 45 f.).

One crucial element, however, is poignantly lacking. Thus far, Wesley has "the faith of a servant," but lacks "the faith of a son." He has not yet experienced "the assurance of faith," which he had seen exemplified by the Moravians on board the *Simmonds* (*Journal*, I, 141–43), and which Peter Böhler would soon press upon him again (*ibid.*, 440–42, 454–62). The doctrine of justification by faith which he had received from his own tradition had not yet been fused with the assurance of faith which he had seen in the Moravians. For the time being, therefore, the well-furnished theologian is caught pathetically in the toils of discontent and self-reproach.

2. Of pride throughout my life past, inasmuch as I thought I had what I find I have not;

3. Of gross irrecollection, inasmuch as in a storm I cry to God every moment; in a calm, not;

4. Of levity and luxuriancy of spirit, recurring whenever the pressure is taken off; and appearing by my speaking words not tending to edify; but most by my manner of speaking of my enemies.

Lord, save, or I perish! Save me:

1. By such a faith as implies peace in life and in death;

2. By such humility as may fill my heart from this hour for ever, with a piercing, uninterrupted sense, *nihil est quod hactenus feci;* [3] having evidently built without a foundation;

3. By such a recollection as may cry to thee every moment, especially when all is calm. Give me faith, or I die; give me a lowly spirit: otherwise, *mihi non sit suave vivere;* [4]

4. By steadiness, seriousness, σεμνότης, sobriety of spirit; avoiding, as fire, every word that tendeth not to edifying, and never speaking of any who oppose me; or sin against God, without all my own sins set in array before my face.

This morning, after explaining these words of St. Paul, "I beseech you, brethren, by the mercies of God, that ye present your bodies a living sacrifice, holy, acceptable to God" [Rom. 12:1], I exhorted my fellow travellers with all my might to comply with the apostle's direction. But leaving them afterwards to themselves, the seriousness they showed at first soon vanished away.

On Monday the 9th, and the following days, I reflected much on that vain desire which had pursued me for so many years: of being in solitude in order to be a Christian. I have now, thought I, solitude enough. But am I therefore the nearer being a Christian? Not if Jesus Christ be the model of Christianity. I doubt, indeed, I am much nearer that mystery of Satan which some writers affect to call by that name. So near that I had probably sunk wholly into it had not the great mercy of God just now thrown me upon reading St. Cyprian's works.[5] "O my soul, come

---

3. [Au.] "I have done nothing hitherto." [Ed.] Cf. *The Imitation of Christ*, Bk. I, chap. 19, sec. i.

4. [Au.] "Let life be a burden to me." [Ed.] But cf. Terence, *The Self-Tormentor*, trans. by John Sargeaunt (Loeb ed., Cambridge, Mass., 1947), I, 164, l. 482.

5. For Wesley, Cyprian's practical piety represented the counterbalance to mys-

not thou into their secret" [Gen. 49:6]! "Stand thou in the good old paths" [cf. Jer. 6:16].

*Fri.* 13 — We had a thorough storm, which obliged us to shut all close, the sea breaking over the ship continually. I was at first afraid, but cried to God and was strengthened. Before ten I lay down, I bless God, without fear. About midnight we were awakened by a confused noise of seas and wind and men's voices, the like to which I had never heard before. The sound of the sea breaking over and against the sides of the ship I could compare to nothing but large cannon or American thunder. The rebounding, starting, quivering motion of the ship much resembled what is said of earthquakes. The captain was upon deck in an instant. But his men could not hear what he said. It blew a proper hurricane, which beginning at southwest, then went west, northwest, north, and, in a quarter of an hour, round by the east to the southwest again. At the same time the sea running (as they term it) mountains high, and that from many different points at once, the ship would not obey the helm; nor indeed could the steersman, through the violent rain, see the compass. So he was forced to let her run before the wind, and in half an hour the stress of the storm was over.

About noon the next day it ceased. But first I had resolved, God being my helper, not only to preach it to all but to apply the Word of God to every single soul in the ship; and if but one, yea, if not one of them will hear, I know "my labour is not in vain" [1 Cor. 15:58].

I no sooner executed this resolution than my spirit revived, so that from this day I had no more of that fearfulness and heaviness which before almost continually weighed me down. I am sensible [that] one who thinks the being *in orco*,[6] as they phrase it, an indispensable preparative for being a Christian, would say I had better have continued in that state, and that this unseasonable relief was a curse, not a blessing. Nay, but who art thou, O man, who, in favour of a wretched hypothesis, thus blasphemest the good gift of God? Hath not he himself said, "This also is the gift of God, if a man have power to rejoice in his labour"? Yea, God setteth his own seal to his weak endeavours, while he thus "answereth him in the joy of his heart" [cf. Eccles. 5:19–20].

*Tues.* 24. — We spoke with two ships, outward-bound, from whom

---

ticism, as his episcopal polity represented a counterweight to papal supremacy. *Cf.* his defense of Cyprian against Conyers Middleton, *Works*, X, 48–52.

6. "In the jaws of death"; (*orcus*, the infernal regions).

we had the welcome news of our wanting but one hundred and sixty leagues of the Land's End. My mind was now full of thought, part of which I writ down as follows:

I went to America to convert the Indians but, oh, who shall convert me? Who, what, is he that will deliver me from this evil heart of unbelief? I have a fair summer religion. I can talk well, nay, and believe myself, while no danger is near. But let death look me in the face, and my spirit is troubled. Nor can I say, "to die is gain" [Phil. 1:21].

> I have a sin of fear, that when I've spun
> My last thread, I shall perish on the shore! [7]

I think, verily, if the gospel be true, I am safe, for I not only have given and do give all my goods to feed the poor; I not only give my body to be burned, drowned, or whatever God shall appoint for me; but I follow after charity (though not as I ought, yet as I can) if haply I may attain it. I *now* believe the gospel is true. "I show my faith by my works" [Jas. 2:18] by staking my all upon it. I would do so again and again a thousand times, if the choice were still to make. Whoever sees me, sees I would be a Christian. Therefore "are my ways not like other men's ways" [*cf.* Is. 55:8]. Therefore, I have been, I am, I am content to be, a "by-word, a proverb of reproach" [*cf.* 2 Chron. 7:20]. But in a storm I think, "What if the gospel be not true? Then thou art of all men most foolish. For what has thou given up thy goods, thy ease, thy friends, thy reputation, thy country, thy life? For what art thou wandering over the face of the earth — a dream, a cunningly devised fable? Oh, who will deliver me from this fear of death? What shall I do? Where shall I fly from it? Should I fight against it by thinking or by not thinking of it?" A wise man advised me some time since, "Be still and go on." Perhaps this is best, to look upon it as my cross; when it comes, to let it humble me and quicken all my good resolutions, especially that of praying without ceasing, and at other times to take no thought about it, but quietly go on in the work of the Lord.

1. For many years [8] I have been tossed by various winds of doctrine. I asked long ago, "What must I do to be saved" [Acts 16:30]? The

7. John Donne, "A Hymn to God the Father," in *Poems*, Herbert J. C. Grierson, ed. (Oxford, 1912), II, 369–70. Cf. *ibid.*, I, 251–53, for evidence that this poem was frequently used as an anthem at St. Paul's.

8. The following six paragraphs were not in the published *Journal*. They were first printed in Whitehead, *Life*, II, 54–56.

Scripture answered, "Keep the commandments, believe, hope, love; follow after these tempers till thou hast fully attained (that is, till death) by all those outward works and means which God hath appointed, by walking as Christ walked."

2. I was early warned against laying, as the papists do, too much stress on outward works — or on a faith without works; which, as it does not include, so it will never lead to, true hope or charity. Nor am I sensible that to this hour I have laid too much stress on either; having from the very beginning valued both faith and the means of grace and good works, not on their own account, but as believing that God, who had appointed them, would by them bring me in due time to the mind that was in Christ [cf. Phil. 2:5].

3. But before God's time was come, I fell among some Lutheran and Calvinist authors, whose confused and indigested accounts magnified faith to such an amazing size that it quite hid all the rest of the commandments. I did not then see that this was the natural effect of their overgrown fear of popery, being so terrified with the cry of merit and good works that they plunged at once into the other extreme. In this labyrinth I was utterly lost, not being able to find out what the error was, nor yet to reconcile this uncouth hypothesis either with Scripture or common sense.

4. The English writers, such as Bishop Beveridge, Bishop Taylor and Mr. Nelson, a little relieved me from these well-meaning, wrong-headed Germans.[9] Their accounts of Christianity I could easily see to be, in the main, consistent both with reason and Scripture. Only when

---

9. The latter part of the seventeenth-century witnessed a vigorous renaissance of patristic studies. Its slogan, as expressed by Thomas Ken, was "the faith professed by the whole Church before the disunion of East and West." William Beveridge (1637–1708), Bishop of St. Asaph, was one of the most scholarly and influential of these "restorers of primitive piety." Wesley had read Beveridge's *Sermons* and *Codex* at Oxford, and had studied his Συνόδικον in Georgia; see above, p. 12. Jeremy Taylor (1613–1667), Bishop of Down and Connor, had already figured in Wesley's conversion of 1725 (see above, p. 7), and was perhaps the century's most eloquent spokesman for an evangelical catholicism both in faith and order. Robert Nelson (1656–1715) was a Nonjuring layman whose lifelong concern for a revival of true religion in the Church of England was in some ways parallel to Wesley's (*cf. Letters*, I, 136). Wesley's chief theological tutor was Bishop George Bull (*Defensor Fidei Nicaenae*), but he numbered amongst his mentors many of the other great spirits of his time: Thomas Ken, John Kettlewell, George Hickes, John Sharp, George Smalridge, and others. The common interest of all these men was their rootage in a Christian tradition more primitive (and, in their eyes, more truly catholic) than the corruptions of the "papists" or the exaggerations of the "protestants."

they interpreted Scripture in different ways I was often much at a loss. And again, there was one thing much insisted on in Scripture — the unity of the Church — which none of them, I thought, clearly explained or strongly inculcated.

5. But it was not long before Providence brought me to those who showed me a sure rule of interpreting Scripture, *viz.: "Consensus veterum: quod ab omnibus, quod ubique, quod semper creditum."* [10] At the same time they sufficiently insisted upon a due regard to the one Church at all times and in all places.

Nor was it long before I bent the bow too far the other way: [11]

1. By making antiquity a co-ordinate rather than subordinate rule with Scripture.

2. By admitting several doubtful writings as undoubted evidences of antiquity.

3. By extending antiquity too far, even to the middle or end of the fourth century.

4. By believing more practices to have been universal in the ancient Church than ever were so.

5. By not considering that the decrees of one provincial synod could bind only that province; and that the decrees of a general synod [bound] only those provinces whose representatives met therein.

6. By not considering that the most of those decrees were adapted to particular times and occasions; and consequently, when these occasions ceased, must cease to bind even those provinces.

These considerations insensibly stole upon me as I grew acquainted with the mystic writers,[12] whose noble descriptions of union with God

10. "The consensus of antiquity: that which has been believed by everyone, everywhere and always." This is Wesley's garbled version of the famous "Canon" of St. Vincent of Lérins, in his *Commonitorium*, Bk. I, sec. ii: *"In ipsa item catholica ecclesia magnopere curandum est ut id teneamus* QUOD UBIQUE, QUOD SEMPER, QUOD AB OMNIBUS CREDITUM EST" [PL, L, 640] "Moreover, in the catholic church herself, all possible care should be taken that we hold fast to what has been believed everywhere, always and by everybody"). Here and elsewhere, Wesley's ecclesiology bears a strong resemblance to that of John Jewel, 1522–1571; *cf.* W. M. Southgate, *John Jewel* (Cambridge, 1962), 192–216.

11. Influenced by such men as William Whiston (*cf. Primitive Christianity* [1711], III) who placed the so-called *Apostolical Constitutions* very nearly on a level with the four Gospels; *cf.* C. J. Abbey and J. H. Overton, *The English Church in the Eighteenth Century*, 202–03; see also 210.

12. In this category Wesley lumped William Law, Michael Molinos, Fénelon, Francke's *Nicodemus*, Gaston de Renty, François de Sales, Madame Guyon and the *Theologia Germanica. Cf.* Jean Orcibal, "Les Spirituels Français et Espagnols chez

and internal religion made everything else appear mean, flat and insipid. But, in truth, they made good works appear so, too; yea, and faith itself, and what not? These gave me an entire new view of religion — nothing like any I had before. But, alas! it was nothing like that religion which Christ and his apostles lived and taught.[13] I had a plenary dispensation from all the commands of God. The form ran thus: "Love is all; all the commands beside are only means of love; you must choose those which you feel are means to you and use them as long as they are so." Thus were all the bands burst at once. And though I could never fully come into this, nor contentedly omit what God enjoined, yet, I know not how, I fluctuated between obedience and disobedience. I had no heart, no vigour, no zeal in obeying; continually doubting whether I was right or wrong and never out of perplexities and entanglements. Nor can I at this hour give a distinct account how or when I came a little back toward the right way. Only, my present sense is this: all the other enemies of Christianity are triflers — the mystics are the most dangerous of its enemies. They stab it in the vitals, and its most serious professors are most likely to fall by them. May I praise him who hath snatched me out of this fire likewise,[14] by warning all others that it is set on fire of hell.

We went on with a small, fair wind till Thursday in the afternoon, and then, sounding, found a whitish sand at seventy-five fathoms; but having had no observation for several days, the captain began to be uneasy, fearing we might either get unawares into the Bristol Channel, or strike in the night on the rocks of Scilly.

*Sat. 28.* — was another cloudy day, but about ten in the morning (the wind continued southerly) the clouds began to fly just contrary to the wind and, to the surprise of us all, sank down under the sun, so that at noon we had an exact observation; and by this we found we were as well as we could desire, about eleven leagues south of Scilly.

*Sun. 29.* — We saw English land once more, which about noon appeared to be the Lizard Point. We ran by it with a fair wind, and at noon the next day made the west end of the Isle of Wight.

---

John Wesley . . . ," *Revue de l'Histoire des Religions*, 139 (1951), 50–109; Green, *Young Wesley*, 275–78; see also R. A. Knox, *Enthusiasm* . . . (Oxford, 1950), 432–35, 378–82.

13. *Cf. Letters*, I, 207–10; VI, 44, 281.

14. An echo of the "brand plucked out of the burning" of the Epworth rectory; see above, p. 6.

Here the wind turned against us and in the evening blew fresh; so that we expected (the tide being likewise strong against us) to be driven some leagues backward in the night: but in the morning, to our great surprise, we saw Beachy Head just before us, and found we had gone forwards near forty miles.

Toward evening was a calm, but in the night a strong north wind brought us safe into the Downs. The day before, Mr. Whitefield had sailed out, neither of us then knowing anything of the other. At four in the morning we took boat and in half an hour landed at Deal, it being Wednesday, February 1, the anniversary festival in Georgia for Mr. Oglethorpe's landing there.

It is now two years and almost four months since I left my native country in order to teach the Georgian Indians the nature of Christianity. But what have I learned myself in the meantime? Why, what I the least of all suspected, that I, who went to America to convert others, was never myself converted to God.[15] "I am not mad," though I thus speak; but "I speak the words of truth and soberness" [cf. Acts 26:25], if haply some of those who still "dream" may "awake" and see that as I am, so are they.

Are they read in philosophy? So was I. In ancient or modern tongues? So was I also. Are they versed in the science of divinity? I too have studied it many years. Can they talk fluently upon spiritual things? The very same could I do. Are they plenteous in alms? Behold, I gave all my goods to feed the poor. Do they give of their labour as well as of their substance? I have laboured more abundantly than they all. Are they willing to *suffer* for their brethren? I have thrown up my friends, reputation, ease, country; I have put my life in my hand, wandering into strange lands; I have given my body to be devoured by the deep, parched up with heat, consumed by toil and weariness or whatsoever God should please to bring upon me. But does all this (be it more or less, it matters not) make me acceptable to God? Does all I ever did or can *know, say, give, do*, or *suffer*, justify me in his sight? Yea, or the "constant use of all the means of grace" (which, nevertheless, is "meet, right and our bounden duty")? [16] Or that "I know nothing of myself" [1 Cor. 4:4]; that I am, as touching outward, moral righteousness, blameless? Or (to come closer yet) the having a "rational conviction" of all the truths of Christianity? Does all this give me a claim to the holy, heavenly, divine character of *a Christian?* By no means, if the oracles of God are true — if we are still to

15. Wesley later quietly corrected this: "I am not sure of this." *Works* (Pine), XXVI (errata).

16. *Cf.* the prayer before the Sanctus, Holy Communion, B.C.P.; see below, p. 65.

abide by "the law and the testimony" [cf. Is. 8:20]. All these things, though, when ennobled by faith in Christ,[17] they are holy and just and good; yet without it are dung and dross, [meet only to be purged away by "the fire that never shall be quenched" (Mk. 9:43, 45)].[18]

This, then, have I learned in the ends of the earth — that I "am fallen short of the glory of God" [Rom. 3:23]; that my whole heart is "altogether corrupt and abominable," and consequently my whole life, seeing it cannot be that an "evil tree" should "bring forth good fruit" [Mt. 7:17–19]; [that, alienated as I am from the life of God, I am "a child of wrath" (Eph. 2:3),[19] an heir of hell;] that my own works, my own sufferings, my own righteousness, are so far from reconciling me to an offended God, so far from making any atonement for the least of those sins (which "are more in number than the hairs of my head" [Ps. 40:12]), that the most specious of them need an atonement themselves, or they cannot abide his righteous judgment; that, "having the sentence of death" [cf. 2 Cor. 1:9] in my heart and having nothing *in* or *of* myself to plead, I have no hope but that of being justified freely, "through the redemption that is in Jesus" [Rom. 3:24]. I have no hope but that if I seek, I shall find Christ and "be found in him, not having my own righteousness, but that which is through the faith of Christ, the righteousness which is of God by faith" [Phil. 3:9].

If it be said that I have faith (for many such things have I heard from many miserable comforters), I answer: "So have the devils — a *sort* of faith — but still they are strangers to the covenant of promise. So the apostles had even at Cana in Galilee, when Jesus first 'manifested forth his glory' [cf. Jn. 2:11]; even then they, in a sort, 'believed on him,' but they had not then 'the faith that overcometh the world' [1 Jn. 5:4]. The faith I want [20] is 'a sure trust and confidence in God, that, through the merits of Christ, my sins are forgiven and I reconciled to the favour of God.' [21] I want that faith which St. Paul recommends to all the world, especially in his Epistle to the Romans, that faith which enables every one

17. Here, too, an added note of Wesley's: "I had even then the faith of a servant though not that of a son." Cf. "The Spirit of Bondage and of Adoption," *Sermons* (Sugden), I, 178–98, and below, Minutes of The Conferences, 1746 (May 13, Q. and A. 11).

18. Bracketed passage omitted in the last edition.

19. In 1774 Wesley added an erratum in contradiction to this: "I believe not." In the last edition, the bracketed portion of the sentence is omitted.

20. Wesley's marginal note: "the faith of a *son*."

21. Cf. "Of the True and Lively Faith," in The Homilies, IV, for this phrase and a development of the contrast between formally orthodox faith and the faith that saves.

that hath it to cry out: 'I live not; but Christ liveth in me; and the life which I now live, I live by faith in the Son of God, who loved me, and gave himself for me' [Gal. 2:20]. I want that faith which none can have without knowing that he hath it (though many *imagine* they have it, who have it not), for whosoever hath it, is 'freed from sin, the whole body of sin is destroyed' [Rom. 6:6, 7] in him; he is freed from fear, 'having peace with God through Christ and rejoicing in hope of the glory of God' [Rom. 5:1–2]. And he is freed from doubt, 'having the love of God shed abroad in his heart through the Holy Ghost which is given unto him' [Rom. 5:5], which 'Spirit itself beareth witness with his spirit that he is a child of God' " [Rom. 8:16].

# II

## THE ALDERSGATE EXPERIENCE[1]

*Editor's introduction.* This is easily the most familiar passage in all Wesley's writings. In the Methodist tradition, it stands as the equivalent of Paul's experience on the Damascus road and Augustine's conversion in the Milanese garden. It is often spoken of as Wesley's "conversion," as if before he had been a heathen or a hypocrite. There are, however, several odd angles to the story. The most striking is the fact that, apart from this one particular account of it, John Wesley makes just one other explicit reference to the Aldersgate event.[2] There are, of course, numerous references to 1738 as the year when the brothers Wesley gained the *assurance* of faith, and there are several instances, both before and after "Aldersgate," where Wesley denies that he was or ever had been a Christian.[3] But, save for an indirect reference to it in Charles Wesley's *Journal* for May 24, 1738, "Aldersgate" simply drops out of sight in the whole of Wesley's subsequent writings. Yet another curiosity is that before May 24 Wesley records moments of equal, or nearly equal, spiritual exaltation; and in the first six months after "Aldersgate" he reports numerous instances of acute spiritual depression, equal in severity to anything preceding.[4]

This account is, therefore, something of an anomaly. Wesley's first biographers took it as his actual conversion to authentic Christianity, and succeeding generations have made of it a pious legend. Moreover, it is plain that Wesley himself here goes to unaccustomed lengths to present the experience as a dramatic climax. Why, then, do we hear of it no more

1. *Journal,* I, 449–84; cf. *Works,* I, 90–106. Amendments or additions are taken from the errata of the text in *Works* (Pine), XXVI, and the edition published by G. Whitefield (1797).

2. In a letter to his brother Samuel, October 30, 1738 (shortly after he had encountered Jonathan Edwards — see above, pp. 15–16. *Letters,* I, 262.

3. *Cf.* below, p. 71 and p. 81.       4. *Cf. Journal,* September 1738 to April 1739.

thereafter? At least a partial explanation comes from the fact that the Aldersgate experience had occurred under Moravian auspices; so that, as "the rift with the Moravians" [5] worsened, Wesley was disinclined to repeat the story of their decisive influence upon his career. Moreover, "Aldersgate" had been followed by further crises of equal, or nearly equal, moment: the German journey, the impact of Edwards's *Faithful Narrative*, the rediscovery of the Homilies on salvation, faith and good works [6] and, finally, the unanticipated response to his revival preaching at Bristol. As his retrospect on this chapter of his autobiography lengthened, it is as if Wesley came to realize that "Aldersgate" had been *one* in a *series* of the "turning points" in his passage from don to missionary to evangelist. Add to this his vivid aversion to the Moravian antinomianism and the independent development of his own societies, and his subsequent silence about "Aldersgate" becomes intelligible.

There can be no doubt, however, that what this experience represented is crucial to an understanding of Wesley's thought. Since his first act of self-dedication to God in 1725, he had striven to pass from faith's threshold to its fullness without a present, personal assurance of God's active grace in his heart. He had fallen in with the prevailing Anglican view — as this had been expressed by Arthur Bedford and others — that distinguished between "the faith of adherence" (to the means of grace) and "the faith of assurance" (inner certitude), the latter being regarded merely as exceptional intensification of the former.[7] And yet, he had experienced many a doubt on this very score and had sought something more vivid and inward in the correlation of his faith and the inner feeling of the assurance of faith. His mother had taught him that the subjective essence of faith was pardon,[8] and he had read the same thing in the Homily "Of the Salvation of All Mankind." The especial role of Peter Böhler in this drama was to force Wesley to a crisis between faith as "hope" and faith as "assurance." "Aldersgate" was the outcome — the fusion of justifying faith with the "sure trust and confidence

---

5. See below, p. 353 ff.                    6. See below, p. 123 ff.

7. *Cf.* Arthur Bedford, *The Doctrine of Assurance* (1738): "The 'faith of adherence' alone is sufficient to bring a man to heaven. . . . And, therefore, to limit salvation to a particular degree of faith ['assurance'] is to destroy all those promises on which thousands of Christians have hitherto depended for their eternal comfort. . . . From which uncharitableness, false doctrine and heresy, Good Lord deliver us" (36–37)!

8. *Cf. Letters,* I, 19–20, 22; *cf.* Martin Schmidt, *John Wesley* (Frankfurt, 1953), 48–63.

in God that by the merits of Christ *his* sins are forgiven and *he* reconciled to the favour of God." [9] From 1738 to 1747 Wesley affirmed the
notion of "degrees in faith," but denied any such relativity in the matter
of assurance. In 1747 he began to distinguish between the objective and
subjective aspects of justification and assurance [10] — to stress both, but in
their correlation rather than identity.

The dramatic structure of the "Aldersgate" account is noteworthy.
Both Paul and Augustine are clearly in Wesley's mind. And yet the stage
of the drama is plainly the Revival itself — that unexpected uprush of
religious vitality into which Wesley had been plunged and whose leader
he was to be for the succeeding half-century.

❖   ❖   ❖   ❖

Sunday [April] 2 [1738] — Being Easter Day, I preached in our college
chapel on "The hour cometh, and now is, when the dead shall hear the
voice of the Son of God, and they that hear shall live" [Jn. 5:25]. I
preached in the afternoon, first at the Castle, and then at Carfax, on the
same words. I see the promise; but it is afar off.

Believing it would be better for me to wait for the accomplishment of
it in silence and retirement, on *Monday* the 3rd I complied with Mr.
Kinchin's desire, and went to him at Dummer, in Hampshire. But I was
not suffered to stay here long; being earnestly pressed to come up to
London, if it were only for a few days. Thither, therefore, I returned,
on *Tuesday* the 18th.

Saturday, [April] 22 [1738] — I met Peter Böhler once more. I had
now no objection to what he said of the nature of faith; viz. that it is (to
use the words of our Church). "a sure trust and confidence which a man
hath in God, that through the merits of Christ his sins are forgiven and
he reconciled to the favour of God." [1] Neither could I deny either the
happiness or holiness which he described as fruits of this living faith.
"The Spirit itself beareth witness with our spirit that we are the children
of God" [Rom. 8:16] and "He that believeth hath the witness in himself"
[*cf.* Acts 10:43] fully convinced me of the former; as "Whosoever is
born of God doth not commit sin" [1 Jn. 3:9] and "Whosover believeth
is born of God" [*cf.* 1 Jn. 5:1] did of the latter. But I could not comprehend what he spoke of "an instantaneous work." I could not understand

9. *Cf.* above, p. 29 n.                    10. *Cf. Letters,* II, 107–08.

1. See below, p. 128.

how this faith should be given in a moment: how a man could at once be thus turned from darkness to light, from sin and misery to righteousness and joy in the Holy Ghost. I searched the Scriptures again touching this very thing, particularly the Acts of the Apostles: but, to my utter astonishment, found scarce any instances there of other than *instantaneous* conversions; scarce any so slow as that of St. Paul, who was three days in the pangs of the new birth. I had but *one* retreat left; viz., "*Thus*, I grant, God wrought in the *first* ages of Christianity; but the times are changed. What reason have I to believe he works in the same manner now?"

But on Sunday the 23rd, I was beat out of this retreat, too, by the concurring evidence of several living witnesses; who testified God "had thus wrought in themselves," giving them in a moment such a faith in the blood of his Son as translated them out of darkness into light, out of sin and fear into holiness and happiness. Here ended my disputing. I could now only cry out, "Lord, help thou my unbelief!"

I asked Peter Böhler again whether I ought not to refrain from teaching others. He said, "No; do not hide in the earth the talent God hath given you." Accordingly, on Tuesday the 25th, I spoke clearly and fully at Blendon to Mr. Delamotte's family of the nature and fruits of faith. Mr. Broughton and my brother were there. Mr. Broughton's great objection was, he could never think that I had not faith, who had done and suffered such things.[2] My brother was very angry, and told me "I did not know what mischief I had done by talking thus." And, indeed, it did please God then to kindle a fire which I trust shall never be extinguished.

On Wednesday the 26th, the day fixed for my return to Oxford, I once more waited on the Trustees for Georgia; but, being straitened for time, was obliged to leave the papers for them which I had designed to give into their own hands. One of these was the instrument whereby they had appointed me minister of Savannah; which, having no more place in those parts, I thought it not right to keep any longer.

Peter Böhler walked with me a few miles, and exhorted me not to stop short of the grace of God. At Gerrard's Cross I plainly declared to those whom God gave into my hands the faith as it is in Jesus; as I did next day to a young man I overtook on the road, and in the evening to our friends at Oxford. A strange doctrine, which some, who did not care to contradict, yet knew not what to make of; but one or two, who

2. Footnote in the edition of 1797: "He was in the right. I certainly then had the faith of a servant, though not the faith of a son."

were thoroughly bruised by sin, willingly heard and received it gladly.

In the day or two following I was much confirmed in the "truth that is after godliness" [Tit. 1:1] by hearing the experiences of Mr. Hutchins, of Pembroke College, and Mrs. Fox; two living witnesses that God *can* (at least, if he *does* not always) give that faith whereof cometh salvation in a moment, as lightning falling from heaven.

Monday, May 1 [1738] — The return of my brother's illness obliged me again to hasten to London. In the evening I found him at James Hutton's, better as to his health than I expected, but strongly averse from what he called "the new faith."

This evening our little society [3] began, which afterwards met in Fetter Lane. Our fundamental rules were as follows:

In obedience to the command of God by St. James, and by the advice of Peter Böhler, it is agreed by us,

1. That we will meet together once a week to "confess our faults to one another, and pray one for another, that we may be healed" [Jas. 5:16].

2. That the persons so meeting be divided into several "bands," or little companies, none of them consisting of fewer than five or more than ten persons.

3. That every one in order speak as freely, plainly, and concisely as he can, the real state of his heart, with his several temptations and deliverances, since the last time of meeting.

4. That all the bands have a conference at eight every Wednesday evening, begun and ended with singing and prayer.

5. That any who desire to be admitted into the society be asked, "What are your reasons for desiring this? Will you be entirely open, using no kind of reserve? Have you any objection to any of our orders?" (which may then be read).

6. That when any new member is proposed, every one present speak clearly and freely whatever objection he has to him.

7. That those against whom no reasonable objection appears be, in order for their trial, formed into one or more distinct bands, and some person agreed on to assist them.

3. Another "religious society" of the sort described by Josiah Woodward (see above, p. 15. At first it was not a Moravian society (this came later), but was heavily influenced by the tone and temper of Moravian quietism. Note the echoes of this in the ensuing account. *Cf.* Daniel Benham, *Memoirs of James Hutton* (1856), and also *Journal*, I, 458.

8. That after two months' trial, if no objection then appear, they may be admitted into the society.

9. That every fourth Saturday be observed as a day of general intercession.

10. That, on the Sunday seven-night following, be a general love-feast from seven till ten in the evening.

11. That no particular member be allowed to act in anything contrary to any order of the society; and that if any persons, after being thrice admonished, do not conform thereto, they be not any longer esteemed as members.

*Wed.* 3 — My brother had a long and particular conversation with Peter Böhler. And it now pleased God to open his eyes; so that he also saw clearly what was the nature of that one true living faith whereby alone, "through grace, we are saved" [*cf.* Eph. 2:5].

*Thur.* 4 — Peter Böhler left London, in order to embark for Carolina. Oh what a work hath God begun, since his coming into England! Such an one as shall never come to an end till heaven and earth pass away.

*Friday* and *Saturday* I was at Blendon. They now "believed our report." Oh may "the arm of the Lord" be speedily "revealed unto them" [Is. 53:1]!

*Sun.* 7 — I preached at St. Lawrence's in the morning, and afterwards at St. Katherine Cree's church. I was enabled to speak strong words at both, and was therefore the less surprised at being informed I "was not to preach any more in either of those churches."

*Tues.* 9 — I preached at Great St. Helen's, to a very numerous congregation, on "he that spared not his own Son, but delivered him up for us all, how shall he not with him also freely give us all things" [Rom. 8:32]? my heart was now so enlarged to declare the love of God to all that were oppressed by the devil, that I did not wonder in the least when I was afterwards told, "Sir, you must preach here no more."

*Wed.* 10 — Mr. Stonehouse, vicar of Islington, was convinced of "the truth as it is in Jesus" [*cf.* Eph. 4:21]. From this time till Saturday 13th, I was sorrowful and very heavy; being neither able to read, nor meditate, nor sing, nor pray, nor do any thing. Yet I was a little refreshed by Peter Böhler's letter, which I insert in his own words:

*Charissime et Suavissime Frater,*
   Intentissimo amore te diligo, multum tui recordans in itinere meo, optando et precando ut quamprimum viscera misericordiae crucifixi

Jesu Christi, tui gratia jam ante sex mille annos commota, menti tuae appareant. Ut gustare et tunc videre possis, quam vehementer te Filius Dei amaverit et hucusque amet, et ut sic confidere possis in eo omni tempore, vitamque ejus in te et in carne tua sentire. Cave tibi a peccato incredulitatis, et si nondum vicisti illud, fac ut proximo die illud vincas, per sanguinem Jesu Christi. Ne differ, quaeso, credere tuum in Jesum Christum; sed potius promissionum ejus quae pertinent ad miserandos peccatores, coram facie ejus benigna sic mentionem fac, ut non aliter possit quam praestare tibi, quod multis aliis praestitit. O quam multus, quam magnus, [quam ineffabilis],[4] quam inexhaustus, est illius amor! Ille certe jamjam paratus est ad auxilium; et nihil potest illum offendere nisi incredulitas nostra. Crede igitur. Fratrem tuum Carolum et Hall, nomine meo saluta multum; et admonete vos invicem ad credendum, et tunc ad ambulandum coram facie Domini ἀκριβῶς, et ad pugnandum contra diabolum et mundum νομίμως, et ad crucifigendum et conculcandum peccatum omne sub pedibus nostris, quantum nobis datum est per gratiam secundi Adami, cujus vita excedit mortem prioris Adami, et cujus gratis antecellit corruptionem et damnationem prioris Adami.

Dominus tibi benedicat. Permane in fide, amore, doctrina, communione sanctorum; et breviter, in omni quod habemus in Novo Foedere. Ego sum et maneo,

*Tuus indignus Frater,*
*Petrus Böhler.*

*In Agris Southamptonianis,*
*Die 8vo Maii, 1738.*

I love you greatly [5] and think much of you in my journey, wishing and praying that the tender mercies of Jesus Christ the crucified, whose bowels were moved towards *you* more than six thousand years ago, may be manifested to your soul: that you may taste and then see how exceedingly the Son of God has loved you and loves you still; and that so you may continually trust in him, and feel his life in *yourself*. Beware of the sin of unbelief; and if you have not conquered it yet, see that you conquer it this very day, through the blood of Jesus Christ. Delay not, I beseech you, to believe in *your* Jesus Christ; but so put him in mind of his promises to poor sinners that he may not be able to refrain from doing for you what he hath done for so many others. Oh how great, how inexpressible, how unexhausted is his love! Surely he is now ready to help, and nothing can offend him but our unbelief. . . .[6]

The Lord bless you! Abide in faith, love, teaching, the commun-

4. Bracketed phrase omitted in the 1797 ed.
5. Wesley's translation and italics.
6. Wesley's translation here skips over the following paragraph:
"Wherefore have faith. Greet ardently in my name your brother Charles and

ion of saints and, briefly, in all which we have in the New Testament. I am [and remain],

> Your unworthy brother,
> Peter Böhler.

*Sun.* 14 — I preached in the morning at St. Ann's, Aldersgate, and in the afternoon at the Savoy chapel, free salvation by faith in the blood of Christ. I was quickly apprised that at St. Ann's likewise I am to preach no more.

So true did I find the words of a friend,[7] wrote to my brother about this time:

> I have seen upon this occasion, more than ever I could have imagined, how intolerable the doctrine of faith is to the mind of man and how peculiarly intolerable to *religious* men. One may say the most unchristian things, even down to deism; the most enthusiastic things, so they proceed but upon mental raptures, lights, and unions; the most severe things, even the whole rigour of ascetic mortification; and all this will be forgiven. But if you speak of faith in such a manner as makes Christ a saviour to the utmost, a most universal help and refuge; in such a manner as takes away glorying, but adds happiness to wretched man; as discovers a greater pollution in the best of us than we could before acknowledge, but brings a greater deliverance from it than we could before expect — if any one offers to talk at this rate, he shall be heard with the same abhorrence as if he was going to rob mankind of their salvation, their mediator, or their hopes of forgiveness. I am persuaded that a "Montanist" or a "Novatian," who from the height of his purity should look down with contempt upon poor sinners and exclude them from all mercy, would not be thought such an overthrower of the gospel as he who should learn from the author of it to be a friend of publicans and sinners, and to sit down upon the level with them as soon as they begin to repent.
>
> But this is not to be wondered at. For all *religious* people have such a quantity of righteousness, acquired by much painful exercise and formed at last into current habits, which is their wealth, both for this world and the next. Now, all other schemes of religion are either

---

[Westley] Hall. Exhort one another in believing and in your walking before God ἀκριβῶs ["carefully"; *cf.* Eph. 5:15] and in your warfare with the devil and the world, νομιμῶs ["lawfully"; *cf.* 2 Tim. 2:5] and in your being crucified [with Christ] and in trampling all sin under foot. We are able to do this, of course, only by the grace of the second Adam [Christ] whose life outweighs the first Adam's death and whose grace cancels the corruption and damnation brought on by the first Adam" [*cf.* 1 Cor. 15:45].

7. John Gambold; *cf.* Moore, *Life*, I, 220 f.

so complaisant as to tell them they are very rich and have enough to triumph in; or else only a little rough but friendly in the main, by telling them their riches are not yet sufficient, but by such arts of self-denial and mental refinement they may enlarge their stock. But the doctrine of faith is a downright robber. It takes away all this wealth, and only tells us it is deposited for us with somebody else, upon whose bounty we must live like mere beggars. Indeed, they that are truly beggars, vile and filthy sinners till very lately, may stoop to live in this dependent condition — it suits them well enough. But they who have long distinguished themselves from the herd of vicious wretches, or have even gone beyond *moral* men: for them to be told that they are either not so well, or but the same needy, impotent, insignificant vessels of mercy with the others — this is more shocking to reason than transubstantiation. For reason had rather resign its pretensions to judge what is bread or flesh than have this honour wrested from it — to be the architect of virtue and righteousness. But where am I running? My design was only to give you warning that, wherever you go, this "foolishness of preaching" will alienate hearts from you and open mouths against you.

*Fri.* 19. My brother had a second return of his pleurisy. A few of us spent Saturday night in prayer. The next day, being Whitsunday — after hearing Dr. Heylin [8] preach a truly Christian sermon (on "They were all filled with the Holy Ghost" [Acts 2:4]; "And so," said he, "may all you be, if it is not your own fault") and assisting him at the Holy Communion (his curate being taken ill in the church) — I received the surprising news that my brother had found rest to his soul.[9] His bodily strength returned also from that hour. "Who is so great a God as our God" [Ps. 77:13]?

I preached at St. John's, Wapping, at three, and at St. Benet's, Paul's Wharf, in the evening. At these churches, likewise, I am to preach no more. At St. Antholin's I preached on the Thursday following.

Monday, Tuesday, and Wednesday, I had continual sorrow and heaviness in my heart; something of which I described in the broken manner I was able, in the following letter to a friend:

Oh, why is it that so great, so wise, so holy a God will use such an instrument as me! Lord, "let the dead bury their dead" [Lk. 9:60]! But wilt thou send the dead to raise the dead? Yea, thou sendest whom thou *wilt send*, and showest mercy by whom thou *wilt* show

8. John Heylin, Rector of St. Mary-le-Strand, author of the *Theological Lectures* which Wesley used in preparing his *Explanatory Notes upon the New Testament.*
9. Cf. *The Journal of the Rev. Charles Wesley*, John Telford, ed. (1909), 138–61.

mercy! Amen! Be it then according to thy will! If thou speak the word, Judas shall cast out devils.

I feel what you say (though not enough), for I am under the same condemnation. I see that the whole law of God is holy, just and good [cf. Rom. 7:12]. I know every thought, every temper of my soul, ought to bear God's image and superscription. But how am I fallen from the glory of God! I feel that "I am sold under sin" [Rom. 7:14]. I know that I too deserve nothing but wrath, being full of all abominations; and having no good thing in me to atone for them, or to remove the wrath of God. All my works, my righteousness, my prayers, need an atonement for themselves; so that my mouth is stopped. I have nothing to plead. God is holy; I am unholy. God is a consuming fire; I am altogether a sinner, meet to be consumed.

Yet I hear a voice (and is it not the voice of God?) saying, "Believe and thou shalt be saved. He that believeth is passed from death unto life. God so loved the world that he gave his only begotten Son, that whosoever believeth in him should not perish but have everlasting life" [cf. Acts 16:31; 1 Jn. 3:14; Jn. 3:16].

Oh, let no one deceive us by vain words, as if we had already attained this faith! [10] By its fruits we shall know. Do we already feel "peace with God" and "joy in the Holy Ghost?" Does his "Spirit bear witness with our spirit that we are the children of God" [cf. Rom. 5:1, 14:17, 8:16]? Alas! with mine he does not. Nor, I fear, with yours. O thou Saviour of men, save us from trusting in anything but thee! Draw us after thee! Let us be emptied of ourselves, and then fill us "with all peace and joy in believing" [Rom. 15:13], and let nothing separate us from thy love in time or in eternity.


What occurred on *Wednesday* 24th, I think best to relate at large, after premising what may make it the better understood. Let him that cannot receive it ask the Father of lights [Jas. 1:17] that he would give more light both to him and me.

1. I believe, till I was about ten years old, I had not sinned away that "washing of the Holy Ghost" [cf. Tit. 3:5] which was given me in baptism, having been strictly educated and carefully taught that I could only be saved "by universal obedience, by keeping all the commandments of God" — in the meaning of which I was diligently instructed. And those instructions, so far as they respected outward duties and sins, I gladly received and often thought of. But all that was said to me of inward obedience or holiness I neither understood nor remembered. So that I was

10. Wesley's note, added later: "That is, the proper Christian faith."

indeed as ignorant of the true meaning of the law as I was of the gospel of Christ.

2. The next six or seven years were spent at school, where, outward restraints being removed, I was much more negligent than before, even of outward duties, and almost continually guilty of outward sins which I knew to be such, though they were not scandalous in the eye of the world. However, I still read the scriptures and said my prayers, morning and evening. And what I now hoped to be saved by was (1) "not being so bad as other people; (2) having still a kindness for religion"; and (3) "reading the Bible, going to church and saying my prayers."

3. Being removed to the university for five years, I still said my prayers both in public and in private, and read with the Scriptures several other books of religion, especially comments on the New Testament. Yet I had not all this while so much as a notion of inward holiness; nay, went on habitually, and for the most part very contentedly, in some or other known sin — indeed, with some intermissions and short struggles, especially before and after the Holy Communion, which I was obliged to receive thrice a year. I cannot well tell what I hoped to be saved by now, when I was continually sinning against that little light I had, unless by those transient fits of what many divines taught me to call "repentance."

4. When I was about twenty-two, my father pressed me to enter into Holy Orders. At the same time, the providence of God directing me to Kempis's *Christian Pattern*, I began to see that true religion was seated in the heart and that God's law extended to all our thoughts as well as words and actions. I was, however, very angry at Kempis for being *too strict*, though I read him only in Dean Stanhope's translation. Yet I had frequently much sensible comfort in reading him, such as I was an utter stranger to before. Meeting likewise with a religious friend, which I never had till now, I began to alter the whole form of my conversation, and to set in earnest upon "a new life." I set apart an hour or two a day for religious retirement. I communicated every week. I watched against all sin, whether in word or deed. I began to aim at, and pray for, inward holiness. So that now, *doing so much and living so good a life*, I doubted not but I was a good Christian.[11]

11. *Cf.* above, pp. 6–7. See also Wesley's alternative accounts of this same crisis in his letter to John Newton (below, pp. 79–80), in *A Plain Account of Christian Perfection*, Pt. II (*Works*, XI, 367 f.), and in the sermon "On Numbers 23:23" (*Works*, VII, 419–30), where he distinguishes between his not being a Christian and his sincere

5. Removing soon after to another college,[12] I executed a resolution which I was before convinced was of the utmost importance — shaking off at once all my trifling acquaintance. I began to see more and more the value of time. I applied myself closer to study. I watched more carefully against actual sins; I advised others to be religious, according to that scheme of religion by which I modelled my own life. But meeting now with Mr. Law's *Christian Perfection* and *Serious Call* [13] (although I was much offended at many parts of both, yet) they convinced me more than ever of the exceeding height and breadth and depth of the law of God. The light flowed in so mightily upon my soul that everything appeared in a new view. I cried to God for help and resolved not to prolong the time of obeying him, as I had never done before. And by my continued *endeavour to keep his whole law*, inward and outward, *to the utmost of my power*, I was persuaded that I should be accepted of him and that I was even then in a state of salvation.[14]

6. In 1730 I began visiting the prisons, assisting the poor and sick in town, and doing what other good I could by my presence or my little fortune to the bodies and souls of all men. To this end I abridged myself of all superfluities, and many that are called necessaries of life. I soon became a "by-word" for so doing, and I rejoiced that "my name was cast out as evil" [*cf*. Lk. 6:22]. The next spring I began observing the Wednesday and Friday fasts commonly observed in the ancient Church,[15] tasting no food till three in the afternoon. And now I knew not how to go any further. I diligently strove against all sin. I omitted no sort of self-denial which I thought lawful. I carefully used, both in public and private, all the means of grace at all opportunities. I omitted no occa-

---

desire to be one. The discrepancies in these various reports reflect the shifting lights in Wesley's memory of his life before Aldersgate. They underscore the fact that *this* particular account here was carefully reconstructed, not directly from the raw text of his diaries or journals, but as a dramatic story to be published *after* the Revival had begun and as an advertisement of his unique initiation into the experience of "assurance." Cf. *Journal*, II, 89 *et seq.*, for three separate memoranda on whether or not he was a "Christian" during this period. See also the letter to James Hervey, below, p. 70 f.

12. See above, p. 8 f.
13. The first of these was published in 1726; the second, in 1728.
14. Wesley's footnote in the 1797 ed.: "And I believe I was."
15. Note that William Beveridge, in Sermon XXXIX (1720) recommends "fasting or abstinence only one day every week, to wit, Friday, which has always been observed in the church." This more rigorous schedule of "the stations" was commended to Wesley by Robert Nelson (*Festivals and Fasts* [1704]).

sion of doing good. I for that reason suffered evil. And all this I knew to be nothing unless as it was directed toward inward holiness. Accordingly this, the image of God, was what I aimed at in all, by doing his will, not my own. Yet when, after continuing some years in this course, I apprehended myself to be near death, I could not find that all this gave me any comfort or any assurance of acceptance with God. At this I was then not a little surprised, not imagining I had been all this time building on the sand,[16] nor considering that "other foundation can no man lay than that which is laid by God, even Christ Jesus" [1 Cor. 3:11].

7. Soon after, a contemplative man [17] convinced me still more than I was convinced before that outward works are nothing, being alone; and in several conversations instructed me how to pursue inward holiness, or a union of the soul with God. But even of his instructions (though I then received them as the words of God) I cannot but now observe (1) that he spoke so incautiously against *trusting* in *outward works* that he discouraged me from *doing* them at all; (2) that he recommended (as it were, to supply what was wanting in them) *mental prayer* and the like exercises, as the most effectual means of purifying the soul and uniting it with God. Now these were, in truth, as much *my own works* as visiting the sick or clothing the naked; and the "union with God" thus pursued was as really *my own righteousness* as any I had before pursued under another name.

8. In this *refined* way of trusting to my own works and my own righteousness (so zealously inculcated by the mystic writers),[18] I dragged on heavily, finding no comfort or help therein till the time of my leaving England. On shipboard, however, I was again active in outward works, where it pleased God of his free mercy to give me twenty-six of the Moravian brethren for companions, who endeavoured to show me a more excellent way [*cf.* 1 Cor. 12:31]. But I understood it not at first. I was too learned and too wise, so that it seemed foolishness unto me. And I continued preaching and following after, and trusting in that righteousness whereby no flesh can be justified.

9. All the time I was at Savannah I was thus "beating the air" [*cf.* 1 Cor.

16. Another amendment by Wesley here: "Not so. I was right, as far as I went."

17. Probably Joseph Hoole, rector of Haxey, near Epworth; *cf.* Moore, *Life*, I, 104.

18. In the second ed. (1743), at the height of the struggle with the Moravians (see below, p. 353 ff.), there is a denunciation of the mystic writers which was dropped from all editions after 1765: "whom I declare in my cool judgment and in the presence of the Most High God, I believe to be the one great anti-Christ."

9:26]. Being ignorant of the righteousness of Christ, which, by a living faith in him, bringeth salvation "to every one that believeth" [Rom. 1:16], I sought to establish my own righteousness, and so laboured in the fire all my days. I was now properly "under the law" [*cf.* Rom. 6:14]. I knew that "the law" of God was "spiritual; I consented to it that it was good." Yea, "I delighted in it after the inner man." Yet was I "carnal, sold under sin." Every day was I constrained to cry out, "What I do, I allow not: for what I would, I do not; but what I hate, that I do. To will is indeed present with me; but how to perform that which is good, I find not. For the good which I would, I do not, but the evil which I would not, that I do. I find a law that when I would do good, evil is present with me, even the law in my members, warring against the law of my mind and still bringing me into captivity to the law of sin" [*cf.* Rom. 7:14–23].

10. In this [vile, abject] state [of bondage to sin] [19] I was indeed fighting continually, but not conquering. Before, I had willingly served sin; now it was unwillingly, but still I served it. I fell and rose and fell again. [20] Sometimes I was overcome and in heaviness: sometimes I overcame and was in joy. For as in the former state I had some foretastes of the terrors of the law, so had I in this of the comforts of the gospel. During this whole struggle between nature and grace which had now continued above ten years, I had many remarkable returns to prayer, especially when I was in trouble. I had many sensible comforts, which are indeed no other than short anticipations of the life of faith. But I was still "under the law," not "under grace" (the state most who are called Christians are content to live and die in), for I was only "striving with," not "freed from, sin" [*cf.* Heb. 12:4; Rom. 6:14]. Neither had I "the witness of the Spirit with my spirit" [*cf.* Rom. 8:16], and indeed could not, for I "sought it not by faith, but as it were by the works of the law" [Rom. 9:32].

11. In my return to England, January 1738, being in imminent danger of death and very uneasy on that account, [21] I was strongly convinced that the cause of that uneasiness was unbelief and that the gaining a true, living faith was the "one thing needful" [*cf.* Lk. 10:42] for me. But still I fixed not this faith on its right object: I meant only faith in God, not faith in or through Christ. Again, I knew not that I was *wholly void of this faith* but only thought *I had not enough* of it. So that when Peter

19. Bracketed words omitted in last edition.
20. *Cf.* Augustine, *Confessions*, Bk. III, chap. xi, sec. 20.
21. See above, p. 43 f.

Böhler, whom God prepared for me as soon as I came to London, affirmed of true faith in Christ (which is but one) that it had those two fruits inseparably attending it, "dominion over sin, and constant peace from a sense of forgiveness," I was quite amazed and looked upon it as a new gospel. If this was so, it was clear I had not faith. But I was not willing to be convinced of this. Therefore I disputed with all my might and laboured to prove that faith might be where these were not, especially where the sense of forgiveness was not; for all the Scriptures relating to this I had been long since taught to construe away and to call all Presbyterians who spoke otherwise. Besides, I well saw no one could, in the nature of things, have such a sense of forgiveness and not *feel* it. But I felt it not. If, then, there was no faith without this,[22] all my pretensions to faith dropped at once.

12. When I met Peter Böhler again, he consented to put the dispute upon the issue which I desired, namely, Scripture and experience. I first consulted the Scripture. But when I set aside the glosses of men and simply considered the words of God, comparing them together, endeavouring to illustrate the obscure by the plainer passages, I found they all made against me and was forced to retreat to my last hold, "that experience would never agree with the *literal interpretation* of those Scriptures. Nor could I therefore allow it to be true, till I found some living witnesses of it." He replied he could show me such at any time; if I desired it, the next day. And, accordingly, the next day he came again with three others, all of whom testified of their own personal experience that a true living faith in Christ is inseparable from a sense of pardon for all past, and freedom from all present, sins. They added with one mouth that this faith was the gift, the free gift of God, and that he would surely bestow it upon every soul who earnestly and perseveringly sought it. I was now thoroughly convinced and, by the grace of God, I resolved to seek it unto the end, first, by absolutely renouncing all dependence, in whole or in part, upon *my own* works or righteousness — on which I had really grounded my hope of salvation, though I knew it not, from my youth up; second, by adding to "the constant use of all the 'other' means of grace," [23] continual prayer for this very thing — justifying, saving faith, a full reliance on the blood of Christ shed for *me*, a trust in him, as *my* Christ, as *my* sole justification, sanctification, and redemption.[24]

---

22. Wesley's later amendment (1747): "There is no *Christian* faith without it."
23. See above, p. 48.
24. This is the doctrine of The Homilies brought home and made intensely personal.

13. I continued thus to seek it (though with strange indifference, dullness and coldness and unusually frequent relapses into sin) till *Wednesday*,
*May* 24. I think it was about five this morning, that I opened my Testament on those words, τὰ μέγιστα ἡμῖν καὶ τίμια ἐπαγγέλματα δεδώρηται, ἵνα
[διὰ τούτων] γένησθε θείας κοινωνοὶ φύσεως, "There are given unto us exceeding great and precious promises, even that ye should be partakers of the
divine nature.²⁵ Just as I went out, I opened it again on those words,
"Thou art not far from the kingdom of God" [Mk. 12:34]. In the afternoon I was asked to go to St. Paul's. The anthem was "Out of the deep
have I called unto thee, O Lord: Lord, hear my voice. O let thine ears
consider well the voice of my complaint. If thou, Lord, will be extreme
to mark what is done amiss, O Lord, who may abide it? For there is
mercy with thee; therefore shalt thou be feared. O Israel, trust in the
Lord, for with the Lord there is mercy and with him is plenteous redemption. And he shall redeem Israel from all his sins." ²⁶

14. In the evening, I went very unwillingly to a society in Aldersgate
Street,²⁷ where one was reading Luther's Preface to the Epistle to the
Romans.²⁸ About a quarter before nine, while he was describing the
change which God works in the heart through faith in Christ, I felt my
heart strangely warmed. I felt I did trust in Christ, Christ alone for salvation; and an assurance was given me that he had taken away *my* sins, even
*mine*, and saved *me* from the law of sin and death.

15. I began to pray with all my might for those who had in a more
especial manner despitefully used me and persecuted me. I then testified
openly to all there what I now first felt in my heart. But it was not long
before the enemy suggested, "This cannot be faith, for where is thy

It became one of the chief distinguishing marks of Wesley's preaching. *Cf.* "The
Scripture Way of Salvation," Pt. III, sec. 18; "Justification by Faith" (Pt. IV, sec. 2),
"The Witness of the Spirit" (Pt. I, sec. i, par. 11), "The Marks of the New Birth" (Pt.
II, sec. 4), "The Nature of Enthusiasm" (sec. 35), *Sermons* (Sugden), II, 442–60; I, 112–
30, 199–218, 280–97; II, 84–103, respectively.

25. [Au.] 2 Pet. 1:4.

26. Ps. 130, *De profundis*, from the B.C.P. Psalter. Wesley habitually quoted the
Psalms from this version.

27. This was a society more heavily dominated by the Moravians than Fetter Lane;
*cf. Journal*, I, 458–59.

28. *Cf.* J. T. McNeill, "Luther at Aldersgate," in *London Quarterly and Holborn
Review* (1939), 200–17, for an analysis of the text of Luther here referred to — viz.
the 1632 edition of the English translation of Luther's *Preface to Romans*, done by
one W. W. (William Wilkinson?) first published in 1594. *Cf.* C. M. Jacob's translation
of the "Prefaces," in *Works of Martin Luther* (Philadelphia, 1932), VI, 447–62, and
especially 452, 456–57.

joy?" Then was I taught that "peace and victory over sin are essential to faith in the Captain of our salvation but that, as to the transports of joy — that usually attend the beginning of it especially in those who have mourned deeply — God sometimes giveth, sometimes withholdest them, according to the counsels of his own will."

16. After my return home, I was much buffeted with temptations, but cried out and they fled away. They returned again and again. I as often lifted up my eyes and he "sent me help from his holy place" [*cf.* Ps. 20:2, B.C.P.]. And herein I found [in what] the difference between this and my former state chiefly consisted. I was striving, yea, fighting with all my might under the law, as well as under grace. But then I was sometimes, if not often, conquered; now, I was always conqueror.

17. *Thur.* May 25. — The moment I awaked, "Jesus, Master," was in my heart and in my mouth; and I found all my strength lay in keeping my eye fixed upon him, and my soul waiting on him continually. Being again at St. Paul's in the afternoon, I could taste the good word of God in the anthem, which began, "My song shall be always of the loving-kindness of the Lord: with my mouth will I ever be showing forth thy truth from one generation to another" [Ps. 89:1, B.C.P.]. Yet the enemy injected a fear, "If thou dost believe, why is there not a more sensible change?" I answered (yet not I): "That I know not. But this I know, I have *now peace with* God. And I *sin not today*, and Jesus my Master has forbid me to take thought for the morrow."

18. "But is not *any* sort of *fear* (continued the tempter) a proof that thou dost not believe?" I desired my Master to answer for me, and opened his book upon those words of St. Paul, "Without were fightings, within were fears" [2 Cor. 7:5]. Then, inferred I, well may fears be within *me*, but I must go on and tread them under my feet.

*Fri.* May 26. — My soul continued in peace, but yet in heaviness because of manifold temptations. I asked Mr. Töltschig, the Moravian, what to do. He said, "You must not fight with them as you did before, but flee from them the moment they appear and take shelter in the wounds of Jesus." The same I learned also from the afternoon anthem, which was, "My soul truly waiteth still upon God: for of him cometh my salvation; he verily is my strength and my salvation, he is my defence, so that I shall not greatly fall. . . . O put your trust in him alway, ye people; pour out your hearts before him, for God is our hope" [Ps. 62:1, 2, 8, B.C.P.].

*Sat.* 27. — Believing one reason of my want of joy was want of time for prayer, I resolved to do no business till I went to church in the morning, but to continue pouring out my heart before him. And this day my spirit was enlarged so that, though I was now also assaulted by many temptations, I was more than conqueror, gaining more power thereby to trust and to rejoice in God my Saviour.

*Sun.* 28. — I waked in peace but not in joy. In the same even, quiet state I was till the evening, when I was roughly attacked in a large company as an enthusiast, a seducer and a setter-forth of new doctrines. By the blessing of God, I was not moved to anger, but after a calm and short reply went away, though not with so tender a concern as was due to those who were seeking death in the error of their life.

This day I preached in the morning at St. George's, Bloomsbury, on "This is the victory that overcometh the world, even our faith" [1 Jn. 5:4], and in the afternoon at the chapel in Long Acre on God's justifying the ungodly; the last time (I understand) I am to preach at either. "Not as I will, but as thou wilt" [Mt. 26:39].

*Mon.* 29. — I set out for Dummer with Mr. Wolf, one of the first-fruits of Peter Böhler's ministry in England. I was much strengthened by the grace of God in him: yet was his state so far above mine that I was often tempted to doubt whether we had one faith. But without much reasoning about it, I held here: "Though his be *strong* and mine *weak*, yet that God hath given *some degree* of faith even to me, I know by its fruits. For I have *constant peace*, not one uneasy thought. And I have *freedom from sin*, not one unholy desire."

Yet on Wednesday did I grieve the Spirit of God not only by not "watching unto prayer" [*cf.* 1 Pet. 4:7] but likewise by speaking with sharpness instead of tender love of one that was not sound in the faith. Immediately God hid his face and I was troubled, and in this heaviness I continued till the next morning, June 1, when it pleased God, while I was exhorting another, to give comfort to *my* soul and, after I had spent some time in prayer, to direct me to those gracious words, "Having therefore boldness to enter into the holiest by the blood of Jesus, let us draw near with a true heart in full assurance of faith. Let us hold fast the profession of our faith without wavering (for he is faithful that promised), and let us consider one another to provoke unto love and to good works" [Heb. 10:22–24].

Saturday, June 3. — I was so strongly assaulted by one of my old enemies that I had scarce strength to open my lips or even to look up for help. But after I had prayed faintly as I could, the temptation vanished away.

*Sun.* 4. — Was indeed a feast-day. For from the time of my rising till past one in the afternoon, I was praying, reading the Scriptures, singing praise, or calling sinners to repentance. All these days I scarce remember to have opened the Testament but upon some great and precious promise [*cf.* 2 Pet. 1:4]. And I saw more than ever that the gospel is in truth but one great promise from the beginning of it to the end.

*Tues.* 6. — I had still more comfort and peace and joy, on which, I fear, I began to presume. For in the evening I received a letter from Oxford which threw me into much perplexity. It was asserted therein that no doubting could consist with the least degree of true faith; that whoever at any time felt any doubt or fear was not "weak in faith" but had *no faith* at all; and that none hath any faith till the law of the Spirit of life has made him *wholly* free from the law of sin and death.[29]

Begging of God to direct me, I opened my Testament on 1 Cor. 3:1 &c., where St. Paul speaks of those whom he terms "babes in Christ," who were "not able to bear strong meat," nay (in a sense), "carnal"; to whom nevertheless he says, "Ye are God's building, ye are the temple of God." Surely, then, these men had *some degree* of faith; though, it is plain, their faith was "weak."

After some hours spent in the Scripture and prayer, I was much comforted. Yet I felt a kind of soreness in my heart, so that I found my wound was not fully healed. O God, save thou me, and all that are "weak in the faith," from "doubtful disputations" [*cf.* Rom. 14:1].

*Wed.* June 7. — I determined, if God should permit, to retire for a short time into Germany. I had fully proposed before I left Georgia so to do, if it should please God to bring me back to Europe. And I now clearly saw the time was come. My weak mind could not bear to be thus sawn asunder. And I hoped the conversing with those holy men who were themselves living witnesses of the full power of faith and yet able to bear with those that are weak, would be a means, under God, of so establishing my soul, that I might "go on from faith to faith and from strength to strength."[30]

29. This was the Moravian contention that finally split the Wesleys from them. See below, pp. 356–58

30. Ps. 84:7; Rom. 1:17. Since 1722 a branch of *Unitas Fratrum* under the leadership of Count Ludwig von Zinzendorf had maintained strongly communal pietistic centers at Herrnhut and Marienborn. *Cf.* Wesley's version of his visit in *Journal*, June 26 to August 28, 1738. But for a Moravian version, see Daniel Benham, *Memoirs of James Hutton* (1856), 40 — a very different account of Wesley's experiences in Germany.

# III

## SELF-IMAGES IN THE LETTERS

*Editor's introduction.* The Telford edition of the *Letters* runs to eight volumes and contains 2,670 letters from Wesley to all sorts and conditions of men — and women. But even this collection was incomplete; materials are now in hand for a ninth volume, which is now being edited by Professor Frank Baker. The single subject of the vast majority of this immense correspondence is the business of the Revival, as this is focused in administrative or pastoral problems, in theological controversy or instruction for his societies and their members. The following samples from so large a collection were selected to illustrate the way in which Wesley regarded himself in his role as leader of the Methodists. Each contains a partial self-portrait, drawn against the background of a specific circumstance or crisis.

❖ ❖ ❖ ❖

## *To James Hervey* [1]

London, March 20, 1739

Dear Sir:

The best return I can make for the kind freedom you use is to use the same to you. O may the God whom we serve sanctify it to us both and teach us the whole truth as it is in Jesus!

---

1. *Journal*, II, 216–18; *Letters*, I, 284–87. James Hervey had been a pupil of Wesley's and one of the original Oxford Methodists. He was later to move over to the Calvinist wing of the Revival and to become one of Wesley's theological critics. At the time of this letter, however, he had recently settled into his first parish — as curate at Weston Favel — and had evidently become alarmed about Wesley's "unusual manner of . . . ministering" and the inevitable tensions this was already beginning to generate. Here, then, was an early foreboding that Wesley was capable

You say you cannot reconcile some parts of my behaviour with the character I have long supported. No, nor ever will. Therefore I have disclaimed that character on every possible occasion. I told all in our ship, all at Savannah, all at Frederica, and that over and over in express terms: "I am not a Christian; I only follow after if haply I may attain it." When they urged my works and self-denial, I answered short, "Though I give all my goods to feed the poor, and my body to be burned, I am nothing: for I have not charity; I do not love God with all my heart." If they added, "Nay, but you could not preach as you do, if you was not a Christian," I again confronted them with St. Paul, "Though I speak with the tongue of men and angels, and have no charity, I am nothing" [cf. 1 Cor. 13:1-3].

Most earnestly, therefore, both in public and private, did I inculcate this: "Be not ye shaken, however I may fall; for the foundation standeth sure" [cf. 2 Tim. 2:19].

If you ask on what principle, then, I acted, it was this: a desire to be a Christian; and a conviction that whatever I judge conducive thereto, that I am bound to do; wherever I judge I can best answer this end, thither it is my duty to go. On this principle, I set out for America; on this I visited the Moravian Church; and on the same am I ready now (God being my helper) to go to Abyssinia or China, or whithersoever it shall please God by this conviction to call me.

As to your advice that I should settle in [Lincoln] college, I have no business there, having now no office and no pupils. And whether the other branch of your proposal be expedient for me (viz. "to accept of a cure of souls"), it will be time enough to consider when one is offered to me.

But in the meantime you think I ought to "sit still" because otherwise I should invade another's office if I interfered with other people's business and intermeddled with souls that did not belong to me. You accordingly ask, "How is it that I assemble Christians who are none of my charge, to

---

of leading a group of his disciples into dissent. In reply, and *before* the actual launching of his career as successful evangelist at Bristol, Wesley develops his concept of a unique calling as *minister extraordinarius*, affirms his freedom to preach wherever he found a responsive hearing and justifies his view of "the world" as his "parish." (See above, pp. 19-21.) Considering its date and its total context, this is one of the most vivid apertures on Wesley's self-understanding that we have. For Wesley's part in a subsequent chapter of their relationship (in connection with Hervey's *Theron and Aspasio* [1755] and the ensuing controversy), see *Works*, X, 298-306, 317-57.

sing psalms and pray and hear the Scriptures expounded?" and think it hard to justify doing this in other men's parishes upon "catholic principles."

Permit me to speak plainly. If by "catholic principles" you mean any other than scriptural, they weigh nothing with *me*. I allow no other rule, whether of faith or practice, than the Holy Scriptures. But on scriptural principles I do not think it hard to justify what I do. God in Scripture commands me, according to my power, to instruct the ignorant, reform the wicked, confirm the virtuous. Man forbids me to do this in another's parish; that is, in effect, [forbids me] to do it at all, seeing I have now no parish of my own, nor probably ever shall. Whom, then, shall I hear, God or man? "If it be just to obey man rather than God, judge you. A dispensation of the gospel is committed to me; and woe is me if I preach not the gospel" [*cf.* Acts 4:19; 1 Cor. 9:16–17]. But where shall I preach it, upon the principles you mention? Why, not in Europe, Asia, Africa, or America; not in any of the Christian parts, at least, of the habitable earth; for all of these are, after a sort, divided into parishes. If it be said, "Go back, then, to the heathens from whence you came," nay, but neither could I now (on your principles) preach to them, for all the heathens in Georgia belong to the parish either of Savannah or Frederica.

Suffer me now to tell you *my* principles in this matter. I look upon *all the world* as *my parish* [2] — thus far I mean, that in whatever part of it I am, I judge it meet, right and my bounden duty [3] to declare unto all that are willing to hear me the glad tidings of salvation. This is the work which I know God has called me to, and sure I am that his blessing attends it. Great encouragement have I, therefore, to be faithful in fulfilling the work he hath given me to do. His servant I am; and, as such, am employed (glory be to him) day and night in his service! I am employed according to the plain direction of his word — "as I have opportunity, doing good unto all men" [*cf.* Gal. 6:10]. And his providence clearly concurs with his word, which has disengaged me from all things else, that I might singly attend on this very thing "and go about doing good" [*cf.* Acts 10:38].

2. See above, p. 21. *Cf.* his discussion of the jurisdiction of his orders with Bishop Potter, who had ordained him (*Letters*, I, 182; IV, 149); see also Whitehead's report of Wesley's exchange with Bishop Butler in *Life*, II, 118–20); *cf. Works*, VIII, 117–19; XIII, 235–38.

3. *Cf.* the prayer following the *Sursum Corda* in the Order of Holy Communion (B.C.P.).

If you ask, "How can this be? How can one do good, of whom 'men say all manner of evil' " [cf. Mt. 5:11]? I will put you in mind (though you once knew this — yea, and much established me in that great truth), the more evil men say of me for my Lord's sake, the more good will he do by me. That it is "for his sake" I know, and he knoweth, and the event agreeth thereto; for he mightily confirms the words I speak, by the Holy Ghost given unto those that hear them. O my friend, my heart is moved toward you. I fear you have herein "made shipwreck of the faith" [cf. 1 Tim. 1:19]; I fear "Satan, transformed into an angel of light" [cf. 2 Cor. 11:14], hath assaulted you and prevailed also. I fear that [the] offspring of hell, *worldly* or *mystic prudence*, has drawn you away from the simplicity of the gospel. How else could you ever conceive that the being reviled and "hated of all men" [cf. Mt. 10:22] should make us less fit for our Master's service? How else could you ever think of "saving yourself and them that hear you" [cf. 1 Tim. 4:16] without being "the filth and offscouring of the world" [cf. 1 Cor. 4:13]. To this hour is this Scripture true. And I therein rejoice — yea, and *will* rejoice. Blessed be God, I enjoy the reproach of Christ! O may you also be vile, exceeding vile, for his sake! God forbid that you should ever be other than *generally* scandalous; I had almost said *universally*. If any man tell you there is a new way of following Christ, "he is a liar, and the truth is not in him" [1 Jn. 2:4]. I am, . . .

## To Samuel Walker [1]

Bristol, September 24, 1755

Reverend Dear Sir,

1. You greatly oblige me by speaking your thoughts so freely, and the more by giving me hopes of seeing your further sentiments on so nice

1. Cf. *Letters*, III, 144-47; cf. Wesley Historical Society *Proceedings*, XXVI, 84. Samuel Walker of Truro in Cornwall was another of several evangelical priests of the Church of England whose ministry was in many ways parallel to Wesley's but who sternly deplored any move that might lead to separation from the Church. Wesley regarded him warmly as colleague and ally, but was prepared to resist his warnings that his societies were necessarily headed into dissent. The date of this letter should be noted. It falls directly after the first annual conference in which the "separatists" among Wesley's preachers had made a massive push to carry the Methodists into outright separation (see above, pp. 21-22). It was from this date that Charles Wesley — as staunch a churchman as Walker — began to pull back from

and important an affair. I did not delay one day to follow your advice
with regard to Mr. Adam, but sent him by the very next post a copy of
those papers; although I am satisfied already as to the publishing them
and have laid aside that design, the reasons you urge against the expediency of it being abundantly sufficient. But you seem a little to misapprehend what we speak of hearing predestinarian preachers. We find by long
experience that this is "deadly poison," not *in itself*, but to *the members
of our Societies*. This we know to be an unquestionable truth; and it was
a truth necessary to be observed, nay, and strongly insisted on (though
without any design of bearing hard on any particular person) when many
were enlarging on the "poisonous doctrines" which they heard at many
of their parish churches.

2. All that you say concerning the inexpediency of a separation from
the Church I readily allow; as likewise that the first and main question
must be, "Is it lawful to separate?" Accordingly, this was debated first,
and that at large, in seven or eight long conversations.[2] And it was then
only, when we could not agree concerning this, that we proceeded to
weigh the expediency of it.

3. As to the grounds on which those who plead for a separation from
the Church proceed, some of them have weighed the point long and
deeply. They have particularly, and with earnest and continued prayer,
considered the lawfulness of it. And they allow, "If it be lawful to abide
therein, then it is not lawful to separate." But they aver, "It is not lawful
to abide therein"; and that for the following reasons:

First. With regard to the liturgy itself: though they allow it is, in the
general, one of the most excellent human compositions that ever was, yet
they think it is both absurd and sinful to declare such an assent and consent as is required to any merely human composition. Again: though they
do not object to the use of forms, yet they dare not confine themselves to

---

his association with the lay preachers and to reduce his activity as his brother's colleague. This was also the time when the slogan, "Separation is *lawful* but not *expedient*," was first invoked against the spirit of revolt. Thus, this letter coincides
with the beginnings of a long struggle in which John Wesley had to stand off opposite pressures and try to hold his movement within the Church of England — sometimes by no more than the sheer weight of his personal authority. It is plain, however, that in these first months after the crisis of 1755 Wesley was nearer the precipice
of "separation" than he had been before or would be thereafter. Hence, the poignant
intensity of this letter to a reproachful ally.
2. In the conference of the previous May 6–11.

them. And in this form (the Book of Common Prayer) there are several things which they apprehend to be contrary to Scripture.

Secondly. As to the laws of the Church, if they include the canons and decretals, both [of] which are received as such in our courts, they think "the latter are the very dregs of popery, and that many of the former, the canons of 1603,[3] are as grossly wicked as absurd." And, over and above the objections which they have to several particular ones, they think "(1) that the spirit which they breathe is throughout truly popish and anti-Christian; (2) that nothing can be more diabolical than the *ipso facto* excommunication so often denounced therein; (3) that the whole method of executing these canons, the process used in our spiritual courts, is too bad to be tolerated, not in a Christian, but in a Mahometan or pagan nation."

Thirdly. With respect to the ministers, they doubt "whether there are not many of them whom God hath not sent, inasmuch as they neither live the gospel nor teach it, neither indeed can, seeing they do not know it." They doubt the more "because they themselves disclaim that inward call to the ministry which is at least as necessary as the outward." And they are not clear "whether it be lawful to attend the ministrations of those whom God has not sent to minister."

Fourthly. The doctrines actually taught by these, and indeed by a great majority of the Church ministers, they think, "are not only wrong, but fundamentally so, and subversive of the whole gospel." They therefore doubt "whether it be lawful to bid them Godspeed or to have any fellowship with them."

I will freely acknowledge that I cannot answer these arguments to my own satisfaction. So that my conclusion, which I cannot yet give up (that it is lawful to continue in the Church), stands, I know not how, almost without any premises that are able to bear its weight.[4]

3. The anti-Puritan canons promulgated by Convocation in July 1604, at the urging of Richard Bancroft, and with the support of King James. They had, however, been framed in 1603 (largely by Bancroft and Thomas Bilson — both strong supporters of divine-right episcopacy). They figured prominently in the debates of the Hampton Court Conference in January 1604. Cf. Edward Cardwell, *A History of the Conferences* . . . (Oxford, 1849), 121–228; Felix Makower, *The Constitutional History and Constitution of the Church of England* (1895), 488–502. See below, p. 416.

4. Cf. *Letters*, III, 131 f.; see also John Wesley, *A Preservative Against Unsettled Notions in Religion* (Bristol, 1758), 237–46, for "Reasons Against a Separation from the Church of England."

My difficulty is very much increased by one of your observations. I know the original doctrines of the Church are sound. I know her worship is (in the main) pure and scriptural. But if "the essence of the Church of England, considered as such, consists in her orders and laws" (many of which I myself can say nothing for) "and not in her worship and doctrines," those who separate from her have a far stronger plea than I was ever sensible of.

4. At present I apprehend those, and those only, to separate from the Church who either renounce her fundamental doctrines or refuse to join her public worship. As yet we have done neither, nor have we taken one step farther than we were convinced was our bounden duty. It is from a full conviction of this that we have (1) preached abroad, (2) prayed extempore, (3) formed Societies, and (4) permitted preachers who were not episcopally ordained. And were we pushed on this side, were there no alternative allowed, we should judge it our bounden duty rather wholly to separate from the Church than to give up any one of these points. Therefore, if we cannot stop a separation without stopping lay preachers, the case is clear — we cannot stop it at all.

5. "But if we permit them, should we not do more? Should we not appoint them rather, since the bare permission puts the matter quite out of our hands and deprives us of all our influence?" In great measure, it does; therefore to appoint them is far more expedient, if it be lawful. But is it lawful for presbyters circumstanced as we are to appoint other ministers? This is the very point wherein we desire advice, being afraid of leaning [on] [5] our own understanding.

It is undoubtedly "needful," as you observe, "to come to some resolution in this point," and the sooner the better. I therefore rejoice to hear that you think "this matter may be better and more inoffensively ordered and that a method may be found which, conducted with prudence and patience, will reduce the constitution of Methodism to due order, and render the Methodists under God more instrumental to the ends of practical religion."

This, sir, is the very thing I want. I must therefore beg your sentiments on this head, and that as particularly as your other engagements will allow. Wishing you more and more of the wisdom from above, I remain, reverend dear sir,

Your obliged and affectionate brother and servant,

5. Telford reads *to*.

## To John Newton [1]

Londonderry, May 14, 1765

Dear Sir:

Your manner of writing needs no excuse. I hope you will always write in the same manner. Love is the plainest thing in the world. I know this dictates what you write; and then what need of ceremony?

You have admirably well expressed what I mean by an *opinion* contradistinguished from an *essential* doctrine. Whatever is "compatible with a love to Christ and a work of grace," I term an opinion.[2] And certainly the holding "particular election" and "final perseverance" is compatible with these. "Yet what fundamental error (you ask) have you opposed with half *that frequency and vehemence* as you have these opinions?" So doubtless you have heard. But it is not true. I have printed near fifty sermons, and only one of these opposes them at all. I preach about eight hundred sermons in a year. And taking one year with another, for twenty years past, I have not preached eight sermons in a year upon the subject. But, "how many of your best preachers have been *thrust out* because they dissented from you in these particulars?" Not one, best or worst, good or bad, was ever "thrust out" on this account. There has been not a single instance of the kind. Two or three (but far from "the best" of our preachers) voluntarily left us after they had embraced those opinions.

1. Copied here from the holograph in the Leete Collection, Southern Methodist University; cf. *Letters*, IV, 297–300. John Newton (1725–1807) was a converted slave trader who was, at the time of this letter, rector of Olney, where he collaborated with William Cowper in what came to be the *Olney Hymns* (1779); cf. John Newton, *Journal of a Slave Trader, 1750–1754*, Bernard Martin and Mark Spurrell, eds. (1962). Under the influence of Whitefield and others, he had adopted a vigorous Calvinism, and although he was a friend of Wesley's and a supporter of the Revival, he was mildly dubious of Wesley's use of lay preachers and strongly opposed to his doctrine of "perfection."

This letter is noteworthy for its autobiographical history of the development of the doctrine in Wesley's thought, for its summary presentation of his prime distinction between "an opinion contradistinguished from an essential doctrine," and for his blunt assertion that "on *justification*" he does not differ from "Mr. Calvin" by "an hair's breadth." Cf. *The Arminian Magazine* (1780), 441–44, for a further incident in the relations between Newton and Wesley.

2. Cf. *Journal*, III, 320; VII, 389; *Letters*, II, 110; IV, 297; *Works*, VI, 199; VIII, 244–46, 249, 340–41; IX, 56–57; X, 347–48.

But it was of their own mere motion. And two I should have expelled for immoral behaviour, but they withdrew and *pretended* "they did not hold our doctrine." Set a mark therefore on him who told you that tale and let his word for the future go for nothing.

"Is a man a believer in Jesus Christ, and is his life suitable to his profession?" are not only the *main* but the *sole* inquiries I make in order to his admission into our Society. If he is a Dissenter, he may be a Dissenter still. But if he is a churchman, I advise him to continue so, and that for many reasons, some of which are mentioned in the tract upon that subject.[3]

When you have read what I have wrote on occasion of the letters lately published, I may say something more on that head.[4] And it will then be time enough to show you why some *part* of those letters *could not* be wrote by Mr. Hervey.

I think on justification just as I have done any time these seven and twenty years, and just as Mr. Calvin does. In this respect I do not differ from him an hair's breadth.

But the main point between you and me is *perfection.* "This," you say, "has no prevalence in these parts. Otherwise I should think it my duty to oppose it with my whole strength, not as an 'opinion,' but as a dangerous mistake which appears to be subversive of the very foundations of Christian experience and which has, in fact, given occasion to the most grievous offences."

Just so my brother and I reasoned thirty years ago: "We think it our duty to oppose predestination with our whole strength, not as an opinion, but as a dangerous mistake which appears to be subversive of the very foundations of Christian experience and which has, in fact, given occasion to the most grievous offences."

That it has given occasion to such offences, I know. I can name time, place and persons. But still another fact stares me in the face: Mr. Haweis and Mr. Newton hold this: and yet I believe these have real Christian experience. But if so, this [doctrine of predestination] is only an "opin-

---

3. *Reasons Against a Separation from the Church of England* (1760), first published as Sec. 13 of *A Preservative Against Unsettled Notions in Religion* (Bristol, 1758).

4. A reference to a controversy that had arisen over *Eleven Letters from the late Rev. Mr. Hervey to the Rev. Mr. John Wesley*, published posthumously in 1764; *cf.* Tyerman, *Life,* II, 526–30. Wesley believed that William Cudworth, erstwhile friend now turned foe, had altered Hervey's text in order to widen the distance between the two former fellow-members of the Oxford Holy Club.

ion." It is not subversive (here is clear proof to the contrary) "of the very foundations of Christian experience." It is "compatible with a love to Christ and a genuine work of grace." Yea, many hold it at whose feet I desire to be found in the day of the Lord Jesus. If, then, I "oppose this with my whole strength," I am a mere bigot *still*. I leave you in your calm and retired moments to make the application.

But how came this opinion [*i.e.* perfection] into my mind? I will tell you with all simplicity. In 1725 I met with Bishop Taylor's *Rules of Holy Living and Dying*. I was struck particularly with the chapter upon *intention*, and felt a fixed intention to "give myself up to God." [5] In this I was much confirmed soon after by the *Christian Pattern*, and longed to "give God all my heart." This is just what I mean by "perfection" now. I sought after it from that hour.

In 1727 I read Mr. Law's *Christian Perfection* and *Serious Call*, and more explicitly resolved to be "all devoted to God in body, soul and spirit."

In 1730 [6] I began to be *homo unius libri*,[7] to study (comparatively) no book but the Bible. I then saw in a stronger light than ever before that only "one thing is needful" [*cf.* Lk. 10:42], even "faith that worketh by that love" [Gal. 5:6] of God and man, all inward and outward holiness. And I groaned to love God with "all my heart," and to serve him with "all my strength."

January 1, 1733, I preached the sermon on "The Circumcision of the Heart," which contains all that I now teach concerning salvation from *all sin* and loving God with an *undivided heart*.[8] In the same year I printed (the first time I ventured to print anything), for the use of my pupils, *A Collection of Forms of Prayer*. And in this I spoke explicitly of giving "the whole heart and the whole life to God." This was then, as it is now, my idea of perfection, though I should have started at the *word*.

In 1735 I preached my farewell sermon at Epworth, in Lincolnshire. In this likewise I spoke with the utmost clearness of having "one design, one desire, one love," and of pursuing the "one end" of our life in *all* our words and actions.

In January 1738 I expressed my desire in those words: [9]

5. See above, p. 7.  6. Manuscript defective here.
7. "A man of only one book"; see below, p. 89.
8. *Cf. Sermons* (Sugden), I, 263–79.
9. Johann Gerhardt, trans. by John Wesley, published in *Hymns and Sacred Poems* (1739).

O grant that nothing in my soul
   May dwell, but Thy *pure love alone!*
O may Thy love *possess me whole.*
   My joy, my treasure, and my crown.
Strange flames far from my heart remove!
   My *every* act, word, thought, be love.

And I am still persuaded, this is what the Lord Jesus hath bought for me with his own blood.

Now, whether *you* desire and expect this blessing or not, is it not an astonishing thing that you or any man living should be disgusted at *me* for expecting it? Is it not more astonishing still that well-nigh all the religious world should be up in arms concerning it? and that they should persuade one another that this hope is "subversive of the very foundations of Christian experience"? Why, then, whoever retains it cannot possibly have any Christian experience at all! Then my brother, Mr. Fletcher and I, and twenty thousand more, who *seem* both to fear and to love God, are in reality children of the devil and in the road to eternal damnation!

In God's name, I entreat you, make me sensible of this! Show me by plain strong reasons what dishonour this hope does to Christ; [10] wherein it opposes justification by faith or any fundamental truth of religion. But do not wrest and wiredraw [11] and colour my words as Mr. Hervey (or Cudworth) has done, in such a manner that when I look in that glass, I do not know my own face! "Shall I call you (says Mr. Hervey) my father or my friend? For you have been both to *me*." So I was. And you have as well requited me! It is well, my reward is with the Most High.

Wishing all happiness to you and yours, I am, dear sir,

                      Your affectionate brother and servant.

## To Charles Wesley [1]

                            Whitehaven, June 27, 1766

Dear Brother,

I think you and I have abundantly too little intercourse with each other. Are we not "old acquaintances"? Have we not known each other for

10. Manuscript defective; this reading conjectural.
11. Wesley first wrote *withdraw*, then amended it to *wiredraw; cf. Oxford English Dictionary,* XII.

---

1. *Letters,* V, 15–17. One of the remarkable features of Wesley's career after 1739

half a century? And are we not jointly engaged in such a work as probably no two other men upon earth are? Why, then, do we keep at such a distance? It is a mere device of Satan. But surely we ought not at this time of day to be ignorant of his devices. Let us therefore make the full use of the little time that remains. *We* at least should *think aloud* and use to the uttermost the light and grace on each bestowed. We should help each other,

> Of little life the best to make,
> And manage wisely the last stake.[2]

In one of my last I was saying I do not feel the wrath of God abiding on me; nor can I believe it does. And yet, this is the mystery: [I do not love God. I never did]. Therefore [I never] believed in the Christian sense of the word. Therefore [I am only an] honest heathen, a proselyte of the Temple, one of the φοβούμενοι τὸν θέον ["God-fearers," Acts 13:16]. And yet to be so employed of God; and so hedged in that I can neither get forward nor backward! Surely there never was such an instance before, from the beginning of the world! If I [ever have had] *that faith*, it would not be so strange. But [I never had any] other ἔλεγχος ["awareness"] of the eternal or invisible world than [I have] now; and that is [none at all], unless such as fairly shines from reason's glimmering

---

is the steadiness of his mood and the near total absence of emotional depressions. This letter reveals one of the most striking exceptions, and carries us back to the patterns of the pre-Revival past. (*Cf. Letters*, I, 269, 270, 292.) It was written in a rare moment of leisure and reflection, after a tour of Scotland that could only be judged a dismal failure (*cf. Journal*, V, 167-72; VI, 240) — and at the height of his marital difficulties, that weighed on him more heavily than he ever publicly acknowledged. It is addressed to his brother, on whom he had depended heavily but who was now quietly slipping into the background of the Revival. The parts in brackets (excepting Scripture references and translations) were written in shorthand. The despair in the second and third paragraphs belongs in Wesley's self-portrait. It was no merely speculative opinion of his that faith is a constant risk and that there is no state of spiritual progress in this life from which one might not lapse — yet also no lapse from which one may not be reclaimed. Here is such a lapse — under grinding pressures and grim frustrations. It reminds one of the old anxieties about the groundlessness of existence that had been so acute in 1738, before and after "Aldersgate."

Yet, as swiftly as the shutters of an anxious heart in crisis open, they close again, and we are back in the affairs of the Revival: — Wesley's difficulties with the preachers, his plans for the future, etc. Other letters dating from the same period have no echo of this depression. The rest of Wesley's summer is serene and the conference (which Charles did not attend) turned out to be something of a triumph (*cf. Journal*, V, 173-84).

2. *Cf.* Abraham Cowley, *Anacreontiques*, Ode V, "Age," in *Works* (1707), I, 51.

ray. [I have no] direct witness (I do not say that [I am a child of God])
but of anything invisible or eternal.

And yet I dare not preach otherwise than I do, either concerning faith,
or love, or justification, or perfection. And yet I find rather an increase
than a decrease of zeal for the whole work of God and every part of it.
I am φερόμενος ["so swept along"] (I know not how) that I can't stand
still. I want all the world to come to ὃν οὐκ οἶδα ["what I do not know
myself"]. Neither am I impelled to this by fear of any kind. I have no
more fear than love. Or if I have [any fear, it is not of falling] into hell,
but of falling into nothing.

I hope you are with Billy Evans. If there is an Israelite indeed, I think
he is one. O insist everywhere on *full* redemption, receivable by *faith
alone;* consequently, to be looked for *now.* You are made, as it were, for
this very thing. Just here you are in your element. In connexion I beat
you, but in strong, pointed *sentences* you beat me. Go on, in your *own
way,* [in] what God has peculiarly called you to. Press the *instantaneous*
blessing. Then I shall have more time for my peculiar calling, enforcing
the *gradual* work.

We must have a thorough *reform of the preachers.* I wish you would
*come to Leeds,*[3] with John Jones in the machine. It comes in two days;
and after staying two days, you might return. I would willingly bear
your expenses up and down. I believe it will help, not hurt, your health.
My love to Sally.

## To "Our Brethren in America"[1]

Bristol, September 10, 1784

1. By a very uncommon train of providences, many of the provinces
of North America are totally disjoined from their mother country and
erected into independent states. The English government has no author-

3. An appeal to Charles to attend the upcoming conference, and to lend a helping
hand.

1. *Letters,* VII, 238–39. This was issued as a broadsheet circular (with which this
text has been collated). This "encyclical" to the American Methodists is as interesting a single document as we have from the tangled affair of Wesley's "ordinations"
for America. Wesley is here conceding American independence with no enthusiasm
and yet without recrimination. He cites Lord King's authority for appointing Coke
and Asbury as "joint superintendents" and Whatcoat and Vasey "to act as elders."

ity over them, either civil or ecclesiastical, any more than over the States of Holland. A civil authority is exercised over them, partly by the Congess, partly by the provincial Assemblies. But no one either exercises or claims any ecclesiastical authority at all. In this peculiar situation some thousands of the inhabitants of these states desire my advice, and in compliance with their desire I have drawn up a little sketch.

2. Lord King's account of *The Primitive Church* [2] convinced me many years ago that bishops and presbyters are the same order and consequently have the same right to ordain. For many years I have been importuned from time to time to exercise this right by ordaining part of our travelling preachers. But I have still refused, not only for peace' sake, but because I was determined as little as possible to violate the established order of the national Church to which I belonged.

3. But the case is widely different between England and North America. Here there are bishops who have a legal jurisdiction. In America there are none, neither any parish ministers, so that for some hundred miles together there is none either to baptize or to administer the Lord's Supper. Here, therefore, my scruples are at an end, and I conceive myself at full liberty, as I violate no order and invade no man's right by appointing and sending labourers into the harvest.

4. I have accordingly appointed Dr. Coke and Mr. Francis Asbury to be joint superintendents over our brethren in North America; as also Richard Whatcoat and Thomas Vasey to act as elders among them, by baptizing and administering the Lord's Supper. And I have prepared a liturgy little differing from that of the Church of England (I think the

---

He reasserts his pastoral authority over the American Methodists and at the same time allows for the separation that was already *de facto*. When Coke arrived in Maryland and broached the idea to Asbury, the latter declined to act as superintendent, "by Mr. Wesley's appointment," unless unanimously elected by the preachers (Francis Asbury, *Journal and Letters,* Elmer T. Clark, ed. [1958], I, 471). Dr. Coke's "ordination certificate" (of Asbury) omits all mention of Wesley's name or authority (*cf. ibid.,* 474). The liturgy mentioned here (the "Sunday Service"), was a more drastic revision of the B.C.P. than Wesley indicates. It was nominally accepted by the Americans, but then quietly dropped from general use. At the same time, however, Wesley's abridgment of the Thirty-nine Articles (the so-called "Twenty-five Articles") was added to his *Sermons on Several Occasions* (1746–60) and *Explanatory Notes on the New Testament* (1755), as comprising what *The Discipline* of 1812 refers to as "our present existing and established standards of doctrine."

2. *An Enquiry into the Constitution, Discipline, Unity and Worship of the Primitive Church* (1691). Wesley never mentions the fact, if he ever knew it, that Lord King had subsequently altered his views in this area, and had repudiated the main thesis of his *Enquiry* long before Wesley had first read it.

best constituted national Church in the world) which I advise all the
travelling preachers to use on the Lord's Day in all their congregations,
reading the Litany only on Wednesdays and Fridays and praying extempore on all other days. I also advise the elders to administer the Supper
of the Lord on every Lord's Day.

5. If any one will point out a more rational and scriptural way of feeding and guiding those poor sheep in the wilderness, I will gladly embrace
it. At present I cannot see any better method than that I have taken.

6. It has, indeed, been proposed to desire the English bishops to ordain
part of our preachers for America. But to this I object: (1) I desired
the Bishop of London to ordain only one but could not prevail; (2) if
they consented, we know the slowness of their proceedings; but the matter admits of no delay; (3) if they would ordain them *now*, they would
likewise expect to govern them. And how grievously would this entangle us! (4) As our American brethren are now totally disentangled
both from the state and from the English hierarchy, we dare not entangle
them again either with the one or the other. They are now at full liberty
simply to follow the Scriptures and the primitive church. And we judge
it best that they should stand fast in that liberty wherewith God has so
strangely made them free.


## *To Freeborn Garrettson* [1]

London, January 24, 1789

My Dear Brother,

It signifies but little where we are, so we are but fully employed for
our good Master. Whether you went, therefore, to the east, it is all one,

---

1. Cf. *Letters*, VIII, 111–12. At eighty-six Wesley's prodigious vitality began finally
to fail. His letters become shorter, his handwriting, barely legible, and something of
a testy temper shows through upon occasion, as it does here. Garrettson was a pio-
neer Methodist preacher from Maryland, who had ranged up and down the Atlantic
seaboard from North Carolina to Nova Scotia in an arduous, effective ministry. At
Wesley's request, he had dispatched his manuscript journal to Wesley for possible
inclusion in *The Arminian Magazine* — and it had been lost in shipwreck! His phrase,
"finding freedom" (*i.e.* in preaching), was in common American speech, denoting the
preacher's experience of charismatic power in utterance. The man who here berates
Garrettson for walking by whim and not rule was the same one who had had to defend himself against charges of "enthusiasm." Despite its symptoms of senility, this
letter serves as an occasion for Wesley to reaffirm yet once again his lifelong ideal:
"a scriptural, rational Christian."

so you were labouring to promote his work. You are following the order of his providence wherever it appeared, as an holy man strongly expressed it, in a kind of holy disordered order. But there is one expression that occurs twice or thrice in yours which gives me some concern: you speak of finding "freedom" to do this or that. This is a word much liable to be abused. If I have plain Scripture or plain reason for doing a thing, well. These are my rules, and my only rules. I regard not whether I have freedom or no. This is an unscriptural expression and a very fallacious rule. I wish to be in every point, great and small, a scriptural, rational Christian.

In one instance formerly you promised to send me your journal. Will you break your word because you do not find "freedom" to keep it? Is not this enthusiasm? O be not of this way of thinking! You know not whither it may lead you. You are called to

> Square your useful life below
> By reason and by grace.[2]

But whatever you do with regard to me you must do quickly, or you will no more in this world.

Your affectionate friend and brother,

## To William Wilberforce [1]

Balam, February 24, 1791

Dear Sir,

Unless the divine power has raised you up to be as *Athanasius contra*

2. *A Collection of Hymns for the Use of the People Called Methodists* (1780), DXII, st. 3.

1. *Cf. Letters,* VIII, 265. This note, written just a week before Wesley's death, re-echoes a long-standing moral concern, first expressed in his vigorous opposition to the introduction of slavery into the Georgia colony. Throughout his ministry he was active in the antislavery campaign in England and threw his weight behind the efforts of Wilberforce, Clarkson, Howard and others to ban it throughout the Empire. (*Cf.* Thomas Clarkson, *History of . . . the Abolition of the African Slave-Trade . . .* [1808], I, 447 ff.) In America, it became a badge of virtue amongst the Methodists for a slaveholding convert to free his slaves. (*Cf.* Abel Stevens, *A Compendious History of American Methodism* [New York, n.d.], 125–26, 135.)

In 1774 Wesley published a tract entitled *Thoughts Upon Slavery* (*Works,* XI, 59–79), which was reprinted and widely distributed in England and America. It was represented to be his own production (*cf. Letters,* VIII, 6, 7, 276) — and its vivid *mundum*,[2] I see not how you can go through your glorious enterprise in opposing that execrable villany [3] which is the scandal of religion, of England, and of human nature. Unless God has raised you up for this very thing, you will be worn out by the opposition of men and devils. But if God be for you, who can be against you? Are all of them together stronger than God? O be not weary of well doing! Go on, in the name of God and in the power of his might, till even American slavery (the vilest that ever saw the sun) shall vanish away before it.

Reading this morning a tract wrote by a poor African, I was particularly struck by that circumstance that a man who has a black skin, being wronged or outraged by a white man, can have no redress; it being a "law" in all our colonies that the *oath* of a black against a white goes for nothing. What villany is this?

That he who has guided you from youth up may continue to strengthen you in this and all things, is the prayer of, dear sir,

Your affectionate servant,

---

sentiments certainly are. Actually, however, it was an abridgment of *Some Historical Account of Guinea*, which had been published in Philadelphia in 1771 by Anthony Benezet, an American Quaker. In judging such a literary "borrowing," it is useful to realize that Wesley and his eighteenth-century colleagues generally understood this as a form of *endorsement*. When he found something that said what he wanted to say, he felt free to make it available to those who might not otherwise have seen it. This is the case, for example, with his *Calm Address to Our American Colonies* (1775), borrowed from Samuel Johnson, *Taxation No Tyranny; A Treatise on Baptism* (see below, p. 317 ff.), and *A Roman Catechism* (1756), abridged from a treatise of a similar title by Bishop John Williams of Chichester (1686), in *Works*, X, 86–128.

2. "Athanasius arrayed against the world"; *cf.* R. Hooker, *Of The Lawes of Ecclesiasticall Politie* (1593–97), V, sec. 42.

3. *Cf. Thoughts Upon Slavery;* see also Wesley's correspondence with the other leaders of the Society for the Abolition of Slavery, in *Letters*, VIII, 6, 17, 23, 194, 207, 275.

## SELF-IMAGES IN THE SERMONS

*Editor's introduction.* In his lifetime Wesley was best known as a preacher, and himself preferred to be known and judged by his sermons. In the *Model Deed*, which he drew up in 1763 to govern the legal arrangements for the Methodist preaching houses, the principal stipulation is a doctrinal one: "Provided always that the persons [admitted to a given pulpit by the Trustees] preach no other doctrine than is contained in Mr. Wesley's *Explanatory Notes Upon the New Testament* and four volumes of sermons." [1] The sermons in these four volumes add up to forty-four. In the first four volumes of his *Works* (1771) Wesley included nine others, making a total of fifty-three. In the last collected edition of his sermons issued in his lifetime (in eight volumes, 1787–88), the first four volumes retain the original forty-four, and these have remained as doctrinal "standards" in Methodist law. [2] Besides the *Sermons on Several Occasions*, Wesley published others in *The Arminian Magazine* and elsewhere, so that the inclusive number of his sermons in the Jackson edition runs to one hundred and fifty-one. [3]

Throughout Wesley's preaching the man and his message illuminate each other. As exemplars of this, the Preface to the first collection of *Sermons* and two of the actual sermons will suffice. "Catholic Spirit" is both a précis of Wesley's ecumenical design and an exhibition of his theological temper. "God's Vineyard" is an autobiographical rehearsal of the history of the Methodist movement, together with a summary appraisal of Methodist doctrine and discipline.

As he himself implies in the Preface, Wesley's *published* sermons were

1. *I.e. Sermons on Several Occasions,* I (1746); II (1748); III (1750); IV (1760). For the text of the *Model Deed,* see *Works,* VIII, 330–31.
2. For a discussion of the historical and legal details of this question, see *Sermons* (Sugden), I, 13–26; II, 331–40.
3. *Works,* V–VII.

not identical with the ones he actually preached. For example, the sermon on "Christian Perfection" was probably never preached in the form in which it appears here; moreover, in his "sermon register" [4] we find the record of hundreds of sermons preached but never published. He usually preached without notes and sometimes for an hour or longer. After a text and theme had fully matured in his preaching of it, he would write out what might well be called a sermonic essay — thus putting his doctrine in this area or that on the record. Read in this light, the published sermons *do* expound "what these doctrines are which I embrace and teach as the essentials of true religion." [5]

✧ ✧ ✧ ✧

## Preface to *Sermons on Several Occasions* [1]

1. The following Sermons contain the substance of what I have been preaching for between eight and nine years last past. During that time I have frequently spoken in public on every subject in the ensuing collection; and I am not conscious that there is any one point of doctrine on which I am accustomed to speak in public which is not here, incidentally if not professedly, laid before every Christian reader. Every serious man who peruses these will therefore see, in the clearest manner, what these doctrines are which I embrace and teach as the essentials of true religion.

2. But I am thoroughly sensible these are not proposed in such a manner as some may expect. Nothing here appears in an elaborate, elegant or oratorical dress. If it had been my desire or design to write thus, my leisure would not permit. But, in truth, I, at present, designed nothing less; for I now write, as I generally speak, *ad populum* ("to the bulk of mankind"), to those who neither relish nor understand the art of speaking, but who, notwithstanding, are competent judges of those truths which are necessary to present and future happiness. I mention this that curious readers may spare themselves the labour of seeking for what they will not find.

3. I design plain truth for plain people. Therefore, of set purpose, I

---

4. See *Journal*, VIII, 171–252.
5. For comments and annotations on Sermons I-LIII, see *Sermons* (Sugden).

---

1. Volume I; written in 1745; published in 1746.

abstain from all nice and philosophical speculations, from all perplexed and intricate reasonings and, as far as possible, from even the show of learning, unless in sometimes citing the original Scriptures. I labour to avoid all words which are not easy to be understood, all which are not used in common life and, in particular, those kinds of technical terms that so frequently occur in bodies of divinity — those modes of speaking which men of reading are intimately acquainted with but which to common people are an unknown tongue. Yet I am not assured that I do not sometimes slide into them unawares; it is so extremely natural to imagine that a word which is familiar to ourselves is so to all the world.

4. Nay, my design is, in some sense, to forget all that ever I have read in my life. I mean to speak, in the general, as if I had never read one author, ancient or modern (always excepting the inspired). I am persuaded that, on the one hand, this may be a means of enabling me more clearly to express the sentiments of my heart while I simply follow the chain of my own thoughts, without entangling myself with those of other men; and that, on the other [hand], I shall come with fewer weights upon my mind, with less of prejudice and prepossession, either to search for myself or to deliver to others the naked truths of the gospel.

5. To candid, reasonable men I am not afraid to lay open what have been the inmost thoughts of my heart. I have thought: "I am a creature of a day, passing through life as an arrow through the air. I am a spirit come from God and returning to God: just hovering over the great gulf till, a few moments hence, I am no more seen, I drop into an unchangeable eternity! I want to know one thing: the way to heaven, how to land safe on that happy shore. God himself has condescended to teach the way; for this very end he came from heaven. He hath written it down in a book. O give me that book! At any price, give me the book of God! I have it: here is knowledge enough for me. Let me be *homo unius libri*.[2] Here then I am, far from the busy ways of men. I sit down alone — only God is here. In his presence I open, I read his book for this end, to find the way to heaven. Is there a doubt concerning the meaning of what I read? Does anything appear dark and intricate? I lift up my heart to the Father of Lights: Lord, is it not thy word, 'If any man lack wisdom, let him ask of God? Thou givest liberally and upbraidest not' [Jas. 1:5]. Thou hast said, 'If any be willing to do thy will, he shall know' [Jn. 7:17]. I am willing to do; let me know thy will." I then search after and consider parallel passages of Scripture, "comparing spiritual things with

2. "A man of only one book"; see above, p. 79; also below, p. 106.

spiritual" [1 Cor. 2:13]. I meditate thereon with all the attention and earnestness of which my mind is capable. If any doubt still remains, I consult those who are experienced in the things of God and then the writings whereby being dead they yet speak. And what I thus learn, that I teach.

6. I have accordingly set down in the following sermons what I find in the Bible concerning the way to heaven, with a view to distinguish this way of God from all those which are the inventions of men. I have endeavoured to describe the true, the scriptural, experimental religion, so as to omit nothing which is a real part thereof and to add nothing thereto which is not. And herein it is more especially my desire, first, to guard those who are just setting their faces toward heaven (and who, having little acquaintance with the things of God, are the more liable to be turned out of the way) from formality, from mere outside religion which has almost driven heart-religion out of the world; and, secondly, to warn those who know the religion of the heart, "the faith which worketh by love" [Gal. 5:6], lest at any time they make void the law through faith [cf. Rom. 3:31] and so fall back into the snare of the devil.

7. By the advice and at the request of some of my friends, I have prefixed to the other sermons contained in this volume three sermons of my own and one of my brother's, preached before the University of Oxford.[3] My design required some discourses on those heads, and I preferred these before any others, as being a stronger answer than any which can be drawn up now to those who have frequently asserted that we have changed our doctrine of late and do not preach now what we did some years ago. Any man of understanding may now judge for himself when he has compared the latter with the former sermons.

8. But some may say I have mistaken the way myself, although I take upon me to teach it to others. It is probable many will think this; and it is very possible that I have. But I trust, whereinsoever I have mistaken, my mind is open to conviction. I sincerely desire to be better informed. I say to God and man, "What I know not, teach thou me!"

9. Are you persuaded you see more clearly than me? It is not unlikely that you may. Then treat me as you would desire to be treated yourself upon a change of circumstances. Point me out a better way than I have yet known. Show me it is so by plain proof of Scripture. And if I linger

3. (1) "Salvation by Faith" (June 11, 1738); (2) "The Almost Christian" (July 25, 1741); (3) "Scriptural Christianity" (August 24, 1744); (4) "Awake, Thou That Sleepest," by Charles Wesley (Apr. 14, 1742).

in the path I have been accustomed to tread and therefore am unwilling to leave it, labour with me a little; take me by the hand and lead me as I am able to bear. But be not displeased if I entreat you not to beat me down in order to quicken my pace. I can go but feebly and slowly at best; then, I should not be able to go at all. May I not request of you, further, not to give me hard names in order to bring me into the right way? Suppose I was ever so much in the wrong, I doubt this would not set me right. Rather, it would make me run so much the farther from you and so get more and more out of the way.

10. Nay, perhaps, if you are angry, so shall I be, too; and then there will be small hopes of finding the truth. If once anger arise, ἠΰτε καπνός (as Homer somewhere expresses it),[4] this smoke will so dim the eyes of my soul that I shall be able to see nothing clearly. For God's sake, if it be possible to avoid it, let us not provoke one another to wrath. Let us not kindle in each other this fire of hell, much less blow it up into a flame. If we could discern truth by that dreadful light, would it not be loss rather than gain? For how far is love, even with many wrong opinions, to be preferred before truth itself without love? We may die without the knowledge of many truths and yet be carried into Abraham's bosom. But if we die without love, what will knowledge avail? Just as much as it avails the devil and his angels.

The God of love forbid we should ever make the trial! May he prepare us for the knowledge of all truth by filling our hearts with all his love and "with all joy and peace in believing" [Rom. 15:13].

## Catholic Spirit

*Editor's introduction.* This sermon appears here as in Volume III of *Sermons on Several Occasions* (1750), collated with the text in Wesley's final revision of the collection in 1787–88 (III, 181–201). It was republished separately in 1755, together with Charles Wesley's hymn, "Catholic Love." The "sermon register" records the text and theme as having been first developed at Newcastle (September 8, 1749), and again later in the same year at Bristol (November 3, 1749); it appears in *Sermons* (Sugden), II, 129–46, and *Works*, V, 492–504.

4. Cf. *The Iliad*, Bk. XVIII, l. 110: "wrath that, far sweeter than trickling honey, *waxeth like smoke* in the breasts of men."

The distinction between "opinion" and essential truth points to the basic difference in Wesley's mind between the fact of faith and all the conceptualizations of faith. In *The Character of a Methodist* [1] he had laid down the rule that, "as to all opinions *which do not strike at the root of Christianity*, we think and let think." [2] In *A Plain Account of the People Called Methodists* [3] he had pushed the point to an extreme — "orthodoxy, or right *opinions*, is at best a slender part of religion, if it can be allowed to be any part at all" — and this had been fiercely disputed by his critics.[4] Ironically enough, some of his defenders have assumed that care for correct doctrine could be safely cast aside — and have suited their actions to this notion. Wesley's point, here and elsewhere, is that religious reality lies deeper than religious conceptuality — as evidenced by those simple but true believers whose "opinions" may be incompetent and those impeccably "orthodox" persons whose hearts nevertheless remain estranged from God and man. Opinions, then, are ways of comprehending (or miscomprehending) reality. The important thing is that reflection upon reality not be confused with reality itself. Wesley is quite specific and quite adamant about the essential doctrines of Christianity — and quite "orthodox"! Yet his "catholic spirit" seeks to find that community of Christians which is constituted by faith and love ("thy 'heart' as my 'heart' "), and which is a necessary precondition to the fruitful negotiation of legitimate differences of opinion and practice.

❖   ❖   ❖   ❖

And when he was departed thence, he lighted on Jehonadab the son of Rechab coming to meet him, and he saluted him, and said to him, Is thine heart right, as my heart is with thy heart? And Jehonadab answered, It is. If it be, give me thine hand (2 Kings 10:15).

1. It is allowed even by those who do not pay this great debt that love is due to all mankind — the royal law, "Thou shalt love thy neighbor as thyself" [Mt. 19:19, 22:39; *cf.* Lev. 19:18], carrying its own evidence to all that hear it — and that not according to the miserable construction put upon it by the zealots of old times: "Thou shalt love thy neighbour (thy relation, acquaintance, friend) and hate thine enemy." Not so. "I

1. *Works*, VIII, 340–47.              2. Italics added.
3. *Works*, VIII, 249–68.
4. *Cf. Works*, VIII, 244–46, 340; IX, 57–58; X, 347–48; XIII, 215–16.

say unto you," saith our Lord, "Love your enemies, bless them that curse you, do good to them that hate you, and pray for them that despitefully use you, and persecute you; that ye may be the children (may appear so to all mankind) of your Father which is in heaven, who maketh his sun to rise on the evil and on the good, and sendeth rain on the just and on the unjust" [Mt. 5:43–45].

2. But it is sure, there is a peculiar love which we owe to those that love God. So David: "All my delight is upon the saints that are in the earth and upon such as excel in virtue" [cf. Ps. 16:3, B.C.P.]. And so a greater than he: "A new commandment I give unto you, that ye love one another: as I have loved you, that ye also love one another. By this shall all men know that ye are my disciples, if ye have love one to another" [Jn. 13:34–35]. This is that love on which the Apostle John so frequently and strongly insists: "This," saith he, "is the message that ye heard from the beginning, that we should love one another" [1 Jn. 3:11]. "Hereby perceive we the love of God, because he laid down his life for us," and we ought, if love should call us thereto, "to lay down our lives for the brethren" [1 Jn. 3:16]. And again: "Beloved, let us love one another, for love is of God. He that loveth not, knoweth not God, for God is love" [1 Jn. 4:7, 8]. "Not that we loved God, but that he loved us and sent his Son to be the propitiation for our sins. Beloved, if God so loved us, we ought also to love one another" [1 Jn. 4:10–11].

3. All men approve of this, but do all men practice it? Daily experience shows the contrary. Where are even the Christians who love one another as he hath given us commandment? How many hindrances lie in the way? The two grand, general hindrances are, first, that they cannot all think alike; and, in consequence of this, secondly, they cannot all walk alike; but in several smaller points their practice must differ in proportion to the difference of their sentiments.

4. But although a difference in opinions or modes of worship may prevent an entire external union, yet need it prevent our union in affection? Though we cannot think alike, may we not love alike? May we not be of one heart, though we are not of one opinion? Without all doubt we may. Herein all the children of God may unite, notwithstanding these smaller differences. These remaining as they are, they may forward one another in love and in good works.

5. Surely in this respect the example of Jehu himself, as mixed a character as he was of, is well worthy both the attention and imitation of every serious Christian. "And when he was departed thence, he lighted

on Jehonadab the son of Rechab coming to meet him. And he saluted him and said to him, 'Is thine heart right, as my heart is with thy heart?' And Jehonadab answered, 'It is.' 'If it be, give me thine hand.' "

The text naturally divides itself into two parts. First, a question proposed by Jehu to Jehonadab: "Is thine heart right, as my heart is with thy heart?" Secondly, an offer made on Jehonadab's answering, "It is." "If it be, give me thine hand."

I. 1. And first, let us consider the question proposed by Jehu to Jehonadab, "Is thine heart right, as my heart is with thy heart?"

The very first thing we may observe in these words is that here is no inquiry concerning Jehonadab's opinions. And yet it is certain he held some which were very uncommon, indeed quite peculiar to himself, and some which had a close influence upon [his] practice; on which, likewise, he laid so great a stress as to entail them upon his children's children, to their latest posterity. This is evident from the account given by Jeremiah, many years after his death:

> I took Jaazaniah and his brethren and all his sons and the whole house of the Rechabites . . . and set before them pots full of wine and cups and said unto them, Drink ye wine. But they said, We will drink no wine, for Jonadab (or Jehonadab) the son of Rechab, our father [1] commanded us, saying, Ye shall drink no wine, neither ye, nor your sons for ever. Neither shall ye build house, nor sow seed, nor plant vineyard, nor have any: but all your days ye shall dwell in tents. . . . And we have obeyed, and done according to all that Jonadab our father commanded us [cf. Jer. 35:3–10].

2. And yet Jehu, although it seems to have been his manner, both in things secular and religious, to "drive furiously" [cf. 2 Kings 9:20], does not concern himself at all with any of these things, but lets Jehonadab abound in his own sense. And neither of them appears to have given the other the least disturbance touching the opinions which he maintained.

3. It is very possible that many good men now also may entertain peculiar opinions, and some of them may be as singular herein as even Jehonadab was. And it is certain, so long as we know but "in part," that all men will not see all things alike. It is an unavoidable consequence of the present weakness and shortness of human understanding that several men will be of several minds, in religion as well as in common life. So it

---

1. [Au.] "It would be less ambiguous if the words were placed thus: 'Jehonadab *our father, the son of Rechab,*' out of love and reverence to whom he probably desired his descendants might be called by that name."

has been from the beginning of the world and so it will be "till the restitu-
tion of all things" [*cf.* Acts 3:21].

4. Nay, farther, although every man necessarily believes that every particular opinion which he holds is true (for to believe an opinion is not
true is the same thing as not to hold it), yet can no man be assured that
all his own opinions, taken together, are true. Nay, every thinking man
is assured they are not, seeing *humanum est errare et nescire* — to be ignorant of many things, and to mistake in some, is the necessary condition of humanity.[2] This, therefore, he is sensible is his own case. He
knows in the general that he himself is mistaken; although in what particulars he mistakes he does not, perhaps he cannot, know.

5. I say, "perhaps he cannot know," for who can tell how far invincible
ignorance may extend or (that comes to the same thing) invincible
prejudice, which is often so fixed in tender minds that it is afterwards impossible to tear up what has taken so deep a root? And who can say unless he knew every circumstance attending it, how far any mistake is
culpable, seeing all guilt must suppose some concurrence of the will, of
which he only can judge who searcheth the heart?

6. Every wise man, therefore, will allow others the same liberty of
thinking which he desires they should allow him; and will no more insist on their embracing his opinions than he would have them to insist on
his embracing theirs. He bears with those who differ from him and only
asks him with whom he desires to unite in love that single question, "Is
thy heart right, as my heart is with thy heart?"

7. We may, secondly, observe that here is no inquiry made concerning
Jehonadab's mode of worship, although it is highly probable there was,
in this respect also, a very wide difference between them. For we may
well believe Jehonadab, as well as his posterity, worshipped God at
Jerusalem, whereas Jehu did not; he had more regard to state-policy than
religion. And, therefore, although he slew the worshippers of Baal and
"destroyed Baal out of Israel," yet from the convenient "sin of Jero-
boam," the worship of "the golden calves, he departed not" [*cf.* 2 Kings
10:25–30].

8. But even among men of an upright heart, men who desire to "have
a conscience void of offence" [Acts 24:16], it must needs be that as long
as there are various opinions, there will be various ways of worshipping
God, seeing a variety of opinions necessarily implies a variety of practice.
And as in all ages men have differed in nothing more than in their opin-

2. *Cf.* Seneca, *Quaestiones Naturales*, Bk. IV, c. 2.

ions concerning the Supreme Being, so in nothing have they more differed from each other than in the manner of worshipping him. Had this
been only in the heathen world, it would not have been at all surprising,
for we know these by their "wisdom knew not God" [cf. 1 Cor. 1:21].
Nor, therefore, could they know how to worship him. But is it not
strange that even in the Christian world, although they all agree in the
general — "God is a Spirit and they that worship him must worship
him in spirit and in truth" [Jn. 4:24] — yet the particular modes of
worshipping God are almost as various as among the heathens?

9. And how shall we choose among so much variety? No man can
choose for or prescribe to another, but every one must follow the dictates of his own conscience in simplicity and godly sincerity. He must be
fully persuaded in his own mind, and then act according to the best
light he has. Nor has any creature power to constrain another to walk by
his own rule. God has given no right to any of the children of men thus
to lord it over the conscience of his brethren. But every man must judge
for himself, as every man must give an account of himself to God.

10. Although, therefore, every follower of Christ is obliged, by the
very nature of the Christian institution, to be a member of some particular congregation or other (some church, as it is usually termed), which
implies a particular manner of worshipping God — for "two cannot
walk together unless they be agreed" [cf. Amos 3:3] — yet none can be
obliged by any power on earth but that of his own conscience to prefer
this or that congregation to another, this or that particular manner of
worship. I know it is commonly supposed that the place of our birth fixes
the church to which we ought to belong; that one, for instance, who is
born in England ought to be a member of that which is styled the Church
of England and, consequently, to worship God in the particular manner
which is prescribed by that church. I was once a zealous maintainer of
this, but I find many reasons to abate of this zeal. I fear it is attended with
such difficulties as no reasonable man can get over — not the least of
which is that if this rule had took place, there could have been no
reformation from popery, seeing it entirely destroys the right of private
judgment on which that whole reformation stands.[3]

11. I dare not, therefore, presume to impose my mode of worship on
any other. I believe it is truly primitive and apostolical. But my belief is
no rule for another. I ask not, therefore, of him with whom I would

3. Cf. Wesley's refutation of Richard Challoner's defense of Rome (The Grounds
of the Old Religion [1742]) in his Journal, III, 72; see also ibid., 243, and An Earnest
Appeal, below, pp. 404–07.

unite in love, "Are you of my church, of my congregation? Do you receive the same form of church government and allow the same church officers with me? Do you join in the same form of prayer wherein I worship God?" I inquire not, "Do you receive the Supper of the Lord in the same posture and manner that I do, nor whether, in the administration of baptism, you agree with me in admitting sureties for the baptized, in the manner of administering it, or the age of those to whom it should be administered?" Nay, I ask not of you (as clear as I am in my own mind) whether you allow baptism and the Lord's Supper at all. Let all these things stand by — we will talk of them, if need be, at a more convenient season. My only question at present is this, "Is thine heart right, as my heart is with thy heart?"

12. But what is properly implied in the question? I do not mean what did Jehu imply therein, but what should a follower of Christ understand thereby when he proposes it to any of his brethren?

The first thing implied is this: Is thy heart right with God? Dost thou believe his being and his perfections, his eternity, immensity, wisdom, power, his justice, mercy and truth? Dost thou believe that he now "upholdeth all things by the word of his power" [cf. Heb. 1:3], and that he governs even the most minute, even the most noxious, to his own glory and the good of them that love him? Hast thou a divine evidence, a supernatural conviction, of the things of God? Dost thou "walk by faith, not by sight," looking not at temporal things but things eternal [cf. 2 Cor. 5:7, 4:18]?

13. Dost thou believe in the Lord Jesus Christ, "God over all, blessed for ever" [cf. Rom. 9:5]? Is he revealed in thy soul? Dost thou "know Jesus Christ and him crucified" [cf. 1 Cor. 2:2]? Does he "dwell in thee and thou in him" [cf. 1 Jn. 4:13, 15]? Is he "formed in thy heart by faith" [cf. Gal. 4:19; Eph. 3:17]? Having absolutely disclaimed all thy own works, thy own righteousness, hast thou "submitted thyself unto the righteousness of God" [cf. Rom. 10:3], which is by faith in Christ Jesus? Art thou "found in him, not having thy own righteousness, but the righteousness which is by faith" [cf. Phil. 3:9]? And art thou, through him, "fighting the good fight of faith, and laying hold of eternal life" [cf. 1 Tim. 6:12]?

14. Is thy faith ἐνεργουμένη δι' ἀγάπης, "filled with the energy of love"? [4] Dost thou love God — I do not say "above all things," for it is both an

---

4. Cf. Gal. 5:6; A.V.: "faith which worketh by love." The Greek reads, πίστις δι' ἀγάπης ἐνεργουμένη. Wesley has reversed the word order to make a rather different point.

unscriptural and an ambiguous expression, but — "with all thy heart, and with all thy mind, and with all thy soul, and with all thy strength" [Lk. 10:27]? Dost thou seek all thy happiness in him alone? And dost thou find what thou seekest? Does thy soul continually "magnify the Lord, and thy spirit rejoice in God thy Saviour" [Lk. 1:46, 47]? Having learned "in everything to give thanks" [1 Thess. 5:18], dost thou find "it is a joyful and pleasant thing to be thankful" [cf. Ps. 147:1, B.C.P.]? Is God the centre of thy soul, the sum of all thy desires? Art thou accordingly "laying up" thy "treasure in heaven" [cf. Mt. 6:20] and "counting all things else dung" and dross [cf. Phil. 3:8]? Hath the love of God cast the love of the world out of thy soul? Then thou art "crucified to the world" [cf. Gal. 6:14]; thou art dead to all below and thy "life is hid with Christ in God" [Col. 3:3].

15. Art thou employed in doing "not thy own will but the will of him that sent thee" [cf. Jn. 7:16], of him that sent thee down to sojourn here awhile, to spend a few days in a strange land, till having finished the work he hath given thee to do, thou return to thy Father's house? Is it thy meat and drink "to do the will of thy Father which is in heaven" [cf. Mt. 7:21]? Is "thine eye single" [Mt. 6:22] in all things? Always fixed on him? Always "looking unto Jesus" [Heb. 12:2]? Dost thou point at him in whatsoever thou doest, in all thy labour, thy business, thy conversation — aiming only at the glory of God in all "whatsoever thou doest, either in word or deed — doing it all in the name of the Lord Jesus, giving thanks unto God, even the Father, through him" [cf. Col. 3:17]?

16. Does the love of God constrain thee to "serve" him "with fear" [cf. Ps. 2:11], to "rejoice unto him with reverence"? Art thou more afraid of displeasing God than either of death or hell? Is nothing so terrible to thee as the thought of offending the eyes of his glory? Upon this ground, dost thou "hate all evil ways," every transgression of his holy and perfect law and herein "exercise thyself to have a conscience void of offence toward God, and toward man" [cf. Acts 24:16]?

17. Is thy heart right toward thy neighbour? Dost thou love as thyself all mankind without exception? "If you love those only that love you, what thank have you" [cf. Lk. 6:32]? Do you "love your enemies" [cf. Lk. 6:27]? Is your soul full of good will, of tender affection, toward them? Do you love even the enemies of God? The unthankful and unholy? Do your bowels yearn over them? Could you "wish yourself" temporally "accursed" [cf. Rom. 9:3] for their sake? And do you show

this by "blessing them that curse you and praying for those that despitefully use you and persecute you" [cf. Mt. 5:44]?

18. Do you show your love by your works? While you have time, as
you have opportunity, do you in fact "do good to all men" [Gal.
6:10], neighbours or strangers, friends or enemies, good or bad? Do you
do them all the good you can, endeavouring to supply all their wants, assisting them both in body and soul to the uttermost of your power? If
thou art thus minded — may every Christian say, "Yea!" — if thou art
but sincerely desirous of it and following on till thou attain, then "thy
heart is right, as my heart is with thy heart."

II. 1. "If it be, give me thy hand." I do not mean, "Be of my opinion."
You need not. I do not expect or desire it. Neither do I mean, "I will be
of your opinion." I cannot; it does not depend on my choice. I can no
more think than I can see or hear as I will. Keep you your opinion; I,
mine, and that as steadily as ever. You need not even endeavour to come
over to me or bring me over to you. I do not desire you to dispute those
points or to hear or speak one word concerning them. Let all opinions
alone on one side and the other: only, "give me thine hand."

2. I do not mean, "embrace my modes of worship" or "I will embrace
yours." This also is a thing which does not depend either on your choice
or mine. We must both act as each is fully persuaded in his own mind.
Hold you fast that which you believe is most acceptable to God and I
will do the the same. I believe the episcopal form of church government
to be scriptural and apostolical. If you think the presbyterian or independent is better, think so still and act accordingly. I believe infants
ought to be baptized, and that this may be done either by dipping or
sprinkling. If you are otherwise persuaded, be so still, and follow your
own persuasion. It appears to me that forms of prayer are of excellent
use, particularly in the great congregation. If you judge extemporary
prayer to be of more use, act suitably to your own judgment. My sentiment is that I ought not to forbid water, wherein persons may be baptized, and that I ought to eat bread and drink wine, as a memorial of my
dying master. However, if you are not convinced of this, act according
to the light you have. I have no desire to dispute with you one moment
upon any of the preceding heads. Let all these smaller points stand aside.
Let them never come into sight. "If thine heart is as my heart," if thou
lovest God and all mankind, I ask no more: "Give me thine hand."

3. I mean, first, love me: and that not only as thou lovest all mankind,
not only as thou lovest thine enemies or the enemies of God, those that

hate thee, that "despitefully use thee, and persecute thee" [Mt. 5:44], not only as a stranger, as one of whom thou knowest neither good nor evil. I am not satisfied with this. No, "if thine heart be right, as mine with thy heart," then love me with a very tender affection, as a friend that is closer than a brother, as a brother in Christ, a fellow citizen of the New Jerusalem, a fellow soldier engaged in the same warfare under the same captain of our salvation. Love me as a companion "in the kingdom and patience of Jesus" [Rev. 1:9] and a joint heir of his glory.

4. Love me (but in a higher degree than thou dost the bulk of mankind) with the love that is "long-suffering and kind," [5] that is patient — if I am ignorant or out of the way, bearing and not increasing my burden — and is tender, soft, and compassionate still; that "envieth not," if at any time it please God to prosper me in this work even more than thee. Love me with the love that "is not provoked," either at my follies or infirmities, or even at my acting (if it should sometimes so appear to thee) not according to the will of God. Love me so as to "think no evil" of me, to put away all jealousy and evil-surmising. Love me with the love that "covereth all things" (that never reveals either my faults or infirmities), that "believeth all things" (is always willing to think the best, to put the fairest construction on all my words and actions), that "hopeth all things," either that the thing related was never done, or not done with such circumstances as are related; or at least that it was done with a good intention, or in sudden stress of temptation. And hope to the end that whatever is amiss will, by the grace of God, be corrected, and whatever is wanting, supplied through the riches of his mercy in Christ Jesus.

5. I mean, secondly, commend me to God in all thy prayers, wrestle with him in my behalf that he would speedily correct what he sees amiss and supply what is wanting in me. In thy nearest access to the throne of grace, beg of him who is then very present with thee that my heart may be more as thy heart, more right both toward God and toward man, that I may have a fuller conviction of things not seen and a stronger view of the love of God in Christ Jesus, may more steadily walk by faith, not by sight [cf. 2 Cor. 5:7], and more earnestly grasp eternal life. Pray that the love of God and of all mankind may be more largely poured into my heart, that I may be more fervent and active in doing the will of my Father which is in heaven, more zealous of good works and more careful to abstain from all appearance of evil.

5. Cf. in this paragraph echoes from 1 Cor. 13:4–7.

6. I mean, thirdly, provoke me to love and to good works. Second thy prayer, as thou hast opportunity, by speaking to me in love whatsoever thou believest to be for my soul's health. Quicken me in the work which God has given me to do and instruct me how to do it more perfectly. Yea, "smite me friendly, and reprove me" [Ps. 141:5, B.C.P.], whereinsoever I appear to thee to be doing rather my own will than the will of him that sent me. O speak and spare not, whatever thou believest may conduce either to the amending my faults, the strengthening my weakness, the building me up in love, or the making me more fit, in any kind, for the Master's use.

7. I mean, lastly, love me not in word only but in deed and in truth. So far as in conscience thou canst (retaining still thy own opinions and thy own manner of worshipping God), join with me in the work of God, and let us go on hand in hand. And thus far, it is certain, thou mayest go. Speak honourably, wherever thou art, of the work of God, by whomsoever he works, and kindly of his messengers. And, if it be in thy power, not only sympathize with them when they are in any difficulty or distress, but give them a cheerful and effectual assistance, that they may glorify God on thy behalf.[6]

8. Two things should be observed with regard to what has been spoken under this last head: the one, that whatsoever love, whatsoever offices of love, whatsoever spiritual or temporal assistance I claim from him whose heart is right as my heart is with his, the same I am ready, by the grace of God, according to my measure, to give him: the other, that I have not made this claim in behalf of myself only, but of all whose heart is right toward God and man, that we may all love one another as Christ hath loved us.

III. 1. One inference we may make from what has been said: we may learn from hence what is a catholic spirit.

There is scarce any expression which has been more grossly misunderstood and more dangerously misapplied than this, but it will be easy for any who calmly consider the preceding observations to correct any such misapprehensions of it and to prevent any such misapplication.

For, from hence we may learn, first, that a catholic spirit is not *speculative* latitudinarianism.[7] It is not an indifference to *all* opinions. This is the

---

6. Edition of 1786 reads: "my behalf."

7. *Cf.* Norman Sykes, *From Sheldon to Secker* (Cambridge, 1959), 146–52, for a brief review of the contemporary latitudinarian controversies that lie back of this disavowal.

spawn of hell, not the offspring of heaven. This unsettledness of thought, this being "driven to and fro and tossed about with every wind of doctrine" [*cf*. Eph. 4:14], is a great curse, not a blessing; an irreconcilable enemy, not a friend, to true catholicism. A man of a truly catholic spirit has not now his religion to seek. He is fixed as the sun in his judgment concerning the main branches of Christian doctrine. It is true he is always ready to hear and weigh whatsoever can be offered against his principles. But as this does not show any wavering in his own mind, so neither does it occasion any. He does not halt between two opinions, nor vainly endeavour to blend them into one. Observe this, you who know not what spirit ye are of, who call yourselves men of a catholic spirit only because you are of a muddy understanding, because your mind is all in a mist, because you have no settled, consistent principles, but are for jumbling all opinions together. Be convinced that you have quite missed your way; you know not where you are. You think you are got into the very spirit of Christ when, in truth, you are nearer the spirit of antichrist. Go first and learn the first elements of the gospel of Christ, and then shall you learn to be of a truly catholic spirit.

2. From what has been said we may learn, secondly, that a catholic spirit is not any kind of *practical* latitudinarianism. It is not indifference as to public worship or as to the outward manner of performing it. This, likewise, would not be a blessing but a curse. Far from being an help thereto, it would, so long as it remained, be an unspeakable hindrance to the worshipping of God in spirit and in truth. But the man of a truly catholic spirit, having weighed all things in the balance of the sanctuary, has no doubt, no scruple at all, concerning that particular mode of worship wherein he joins. He is clearly convinced that *this* manner of worshipping God is both scriptural and rational. He knows none in the world which is more scriptural, none which is more rational. Therefore, without rambling hither and thither, he cleaves close thereto and praises God for the opportunity of so doing.

3. Hence we may, thirdly, learn that a catholic spirit is not indifference to all congregations. This is another sort of latitudinarianism, no less absurd and unscriptural than the former. But it is far from a man of a truly catholic spirit. He is fixed in his congregation as well as his principles. He is united to one, not only in spirit but by all the outward ties of Christian fellowship. There he partakes of all the ordinances of God. There he receives the Supper of the Lord. There he pours out his soul in public prayer, and joins in public praise and thanksgiving.

There he rejoices to hear the word of reconciliation, the gospel of the grace of God. With these his nearest, his best-beloved brethren, on solemn occasions he seeks God by fasting. These particularly he watches over in love, as they do over his soul, admonishing, exhorting, comforting, reproving and every way building up each other in the faith. These he regards as his own household, and therefore, according to the ability God has given him, naturally cares for them and provides that they may have all the things that are needful for life and godliness.

4. But while he is steadily fixed in his religious principles, in what he believes to be the truth as it is in Jesus, while he firmly adheres to that worship of God which he judges to be most acceptable in his sight, and while he is united by the tenderest and closest ties to one particular congregation, his heart is enlarged toward all mankind, those he knows and those he does not; he embraces with strong and cordial affection neighbours and strangers, friends and enemies. This is catholic or universal love. And he that has this is of a catholic spirit. For love alone gives the title to this character: catholic love is a catholic spirit.

5. But if we take this word in the strictest sense, a man of a catholic spirit is one who, in the manner above-mentioned, gives his hand to all whose hearts are right with his heart: one who knows how to value and praise God for all the advantages he enjoys with regard to the knowledge of the things of God, the true scriptural manner of worshipping him, and, above all, his union with a congregation fearing God and working righteousness; one who, retaining these blessings with the strictest care, keeping them as the apple of his eye, at the same time loves — as friends, as brethren in the Lord, as members of Christ and children of God, as joint partakers now of the present kingdom of God and fellow heirs of his eternal kingdom — all, of whatever opinion or worship or congregation, who believe in the Lord Jesus Christ, who love God and man, who, rejoicing to please and fearing to offend God, are careful to abstain from evil and zealous of good works. He is the man of a truly catholic spirit who bears all these continually upon his heart; who, having an unspeakable tenderness for their persons and longing for their welfare, does not cease to commend them to God in prayer as well as to plead their cause before men; who speaks comfortably to them and labours by all his words to strengthen their hands in God. He assists them to the uttermost of his power in all things, spiritual and temporal. He is ready "to spend and be spent for them" [cf. 2 Cor. 12:15], yea, "to lay down his life for" their sake [Jn. 15:13].

6. Thou, O man of God, think on these things! If thou art already in this way, go on. If thou has heretofore mistook the path, bless God who hath brought thee back! And now run the race which is set before thee, in the royal way of universal love. Take heed, lest thou be either wavering in thy judgment or straitened in thy bowels. But keep an even pace, rooted in the faith once delivered to the saints [cf. Jude 3], and grounded in love, in true catholic love, till thou art swallowed up in love for ever and ever!

## On God's Vineyard

*Editor's introduction.* This sermon was first published in the eighth volume of *Sermons on Several Occasions* (1788), pp. 251–72, and then reprinted in *The Arminian Magazine* for 1789, pp. 6–14, 62–68 — there dated "Witney, October 17, 1787." It appears in *Works*, VII, 202–13. In the *Journal* we note that on October 9 Wesley had returned to London after an arduous and extended visitation of the Methodist societies in England, Ireland and the Channel Islands, a journey which had begun the previous February 25: [1]

> Wed. [October] 10. — I retired and spent the rest of the week in answering letters and preparing matter for the Magazine.
> Mon. 15. — I began a little tour through Oxfordshire. I preached at Wallingford in the evening, with much enlargement of heart.
> Tues. 16. — . . . About one I preached at Oxford to a very quiet, deeply serious congregation. The house at Witney would nothing near contain the people in the evening; it was well filled at five on Wednesday morning [Oct. 17th]. I dearly love this people; they are so simple of heart and so much alive to God. After dinner we returned to Oxford. . . .

Nothing in the *Journal, Diary* or *Letters* suggests any particular "occasion" for this sermon — save the recent experience of having completed an intensive survey of the entire scope and spread of British Methodism. What he had found in his journeyings had left him with mixed feelings. The annual conference at Manchester (July 31–Aug. 4) had been marred by a struggle over the perennial issue of the ministerial status of the Methodist preachers and further bickerings about the hymnbook.[2]

One can, therefore, imagine the eighty-four-year-old evangelist, in

1. *Journal*, VII, 333–34.                    2. *Cf.* Tyerman, *Life*, III, 496–99.

a brief but pleasant interlude in a charming Oxfordshire village, casting his mind back over the vicissitudes of Methodism in *time*, just as he had recently done in *space*. This sermon-essay, "On God's Vineyard," with its peculiar limitation of reference to "the body of people commonly called Methodists" and to "that Society only which began at Oxford in the year 1729, and remains united at this day," is the result. Save for the hortatory ending, it is an exercise in autobiographical retrospect, aimed at describing and assessing the Revival after fifty years, with a view to its further renewal by recalling it to its origins and essentials — and this by the one man who could speak of both with definitive authority.

Especially noteworthy are Wesley's comments on the correlations between the doctrines of justification and sanctification, as well as his insistence that, next to Scripture, the principal source of the Wesleyan notion of justification was, and always had been, The Homilies. Most of the motifs which Wesley had elaborated elsewhere are restated here in what is, in effect, a valedictory.

❖   ❖   ❖   ❖

What could have been done more to my vineyard, that I have not done in it? Wherefore, when I looked that it should bring forth grapes, brought it forth wild grapes (Is. 5:4)?

The "vineyard of the Lord" [*cf.* Is. 5:7], taking the word in its widest sense, may include the whole world. All the inhabitants of the earth may, in some sense, be called "the vineyard of the Lord," who "hath made all nations of men to dwell on all the face of the earth that they might seek the Lord, if haply they may feel after him, and find him" [*cf.* Acts 17:26–27]. But, in a narrower sense, "the vineyard of the Lord" may mean the Christian world; that is, all that name the name of Christ, and profess to obey his word. In a still narrower sense, it may be understood of what is termed the Reformed part of the Christian Church. In the narrowest of all, one may by that phrase, "the vineyard of the Lord," mean the body of people commonly called Methodists. In this sense I understand it now, meaning thereby that Society only which began at Oxford in the year 1729, and remains united at this day. Understanding the word in this sense, I repeat the question which God proposes to the prophet: "What could have been done more to my vineyard, that I have not done in it? Wherefore, when I looked that it should bring forth grapes, brought it forth wild grapes?"

What could God have done more in this his vineyard (supposing he had designed it should put forth great branches and spread over the earth) which he hath not done in it,

First, with regard to doctrine?
Secondly, with regard to spiritual helps?
Thirdly, with regard to discipline? And,
Fourthly, with regard to outward protection?

These things being considered, I would then briefly inquire, "Wherefore, when he looked it should bring forth grapes, brought it forth wild grapes?"

I. 1. First. What could have been done in this his vineyard which God hath not done in it? What could have been done more, with regard to doctrine? From the very beginning, from the time that four young men united together, each of them was *homo unius libri* — "a man of one book." God taught them all to make his "word a lantern unto their feet, and a light in all their paths" [Ps. 119:105, B.C.P.]. They had one, and only one, rule of judgment: namely, the oracles of God [*cf.* Rom. 3:2; Heb. 5:12]. They were one and all determined to be "Bible-Christians." They were continually reproached for this very thing; some terming them in derision "Bible-bigots," others, "Bible-moths" (feeding, they said, upon the Bible as moths do upon cloth). And indeed, unto this day, it is their constant endeavour to think and speak as the oracles of God.

2. It is true, a learned man, Dr. Trapp,[1] soon after their setting out, gave a very different account of them. "When I saw," said the Doctor, "these two books, *The Treatise on Christian Perfection,* and *The Serious Call to a Holy Life,* I thought, 'These books will certainly do mischief.' And so it proved; for presently after, up sprung the Methodists. So he (Mr. Law) was their parent." Although this was not entirely true, yet there was some truth in it. All the Methodists carefully read these books and were greatly profited thereby. Yet they did by no means spring from them, but from the Holy Scriptures, being "born again," as St. Peter speaks, "by the word of God, which liveth and abideth for ever" [*cf.* 1 Pet. 1:23].

3. Another learned man, the late Bishop Warburton,[2] roundly affirms

1. Joseph Trapp (1679–1747); poet and pamphleteer; ally of Henry Sacheverell; first professor of poetry at Oxford. His anti-Methodist pamphlet (directed largely at Whitefield) was entitled *The Nature, Folly, Sin and Danger of Being Righteous Overmuch, with a Particular View to the Doctrines and Practices of Certain Modern Enthusiasts* (1739).

2. William Warburton (1698–1779), bishop of Gloucester, 1759–79. *His Divine*

that "they were the offspring of Mr. Law and Count Zinzendorf together." But this was a greater mistake still. For they had met together
several years before they had the least acquaintance with Count Zinzendorf, or even knew there was such a person in the world. And when they
did know him, although they esteemed him very highly in love, yet they
did not dare to follow him one step farther than they were warranted
by the Scripture.[3]

4. The book which, next to the Holy Scripture, was of the greatest
use to them in settling their judgment as to the grand point of justification by faith was the book of Homilies.[4] They were never clearly convinced that we are justified by faith alone till they carefully consulted
these and compared them with the sacred writings, particularly St.
Paul's Epistle to the Romans.[5] And no minister of the Church can, with
any decency, oppose these, seeing at his ordination he subscribed to them
in subscribing the Thirty-sixth Article of the Church.

5. It has been frequently observed that very few were clear in their
judgment both with regard to justification and sanctification. Many who
have spoken and written admirably well concerning justification had no
clear conception, nay, were totally ignorant, of the doctrine of sanctification. Who has wrote more ably than Martin Luther on justification by
faith alone? And who was more ignorant of the doctrine of sanctification, or more confused in his conceptions of it? In order to be thoroughly
convinced of this, of his total ignorance with regard to sanctification,
there needs no more than to read over, without prejudice, his celebrated
comment on the Epistle to the Galatians.[6] On the other hand, how many
writers of the Romish Church (as Francis Sales[7] and Juan de Castaniza,[8]

---

*Legation of Moses* (1737-41) was an apology for orthodoxy against the deists; his
*Doctrine of Grace: or, the Office and Operations of the Holy Spirit vindicated from
the Insults of Infidelity and the Abuses of Fanaticism* . . . (1763), was a vigorous
polemic against the Methodists.

   3. See below, p. 367 ff.             4. See below, pp. 123-33.

   5. Cf. *Journal*, II, 101 (for Sunday, Nov. 12, 1738); see above, p. 16.

   6. Cf. *Journal*, II, 467 (June 15, 1741); see below, p. 366. See also *Journal*, II, 174;
III, 409, for other references to Luther in this same vein. Wesley nowhere acknowl-
edges Luther as a principal theological influence.

   7. François de Sales, 1567-1622, leader of the Counter Reformation in Savoy and
a great teacher of the devotional life. His chief writings, which Wesley had read, are
*Introduction to the Devout Life* (1608; Westminster, 1948) and *A Treatise on the
Love of God* (1616; Westminster, 1942).

   8. A Spanish Benedictine monk (*c.* 1536-99). In Wesley's time he was credited
with a then highly esteemed devotional treatise, *De pugna spiritualis; tractatus vere
aureus de perfectione vitae christianae* (1599). It was translated into English in 1698

in particular) have wrote strongly and scripturally on sanctification, who, nevertheless, were entirely unacquainted with the nature of justification! Insomuch that the whole body of their Divines at the Council of Trent, in their *Catechismus ad Parochos* [9] (the catechism which every parish priest is to teach his people), totally confound sanctification and justification together. But it has pleased God to give the Methodists a full and clear knowledge of each, and the wide difference between them.

6. They know, indeed, that at the same time a man is justified, sanctification properly begins. For when he is justified, he is "born again," "born from above," "born of the Spirit" [cf. Jn. 3:3, 6]; which, although it is not (as some suppose) the whole process of sanctification, is doubtless the gate of it. Of this, likewise, God has given them a full view. They know, the new birth implies as great a change in the soul, in him that is "born of the Spirit," as was wrought in his body when he was born of a woman. Not an outward change only, as from drunkenness to sobriety, from robbery or theft to honesty — this is the poor, dry, miserable conceit of those that know nothing of real religion — but an inward change from all unholy to all holy tempers: from pride to humility, from passionateness to meekness, from peevishness and discontent to patience and resignation; in a word, from an earthly, sensual, devilish mind to the mind that was in Christ Jesus [cf. Phil. 2:5].

7. It is true, a late very eminent author, in his strange treatise on regeneration [10] proceeds entirely on the supposition that it is the whole gradual progress of sanctification. No; it is only the threshold of sanctification, the first entrance upon it. And as, in the natural birth, a man is born at once and then grows larger and stronger by degrees, so in the spiritual birth, a man is born at once and then gradually increases in

---

(by Richard Lucas), under the title *The Spiritual Combat; or the Christian Pilgrim in His Spiritual Conflict and Conquest.* Nowadays, it is attributed to Lorenzo Scupoli; *cf.* Lawrence Scupoli, *The Spiritual Combat and a Treatise on Peace of the Soul* (Westminster, 1945). See also Martin Schmidt, *John Wesley* (Frankfurt, 1953), 48–53; M. Alamo, in *Dictionnaire d'histoire et de geographique ecclesiastique*, XI, 1414–15; and the *Lexikon für Theologie und Kirche*, IX, 389.

9. *Cf. The Catechism of the Council of Trent*, translated into English; with notes by T. A. Buckley (1852).

10. *Cf.* Daniel Waterland, *Regeneration Stated and Explained, according to Scripture and Antiquity* (1740), which was by all odds the most famous of the eighteenth century's essays in this field, just as Waterland was himself one of the few truly eminent Anglican theologians of the period. But it is possible that Wesley *may* have had in mind William Law, *Grounds and Reasons of Christian Regeneration* (1739). *Cf.* Sermon XLV, "The New Birth" (*Works*, VI, 74–75).

spiritual stature and strength. The new birth, therefore, is the first point of sanctification, which may increase "more and more unto the perfect day" [Prov. 4:18].

8. It is, then, a great blessing given to this people, that as they do not think or speak of justification so as to supersede sanctification, so neither do they think or speak of sanctification so as to supersede justification. They take care to keep each in its own place, laying equal stress on one and the other. They know God has joined these together and it is not for man to put them asunder. Therefore they maintain, with equal zeal and diligence, the doctrine of free, full, present justification, on the one hand, and of entire sanctification both of heart and life, on the other — being as tenacious of inward holiness as any mystic, and of outward, as any Pharisee.

9. Who then is a Christian, according to the light which God hath vouch-safed to this people? He that, being "justified by faith, hath peace with God through our Lord Jesus Christ" [Rom. 5:1]; and, at the same time, is "born again," "born from above," "born of the Spirit"; inwardly changed from the image of the devil, to that "image of God wherein he was created" [cf. Col. 3:10]; he that finds the love of God shed abroad in his heart by the Holy Ghost which is given unto him [cf. Rom. 5:5], and whom this love sweetly constrains to "love his neighbour (every man) as himself"; he that has learned of his Lord to be meek and lowly in heart and in every state to be content; he in whom is that whole mind, all those tempers, which were also in Christ Jesus; he that abstains from all appearance of evil [cf. 1 Thess. 5:22] in his actions and that "offends not" with "his tongue" [cf. Jas. 3:2, 5]; he that walks in all the commandments of God and in all his ordinances blameless; he that, in all his intercourse with men, does to others as he would they should do to him; and in his whole life and conversation, whether he eats or drinks or whatsoever he doeth, doeth all to the glory of God [cf. 1 Cor. 10:31].

Now, what could God have done more for this his vineyard which he hath not done in it, with regard to *doctrine?*

II. We are to inquire, secondly, what could have been done which he hath not done in it, with regard to *spiritual helps?*

1. Let us consider this matter from the very beginning. Two young clergymen, not very remarkable in any way, of middle age, having a toler-able measure of health (though rather weak than strong), began, about fifty years ago, to call sinners to repentance. This they did, for a time, in many of the churches in and about London. But two difficulties arose:

first, the churches were so crowded that many of the parishioners could not get in; secondly, they preached new doctrines — that we are saved by faith and that "without holiness no man could see the Lord" [cf. Heb. 12:14]. For one or other of these reasons, they were not long suffered to preach in the churches. They then preached in Moorfields, Kennington Common and in many other public places.[11] The fruit of their preaching quickly appeared. Many sinners were changed both in heart and life. But, it seemed, this could not continue long. For every day one clearly saw these preachers would quickly wear themselves out; and no clergyman dared to assist them. But soon one and another, though not ordained, offered to assist them. God gave a signal blessing to their word [work?]. Many sinners were thoroughly convinced of sin, and many truly converted to God. Their assistants increased, both in number and in the success of their labours. Some of them were learned, some unlearned. Most of them were young, a few middle-aged. Some of them were weak; some, on the contrary, of remarkably strong understanding. But it pleased God to own them all, so that more and more brands were plucked out of the burning.[12]

2. It may be observed that these clergymen, all this time, had no plan at all. They only went hither and thither, wherever they had a prospect of saving souls from death. But when more and more asked, "What must I do to be saved?" they were desired to meet all together. Twelve came the first Thursday night; forty the next; soon after, a hundred. And they continued to increase, till, three or four and twenty years ago, the London society amounted to about twenty-eight hundred.

3. But how should this multitude of people be kept together? And how should it be known whether they walked worthy of their profession? They were providentially led, when they were thinking on another thing, namely, paying the public debt, to divide all the people into little companies, or classes, according to their places of abode, and appoint one person in each class to see all the rest weekly. By this means it was quickly discovered if any of them lived in any known sin. If they did, they were first admonished and, when judged incorrigible, excluded from the society.

4. This division of the people, and the exclusion of those that walked

11. Notice that there is no mention here that the first field preaching was in Bristol (see above, pp. 16–17). There is a similar silence in the sermon "On Numbers 23:23," *Works*, VII, 419–30.

12. Cf. Zech. 3:2; see also above, p. 6.

disorderly without any respect of persons, were helps which few other communities had. To these, as the societies increased, was soon added another. The "stewards" of the societies in each district were desired to meet the preachers once a quarter, in some central place, to give an account of the spiritual and temporal state of their several societies.[13] The use of these quarterly-meetings was soon found to be exceeding great; in consideration of which, they were gradually spread to all the societies in the kingdom.

5. In order to increase the union between the preachers, as well as that of the people, they were desired to meet all together in London; and, some time after, a select number of them. Afterwards, for more convenience, they met at London, Bristol, and Leeds, alternately. They spent a few days together in this general conference,[14] in considering what might most conduce to the general good. The result was immediately signified to all their brethren. And they soon found that what St. Paul observes of the whole Church, may be, in a measure, applied to every part of it: "The whole body being fitly framed together and compacted by that which every joint supplieth, maketh increase of the body to the edifying of itself in love" [Eph. 4:16].

6. That this may be the more effectually done, they have another excellent help in the constant change of preachers; it being their rule that no preacher shall remain in the same circuit more than two years together, and few of them more than one year. Some, indeed, have imagined that this was a hindrance to the work of God, but long experience in every part of the kingdom proves the contrary. This has always shown that the people profit less by any one person than by a variety of preachers, while they

> Used the gifts on each bestow'd,
> Tempered by the art of God.[15]

7. Together with these helps, which are peculiar to their own society, they have all those which are enjoyed in common by the other members of the Church of England. Indeed, they have been long pressed to separate from it — to which they have had temptations of every kind.

13. See below, p. 146.                    14. See below, pp. 134-37.
15. Cf. *Collection of Hymns* . . . (1780), 481 (DIV, st. 6):
> Never from our office move:
> Needful to each other prove:
> Use the grace on *earth* bestow'd;
> Temper'd by the *heart* of God.

But they cannot, they dare not, they will not, separate from it while they can remain therein with a clear conscience. It is true, if any sinful terms of communion were imposed upon them, then they would be constrained to separate; but as this is not the case at present, we rejoice to continue therein.

8. What then could God have done more for his vineyard, which he hath not done in it, with regard to spiritual helps? He has hardly dealt so with any other people in the Christian world. If it be said, "He could have made them a separate people, like the Moravian Brethren," I answer: "This would have been a direct contradiction to his whole design in raising them up: namely, to spread scriptural religion throughout the land, among people of every denomination, leaving every one to hold his own opinions and to follow his own mode of worship." This could only be done effectually by leaving these things as they were and endeavouring to leaven the whole nation with that "faith that worketh by love" [Gal. 5:6].

III. 1. Such are the *spiritual helps* which God has bestowed on this vineyard with no sparing hand. *Discipline* might be inserted among these, but we may as well speak of it under a separate head. It is certain that, in this respect, the Methodists are a highly favoured people. Nothing can be more simple, nothing more rational, than the Methodist discipline. It is entirely founded on common sense, particularly applying the general rules of Scripture. Any person determined to save his soul may be united (this is the only condition required) with them. But this desire must be evidenced by three marks: avoiding all known sin; doing good after his power; and, attending all the ordinances of God.[16] He is then placed in such a class as is convenient for him, where he spends about an hour in a week. And, the next quarter, if nothing is objected to him, he is admitted into the society, and therein he may continue as long as he continues to meet his brethren and walks according to his profession.

2. Their public service is at five in the morning, and six or seven in the evening, that their temporal business may not be hindered. Only on Sunday it begins between nine and ten and concludes with the Lord's Supper. On Sunday evening the society meets; but care is taken to dismiss them early, that all the heads of families may have time to instruct their several households. Once a quarter, the principal preacher in every circuit examines every member of the societies therein. By this means, if the behaviour of any one is blameable, which is frequently to be expected in

16. *Cf.* the three "General Rules," below, pp. 177–79.

so numerous a body of people, it is easily discovered, and either the offence or the offender removed in time.

3. Whenever it is needful to exclude any disorderly member out of the society, it is done in the most quiet and inoffensive manner — only by not renewing his ticket at the quarterly visitation. But in some cases where the offence is great and there is danger of public scandal, it is judged necessary to declare, when all the members are present: "A. B. is no longer a member of our society." Now, what can be more rational or more scriptural than this simple discipline — attended from the beginning to the end with no trouble, expense, or delay?

IV. 1. But was it possible that all these things should be done without a flood of opposition? The prince of this world was not dead nor asleep, and would he not fight that his kingdom might not be delivered up? If the word of the apostle be found true, in all ages and nations, "all they that will live godly in Christ Jesus shall suffer persecution" [2 Tim. 3:12]. If this be true with regard to every individual Christian, how much more with regard to bodies of men visibly united together with the avowed design to overthrow his kingdom? And what could withstand the persecution he would not fail to stir up against a poor, defenceless, despised people, without any visible help, without money, without power, without friends?

2. In truth, the god of this world was not asleep, neither was he idle. He *did* fight, and that with all his power, that his kingdom might not be delivered up. He "brought forth all his hosts to war." First, he stirred up the beast of the people. They roared like lions, they encompassed the little and defenceless on every side. And the storm rose higher and higher, till deliverance came in a way that none expected. God stirred up the heart of our late gracious sovereign to give such orders to his magistrates as, being put in execution, effectually quelled the madness of the people. It was about the same time that a great man applied personally to his Majesty, begging that he would please to "take a course to stop these run-about preachers." His Majesty, looking sternly upon him, answered without ceremony, like a king, "I tell you, while I sit on the throne, no man shall be persecuted for conscience' sake." [17]

3. But in defiance of this, several who bore his Majesty's commission have persecuted them from time to time, and that under colour of law, availing themselves of what is called the Conventicle Act — one in particular, in Kent, who some years since took upon him to fine one of the

17. See above, p. 21.

preachers and several of his hearers. But they thought it their duty to appeal to his Majesty's Court of King's Bench. The cause was given for the plaintiffs, who have ever since been permitted to worship God according to their own conscience.

4. I believe this is a thing wholly without precedent. I find no other instance of it, in any age of the Church, from the day of Pentecost to this day. Every opinion, right and wrong, has been tolerated, almost in every age and nation. Every mode of worship has been tolerated, however superstitious or absurd. But I do not know that true, vital, scriptural religion was ever tolerated before. For this the people called Methodists have abundant reason to praise God. In their favour he hath wrought a new thing in the earth: "he hath stilled the enemy and the avenger" [Ps. 8:2]. This, then, they must ascribe unto him, the author of their outward as well as inward peace.

V. 1. What indeed could God have done more for this his vineyard which he hath not done in it? This having been largely showed, we may now proceed to that strong and tender expostulation: "After all that I had done, might I not have looked for the most excellent grapes? Wherefore, then, brought it forth wild grapes?" "Might I not have expected a general increase of faith and love, of righteousness and true holiness; yea, and of the fruit of the Spirit — love, joy, peace, long-suffering, meekness, gentleness, fidelity, goodness, temperance" [cf. Gal. 5:22–23]? Was it not reasonable to expect that these fruits would have overspread his whole church? Truly, when I saw what God had done among his people between forty and fifty years ago, when I saw them warm in their first love, magnifying the Lord and rejoicing in God their Saviour, I could expect nothing less than that all these would have lived like angels here below, that they would have walked as continually seeing him that is invisible, having constant communion with the Father and the Son — living in eternity and walking in eternity. I looked to see "a chosen generation, a royal priesthood, a holy nation, a peculiar people"; in the whole tenor of their conversation "showing forth his praise, who had called them into his marvellous light" [1 Pet. 2:9].

2. But, instead of this, it brought forth wild grapes — fruit of a quite contrary nature. It brought forth error in ten thousand shapes, turning many of the simple out of the way. It brought forth enthusiasm, imaginary inspiration, ascribing to the all-wise God all the wild, absurd, self-inconsistent dreams of a heated imagination. It brought forth pride, robbing the giver of every good gift of the honour due to his name. It

brought forth prejudice, evil-surmising, censoriousness, judging and condemning one another — all totally subversive of that brotherly love which
is the very badge of the Christian profession, without which whosoever
liveth is counted dead before God. It brought forth anger, hatred, malice,
revenge, and every evil word and work — all direful fruits, not of the
Holy Spirit, but of the bottomless pit!

3. It brought forth likewise in many, particularly those that are increased in goods, that grand poison of souls: the love of the world, and
that in all its branches — "the desire of the flesh," that is, the seeking
happiness in the pleasures of sense; "the desire of the eyes," that is, seeking happiness in dress, or any of the pleasures of imagination; and "the
pride of life," that is, seeking happiness in the praise of men; or in that
which ministers to all these, laying up treasures on earth [cf. 1 Jn. 2:16].
It brought forth self-indulgence of every kind — delicacy, effeminacy,
softness — but not softness of the right kind, that melts at human woe. It
brought such base, grovelling affections, such deep earthly-mindedness, as
that of the poor heathens, which occasioned the lamentation of their own
poet over them — O curvae in terras animae et caelestium inanes! [18] —
O souls bowed down to earth and void of God!

4. O ye that have riches in possession, once more hear the word of
the Lord! Ye that are rich in this world, that have food to eat and raiment
to put on, and something over, are you clear of the curse of loving the
world? Are you sensible of your danger? Do you feel, "How hardly
will they that have riches enter into the kingdom of heaven" [Lk. 18:24]?
Do you continue unburned in the midst of the fire? Are you untouched
with the love of the world? Are you clear from the desire of the flesh,
the desire of the eyes, and the pride of life? Do you "put a knife to your
throat" [cf. Prov. 23:2] when you sit down to meat, lest your "table
should be a snare to you" [cf. Ps. 69:22]? Is not your belly your god?
Is not eating and drinking, or any other pleasure of sense, the greatest
pleasure you enjoy? Do not you seek happiness in dress, furniture, pictures, gardens, or anything else that pleases the eye? Do not you grow
soft and delicate, unable to bear cold, heat, the wind or the rain as you
did when you were poor? Are you not increasing in goods, laying up
treasures on earth, instead of restoring to God in the poor, not so much,

18. Wesley may have read this in Lactantius, Divinarum Institutionum, Bk. II,
chap. ii (which has terras in place of terris, etc.; cf. PL, VI, 261). Its original source
is Perseus, Satura II, l. 61 (cf. S. G. Owen's edition of Perseus in Scriptorum Classi-
corum Bibliotheca Oxoniensis [Oxford, 1908]).

or so much, but all that you can spare? Surely, "it is easier for a camel to go through the eye of a needle, than for a rich man to enter into the kingdom of heaven" [Mt. 19:24]!

5. But why will ye still bring forth wild grapes? What excuse can ye make? Hath God been wanting on *his* part? Have you not been warned over and over? Have ye not been fed with "the sincere milk of the word" [*cf.* 1 Pet. 2:2]? Hath not the whole word of God been delivered to you, and without any mixture of error? Were not the fundamental doctrines both of free, full, present justification delivered to you, as well as sanctification, both gradual and instantaneous? Was not every branch both of inward and outward holiness clearly opened and earnestly applied, and that by preachers of every kind, young and old, learned and unlearned? But it is well if some of you did not despise the helps which God had prepared for you. Perhaps you would hear none but clergymen or, at least, none but men of learning. Will you not then give God leave to choose his own messengers — to send by whom he *will* send? It is well if this bad wisdom was not one cause of your "bringing forth wild grapes"!

6. Was not another cause of it your despising that excellent help, union with a Christian society? Have you not read, "How can one be warm alone?" and, "Woe be unto him that is alone when he falleth" [*cf.* Eccles. 4:10–11]? "But you have companions enough" [you say]. Perhaps more than enough, more than are helpful to your soul. But have you enough that are athirst for God and that labour to make *you* so? Have you companions enough that watch over your soul, as they that must give account, and that freely and faithfully warn you if you take any false step or are in danger of doing so? I fear you have few of these companions, or else you would bring forth better fruit!

7. If you are a member of the society, do you make a full use of your privilege? Do you never fail to meet your class, and that not as matter of form, but expecting that when you are met together in his name, your Lord will be in the midst of you? Are you truly thankful for the amazing liberty of conscience which is vouchsafed to you and your brethren, such as never was enjoyed before by persons in your circumstances? And are you thankful to the giver of every good gift for the general spread of true religion? Surely, you can never praise God enough for all these blessings, so plentifully showered down upon you, till you praise him with angels and archangels and all the company of heaven! [19]

19. *Cf.* the Sanctus, in the Order for Holy Communion. B.C.P.

PART TWO

❖

*Theological Foundations*

# Introduction to Part Two

IN THE HISTORY of Christian doctrine the front rank is rightly reserved for the great speculative theologians — that select company of systematic thinkers who have managed to effect major mutations in the Christian mind. Wesley has no place in this company — nor did he aspire to one. He was, by talent and intent, a *folk*-theologian: an eclectic who had mastered the secret of plastic synthesis, simple profundity, the common touch. He was an effective evangelist guided by a discriminating theological understanding, a creative theologian practically involved in the application of his doctrine in the renewal of the church.

Few of his doctrinal views are abstruse and none is original. It is their sum and balance that is unique, that gives him a distinctive theological stance. The elements of his theology were adapted from many sources: the prime article of justification by faith, from the reformers (Anglican) of the sixteenth century; the emphasis on the assurance of faith, from the Moravian pietists; the ethical notions of divine-human synergism, from the ancient Fathers of the Church; the idea of the Christian life as devotion, from Taylor, a Kempis, Law (and Scougal), the vision and program of "perfection" ($\tau\epsilon\lambda\epsilon i\omega\sigma\iota s$), from Gregory of Nyssa via "Macarius." These diverse motifs — mildly incongruous in the theological climate of the early eighteenth century — he brought and held together within the liturgical frame of the Book of Common Prayer, the Articles and The Homilies. But their development in his mind was ordered by the practical exigencies of the Revival itself. Wesley's theology is self-consciously Anglican, but its exact counterpart is not to be found anywhere else in that tradition. There are features in his position derived from left-wing Protestantism — field preaching, lay preaching, "the witness of the Spirit," extempore prayer in the congregation, etc. — and these greatly alarmed his fellow Anglicans, who saw in them the fatal flaw of "enthusiasm." Yet his violent aversion to antinomianism is clearly catholic — and so are his basic arguments against Calvinistic predestinarianism. There are a few instructive parallels between Wesley in the eighteenth century and Luther and Calvin in the sixteenth, but it is highly misleading to interpret him as

their conscious debtor.[1] Indeed, the bulk of his references to them are
largely negative.

For all this borrowing and mixing under the pressures and heat of a
great popular movement, Wesley's theology emerges clear and consistent
and integral. It is at this level that a claim to originality may be registered
for him — and tested. Many other theological systems are bolder, subtler,
more massive — but none has a more intense and sustained evangelical
concern. He seems to have been aware that the strength of his position
lay in its simple profundity, and this prompted him to make frequent
summaries of it — usually with a clearly drawn boundary line between
essential doctrine and "opinions." [2] This makes for a certain repetitiousness — and yet also a certain cumulative impact of his thought upon the
attentive reader.

The following PART TWO consists of a representative sampling of Wesley's basic theological statements. Each is comparatively short. They are
all plainly circumstantial and practical; they spread out over the principal topics of his message: the fact of faith, the assurance of faith, the faith
that works by love, the faith that ripens to fulfillment.

The selections here range from the bleak dawn before the Revival was
actually under way down to its heyday of real success. They vary in
form from his abridgment of the Edwardian Homilies, through his minutes of the early "conferences" between himself and his preachers, to
doctrinal "sermons" and theological essays. Everything here was written
for common people to read — or to hear read in the meetings of the
Methodist societies. And yet, the life of faith which they describe and
"enforce" is quite uncommon. Thus the reader may examine for himself
a cross section of Wesley's interpretations of the Christian faith and its
expression in witness, discipline and nurture.

1. But *cf.* G. C. Cell, *The Rediscovery of John Wesley* (New York, 1935), Franz
Hildebrandt, *From Luther to Wesley* (1951), and Colin Williams, *John Wesley's
Theology Today* (New York, 1960) — all of whom make him out as the theological
heir of *Continental* Protestantism (a notion that would have astonished Wesley).

2. *E.g. Journal*, III, 534; IV, 419; *Letters*, IV, 146; V, 225–29; VI, 28; *Works*, VIII,
46–49, 67, 472; IX, 174.

# I

## DOCTRINAL SUMMARIES

*Editor's introduction.* Mid-November of 1738 found Wesley just past the halfway mark between his Aldersgate experience and his first real success as an evangelist. He had already visited the Moravians in Germany; he had just recently discovered Jonathan Edwards and the Great Awakening; [1] he was currently immersed in the life of the religious societies in London (especially Fetter Lane). It was in this pregnant time that he "began more narrowly to inquire what the doctrine of the Church of England is concerning the much controverted point of justification by faith." [2] The following tract is one of the results of that inquiry: his first published doctrinal manifesto. [3] It went through nineteen editions in his lifetime and was a staple item in Methodist instruction.

In it Wesley condensed thirty-six pages of an octavo copy of *Certain Sermons or Homilies, Appointed to Be Read in Churches*, [4] into a twelve-page duodecimo pamphlet, with very few editorial changes and still fewer gaps in style or argument. It is a good example of Wesley's way of working: his material is borrowed, but its form and use are distinctively his own.

The history and form-criticism of The Homilies is on the murky side, [5] but Wesley regarded them as typical of the Anglican consensus — the

1. See above, pp. 15–16.    2. *Journal*, II, 101.

3. Green, *Bibliography*, #9, dates the first edition as 1739. But there is an authentic text in the Library of Wesley Theological Seminary, Washington, D.C., dated 1738. This fits the evidence of the *Journal* entry, plus the reference in "On God's Vineyard" (above, p. 107), and must be reckoned as the first edition. See above, pp. 16–17.

4. His own copy of The Homilies (now in the Leete Collection, Southern Methodist University) was printed at Oxford and dated 1683 — *i.e.* the last reprint authorized by Charles II.

5. *Cf.* J. T. Tomlinson, *The Prayer Book, Articles and Homilies* (1897), a somewhat crotchety exception to the general neglect of this subject in the literature of English church history.

more so because Homily III is invoked by Article XI as authoritative. He himself often speaks of "the words of our Church," [6] referring to The Homilies, and, usually, to the passages from which this "extract" was taken.

His choice of the first five Edwardian Homilies to digest is significant because it locates the core of his own doctrinal position. One should remember that the idea of a book of homilies had been forced on the Convocation of 1542 by the fact that a large number of erstwhile Roman priests and monks were newly required to preach regularly in their churches without adequate training or practice. The remedy for this — twelve "model" sermons touching the main points of disagreement with Rome and The Council of Trent (already convoked) — was completed within a year, but was then suppressed by Henry VIII. Edward VI authorized publication in 1547.

It is reasonably clear that the author of the particular Homilies which Wesley chose to extract was Thomas Cranmer — Archbishop of Canterbury under Henry VIII and Edward VI (1532–53). In his own way, he, too, was something of a folk-theologian, albeit with an incomparably greater talent for liturgical English. Again like Wesley, Cranmer was open to the influences of both the Protestant and Catholic traditions, more concerned with an evangelical catholicism than with a radical either/or. For example, it is a moot question whether the chief "source" for Homily III ("Of the Salvation of All Mankind") was Cajetanus's commentary on the New Testament [7] or Melanchthon's *locus* on "The Vocabulary of Grace." [8] It could have been either or both. The point is that the taproot of Wesley's theology was sunk into the rich original stratum of the English Reformation: fiercely anti-Roman in polity, yet also instinctively opposed to the extremes of the Continental Protestants; ecumenical in tone and temper; devoted to the dynamic balance of Christian worship and Christian behavior.

It is interesting to compare Cranmer's text and Wesley's abridgment of it. What the latter did was simply to excise every passage in Cranmer that could be eliminated without mangling the nerve of the argument. The result is that a great deal of splendid rhetoric is discarded, but every main idea retained. The impact of the shortened piece upon a reader is, if anything, heightened. There is only one shift of emphasis, and this is

6. *Cf.* Article XXXV, "Of the Homilies," B.C.P.
7. Cranmer's autographed copy of this is in the British Museum.
8. *Cf.* Tomlinson, *Prayer Book*, 238–40.

readily understood if the context be taken into account: Wesley reduced Cranmer's accent on the *necessity* of "good works annexed to faith" in the direction of a more explicit emphasis upon their spontaneous character as the *fruits* of faith.

He reprinted this "extract" in Vol. IX (pp. 37–53) of his collected *Works* (Pine), from which our text is taken (collated, of course, against the earlier editions). His subsequent editors quietly dropped it from their editions; yet if ever Wesley made another man's words his very own, he did so in this instance. *Salvation, Faith and Good Works* is, therefore, a genuine fundament of the Wesleyan theology.

✢ ✢ ✢ ✢

## The Doctrine of Salvation, Faith and Good Works, Extracted from the Homilies of the Church of England [1]

### TO THE READER

[He that desires more perfectly to understand these great doctrines of Christianity ought diligently to read the Holy Scriptures, especially St. Paul's Epistles to the Romans and the Galatians.] [2] And whosoever giveth his mind to Holy Scriptures with diligent study and burning desire, it cannot be that he should be left without help. For either God will send him some godly doctor to teach him or God himself from above will give light unto [his] mind and teach [him] those things which are necessary for [him]. Man's human and worldly wisdom or science is not needful to the understanding of Scripture but the revelation of the Holy Ghost who inspireth the true meaning unto them that with humility and diligence search [for it]. [3]

1. Cf. *Certain Sermons or Homilies, Appointed to Be Read in Churches* (Oxford, 1683), 5–35.

2. Wesley's prefatory sentence; throughout this section brackets denote his interpolations, except for Scripture citations, which have been added by the editor.

3. [Au.] *Homily of Reading the Holy Scriptures.* [Ed.] "The Second Part of the Sermon of the Knowledge of Holy Scripture," p. 5. As a sample for checking Wesley's method of abridgment, the following is Cranmer's first paragraph with Wesley's resulting abridgment picked out in small caps.

AND WHOSOEVER GIVETH HIS MIND TO HOLY SCRIPTURES WITH DILIGENT STUDY AND BURNING DESIRE, IT CANNOT BE (saith St. Chrysostom) THAT HE SHOULD BE LEFT WITHOUT HELP. FOR EITHER GOD Almighty WILL SEND HIM SOME GODLY DOCTOR TO TEACH HIM, as he did to instruct the eunuch, a noble man of Ethiope and treasurer unto

## Of the Salvation of Mankind

1. Because all men are sinners against God and breakers of his law,
therefore can no man by his works be justified and made righteous before
God. But every man is constrained to seek for another righteousness or
justification, to be received at God's own hands. And this justification or
righteousness which we receive of God's mercy and Christ's merits, embraced by faith, is taken, accepted and allowed of God for our perfect
and full justification. For the more [clear and] full understanding hereof,
it is our part ever to remember how that, all the world being wrapped in
sin, God sent his only Son into the world to fulfil the law for us and, by
shedding his blood, to make satisfaction to his Father for our sins, to
assuage his indignation conceived against us.

2. Insomuch that infants, being baptized and dying in their infancy,
are by this sacrifice washed from their sins. And they who in act or deed
sin after their baptism, when they turn again to God unfeignedly, are
likewise washed by this sacrifice from their sins in such sort that there
remaineth not any spot of sin that shall be imputed to their damnation.
This is that justification [4] which St. Paul speaketh of when he saith, "No
man is justified by the works of the law but by faith in Jesus Christ." And
again, "We are justified by the faith of Christ and not by the works of
the law, for by the works of the law shall no flesh be justified" [cf. Gal.
2:16].

3. The great wisdom of God in this mystery of our redemption [hath

---

Queen Candace, who having affection to read the Scripture (although he under-
stood it not) yet for the desire he had unto God's Word, God sent his Apostle
Philip to declare unto him the true sense of the Scripture that he read; or else,
if we lack a learned man to instruct and teach us, yet GOD HIMSELF FROM ABOVE
WILL GIVE LIGHT UNTO our minds [HIS MIND] AND TEACH US [HIM] THOSE THINGS
WHICH ARE NECESSARY FOR us [HIM] and wherein we be ignorant. And in another
place Chrysostom saith that MAN'S HUMAN AND WORLDLY WISDOM OR SCIENCE IS NOT
NEEDFUL TO THE UNDERSTANDING OF SCRIPTURE BUT THE REVELATION OF THE HOLY
GHOST WHO INSPIRETH THE TRUE MEANING UNTO THEM THAT WITH HUMILITY AND DILI-
GENCE do SEARCH therefore [FOR IT]. "He that asketh shall have and he that seeketh
shall find and he that knocketh shall have the door opened" [cf. Lk. 11:10].
If we read once, twice or thrice, and understand not, let us not cease so, but still
continue reading, praying, asking of others and so by still knocking (at the last)
the door shall be opened, as St. Augustine saith — "Although many things in the
Scripture be spoken of in obscure mysteries, yet there is nothing spoken under
dark mysteries in one place but the selfsame thing in other places is spoken of
more familiarly and plainly, to the capacity both of learned and unlearned."
4. Wesley's first edition adds, "or righteousness."

tempered his justice and mercy together]. His mercy he showeth in delivering us from our captivity without requiring any ransom to be paid or amends to be made on [5] our parts, which thing by us had been impossible to be done. And whereas it lay not in us to do that, he provided a ransom for us: that was the precious body and blood of his own son.[6] And so the justice of God and his mercy embraced together,[7] and fulfilled the great mystery of our redemption.

4. Of this justice and mercy of God knit together, speaketh St. Paul in the third chapter to the Romans, "All have [sinned and come short] of the glory of God, but are justified freely by his grace through [the] redemption that is in Jesus Christ, whom God hath [set forth to be a propitiation] through faith in his blood" [v. 23–25]. And in the tenth, "Christ is the end of the law [for] righteousness to every [one] that believeth" [v. 4]. And in the eighth chapter, "That which was impossible by the law, inasmuch as it is weak [through] the flesh, God sending his own son in the [likeness] of sinful flesh, [and for] sin, condemned sin in the flesh, that the righteousness of the law might be fulfilled in us [who] walk not after the flesh but after the Spirit" [v. 3–4].[8]

5. In these places the apostle toucheth especially three things which must go together in our justification: upon God's part, his great mercy and grace; upon Christ's part, the satisfaction of God's justice by the offering his body and shedding his blood, with the fulfilling of the law perfectly and thoroughly; and upon our part, true and lively faith in the merits of Jesus Christ, so that in our justification there is not only God's mercy and grace, but his justice also. And so the grace of God doth not shut out the [righteousness] of God in our justification, but only shutteth out the [righteousness] of man, that is to say, the [righteousness] of our works.

6. And therefore St. Paul declareth nothing on the behalf of man concerning his justification but only a true and lively faith, which [itself] is the gift of God. And yet that faith doth not shut out repentance, hope, love and the fear of God, to be joined with faith in every man that is justified. But it shutteth them out from the office of justifying, so that although they be all present together in him that is justified, yet they justify not all together.

5. First edition: "upon."
6. First edition adds, "who besides this ransom fulfilled the Law for us perfectly."
7. Homily text, "did embrace together."
8. Note that Wesley substitutes the A.V. for Cranmer's translations.

7. Neither doth faith shut out good works, necessary to be done afterwards, of duty towards God [9] (for we are most bounden to serve God in
doing good works commanded in Scripture all the days of our life). But
we may not do them to this intent, to be [justified] by doing them. For
all the good works we can do are not able to deserve our justification.
But our justification cometh freely [of] the mere mercy of God, and of
so great and free mercy that, whereas all the world was not able to pay
any part towards their ransom, it pleased [him], without any of our
deserving, to prepare for us the most precious jewels of Christ's body
and blood whereby our ransom might be paid, the law fulfilled and his
justice satisfied. So that Christ is now the righteousness of all them that
truly believe in him.[10] He for them fulfilled the law in his life, so that
now in him and by him every Christian may be called a fulfiller of the
law, forasmuch as that which their infirmity lacked, Christ's [righteous-
ness] hath supplied.

8.[11] Ye have heard that no man can be justified by his own works
[inasmuch as] no man fulfilleth the law. And St. Paul, in his Epistle to the
Galatians, proveth the same, saying, "If there had been a law given which
could have justified, verily righteousness should have been by the law"
[Gal. 3:21]. And again, "If righteousness come by the law, then is
Christ dead in vain" [Gal. 2:21]. And to the Ephesians he saith, "By
grace are ye saved through faith and that not of yourselves. It is
the gift of God, not of works, lest any man should boast" [Eph.
2:8–9]. And to be short, the sum of all Paul's disputation is this: "If
[righteousness] come of works then it cometh not of grace, and if it
come of grace then it cometh not of works" [cf. Rom. 11:6]. And
to this end tend all the prophets, as St. Peter saith, "[To him give] all
the prophets witness that, through this name, whosoever believeth in him
shall receive remission of sins" [Acts 10:43].

9. And [that we are] justified only by this true and lively faith in
Christ speak all the ancient authors, especially Origen, St. Cyprian, St.
Chrysostom, Hilary, Basil, St. Ambrose and St. Augustine,[12] by which
they take away clearly all merit of our works and wholly ascribe our

9. The Homily text reads: "Neither doth faith shut out the justice of our good
works, necessarily to be done afterwards of duty towards God. . . ."
10. First edition adds, "*He for them paid their ransom by his death.*"
11. *Cf.* "The Second Part of the Sermon of Salvation."
12. *Cf.* the text of Homily III for references to these and other patristic authors,
with several representative quotations; notice Wesley's *selection* from Cranmer's
catena.

justification unto Christ only. This faith, the Holy Scripture teacheth us, is the strong rock and foundation of the Christian religion. This doctrine all ancient authors of Christ's church do approve. This doctrine setteth forth the true glory of Christ and beateth down the vainglory of man. This whosoever denieth is not to be accounted for a Christian man, nor for a setter-forth of Christ's glory, but for an adversary to Christ and his gospel and for a setter-forth of man's vainglory.

10. But that this true doctrine of justification by faith may be truly understood, [observe that] justification is the office of God only and is not a thing which we render unto him but which we receive of him by his free mercy, through the only merits of his beloved Son. [And the true sense] of this doctrine — *we are justified freely by faith without works*, or, *we are justified by faith in Christ only* — is not that this our own act, *to believe in Christ*, or that this our faith in Christ, which is within us, doth justify us (for that were to account ourselves to be justified by some act or virtue that is within ourselves), but that although we have faith, hope and charity within us and do never so many works thereunto, yet we must renounce the merit of all, of faith, hope, charity and all other virtues and good works which we either have done, shall do, or can do, as far too weak to deserve our justification. [For which] therefore we must trust only in God's mercy and the sacrifice which Christ offered for us on the Cross.

11. As [then] John Baptist [as great and godly a man as he was], yet in this matter of forgiving sin, put the people from him, and [pointed] them to Christ, saying, "Behold the Lamb of God, which taketh away the sins of the world" [Jn. 1:29]: even so, as great and godly a virtue as faith is, it putteth us from itself and [pointeth] us to Christ, to have only by him remission of sins, or justification. So that our faith, as it were, saith unto us thus: "It is not I that taketh away your sins. It is Christ only and to him alone I send you for that purpose, forsaking all your good virtues, words, thoughts and works and putting your trust in Christ only."

12.[13][And in truth, neither our faith nor our works do justify us — that is, deserve remission of our sins — but God himself doth justify us] of his own mercy, through the merits of his Son only. Nevertheless [because] by faith given us of God we embrace the promise of God's mercy and the remission of our sins, therefore the Scripture [saith] that "faith doth justify"; yea, "faith without works." [And as it is all one] to say, "faith without works" and "only faith doth justify us," therefore the ancient

13. *Cf.* "The Third Part of the Sermon of Salvation."

fathers from time to time [speak thus], "Only faith justifieth us," meaning no other than St. Paul meant when he said, "Faith without works justifieth us" [*cf.* Gal. 2:16]. And because this is [wrought] through the only merits of Christ, and not through our merits or through the merit of any virtue we have within us or of any work that cometh from us, therefore, in that respect we renounce, as it were again, faith, works and all other virtues. For our [corruption] through original sin is so great that *all [our] faith, charity, words and works [cannot] merit or deserve any part of our justification for us.* And [therefore we thus speak], humbling ourselves to God [and giving to our Saviour Christ all the glory of our justification].

13. [To justify, then, is the office of God to man.] Our office [and duty to God] is not to pass our time [sinfully or unfruitfully, for this were to] serve the devil and not God. For that faith which bringeth [not forth repentance but] either evil works or no good works, is not a right, pure and living faith, but a dead and devilish one, as St. Paul and St. James call it. For even the devils believe "that Christ was born of a virgin, that he wrought all kind of miracles, declaring himself very God, that for our sakes [he] suffered a most painful death to redeem us from death everlasting, that he rose again the third day, that he ascended into heaven and sitteth at the right hand of the Father, and at the end of the world shall come again [to] judge both the quick and the dead." These articles of our faith the devils believe, and so they believe all that is written in the Old and New Testament. And yet for all this faith, *they be but devils.* [They remain] still in their damnable estate, *lacking the very true Christian faith.*

14. *The right and true Christian faith is not only to believe that Holy Scripture and the articles of our faith are true, but also to have a sure trust and confidence to be saved from everlasting damnation by Christ, whereof doth follow a loving heart to obey his commandments.*

15. And this true Christian faith neither any devil hath, nor yet any man who,[14] in his receiving the sacraments, in coming to church and in all other outward appearances, seemeth to be a Christian, and yet in his [life] showeth the contrary. For how can a man have this "true faith, this sure confidence in God that, by the merits of Christ, his sins [are] forgiven, and he reconciled to the favour of God," when he denieth Christ in his [works]? Surely no ungodly man can have this faith and trust in God!

14. First edition adds, "in outward profession."

16. [If we do truly believe that] whereas we were condemned to hell and death everlasting, God hath given his own Son to take our nature upon him and to suffer death for our offences, to justify us and to restore us to life everlasting; [if we truly believe that he hath made] us his dear children, brethren unto his only Son and inheritors with him of his eternal kingdom of heaven, these great and merciful benefits of God [will] move us to render ourselves unto God wholly, with all our hearts, might and power, to serve him in all good [works], to seek in all things his glory, evermore dreading to offend in word, thought or deed such a merciful God and loving Redeemer. [They will also] move us to be ever ready for his sake to give ourselves to our neighbours and, as much as lieth in us, to study with all our endeavour to do good to every man. These [are] the fruits of true faith: to do good, as much as lieth in us, to every man and above all things and in all things to advance the glory of God, to whom be praise and honour, world without end.

## Of True Christian Faith [15]

1. The first coming unto God is through faith, whereby we [are] justified before God. [But] lest any man should be deceived for [want] of a right understanding thereof, it is diligently to be noted that faith is taken in Scripture two ways. There is one faith which the Scripture [calleth] a dead faith; and this by St. James is compared to the faith of devils [who] "believe and tremble" [2:19] [and] yet do nothing well. And such a faith [as this] have wicked Christians who [*profess they know God but in works deny him*].

2. This faith is a persuasion that there is a God and a belief [of all the truths contained in his Word]; so that it consisteth only in believing that the Word of God is true. And *this is not properly called faith*. But as he that readeth Caesar's *Commentary*, [though he believeth it] to be true, yet [he] is not properly said [to believe] in Caesar;[16] even so he that believeth all the Bible [to be] true and yet liveth ungodly is not properly said [to believe] in God.[17] For inasmuch as faith without works is dead, it is not faith — as a dead man is not a man.[18]

15. *Cf.* "A Short Declaration of the True, Lively and Christian Faith."
16. Wesley's interpolation in first edition: "Of whom he looketh for no benefit."
17. First edition adds, "For he hath not such a faith and trust in God whereby he surely looketh for grace, mercy and everlasting life at God's hand."
18. A quotation from Didymus Alexandrinus, *Enarratio in Epistolam Beati Jacobi,* PG, XXXIX, 1752. This is the so-called "Didymus the Blind" (*c.* 313-398), teacher

3. Another faith there is in Scripture which is not idle [or] unfruitful but (as St. Paul declares) "worketh by love" [Gal. 5:6]. And as that is called a dead faith, so this may be called a quick or [living] faith. This is not only a belief of the articles of our faith but also "a true trust and confidence of the mercy of God through our Lord Jesus Christ and a steadfast hope of all good things at God's hand," [19] called by St. Paul, "The full assurance of faith" [cf. Heb. 10:22]; a confidence [that though we should] fall from him by sin, yet if we return to him by true repentance, he will forgive our offences for his Son's sake and make us inheritors of his everlasting Kingdom; that, in the meantime, he will be our protector and defender, [and not withdraw] his mercy finally from us, if we commit ourselves wholly unto him, hang only upon him and call upon him, ready to obey and serve him.[20] This is the true, [living] Christian faith, [which] is not in the mouth and outward profession only, but it liveth and stirreth inwardly in the heart. And this faith is not without hope and trust in God nor without the love of God and of our neighbour, nor without the fear of God, nor without the desire to hear God's Word and to follow the same in [avoiding] evil and gladly doing all good works.

4. Of this faith three things are specially to be noted. First, that [it] is fruitful in bringing forth good works; secondly, that without it can no good works be done; thirdly, what good works this faith doth bring forth.

5. For the first, as light cannot be hid but will show itself at one place or other, so true faith cannot be [hid] but will break out and show itself by good works. And as the living body of a man ever exerciseth such things as belong to a living body, for nourishment and preservation of the same, even so the soul that hath a [living] faith will be always doing some good work, which shall declare that it is living. Therefore, if [any man fancy he is] set at liberty from doing good works, it is a manifest token [he hath no true faith; yea, he knoweth not] what true faith meaneth. For [true] Christian faith is not only [a belief of] all the things of God which are contained in Holy Scripture, but also an earnest trust and

---

of Gregory Nazianzus, Jerome, Rufinus; cf. J. Quasten, *Patrology* (Utrecht, 1950), III, 85–100; see also *Oxford Dictionary of the Christian Church,* F. L. Cross, ed. (1958), 398.

19. [Au.] It is the doctrine of the Church of England to which every minister of our Church hath subscribed, in subscribing the Thirty-fifth Article, that "without or before this [faith] can no good work be done."

20. Cf. *Minutes* (1744), Q. 4–10 (pp. 137–38). See also the sermon "Justification by Faith" (below, pp. 198–209).

confidence in God that he is careful over us as the father is over the child whom he [loveth] and that he will be merciful to us for his son's sake. [And this true faith, when we consider] what God hath done for us, is also moved through continual assistance of the Spirit of God to serve and please him, to keep his favour, to fear his displeasure, to continue his obedient children, showing thankfulness by observing his commandments;[21] considering how, clearly without [our] deservings, we have freely received his mercy and pardon.

6.[22] [Therefore if it do not appear in] our conversation, the faith we pretend to have is but feigned, because true faith is manifestly shown by good living and not by words only. As St. Augustine saith, "Good living cannot be separated from true faith which worketh by love."[23] And St. Chrysostom, "Faith is full of good works, and as soon as a man believeth he shall be [adorned] with them."[24] How plentiful [it] is of good works St. Paul teacheth at large in the eleventh chapter To the Hebrews, [evidently declaring] that true faith is no unfruitful thing but a thing of perfect virtue, of wonderful operation and strength, bringing forth all good motions and good works.

7.[25] [Every man therefore must diligently examine himself whether he hath this faith in his heart or not.] He that feeleth his heart set to seek God's honour and leadeth not his life after [his own desire] but setteth his mind to serve God, and for his sake to love all his neighbours, whether they be friends or adversaries, doing good to every man (as opportunity serveth) and willingly hurting no man — such a man may well rejoice in God, perceiving by his life that he hath a [living] faith. [But he that doth not live according to God's words deceiveth himself if he think he believeth in him.]

8. [Let us then by our works declare] our faith to be the [living] Christian faith; and by such virtues as ought to spring out of faith, "let us add to (or in) [our] faith, virtue; in [our] virtue, knowledge; in [our] knowledge, temperance; in [our] temperance, patience; in [our] patience, godliness; in [our] godliness, brotherly [kindness]; and in brotherly [kindness], charity" [cf. 2 Pet. 1:19]. So shall we both certify our conscience [that we are in the right faith] and also confirm other men. If you

---

21. First edition adds here: ". . . that freely for true love chiefly, and not for dread of punishment, or love of temporal reward, . . ."
22. Cf. "The Second Part of the Sermon of Faith."
23. Cf. De fide et operibus, XIV, 21; PL, XL, 211; CSEL, XLI, 62.
24. Cf. Homily XXIV, on "The Gospel of St. Matthew"; NPNF[1], X, 167.
25. Cf. "The Third Part of the Sermon of Faith."

feel and perceive such a faith in you, rejoice in it and be diligent to maintain it. Let it be daily increasing more and more by [good works]. So shall you be sure that you shall please God and, when his will is, "receive the end of your faith, [even] the salvation of your souls" [1 Pet. 1:9].

9.[26] The second thing that was noted of true faith was that without it can no good works be done; "for as the branch cannot bear fruit of itself," saith our Saviour Christ, "except it abide in the vine, no more can ye, except ye abide in me. I am the vine; ye are the branches. He that abideth in me and I in him, he bringeth forth much fruit. For without me ye can do nothing" [Jn. 15:4-5]. And St. Paul proveth that Enoch had faith, because "he pleased God. For without faith," saith he, "it is impossible to please him." [27]

10. Faith giveth life to the soul; and they [are] as much dead to God [who want] faith as they are to the world whose bodies [want] souls. Without faith all [we do] is but dead before God, be it ever so glorious before man; even as a picture is but a dead representation of the thing itself, so [are] the works of [those who have not faith] before God. They [are] but shadows of good and [living] things, and not good and [living] things indeed. For without faith no work is good before God. "We must set no good works before faith. . . . Let no man," saith St. Augustine, "reckon upon his good works before his faith, for where faith was not, good works were not. . . . There is one work in which are all good works, that is faith which worketh by love. If thou hast this, thou hast the ground of all good works. Without this, thou hast only the shadows of them." [28]

11. To the same purpose [saith] St. Chrysostom, "[You shall find] many who have not the true faith, yet [29] flourish in works of mercy. But the chief work is lacking: to believe in him whom God hath sent. So soon as a man hath faith, he shall flourish in good works. For faith is full of good works and nothing is good without faith. They that shine in good works without faith are like dead men who have goodly and precious tombs. Faith [cannot] be [30] without good works, for then it is no true faith. And when it is adjoined to works, yet it is above the works. For as men first have life and after [are] nourished, so must our faith in Christ

26. Cf. "A Sermon of Good Works Annexed to Faith."
27. Cf. Heb. 11:6; here the Homily reads "the Eunuch" for "Enoch."
28. Cf. The Homilies text here (1683 ed., 27-28), and note Wesley's revisions.
29. Second edition reads, "*appear* to flourish."        30. First edition adds, "naked."

go before, and after be nourished with good works. And life may be without nourishment, but nourishment cannot be without life. A man must needs be nourished by good works, but first he must have faith. He that doth good [works], yet without faith, he hath no life. I can show a man that, by faith without works, lived and came to heaven. But without faith never man had life. The thief that was hanged when Christ suffered did believe only, and the most merciful God justified him. Faith by itself saved him, but works by themselves never justified any man." [31]

12.[32] [The third thing to be noted of true faith is *what* good works it doth bring forth. And this Christ himself hath plainly declared]: "If thou wilt enter into life, keep the commandments." So that [we are] taught by Christ's own mouth that the works of the commandments of God [are the true works of faith, the very way that doth lead to everlasting life] [*cf.* Mt. 19:16–19].

13.[33] Wherefore, as ye have any [regard for everlasting life], apply yourselves above all things to read and hear God's Word, mark diligently what his [commandments are] and with all your endeavour follow the same. First, you must have an assured faith in God and give yourselves wholly unto him; love him in prosperity and adversity and dread to offend him evermore. Then, for his sake, love all men, friends and foes, because they [are] his [creatures] and image, and redeemed by Christ as ye are. Cast in your minds how you may do good unto all men, unto your powers, and hurt [none]. Obey all your superiors and governors. Serve your masters faithfully and diligently, disobey not your fathers and mothers but honour, help, and please them to your power. Oppress not, kill not, beat not, neither slander nor hate any man; but love all men, speak well of all men, help and succour every man as you may, yea, even your enemies that hate you, that speak evil of you and hurt you. Take no man's goods nor covet your neighbour's goods, but [be content with your own] and bestow [them] charitably, as need requireth. Flee all idolatry, witchcraft, perjury; commit no manner of adultery, fornication or other [unchastity] in will or deed. And [labouring] continually in thus keeping the commandments [which, wrought in faith, God hath ordained to be the pathway unto heaven], you shall not fail to come to that everlasting life where you shall live in glory and joy with God for ever.

31. *Cf.* The Homilies (1683 ed., 28–29).
32. *Cf.* "The Second Part of the Sermon of Good Works" (*ibid.*, 29).
33. "The Third Part of the Sermon of Good Works" (*ibid.*, 35–36).

## Doctrines and Discipline in the Minutes
## of the Conferences, 1744–47

*Editor's introduction.* In 1785, defending himself in face of the furor lately stirred by his "Deed of Declaration," which had given the annual conference a legal basis for continuing after his death, Wesley felt called upon to review the origins of this unique agency in Methodist polity: [1]

> In June 1744, I desired my brother and a few other clergymen to meet me in London, to consider how we should proceed to save our own souls and those that heard us. After some time, I invited the lay preachers that were in the house to meet with us. We conferred together for several days and were much comforted and strengthened thereby.
>
> The next year I not only invited most of the "travelling preachers" but several others to confer with me in Bristol. And from that time for some years, though I invited only a part of the "travelling preachers," yet I permitted any that desired it, to be present, not apprehending any ill consequences therefrom.
>
> But two ill consequences soon appeared: one, that the expense was too great to be borne; the other, that many of our people were scattered while they were left without a shepherd. I therefore determined first, that for the time to come, none should be present but those whom I invited; and second, that I would only invite a select number out of every circuit.
>
> This I did for many years, and all that time the term "Conference" meant not so much the conversation we had together as the persons that conferred — namely, those whom I invited to confer with me from time to time. So that all this time it depended on me alone, not only what persons should constitute the Conference, but whether there should be any Conference at all. This lay wholly in my own breast; neither the preachers nor the people having any part or lot in the matter.

Besides the light this passage sheds on Wesley's concept of his own special authority as leader of the Revival, whose ministry was represented and multiplied by those in voluntary connection with him, it also gives us a valuable clue as to the nature and function of the early conferences.

By 1744 the Revival was beginning to lose something of its novelty and to attract both persecutors and misinterpreters. It seems certain that

---

1. "Thoughts Upon Some Late Occurrences," *Works*, XIII, 248.

it would have been largely dissipated (as Whitefield's movement was) had it not been for the patterns of polity and discipline which Wesley adopted and enforced. The annual "conference" was one of those strokes of practical genius that marked off Wesleyan Methodism from the other vectors of the Evangelical Revival.

What the Methodist preachers needed was an elementary doctrinal compend and an administrative charter. Both of these were hammered out "in conference," and published in the *Minutes*. The procedure was that of group interrogation and debate. Questions might be posed by anyone and discussed by everyone. But the final answers were always pronounced by Wesley himself, in the light of the discussion. The questions and the answers were then minuted and published. No stronger evidence of Wesley's primary concern for sound doctrine in the guidance of his Societies exists than the records of these early "conferences."

The "minutes" printed here are from the text first published in *Publications of the Wesley Historical Society*, No. 1 (1896). This text should be compared — and contrasted — with that of the so-called "Doctrinal Minutes" of *Works*, VIII, pp. 275–98, or the "Large Minutes" in the same volume, pp. 299–338. For the years 1744, 1745, and 1747, the text is based on John Bennet's record, which is somewhat more complete than the only copy by Wesley which has survived. Bennet missed the Conference of 1746, however, and its record is here supplied from Wesley's copy. Both texts have been compared and their variations indicated by brackets [2] (bracketed scriptural references and translations are, however, editorial additions). Intervals and omissions (of doctrinally irrelevant material) are shown by ellipses, with bracketed notations following.

Clumsy and laconic as these "minutes" are in their form and style, they constitute the most important single exhibition of the manner and the substance of Wesley's theologizing — in the midst of a surging revival, in response to actual, urgent questions, in vigorous conversation with his assistants, whose own views spanned most of the live options extant in the theological forum of the time. The distillate of it presented here provides us with an unequaled access to the mind and methodology of this evangelist-theologian.

❖   ❖   ❖   ❖

2. For details concerning the manuscript backgrounds of the texts involved, *cf.* Wesley Historical Society, *Proceedings* (Burnley, 1896), I, 3–6.

## THE FIRST ANNUAL CONFERENCE

### Monday, June 25, 1744

The following persons being met at the Foundery — John Wesley, Charles Wesley, John Hodges,[1] Henry Piers,[2] Samuel Taylor [3] and John Meriton — after some time spent in prayer, the design of our meeting was proposed, namely, to consider,

1. What to teach;
2. How to teach; and
3. What to do, *i.e.* how to regulate our doctrine, discipline and practice.

But first it was inquired whether any of our lay brethren should be present at this conference, and it was agreed to invite from time to time such of them as we should think proper. 'Twas then asked, "Which of them shall we invite today?" The answer was, "Thomas Richards, Thomas Maxfield, John Bennet and John Downes," who were accordingly brought in. Then was read as follows:

> It is desired that all things may be considered as in the immediate presence of God, that we may meet with a single eye and as little children who have everything to learn, that every point may be examined from the foundation, that every person may speak freely whatever is in his heart and that every question proposed may be fully debated and bolted to the bran.

The first preliminary question was then proposed; namely, how far does each of us agree to submit to the unanimous judgment of the rest? It was answered: in speculative things each can only submit so far as his judgment shall be convinced; in every practical point, so far as we can without wounding our consciences. To the second preliminary question, namely, how far should any of us mention to others what may be mentioned here, it was replied: "Not one word which may be here spoken of persons should be mentioned elsewhere; nothing at all, unless so far as we may be convinced the glory of God requires it. And from time to time we will consider on each head, is it for the glory of God that what we have now spoken should be mentioned again?"

About seven o'clock we began to consider the doctrine of Justification, the questions relating to which were as follows, with the substance of the answers thereto:

Q. 1. What is it to be justified?

1. Rector of Wenvoe.        2. Vicar of Bexley.        3. Vicar of Quinton.

A. To be pardoned and received into God's favour and into such a state that, if we continue therein, we shall be finally saved.

Q. 2. Is faith the condition of justification?

A. Yes, for everyone who believeth not is condemned and everyone who believes is justified.

Q. 3. But must not repentance and works meet for repentance go before faith?

A. Without doubt, if by repentance you mean conviction of sin, and by works meet for repentance, obeying God as far as we can, forgiving our brother, leaving off from evil, doing good and using his ordinances according to the power we have received.

Q. 4. What is faith?

A. Faith, in general, is a divine supernatural ἔλεγχος ["evidence," "manifestation"] of things not seen, *i.e.* of past, future, or spiritual things. 'Tis a spiritual sight of God and the things of God.[4] Therefore, repentance is a low species of faith, *i.e.* a supernatural sense of an offended God. Justifying faith is a supernatural inward sense or sight of God in Christ reconciling the world unto himself. First, a sinner is convinced by the Holy Ghost: "Christ loved me and gave himself for me." This is that faith by which he is justified, or pardoned, the moment he receives it. Immediately the same Spirit bears witness, "Thou art pardoned, thou hast redemption in his blood." And this is saving faith, whereby the love of God is shed abroad in his heart.

Q. 5. Have all true Christians this faith? May not a man be justified and not know it?

A. That all true Christians have this faith, even such a faith as implies an assurance of God's love, appears from Rom. 8:15, Eph. 4:32, 2 Cor. 13:5, Heb. 8:10, 1 Jn. 4:10 and 19.[5] And that no man can be justified and not know it appears farther from the very nature of things — for faith after repentance is ease after pain, rest after toil, light after darkness — and from the immediate as well as distant fruits.

Q. 6. But may not a man go to heaven without it?

A. It doth not appear from Holy Writ that a man who hears the gospel can,[6] whatever a heathen may do.[7]

---

4. This is Wesley's standard definition, often repeated with only slight variations. For examples, see *The Scripture Way of Salvation*, Pt. II, par. 1 (below, pp. 275–76), *An Earnest Appeal*, par. 6 (below, p. 386), *A Farther Appeal*, Pt. I; cf. *Works*, VIII, 48; *Letters*, II, 48–50; III, 162, 174.

5. This corrects the text, which actually reads: "and last 1 John v. 19."

6. [Au.] Mk. 16:16.

7. [Au.] Rom. 2:14.

Q. 7. What are the immediate fruits of justifying faith?

A. Peace, joy, love, power over all outward sin and power to keep down all inward sin.

Q. 8. Does any one believe who has not the witness in himself or any longer than he sees, loves and obeys God?

A. We apprehend not: "seeing God" being the very essence of faith; love and obedience, the inseparable properties of it.

Q. 9. What sins are consistent with justifying faith?

A. No wilful sin. If a believer wilfully sins, he thereby forfeits his pardon. Neither is it possible he should have justifying faith again without previously repenting.

Q. 10. Must every believer come into a state of doubt or fear or darkness? Will he do so unless by ignorance or unfaithfulness? Does God otherwise withdraw himself?

A. It is certain a believer need never again come into condemnation. It seems he need not come into a state of doubt or fear or darkness, and that (ordinarily at least) he will not, unless by ignorance and unfaithfulness. Yet it is true that the first joy does seldom last long, that it is commonly followed by doubts and fears, and that God usually permits very great heaviness before any large manifestation of himself.

Q. 11. Are works necessary to the continuance of faith?

A. Without doubt, for a man may forfeit the gift of God either by sins of omission or commission.

Q. 12. Can faith be lost but for want of works?

A. It cannot but through disobedience.

Q. 13. How is faith made perfect by works?

A. The more we exert our faith, the more 'tis increased. To him that hath, more and more is given.

Q. 14. St. Paul says Abraham was not justified by works; St. James, he was justified by works. Do they not then contradict each other?

A. No, first, because they do not speak of the same justification. St. Paul speaks of that justification which was when Abraham was seventy-five years old,[8] above twenty years before Isaac was born; St. James,[9] of that justification which was when he offered up Isaac on the altar.

No, secondly, because they do not speak of the same works. St. Paul speaks of works that precede faith, St. James, of works that spring from faith.

Q. 15. In what sense is Adam's sin imputed to all mankind?

8. Cf. Rom. 4:1–25.                              9. Cf. Jas. 2:21–26.

A. In Adam all died — *i.e.* (1) our bodies then became mortal; (2) our souls died — *i.e.* were disunited from God; (3) and hence we are all born with a sinful, devilish nature, by reason whereof (4) we all are children of wrath, liable to death eternal.[10]

Q. 16. In what sense is the righteousness of Christ imputed to believers, or to all mankind?

A. We do not find it affirmed expressly in Scripture that God imputes the righteousness of Christ to any, although we do find that faith is imputed unto us for righteousness. That text, "As by one man's disobedience all men were made sinners, so by the obedience of one all were made righteous" [Rom. 5:19], we conceive means, by the merits of Christ all men are cleared from the guilt of Adam's actual sin. We conceive farther that, through the obedience and death of Christ:

1. The bodies of all men become immortal after the resurrection;
2. Their souls recover a capacity of spiritual life;
3. And an actual seed or spark thereof;
4. All believers become children of grace;
5. Are re-united to God; and
6. Made partakers of the divine nature.

Q. 17. Have we not then unawares leaned too much towards Calvinism?
A. It seems we have.
Q. 18. Have we not also leaned towards antinomianism?
A. We are afraid we have.
Q. 19. What is antinomianism?
A. The doctrine which makes void the law through faith.
Q. 20. What are the main pillars thereof?
A. 1. That Christ abolished the moral law:
2. That Christians therefore are not obliged to observe it;
3. That one branch of Christian liberty is liberty from obeying the commandments of God;
4. That it is bondage to do a thing because it is commanded or forbear it because it is forbidden;
5. That a believer is not obliged to use the ordinances of God or to do good works;
6. That a preacher ought not to exhort to good works — not unbelievers because it is hurtful, not believers because it is needless.

10. [Au.] Rom. 5:18; Eph. 2:3.

Q. 21. What was the occasion of St. Paul writing his Epistle to the Galatians?

A. The coming of certain men among the Christians who taught, "Except ye be circumcised and keep the whole law of Moses, ye cannot be saved."

Q. 22. What is his main design therein?

A. To prove, (1) that no man can be justified or saved by the works of the law, either moral or ritual; (2) that every believer is justified by faith in Christ without the works of the law.

Q. 23. What does he mean by "the works of the law" [cf. Gal. 2:16; 3:5, 10]?

A. All works that do not spring from faith in Christ.

Q. 24. What is meant by being under the law?

A. Under the Mosaic dispensation.

Q. 25. What law has Christ abolished?

A. The ritual law of Moses.

Q. 26. What is meant by liberty?

A. Liberty (1) from the law; (2) from sin.


On Tuesday morning, June the 26th, was considered the doctrine of Sanctification, with regard to which the questions asked and the substance of the answers given were as follows:

Q. 1. What is it to be sanctified?

A. To be renewed in the image of God, in righteousness and true holiness.

Q. 2. Is faith the condition or the instrument of sanctification, or present salvation?

A. It is both the condition and the instrument of it. When we begin to believe, then salvation begins. And as faith increases, holiness increases till we are created anew.

Q. 3. Is not every believer a new creature?

A. Not in the sense of St. Paul, 2 Cor. 5:17, "All old things are passed away in him who is so a new creature and all things become new."

Q. 4. But has every believer a new heart?

A. A great change is wrought in the heart or affections of every one as soon as he believes; yet he is still full of sin, so that he has not then a new heart in the full sense.

Q. 5. Is not every believer born of God, a temple of the Holy Ghost?

A. In a low sense he is. But he that is in the proper sense born of God cannot commit sin.

Q. 6. What is implied in being made perfect in love?

A. The loving the Lord our God with all our mind and soul and strength.[11]

Q. 7. Does this imply that he who is thus made perfect cannot commit sin?

A. St. John affirms it expressly. He cannot commit sin because he is born of God.[12] And, indeed, how should he, seeing there is now none occasion of stumbling in him? [13]

Q. 8. Does it imply that all inward sin is taken away?

A. Without doubt, or how should he be said to be saved from all his uncleannesses? [14]

Q. 9. Can we know one who is thus saved? What is a reasonable proof of it?

A. We cannot, without the miraculous discernment of spirits, be infallibly certain of those who are thus saved. But we apprehend these would be the best proofs which the nature of the thing admits (unless they should be called to resist unto blood):

(1) if we had sufficient evidence of their unblameable behaviour, at least from the time of their justification;

(2) if they give a distinct account of the time and manner wherein they were saved from sin and of the circumstances thereof with such sound speech as could not be reproved; and

(3) [if] upon a strict inquiry from time to time, for two or three years following, it appeared that all their tempers, words, and actions were holy and unreprovable.

Q. 10. How should we treat those who think they have attained?

A. Exhort them to forget the things that are behind, to watch and pray always that God may search the ground of their hearts.


Wednesday, June the 27th, we began to consider points of discipline, with regard to which the questions asked and the substance of the answers given were as follows:

Q. 1. What is the Church of England?

11. [Au.] Deut. 6:5, 30:6; Ezek. 36 [25–29].          12. [Au.] 1 John 3:9.
13. [Au.] 1 John 2:10.
14. [Au.] 1 John 2:29. [Ed.] But see 1 Jn. 1:9; cf. Ezek. 36:29.

A. According to the 20th Article, the visible Church of England is the congregation of English believers in which the pure word of God is preached and the sacraments duly administered. But the word church is sometimes taken in a looser sense for a congregation professing to believe. So it is taken in the 26th Article and in the first, second, and third chapters of Revelations [sic].

Q. 2. What is a member of the Church of England?

A. A believer hearing the pure word preached and partaking of the sacraments duly administered in this Church.

Q. 3. What is it to be zealous for the Church?

A. To be earnestly desirous of its welfare [and increase: of its welfare] [15] by the confirmation of its present members in faith, hearing and communicating; [and] of its increase, by the addition of new members.

Q. 4. How are we to defend the doctrine of the Church?

A. Both by our preaching and living.

Q. 5. Do the 8th, 13th, 15th, 16th, 17th, 21st, 23rd, and 27th Articles agree with Scripture?

A. We will consider.

Q. 6. How shall we bear the most effectual testimony against that part of the clergy who either preach or live contrary to the doctrine of the Church of England?

A. Not by preaching, for they do not hear us; but by an earnest and tender address from the press.

Q. 7. How should we behave at a false or railing sermon?

A. If it only contain personal reflections we may quietly suffer it. If it blaspheme the work and Spirit of God, it may be better to go out of church. In either case, if opportuny serve, it would be well to speak or write to the minister.

Q. 8. How far is it our duty to obey the bishops?

A. In all things indifferent. And on this ground of obeying them, we should observe the canons so far as we can with a safe conscience.

Q. 9. Do we separate from the Church?

A. We conceive not. We hold communion therewith for conscience sake, by constant attending both the word preached and the sacraments administered therein.

Q. 10. What then do they mean who say, "You separate from the Church"?

A. We cannot certainly tell. Perhaps they have no determinate mean-

15. Brackets denote Wesley's amendments in Minutes (Works, VIII, 280).

ing, unless by the Church they mean themselves, *i.e.* that part of the clergy who accuse us of preaching false doctrine. And it is sure we do herein separate from them by maintaining the doctrine which they deny.

Q. 11. But do you not weaken the Church?

A. Do not they who ask this by the Church mean themselves? We do not purposely weaken any man's hands, but accidentally we may thus far: they who come to know the truth by us will esteem such as deny it less than they did before. But the Church in the proper sense, the congregation of English believers, we do not weaken at all.

Q. 12. Do not you entail a schism on the Church? That is, is it not probable that your hearers after your death will be scattered into all sects and parties, or that they will form themselves into a distinct sect?

A. 1. We are persuaded the body of our hearers will even after our death remain in the Church, unless they be thrust out.

2. We believe, notwithstanding, either that they will be thrust out or that they will leaven the whole Church.

3. We do, and will do, all we can to prevent those consequences which are supposed likely to happen after our death.

4. But we cannot with good conscience neglect the present opportunity of saving souls while we live for fear of consequences which may possibly or probably happen after we are dead.

Thursday, June the 28th, were considered other points of discipline. The substance of the questions and answers was as follows:

Q. 1. How are the people divided who desire to be under your care?

A. Into the United Societies, the Bands, the Select Societies, and the Penitents.

Q. 2. How do these differ from each other?

A. The United Societies (which are the largest of all) consist of awakened persons. Part of these, who are supposed to have remission of sins, are more closely united in the Bands. Those in the Bands who seem to walk in the light of God compose the Select Societies. Those of them who have made shipwreck of the faith meet apart as Penitents.

Q. 3. What are the Rules of the United Societies?

A. Those that follow. (Then they were read.) [16]

Q. 4. What are the Rules of the Bands?

A. They are these (which were read and considered).[17]

16. See below, p. 177 ff.                    17. See below, p. 180 f.

Q. 5. What are the Rules of the Select Societies?

A. The same [as above], and these three:

1. Let nothing spoken in this Society be spoken again; no, not even to the members of it.

2. Every member agrees absolutely to submit to his minister in all indifferent things.

3. Every member, till we can have all things common, will bring once a week, *bona fide*, all he can spare towards a common stock. . . . [Q. 6–11 omitted.]

Q. 12. What is the best way of spreading the gospel?

A. To go a little and a little farther from London, Bristol, St. Ives, Newcastle or any other Society. So a little leaven would spread with more effect and less noise, and help would always be at hand.

Q. 13. What is the best general method in preaching?

A. 1. To invite.

2. To convince.

3. To offer Christ; and, lastly,

4. To build up — and to do this (in some measure) in every sermon.


Friday, June the 29th, we considered:

Q. 1. Are Lay Assistants allowable?

A.      Only in cases of necessity.

Q. 2. What is the office of our Assistants?

A.      In the absence of the minister,[18] to feed and guide, to teach and govern the flock:

1. To expound every morning and evening.

2. To meet the United Societies, the Bands, the Select Societies, and the Penitents every week.

3. To visit the classes (London [19] excepted) once a month.

4. To hear and decide all differences.

5. To put the disorderly back on trial, and to receive on trial for the Bands or Society.

6. To see that the Stewards and the Leaders, schoolmasters and housekeepers, faithfully discharge their several offices.

18. *I.e.* the *ordained* rector or curate; *cf.* Wesley's distinction between "priests" and "preachers" in his sermon "On the Ministerial Office," *Works*, VII, 273–77.

19. A later note of Wesley's adds, "and Bristol."

7. To meet the Stewards, the Leaders of the Bands and Classes weekly, and overlook their accounts.

Q. 3. What are the Rules of an Assistant?

A. 1. Be diligent. Never be unemployed a moment, never be triflingly employed, never while away time; spend no more time at any place than is strictly necessary.

2. Be serious. Let your motto be, "holiness unto the Lord." Avoid all lightness as you would avoid hell-fire, and laughing as you would cursing and swearing.

3. Touch no woman. Be as loving as you will but hold your hands off 'em. Custom is nothing to us.

4. Believe evil of no one. If you see it done, well. Else take heed how you credit it. Put the best construction on every thing. You know the judge is always supposed to be on the prisoner's side.

5. Speak evil of no one, else your word especially would eat as doth a canker. Keep your thoughts within your own breast till you come to the person concerned.

6. Tell everyone what you think wrong in him and that plainly and as soon as may be; else it will fester in your heart. Make all haste, therefore, to cast the fire out of your bosom.

7. Do nothing "as a gentleman." You have no more to do with this character than with that of a dancing-master. You are the servant of all; therefore

8. Be ashamed of nothing but sin; not of fetching wood or drawing water, if time permit; not of cleaning your own shoes or your neighbour's.

9. Take no money of any one. If they give you food when you are hungry or clothes when you need them, it is good. But not silver or gold. Let there be no pretence to say we grow rich by the gospel.

10. Contract no debt without my knowledge.

11. Be punctual: do everything exactly at the time. And, in general, do not mend our rules but keep them, not for wrath but for conscience' sake.

12. Act in all things not according to your own will but as a son in the gospel. As such, it is your part to employ your time in the manner which we direct: partly in visiting the flock from house to house (the sick in particular); partly, in such a course of reading, meditation and prayer as we advise from time to time.

Above all, if you labour with us in our Lord's vineyard, it is
needful you should do that part of the work which we direct,
at those times and places which we judge most for his glory.
. . . [Q. 4–5 omitted.]

Q. 6. What is the office of a Steward?

A. 1. To manage the temporal things of the Society.

2. To receive the weekly contributions of the Leaders of the classes.

3. To expend what is needful from time to time.

4. To send relief to the poor.

5. To see that the public buildings be kept clean and in good repair.

6. To keep an exact account of receipts and expenses.

7. To inform the Helpers if the rules of the house, of the school, of
the Bands, or of the Society, be not punctually observed: and

8. If need be, to inform the minister hereof.

9. To tell the Helpers in love if they think anything amiss in their
doctrine or life.

10. If it be not removed, to send timely notice to the minister.

11. To meet his fellow Steward weekly, in order to consult together
on the preceding heads.

Q. 7. What are the Rules of a Steward?

A. 1. Be frugal. Save everything that can be saved honestly.

2. Spend no more than you receive. Contract no debt.

3. Do nothing rashly. Let every design be thoroughly weighed before you begin to execute it.

4. Have no long accounts. Pay everything within the week.

5. Give none that ask relief an ill word or ill look. Do not hurt
them if you cannot help them.

6. Expect no thanks from man.

7. Remember you are a servant of the Helper, not his master; therefore speak to him always as such. . . . [Q. 8–13 omitted.]

Q. 14. What books may an Assistant read?

A. Sallust, Caesar, Tully,[20] Erasmus, Castellio,[21] Terence, Virgil, Horace, Vida,[22] Buchanan,[23] G. Test.,[24] Epictetus, Plato, Ignatius, Ephraim

20. Marcus Tullius Cicero.

21. Sebastian Castellio (1515–1563); cf. his De haereticis, an sint persequendi
(1554).

22. Marco Giralomo Vida (c. 1489–1566); cf. his Ars Poetica (1527).

23. George Buchanan (1506–1582), Scottish humanist and jurist whose Latin
translations of the Psalms were much admired in the eighteenth century.

24. Greek Testament; cf. Wesley Historical Society, Proceedings, I, 29.

Syrus, Homer, *Greek Epigrams*, Duport,[25] Bp. Ussher's *Sermons*, Arndt,[26] Boehm,[27] Nalson,[28] Pascal, Francke,[29] R. Gell,[30] our *Tracts*.[31] . . . [Q. 15–18 omitted, as well as minutes for Saturday, June 30.]

✣ ✣

## THE SECOND ANNUAL CONFERENCE

### *Bristol, Thursday, August 1, 1745*

The following persons being met together at the New Room — John Wesley, Charles Wesley, John Hodges, Thomas Richards, Samuel Larwood, Thomas Meyrick, James Wheatley, Richard Moss, John Slocombe, Herbert Jenkins, Marmaduke Gwynne — it was inquired:

Q. 1. Should we still consider ourselves as little children, who have everything to learn?

A. Yes, so far as to have our minds always open to any farther light which God may give us.

Q. 2. What general method may we observe in our following conferences?

A. 1. To read and weigh at every conference each article of those preceding.

2. To speak freely and hear calmly touching each, that we may either retract, amend or enlarge it.

Q. 3. Should not the time of this conference be a time of particular watching and self-denial?

25. James Duport (1606–1679), Cambridge classical scholar, best known for his collection of Homeric aphorisms, *Homeri gnomologia* (1660).

26. Johann Arndt (1555–1621), early and influential Lutheran pietist; *cf.* his *Wahre Christentum* (1606–1610); in English, *True Christianity*, trans. by A. W. Boehm (1712).

27. Anthony William Boehm (1673–1722), German chaplain at St. James; author of *Discourses and Tracts* (1716). See below, p. 162.

28. Valentine Nalson (1683–1723), vicar of St. Martin's York; author of *Twenty Sermons preached in the Cathedral of York* (1724; 2d ed., 1737). See below, p. 163.

29. August Hermann Francke (1663–1727), greatest of the German pietists. Cf. his *Nicodemus, or a Treatise on the Fear of Man* (1706) and *The Marvellous Footsteps of Divine Providence* (1706).

30. Robert Gell (1595–1665), chaplain to Archbishop of Canterbury, Rector of St. Mary, Aldermanbury, London; author of *Remains; or Select Scriptures of the New Testament* (1676).

31. *Cf.* a newly discovered letter from Wesley to Peard Dickinson, in Mrs. John Warnick, "Four Unpublished Letters of John Wesley," *The Perkins School of Theology Journal*, XIII (1960), No. 2, 28–32. See also Wesley Historical Society, *Proceedings*, I, 28–29.

A. It should.

Q. 4. Should we not desire all who can of the Society to join with us tomorrow in fasting and prayer?

A. We will desire them so to do.

Q. 5. Ought not every question which shall be proposed to be examined from the foundation?

A. Without question it ought. If there was any defect herein at the last conference, let us amend it now.

Q. 6. How can we effectually provide that everyone may speak freely whatever is in his heart?

A. By taking care to check no one either by word or look, even though he should say what was quite wrong.

Q. 7. How shall we provide that every point may be fully and thoroughly settled?

A. Let us beware of making haste or showing any impatience, whether of delay or of contradiction.

About seven, it was proposed to review the Minutes of the last conference with regard to justification:

Q. 1. How comes what is written on this subject to be so intricate and obscure. Is this obscurity from the nature of the thing itself, or from the fault or weakness of those who have generally treated of it?

A. We apprehend this obscurity does not arise from the nature of the subject, but perhaps partly from hence: that the devil peculiarly labours to perplex a subject of the greatest importance; and partly from the extreme warmth of most writers who have treated of it.

Q. 2. We affirm faith is the sole condition of justification. But does not repentance go before that faith? Yea, and (supposing there be an opportunity for them) fruits or works meet for repentance?

A. Without doubt they do.

Q. 3. How then can we deny them to be conditions of justification? Is not this a mere strife of words? But is it worth while to continue a dispute on the term "condition"?

A. It seems not, though it has been generally abused. But so the abuse cease, let the use remain.

Q. 4. Shall we read over together Mr. Baxter's *Aphorisms* concerning justification? [32]

32. Cf. *An Extract of Mr. Richard Baxter's Aphorisms of Justification*, published by John Wesley, etc. (1745). The original had been published in 1649 and represents

A. By all means (which were accordingly read). And it was desired that each present would in the afternoon consult the Scriptures cited therein and bring what objections might occur the next morning.

Friday, August 2nd, the question was proposed:

Q. 1. Is an assurance of God's love absolutely necessary to our being in his favour, or may there possibly be some exempt cases?

A. We dare not positively say there are not.

Q. 2. Is such an assurance absolutely necessary to inward and outward holiness?

A. To inward, we apprehend it is: to outward holiness, we incline to think it is not.

Q. 3. Is it indispensably necessary to final salvation? Suppose in a papist or a Quaker, or, in general, among those who never heard it preached?

A. Love hopeth all things. We know not how far any of those may fall under the case of invincible ignorance.

Q. 4. But what can we say of one of our own Society who dies without it, as John Warr at London?

A. It may possibly be an exempt case (if the fact was really so). But we determine nothing. We leave his soul in the hands of him that made it.

Q. 5. Does a man believe any longer than he "sees" God?

A. We conceive not. But we allow there may be infinite degrees in seeing God; even as many as there are between him who sees the sun when it shines on his eyelids closed and him who stands with his eyes wide open in the full blaze of its beams.

Q. 6. Does a man believe any longer than he loves God?

A. In no wise. For neither circumcision nor uncircumcision avails without "faith working by love" [Gal. 5:6].

Q. 7. Have we duly considered the case of Cornelius? Was not he in the favour of God when his prayers and his alms came up for a memorial before God, *i.e.* before he believed in him [*cf.* Acts 10:2]?

A. It does seem that he was. But we speak not of those who have not heard the gospel.

---

a principal source of Wesley's covenantal theology in opposition to "high" Calvinism. See Richard Baxter, *Aphorisms*, No. XIX-XLV, and compare them with Wesley, *Predestination Calmly Considered*, below, pp. 456–58.

Q. 8. But were those works of his "splendid sins"? [33]

A. No, nor were they done without the grace of Christ.

Q. 9. How then can we maintain that all works done before we have a sense of the pardoning love of God are sin, and as such, an abomination to him?

A. The works of him who has heard the gospel and does not believe are not done as God hath willed and commanded them to be done. Therefore, they are sinful. And yet we know not how to say that they are an abomination to the Lord in him who feareth God and, from that principle, does the best he can.

Q. 10. Seeing there is so much difficulty in this subject, can we deal too tenderly with them that oppose us?

A. We cannot unless we give up any part of the truth of God.

Q. 11. Is a believer constrained to obey God?

A. At first he is. "The love of Christ constraineth him" [cf. 2 Cor. 5:14]. After this he may obey or he may not, no necessity being laid upon him.

Q. 12. Can faith be lost but through disobedience?

A. It cannot. A believer first inwardly disobeys — inclines to sin with his heart. Then his intercourse with God is lost, i.e. his faith is lost, and after this he may fall into outward sin, being now weak and like unto another man.

Q. 13. How can such a man recover faith?

A. By repenting and doing the first works. [34]

Q. 14. Whence is it that the majority of those that believe fall more or less into doubt or fear?

A. Chiefly from their own ignorance or unfaithfulness, often from their not watching unto prayer; perhaps sometimes from some defect or want of the power of God in the preaching they hear.

Q. 15. Is there not a defect in us? Do we preach as we did at the first? Have we not changed our doctrines?

A. 1. At first we preached almost wholly to unbelievers. To these, therefore, we spake almost continually of remission of sins through the death of Christ and the nature of faith in his blood. And so we do still, among those who need to be taught the first elements of the gospel of Christ.

33. See below, p. 440; cf. Oxford English Dictionary, X, for a citation of this phase from Richard Fiddes (1714).
34. [Au.] Rev. 2:5.

2. But those in whom the foundation is already laid we exhort to go on to perfection; which we did not see so clearly at first, although we occasionally spake of it from the beginning.

3. Yet we now preach, and that continually, faith in Christ as Prophet, Priest and King,[35] at least as clearly, as strongly and as fully as we did six years ago.

Q. 16. Do we not discourage visions and dreams too much, as if we condemned them *toto genere?*

A. We do not intend to do this. We neither discourage nor encourage them. We learn from Acts 2:19, &c., to expect something of this kind "in the last days." And we cannot deny that saving faith is often given in dreams or visions in the night, which faith we account neither better nor worse than if it come by any other means.

Q. 17. Do not our Assistants preach too much of the wrath and too little of the love of God?

A. We fear that they have leaned to that extreme and hence some may have lost the joy of faith.

Q. 18. Need we ever preach the terror of the Lord to those who know they are accepted of him?

A. No. It is folly so to do, for love is to them the strongest of all motives.

Q. 19. Do we ordinarily represent a justified state so great and happy as it is?

A. Perhaps not. A believer walking in the light is inexpressibly great and happy.

Q. 20. Should we not have a care of depreciating justification in order to exalt the state of full sanctification?

A. Undoubtedly we should beware of this, for one may insensibly slide into it.

Q. 21. How shall we effectually avoid it?

A. When we are going to speak of entire sanctification, let us first describe the blessings of a justified state as strongly as possible.

Q. 22. Does not the truth of the gospel lie very near both to Calvinism and antinomianism?

A. Indeed it does; as it were, within a hair's breadth. So that 'tis altogether foolish and sinful, because we do not quite agree either with one or the other, to run from them as far as ever we can.

35. Cf. John Deschner, *Wesley's Christology, an Interpretation* (Dallas, 1960), chap. IV–VI.

Q. 23. Wherein may we come to the very edge of Calvinism?

A. 1. In ascribing all good to the free grace of God.

   2. In denying all natural free-will and all power antecedent to grace.
   And,

   3. In excluding all merit from man, even for what he has or does by
   the grace of God.

Q. 24. Wherein may we come to the very edge of antinomianism?

A. 1. In exalting the merits and love of Christ.

   2. In rejoicing evermore.

Q. 25. What can we do to stop the progress of antinomianism?

A. 1. Pray without ceasing that God would speak for himself.

   2. Write one or two more dialogues.

Q. 26. Doth faith supersede (set aside the necessity of) holiness or good
works?

A. In no wise. So far from it, that it implies both, as a cause does its
effects.


About ten, we began to speak of Sanctification, with regard to which it
was enquired:

Q. 1. When does inward sanctification begin?

A. In the moment we are justified, the seed of every virtue is then instantaneously sown in the soil. From that time the believer gradually dies
to sin and grows in grace. Yet sin remains in him, yea, the seed of all sin,
till he is sanctified throughout in spirit, soul and body.

Q. 2. What will become of a heathen, a papist, or a Church of England man, if he dies without being thus sanctified?

A. He cannot see the Lord. But none who seeks it sincerely shall or can
die without it, though possibly he may not attain it till the very article
of death.

Q. 3. Is it ordinarily not given till a little before death?

A. It is not to those who expect it no sooner nor probably ask for it.

Q. 4. But ought we to expect it sooner?

A. Why not? Although we grant:

   1. That the generality of believers [whom we have hitherto
   known] [36] are not so sanctified till near death;

   2. That few of those to whom St. Paul wrote his Epistles were so
   at that time he wrote;

36. Wesley's handwritten interpolation.

3. Nor he himself at the time of writing his former Epistles. Yet this does not prove that we may not today.

Q. 5. But would not one who was thus sanctified be incapable of worldly business?

A. He would be far more capable of it than ever, as going through all without distraction.

Q. 6. Would he be capable of marriage?

A.[37] We cannot well judge. But supposing he were not, the number of those in that state is so small, it would produce no inconvenience.

Q. 7. Does the Scripture mention any living men who were wholly sanctified?

A. Yes: St. John and all those then with the apostle in whose name he speaks those words, 1 Jn. 4:17: "Herein (or through him) is our love made perfect, that we may have boldness in the day of judgment; because as he is, so are we in this world."

Q. 8. Can a justified person judge of a sanctified?

A. Not without a peculiar gift of God, for the spiritual man is judged of no man.

Q. 9. Should we not then beware of bearing hard on those who think they have attained?

A. We should, and the rather, because if they are faithful to the grace they have received, they are in no danger of perishing at last — no, not even if they remain in luminous faith for many months or years, perhaps till within a little of their spirits returning to God.

Q. 10. In what manner should we preach entire sanctification?

A. Scarce at all to those who are not pressing forward; to those who are, always by way of promise, always drawing rather than driving.

Q. 11. How should we wait for the fulfilling of this promise?

A. In universal obedience, in keeping all the commandments, in denying ourselves and taking up our cross daily. These are the general means which God hath ordained for our receiving his sanctifying grace. The particular are prayer, searching the Scripture, communicating and fasting.


On Saturday, August 3rd, were considered points of discipline:

Q. 1. Can he be a spiritual governor of the Church who is not a believer, not a member of it?

---

37. Later Wesley added this note: "Mᵉ is H in all," a cryptic reference to Heb. 13:4: "Marriage is honorable in all."

A. It seems not, though he may be a governor in outward things by a power derived from the King.

Q. 2. What are properly the laws of the Church of England?

A. The rubrics; and to those we submit, as the ordinance of man, for the Lord's sake.

Q. 3. But is not the will of our governors a law?

A. No; not of any governor, temporal or spiritual. Therefore, if any bishop wills that I should not preach the gospel, his will is no law to me.

Q. 4. But what if he produce a law against your preaching?

A. I am to obey God rather than man.

Q. 5. Is Episcopal, Presbyterian, or Independent church-government most agreeable to reason?

A. The plain origin of church-government seems to be this. Christ sends forth a preacher of the gospel. Some who hear him repent and believe the gospel. They then desire him to watch over them, to build them up in the faith and to guide their souls in the paths of righteousness. Here then is an independent congregation, subject to no pastor but their own, neither liable to be controlled in things spiritual by any other man or body of men whatsoever. But soon after some from other parts, who are occasionally present while he speaks in the name of him that sent him, beseech him to come over and help them, also. Knowing it to be the will of God, he complies, yet not till he has conferred with the wisest and holiest of his congregation and, with their advice, appointed one who has gifts and grace to watch over the flock till his return.

If it please God to raise another flock in the new place, before he leaves them he does the same thing, appointing one whom God has fitted for the work to watch over these souls also. In like manner, in every place where it pleases God to gather a little flock by his Word, he appoints one in his absence to take the oversight of the rest and to assist them of the ability which God giveth. These are deacons, or servants of the church, and look on their first pastor as their common father. And all these congregations regard him in the same light and esteem him still as the shepherd of their souls.

These congregations are not strictly independent. They depend on one pastor, though not on each other.

As these congregations increase, and as the deacons grow in years and grace, they need other subordinate deacons or helpers, in respect of whom they may be called "Presbyters," or elders, as their father in the Lord may be called the "Bishop" or Overseer of them all.

Q. 6. Is mutual consent absolutely necessary between the pastor and his flock?

A. No question. I cannot guide any soul unless he consents to be guided by me. Neither can any soul force me to guide him if I consent not.

Q. 7. Does the ceasing of this consent on either side dissolve the relation?

A. It must in the nature of things. If a man no longer consent to be guided by me, I am no longer his guide; I am free. If one will not guide me any longer, I am free to seek one who will.

Q. 8. But is the shepherd free to leave his sheep, or the sheep to leave their shepherd?

A. Yes, if one or the others are convinced it is for the glory of God and the superior good of their souls.

Q. 9. How shall we treat those who leave us?

A. 1. Beware of all sharpness, or bitterness, or resentment.

2. Talk with them once or twice at least.

3. If they persist in their design, consider them as "dead" and name them not unless in prayer. . . .[38]

✤ ✤

## The Third Annual Conference
### Monday, May 12, 1746

The following persons being met at the New Room in Bristol — John Wesley, Charles Wesley, John Hodges, Jonathan Reeves, Thos. Maxfield, Thos. Westell and Thos. Willis — it was inquired:

Q. 1. Who are the properest persons to be present at any conference of this nature?

A. 1. As many of the preachers as conveniently can.

2. The most earnest and most sensible of the Band Leaders where the conference is. And,

3. Any pious and judicious stranger who may be occasionally in the place.

Q. 2. Might it not be useful to read over one or more of our Tracts at each conference?

---

38. The remaining questions and answers (Q. 10-19), plus a section on the role of the "assistants," Q. 1-14, are omitted, as having more to do with practical details than with any significant doctrinal issues.

A. Doubtless it might, were it only to correct what is amiss and explain what is obscure in each.

Q. 3. Which shall we read now?

A. The *New England Narrative* and the *Distinguishing Marks of a Work of the Spirit of God* (which were read).[39]

Q. 4. Would it not be proper to send these to each of the Bishops?

A. Let them be sent as soon as possible.

Tuesday, May 13, 1746, the same persons being present, it was inquired:

Q. 1. Can any unbeliever (whatever he be in other respects) challenge anything of God's justice?

A. Absolutely nothing but hell. And this is a point which we cannot too much insist on.

Q. 2. Do we empty men of their own righteousness, as we did at first? Do we sufficiently labour when they begin to be convinced of sin, to take away all they lean upon? Should we not then endeavour with all our might to overturn their false foundations?

A. This was at first one of our principal points, and it ought to be so still, for till all other foundations are overturned, they cannot build upon Christ.

Q. 3. Did we not then purposely throw them into convictions, into strong sorrow and fear? Nay, did we not strive to make them inconsolable, refusing to be comforted?

A. We did, and so we should do still. For the stronger the conviction, the speedier is the deliverance; and none so soon receives the peace of God as those who steadily refuse all other comfort.

Q. 4. Let us consider a particular case. Was you, Jonathan Reeves, before you received the peace of God, convinced that, notwithstanding all you did or could do, you was in a state of damnation?

A. J. R. I was convinced of it as fully as that I am now alive.

Q. 5. Are you sure that conviction was from God?

A. J. R. I can have no doubt but it was.

Q. 6. What do you mean by a state of damnation?

A. J. R. A state wherein if a man dies, he perishes for ever.

Q. 7. How did that conviction end?

A. J. R. I had first a strong hope that God would deliver me, and this

---

39. See above, pp. 15-16.

brought a degree of peace. But I had not that solid peace of God till Christ was revealed in me.

Q. 8. But is not such a trust in the love of God, though it be as yet without a distinct sight of God reconciled through Christ Jesus, a low degree of justifying faith?

A. Perhaps it is. But this abides for a short time only: nor is this the proper Christian faith.

Q. 9. By what faith were the apostles clean before Christ died?

A. By such a faith as this, by a Jewish faith, for the Holy Ghost was not then given.

Q. 10. Of whom then do you understand those words "Who is there among you that feareth the Lord, that obeyeth the voice of his servant, that walketh in darkness and hath no light?" [40]

A. Of a believer under the Jewish dispensation; one in whose heart God hath not yet shined to give him the light of the glorious love of God in the face of Jesus Christ.

Q. 11. Who is a Jew (inwardly)?

A. A servant of God,[41] one who sincerely obeys him out of fear. Whereas a Christian (inwardly) is a child of God, one who sincerely obeys him out of love.

Q. 12. But was you not sincere before Christ was revealed in you?

A. J. R. It seemed to me that I was in some measure.

Q. 13. What is sincerity?

A. Willingness to know and do the will of God. The lowest species thereof seems to be "faithfulness in that which is little" [cf. Lk. 19:17].

Q. 14. Has God any regard to man's sincerity?

A. So far that no man in any state can possibly be accepted without it, neither indeed in any moment wherein he is not sincere.

Q. 15. But can it be received that God has any regard to the sincerity of an unbeliever?

A. Yes, so much that if he persevere therein, God will infallibly give him faith.

Q. 16. What regard may we conceive him to have to the sincerity of a believer?

A. So much that in every sincere believer he fulfills all the great and precious promises.

40. [Au.] Isaiah 50:10.
41. For the distinction between the "faith of a *servant*" and the "faith of a *son*," *cf.* sermon "On Faith" (*Works*, VII, 199–200).

Q. 17. Whom do you term a sincere believer?

A. One that walks in the light as God is in the light.

Q. 18. Is sincerity the same with "a single eye" [*cf*. Mt. 6:22]?

A. Not altogether. The latter refers to our intention, the former to our will or desires.

Q. 19. Is it not all in all?

A. All will follow persevering sincerity. God gives everything with it, nothing without it.

Q. 20. Are not then sincerity and faith equivalent terms?

A. By no means. It is at least as nearly related to works as it is to faith. For example, who is sincere before he believes? He that then does all he can; he that, according to the power he has received, brings forth "works meet for repentance" [Acts 26:20]. Who is sincere after he believes? He that, from a sense of God's love, is zealous of all good works.

Q. 21. Is not sincerity what St. Paul terms a willing mind, προθυμία, 2 Cor. 8:12?

A. Yes, if that word be taken in a general sense, for it is a constant disposition to use all the grace given.

Q. 22. But do we not then set sincerity on a level with faith?

A. No, for we allow a man may be sincere and not be accepted, as he may be penitent and not be accepted (not as yet); but [he] cannot have faith and not be accepted. The very moment he believes, he is justified.

Q. 23. But do we not give up faith and put sincerity in its place, as the condition of our acceptance with God?

A. We believe it is one condition of our acceptance, as repentance likewise is. And we believe it a condition of our continuing in a state of acceptance. Yet we do not put it in the place of faith. It is by faith [that] the merits of Christ are applied to my soul; but if I am not sincere, they are not applied.

Q. 24. Is not this that "going about to establish your own righteousness" whereof St. Paul speaks: Rom. 10:3?

A. St. Paul there manifestly speaks of unbelievers who sought to be accepted for the sake of their own righteousness. We do not seek to be accepted for the sake of our sincerity but through the merits of Christ alone. Indeed, as long as any man believes, he cannot go about (in St. Paul's sense) to "establish his own righteousness."

Q. 25. But do you consider that we are under the covenant of grace and that the covenant of works is now abolished?

A. All mankind were under the covenant of grace from the very hour that the original promise was made. If by the covenant of works you mean that of unsinning obedience made with Adam before the fall, no man but Adam was ever under that covenant, for it was abolished before Cain was born. Yet it is not so abolished but that it will stand, in a measure, even to the end of the world: *i.e.* if "we do thus," we shall live; if not, we shall die eternally. If we do well, we shall live with God in glory; if evil, we shall die the second death [*cf.* Rev. 20:6, 14; 21:8]. For every man shall be judged in that day and rewarded according to his works.

Q. 26. What means then, "To him that believeth, his faith is counted for righteousness" [*cf.* Gal. 3:6; Rom. 4:5]?

A. That God forgives him that is unrighteous as soon as he believes, accepting his faith instead of perfect righteousness. But then observe, universal righteousness follows, though it did not precede, faith.

Q. 27. But is faith thus "counted to us for righteousness" at whatsoever time we believe?

A. Yes. In whatsoever moment we believe, all our past sins vanish away. They are as though they had never been, and we stand clear in the sight of God.

Tuesday, ten o'clock, Mr. Taylor of Quinton being added, it was inquired:

Q. 1. Are not the assurance of faith, the inspiration of the Holy Ghost, and revelation of Christ in us, terms nearly of the same import?

A. He that denies one of them must deny all, they are so closely connected together.

Q. 2. Are they ordinarily, where the pure gospel is preached, essential to our acceptance?

A. Undoubtedly they are, and as such, to be insisted on in the strongest terms.

Q. 3. Is not the whole dispute of salvation by faith or by works a mere "strife of words" [*cf.* 1 Tim. 6:4]?

A. In asserting salvation by faith we mean this:

1. That pardon (salvation begun) is received by faith producing works;
2. That holiness (salvation continued) is faith working by love;
3. That heaven (salvation finished) is the reward of this faith. If you, who assert salvation by works, or by faith and works, mean the same thing (understanding by faith, the revelation of Christ

in us — by salvation, pardon, holiness, glory), we will not strive with you at all. If you do not, this is not a "strife of words," but the very vitals; the essence of Christianity is the thing in question.

Q. 4. Wherein does our doctrine now differ from that we preached when at Oxford?

A. Chiefly in these two points:

1. We then knew nothing of the righteousness of faith in justification; nor

2. Of the nature of faith itself as implying consciousness of pardon.[42]

Q. 5. May not some degree of love of God go before a distinct sense of justification?

A. We believe it may.

Q. 6. Can any degree of sanctification or holiness?

A. Many degrees of outward holiness may; yea, and some of meekness and several other tempers which would be branches of Christian holiness. But they do not spring from Christian principles. For the abiding love of God cannot spring but from faith in a pardoning God, and no true Christian holiness can exist without that love of God for its foundation.

Q. 7. Is every man as soon as he believes a new creature, sanctified, born again, pure in heart? Has he then a new heart? Does Christ dwell therein? And is he a temple of the Holy Ghost?

A. All those things may be affirmed of every believer, in a low sense. Let us not therefore contradict those who maintain it. Why should we contend about words?

On Wednesday, 14th, were considered points relating to discipline. . . . [Q. 1–7 are omitted, having to do with practical details and local circumstances.]

Q. 8. How shall we try those who believe they are moved by the Holy Ghost and called of God to preach?

A. Inquire:

1. Do they know in whom they have believed? Have they the love

42. Cf. *Journal*, V, 338; Tyerman, *Life*, I, 193; *Letters*, III, 305; *Justification by Faith*, Pt. II, par. 4; Pt. IV, par. 2 (below, pp. 201, 205); *The Scripture Way of Salvation*, Pt. II, par. 1 (below, p. 275); "The Law Established by Faith," Discourse II, Pt. III, par. 3 (below, pp. 229–30).

of God in their hearts? Do they desire and seek nothing but God? And are they holy in all manner of conversation?

2. Have they *gifts* (as well as *grace*) for the work? Have they (in some tolerable degree) a clear, sound understanding? Have they a right judgment in the things of God? Have they a just conception of the *salvation by faith?* And has God given them any degree of utterance? Do they speak justly, readily, clearly?

3. Have they success? Do they not only so speak as generally either to convince or affect the hearts, but have any received remission of sins by their preaching — a clear and lasting sense of the love of God? As long as these three marks undeniably concur in any, we allow him to be called of God to preach. These we receive as sufficient reasonable evidence that he is moved thereto by the Holy Ghost.

Q. 9. But how shall we know, in the case of a particular person, whether there is this evidence or no?

A. 1. We will send one of our helpers to hear him preach and to talk with him on the preceding heads.

2. We will hear him preach and talk with him ourselves.

3. We will examine thoroughly those who think they have received remission of sins by his preaching.

4. We will desire him to relate or to write down the reasons why he believes he is called of God to preach.

5. We will desire the congregation to join with us in fasting and prayer, that we may judge and act according to the will of God.

Q. 10. Should we not use the same method of fasting and prayer on other occasions also?

A. Without doubt we should use it:

1. At the receiving any fellow labourer in our Lord's vineyard;

2. At going ourselves, or sending any, to a new place;

3. Before publishing any book.

Q. 11. Why do we not use more form and solemnity in receiving a new labourer?

A. We purposely decline it:

1. Because there is something of stateliness in it, whereas we would be little and inconsiderable;

2. Because we would not make haste. We desire barely to follow Providence as it gradually opens. . . . [Q. 12–13 omitted.]

Q. 14. In what light should your assistants consider themselves?

A. As learners rather than teachers, as young students at the university for whom, therefore, a method of study is expedient in the highest degree.

Q. 15. What method would you advise them to?

A. We would advise them:

1. Always to rise at 4.

2. From 4 to 5 in the morning and from 5 to 6 in the evening, partly to use meditation and private prayer, partly to read the Scripture (2 or 3 verses, or 1 or 2 chapters), partly some close practical book of divinity, in particular *The Life of God in the Soul of Man*,[43] Kempis,[44] *The Pilgrim's Progress*,[45] Mr. Law's *Tracts*,[46] Beveridge's *Private Thoughts*,[47] Heylin's *Devotional Tracts*,[48] *The Life of Mr. Halyburton*[49] and *Monsieur De Renty*.[50]

3. From 6 in the morning (allowing one hour for breakfast) to 12 to read in order slowly, and with much prayer, Bishop Pearson *On the Creed*,[51] Bishop Fell *On the Epistles*,[52] Mr. Boehm's and

43. Henry Scougal (1650–1678), Scottish theologian and mystic. Cf. Wesley's abridgment of *The Life of God in the Soul of Man* (1744); see also Winthrop S. Hudson's modern edition (Philadelphia, 1948).

44. Wesley's third publication was an English edition of a Kempis's *De Imitatione Christi*, under the title, *The Christian Pattern* (1735). Cf. Green, *Bibliography*, #3, #26.

45. John Bunyan (1628–1688); cf. *Works*, X, 385, 387.

46. William Law (1686–1761); see above, p. 7.

47. William Beveridge (1637–1708); see above, p. 12.

48. John Heylyn (1685?–1759), rector of St. Mary-le-Strand, London, and later prebend of Westminster; author of *Theological Lectures . . . to which are added Select Discourses . . .* (1749).

49. Thomas Halyburton (1674–1712), Scottish theologian and professor at St. Andrews; author of a famous autobiography (*Memoirs . . .* [Edinburgh, 1715; London, 1718]), abstracted and published by Wesley in 1739. In his Preface Wesley says: ". . . I cannot but value it next to the Holy Scriptures, above any other human composition, excepting only *The Christian Pattern* and the small remains of Clemens Romanus, Polycarp and Ignatius."

50. *The Holy Life of M. de Renty, a late Nobleman of France . . .* , *Written in French by John Baptiste Saint-Jure and faithfully translated into English*, by "E. S., Gent." (1658). Wesley published an "extract" of this in 1741; later, he included it in *A Christian Library* (1749–55), XXIX, 212–75.

51. John Pearson (1613–1686), bishop of Chester, adjudged by Gilbert Burnet "the greatest divine of the age." His *An Exposition of the Creed* (1659; 9th ed., 1710) remains a landmark in Anglican theology.

52. John Fell (1625–1686), dean of Christ Church, bishop of Oxford. His greatest work was a critical edition of the epistles of St. Cyprian (Oxford, 1682) but he also had an editorial hand in *A Paraphrase and Annotations upon the Epistles of St. Paul* (1675; 3d ed. 1684). The reference here might be to either book, since we know that Wesley set great store by Cyprian.

Mr. Nalson's *Sermons*,[53] Mr. Pascal's *Thoughts*, our other tracts and poems, Milton's *Paradise Lost*, Cave['s],[54] and Fleury's *Primitive Christianity*,[55] and Mr. Echard's *Ecclesiastical History*.[56]

Q. 16. Have we in anything altered our manner of preaching for the worse since we set out?

A. Perhaps we do not preach so much concerning the blood of atonement as we did at first.

Q. 17. What inconvenience is there in speaking much of the wrath and little of the love of God?

A. It generally hardens them that believe not and discourages them that do.

Q. 18. What sermons do we find by experience to be attended with the greatest blessing?

A. 1. Such as are most close, convincing and practical.

2. Such as have most of Christ the Priest — the atonement.

3. Such as urge the heinousness of men living in contempt or ignorance of him.

Q. 19. Should we preach in Moorfields?

A. It is not clear to us that we should, as we have a more convenient place [57] which contains as many as can hear. . . . [Questions for Thursday, May 15, are omitted.]

❖ ❖

THE FOURTH ANNUAL CONFERENCE

*Monday, June 15, 1747*

The following persons being met at the Foundery — John Wesley, Charles Wesley, Westley Hall and Charles Manning — it was inquired:

53. See above, p. 147.

54. William Cave (1637–1713), rector of Allhallows, London, canon of Windsor; author of *Primitive Christianity, or the Religion of the Ancient Christians in the First Ages of the Gospel* (1672).

55. Claude Fleury (1640–1723), French court chaplain and distinguished church historian. The reference here is to an English translation of the first two volumes of his *Histoire ecclesiastique* (Paris, 1691–1721, in 20 v.), *Discourses on Ecclesiastical History* (1721).

56. Laurence Echard (1670?–1730), prebend of Lincoln; author of a controversial *History of England* (1707, 1718). The reference here is to *A General Ecclesiastical History from the Nativity of Our Blessed Saviour to the First Establishment of Christianity by Human Laws under the Emperor Constantine the Great* . . . (1702; 5th ed., 1719).

57. The Foundery, near Finsbury Square; cf. *Journal*, II, 316, 371; see also citations in Wesley's diaries in *ibid.*, 349, 351–52, 418, 438.

Q. 1. Which of our brethren shall we invite to be present at this conference?

A. John Jones, Thomas Maxfield, Jonathan Reeves, John Nelson, John Bennet, John Downes, Thomas Crouch, Robert Swindells and John Maddern (who were accordingly brought in).

Q. 2. How may the time of this conference be made more eminently a time of prayer, watching and self-denial?

A. 1. While we are in conference, let us have an especial care to set God always before us.

2. In the intermediate hours, let us visit none but the sick and spend all our time that remains in retirement.

3. Let us then give ourselves unto prayer for one another, and for the blessing of God on this our labour.

Q. 3. Should we at every conference read over all the conferences we have had from the beginning?

A. That immediately preceding, and so much of the rest as we may find needful from time to time.

Q. 4. In our first conference it was agreed to examine every point from the foundation. Have we not been someway fearful of doing this? What were we afraid of? Of overturning our first principles?

A. Whoever was afraid of this, it was a vain fear. For if they are true, they will bear the strictest examination. If they are false, the sooner they are overturned the better. Let us all pray for the willingness to receive light, an invariable desire to know of every doctrine whether it be of God.

Q. 5. [a.] It was then inquired, "How far does each of us agree to submit to the unanimous judgment of the rest?

[A.] And it was answered, "In speculative things, each can only submit as far as his judgment shall be convinced; in every practical point, as far as we can without wounding our several consciences." [58]

[Q. 5. b.] Can a Christian submit any farther than this to any man, or number of men, upon earth?

[A.] It is undeniably plain he cannot: either to pope, council, bishop or convocation. And this is the grand principle of every man's right to private judgment — in opposition to implicit faith in man — on which Calvin, Luther, Melanchthon and all the ancient Reformers, both at home and abroad, proceeded: "Every man must think for himself, since every man must give an account for himself to God."

58. *Cf.* above, p. 136.

Q. 6. Shall each of us read over all the tracts which have been published before our next conference, and write down every passage we do not approve, or do not fully understand?

A. Every one answered in [order]: "I will endeavour so to."


Tuesday, [June] 16th, Mr. [Richard] Bateman of St. Bartholomew's, Mr. [Henry] Piers, Howel Harris and Thomas Hardwick [59] being added, it was inquired:

Q. 1. Is justifying faith a divine assurance that Christ loved me and gave himself for me?

A. We believe it is.

Q. 2. What is the judgment of most of the serious Dissenters concerning this?

A. They generally allow that many believers have such an assurance and that it is to be desired and prayed for by all. But then they affirm that this is the highest species or degree of faith, that it is not the common privilege of believers. Consequently, they deny that this is justifying faith, or necessarily implied therein.

Q. 3. And are there not strong reasons for this opinion? For instance, if the true believers of old had not this assurance, then it is not necessarily implied in justifying faith. But the true believers of old had not this assurance.

A. David and many more of the believers of old had undeniably this assurance. But even if the Jews had it not, it would not follow that this is not implied in Christian faith.

Q. 4. But do you not know that the apostles themselves had it not till the day of Pentecost?

A. The apostles themselves had not the proper Christian faith till after the day of Pentecost.

Q. 5. But were not those Christian believers in the proper sense, to whom St. John wrote his first Epistle? Yet to these he says, "These things have I written unto you that believe on the name of the Son of God; that ye may [know that ye] have eternal life, and that ye may believe on the name of the Son of God." [60]

59. All these men disagreed with Wesley on the point of "assurance" and each eventually went his separate way apart from the Wesleyan Revival. This accounts for the change in form and tone of the "minutes" of this session.

60. [Au.] 1 Jn. 5:13.

A. This does not prove that they did not know they had eternal life any more than that they did not believe. His plain meaning is, "I have written unto you that you may be the more established in the faith." Therefore it does not follow from hence that they had not this assurance, but only that there are degrees therein.

Q. 6. But were not the Thessalonians true believers? Yet they had not this assurance; they had only a good hope.[61]

A. The text you refer to runs thus, "Now our Lord Jesus Christ himself, and God, even our Father, which hath loved us and given us everlasting consolation and good hope through grace, comfort your hearts, and stablish you in every good word and work." This good hope does not exclude, but necessarily implies, a strong assurance of the love of God.

Q. 7. But does not St. Paul say of himself,[62] "I know nothing by myself, yet am I not hereby justified"?

A. He does not say of himself here that he was not justified or that he did not know it, but only that though he had a conscience void of offence, yet this did not justify him before God. And must not every believer say the same? This therefore is wide of the point.

Q. 8. But does he not disclaim any such assurance in those words,[63] "I was with you in weakness and in fear and in much trembling"?

A. By no means. For these words do not imply any fear either of death or hell. They express only a deep sense of his utter insufficiency for the great work wherein he was engaged.

Q. 9. However, does he not exclude Christians in general from such an assurance when he bids them work out their salvation with fear and trembling?[64]

A. No more than from love, which is always joined with filial fear and reverential trembling. And the same answer is applicable to all those texts which exhort a believer to fear.

Q. 10. But does not matter of fact prove that justifying faith does not necessarily imply assurance? For can you believe that such a person as J. A. or E. V. — who have so much integrity, zeal and fear of God and walk so unblamably in all things — is void of justifying faith? Can you suppose such as these to be under the wrath and under the curse of God, especially if you add to this that they are continually longing, striving, praying, for the assurance which they have not?

A. This contains the very strength of the cause and sometimes inclines

61. [Au.] 2 Thess. 2:16.        62. [Au.] 1 Cor. 4:4.        63. [Au.] 1 Cor. 2:3.
64. [Au.] Phil. 2:12.

us to think that some of these may be exempt cases. But however that be, we answer:

1. It is dangerous to ground a general doctrine on a few particular experiments.
2. Men may have many good tempers and a blameless life (speaking in a loose sense) by nature and habit, with preventing grace, and yet be utterly void of faith and the love of God.
3. 'Tis scarce possible for us to know all the circumstances relating to such persons, so as to judge certainly concerning them.
4. But this we know that [if] Christ is not revealed in them, they are not yet Christian believers.

Q. 11. But what becomes of them then, suppose they die in this state?

A. That is a supposition not to be made. They *cannot* die in this state. They must go backward or forward. If they continue to seek, they will surely find righteousness, peace and joy in the Holy Ghost [cf. Rom. 14:17]. We are confirmed in this belief by the many instances we have seen of such as these finding peace at the last hour. And it is not impossible but others may then be made partakers of like precious faith and yet go hence without giving any outward proof of the change which God hath wrought.

## Wednesday, [June] 17.

Q. 1. How much is allowed by our brethren who differ from us with regard to entire sanctification?

A. They grant:

1. That every one must be entirely sanctified in the article of death;
2. That till then a believer daily grows in grace, and comes nearer and nearer to perfection;
3. That we ought to be continually pressing after this, and to exhort all others so to do.

Q. 2. But what do we allow them?

A. We grant:

1. That many of those who have died in the faith, yea, the greater part of them we have known, were not sanctified throughout — not made perfect in love — till a little before death.
2. That the term "sanctified" is continually applied by St. Paul to all that were justified — were true believers.

3. That by this term alone he rarely (if ever) means saved from all sin.

4. That consequently it is not proper to use it in this sense, without adding the word "wholly," "entirely," or the like.

5. That the inspired writers almost continually spoke of or to those who are justified but very rarely either of or to those who were wholly sanctified.

6. That consequently it behooves us to speak almost continually of the state of justification, but rarely, at least in full and explicit terms, concerning entire sanctification.

Q. 3. What then is the point wherein we divide?

A. It is this — whether we should expect to be saved from all sin before the article of death?

Q. 4. Is there any clear Scripture promise of this — that God will save us from all sin?

A. There is. "He shall redeem Israel from all his sins." [65] This is more largely expressed in the prophecy of Ezekiel, "Then will I sprinkle clean water upon you and ye shall be clean; from all your filthiness and from all your idols will I cleanse you. . . . I will also save you from all your uncleannesses." [66] No promise can be more full and clear. And to this the apostle plainly refers in that exhortation, "Having these promises, let us cleanse ourselves from all filthiness of flesh and spirit, perfecting holiness in the fear of God." [67] Equally clear and express is that ancient promise, "The Lord thy God will circumcise thy heart, and the heart of thy seed, to love the Lord thy God with all thy heart and with all thy soul." [68]

Q. 5. But does any assertion answerable to this occur in the New Testament?

A. There does, and that laid down in the plainest terms. So 1 John 3:8: "For this purpose the Son of God was manifested, that he might destroy the works of the devil" — the works of the devil without any limitation or restriction. But all sin is the work of the devil. Parallel to which is that assertion of St. Paul,[69] "Christ loved the church, and gave himself for it, that he might present it to himself a glorious church, not having spot, or wrinkle or any such thing, but that it should be holy and without blemish." And to the same effect is his assertion in the eighth of the Romans, 3–4, "God sent his Son . . . that the righteousness of the law might be fulfilled in us who walk not after the flesh but after the Spirit."

65. [Au.] Ps. 130:8.          66. [Au.] Ezek. 36:25, 29.          67. [Au.] 2 Cor. 7:1.
68. [Au.] Deut. 30:6.          69. [Au.] Eph. 5:25, 27.

Q. 6. Does the New Testament afford any further ground for expecting to be saved from all sin?

A. Undoubtedly it does, both in those prayers and commands which are equivalent to the strongest assertions.

Q. 7. What prayers do you mean?

A. Prayers for entire sanctification, which, were there no such thing, would be mere mockery of God. Such in particular, are, "Deliver us from evil," or rather "from the evil one" [cf. Mt. 6:13]. Now when this is done, when we are delivered from all evil, there can be no sin remaining. "Neither pray I for these alone, but for them also which shall believe on me through their word: that they all may be one, as thou, Father, art in me, and I in thee; that they also may be one in us . . . I in them, and thou in me, that they may be made perfect in one." [70] . . . "I bow my knees unto the God and Father of our Lord Jesus Christ . . . that he would grant you . . . that ye, being rooted and grounded in love, may be able to comprehend with all saints what is the breadth and length and depth and height, and to know the love of Christ which passeth knowledge that ye might be filled with all the fulness of God." [71] "The very God of peace sanctify you wholly; and I pray God your whole body, spirit, soul, be preserved blameless unto the coming of our Lord Jesus Christ." [72]

Q. 8. What command is there to the same effect?

A. "Be ye perfect, as your Father which is in heaven is perfect." [73] "Thou shalt love the Lord thy God with all thy heart, and with all thy soul, and with all thy mind." [74] But if the love of God fill all the heart, there can be no sin there.

Q. 9. But how does it appear that this is to be done before the article of death?

A. First: from the very nature of a command, which is not given to the dead but unto the living. Therefore, "Thou shalt love the Lord thy God with all thy heart" cannot mean, "Thou shalt do this when thou diest, but not while thou livest."

Secondly: from express texts of Scripture. "The grace of God that bringeth salvation hath appeared unto all men, teaching us that, having renounced (ἀρνησάμενοι) ungodliness and worldly lusts, we should live soberly, righteously, and godly in this present world, looking for the

70. [Au.] Jn. 17:20-23.    71. [Au.] Eph. 3:14, 16-19.
72. [Au.] 1 Thess. 5:23.
73. [Au.] Mt. 6, last. [Ed.] Intended citation: Mt. 5:48.    74. [Au.] Mt. 22:37.

glorious appearing of our Lord Jesus Christ, who gave himself for us, that he might redeem us from all iniquity, and purify unto himself a peculiar people, zealous of good works." [75] "He hath raised up an horn of salvation for us . . . to perform the mercy promised to our fathers . . . the oath which he sware to our father Abraham, that he would grant unto us, that we being delivered out of the hands of our enemies should serve him without fear, in holiness and righteousness before him all the days of our life." [76]

Q. 10. Is there any example in Scripture of persons who had attained this?

A. Yes. St. John and all those of whom he says in his first Epistle [4:17]: "Herein is our love made perfect, that we may have confidence in the day of judgment; because as he is, so are we in this world."

Q. 11. But why are there not more examples of this kind recorded in the New Testament?

A. It does not become us to be peremptory in this matter. One reason might possibly be because the apostles wrote to the church while it was in a state of infancy. Therefore they might mention such persons the more sparingly, lest they should give strong meat to babes.

Q. 12. Can you show one such example now? Where is he that is thus perfect?

A. To some that make this inquiry one might answer, "If I knew one here, I would not tell you. You are like Herod, you only seek the young child to destroy it" [cf. Mt. 2:8, 16–18]. But to the serious we answer, "There are numberless reasons why there should be few, if any, indisputable examples. What inconveniences would this bring on the person himself, set as a mark for all to shoot at! What a temptation would it be to others, not only to men who knew not God, but to believers themselves! How hardly would they refrain from idolizing such a person! And yet how unprofitable to gainsayers! For if they hear not Moses and the prophets, Christ and his apostles, neither would they be persuaded, though one rose from the dead" [cf. Lk. 16:31].

Q. 13. Suppose one had attained to this, would you advise him to speak of it?

A. Not to them who know not God: it would only provoke them to contradict and blaspheme. Nor to any without some particular reason,

75. [Au.] Tit. 2:11–14.
76. [Au.] Lk. 1:69–75. [Ed.] This was doubly familiar to Wesley as the Benedictus in The Order of Morning Prayer, B.C.P.

without some particular good in view, and then they should have an especial care to avoid all appearance of boasting — and to speak more loudly and convincingly by their lives than they can do by their tongues.

Q. 14. Is it a sin not to believe those who say they have attained?

A. By no means; even though they said true, we ought not hastily to believe but to suspend our judgment till we have farther and stronger proof.

Q. 15. But are we not apt to have a secret distaste to any who say they are saved from all sin?

A. 'Tis very possible we may, and that on several grounds — partly from a concern for the honour of God and the good of souls who may be hurt, yea, or turned out of the way, if these are not what they profess; partly from a kind of implicit envy at those who speak of higher attainments than our own; and partly from our slowness and unreadiness of heart to believe the works of God.

Q. 16. Does not the harshly preaching perfection tend to bring believers into a kind of bondage of slavish fear?

A. It does. Therefore we should always place it in the most amiable light, so that it may excite only hope, joy and desire.

Q. 17. Why may we not continue in the joy of faith even till we are made perfect?

A. Why not indeed? — since holy grief does not quench this joy; since even while we are under the cross, while we deeply partake of the sufferings of Christ, we may rejoice with joy unspeakable.

Q. 18. Do we not discourage believers from rejoicing evermore?

A. We ought not so to do. Let them all their life long rejoice unto God, so it be with reverence. And even if lightness or pride should mix with their joy, let us not strike at the joy itself (this is the gift of God) but at the lightness or pride, that the evil may cease and the good remain.

Q. 19. Ought we to be anxiously careful about perfection, lest we should die before we have attained it?

A. In no wise. We ought to be thus careful for nothing, neither spiritual nor temporal.

Q. 20. But ought we not to be troubled on account of the sinful nature which still remains in us?

A. It is good for us to have a deep sense of this and to be much ashamed before the Lord. But this should only incite us the more earnestly to turn unto Christ every moment and to draw light and life and strength from him, that we may go on, conquering and to conquer [cf. Rev. 6:2].

And therefore, when a sense of our sins most abounds, the sense of his love should much more abound.[77]

Q. 21. Will our joy or our trouble increase as we grow in grace?

A. Perhaps both. But without doubt our joy in the Lord will increase as our love increases.

Q. 22. Is not the teaching believers to be continually poring upon their inbred sin the ready way to make them forget that they are purged from their former sins?

A. We find by experience that it is; or to make them undervalue and account it a little thing: whereas, indeed — though there are still greater gifts beyond — this is inexpressibly great and glorious.

About ten (Mr. Perronet, Vicar of Shoreham, being added), we began to consider points of discipline.

Q. 1. What is schism in the Scripture sense of the word?

A. The word only occurs twice in the New Testament: 1 Cor. 1:10, where St. Paul exhorts them that there may be no "schisms" among them (σχισμάτα is the word, which we render "divisions"), and 12:25, "God hath mingled the body together, having given the more abundant honour to that part which lacked, that there may be no 'schism' in the body," *i.e.* in the Church, the body of Christ. In both these places the word undeniably means (which consequently is the true spiritual notion of "schism") a causeless breach, rupture, or division, made amongst the members of Christ, among those who are the living body of Christ, and members in particular.[78]

Q. 2. Are not the Methodists guilty of making such a schism?

A. No more than rebellion or murder. They do not divide themselves at all from the living body of Christ. Let any prove it if they can.

Q. 3. But do not they divide themselves from the Church of England?

A. No. They hold communion therewith now in the same manner as they did twenty years ago, and hope to do so until their lives' end.

Q. 4. You profess to obey both the governors and rules of the Church; yet in many instances you do not obey them. How is this consistent? Upon what principles do you act while you sometimes obey and sometimes not?

A. It is entirely consistent. We act at all times on one plain, uniform

---

77. Cf. "Wandering Thoughts" (*Sermons* [Sugden], II, 178 ff.); "On Sin in Believers" (*ibid.*, 360 ff.); "The Repentance of Believers" (*ibid.*, 379 ff.).
78. Cf. The sermon "On Schism," *Works*, VI, 406.

principle: "We will obey the rules and governors of the Church whenever we can, consistently with our duty to God. Whenever we cannot, we will quietly obey God rather than men."

Q. 5. But why do you say you are thrust out of the Church? Has not every minister a right to dispose of his own church?

A. He ought to have, but in fact he has not. A minister desires I should preach in his church, but the bishop forbids him. That bishop then injures him and thrusts me out of that church.

Q. 6. Does a church in the New Testament always mean "a single congregation"?

A. We believe it does. We do not recollect any instance to the contrary.

Q. 7. What instance or ground is there in the New Testament for a national church?

A. We know none at all. We apprehend it [a national church] to be a mere political institution.

Q. 8. Are the three orders of bishops, priests and deacons plainly described in the New Testament?

A. We think they are, and believe they generally obtained in the churches of the apostolic age.

Q. 9. But are you assured, God designed the same plan should obtain in all churches throughout all ages?

A. We are not assured of this because we do not know that it is asserted in Holy Writ.

Q. 10. If this plan were essential to a Christian church, what must become of all the foreign Reformed Churches?

A. It would follow they are no parts of the Church of Christ — a consequence full of shocking absurdity.

Q. 11. In what age was the divine right of episcopacy first asserted in England?

A. About the middle of Queen Elizabeth's reign.[79] Till then all the bishops and clergy in England continually allowed and joined in the ministrations of those who were not episcopally ordained.

Q. 12. Must there not be numberless accidental variations in the government of various churches?

A. There must, in the nature of things. As God variously dispenses his

79. By Hadrian Saravia and Thomas Bilson. Cf. A. J. Mason, The Church of England and Episcopacy (Cambridge, 1914), 31-40, 44-52. See also N. Sykes, Old Priest New Presbyter (Cambridge, 1956), 101; and P. M. Dawley, John Whitgift and the Reformation (New York, 1954), 140-41.

gifts of nature, providence and grace, both the offices themselves and the officers in each ought to be varied from time to time.

Q. 13. Why is it that there is no determinate plan of church-government appointed in Scripture?

A. Without doubt because the wisdom of God had a regard to this necessary variety.

Q. 14. Was there any thought of uniformity in the government of all churches until the time of Constantine?

A. It is certain there was not, and would not have been then had men consulted the word of God only.

### Thursday, [June] the eighteenth

Q. 1. Have we not limited field preaching too much?

A. It seems we have:

1. Because our calling is to save that which is lost. Now, we cannot expect the wanderers from God to seek us. It is our part to go and seek them.

2. Because we are more peculiarly called, by going out into the highways and hedges (which none will do if we do not) to compel them to come in [cf. Lk. 14:23].

3. Because that reason against it is not good, "The house will hold all that come." The house may hold all that will come to the house, but not all that will come into the field.

4. Because we have always found a greater blessing in field preaching than in any other preaching whatever.

Q. 2. What is "respect of persons" [Jas. 2:1]?

A. The regarding one person more than another on account of some outward circumstances, particularly riches.

Q. 3. Have we not fallen into this by allowing more of our time to the rich than to the poor, by not speaking so plain and home to them and by admitting them into the Bands or Society, though they had never received remission of sins, or had met in Band at all?

A. These are instances of such a respect of persons as we will endeavour to avoid for the time to come.

Q. 4. Would it not be well for the minister to visit the sick on Monday, Thursday, Friday, Saturday?

A. It seems no time could be more profitably employed, either for them or us.

Q. 5. How shall we keep off unworthy communicants?

A. 1. By being exactly careful whom we admit into the society; and

2. By giving notes [tokens] to none but those who come to us on the days appointed in each quarter.

Q. 6. How shall we thoroughly purge the Bands?

A. 1. In visiting the classes, meet those who are in the Bands every morning before the rest and examine them as strictly as you can both as to their heart and life.

2. Meet the married men and married women apart, the first Wednesday and Sunday after each visitation; the single men and single women apart on the second Wednesday and Sunday.[80] . . .

Q. 10. Are our assistants exemplary in their lives? Do we inquire enough into this?

A. Perhaps not. We should consider each of them who is with us as a pupil at the university, into whose behaviour and studies we should therefore make a particular inquiry every day. Might we not particularly inquire: Do you rise at four? Do you study in the method laid down at the last conference? Do you read the books we advise and no other? Do you see the necessity of regularity in study? What are the chief temptations to irregularity? Do you punctually observe the evening hour of retirement? Are you exact in writing your journal? Do you fast on Friday? Do you converse seriously, usefully and closely? Do you pray before, and have you a determinate end in, every conversation?

Q. 11. How often should our assistants preach?

A. Never more than twice a day, unless on a Sunday or an extraordinary occasion, of which themselves are to be the judges.

Q. 12. Are there any smaller advices concerning preaching, which it may be useful for them to observe?

A. Perhaps these that follow:

1. Be sure to begin and end precisely at the time appointed.

2. Sing no hymns of your own composing.

3. Endeavour to be serious, weighty and solemn in your whole deportment before the congregation.

4. Choose the plainest text you can.

5. Take care not to ramble from your text, but keep close to it, and make out what you undertake.

6. Always suit the subject to the audience.

80. Q. 7–9 omitted; they concern the rosters of the assistants and their appointments.

   7. Beware of allegorizing or spiritualizing too much.

   8. Take care of anything awkward or affected, either in your gesture or pronunciation.

   9. Tell each other if you observe anything of this kind.

Q. 13. Is there any part of the work of an assistant wherein only some of our assistants need be employed?

A. There is. Let those and those only to whom we shall write from time to time:

   1. Visit the classes in each place and write new lists of all the members.

   2. Regulate the Bands.

   3. Deliver new tickets [tokens].

   4. Keep watch-nights and lovefeasts.

   5. Take and send us up an exact account of the behaviour of the stewards, housekeepers, schoolmasters and leaders.[81] . . .

*Editor's postscript.* Because they have nothing of distinctive doctrinal interest in them, the Minutes for the Conference of 1748 are omitted. There were no further published minutes until 1765, when annual publication was begun — and has been continued ever since. Wesley's manuscript copies of the minutes of the conferences of 1749, 1755 and 1758 were preserved and were published by the Wesley Historical Society in its *Proceedings,* Vol. IV (Pt. 5), 1904, pp. 63–73. Of these, a passage from the Bristol Conference of 1758 records a brief review of the doctrine of Christian perfection, then being agitated more actively than before both by the Methodists and their critics. The following short passage from the sessions of Monday, August 14, and Tuesday, August 15, is reprinted here (and should be compared with the sermon and "thoughts" on that topic, below, pp. 252 ff.; 283 ff.):

❖ ❖

### Monday, August 14, 1758

We revised that part of our former conferences [minutes] which relates to Justification and all agreed that there was no need of retracting or altering anything.

81. Q. 14–16 omitted; they cover the appointments and calendar for the ensuing year.

### Tuesday, August 15, 1758

Q. Did you affirm that perfection excludes all infirmities, ignorance and mistake?

A. We continually affirm just the contrary.

Q. Do you say: "Every one who is not saved from all sin is in a state of damnation"?

A. So far from it that we will not say any one is in a state of damnation that fears God and really strives to please him.

Q. In what manner would you advise those who think they have attained to speak of their own experience?

A. With great wariness and with the deepest humility and self-abasement before God.

Q. How should young preachers especially speak of perfection in public?

A. Not too minutely or circumstantially, but rather in general and scriptural terms.

Q. Have they that are perfect need of the merits of Christ? Can they pray for forgiveness?

A. 1. Every one may *mistake* as long as he lives.

2. A *mistake* in *opinion* may *occasion* a mistake in *practice* (as in [the case of] Mr. De Renty).

3. Every *such mistake* is a transgression of the perfect law.

4. Therefore every such mistake, were it not for the blood of atonement, would expose to eternal damnation.

5. It follows that the most perfect have continual need of the merits of Christ, even for their actual transgressions, and may well say, for themselves as well as their brethren, "Forgive us our trespasses" [*cf.* Mt. 6:12, as in B.C.P. version of the Lord's Prayer].

Q. What then does Christian perfection imply?

A. The loving God with all the heart, so that every evil temper is destroyed and every thought and word and work springs from and is conducted to that end by the pure love of God and our neighbour.

❖ ❖

## THE RULES OF THE UNITED SOCIETIES [82]

1. In the latter end of the year 1739, eight or ten persons came to me

---

82. See reference to these rules above, p. 143. The copy text here is the first edition, 1743 (*cf.* Green, *Bibliography*, #43); see also *Works*, VIII, 269–71.

in London, who appeared to be deeply convinced of sin, and earnestly groaning for redemption. They desired (as did two or three more the next day) that I would spend some time with them in prayer and advise them how to flee from the wrath to come, which they saw continually hanging over their heads. That we might have more time for this great work, I appointed a day when they might all come together, which from thenceforward they did every week, namely, on Thursday in the evening. To these, and as many more as desired to join with them (for their number increased daily) I gave those advices from time to time which I judged most needful for them; and we always concluded our meeting with prayer suited to their several necessities.

2. This was the rise of the United Society, first at London and then in other places. Such a society is no other than *a company of men having the form and seeking the power of godliness, united in order to pray together, to receive the word of exhortation, and to watch over one another in love, that they may help each other to work out their salvation.*

3. That it may the more easily be discerned whether they are indeed working out their own salvation, each society is divided into smaller companies called "classes," according to their respective places of abode. There are about twelve persons in every class, one of whom is styled the Leader. It is his business: (1) To see each person in his class once a week at least, in order to inquire how their souls prosper; to advise, reprove, comfort, or exhort, as occasion may require; to receive what they are willing to give toward the relief of the poor; (2) To meet the minister and the stewards of the society once a week; to pay to the stewards what they have received of their several classes in the week preceding; and to show their account of what each person has contributed.

4. There is one only condition previously required in those who desire admission into these societies — "a desire to flee from the wrath to come, to be saved from their sins." But wherever this is really fixed in the soul, it will be shown by its fruits. It is therefore expected of all who continue therein, that they should continue to evidence their desire of salvation:

First, by doing no harm, by avoiding evil in every kind; especially that which is most generally practised. Such is the taking the name of God in vain; the profaning the day of the Lord, either by doing ordinary work thereon, or by buying or selling; drunkenness, *buying or selling spirituous liquors*, or *drinking them*, unless in cases of extreme necessity; *fighting*, quarreling, brawling; going to law; returning evil for evil, or railing for railing; the *using many words* in buying or selling; the *buying or selling uncustomed goods;* the giving or taking things on usury; *uncharitable* or *unprofitable* conversation; doing to others as we would not they should do unto us; doing what we know is not for the glory of God, as the *putting on of gold or costly apparel;* the *taking such diversions* as cannot be used in the name of the Lord Jesus, the *singing* those *songs* or *reading* those *books* which do not tend to the knowledge or love of God; softness and needless self-indulgence; laying up treasures upon earth.

5. It is expected of all who continue in these societies, that they should continue to evidence their desire of salvation:

Secondly, by doing good, by being in every kind merciful after their power; as they have opportunity, doing good of every possible sort, and as far as is possible, to all men: to their bodies, of the ability which God giveth, by giving food to the hungry, by clothing the naked, by visiting or helping them that are sick, or in prison; to their souls by instructing, reproving, or exhorting all they have any intercourse with; trampling under foot that enthusiastic doctrine of devils, that we are not to do good unless "our heart be free to it": by doing good especially to them that are of the household of faith, or groaning so to be; employing them, preferably to others, buying one of another, helping each other in business (and that so much the more, because the world will love its own, and them only); by all possible diligence and frugality, that the gospel be not blamed; by running with patience the race that is set before them, "denying themselves and taking up their cross daily" [*cf.* Lk. 9:23]: submitting to bear the reproach of Christ, to be as the filth and offscouring of the world; and looking that men should "say all manner of evil of them falsely for the Lord's sake" [*cf.* Mt. 5:11].

6. It is expected of all who desire to continue in these societies, that they should continue to evidence their desire of salvation: thirdly, *by attending upon all the ordinances of God.* Such are the public worship of God; the ministry of the word, either read or expounded, the Supper of the Lord; private prayer; searching the Scriptures; and fasting, or abstinence.

7. These are the General Rules of our societies, all [of] which we are taught of God to observe, even in his written word — the only rule, and the sufficient rule, both of our faith and practice. And all these, we know, his Spirit writes on every truly awakened heart. If there be any among us who observe them not, who habitually break any of them, let it be made known unto him who watches over that soul as one that must

give account. I will admonish him of the error of his ways. I will bear with him for a season. But if he repent not, he hath no more place among us. We have delivered our own souls.

## RULES OF THE BANDS [83]

The design of our meeting is to obey that command of God, "Confess your faults one to another, and pray one for another, that ye may be healed" (Jas. 5:16).

To this end, we intend:

1. To meet once a week, at the least.

2. To come punctually at the hour appointed, without some extraordinary reason.

3. To begin (those of us who are present) exactly at the hour, with singing or prayer.

4. To speak each of us in order, freely and plainly, the true state of our souls, with the faults we have committed in thought, word, or deed, and the temptations we have felt since our last meeting.

5. To end every meeting with prayer suited to the state of each person present.

6. To desire some person among us to speak his own state first, and then to ask the rest, in order, as many and as searching questions as may be, concerning their state, sins and temptations.

Some of the questions proposed to every one before he is admitted among us may be to this effect:

1. Have you the forgiveness of your sins?

2. Have you peace with God through our Lord Jesus Christ?

3. Have you the witness of God's Spirit with your spirit that you are a child of God?

4. Is the love of God shed abroad in your heart?

5. Has no sin, inward or outward, dominion over you?

6. Do you desire to be told of your faults?

7. Do you desire to be told of all your faults, and that plain and home?

8. Do you desire that every one of us should tell you, from time to time, whatsoever is in his heart concerning you?

9. Consider! Do you desire we should tell you whatsoever we think, whatsoever we fear, whatsoever we hear concerning you?

10. Do you desire that, in doing this, we should come as close as possi-

83. See reference above, p. 143. The copy text here is the first edition (1744); see also *Works*, VIII, 272–73.

ble; that we should cut to the quick, and search your heart to the bottom?

11. Is it your desire and design to be, on this and all other occasions, entirely open, so as to speak everything that is in your heart without exception, without disguise and without reserve?

Any of the preceding questions may be asked as often as occasion offers; the five following at every meeting:

1. What known sins have you committed since our last meeting?
2. What temptations have you met with?
3. How were you delivered?
4. What have you thought, said, or done, of which you doubt whether it be sin or not?
5. Have you nothing you desire to keep secret?

## A Plain Account of Genuine Christianity [1]

*Editor's introduction.* Wesley was fond of dilating on the Christian ideal. In *The Character of a Methodist* and *The Principles of a Methodist* (1742), in the *Appeals* (1744–45) and in his sermons he frequently undertook to delineate the character of the perfect Christian — without, however, claiming this character for himself or ascribing it to other living persons. Here, in this *Plain Account of Genuine Christianity*, he again invokes the ideal, now to turn it to apologetic purposes.

In 1749 Dr. Conyers Middleton (1683–1750), a Cambridge don who was essentially a deist, published *A Free Inquiry into the Miraculous Powers which Are Supposed to Have Subsisted in the Christian Church from the Earliest Ages through Several Successive Centuries: By Which It Is Shown that We Have No Sufficient Reason to Believe, Upon the Authority of the Primitive Fathers, that Any Such Powers Were Continued to the Church After the Days of the Apostles.* His ostensible aim was to reject the doctrinal authority of "Christian antiquity" and "to fix the religion of Protestants on its proper basis, that is, on the sacred Scriptures . . ." (p. cxi). But an orthodox reader could scarcely miss the point that Middleton's sweeping rejection of the "miraculous powers" in the period immediately following the apostolic age might readily be

1. The copy text is the first edition (Dublin, 1753), collated with the third edition (Bristol, 1761), *Works* (Pine), XVIII, 252–75, and the sixth (1779).

extended to exclude them from the age of the Apostles and from the New Testament itself. Conversely, the counterargument that it would take an infallible church to validate both Scripture and antiquity seemed to deliver the church of the Fathers into the hands of an infallible magisterium — and this way lay popery! Indeed, Middleton's book was one of the decisive factors in Edward Gibbon's "conversion" to Rome (transient though it was).[2]

Wesley read the *Inquiry* in loose sheets in late December 1748. "January 2, Monday [1749] — I had designed to set out with a friend for Rotterdam; but being much pressed to answer Dr. Middleton's book against the Fathers, I postponed my voyage and spent almost twenty days in that unpleasing employment." [3] The result was *A Letter to the Reverend Doctor Conyers Middleton, Occasioned by His Late Free Enquiry*.[4] It is an extended and detailed refutation, involving much analysis of the patristic texts invoked by Middleton and a discussion of their exegesis and interpretation. It failed, however, to make much of an impression either on Middleton, or on the other orthodox critics who quickly ranged themselves alongside Wesley. This was partly because of Wesley's careless handling of Middleton's text,[5] and partly because his deepest concern was not with the scholarly issues involved, but with the practical threat to piety posed by Middleton's clever sophistries — despite all his straight-faced profession of loyalty to "the sacred Scriptures"!

It is quite in character, therefore, that after some sixty pages of academic disputation, Wesley switches his argument from the analysis of patristic texts over to a quite different line. The one point he really cared to make is that actual Christian faith and life, not only in apostolic and patristic, but also still in modern times, reflects the supernatural power of God and the miraculous presence of the Holy Spirit. If *this* thesis is acknowledged, then the rest of Middleton's case collapses, in Wesley's view, as just another pointless distortion of the Christian message. He turns, therefore, to the familiar task of describing the ideal Christian and genuine Christianity, in terms which are meant to undercut Middleton's appeal to church history. The miracle of Christian living is the really essential miraculous power which *has* "subsisted in the Church" in

2. *Cf.* Edward Gibbon, *Memoirs of The Life of Edward Gibbon*, G. Birkbeck Hill, ed. (1900), 67–69.

3. *Journal*, III, 390.

4. Reprinted in *Works* (Pine), XVIII, 140–276, and *Works*, X, 1–79.

5. A collation of Middleton's and Wesley's texts indicates that more than three-fourths of the latter's citations are inexact and garbled.

*all* ages, and is still present and active in the Christian community. The delineation of this power of Christian experience and life becomes the concluding section (VI) of his open letter to Middleton.

As if aware that the scholars would neglect his homiletical conclusion and that some of his Methodist readers might not wade through his disputation with the scholar to get to his homily on the Christian life, Wesley issued it as a separate sixteen-page pamphlet in 1753 (Dublin), under the title, *A Plain Account of Genuine Christianity*. In this form it was widely circulated for the rest of the century. It is this tract — with its echoes of its controversial context but with its main stress on the vitality of Christian experience — that we have chosen to represent Wesley's vision of the Christian ideal.

❖  ❖  ❖  ❖

We [Middleton and Wesley] have been long disputing about "Christians," about "Christianity" and the "evidence" whereby it is supported. But what do these terms mean? Who is a Christian indeed? What is real, genuine Christianity? And what is the surest and most accessible evidence (if I may so speak) whereby I may know that it is of God? May the God of the Christians enable me to speak on these heads in a manner suitable to the importance of them!

### SECTION I

1. I would consider, first, who is a Christian indeed? What does that term properly imply? It has been so long abused, I fear, not only to mean nothing at all, but what was far worse than nothing, to be a cloak for the vilest hypocrisy, for the grossest abominations and immoralities of every kind, that it is high time to rescue it out of the hands of wretches that are a reproach to human nature, to show determinately what manner of man he is to whom this name of right belongs.

2. A "Christian" cannot think of the Author of his being without abasing himself before him, without a deep sense of the distance between a worm of earth and him that "sitteth on the circle of the heavens" [*cf.* Is. 40:22]. In his presence he sinks into the dust, knowing himself to be less than nothing in his eye and being conscious, in a manner words cannot express, of his own littleness, ignorance, foolishness. So that he can only cry out, from the fulness of his heart, "O God, what is man? What am I?"

3. He has a continual sense of his dependence on the parent of good,[1] for his being and all the blessings that attend it. To him he refers every natural and every moral endowment, with all that is commonly ascribed either to fortune or to the wisdom, courage, or merit of the possessor. And hence he acquiesces in whatsoever appears to be his will, not only with patience but with thankfulness. He willingly resigns all he is, all he has, to his wise and gracious disposal. The ruling temper of his heart is the most absolute submission and the tenderest gratitude to his sovereign benefactor. And this grateful love creates filial fear, an awful reverence toward him and an earnest care not to give place to any disposition, not to admit an action, word or thought which might in any degree displease that indulgent power to whom he owes his life, breath and all things [cf. Acts 17:25].

4. And as he has the strongest affection for the fountain of all good, so he has the firmest confidence in him; a confidence which neither pleasure nor pain, neither life nor death, can shake. But yet this, far from creating sloth or indolence, pushes him on to the most vigorous industry. It causes him to put forth all his strength in obeying him in whom he confides; so that he is never faint in his mind, never weary of doing whatever he believes to be his will. And as he knows the most acceptable worship of God is to imitate him he worships, so he is continually labouring to transcribe into himself all his imitable perfections: in particular, his justice, mercy and truth, so eminently displayed in all his creatures.

5. Above all, remembering that God is love, he is conformed to the same likeness. He is full of love to his neighbour: of universal love, not confined to one sect or party, not restrained to those who agree with him in opinions, or in outward modes of worship, or to those who are allied to him by blood or recommended by nearness of place. Neither does he love those only that love him, or that are endeared to him by intimacy of acquaintance. But his love resembles that of him whose mercy is over all his works [cf. Ps. 145:9, B.C.P.]. It soars above all these scanty bounds, embracing neighbours and strangers, friends and enemies; yea, not only the good and gentle but also the froward, the evil and unthankful. For he loves every soul that God has made, every child of man, of whatever place or nation. And yet this universal benevolence does in nowise interfere with a peculiar regard for his relations, friends and benefactors, a fervent love for his country and the most endeared affection to all men of integrity, of clear and generous virtue.

6. His love to these, so to all mankind, is in itself generous and dis-

1. Cf. John Milton, *Paradise Lost*, Bk. V, l. 153; see below, p. 186 and 388.

interested, springing from no view of advantage to himself, from no regard to profit or praise; no, nor even the pleasure of loving. This is the daughter, not the parent, of his affection. By experience he knows that *social love* (if it mean the love of our neighbour) is absolutely, essentially different from *self-love*, even of the most allowable kind, just as different as the objects at which they point. And yet it is sure that, if they are under due regulations, each will give additional force to the other, 'till they mix together never to be divided.

7. And this universal, disinterested love is productive of all right affections. It is fruitful of gentleness, tenderness, sweetness; of humanity, courtesy and affability. It makes a Christian rejoice in the virtues of all, and bear a part in their happiness at the same time that he sympathizes with their pains and compassionates their infirmities. It creates modesty, condescension, prudence — together with calmness and evenness of temper. It is the parent of generosity, openness and frankness, void of jealousy and suspicion. It begets candor and willingness to believe and hope whatever is kind and friendly of every man; and invincible patience, never overcome of evil, but overcoming evil with good [*cf*. Rom. 12:21].

8. The same love constrains him to converse, not only with a strict regard to truth but with artless sincerity and genuine simplicity, as one in whom there is no guile. And not content with abstaining from all such expressions as are contrary to justice or truth, he endeavours to refrain from every unloving word, either to a present or of an absent person; in all his conversation aiming at this, either to improve himself in knowledge or virtue, or to make those with whom he converses some way wiser, or better, or happier than they were before.

9. The same love is productive of all right actions. It leads him into an earnest and steady discharge of all social offices, of whatever is due to relations of every kind: to his friends, to his country and to any particular community whereof he is a member. It prevents his willingly hurting or grieving any man. It guides him into an uniform practice of justice and mercy, equally extensive with the principle whence it flows. It constrains him to do all possible good, of every possible kind, to all men; and makes him invariably resolved in every circumstance of life to do that, and that only, to others, which supposing he were himself in the same situation, he would desire they should do to him.

10. And as he is easy to others, so he is easy in himself. He is free from the painful swellings of pride, from the flames of anger, from the impetuous gusts of irregular self-will. He is no longer tortured with envy or malice, or with unreasonable and hurtful desire. He is no more

enslaved to the pleasures of sense, but has the full power both over his mind and body, in a continued cheerful course of sobriety, of temperance and chastity. He knows how to use all things in their place and yet is superior to them all. He stands above those low pleasures of imagination which captivate vulgar minds, whether arising from what mortals term greatness, or novelty or beauty. All these too he can taste and still look upward, still aspire to nobler enjoyments. Neither is he a slave to fame: popular breath affects not him; he stands steady and collected in himself.

11. And he who seeks no praise cannot fear dispraise. Censure gives him no uneasiness, being conscious to himself that he would not willingly offend and that he has the approbation of the Lord of all. He cannot fear want, knowing in whose hand is the earth and the fulness thereof and that it is impossible for him to withhold from one that fears him any manner of thing that is good. He cannot fear pain, knowing it will never be sent unless it be for his real advantage, and that then his strength will be proportioned to it, as it has always been in times past. He cannot fear death, being able to trust him he loves with his soul as well as his body, yea, glad to leave the corruptible body in the dust, 'till it is raised, incorruptible and immortal. So that, in honour or shame, in abundance or want, in ease or pain, in life or in death, always and in all things, he has learned to be content, to be easy, thankful, joyful, happy.

12. He is happy in knowing there is a God — an intelligent Cause and Lord of all — and that he is not the produce either of blind chance or inexorable necessity. He is happy in the full assurance he has, that this Creator and End of all things is a being of boundless wisdom, of infinite power to execute all the designs of his·wisdom and of no less infinite goodness to direct all his power to the advantage of all his creatures. Nay, even the consideration of his immutable justice, rendering to all their due, of his unspotted holiness, of his all-sufficiency in himself and of that immense ocean of all perfections which center in God from eternity to eternity, is a continual addition to the happiness of a Christian.

13. A farther addition is made thereto while, in contemplating even the things that surround him, that thought strikes warmly upon his heart —

These are thy glorious works, Parent of Good! [2]

while he takes knowledge of the invisible things of God, even his eternal power and wisdom in the things that are seen, the heavens, the earth,

2. John Milton, *Paradise Lost*, Bk. V, l. 153; see above, p. 184, and below, p. 388.

the fowls of the air, the lilies of the field. How much more, while, rejoicing in the constant care which he still takes of the work of his own hand, he breaks out in a transport of love and praise, "O Lord our Governor! How excellent is thy Name in all the earth; thou that hast set thy glory above the heavens" [Ps. 8:1, B.C.P.]! — while he, as it were, sees the Lord sitting upon his throne and ruling all things well; while he observes the general providence of God co-extended with his whole creation and surveys all the effects of it in the heavens and earth, as a well-pleased spectator; while he sees the wisdom and goodness of his general government descending to every particular, so presiding over the whole universe as over a single person, so watching over every single person as if he were the whole universe — how does he exult when he reviews the various traces of the Almighty Goodness in what has befallen himself in the several circumstances and changes of his own life, all which he now sees have been allotted to him and dealt out in number, weight and measure. With what triumph of soul, in surveying either the general or particular providence of God, does he observe every line pointing out an hereafter, every scene opening into eternity?

14. He is peculiarly and inexpressibly happy in the clearest and fullest conviction: "This all-powerful, all-wise, all-gracious Being, this Governor of all, loves *me*. This lover of my soul is always with me, is never absent; no, not for a moment. And I love him: there is none in heaven but thee, none on earth that I desire beside thee [*cf*. Ps. 73:25]! And he has given me to resemble himself; he has stamped his image on my heart. And I live unto him; I do only his will; I glorify him with my body and my spirit. And it will not be long before I shall die unto him, I shall die into the arms of God. And then farewell sin and pain, then it only remains that I should live with him for ever."

15. This is the plain, naked portraiture of a Christian. But be not prejudiced against him for his name. Forgive his particularities of opinion and (what you think) superstitious modes of worship. These are circumstances but of small concern and do not enter into the essence of his character. Cover them with a veil of love and look at the substance: his tempers, his holiness, his happiness. Can calm reason conceive either a more amiable or a more desirable character?

Is it your own? Away with names! Away with opinions! I care not what you are called. I ask not (it does not deserve a thought) what opinion you are of, so you are conscious to yourself that you are the man whom I have been (however faintly) describing.

Do not you know you ought to be such? Is the Governor of the world well pleased that you are not?

Do you at least desire it? I would to God that desire may penetrate your inmost soul and that you may have no rest in your spirit 'till you are not only almost but altogether a Christian! [3]

SECTION II

1. The second point to be considered is what is real, genuine Christianity — whether we speak of it as a principle in the soul or as a scheme or system of doctrine?

Christianity, taken in the latter sense, is that system of doctrine which describes the character above recited, which promises it shall be mine (provided I will not rest till I attain) and which tells me how I may attain it.

2. First, it *describes* this character in all its parts, and that in the most lively and affecting manner. The main lines of this picture are beautifully drawn in many passages of the Old Testament. These are filled up in the New, retouched and finished with all the art of God.

The same we have in miniature more than once; particularly in the thirteenth chapter of the former Epistle to the Corinthians, and in that discourse which St. Matthew records as delivered by our Lord at his entrance upon his public ministry.

3. Secondly, Christianity *promises* this character shall be mine if I will not rest till I attain it. This is promised both in the Old Testament and the New. Indeed the New is, in effect, all a promise, seeing every description of the servants of God mentioned therein has the nature of a command, in consequence of those general injunctions: "Be ye followers of me, as I am of Christ;" [4] "Be ye followers of them who through faith and patience inherit the promises." [5] And every command has the force of a promise, in virtue of those general promises: "A new heart will I give you, and I will put my Spirit within you, and cause you to walk in my statutes, and ye shall keep my judgments, and do them." [6] "This is the covenant that I will make after those days, saith the Lord; I will put my laws into their minds and write them in their hearts." [7] Accordingly, when it is said, "Thou shalt love the Lord thy God with all thy heart, and with all thy soul, and with all thy mind"; [8] it is not only a

---

3. *Cf.* "The Almost Christian," *Sermons* (Sugden), I, 53–67.
4. [Au.] 1 Cor. 11:1.          5. [Au.] Heb. 6:12.          6. [Au.] Ezek. 36:26–27.
7. [Au.] Heb. 8:10.          8. [Au.] Mt. 22:37.

direction what I shall do, but a promise of what God will do in me, exactly equivalent with what is written elsewhere: "The Lord thy God will circumcise thy heart, and the heart of thy seed" (alluding to the custom then in use) "to love the Lord thy God with all thy heart, and with all thy soul." [9]

4. This being observed, it will readily appear to every serious person who reads the New Testament with that care which the importance of the subject demands that every particular branch of the preceding character is manifestly promised therein, either explicitly, under the very form of a promise, or virtually, under that of a description or command.

5. Christianity tells me, in the third place, how I may attain the promise, namely, by faith.

But what is faith? Not an opinion, no more than it is a form of words; not any number of opinions put together, be they ever so true. A string of opinions is no more Christian faith than a string of beads is Christian holiness.

It is not an assent to any opinion, or any number of opinions. A man may assent to three or three-and-twenty creeds; he may assent to all the Old and New Testament (at least, as far as he understands them) and yet have no Christian faith at all.

6. The faith by which the promise is attained is represented by Christianity as a power wrought by the Almighty in an immortal spirit inhabiting an house of clay, to see through that veil into the world of spirits, into things invisible and eternal; a power to discern those things which with eyes of flesh and blood no man hath seen or can see, either by reason of their nature, which (though they surround us on every side) is [are?] not perceivable by these gross senses, or by reason of their distance, as being yet afar off in the bosom of eternity.[10]

7. This is Christian faith in the general notion of it. In its more particular notion, it is a divine evidence or conviction wrought in my heart that God is reconciled to *me* through his Son, inseparably joined with a confidence in him as a gracious, reconciled Father, as for all things, so especially for all those good things which are invisible and eternal.[11]

9. [Au.] Deut. 30:6.

10. *Cf.* This analogy between physical and spiritual sensation with *An Earnest Appeal*, below, p. 386 ff.

11. *Cf.* "Justification by Faith," below, p. 204 ff. See also "The Scripture Way of Salvation," below, p. 275 ff.; and *The Doctrine of Salvation, Faith and Good Works,* above, p. 125 f.

To believe (in the Christian sense) is, then, to walk in the light of eternity and to have a clear sight of, and confidence in, the Most High, reconciled to me through the Son of his love.

8. Now, how highly desirable is such a faith, were it only on its own account? For how little does the wisest of men know of anything more than he can see with his eyes? What clouds and darkness cover the whole scene of things invisible and eternal? What does he know even of himself as to his invisible part, what of his future manner of existence? How melancholy an account does the prying, learned philosopher (perhaps the wisest and best of all heathens), the great, the venerable Marcus [Aurelius] Antoninus,[12] give of these things? What was the result of all his serious researches, of his high and deep contemplations? "Either dissipation (of the soul as well as the body) into the common, unthinking mass or reabsorption into the universal fire (the unintelligent source of all things) or some unknown manner of conscious existence, after the body sinks to rise no more." One of these three he supposed must succeed death; but which, he had no light to determine. Poor Antoninus — with all his wealth, his honour, his power, with all his wisdom and philosophy!

> What points of knowledge did he gain?
> That life is sacred all — and vain!
> Sacred how high, and vain how low?
> He could not tell — but died to know.[13]

9. He died to know! And so must you, unless you are now a partaker of Christian faith. O consider this! Nay, and consider, not only how little you know of the immensity of the things that are beyond sense and time, but how uncertainly do you know even that little! How faintly glimmering a light is that you have? Can you properly be said to *know* any of these things? Is that knowledge any more than bare conjecture? And the reason is plain. You have no senses suited to invisible or eternal objects. What *desiderata* then, especially to the rational, the reflecting part of mankind, are these: a more extensive knowledge of things invisible and eternal, a greater certainty in whatever knowledge of them we have, and, in order to both, faculties capable of discerning things invisible?

12. Roman Emperor and Stoic philosopher (121–180) whose *Meditations* Wesley read (or reread?) in October 1745; *cf. Journal*, III, 215.

13. *Cf.* John Gambold (member of the Oxford Holy Club; rector of Stanton Harcourt), *Works* (Bath, 1789), 276, where the last line reads: "He knew not here — but died to know."

10. Is it not so? Let impartial reason speak. Does not every thinking man want a window, not so much in his neighbour's as in his own breast? He wants an opening there of whatever kind that might let in light from eternity. He is pained to be thus feeling after God so darkly, so uncertainly; to know so little of God and indeed so little of any beside material objects. He is concerned that he must see even that little, not directly, but in the dim, sullied glass of sense and, consequently, so imperfectly and obscurely that 'tis all a mere enigma still.

11. Now, these very *desiderata* faith supplies. It gives a more extensive knowledge of things invisible, showing what eye had not seen, nor ear heard, neither could it before enter into our heart to conceive. And all these it shows in the clearest light, with the fullest certainty and evidence, ἔλεγχος. For it does not leave us to receive our notices of them by mere reflection from the dull glass of sense, but resolves a thousand enigmas of the highest concern by giving faculties suited to things invisible. O who would not wish for such a faith, were it only on these accounts? How much more, if by this I may receive the promise, I may attain all that holiness and happiness?

12. So Christianity tells me and so I find it. May every real Christian say, "I now am assured that these things are so; I experienced them in my own breast. What Christianity (considered as a doctrine) promised, is accomplished in my soul." And Christianity, considered as an inward principle, is the completion of all those promises. It is holiness and happiness, the image of God impressed on a created spirit; a fountain of peace and love springing up into everlasting life.

### SECTION III

1. And this I conceive to be the strongest evidence of the truth of Christianity. I do not undervalue traditional evidence. Let it have its place and its due honour. It is highly serviceable in its kind and in its degree. And yet I cannot set it on a level with this.

It is generally supposed that traditional evidence is weakened by length of time, as it must necessarily pass through so many hands in a continued succession of ages. But no length of time can possibly affect the strength of this internal evidence. It is equally strong, equally new, through the course of seventeen hundred years. It passes now, even as it has done from the beginning, directly from God into the believing soul. Do you suppose time will ever dry up this stream? O, no! It shall never be cut off.

*Labitur et labetur in omne volubilis aevum* [14]

2. Traditional evidence is of an extremely complicated nature, necessarily including so many and so various considerations that only men of strong and clear understanding can be sensible of its full force. On the contrary, how plain and simple is this and how level to the lowest capacity? Is not this the sum: "One thing I know; I was blind, but now I see" [*cf.* Jn. 9:25]? — an argument so plain that a peasant, a woman, a child, may feel all its force.

3. The traditional evidence of Christianity stands, as it were, a great way off, and therefore, although it speaks loud and clear, yet makes a less lively impression. It gives us an account of what was transacted long ago, in far distant times as well as places; whereas the inward evidence is intimately present to all persons, at all times and in all places. It is nigh thee, in thy mouth, and in thy heart [*cf.* Deut. 30:14; Rom. 10:8], if thou believest in the Lord Jesus Christ. "This," then, "is the record," this is the evidence, emphatically so called, "that God hath given unto us eternal life and this life is in his Son" [1 Jn. 5:11].

4. If, then, it were possible (which I conceive it is not) to shake the traditional evidence of Christianity, still he that has the internal evidence (and every true believer hath the witness or evidence in himself) would stand firm and unshaken. Still he could say to those who were striking at the external evidence, "Beat on the sack of Anaxagoras," [15] but you can no more hurt *my* evidence of Christianity than the tyrant could hurt the spirit of that wise man.

5. I have sometimes been almost inclined to believe that the wisdom of God has, in most later ages, permitted the external evidence of Christianity to be more or less clogged and encumbered for this very end, that men (of reflection especially) might not altogether rest there, but be constrained to look into themselves also and attend to the light shining in their hearts.

Nay, it seems (if it may be allowed for us to pry so far into the rea-

14. "It flows and goes on flowing through all the circling years." *Cf.* Horace, *Epistles*, BK. I, Epistle ii, l. 43; Wesley quotes it again, *Letters*, II, 384.

15. Wesley's point here is obvious enough, but his citation is not, nor does it fit the records we have of the life and sayings of Anaxagoras. If, however, we read Epictetus, we would have abundant documentation for the idea, if not the actual aphorism; *cf. Discourses*, Bk. I, chap. xix (Loeb ed. [Cambridge, Mass., 1946], I, 128–35); Bk. III, chap. vi (*ibid.*, II, 46–47); chap. x (*ibid.*, 76–77); Bk. IV, chap. i (*ibid.*, 295–99); *Fragments*, sec. 23 (Loeb ed., II, 466–67), and sec. 26 (470–71); and *Manual*, sec. 20 (Loeb ed., II, 498–99).

sons of the divine dispensations) that, particularly in this age, God suffers all kind of objections to be raised against the traditional evidence of Christianity that men of understanding (though unwilling to give it up, yet, at the same time they defend this evidence) may not rest the whole strength of their cause thereon but seek a deeper and firmer support for it.

6. Without this, I cannot but doubt whether they can long maintain their cause; whether, if they do not obey the loud call of God and lay far more stress than they have hitherto done on this internal evidence of Christianity, they will not, one after another, give up the external, and (in heart at least) go over to those whom they are now contending with; so that, in a century or two, the people of England will be fairly divided into real deists and real Christians. And I apprehend this would be no loss at all, but rather an advantage to the Christian cause. Nay, perhaps it would be the speediest, yea, the only effectual way of bringing all reasonable deists to be Christians.

7. May I be permitted to speak freely? May I, without offence, ask of you that are called Christians what real loss would you sustain in giving up your present opinion that the Christian system is of God? Though you bear the name, you are not Christians now: you have neither Christian faith nor love. You have no divine evidence of things unseen, you have not entered "into the holiest by the blood of Jesus" [cf. Heb. 10:19]. You do not love God with all your heart; neither do you love your neighbour as yourself. You are neither happy nor holy. You have not learned in every state therewith to be content; to rejoice evermore, even in want, pain, death and in everything to give thanks. You are not holy in heart: superior to pride, to anger, to foolish desires. Neither are you holy in life; you do not walk as Christ also walked. Does not the main of your Christianity lie in your opinion, decked with a few outward observances? For as to morality, even honest heathen morality — O let me utter a melancholy truth! — many of those whom you style deists, there is reason to fear, have far more of it than you.

8. Go on, gentlemen, and prosper! Shame these nominal Christians out of that poor superstition which they call Christianity. Reason, rally, laugh them out of their dead, empty forms, void of spirit, of faith, of love. Convince them that such unmeaning pageantry — for such it manifestly is if there is nothing in the heart correspondent with the outward show — is absolutely unworthy, you need not say of God, but even of any man that is endued with common understanding. Show them that while they are endeavouring to please God thus, they are only beating the

air. Know your time; press on; push your victories 'till you have conquered all that know not God. And then he, whom neither they nor you know now, shall rise and gird himself with strength and go forth in his almighty love, and sweetly conquer you all together.

9. O that the time were come! How do I long for you to be partakers of the exceeding great and precious promises! How am I pained when I hear any of you using those silly terms which the men of form have taught you: calling the mention of the only thing you want "cant"; the deepest wisdom, the highest happiness, "enthusiasm"! What ignorance is this? How extremely despicable would it make you in the eyes of any but a Christian? But he cannot despise you, who loves you as his own soul, who is ready to lay down his life for your sake.

10. Perhaps you will say, "But this internal evidence of Christianity affects only those in whom the promise is fulfilled. It is no evidence to *me*." There is truth in this objection. It does affect them chiefly, but it does not affect them only. It cannot, in the nature of things, be so strong an evidence to others as it is to them. And yet it may bring a degree of evidence. It may reflect some light on you also.

For, first, you see the beauty and loveliness of Christianity, when it is rightly understood, and you are sure there is nothing to be desired in comparison of it.

Secondly, you know the Scripture promises this and says it is attained by faith, and by no other way.

Thirdly, you see clearly how desirable Christian faith is, even on account of its own intrinsic value.

Fourthly, you are a witness that the holiness and happiness above described can be attained no other way. The more you have laboured after virtue and happiness, the more convinced you are of this. Thus far, then, you need not lean upon other men; thus far you have personal experience.

Fifthly, what reasonable assurance can you have of things whereof you have not personal experience? Suppose the question were, can the blind be restored to sight? This you have not yourself experienced. How then will you know that such a thing ever was? Can there be an easier or surer way than to talk with one or some number of men who were blind but are now restored to sight? They cannot be deceived as to the fact in question; the nature of the thing leaves no room for this. And if they are honest men (which you may learn from other circumstances), they will not deceive you.

Now transfer this to the case before us. And those who were blind, but now see — those who were sick many years, but now are healed; those who were miserable, but now are happy — will afford *you* also a very strong evidence of the truth of Christianity; as strong as can be in the nature of things 'till you experience it in your own soul. And this, though it be allowed they are but plain men, and, in general, of weak understanding; nay, though some of them should be mistaken in other points and hold opinions which cannot be defended.[16]

11. All this may [also] be allowed concerning the primitive Fathers. I mean particularly Clemens Romanus, Ignatius, Polycarp, Justin Martyr, Irenaeus, Origen, Clemens Alexandrinus, Cyprian; to whom I would add Macarius and Ephraim Syrus.[17]

I allow that some of these had not strong natural sense, that few of them had much learning, and none the assistances which our age enjoys in some respects above all that went before.

Hence I doubt not but whoever will be at the pains of reading over their writings for that poor end will find many mistakes, many weak suppositions, and many ill-drawn conclusions.

12. And yet I exceedingly reverence them, as well as their writings, and esteem them very highly in love. I reverence them, because they were Christians, such Christians as are above described. And I reverence their writings, because they describe true, genuine Christianity, and direct us to the strongest evidence of the Christian doctrine.

Indeed, in addressing the heathens of those times, they intermix other arguments — particularly, that drawn from the numerous miracles which were then performed in the church, which they needed only to open their eyes and see daily wrought in the face of the sun.

But still they never relinquish this: "What the Scripture promises, I enjoy. Come and see what Christianity has done here; and acknowledge it is of God."

I reverence these ancient Christians (with all their failings) the more, because I see so few Christians now; because I read so little in the writings of later times, and hear so little, of genuine Christianity; and because most of the modern Christians (so called), not content with be-

16. The separate text of *A Plain Account* . . . ends here. The added sections form the conclusion of the "Letter" to Dr. Middleton; see above, p. 181 f.; and *Works*, X, 79.

17. See above, p. 9 f.

ing wholly ignorant of it, are deeply prejudiced against it, calling it "enthusiasm," and I know not what.

That the God of power and love may make both them, and you, and me, such Christians as those Fathers were, is the earnest prayer of, Reverend Sir,

Your real friend and servant,

# II

## FAITH AND THE ASSURANCE OF FAITH

*Editor's introduction.* The following essay first appeared in print (as Sermon V) in *Sermons on Several Occasions* (1746), but its theme had served Wesley as the touchstone of evangelical Christianity from the beginning of the Revival, and he preached on it in season and out. (*Cf. Journal*, III, 20; see also "sermon register" in *Journal*, VIII, 171–252. See also *Sermons* [Sugden], I, v, 112–30.) The "sermon" was probably never preached as it was published. What we have here is plainly a popular theological tract. Its primary concerns are to undercut every ground of human self-sufficiency, to depict the human predicament in genuinely desperate terms and to offer to men aware of their radical need the good news of the gospel *by faith alone*. Justification is *pardon* — God's gracious forgiveness to those who cannot claim or expect it. But the crux of the problem of pardon is our acceptance of it and this is the essence of the act of faith, from its human side. This requires Wesley to develop his standard definition of faith (see above, pp. 128–33, and below, pp. 386–88) and to exhort his hearers to seek and receive their justification by faith, thus understood. It is important to notice that Wesley here grounds his doctrine of *sola fide* directly upon "the words of our own Church" in support of his doctrine. His references, in this instance, are to the Elizabethan Homilies: XXV, "Of the Passion" (Richard Taverner), and XXVII, "Of the Worthy Receiving of the Sacrament" (John Jewel). One might expect some mention of Luther or Calvin. There is none. Evidently, Wesley was convinced that he had received the good essence of their doctrine *through his own tradition*. The copy text used here is the edition of 1787, I, 81–101, collated with the first edition and *Sermons* (Sugden).

❖ ❖ ❖ ❖

## Justification by Faith

To him that worketh not, but believeth on him that justifieth the ungodly, his faith is counted to him for righteousness (Rom. 4:5).

1. How a sinner may be justified before God, the Lord and Judge of all, is a question of no common importance to every child of man. It contains the foundation of all our hope, inasmuch as while we are at enmity with God, there can be no true peace, no solid joy, either in time or in eternity. What peace can there be while our own heart condemns us; and, much more, he [also] that is "greater than our heart, and knoweth all things" [1 Jn. 3:20]? What solid joy, either in this world or that to come, while "the wrath of God abideth on us" [Jn. 3:36]?

2. And yet how little hath this important question been understood? What confused notions have many had concerning it? Indeed, not only confused, but often utterly false, contrary to the truth as light to darkness — notions absolutely inconsistent with the oracles of God, and with the whole analogy of faith. And hence erring concerning the very foundation, they could not possibly build thereon; at least, not "gold, silver, or precious stones," which would endure when tried as by fire, but only "hay and stubble" [cf. 1 Cor. 3:12], neither acceptable to God nor profitable to man.

3. In order to do justice, as far as in me lies, to the vast importance of the subject, to save those that seek the truth in sincerity from "vain jangling and strifes of words" [cf. 1 Tim. 1:6, 6:4], to clear the confusedness of thought into which so many have already been led thereby and to give them true and just conceptions of this great mystery of godliness, I shall endeavour to show:

First, what is the general ground of the whole doctrine of justification;

Secondly, what justification is;

Thirdly, who they are that are justified; and,

Fourthly, on what terms they are justified.

I. I am first to show what is the general ground of this whole doctrine of justification.

1. In the image of God was man made: holy as he that created him is holy, merciful as the Author of all is merciful, perfect as his Father in heaven is perfect [cf. Mt. 5:48]. As God is love, so man, dwelling in love, dwelt in God, and God in him [cf. 1 Jn. 4:16]. God made him to be "an

image of his own eternity" [Wisd. of Sol. 2:23], an incorruptible picture of the God of glory. He was accordingly pure, as God is pure, from every spot of sin. He knew not evil in any kind or degree, but was inwardly and outwardly sinless and undefiled. He "loved the Lord his God with all his heart and with all his mind and soul and strength" [Mk. 12:30].

2. To man, thus upright and perfect, God gave a perfect law, to which he required full and perfect obedience. He required full obedience in every point, and this to be performed without any intermission, from the moment man became a living soul till the time of his trial should be ended. No allowance was made for any falling short; as, indeed, there was no need of any, man being altogether equal to the task assigned and thoroughly furnished for every good word and work [cf. 2 Tim. 3:17; 2 Thess. 3:17].

3. To the entire law of love which was written in his heart (against which, perhaps, he could not sin directly), it seemed good to the sovereign wisdom of God to superadd one positive law: "Thou shalt not eat of the fruit of the tree that groweth in the midst of the garden" [Gen. 3:3]; annexing that penalty thereto, "In the day that thou eatest thereof thou shalt surely die" [cf. Gen. 3:3–5].

4. Such then was the state of man in Paradise. By the free, unmerited love of God, he was holy and happy. He knew, loved, enjoyed God, which is (in substance) life everlasting. And in this life of love he was to continue for ever, if he continued to obey God in all things. But if he disobeyed in any, he was to forfeit all. "In that day," said God, "thou shalt surely die."

5. Man did disobey God. He "ate of the tree of which God commanded him, saying, 'Thou shalt not eat of it.'" And in that day he was condemned by the righteous judgment of God. Then also the sentence, whereof he was warned before, began to take place upon him. For the moment he tasted that fruit, he died. His soul died, was separated from God, separate from whom the soul has no more life than the body has when separate from the soul. His body, likewise, became corruptible and mortal, so that death then took hold on this also. And being already dead in spirit, dead to God, dead in sin, he hastened on to death everlasting, to the destruction both of body and soul, in the fire never to be quenched.

6. Thus, "by one man sin entered into the world, and death by sin. And so death passed upon all men," as being contained in him who was the common father and representative of us all. Thus, "through the offence of one," all are dead, dead to God, dead in sin, dwelling in a corruptible, mortal body, shortly to be dissolved and under the sentence of death

eternal. For, as "by one man's disobedience all were made sinners," so, by that offence of one, "judgment came upon all men to condemnation." [1]

7. In this state we were, even all mankind, when "God so loved the world that he gave his only begotten Son, to the end we might not perish, but have everlasting life" [Jn. 3:16]. In the fullness of time he was made man, another common head of mankind, a second general parent and representative of the whole human race. And as such it was that "he bore our griefs," "the Lord laying upon him the iniquities of us all." Then "was he wounded for our transgressions and bruised for our iniquities. He made his soul an offering for sin" [cf. Is. 53:4–6, 10]. He poured out his blood for the transgressors. He "bare our sins in his own body on the tree" [1 Pet. 2:24], that "by his stripes we might be healed" and by that "one oblation of himself, once offered," *he hath redeemed me and all mankind,* having thereby "made a full, perfect and sufficient sacrifice and satisfaction for the sins of the whole world." [2]

8. In consideration of this, that the Son of God hath "tasted death for every man" [Heb. 2:9], God hath now "reconciled the world to himself, not imputing to them their former trespasses" [cf. 2 Cor. 5:19]. And thus, "as, by the offence of one, judgment came upon all men to condemnation, even so by the righteousness of one, the free gift came upon all men unto justification" [Rom. 5:18]. So that, for the sake of his well-beloved Son, of what he hath done and suffered for us, God now vouchsafes on one only condition (which [he] himself also enables us to perform) both to remit the punishment due to our sins, to reinstate us in his favour and to restore our dead souls to spiritual life, as the earnest of life eternal.

9. This, therefore, is the general ground of the whole doctrine of justification. By the sin of the first Adam, who was not only the father but likewise the representative of us all, we all fell short of the favour of God, we all became children of wrath, or, as the apostle expresses it, "judgment came upon all men to condemnation." Even so, by the sacrifice for sin made by the second Adam, as the representative of us all, God is so far reconciled to all the world that he hath given them a new covenant — the plain condition whereof being once fulfilled, "there is . . . no more condemnation" [Rom. 8:1] for us, but "we are justified freely by his grace through the redemption that is in Jesus Christ" [Rom. 3:24].

II. 1. But what is it to be "justified"? What is "justification": This was

---

1. [Au.] Rom. 5:12–18.
2. The Prayer of Consecration, in the Order for Holy Communion, B.C.P.

the second thing which I proposed to show. And it is evident, from what has been already observed, that it is not the being made actually just and righteous. This is *sanctification*, which is, indeed, in some degree, the immediate *fruit* of justification, but nevertheless is a distinct gift of God and of a totally different nature. The one implies what God *does for* us through his Son; the other, what he *works in* us by his Spirit. So that, although some rare instances may be found, wherein the term "justified" or "justification" is used in so wide a sense as to include "sanctification" also, yet in general use they are sufficiently distinguished from each other, both by St. Paul and the other inspired writers.

2. Neither is that far-fetched conceit that justification is the clearing us from accusation, particularly that of Satan, easily provable from any clear text of Holy Writ. In the whole scriptural account of this matter, as above laid down, neither that accuser nor his accusation appears to be at all taken in. It cannot indeed be denied, that he is "the accuser of men" [*cf.* Rev. 12:10], emphatically so called. But it does in no wise appear that the great apostle hath any reference to this, more or less, in all that he hath written touching justification, either to the Romans or the Galatians.

3. It is also far easier to take for granted, than to prove from any clear Scripture testimony, that justification is the clearing us from the accusation brought against us by the Law; at least if this forced, unnatural way of speaking mean either more or less than this, that whereas we have transgressed the Law of God and thereby deserved the damnation of hell, God does not inflict on those who are justified the punishment which they had deserved.

4. Least of all does justification imply that God is deceived in those whom he justifies, that he thinks them to be what, in fact, they are not; that he accounts them to be otherwise than they are. It does by no means imply that God judges concerning us contrary to the real nature of things, that he esteems us better than we really are, or believes us righteous when we are unrighteous. Surely no. The judgment of the all-wise God is always according to truth. Neither can it ever consist with his unerring wisdom to think that I am innocent, to judge that I am righteous or holy, because another is so. He can no more, in this manner, confound me with Christ than with David or Abraham. Let any man to whom God hath given understanding weigh this without prejudice and he cannot but perceive that such a notion of justification is neither reconcilable to reason or Scripture.

5. The plain scriptural notion of justification is pardon — the forgiveness of sins. It is that act of God the Father, whereby, for the sake of
the propitiation made by the blood of his Son, he "showeth forth his
righteousness (or mercy) by the remission of the sins that are past" [Rom.
3:25]. This is the easy, natural account of it given by St. Paul, throughout
this whole Epistle. So he explains it himself more particularly in this and
in the following chapter. Thus, in the next verses but one to the text,
"Blessed are they," saith he, "whose iniquities are forgiven, and whose
sins are covered. Blessed is the man to whom the Lord will not impute
sin" [cf. Ps. 32:1–2]. To him that is justified or forgiven, God "will not
impute sin" to his condemnation. He will not condemn him on that account, either in this world or in that which is to come. His sins — all his
past sins, in thought, word and deed — are covered, are blotted out, shall
not be remembered or mentioned against him, any more than if they had
not been. God will not inflict on that sinner what he deserved to suffer,
because the Son of his love hath suffered for him. And from the time we
are "accepted through the beloved," "reconciled to God through his
blood" [cf. Eph. 1:6; cf. Rom. 5:9, 10], he loves and blesses and watches
over us for good, even as if we had never sinned.

Indeed, the apostle in one place seems to extend the meaning of the
word much farther, where he says, "Not the hearers of the law, but the
doers of the law, shall be justified" [Rom. 2:13]. Here he appears to refer
our justification to the sentence of the Great Day. And so our Lord himself unquestionably doth when he says, "By thy words thou shalt be
justified" [Mt. 12:37], proving thereby that "for every idle word men
shall speak, they shall give an account in the day of judgment" [Mt.
12:36]; but perhaps we can hardly produce another instance of St. Paul's
using the word in that distant sense. In the general tenor of his writings, it
is evident he doth not, and least of all in the text before us, which undeniably speaks, not of those who have already "finished their course"
[cf. 2 Tim. 4:7], but of those who are now just "setting out," just beginning to "run the race which is set before them" [Heb. 12:1].

III. 1. But this is the third thing which was to be considered, namely,
who are they that are justified? And the apostle tells us expressly: "the
ungodly." "He (that is, God) justifieth the ungodly" [Rom. 4:5]; the
ungodly of every kind and degree and none but the ungodly. As they
"that are righteous need no repentance," so they need no forgiveness
[cf. Mt. 9:13]. It is only sinners that have any occasion for pardon. It is
sin alone which admits of being forgiven. Forgiveness, therefore, has an

immediate reference to sin, and, in this respect, to nothing else. It is our *unrighteousness* to which the pardoning God is *merciful*. It is our *iniquity* which he *remembereth no more*.

2. This seems not to be at all considered by those who so vehemently contend that a man must be sanctified (that is, holy) before he can be justified, especially by such of them as affirm that universal holiness or obedience must precede justification (unless they mean that justification at the last day, which is wholly out of the present question).[3] So far from it, that the very supposition is not only flatly impossible — for where there is no love of God, there is no holiness; and there is no love of God but from a sense of his loving us — but also grossly, intrinsically absurd, contradictory to itself. For it is not a *saint* but a *sinner* that is *forgiven*, and under the notion of a sinner. God *justifieth* not the godly but the *ungodly*, not those that are holy already but the unholy. Upon what condition he doth this will be considered quickly; but whatever it is, it cannot be holiness. To assert this is to say the Lamb of God takes away only those sins which were taken away before.

3. Does, then, the Good Shepherd seek and save only those that are found already? No. He seeks and saves that which is lost. He pardons those who need his pardoning mercy. He saves from the guilt of sin — and, at the same time, from the power — sinners of every kind, of every degree; men who, till then, were altogether ungodly, in whom the love of the Father was not and, consequently, in whom dwelt no good thing, no good or truly Christian temper, but all such as were evil and abominable: pride, anger, love of the world, the genuine fruits of that "carnal mind" which is "enmity against God" [Rom. 8:7].

4. These who are sick, "the burden of whose sins is intolerable," [4] are they that need a physician; these who are guilty, who groan under the wrath of God, are they that need a pardon. These who are "condemned already" [Jn. 3:18], not only by God, but also by their own conscience, as by a thousand witnesses of all their ungodliness, both in thought and word and work, cry aloud for him that "justifieth the ungodly," "through the redemption that is in Jesus — the ungodly, and him that worketh not" [*cf*. Rom. 4:5] — that worketh not, before he is justified, anything that is good, that is truly virtuous or holy, but only evil continually. For his heart is necessarily, essentially, evil till the love of God is shed abroad

3. [Ed.] For a suggestion that Wesley held a notion of *double* justification, *cf*. John Deschner, *Wesley's Christology* (Dallas, 1960), 181–96.

4. *Cf*. The General Confession, in the Order for the Holy Communion, B.C.P.

therein. And while the tree is corrupt, so are the fruits; "for an evil tree cannot bring forth good fruit" [Mt. 7:18].

5. If it be objected, "Nay, but a man, before he is justified, may feed the hungry, or clothe the naked, and these are good works," the answer is easy. He may do those even before he is justified; and these are, in one sense, "good works"; they are "good and profitable to men." But it does not follow that they are, strictly speaking, good in themselves or good in the sight of God. All truly "good works" (to use the words of our Church) [5] "follow after justification." And they are therefore good and "acceptable to God in Christ" [1 Pet. 2:5] because they "spring out of a true and living faith." By a parity of reason, all "works done before justification" are not good, in the Christian sense, "forasmuch as they spring not of faith in Jesus Christ" (though often from some kind of faith in God they may spring). "Yea rather, for that they are not done as God hath willed and commanded them to be done, we doubt not," how strange soever it may appear to some, "but they have the nature of sin." [6]

6. Perhaps those who doubt of this have not duly considered the weighty reason which is here assigned, why no works done before justification can be truly and properly good. The argument plainly runs thus:

No works are good which are not done as God hath willed and commanded them to be done:

But no works done before justification are done as God hath willed and commanded them to be done:

Therefore, no works done before justification are good.

The first proposition is self-evident. And the second, that no works done before justification are done as God hath willed and commanded them to be done, will appear equally plain and undeniable if we only consider that God hath willed and commanded that "all our works" should "be done in charity" ἐν ἀγάπῃ [cf. 1 Cor. 16:14] (in love), in that love to God which produces love to all mankind. But none of our works can be done in this love while the love of the Father (of God as our Father) is not in us. And this love cannot be in us till we receive the "Spirit of adoption, crying in our hearts, 'Abba, Father'" [Rom. 8:15]. If, therefore, God doth not "justify the ungodly," and him that (in this sense) "worketh not" [Rom. 4:5], then hath Christ died in vain; then, notwithstanding his death, can no flesh living be justified.

IV. 1. But on what terms, then, is he justified, who is altogether "un-

5. Cf. Homily V, "Of Good Works," Pt. II.        6. Articles of Religion, XII, B.C.P.

godly," and till that time "worketh not"? On one alone, which is faith: he "believeth in him that justifieth the ungodly." And "he that believeth is not condemned" [*cf.* Jn. 3:18]; yea, he "is passed from death unto life" [*cf.* 1 Jn. 3:14]. For "the righteousness" (or mercy) "of God is by faith of Jesus Christ, unto all and upon all them that believe — whom God hath set forth for a propitiation, through faith in his blood that he might be just and" (consistently with his justice) "the justifier of him which believeth in Jesus" [*cf.* Rom. 3:22–26]. *Therefore, we conclude that a man is justified by faith, without the deeds of the law,* without previous obedience to the moral law, which, indeed, he could not, till now, perform. That it is the moral law, and that alone, which is here intended, appears evidently from the words that follow: "Do we then make void the law through faith? God forbid! Yea, we establish the law" [Rom. 3:31]. What law do we establish by faith? Not the ritual law, not the ceremonial law of Moses — in no wise — but the great, unchangeable law of love, the holy love of God and of our neighbour.

2. Faith in general is a divine, supernatural ἔλεγχος, "evidence" or conviction "of things not seen," not discoverable by our bodily senses, as being either past, future, or spiritual.[7] Justifying faith implies, not only a divine evidence or conviction that "God was in Christ, reconciling the world unto himself" [2 Cor. 5:19], but a sure trust and confidence that Christ died for *my* sins, that he loved *me* and gave himself for *me*. And at what time soever a sinner thus believes, be it in early childhood, in the strength of his years, or when he is old and hoary-haired, God justifieth that ungodly one. God, for the sake of his Son, pardoneth and absolveth him who had in him, till then, no good thing. Repentance, indeed, God had given him before, but that repentance was neither more nor less than a deep sense of the want of all good, and the presence of all evil. And whatever good he hath or doth from that hour when he first believes in God through Christ, faith does not *find*, but *bring*. This is the fruit of faith. First the tree is good and then the fruit is good also.

3. I cannot describe the nature of this faith better than in the words of our own Church:

The only instrument of salvation (whereof justification is one branch) is faith; that is, a sure trust and confidence that God both hath and will forgive our sins, that he hath accepted us again into his favour, for the merits of Christ's death and passion. . . . But here we must take heed that we do not halt with God through an

7. See above, p. 386.

inconstant, wavering faith. . . . Peter, coming to Christ upon the water, because he fainted in faith, was in danger of drowning. So we, if we begin to waver or doubt, it is to be feared that we should sink as Peter did, not into the water, but into the bottomless pit of hell-fire.[8]

[Therefore, have] [9] a sure and constant faith, not only that the death of Christ is available for all the world, but that he hath made a full and sufficient sacrifice for *thee*, a perfect cleansing of *thy* sins, so that thou mayest say with the apostle, "he loved *thee*, and gave himself for *thee*" [Gal. 2:20]. For this is to make Christ *thine own* and to apply his merits unto *thyself*.[10]

4. By affirming that this faith is the term or condition of justification, I mean, first, that there is no justification without it. "He that believeth not is condemned already" [Jn. 3:18]. And, so long as he believeth not, that condemnation cannot be removed, but "the wrath of God abideth on him" [Jn. 3:36]. As "there is no other name given under heaven than that of Jesus of Nazareth," no other merit "whereby" a condemned sinner can ever "be saved" from the guilt of sin, so there is no other way of obtaining a share in his merit than "by faith in his name" [*cf.* Acts 3:16]. So that as long as we are without this faith, we are "strangers to the covenant of promise," we are "aliens from the commonwealth of Israel, and without God in the world" [Eph. 2:12]. Whatsoever virtues (so-called) a man may have — I speak of those unto whom the gospel is preached, for "what have I to do to judge them that are without" [1 Cor. 5:12]? — whatsoever good works (so accounted) he may do, it profiteth not. He is still a "child of wrath" [*cf.* Eph. 2:3], still under the curse, till he believes in Jesus.

5. Faith, therefore, is the *necessary* condition of justification; yea, and the *only necessary* condition thereof. This is the second point carefully to be observed: that the very moment God giveth faith (for "it is the gift of God") to the "ungodly that worketh not," that "faith is counted to him for righteousness" [Rom. 4:5]. He hath no righteousness at all antecedent to this; not [even] so much as negative righteousness, or innocence. But "faith is imputed to him for righteousness" the very mo-

---

8. [Au.] "Second Sermon on the Passion." [Ed.] *Cf. Certain Sermons or Homilies, Appointed to Be Read in Churches* . . . (Oxford, 1683), 272–73; this is the "second book" of Homilies, issued under Elizabeth I, in 1571. Note how severely Wesley abridges Jewel's text.

9. Brackets indicate words added by Wesley.

10. [Au.] "Sermon on The Sacrament, First Part"; [Ed.] *cf. Certain Sermons or Homilies*, 284. The italics are supplied by Wesley.

ment that he believeth. Not that God (as was observed before) thinketh him to be what he is not. But as "he made Christ to be sin for us" [cf. 2 Cor. 5:21], that is, treated him as a sinner, punished him for our sins, so he counteth us righteous from the time we believe in him — that is, he doth not punish us for our sins; yea, treats us as though we were guiltless and righteous.

6. Surely the difficulty of assenting to the proposition that faith is the *only condition* of justification must arise from not understanding it. We mean thereby thus much: that it is the only thing without which none is justified; the only thing that is immediately, indispensably, absolutely requisite in order to pardon. As, on the one hand, though a man should have everything else without faith, yet he cannot be justified; so, on the other, though he be supposed to want everything else, yet if he hath faith, he cannot but be justified. For suppose a sinner of any kind or degree, in a full sense of his total ungodliness, of his utter inability to think, speak, or do good, and his absolute meetness for hell-fire; suppose, I say, this sinner, helpless and hopeless, casts himself wholly on the mercy of God in Christ (which indeed he cannot do but by the grace of God), who can doubt but he is forgiven in that moment? Who will affirm that any more is *indispensably required* before that sinner can be justified?

Now, if there ever was one such instance from the beginning of the world (and have there not been, and are there not, ten thousand times ten thousand?) it plainly follows that faith is, in the above sense, the sole condition of justification.

7. It does not become poor, guilty, sinful worms who receive whatsoever blessings they enjoy — from the least drop of water that cools our tongue to the immense riches of glory in eternity: of grace, of mere favour and not of debt — to ask of God the reasons of his conduct. It is not meet for us to call him in question "who giveth account to none of his ways" [cf. Job 33:13]; to demand "why didst thou make faith the condition, the only condition, of justification?" "Wherefore didst thou decree, 'he that believeth, *and he only*, shall be saved'?" This is the very point on which St. Paul so strongly insists in the ninth chapter of this Epistle, viz. that the terms of pardon and acceptance must depend, not on us, but "on him that calleth" us; that there is no "unrighteousness with God" in fixing his own terms, not according to ours, but his own good pleasure — who may justly say, "I will have mercy on whom I will have mercy," namely, on him who believeth in Jesus. "So then it is not of him that willeth, nor of him that runneth," to choose the condition on which

he shall find acceptance, "but of God that showeth mercy," that accept-eth none at all but of his own free love, his unmerited goodness. "There-fore hath he mercy on whom he will have mercy," viz. on those who be-lieve on the Son of his love. "And whom he will" that is, those who believe not, "he hardeneth," leaves at last to the hardness of their hearts [*cf.* Rom. 9:14–18].

8. One reason, however, we may humbly conceive of God's fixing this condition of justification — "if thou believest in the Lord Jesus Christ, thou shalt be saved" [*cf.* Acts 16:31] — was to *hide pride from man*. Pride had already destroyed the very angels of God, had cast down "a third part of the stars of heaven" [Rev. 8:12]. It was likewise in great meas-ure owing to this, when the tempter said, "Ye shall be as gods" [Gen. 3:5], that Adam fell from his own steadfastness and brought sin and death into the world. It was therefore an instance of wisdom worthy of God to appoint such a condition of reconciliation for him and all his posterity as might effectually humble, might abase them to the dust. And such is faith. It is peculiarly fitted for this end, for he that cometh unto God by this faith must fix his eye singly on his own wickedness, on his guilt and helplessness, without having the least regard to any supposed good in himself, to any virtue or righteousness whatsoever. He must come as a *mere sinner*, inwardly and outwardly, self-destroyed and self-condemned, bringing nothing to God but ungodliness only, pleading nothing of his own but sin and misery. Thus it is, and thus alone, when his "mouth is stopped," and he stands utterly "guilty before God" [*cf.* Rom. 3:19], that he can "look unto Jesus," as the whole and sole "propitiation for his sins" [Rom. 3:25; 1 Jn. 4:10]. Thus only can he be "found in him," and receive the "righteousness which is of God by faith" [Rom. 3:22].

9. Thou ungodly one, who hearest or readest these words — thou vile, helpless, miserable sinner! — I charge thee before God the Judge of all, go straight unto him with all thy ungodliness. Take heed thou destroy not thy own soul by pleading thy righteousness, more or less. Go as altogether ungodly, guilty, lost, destroyed, deserving and dropping into hell, and thou shalt then find favour in his sight and know that he justifieth the ungodly. As such thou shalt be brought unto the "blood of sprinkling" [Heb. 12:24], as an undone, helpless, damned sinner. Thus "look unto Jesus!" There is "the Lamb of God," who "taketh away *thy* sins" [*cf.* Jn. 1:29]! Plead thou no works, no righteousness of thine own, no hu-mility, contrition, sincerity! In no wise. That were, in very deed, to deny the Lord that bought thee. No. Plead thou singly the blood of the cove-

nant, the ransom paid for thy proud, stubborn, sinful soul. Who art thou
that now seest and feelest both thine inward and outward ungodliness?
Thou art the man! I want *thee* for my Lord! I challenge *thee* for a child
of God by faith! The Lord hath need of *thee*. Thou who feelest thou art
just fit for hell, art just fit to advance his glory: the glory of his free
grace justifying "the ungodly and him that worketh not." O come
quickly! Believe in the Lord Jesus, and thou, even thou, art reconciled
to God.


## The Witness of the Spirit; Discourse II


*Editor's introduction.* Wesley published a *first* essay on "The Witness of
the Spirit" in the first edition of *Sermons on Several Occasions* ([1746],
I, x; *cf. Sermons* [Sugden], I, 202–18). In it he argued that God's gift of
faith is accompanied by an *assurance* of God's favor, as light stimulates
sight, as consciousness prompts self-consciousness. Here, unmistakably,
was the doctrine which John Smith had deplored as "perceptible inspiration." (See above, pp. 3–4.) It was this idea — of the immediate intuition of
God's pardoning love — which raised the shout of "enthusiasm" against
the Methodists. In reaction, Wesley quietly dropped his earlier insistence
(borrowed from the Moravians) that without "assurance" there is *no*
valid justifying faith. He continued, however, to insist on their correlation — only urging now that they ought *normally* to concur and re-
enforce each other. In 1767 he wrote and published a second sermon on
the same text, with the same title. In the collected *Works* (Pine), Vol. I,
*both* sermons appear (pp. 195–235), with the second entitled "Discourse
II on The Witness of the Spirit" (pp. 216–35). It was not reprinted in
the last edition of the *Sermons* (1787–88). We present it here from the
text of the Pine edition, collated with that of 1767. See also *Sermons*
(Sugden), Vol. II, 343–59, and *Works*, Vol. V, 123–34. Among other
things, it includes a simplified sketch of Wesley's religious epistemology
— a theory centering in the notion of the believer's immediate awareness of the reality of God's gracious presence in the inmost self ("the
heart"). Wesley appeals to "experience" as decisive — but it should be
noted that, by "experience," he normally means *religious* intuition —
not perception or feelings in general. This distinction enables him to

differentiate "experience" from "enthusiasm," and thus to deny the charge that the Methodists are enthusiasts.

There is more behind this doctrine of the inner assurance of faith than meets the eye. It is worth noting that on most of Wesley's reading lists the names of such Christian Platonists as Malebranche and John Norris turn up; he had read Berkeley at Oxford. He never took the time to master the speculative outreach of the idealistic philosophy which these men shared. But he grasped its practical import for religious thought and he adopted it (consistently, if not critically) as a major resource for communicating the gospel — in bringing faith home to the heart, in accenting the deeply personal character of true religion.

❖   ❖   ❖   ❖

The Spirit itself beareth witness with our Spirit, that we are the children of God (Rom. 8:16).

I. 1. None who believes the Scriptures to be the Word of God can doubt the importance of such a truth as this; a truth revealed therein not once only, not obscurely, not incidentally; but frequently and that in express terms — but solemnly and of set purpose as denoting one of the peculiar privileges of the children of God.

2. And it is the more necessary to explain and defend this truth because there is a danger on the right hand and on the left. If we deny it, there is a danger lest our religion degenerate into mere formality; lest, having "a form of godliness," we neglect, if not "deny, the power of it" [cf. 2 Tim. 3:5]. If we allow it but do not understand what we allow, we are liable to run into all the wildness of enthusiasm. It is therefore needful, in the highest degree, to guard those who fear God from both these dangers by a scriptural and rational illustration and confirmation of this momentous truth.

3. It may seem something of this kind is the more needful because so little has been wrote on the subject with any clearness, unless some discourses on the wrong side of the question which explain it quite away. And it cannot be doubted but these were occasioned, at least in great measure, by the crude, unscriptural, irrational explications of others, who "knew not what they spake nor whereof they affirmed" [cf. 1 Tim. 1:7].

4. It more nearly concerns the Methodists, so-called, clearly to understand, explain and defend this doctrine because it is one grand part of the

testimony which God has given them to bear to all mankind. It is by his peculiar blessing upon them, in searching the Scriptures, confirmed by the experience of his children, that this great evangelical truth has been recovered, which had been for many years well-nigh lost and forgotten.

II. 1. But what is "the witness of the Spirit"? The original word, ἡ μαρτυρία, may be rendered either (as it is in several places) "the witness," or less ambiguously, "the testimony" or "the record." So it is rendered in our translation, "This is the record"[1] (the testimony, the sum of what God testifies in all the inspired writings) "that God hath given unto us eternal life, and this life is in his Son." The testimony now under consideration is given by the Spirit of God to and with our spirit: he is the person testifying. What he testifies to us is "that we are the children of God." The immediate result of this testimony is "the fruit of the Spirit": namely, "love, joy, peace, long-suffering, gentleness, goodness" [Gal. 5:22] — and without these, the testimony itself cannot continue. For it is inevitably destroyed, not only by the commission of any outward sin or the omission of [any] known duty, but by giving way to any inward sin — in a word, by whatever grieves the Holy Spirit of God.

2. I observed many years ago:[2]

It is hard to find words in the language of men to explain the deep things of God. Indeed, there are none that will adequately express what the Spirit of God works in his children.[3] But perhaps one might say — desiring any who are taught of God to correct, soften or strengthen the expression — by "the testimony of the Spirit" I mean an inward impression on the soul, whereby the Spirit of God immediately and directly witnesses to my spirit that I am a child of God; that "Jesus Christ hath loved me and given himself for me"; that all my sins are blotted out, and I, even I, am reconciled to God.

3. After twenty years' further consideration, I see no cause to retract any part of this. Neither do I conceive how any of these expressions may be altered so as to make them more intelligible. I can only add that if any of the children of God will point out any other expressions which are more clear, or more agreeable to the Word of God, I will readily lay these aside.

4. Meantime, let it be observed, I do not mean hereby that the Spirit of God testifies this by any outward voice; no, nor always by an inward

1. [Au.] 1 Jn. 5:11.
2. Cf. "The Witness of the Spirit"; Discourse I, Pt. IV, par. 7; cf. Sermons (Sugden), I, 207–08.
3. The original reads, ". . . what the children of God experience."

voice, although he may do this sometimes. Neither do I suppose that he always applies to the heart (though he often may) one or more texts of Scripture. But he so works upon the soul by his immediate influence and by a strong, though inexplicable, operation that the stormy wind and troubled waves subside and there is a sweet calm, the heart resting as in the arms of Jesus, and the sinner being clearly satisfied that God is reconciled, that all his "iniquities are forgiven, and his sins covered" [*cf*. Ps. 32:1–2; Rom. 4:7].

5. Now, what is the matter of dispute concerning this? Not whether there be a witness or testimony of the Spirit. Not whether the Spirit does testify with our spirit that we are the children of God. None can deny this without flatly contradicting the Scriptures and charging a lie upon the God of truth. Therefore, that there is a testimony of the Spirit is acknowledged by all parties.

6. Neither is it questioned whether there is an *indirect* witness, or testimony, that we are the children of God. This is nearly, if not exactly the same with "the testimony of a good conscience towards God" and is the result of reason, or reflection on what we feel in our own souls. Strictly speaking, it is a conclusion drawn partly from the Word of God and partly from our own experience. The Word of God says every one who has the fruit of the Spirit is a child of God; experience, or inward consciousness, tells me that I have the fruit of the Spirit; and hence I rationally conclude: therefore, I am a child of God. This is likewise allowed on all hands, and so is no matter of controversy.

7. Nor do we assert that there can be any real testimony of the Spirit without the fruit of the Spirit. We assert, on the contrary, that the fruit of the Spirit immediately springs from this testimony; not always indeed in the same degree, even when the testimony is first given, and much less afterwards. Neither joy nor peace is always at one stay; no, nor love, as neither is the testimony itself always equally strong and clear.

8. But the point in question is whether there be any *direct testimony* of the Spirit at all; whether there be any other testimony of the Spirit than that which arises from a consciousness of the fruit.

III. 1. I believe there is because that is the plain, natural meaning of the text, "The Spirit itself beareth witness with our spirit, that we are the children of God." It is manifest: here are two witnesses mentioned, who together testify the same thing, the Spirit of God, and our own spirit. The late Bishop of London,[4] in his sermon on this text, seems

4. Edmund Gibson (1669–1748), noted canonist and editor of *Codex Iuris Ecclesiastici Anglicani* (1713).

astonished that any one can doubt of this, which appears upon the very face of the words. Now, "the testimony of our own spirit," says the Bishop, "is one, which is the consciousness of our own sincerity"; or, to express the same thing a little more clearly, the consciousness of the fruit of the Spirit. When our spirit is conscious of this — of love, joy, peace, long-suffering, gentleness, goodness — it easily infers from these premises that we are the children of God.

2. It is true, that great man supposes the other witness to be "the consciousness of our own good works." This, he affirms, is "the testimony of God's Spirit." But this is included in the testimony of our own spirit; yea, and in sincerity, even according to the common sense of the word. So the apostle: "Our rejoicing is this, the testimony of our conscience, that in simplicity and godly sincerity we have had our conversation in the world" [2 Cor. 1:12] — where, it is plain, sincerity refers to our words and actions at least as much as to our inward dispositions. So that this is not another witness but the very same that he mentioned before: the consciousness of our good works being only one branch of the consciousness of our sincerity. Consequently here is only one witness still. If, therefore, the text speaks of two witnesses, one of these is not the consciousness of our good works, neither of our sincerity — all this being manifestly contained in the testimony of our spirit.

3. What then is the other witness? This might easily be learned, if the text itself were not sufficiently clear, from the verse immediately preceding: "Ye have received, not the spirit of bondage, but the spirit of adoption, whereby we cry, 'Abba, Father'" [Rom. 8:15]. It follows, "The Spirit itself beareth witness with our spirit, that we are the children of God."

4. This is farther explained by the parallel text, "Because ye are sons, God hath sent forth the Spirit of his Son into your hearts, crying, 'Abba, Father.'" [5] Is not this something *immediate* and *direct*, not the result of reflection or argumentation? Does not this Spirit cry, "Abba, Father," in our hearts the moment it is given, antecedently to any reflection upon our sincerity; yea, to any reasoning whatsoever? And is not this the plain, natural sense of the words which strikes any one as soon as he hears them? All these texts then, in their most obvious meaning, describe a direct testimony of the Spirit.

5. That the testimony of the Spirit of God must, in the very nature of things, be antecedent to the testimony of our own spirit, may appear from this single consideration: We must be holy in heart and life before we

5. [Au.] Gal. 4:6.

can be conscious that we are so. But we must love God before we can be holy at all, this being the root of all holiness. Now, we cannot love God till we know he loves us — "We love him, because he first loved us" [1 Jn. 4:19] — and we cannot know his love to us till his Spirit witnesses it to our spirit. Till then we cannot believe it; we cannot say, "The life which I now live, I live by faith in the Son of God, who loved me, and gave himself for me" [Gal. 2:20].

> Then, only then, we feel
> Our interest in his blood,
> And cry, with joy unspeakable,
> "Thou art my Lord, my God!" [6]

Since, therefore, the testimony of his Spirit must precede the love of God and all holiness, of consequence it must precede our consciousness thereof.

6. And here, properly, comes in to confirm this scriptural doctrine the experience of the children of God, the experience not of two or three, not of a few, but of a great multitude which no man can number. It has been confirmed both in this and in all ages, by "a cloud of" living and dying "witnesses." It is confirmed by *your* experience and *mine*. The Spirit itself bore witness to my spirit that I was a child of God, gave me an *evidence* hereof, and I immediately cried, "Abba, Father!" And this I did (and so did you) before I reflected on, or was conscious of, any fruit of the Spirit. It was from this testimony received that love, joy, peace, and the whole fruit of the Spirit flowed. First, I heard,

> Thy sins are forgiven! Accepted thou art!
> I listen'd, and heaven sprung up in my heart.[7]

7. But this is confirmed not only by the experience of the children of God — thousands of whom can declare that they never did know themselves to be in the favour of God till it was directly witnessed to them by his Spirit — but by all those who are convinced of sin, who feel the wrath of God abiding on them. These cannot be satisfied with anything less than a direct testimony from his Spirit — that he is "merciful to their unrighteousness, and remembers their sins and iniquities no more" [*cf.* Heb. 8:12]. Tell any of these, "You are to know you are a child [of God], by reflecting on what he has wrought in you, on your love, joy,

6. "Spirit of Faith, Come Down"; *cf. The Methodist Hymnal* (New York, 1932), 183; *The Methodist Hymn Book* (1933), 363.
7. Cf. *Hymns and Sacred Poems* (1739), "cxcvi," in G. Osborn, ed., *Poetical Works of John and Charles Wesley* (1872), V, 116, st. 9.

and peace"; and will he not immediately reply, "By all this I know I am a child of the devil. I have no more love to God than the devil has; my carnal mind is enmity against God. I have no joy in the Holy Ghost; my soul is sorrowful even unto death. I have no peace; my heart is a troubled sea; I am all storm and tempest." And which way can these souls possibly be comforted but by a divine testimony (not that they are good, or sincere, or conformable to the Scripture in heart and life, but) that God "justifieth the ungodly?" — him that, till the moment he is justified, is all ungodly, void of all true holiness; "him that worketh not" [Rom. 4:5], that worketh nothing that is truly good, till he is conscious that he is accepted, not for any works of righteousness which he hath done, but by the mere free mercy of God, wholly and solely for what the Son of God hath done and suffered for him. And can it be any otherwise if "a man is justified by faith, without the works of the law" [Rom. 3:28]? If so, what inward or outward goodness can he be conscious of, antecedent to his justification? Nay, is not the "having nothing to pay," that is, the being conscious that "there dwelleth in us no good thing" [Rom. 7:18] — neither inward nor outward goodness — essentially, indispensably, necessary before we can be "justified freely through the redemption that is in Jesus Christ" [Rom. 3:24]? Was ever any man justified since his coming into the world, or can any man ever be justified, till he is brought to that point,

> I give up every plea beside,
> Lord, I am damn'd; but thou hast died? [8]

8. Every one, therefore, who denies the existence of such a testimony does, in effect, deny justification by faith. It follows, that either he never experienced this, either he never was justified, or that he has forgotten (as St. Peter speaks τοῦ καθαρισμοῦ τῶν πάλαι αὐτοῦ ἁμαρτιῶν, "the purification from his former sins" [2 Pet. 1:9]) the experience he then had himself, the manner wherein God wrought in his own soul, when his former sins were blotted out.

9. And the experience even of the children of the world here confirms that of the children of God. Many of these have a desire to please God. Some of them take much pains to please him. But do they not, one and all, count it the highest absurdity for any to talk of *knowing* his sins are forgiven? Which of *them* even pretends to any such thing? And yet many of them are conscious of their own sincerity. Many of them un-

8. "Gal. iii, 22," in *ibid.*, I, 85, st. 12.

doubtedly have, in a degree, the testimony of their own spirit, a consciousness of their own uprightness. But this brings them no consciousness that they are forgiven; no knowledge that they are the children of God. Yea, the more sincere they are, the more uneasy they generally are for want of knowing it, plainly showing that this cannot be known in a satisfactory manner by the bare testimony of our own spirit, without God's directly testifying that we are his children.

IV. But abundance of objections have been made to this, the chief of which it may be well to consider.

1. It is objected, first: "Experience is not sufficient to prove a doctrine which is not founded on Scripture." This is undoubtedly true, and it is an important truth; but it does not affect the present question, for it has been shown that this doctrine is founded on Scripture. Therefore experience is properly alleged to confirm it.

2. "But madmen, French prophets, and enthusiasts of every kind, have imagined they experienced this witness." They have so, and perhaps not a few of them did, although they did not retain it long. But if they did not, this is no proof at all that others have not experienced it, as a madman's *imagining* himself a king does not prove that there are no *real* kings.

"Nay, many who pleaded strongly for this have utterly decried the Bible." Perhaps so; but this was no necessary consequence. Thousands plead for it who have the highest esteem for the Bible.

"Yea, but many have fatally deceived themselves hereby and got above all conviction." And yet a scriptural doctrine is no worse though men abuse it to their own destruction.

3. "But I lay it down as an undoubted truth, the fruit of the Spirit is the witness of the Spirit." Not undoubted; thousands doubt of, yea, flatly deny it. But let that pass.

"If this witness be sufficient, there is no need of any other. But it is sufficient, unless in one of these cases: 1. The *total absence* of the fruit of the Spirit. And this is the case when the direct witness is first given. 2. The *not perceiving it*. But to contend for it, in this case, is to contend for being in the favour of God and not knowing it." True; not knowing it at that time any otherwise than by the testimony which is given for that end. And this we do contend for. We contend that the direct witness may shine clear, even while the indirect one is under a cloud.

4. It is objected, secondly, "The design of the witness contended for is to prove that the profession we make is genuine. But it does not prove this." I answer, the proving this is not the design of it. It is antecedent to

our making any profession at all but that of being lost, undone, guilty, helpless sinners. It is designed to assure those to whom it is given that they are children of God, that they are "justified freely by his grace, through the redemption that is in Jesus Christ" [Rom. 3:24]. And this does not suppose that their preceding thoughts, words, and actions are conformable to the rule of Scripture. It supposes quite the reverse, namely, that they are sinners all over, sinners both in heart and life. Were it otherwise, God would "justify the godly"; [9] and "their own works" would be "counted to them for righteousness." And I cannot but fear that a supposition of our being justified by works is at the root of all these objections, for whoever cordially believes that God *imputes* to all that are justified "righteousness without works" will find no difficulty in allowing the witness of his Spirit preceding the fruit of it.

5. It is objected, thirdly, "One evangelist says, 'Your heavenly Father will give the Holy Spirit to them that ask him.' The other evangelist calls the same thing 'good gifts' [*cf.* Lk. 11:13; Mt. 7:11], abundantly demonstrating that the Spirit's way of bearing witness is by giving good gifts." Nay, here is nothing at all about "bearing witness" either in the one text or the other. Therefore till this demonstration is better demonstrated, I let it stand as it is.

6. It is objected, fourthly, "The Scripture says, 'The tree is known by its fruits' [*cf.* Mt. 12:33]; 'prove all things' [*cf.* 1 Thess. 5:21]; 'try the spirits' [*cf.* 1 Jn. 4:1]; 'examine yourselves' " [*cf.* 2 Cor. 13:5]. Most true. Therefore, let every man who believes he "hath the witness in himself," try whether it be of God. If the fruit follow, it is; otherwise, it is not. For certainly "the tree is known by its fruit." Hereby we *prove* if it be "of God." "But the direct witness is never referred to in the book of God." Not as standing alone, not as a single witness, but as connected with the other, as giving a "joint testimony," testifying *with our spirit* that we are children of God. And who is able to prove that it is not *thus* referred to in this very Scripture, "Examine yourselves whether ye be in the faith; prove your own selves. Know ye not your own selves that Jesus Christ is in you" [*cf.* 2 Cor. 13:5]? It is by no means clear that they did not know this by a *direct* as well as a *remote* witness. How is it proved that they did not know it — first, by an inward consciousness, and then by "love, joy, and peace?"

7. "But the testimony arising from the internal and external change is constantly referred to in the Bible." It is so; and we constantly refer thereto to confirm the testimony of the Spirit.

9. The 1788 edition here reads, "justify the ungodly."

"Nay, all the marks *you* have given, whereby to distinguish the operations of God's Spirit from delusion, refer to the change wrought in us and upon us." This, likewise, is undoubtedly true.

8. It is objected, fifthly, that "the direct witness of the Spirit does not secure us from the greatest delusions. And is that a witness fit to be trusted whose testimony cannot be depended on, that is forced to fly to something else to prove what it asserts?" I answer: to secure us from all delusion, God gives us two witnesses that we are his children. And this they testify conjointly. Therefore, "what God hath joined together, let not man put asunder" [Mk. 10:9; Mt. 19:6]. And while they are joined, we cannot be deluded; their testimony can be depended on. They are fit to be trusted in the highest degree, and need nothing else to prove what they assert.

"Nay, the direct witness only asserts, but does not prove anything." By two witnesses shall every word be established [*cf.* Mt. 18:16]. And when the Spirit "witnesses with our Spirit," as God designs it to do, then it fully proves that we are children of God.

9. It is objected, sixthly, "You own the change wrought is a sufficient testimony, unless in the case of severe trials, such as that of our Saviour upon the cross. But none of us can be tried in that manner." But you or I may be tried in such a manner, and so may any other child of God, that it will be impossible for us to keep our filial confidence in God without the direct witness of his Spirit.

10. It is objected, lastly, "The greatest contenders for it are some of the proudest and most uncharitable of men." Perhaps some of the *hottest* contenders for it are both proud and uncharitable, but many of the *firmest* contenders for it are eminently meek and lowly in heart, and, indeed, in all other respects also,

True followers of their lamb-like Lord.[10]

The preceding objections are the most considerable that I have heard and I believe contain the strength of the cause. Yet I apprehend whoever calmly and impartially considers those objections and the answers together, will easily see that they do not destroy, no, nor weaken, the evidence of that great truth, that the Spirit of God does, *directly* as well as *indirectly*, testify that we are children of God.

V. 1. The sum of all is this: the testimony of the Spirit is an inward

10. *Cf.* similar phrases in Osborn, *Poetical Works*, III, 323; V, 86; X, 426.

impression on the souls of believers, whereby the Spirit of God directly testifies to their spirit that they are children of God. And it is not questioned whether there is a testimony of the Spirit, but whether there is any *direct testimony*, whether there is any other than that which arises from a consciousness of the fruit of the Spirit. We believe there is because this is the plain natural meaning of the text, illustrated both by the preceding words and by the parallel passage in the Epistle to the Galatians; because, in the nature of the thing, the testimony must precede the fruit which springs from it; and because this plain meaning of the Word of God is confirmed by the experience of innumerable children of God, yea, and by the experience of all who are convinced of sin, who can never rest till they have a direct witness — and even of the children of the world, who, not having the witness in themselves, one and all declare, none can *know* his sins forgiven.

2. And whereas it is objected that experience is not sufficient to prove a doctrine unsupported by Scripture; that madmen and enthusiasts of every kind have imagined such a witness; that the design of that witness is to prove our profession genuine, which design it does not answer; that the Scripture says, "The tree is known by its fruit" [Mt. 12:33], "examine yourselves, prove your own selves" [2 Cor. 13:5], and meantime, the direct witness is never referred to in all the book of God; that it does not secure us from the greatest delusions; and, lastly, that the change wrought in us is a sufficient testimony, unless in such trials as Christ alone suffered, we answer: 1. Experience is sufficient to *confirm* a doctrine which is grounded on Scripture. 2. Though many fancy they experience what they do not, this is no prejudice to real experience. 3. The design of that witness is to assure us we are children of God, and this design it does answer. 4. The true witness of the Spirit is known by its fruit, "love, peace, joy," not indeed preceding but following it. 5. It cannot be proved that the direct as well as the indirect witness is not referred to in that very text, "Know ye not your own selves that Jesus Christ is in you?" 6. The Spirit of God, "witnessing with our spirit," does secure us from all delusion; and, lastly, we are all liable to trials wherein the testimony of our own spirit is not sufficient, wherein nothing less than the direct testimony of God's Spirit can assure us that we are his children.

3. Two inferences may be drawn from the whole. The first: let none ever presume to rest in any supposed testimony of the Spirit which is separate from the fruit of it. If the Spirit of God does really testify that we are children of God, the immediate consequence will be the fruit of

the Spirit, even "love, joy, peace, long-suffering, gentleness, goodness, fidelity, meekness, temperance" [Gal. 5:22–23]. And however this fruit may be clouded for a while, during the time of strong temptation, so that it does not appear to the tempted person while "Satan is sifting him as wheat" [*cf.* Lk. 22:31], yet the substantial part of it remains even under the thickest cloud. It is true, joy in the Holy Ghost may be withdrawn during the hour of trial, yea, the soul may be "exceeding sorrowful" [*cf.* Mt. 26:38], while "the hour and power of darkness" [*cf.* Lk. 22:53] continue; but even this is generally restored with increase, till we rejoice "with joy unspeakable and full of glory" [*cf.* 1 Pet. 1:8].

4. The second inference is: let none rest in any supposed fruit of the Spirit without the witness [of the Spirit]. There may be foretastes of joy, of peace, of love — and those not delusive, but really from God — long before we have the witness in ourselves, before the Spirit of God witnesses with our spirits that we have "redemption in the blood of Jesus, even the forgiveness of sins" [*cf.* Eph. 1:7]. Yea, there may be a degree of long-suffering, of gentleness, of fidelity, meekness, temperance (not a shadow thereof, but a real degree, by the preventing grace of God), before we "are accepted in the beloved" [*cf.* Eph. 1:6], and, consequently, before we have a testimony of our acceptance. But it is by no means advisable to rest here. It is at the peril of our souls if we do. If we are wise, we shall be continually crying to God, until his Spirit cry in our heart, "Abba, Father!" This is the privilege of all the children of God, and without this we can never be assured that we are his children. Without this we cannot retain a steady peace, nor avoid perplexing doubts and fears. But when we have once received this "Spirit of adoption," that "peace which passes all understanding" and which expels all painful doubt and fear will "keep our hearts and minds in Christ Jesus" [Phil. 4:7]. And when this has brought forth its genuine fruit (all inward and outward holiness), it is undoubtedly the will of him that calleth us to give us always what he has once given — so that there is no need that we should ever more be deprived of either the testimony of God's Spirit or the testimony of our own: the consciousness of our walking in all righteousness and true holiness.

# III

## FAITH AT WORK

*Editor's introduction.* **One** of Wesley's favorite texts was Gal. 5:6: "For in Jesus Christ neither circumcision availeth any thing, nor uncircumcision; but *faith which worketh by love*." For, as strongly as he stressed faith as the foundation of the Christian life, he was equally intent upon love as the fruition of that life. Faith is not an end in itself, but rather a necessary means. Faith is in order to love. Thus, the life of faith is a life of discipline, nurture, effort; faith actively promotes the good essence of the law. Wesley's radical insistence on *justification by faith alone* estranged the legalists; his equally insistent demand for Christian morality provoked the antinomians. Wesley finds both intolerable: he is stern with the legalists, downright fierce with the antinomians. The genius of the gospel, in his eyes, is its power to generate a faith that impels the believer to the quality of love that *works* for righteousness.

Many of the Methodists had felt the pull of pietism, the pall of what Wesley called "the German stillness." It was their glib disjunction between "law" and "gospel" that roused Wesley to lay out his own alternative, in defense of the integrity of grace and goodness.

In response to an appeal from the Conference of 1745 (see above, p. 151), he published in rapid succession *A Dialogue Between an Antinomian and His Friend* and *A Second Dialogue . . .* (both in 1745). These were aimed directly at the Moravians as well as Dissenters like William Cudworth, who were denouncing what they termed Wesley's "legal preaching" as "an abomination" (*cf.* Tyerman, *Life*, I, 482). These were soon afterwards joined by James Relly, at whom *A Blow at the Root* (see below, p. 377 ff.) was aimed. As part of this earnest and relentless campaign against antinomians of every sort, Wesley published in *Sermons on Several Occasions*, Vol. III (1750), a tripartite essay on faith and good works: "The Original Nature, Property and Use of the Law"; "The Law Established by Faith, I"; and "The Law Established by Faith,

II." This trilogy was afterward reprinted as a separate tract (1751). Its third part, reprinted here, is the culmination and climax of the whole argument. Our copy text is *Sermons on Several Occasions* (1787), Vol. III, pp. 121–36, collated with the first edition (1750). See also *Sermons* (Sugden), Vol. II, pp. 38–83.

It would be useful to compare this statement of the moral implications of faith with *The Doctrine of Salvation, Faith and Good Works* (above, p. 124 ff.) and with the essays on "Christian Perfection" (below, pp. 251–305). There is something quite distinctive in Wesley's vision of the Christian life as an organic fusion of justification *and* sanctification as reciprocals.

✢   ✢   ✢   ✢

## The Law Established by Faith; Discourse II

Do we then make void the law through faith? God forbid! Yea, we establish the law (Rom. 3:31).

1. It has been shown in the preceding discourse which are the most usual ways of "making void the law through faith":

Namely, first, the not preaching it at all, which effectually makes it all void at a stroke, and this under colour of "preaching Christ" and magnifying the gospel — though it be, in truth, destroying both the one and the other.

Secondly, the teaching (whether directly or indirectly) that faith supersedes the necessity of holiness, that this is less necessary now or a less degree of it necessary than before Christ came, that it is less necessary to us because we believe than otherwise it would have been, or, that Christian liberty is a liberty from any kind of degree of holiness — so perverting those great truths that we are now under the "covenant of grace" and not "of works"; that "a man is justified by faith without the works of the law" and that "to him that worketh not but believeth, his faith is counted for righteousness" [Rom. 4:5].

Or, thirdly, the doing this practically: the making void the law in practice, though not in principle; the living or acting as if faith was designed to excuse us from holiness; the allowing ourselves in sin "because we are not under the law, but under grace" [Rom. 6:14].

It remains to inquire how we may follow a better pattern, how we may be able to say with the apostle, "Do we then make void the law through faith? God forbid! Yea, we establish the law."

2. We do not, indeed, establish the old ceremonial law; we know that is abolished for ever. Much less do we establish the whole Mosaic dispensation; this we know our Lord has "nailed to his cross" [*cf.* Col. 2:14]. Nor yet do we so establish the *moral* law (which it is to be feared, too many do) as if the fulfilling it — the keeping all the commandments — were the condition of our justification. If it were so, surely "in his sight should no man living be justified" [*cf.* Rom. 3:20]. But all this being allowed, we still, in the apostle's sense, "establish the law": the moral law.

I. 1. We establish the law, first, by our doctrine: by endeavouring to preach it in its whole extent, to explain and enforce every part of it, in the same manner as our great Teacher did while upon earth. We establish it by following St. Peter's advice: "If any man speak, let him speak as the oracles of God" [1 Pet. 4:11]; as the holy men of old, moved by the Holy Ghost, spoke and wrote for our instruction, and as the apostles of our blessed Lord by the direction of the same Spirit. We establish it whenever we speak in his Name, by keeping back nothing from them that hear; by declaring to them, without any limitation or reserve, the whole counsel of God. And in order the more effectually to establish it, we use herein great plainness of speech. "We are not as many that *corrupt* the word of God," καπηλεύουσι [*cf.* 2 Cor. 2:17] (as artful men their bad wines).[1] We do not cauponize, mix, adulterate, or soften it to make it suit the taste of the hearers — "but as of sincerity, but as of God in the sight of God, speak we in Christ," as having no other aim than, "by manifestation of the truth, to commend ourselves to every man's conscience in the sight of God" [2 Cor. 4:2].

2. We then, by our doctrine, establish the law when we thus openly declare it to all men and that in the fulness wherein it is delivered by our blessed Lord and his apostles, when we publish it in the height and depth and length and breadth thereof. We then establish the law when we declare every part of it, every commandment contained therein, not

---

1. Wesley here changes the participle in the New Testament text, καπηλεύοντες, to the contract form of the present indicative. In his *Explanatory Notes Upon the New Testament*, Wesley borrows Bengel's idea that καπηλεύοντες implies dishonesty. However, the usual meaning of καπηλεύω is simply "to sell" or "drive a bargain." *Cf.* this passage in R.S.V.: "peddlers of God's word"; and in N.E.B.: "hawking the word of God about."

only in its full, literal sense but likewise in its spiritual meaning, not only with regard to the outward actions which it either forbids or enjoins, but also with respect to the inward principle, to the thoughts, desires and intents of the heart.

3. And indeed this we do the more diligently, not only because it is of the deepest importance — inasmuch as all the fruit (every word and work) must be only evil continually if the tree be evil, if the dispositions and tempers of the heart be not right before God — but likewise because, as important as these things are, they are little considered or understood; so little, that we may truly say of the law, too, when taken in its full spiritual meaning, it is "a mystery which was hid from ages and generations since the world began" [*cf.* Rom. 16:25]. It was utterly hid from the heathen world. They, with all their boasted wisdom, neither "found out God" nor the law of God: not in the letter, much less in the spirit of it. "Their foolish hearts were" more and more "darkened"; while "professing themselves wise, they became fools" [*cf.* Rom. 1:21–22]. And it was almost equally hid, as to its spiritual meaning, from the bulk of the Jewish nation. Even these, who were so ready to declare concerning others, "this people that knoweth not the law is accursed" [*cf.* Jn. 7:49], pronounced their own sentence therein, as being under the same curse, the same dreadful ignorance. Witness our Lord's continual reproof of the wisest among them, for their gross misinterpretations of it. Witness the supposition, almost universally received among them, that they needed only to make clean the outside of the cup, that the paying tithe of mint, anise, and cummin (outward exactness) would atone for inward unholiness, for the total neglect both of justice and mercy, of faith and the love of God. Yea, so absolutely was the spiritual meaning of the law hidden from the wisest of them that one of their most eminent rabbis comments thus on those words of the Psalmist, "If I incline unto iniquity with my heart, the Lord will not hear me" [Ps. 66:16, B.C.P.]: "That is, saith he, if it be only in my heart, if I do not commit outward wickedness, the Lord will not regard it. He will not punish me, unless I proceed to the outward act!" [2]

4. But, alas, the law of God, as to its inward, spiritual meaning, is

---

2. It is probable that Wesley is here following Matthew Henry, whose commentary on the Psalms makes this point for Psalm 66:18: "The Jewish writers, some of them that have the leaven of the Pharisees, which is hypocrisy, put a very corrupt gloss upon these words . . . if I allow myself only heart-sins and iniquity

not hid from the Jews or heathens only, but even from what is called the Christian world, at least from a vast majority of them. The spiritual sense of the commandments of God is still a mystery to these also. Nor is this observable only in those lands which are overspread with Romish darkness and ignorance. But this is too sure, that the far greater part even of those who are called "reformed Christians" are utter strangers at this day to the law of Christ, in the purity and spirituality of it.

5. Hence it is that to this day, "the scribes and Pharisees" — the men who have the form but not the power of religion, and who are generally wise in their own eyes and righteous in their own conceits — "hearing these things, are offended," are deeply offended, when we speak of the religion of the heart, and particularly when we show that, without this, were we to "give all our goods to feed the poor," it would profit us nothing [cf. 1 Cor. 13:3]. But offended they must be, for we cannot but speak the truth as it is in Jesus. It is our part, whether they will hear or whether they will forbear, to deliver our own soul. All that is written in the book of God we are to declare, not as pleasing men, but the Lord. We are to declare, not only all the promises, but all the threatenings, too, which we find therein. At the same time that we proclaim all the blessings and privileges which God had prepared for his children, we are likewise to "teach all the things whatsoever he hath commanded" [cf. Mt. 28:20]. And we know that all these have their use, either for the awakening those that sleep, the instructing the ignorant, the comforting the feebleminded, or the building up and perfecting of the saints. We know that "all Scripture, given by inspiration of God, is profitable," either "for doctrine" or "for reproof," either "for correction" or "for

---

does not break out in my words and actions, God . . . will take no notice of it . . . , as if heart-sins were no sins in God's account." But David Kimchi (1160–1235), the most famous of the medieval Jewish exegetes, and the probable reference here, says just the opposite in his commentary on this same passage: "If I incline to an iniquity in my heart to do it, it is as if I had announced my intention with my lips. The sin lives in the evil thought." Cf. *Sepher Tehillim 'im pirush rabbenu David Kim'hi (The Book of Psalms with Commentary of our Rabbi David Kim'hi)* (Berlin, 1767), 37.

There is in the Library of Christ Church (and was in Wesley's time) a copy of Dom Ambrose Janvier, *Rabbi Davidis Kimchi Commentarii in Psalmos Davidis . . . ex Hebraeo Latiné Redditi* (1702), and to Kimchi's comment on Ps. 66:18 Janvier adds a footnote in the same vein as Wesley's alleged quotation — viz. turning Kimchi's thought upside down.

instruction in righteousness"; and "that the man of God," in the process of the work of God in his soul, has need of every part thereof, that he "may at length be perfect, thoroughly furnished unto all good works" [2 Tim. 3:16–17].

6. It is our part thus to "preach Christ" by preaching all things whatsoever he hath revealed. We may indeed, without blame, yea, and with a peculiar blessing from God, declare the love of our Lord Jesus Christ. We may speak in a more especial manner, of "the Lord our righteousness" [cf. Jer. 23:6]; [3] we may expatiate upon the grace of "God in Christ reconciling the world unto himself" [2 Cor. 5:19]; we may, at proper opportunities, dwell upon his praise, as bearing "the iniquities of us all," as "wounded for our transgressions" and "bruised for our iniquities," that "by his stripes we" might "be healed" [cf. Is. 53:4–5]. But still we should not preach Christ according to his Word if we were wholly to confine ourselves to this. We are not ourselves clear before God, unless we proclaim him in all his offices. To preach Christ as a workman that needeth not to be ashamed [cf. 2 Tim. 2:15] is to preach him not only as our great "High Priest, taken from among men, and ordained for men, in things pertaining to God" [Heb. 5:1], as such "reconciling us to God by his blood" [cf. Rom. 5:9, 10], and "ever living to make intercession for us" [cf. Heb. 7:25], but likewise as the Prophet of the Lord, "who of God is made unto us wisdom" [1 Cor. 1:30], who, by his word and his Spirit, "is with us always, guiding us into all truth" [cf. Jn. 16:13]; yea, and as remaining a King for ever, as giving laws to all whom he has bought with his blood, as restoring those to the image of God whom he had first reinstated in his favour, as reigning in all believing hearts until he has "subdued all things to himself" [cf. Phil. 3:21], until he hath utterly cast out all sin, and "brought in everlasting righteousness" [cf. Dan. 9:24].

II. 1. "We establish the law," secondly, when we so preach faith in Christ as not to supersede but produce holiness: to produce all manner of holiness, negative and positive, of the heart and of the life.

In order to this, we continually declare (what should be frequently and deeply considered by all who would not "make void the law through faith") that faith itself — even Christian faith, the faith of God's elect, the faith of the operation of God — still is only the handmaid of love. As glorious and honourable as it is, it is not the end of the commandment. God hath given this honour to love alone. Love is the end of all the com-

3. Cf. Wesley's sermon by this title; *Sermons* (Sugden), II, 420–41.

mandments of God. Love is the end, the sole end, of every dispensation of God, from the beginning of the world to the consummation of all things. And it will endure when heaven and earth flee away; for "love" alone "never faileth" [1 Cor. 13:8]. Faith will totally fail; it will be swallowed up in sight, in the everlasting vision of God. But even then, love,

> Its nature and its office still the same,
> Lasting its lamp, and unconsumed its flame,
> Its deathless triumph shall for ever live,
> And endless good diffuse, and endless praise receive.[4]

2. Very excellent things are spoken of faith, and whosoever is a partaker thereof may well say with the apostle, "thanks be to God for his unspeakable gift" [2 Cor. 9:15]. Yet still it loses all its excellence when brought into a comparison with love. What St. Paul observes concerning the superior glory of the gospel above that of the law, may, with great propriety, be spoken of the superior glory of love above that of faith: "Even that which was made glorious hath no glory in this respect, by reason of the glory that excelleth. For if that which is done away is glorious, much more doth that which remaineth exceed in glory" [cf. 2 Cor. 3:9–10]. Yea, all the glory of faith, before it is done away, arises hence, that it ministers to love. It is the great temporary means which God has ordained to promote that eternal end.

3. Let those who magnify faith beyond all proportion so as to swallow up all things else, and who so totally misapprehend the nature of it as to imagine it stands in the place of love, consider farther that as love will exist after faith, so it did exist long before it. The angels who, from the moment of their creation, beheld the face of their Father that is in heaven had no occasion for faith in its general notion (as it is the evidence of things not seen). Neither had they need of faith, in its more particular acceptation (faith in the blood of Jesus); for he took not upon him the nature of angels but only the seed of Abraham. There was, therefore, no place before the foundation of the world for faith, either in the general or particular sense. But there was for love. Love existed from eternity in God, the great ocean of love. Love had a place in all the children of God, from the moment of their creation. They received at once, from their gracious Creator, to exist and to love.

4. A paraphrase of a stanza of Matthew Prior's poem "Charity"; cf. *The Literary Works of Matthew Prior*, H. B. Wright and M. K. Spears, eds. (Oxford, 1959), I, 207–09.

4. Nor is it certain (as ingeniously and plausibly as many have descanted upon this) that faith, even in the general sense of the word, had any place in paradise. It is highly probable, from that short and uncircumstantial account which we have in Holy Writ, that Adam, before he rebelled against God, walked with him by sight and not by faith.

> For then his reason's eye was strong and clear,
> And, as an eagle can behold the sun,
> Might have beheld his Maker's face as near
> As th' intellectual angels could have done.[5]

He was then able to talk with him face to face, whose face we cannot now see and live; and, consequently had no need of that faith whose office it is to supply the want of sight.

5. On the other hand, it is absolutely certain, faith, in its particular sense, had then no place. For in that sense, it necessarily presupposes sin, and the wrath of God declared against the sinner, without which there is no need of an atonement for sin in order to the sinner's reconciliation with God. Consequently, as there was no need of an atonement before the fall, so there was no place for faith in that atonement, man being then pure from every stain of sin, holy as God is holy. But love even then filled his heart. It reigned in him without a rival. And it was only when love was lost by sin that faith was added, not for its own sake, nor with any design that it should exist any longer than until it had answered the end for which it was ordained — namely, to restore man to the love from which he was fallen. At the fall, therefore, was added this evidence of things unseen which before was utterly needless, this confidence in redeeming love, which could not possibly have any place till the promise was made, that the seed of the woman should bruise the serpent's head [*cf.* Gen. 3:15].

6. Faith, then, was originally designed of God to re-establish the law of love. Therefore, in speaking thus, we are not undervaluing it or robbing it of its due praise but, on the contrary, showing its real worth, exalting it in its just proportion and giving it that very place which the wisdom of God assigned it from the beginning. It is the grand means of restoring that holy love wherein man was originally created. It follows, that although faith is of no value in itself (as neither is any other means what-

5. Another paraphrase, this time of Sir John Davies's *Nosce teipsum,* "Of humane knowledge," v. 3. Cf. *The Poems of Sir John Davies,* C. Howard, ed. (New York, 1941), 113. There are striking parallels between Davies's and Wesley's ideas of religious intuition.

soever), yet as it leads to that end — the establishing anew the law of love in our hearts — and as, in the present state of things, it is the only means under heaven for effecting it, it is on that account an unspeakable blessing to man and of unspeakable value before God.

III. 1. And this naturally brings us to observe, thirdly, the most important way of "establishing the law"—namely, the establishing it in our own hearts and lives. Indeed, without this, what would all the rest avail? We might establish it by our doctrine; we might preach it in its whole extent; might explain and enforce every part of it; we might open it in its most spiritual meaning and declare the mysteries of the kingdom; we might preach Christ in all his offices and faith in Christ as opening all the treasures of his love — and yet, all this time, if the law we preached were not established in our hearts, we should be of no more account before God than "sounding brass or tinkling cymbals" [cf. 1 Cor. 13:1]. All our preaching would be so far from profiting ourselves that it would only increase our damnation.

2. This is, therefore, the main point to be considered: how may we establish the law in our own hearts so that it may have its full influence on our lives? And this can only be done by faith.

Faith alone it is which effectually answers this end, as we learn from daily experience. For so long as we walk by faith, not by sight, we go swiftly on in the way of holiness. While we steadily look, not at the things which are seen, but at those which are not seen, we are more and more crucified to the world and the world crucified to us. Let but the eye of the soul be constantly fixed, not on the things which are temporal but on those which are eternal, and our affections are more and more loosened from earth and fixed on things above. So that faith in general is the most direct and effectual means of promoting all righteousness and true holiness, of establishing the holy and spiritual law in the hearts of them that believe.

3. And by faith, taken in its more particular meaning for a confidence in a pardoning God, we establish his law in our own hearts in a still more effectual manner. For there is no motive which so powerfully inclines us to love God as the sense of the love of God in Christ. Nothing enables us like a piercing conviction of this to give our hearts to him who was given for us. And from this principle of grateful love to God arises love to our brother also. Neither can we avoid loving our neighbour, if we truly believe the love wherewith God hath loved us. Now this love to man, grounded on faith and love to God, "worketh no ill" to our "neigh-

bour." Consequently it is, as the apostle observes, the fulfilling of the "whole (negative) law" [Rom. 13:10] — for this: "thou shalt not commit adultery; thou shalt not kill; thou shalt not steal; thou shalt not bear false witness; thou shalt not covet" — and if there be any other commandment, it is briefly comprehended in this saying, "thou shalt love thy neighbour as thyself" [cf. Rom. 13:9]. Neither is love content with barely working no evil to our neighbour. It continually incites us to do good as we have time and opportunity; to do good, in every possible kind and in every possible degree, to all men. It is, therefore, the fulfilling of the positive, likewise, as well as of the negative, law of God.

4. Nor does faith fulfil either the negative or positive law as to the external part only, but it works inwardly by love to the purifying of the heart, the cleansing it from all vile affections. "Every one that hath this 'faith' in himself, purifieth himself even as he is pure" [1 Jn. 3:3] — purifieth himself from every earthly, sensual desire, from all vile and inordinate affections, yea, from the whole of that carnal mind which is enmity against God. At the same time, if it have its perfect work, it fills him with all goodnesss, righteousness and truth. It brings all heaven into his soul and causes him to walk in the light, even as God is in the light [cf. 1 Jn. 1:7].

5. Let us thus endeavour to establish the law in ourselves, not sinning "because we are under grace" [cf. Rom. 6:14–15], but rather using all the power we receive thereby "to fulfil all righteousness." Calling to mind what light we received from God while his Spirit was convincing us of sin, let us beware we do not put out that light. What we had then attained, let us hold fast. Let nothing induce us to build again what we have destroyed; to resume anything, small or great, which we then clearly saw was not for the glory of God or the profit of our own soul; or to neglect anything, small or great, which we could not then neglect without a check from our own conscience. To increase and perfect the light which we had before, let us now add the light of faith. Confirm we the former gift of God by a deeper sense of whatever he had then shown us, by a greater tenderness of conscience and a more exquisite sensibility of sin. Walking now with joy and not with fear, in a clear, steady sight of things eternal, we shall look on pleasure, wealth, praise, all the things of earth, as on bubbles upon the water, counting nothing important, nothing desirable, nothing worth a deliberate thought but only what is "within the veil," where Jesus "sitteth at the right hand of God" [cf. Heb. 6:19; Col. 3:1].

6. Can *you* say, "thou art merciful to *my* unrighteousness; my sins thou rememberest no more" [*cf.* Heb. 8:12]? Then, for the time to come, see that you fly from sin, as from the face of a serpent! For how exceeding sinful does it appear to you now, how heinous above all expression! On the other hand, in how amiable a light do you now see the holy and perfect will of God? Now, therefore, labour that it may be fulfilled, both in you, by you and upon you! Now watch and pray that you may sin no more, that you may see and shun the least transgression of his law! You see the motes which you could not see before, as when the sun shines into a dark place. In like manner, you see the sins which you could not see before, now that the sun of righteousness shines in your heart. Now, then, do all diligence to walk in every respect according to the light you have received! Now be zealous to receive more light daily, more of the knowledge and love of God, more of the Spirit of Christ, more of his life and of the power of his resurrection. Now use all the knowledge and love and life and power you have already attained. So shall you continually go on from faith to faith. So shall you daily increase in holy love, till faith is swallowed up in sight and the law of love established to all eternity!

## Of Preaching Christ

*Editor's introduction.* This was an "open letter," first published in *The Arminian Magazine* in 1779 (310–17), addressed to "My dear friend," but also entitled "Of Preaching Christ." It is another analysis of the reciprocal balance between law and gospel in evangelical preaching, yet another exhortation to good works as the fruitage of faith, another denunciation of antinomianism. John Telford suggests that it might have been written to Ebenezer Blackwell — a merchant-banker in London who had befriended Wesley and the Revival since the early days (*cf. Letters*, III, 78–85; see also II, 114, 131, 151). This seems most unlikely; it bears no resemblance in form and mood to the other letters to Blackwell. Whoever it was had fallen under the bad influence of James Wheatley (*cf.* Tyerman, *Life*, II, 121–30), a former Methodist preacher who had put his antinomian theories into scandalous practice, for which he had been expelled by the Wesleys. Wesley takes this outward scandal as the natural consequence of a deeper confusion which fails to divide merit from faith and yet also to unite grace and goodness. In response, Wesley explains the dialectical character of "preaching Christ," according to the situation *of the hearer*. The gospel attracts the contrite and humble; the law convicts the proud and self-sufficient. The gospel saves, the law is for discipline — "both at once, or both in one." Thus, we have yet another statement of Wesley's conviction that the genius of authentic Christianity lies in its power to hold together, in their right order, faith *and* righteousness, against the legalists on the one side and the libertines on the other. Here he applies his formula to its crucial test case — evangelistic preaching!

❖    ❖    ❖    ❖

*London, December 20, 1751.*

My dear friend,

The point you speak of in your letter of September 21 is of a very important nature. I have had many serious thoughts concerning it, particularly for some months last past. Therefore, I was not willing to speak hastily or slightly of it, but rather delayed till I could consider it thoroughly.

I mean by "preaching the gospel," preaching the love of God to sinners, preaching the life, death, resurrection and intercession of Christ, with all the blessings which in consequence thereof are freely given to true believers.

By "preaching the law" I mean explaining and enforcing the commands of Christ briefly comprised in the Sermon on the Mount.

Now it is certain, preaching the gospel to penitent sinners "begets faith," that it "sustains and increases spiritual life in true believers."

Nay, sometimes it "teaches and guides" them that believe; yea, and "convinces them that believe not."

So far all are agreed. But what is the stated means of "feeding and comforting" believers? What is the means, as of "begetting spiritual life" where it is not, so of "sustaining and increasing" it where it is?

Here they divide. Some think [of] preaching the law only; others, preaching the gospel only. I think neither the one nor the other, but duly mixing both, in every place if not in every sermon.

I think the right method of preaching is this. At our first beginning to preach at any place — after a general declaration of the love of God to sinners and his willingness that they should be saved — to preach the law in the strongest, the closest, the most searching manner possible, only in--

termixing the gospel here and there and showing it, as it were, afar off.

After more and more persons are convinced of sin, we may mix more and more of the gospel in order to "beget faith," to raise into spiritual life those whom the law hath slain; but this is not to be done too hastily neither. Therefore it is not expedient wholly to omit the law; not only because we may well suppose that many of our hearers are still unconvinced, but because otherwise there is danger that many who are convinced will heal their own wounds slightly. Therefore it is only in private converse with a thoroughly convinced sinner that we should preach nothing but the gospel.

If, indeed, we could suppose a whole congregation to be thus convinced, we should need to preach only the gospel. And the same we might do if our whole congregation were supposed to be newly justified. But when these grow in grace and in the knowledge of Christ, a wise builder would preach the law to them again, only taking particular care to place every part of it in a gospel light as not only a command but a privilege also, as a branch of the glorious liberty of the sons of God. He would take equal care to remind them that this is not the cause but the fruit of their acceptance with God; that other cause, "other foundation, can no man lay than that which is laid, even Jesus Christ" [1 Cor. 3:11]; that we are still forgiven and accepted only for the sake of what he hath done and suffered for us; and that all true obedience springs from love to him, grounded on his first loving us. He would labour, therefore, in preaching any part of the law, to keep the love of Christ continually before their eyes, that thence they might draw fresh life, vigour and strength to run the way of his commandments.

Thus would he preach the law even to those who were pressing on to the mark. But to those who were careless or drawing back he would preach it in another manner, nearly as he did before they were convinced of sin. To those meanwhile who were earnest but feebleminded, he would preach the gospel chiefly, yet variously intermixing more or less of the law according to their various necessities.

By preaching the law in the manner above described, he would teach them how to walk in him whom they had received. Yea, and the same means (the main point wherein it seems your mistake lies) would both *sustain and increase their spiritual life*. For the commands are food as well as the promises: food equally wholesome, equally substantial. These also, duly applied, not only direct but likewise *nourish and strengthen* the soul.

Of this you appear not to have the least conception; therefore I will

234 THEOLOGICAL FOUNDATIONS

endeavour to explain it. I ask, then, "Do not all the children of God experience that, when God gives them to see deeper into his blessed law, whenever he gives a new degree of light, he gives likewise a new degree of strength?" Now I see, he that loves me bids me do this. And now I feel, I can do it through Christ strengthening me.

Thus light and strength are given by the same means and frequently in the same moment, although sometimes there is a space between. For instance, I hear the command, "Let your communication be always in grace, meet to minister grace to the hearers." God gives me more light into this command. I see the exceeding height and depth of it. At the same time I see (by the same light from above) how far I have fallen short. I am ashamed; I am humbled before God. I earnestly desire to keep it better; I pray to him that hath loved me for more strength, and I have the petition I ask of him. Thus the law not only convicts the unbeliever and enlightens the believing soul, but also conveys food to a believer, sustains and increases his spiritual life and strength.

And if it increases his spiritual life and strength, it cannot but increase his comfort also. For doubtless the more we are alive to God, the more we shall rejoice in him; the greater measure of his strength we receive, the greater will be our consolation also.

And all this, I conceive, is clearly declared in one single passage of Scripture: "The law of the Lord is perfect, *converting the soul;* the testimony of the Lord is sure, *making wise the simple.* The statutes of the Lord are right, *rejoicing the heart;* the commandment of the Lord is pure, *enlightening the eyes.* . . . More to be desired are they than gold, yea, than much fine gold; sweeter also than honey and the honeycomb" [Ps. 19:7–8, 10]. They are both food and medicine; they both refresh, strengthen, and nourish the soul.

Not that I would advise to preach the law without the gospel any more than the gospel without the law. Undoubtedly both should be preached in their turns; yea, both at once, or both in one. All the conditional promises are instances of this. They are law and gospel mixed together.

According to this model, I should advise every preacher continually to preach the law — the law grafted upon, tempered by and animated with the spirit of the gospel. I advise him to declare, explain and enforce every command of God. But meantime to declare in every sermon (and the more explicitly the better) that the first and great command to a Christian is, "Believe in the Lord Jesus Christ" [*cf.* Acts 16:31]: that Christ is all in all, our "wisdom, righteousness, sanctification and redemption"; [1] that all life, love, strength are from him alone, and all freely given to us through faith. And it will ever be found that the law thus preached both enlightens and strengthens the soul, that it both nourishes and teaches, that it is the guide, "food, medicine and stay" of the believing soul.

Thus all the apostles built up believers — witness all the epistles of St. Paul, James, Peter and John. And upon this plan all the Methodists first set out. In this manner, not only my brother and I, but Mr. Maxfield, [John] Nelson, James Jones, [Thomas] Westell and [Jonathan] Reeves all preached at the beginning.

By this preaching it pleased God to work those mighty effects in London, Bristol, Kingswood, Yorkshire and Newcastle. By means of this twenty-nine persons received remission of sins in one day at Bristol only, most of them while I was opening and enforcing in this manner our Lord's Sermon upon the Mount.[2]

In this manner John Downes, John Bennet, John Haughton and all the other Methodists preached, till James Wheatley came among them, who never was clear, perhaps not sound, in the faith. According to his understanding was his preaching — an unconnected rhapsody of unmeaning words, like Sir John Suckling's

> Verses, smooth and soft as cream,
> In which was neither depth nor stream.[3]

Yet (to the utter reproach of the Methodist congregations) this man became a most popular preacher. He was admired more and more wherever he went, till he went over the second time into Ireland and conversed more intimately than before with some of the Moravian preachers.

The consequence was that he leaned more and more both to their doctrine and manner of preaching. At first several of our preachers complained of this; but in the space of a few months (so incredible is the force of soft words) he by slow and imperceptible degrees brought almost all the preachers then in the kingdom [Ireland] to think and speak like himself.

These, returning to England, spread the contagion to some others of their brethren. But still the far greater part of the Methodist preachers thought and spoke as they had done from the beginning.

1. 1 Cor. 1:30. This appears to have been Wesley's most frequently used text.
2. Cf. Sermons XVI–XXVIII, *Sermons* (Sugden), I, 315–542; II, 9–36.
3. Not Suckling but Ben Jonson, *paraphrased* from *Explorata Ingeniorum*, sec. 5.

This is the plain fact. As to the fruit of this *new* manner of preaching (entirely new to the *Methodists*), speaking much of the promises, little of the commands (even to unbelievers and still less to believers) — you think it has done great good; I think it has done great harm.

I think it has done great harm to the preachers, not only to James Wheatley himself, but to those who have learned of him: David Trathen, Thomas Webb, Robert Swindells and John Maddern — I fear to others also, all of whom are but shadows of what they were. Most of them have exalted themselves above measure, as if they only "preached Christ, preached the gospel." And as highly as they have exalted themselves, so deeply have they despised their brethren, calling them "legal preachers, legal wretches" and — by a cant name — "doctors," or "doctors of divinity." They have not a little despised their ministers also for "countenancing the doctors," as they termed them. They have made their faults (real or supposed) common topics of conversation, hereby cherishing in themselves the very spirit of Ham; yea of Korah, Dathan and Abiram.[4]

I think it has likewise done great harm to their hearers, diffusing among them their own prejudice against the other preachers, against their ministers, me in particular (of which *you* have been an undeniable instance), against the scriptural, Methodist, manner of preaching Christ, so that they could no longer bear sound doctrine — they could no longer hear the plain old truth with profit or pleasure, nay hardly with patience.

After hearing such preachers for a time, you yourself — need we farther witnesses? — could find in my preaching "no food for your soul," nothing to "strengthen you in the way," no "inward experience of a believer"; "it was all barren and dry." That is, you had no taste for mine or John Nelson's preaching; it neither refreshed nor nourished you.

Why, this is the very thing I assert — that the "gospel preachers" (so called) corrupt their hearers. They vitiate their taste so that they cannot relish sound doctrine, and spoil their appetite so that they cannot turn it into nourishment. They, as it were, feed them with sweetmeats till the genuine wine of the kingdom seems quite insipid to them. They give them cordial upon cordial, which make them all life and spirit for the present; but meantime their appetite is destroyed, so that they can neither retain nor digest the pure milk of the Word.

4. *Cf.* Num. 16:1–50; 26:9–11. See also Wesley's sermon "The Ministerial Office," where he insists upon the propriety of laymen being appointed to the "prophetic" ministry of preaching and yet sharply distinguishes this from the "priestly" office which is conferred only by clerical ordination; *Works,* VII, 273–81.

Hence it is that — according to the constant observation I have made in all parts both of England and Ireland — preachers of this kind (though quite the contrary appears at first) spread death, not life, among their hearers. As soon as that flow of spirits goes off, they are without life, without power, without any strength or vigour of soul, and it is extremely difficult to recover them because they still cry out, "Cordials, cordials!" — of which they have had too much already, and have no taste for the food which is convenient for them. Nay, they have an utter aversion to it, and that confirmed by principle, having been taught to call it husks, if not poison. How much more [aversion] to those bitters which are previously needful to restore their decayed appetite?

This was the very case when I went last into the North. For some time before my coming John Downes had scarce been able to preach at all. The three others in the Round [5] were such as styled themselves "gospel preachers." When I came to review the societies, with great expectation of finding a vast increase, I found most of them lessened by one-third, one entirely broken up. That of Newcastle itself was less by an hundred members than when I visited it before, and of those that remained, the far greater number in every place were cold, weary, heartless and dead. Such were the blessed effects of this "gospel-preaching," of this *new* method of "preaching Christ"!

On the other hand, when in my return, I took an account of the societies in Yorkshire, chiefly under the care of John Nelson (one of the *old* way, in whose preaching you could find no life, no food), I found them all alive, strong and vigorous of soul — believing, loving and praising God their Saviour, and increased in number from eighteen or nineteen hundred to upwards of three thousand. These had been continually fed with that wholesome food which *you* could neither relish nor digest. From the beginning they had been taught both the law and the gospel. "God loves *you:* therefore love and obey him. Christ died for *you:* therefore die to sin. Christ is risen: therefore rise in the image of God. Christ liveth evermore: therefore live to God, till you live with him in glory."

So *we* preached; and so *you* believed. This is the scriptural way, the Methodist way, the true way. God grant we may never turn therefrom, to the right hand or to the left.

5. An administrative unit of the Methodist preachers in a given area; called a "round" because of the way in which each preacher rotated among the societies under his care.

238

THEOLOGICAL FOUNDATIONS

# The Use of Money

*Editor's introduction.* This sermonic essay (*cf. Sermons* [Sugden], II, 309–27) exhibits Wesley's practical understanding of the reciprocity of Christian faith and social responsibility. It is presented as a single sample of Wesley's numerous but scattered writings in the area of Christian social ethics — since it conveys, better than any other, his distinctive approach to the moral and religious issues involved in the revolution in economic and social theory that was taking place in eighteenth-century Britain. (*Cf.* G. M. Trevelyan, *History of England,* 3d ed. [New York, 1945], III, 11–41.)

Wesley placed it at the very end of *Sermons on Several Occasions,* Vol. IV (1760), pp. 129–44 (pp. 127–47 in the edition of 1787). In the first period of the Revival the majority of Methodists had come from the dispossessed and depressed segments of English society. But in a time of vigorous, albeit irregular, economic growth it was natural enough that the Methodist version of the classical Puritan virtues of industry, thrift and sobriety should result in a general increase of economic competence and some instances of actual affluence. In 1744, when this sermon was first written, the trend was already set which would, in another generation or so, firmly fix the Methodists in the rising English middle class. The Minutes of the Conference of 1766 lament that "many Methodists grow rich and thereby lovers of the present world"; and in his sermon on "The Causes of the Inefficacy of Christianity" (CXVI, in *Works,* VII, 281–90), Wesley comments: "The Methodists grow more and more self-indulgent *because they grow rich.*" "The Use of Money" is a direct attack upon the problem of Christian economic responsibility; an indirect explication of that oft-reiterated text of Wesley's: "the faith which *worketh* by love" (Gal. 5:6).

Wesley was neither Leveller nor Luddite. His foreseeing of the consequences of the First Industrial Revolution was no more expert than that of any other shrewd (and conservative) observer. The formal premises of his economic doctrine rest partly on medieval notions of just price and general welfare; partly on the then current mercantilist theories of money and wealth. Yet his appraisals of this domain of man's life — the relationships between economic and moral values, between individual and society — are based on a clear, firm concept of the Christian stewardship in the ordering of human affairs, in obedience to God's righteous rule in the lives of men (*cf.* his sermon "The Good Steward," *Sermons* [Sugden], II, 461–80). To strike a creative balance between frugality and generosity and to come as near as this essay does to a successful fusion of the monastic spirit *and* the mercantile system is an achievement still worth remarking, even in a time when the parameters of economic decision and responsibility have changed out of all recognition from those in Wesley's time and circumstances.

❖ ❖ ❖ ❖

I say unto you, "Make to yourselves friends of the mammon of unrighteousness; that, when ye fail, they may receive you into the everlasting habitations" (Lk. 16:9).

1. Our Lord, having finished the beautiful parable of the Prodigal Son, which he had particularly addressed to those who murmured at his receiving publicans and sinners, adds another relation of a different kind, addressed rather to the children of God. "He said unto his disciples" — not so much to the scribes and Pharisees to whom he had been speaking before — "There was a certain rich man who had a steward, and he was accused to him of wasting his goods. And calling him, he said, 'Give an account of thy stewardship, for thou canst be no longer steward.'" [1] After reciting the method which the bad steward used to provide against the day of necessity, our Saviour adds, "His lord commended the unjust steward" — namely in this respect, that he used timely precaution — and subjoins this weighty reflection, "The children of this world are wiser in their generation than the children of light" [Lk. 16:8]. Those who seek no other portion than "this world are wiser" (not absolutely, for they are, one and all, the veriest fools, the most egregious madmen under heaven, but) "in their generation," in their own way, they are more consistent with themselves, they are truer to their acknowledged principles, they more steadily pursue their end "than the children of light," than they who see "the light of the glory of God in the face of Jesus Christ" [*cf.* 2 Cor. 4:6]. Then follow the words above recited: "And I" — the only-begotten Son of God, the Creator, lord, and possessor of heaven and earth, and all that is therein, the judge of all, to whom ye are to "give an account of your stewardship" when ye "can be no longer stewards" — "*I* say unto you," learn in this respect even of the unjust steward, "make your-

1. [Au.] Lk. 16:1–2.

selves friends," by wise, timely precaution, "of the mammon of unrighteousness." "Mammon" means riches or money. It is termed "the mammon of unrighteousness" because of the unrighteous manner wherein it is
frequently procured and wherein even that which was honestly procured
is generally employed. "Make yourselves friends" of this by doing all
possible good, particularly to the children of God, "that, when ye fail"
(when ye return to dust, when ye have no more place under the sun),
those of them who are gone before "may receive you," (may welcome
you) into "the everlasting habitations."

2. An excellent branch of Christian wisdom is here inculcated by our
Lord on all his followers — namely, the right use of money — a subject
largely spoken of, after their manner, by men of the world, but not
sufficiently considered by those whom God hath chosen out of the world.
These, generally, do not consider as the importance of the subject requires,
the use of this excellent talent. Neither do they understand how to employ it to the greatest advantage, the introduction of which into the world
is one admirable instance of the wise and gracious providence of God.
It has, indeed, been the manner of poets, orators, and philosophers, in almost all ages and nations, to rail at this as the grand corrupter of the
world, the bane of virtue, the pest of human society. Hence, nothing is
so commonly heard as

> *Ferrum, ferroque nocentius aurum* . . .
> And gold, more mischievous than keenest steel . . .[2]

Hence also the lamentable complaint,

> *Effodiuntur opes, irritamenta malorum.*[3]

Nay, one celebrated writer gravely exhorts his countrymen, in order to
banish all vice at once, to "throw all their money into the [nearby] sea":

> *In mare proximum,*
> *Summi materiem mali!* [4]

But is not all this mere empty rant? Is there any solid reason therein? By
no means. For let the world be as corrupt as it will, is gold or silver to
blame? "The love of money," we know, "is the root of all evil" [1 Tim.
6:10], but not the thing itself. The fault does not lie in the money but in
them that use it. It may be used ill; and what may not? But it may like-

2. *Cf.* Ovid, *Metamorphoses*, Bk. I, ch. i, l. 141; the second quotation is from l. 140.
3. Wealth is dug up, a stimulus to all sorts of evil . . .
4. A misleading paraphrase of Horace, *Carminum*, III, ch. xxiv, l. 45–50.

wise be used well; it is full as applicable to the best as to the worst uses. It is of unspeakable service to all civilized nations in all the common affairs of life. It is a most compendious instrument of transacting all manner of business and (if we use it according to Christian wisdom) of doing all manner of good. It is true, were man in a state of innocence, or were all men "filled with the Holy Ghost" [cf. Acts 4:31], so that, like the infant church at Jerusalem, "no man counted anything he had his own," but "distribution was made to every one as he had need" [cf. Acts 4:32, 35], the use of it would be superseded, as we cannot conceive there is anything of the kind among the inhabitants of heaven. But, in the present state of mankind, it is an excellent gift of God, answering the noblest ends. In the hands of his children, it is food for the hungry, drink for the thirsty, raiment for the naked. It gives to the traveller and the stranger where to lay his head. By it we may supply the place of an husband to the widow and of a father to the fatherless. We may be a defence for the oppressed, a means of health to the sick, of ease to them that are in pain. It may be as eyes to the blind, as feet to the lame, yea, a lifter up from the gates of death [cf. Ps. 9:13, B.C.P.].

3. It is, therefore, of the highest concern that all who fear God know how to employ this valuable talent, that they be instructed how it may answer these glorious ends and in the highest degree. And, perhaps, all the instructions which are necessary for this may be reduced to three plain rules, by the exact observance whereof we may approve ourselves faithful stewards of "the mammon of unrighteousness."

I. 1. The first of these is — he that heareth, let him understand! — *Gain all you can.* Here we may speak like the children of the world. We meet them on their own ground. And it is our bounden duty to do this. We ought to gain all we can gain without buying gold too dear, without paying more for it than it is worth. But this, it is certain, we ought not to do: we ought not to gain money at the expense of life nor — which is in effect the same thing — at the expense of our health. Therefore, no gain whatsoever should induce us to enter into, or to continue in, any employ which is of such a kind or is attended with so hard or so long labour, as to impair our constitution. Neither should we begin or continue in any business which necessarily deprives us of proper seasons for food and sleep, in such a proportion as our nature requires. Indeed, there is a great difference here. Some employments are absolutely and totally unhealthy — as those which imply the dealing much with arsenic or other equally hurtful minerals, or the breathing an air tainted with streams of melting lead, which must at length destroy the firmest constitution. Others may not be absolutely unhealthy, but only to persons of a weak constitution. Such are those which require many hours to be spent in writing, especially if a person write sitting and lean upon his stomach or remain long in an uneasy posture. But whatever it is which reason or experience shows to be destructive of health or strength, that we may not submit to, seeing "the life is more" valuable "than meat and the body than raiment" [Lk. 12:23]. And, if we are already engaged in such an employ, we should exchange it as soon as possible for some which, if it lessen our gain, will however not lessen our health.

2. We are, secondly, to *gain all we can* without hurting our mind any more than our body; for neither may we hurt this. We must preserve, at all events, the spirit of an healthful mind. Therefore, we may not engage or continue in any sinful trade, any that is contrary to the law of God, or of our country. Such are all that necessarily imply our robbing or defrauding the king of his lawful customs.[5] For is it at least as sinful to defraud the king of his right as to rob our fellow subjects. And the king has full as much right to his customs as we have to our houses and apparel. Other businesses there are which, however innocent *in themselves*, cannot be followed with innocence now, at least not in England: such, for instance, as will not afford a competent maintenance without cheating or lying or conformity to some custom which is not consistent with a good conscience. These, likewise, are sacredly to be avoided, whatever gain they may be attended with, provided we follow the custom of the trade. For, to gain money, we must not lose our souls. There are yet others which many pursue with perfect innocence, without hurting either their body or mind. And yet perhaps you cannot — either they may entangle you in that company which would destroy your soul (and by repeated experiments it may appear that you cannot separate the one from the other) or there may be an idiosyncrasy, a peculiarity in your constitution of soul (as there is in the bodily constitution of many) by reason whereof that employment is deadly to you which another may safely follow. So I am convinced, from many experiments, I could not study to any degree of perfection either mathematics, arithmetic or algebra without being a

5. Smuggling was a major problem in Hanoverian Britain and a major vice in Wesley's eyes. He mobilized the full weight of his movement against it. *Cf.* its prohibition in the first of the General Rules (above, pp. 178–79). See also *A Word to a Smuggler* (*Works*, XI, 174–78); *The Doctrine of Original Sin* (*Works*, IX, 225–26); *Letters*, VI, 238, 240, 244; *Journal*, IV, 76, 220, 325, 530; V, 151; VI, 6; VIII, 113).

deist, if not an atheist. And yet others may study them all their lives without sustaining any inconvenience. None, therefore, can here determine for another, but every man must judge for himself and abstain from whatever he in particular finds to be hurtful to his soul.

3. We are, thirdly, to *gain all we can* without hurting our neighbour. But this we may not, cannot do, if we love our neighbour as ourselves. We cannot, if we love every one as ourselves, hurt any one *in his substance*. We cannot devour the increase of his lands (and perhaps the lands and houses themselves) by gaming, by overgrown bills (whether on account of physic, or law, or anything else) or by requiring or taking such interest as even the laws of our country forbid. Hereby all pawnbroking is excluded, seeing whatever good we might do thereby, all unprejudiced men see with grief to be abundantly overbalanced by the evil. And if it were otherwise, yet we are not allowed to "do evil that good may come" [Rom. 3:8]. We cannot, consistent with brotherly love, sell our goods below the market price. We cannot study to ruin our neighbour's trade in order to advance our own, much less can we entice away or receive any of his servants or workmen whom he has need of. None can gain by swallowing up his neighbour's substance without gaining the damnation of hell!

4. Neither may we gain by hurting our neighbour *in his body*. Therefore we may not sell anything which tends to impair health. Such is, eminently, all that liquid fire commonly called drams, or spirituous liquors. It is true, these may have a place in medicine. They may be of use in some bodily disorders, although there would rarely be occasion for them were it not for the unskillfulness of the practitioner. Therefore, such as prepare and sell them *only for this end* may keep their conscience clear. But who are they? Who prepare and sell them *only for this end?* Do you know ten such distillers in England? Then excuse these. But all who sell them in the common way to any that will buy are poisoners-general. They murder his Majesty's subjects by wholesale, neither do their eyes pity or spare. They drive them to hell like sheep. And what is their gain? Is it not the blood of these men? Who then would envy their large estates and sumptuous palaces? A curse is in the midst of them! The curse of God cleaves to the stones, the timber, the furniture of them! The curse of God is in their gardens, their walks, their groves — a fire that burns to the nethermost hell. Blood, blood is there — the foundation, the floor, the walls, the roof, are stained with blood! And canst thou hope — O thou man of blood, though thou art "clothed in scarlet and fine

linen, and farest sumptuously every day" [cf. Lk. 16:19] — canst thou hope to deliver down thy "fields of blood" [cf. Mt. 27:8] to the third generation? Not so, for there is a God in heaven. Therefore, thy name shall soon be rooted out. Like as those whom thou hast destroyed, body and soul, "thy memorial shall perish with thee" [cf. Ps. 9:6, B.C.P.]!

5. And are not they partakers of the same guilt, though in a lower degree, whether surgeons, apothecaries, or physicians, who play with the lives or health of men to enlarge their own gain, who purposely lengthen the pain or disease which they are able to remove speedily, who protract the cure of their patient's body in order to plunder his substance? Can any man be clear before God who does not shorten every disorder *as much as he can* and remove all sickness and pain *as soon as he can?* He cannot. For nothing can be more clear than that he does not [love his neighbour as himself; than that he does not] [6] "do unto others, as he would they should do unto himself." [7]

6. This is dear-bought gain. And so is whatever is procured by hurting our neighbor *in his soul:* by ministering, suppose, either directly or indirectly to his unchastity or intemperance, which certainly none can do who has any fear of God or any real desire of pleasing him. It nearly concerns all those to consider this, who have anything to do with taverns, victualling-houses, opera-houses, play-houses, or any other places of public, fashionable diversion. If these profit the souls of men, you are clear; your employment is good and your gain innocent. But if they are either sinful in themselves, or natural inlets to sin of various kinds, then, it is to be feared, you have a sad account to make. O beware, lest God say in that day, "These have perished in their iniquity, but their blood do I require at thy hands" [cf. Ezek. 3:18]!

7. These cautions and restrictions being observed, it is the bounden duty of all who are engaged in worldly business to observe that first and great rule of Christian wisdom with respect to money: *Gain all you can.* Gain all you can by honest industry. Use all possible diligence in your calling. Lose no time. If you understand yourself and your relation to God and man, you know you have none to spare. If you understand your particular calling, as you ought, you will have no time that hangs upon your hands. Every business will afford some employment sufficient for every day and every hour. That wherein you are placed, if you follow it in earnest, will leave you no leisure for silly, unprofitable diversions.

6. Words in brackets added in the editions of 1750 and 1829.
7. Cf. Lk. 6:31; Mt. 7:12; see also Wesley, Preface, *Primitive Physick* (1747).

You have always something better to do, something that will profit you, more or less. And "whatsoever thy hand findeth to do, do it with thy might" [Eccles. 9:10]. Do it as soon as possible: no delay! No putting off from day to day, or from hour to hour! Never leave anything till tomorrow which you can do today. And do it as well as possible. Do not sleep or yawn over it. Put your whole strength to the work. Spare no pains. Let nothing be done by halves, or in a slight and careless manner. Let nothing in your business be left undone if it can be done by labour or patience.

8. *Gain all you can* by common sense, by using in your business all the understanding which God has given you. It is amazing to observe how few do this, how men run on in the same dull track with their forefathers. But whatever they do who know not God, this is no rule for *you*. It is a shame for a Christian not to improve upon *them* in whatever he takes in hand. *You* should be continually learning from the experience of others or from your own experience, reading and reflection, to do everything you have to do better today than you did yesterday. And see that you practice whatever you learn, that you may make the best of all that is in your hands.

II. 1. Having gained all you can by honest wisdom and unwearied diligence, the second rule of Christian prudence is: *Save all you can*. Do not throw the precious talent into the sea. Leave that folly to heathen philosophers. Do not throw it away in idle expenses, which is just the same as throwing it into the sea. Expend no part of it merely to gratify the desire of the flesh, the desire of the eye, or the pride of life.

2. Do not waste any part of so precious a talent merely in gratifying the desires of the flesh, in procuring the pleasures of sense of whatever kind, particularly in enlarging the pleasure of tasting. I do not mean, avoid gluttony and drunkenness only. An honest heathen would condemn these. But there is a regular, reputable kind of sensuality, an elegant epicurism, which does not immediately disorder the stomach nor (sensibly, at least) impair the understanding. And yet (to mention no other effects of it now) it cannot be maintained without considerable expense. Cut off all this expense! Despise delicacy and variety and be content with what plain nature requires.

3. Do not waste any part of so precious a talent, merely in gratifying the desire of the eye by superfluous or expensive apparel, or by needless ornaments. Waste no part of it in curiously adorning your houses, in superfluous or expensive furniture, in costly pictures, painting, gilding,

books, in elegant (rather than useful) gardens. Let your neighbours who know nothing better do this. "Let the dead bury their dead" [Mt. 8:22; Lk. 9:60]. But "what is that to thee?" says our Lord: "Follow thou me" [*cf.* Jn. 21:22]. Are you willing? Then you are able so to do!

4. Lay out nothing to gratify the pride of life, to gain the admiration or praise of men. This motive of expense is frequently interwoven with one or both of the former. Men are expensive in diet, or apparel, or furniture, not barely to please their appetite, or to gratify their eye or their imagination, but their vanity too. "So long as thou dost well unto thyself, men will speak good of thee." So long as thou art "clothed in purple and fine linen and farest sumptuously every day," no doubt many will applaud thy elegance of taste, thy generosity and hospitality. But do not buy their applause so dear. Rather be content with the honour that cometh from God.

5. Who should expend anything in gratifying these desires if he considered that to gratify them is to increase them? Nothing can be more certain than this. Daily experience shows, the more they are indulged, they increase the more. Whenever, therefore, you expend anything to please your taste or other senses, you pay so much for sensuality. When you lay out money to please your eye, you give so much for an increase of curiosity, for a stronger attachment to these pleasures which perish in the using. While you are purchasing anything which men use to applaud, you are purchasing more vanity. Had you not then enough of vanity, sensuality, curiosity, before? Was there need of any addition? And would you pay for it, too? What manner of wisdom is this? Would not the literally throwing your money into the sea be a less mischievous folly?

6. And why should you throw away money upon your children any more than upon yourself — in delicate food, in gay or costly apparel, in superfluities of any kind? Why should you purchase for them more pride or lust, more vanity, or foolish and hurtful desires? They do not want any more; they have enough already, nature has made ample provisions for them. Why should you be at farther expense to increase their temptations and snares and to pierce them through with many sorrows [*cf.* 1 Tim. 6:10]?

7. Do not leave it to them to throw away. If you have good reason to believe they would waste what is now in your possession in gratifying and thereby increasing the desire of the flesh, the desire of the eye, or

the pride of life, at the peril of theirs and your own soul, do not set these traps in their way. Do not offer your sons or your daughters unto Belial any more than unto Moloch [*cf.* 1 Sam. 1:16 ff.].[8] Have pity upon them and remove out of their way what you may easily foresee would increase their sins and consequently plunge them deeper into everlasting perdition! How amazing, then, is the infatuation of those parents who think they can never leave their children enough! What! Cannot you leave them enough of arrows, firebrands and death? Not enough of foolish and hurtful desires? Not enough of pride, lust, ambition, vanity? Not enough of everlasting burnings? Poor wretch! Thou fearest where no fear is. Surely both thou and they, when ye are lifting up your eyes in hell, will have enough both of "the worm that never dieth" [*cf.* Mk. 9:44], and of "the fire that never shall be quenched" [Mk. 9:43, 45]!

8. "What then would you do, if you was in my case, if you had a considerable fortune to leave?" Whether I *would* do it or no, I know what I *ought* to do. This will admit of no reasonable question. If I had one child, elder or younger, who knew the value of money — one who, I believed, would put it to the true use — I should think it my absolute, indispensable duty to leave that child the bulk of my fortune, and to the rest just so much as would enable them to live in the manner they had been accustomed to do. "But what if all your children were equally ignorant of the true use of money?" I ought then — hard saying! who can hear it? — to give each what would keep him above want and to bestow all the rest in such a manner as I judged would be most for the glory of God.

III. 1. But let not any man imagine that he has done anything barely by going thus far (by *gaining* and *saving all he can*) if he were to stop here. All this is nothing if a man go not forward, if he does not point all this at a farther end. Nor, indeed, can a man properly be said to *save* anything if he only *lays it up*. You may as well throw your money into the sea as bury it in the earth. And you may as well bury it in the earth as in your chest or in the Bank of England. Not to use is effectually to throw it away. If, therefore, you would indeed "make yourselves friends of the mammon of unrighteousness," add the third rule to the two preceding. Having first gained all you can and, secondly, saved all you can, then *give all you can*.

2. In order to see the ground and reason of this, consider: when the

8. A god whose worship involved child sacrifice; *cf.* Lev. 20:2; Jer. 32:35.

possessor of heaven and earth brought you into being and placed you in this world, he placed you here not as a proprietor but a steward.[9] As such he entrusted you for a season with goods of various kinds, but the sole property of these still rests in him, nor can ever be alienated from him. As you yourself are not your own, but his, such is likewise all that you enjoy. Such is your soul and your body, not your own but God's. And so is your substance in particular. And he has told you, in the most clear and express terms, how you are to employ it for him in such a manner than it may be all an holy sacrifice, acceptable through Christ Jesus. And this light, easy service he hath promised to reward with an eternal weight of glory [cf. 2 Cor. 4:17].

3. The directions which God has given us touching the use of our worldly substance may be comprised in the following particulars. If you desire to be a faithful and a wise steward, out of that portion of your Lord's goods which he has for the present lodged in your hands (but with the right of resuming whenever it pleases him), first provide things needful for yourself: food to eat, raiment to put on, whatever nature moderately requires for preserving the body in health and strength. Secondly, provide these for your wife, your children, your servants, or any others who pertain to your household. If, when this is done, there be an overplus left, then "do good to them that are of the household of faith." If there be an overplus still, "as you have opportunity, do good unto all men" [cf. Gal. 6:10]. In so doing, you give all you can; nay, in a sound sense, all you have. For all that is laid out in this manner is really given to God. You "render unto God the things that are God's" [Mt. 22:21], not only by what you give to the poor, but also by that which you expend in providing things needful for yourself and your household.

4. If, then, a doubt should at any time arise in your mind concerning what you are going to expend, either on yourself or any part of your family, you have an easy way to remove it. Calmly and seriously inquire:

1. In expending this, am I acting according to my character? Am I acting herein, not as a proprietor, but as a steward of my Lord's goods?

2. Am I doing this in obedience to his Word? In what Scripture does he require me so to do?

3. Can I offer up this action, this expense, as a sacrifice to God through Jesus Christ?

9. Cf. Wesley's amplification of this theme in his sermon "The Good Steward," *Sermons* (Sugden), II, 461-80.

4. Have I reason to believe that for this very work I shall have a re-ward at the resurrection of the just?

You will seldom need anything more to remove any doubt which arises on this head; but by this fourfold consideration you will receive clear light as to the way wherein you should go.

5. If any doubt still remain, you may farther examine yourself by prayer, according to those heads of inquiry. Try whether you can say to the searcher of hearts, your conscience not condemning you, "Lord, thou seest I am going to expend this sum on that food, apparel, furniture. And thou knowest I act therein with a single eye as a steward of thy goods, expending this portion of them thus in pursuance of the de-sign thou hadst in entrusting me with them. Thou knowest I do this in obedience to thy Word, as thou commandest, and because thou com-mandest it. Let this, I beseech thee, be an holy sacrifice, acceptable through Jesus Christ! And give me a witness in myself that for this labour of love I shall have a recompense when thou rewardest every man according to his works." Now, if your conscience bear you witness in the Holy Ghost that this prayer is well pleasing to God, then have you no reason to doubt but that expense is right and good and such as will never make you ashamed.

6. You see, then, what it is to "make yourselves friends of the mammon of unrighteousness," and by what means you may procure, "that, when ye fail, they may receive you into the everlasting habitations." You see the nature and extent of truly Christian prudence so far as it relates to the use of that great talent, money. *Gain all you can,* without hurting either yourself or your neighbour, in soul or body, by applying hereto with unintermitted diligence and with all the understanding which God has given you. *Save all you can,* by cutting off every expense which serves only to indulge foolish desire, to gratify either the desire of the flesh, the desire of the eye, or the pride of life [*cf.* 1 Jn. 2:16]. Waste nothing, liv-ing or dying on sin or folly, whether for yourself or your children. And then *give all you can;* or, in other words, give all you have to God. Do not stint yourself, like a Jew rather than a Christian, to this or that propor-tion. Render unto God not a tenth, not a third, not half, but all that is God's (be it more or less) by employing all on yourself, your household, the household of faith and all mankind, in such a manner that you may give a good account of your stewardship when ye can be no longer stewards; in such a manner as the oracles of God direct, both by gen-eral and particular precepts; in such a manner, that whatever ye do

may be "a sacrifice of a sweet-smelling savour to God" [cf. Lev. 8:21], and that every act may be rewarded in that day when the Lord cometh with all his saints.

7. Brethren, can we be either wise or faithful stewards unless we thus manage our Lord's goods? We cannot, as not only the oracles of God but our own conscience beareth witness. Then why should we delay? Why should we confer any longer with flesh and blood, or men of the world? Our kingdom, our wisdom, "is not of this world" [cf. Jn. 18:36, 1 Cor. 2:6]. Heathen custom is nothing to us. We follow no men any farther than they are followers of Christ. Hear ye him! Yea, today, while it is called today, hear and obey his voice [cf. Heb. 3:13]! At this hour and from this hour, do his will! Fulfill his word, in this and in all things! I entreat you, in the name of the Lord Jesus, act up to the dignity of your calling! No more sloth! Whatsoever your hand findeth to do, do it with your might! No more waste! Cut off every expense which fashion, caprice, or flesh and blood demand! No more covetousness! But employ whatever God has entrusted you with in doing good, all possible good, in every possible kind and degree, to the household of faith, to all men! This is no small part of "the wisdom of the just" [cf. Lk. 1:17]. Give all ye have, as well as all ye are, a spiritual sacrifice to him who withheld not from you his Son, his only Son — so, "laying up in store for yourselves a good foundation against the time to come, that ye may attain eternal life" [cf. 1 Tim. 6:19]!

## IV

### THE FULLNESS OF FAITH

*Editor's introduction.* In 1767 Wesley wrote and published *A Plain Account of Christian Perfection as Believed and Taught by the Rev. Mr. John Wesley from the Year 1725 to 1765*. It was a mildly truculent re-action to the charge that he had changed his teaching on the topic of "perfection" in the course of the Revival — more specifically in the face of the rash of professions of "entire sanctification" amongst the Methodists in the late fifties and early sixties. In form, the *Plain Account* is a history of his thoughts and writings on the subject over the course of forty years. It begins with a reference to the sermon "The Circumcision of the Heart," [1] preached in St. Mary's, Oxford, January 1, 1733, as "the first [composed] of all my writings which have been published." At a dis-tance of three decades and a tumult, Wesley then insists: "This was the view of religion I then had, which even then I scrupled not to term 'perfection.' This is the view I have of it now, without any material addi-tion or diminution." In this way, and in many others, Wesley asserted that his doctrine of "Christian perfection" had been the creative focus of his understanding of the Christian life from his first conversion to "serious" religion in 1725, and that it had continued as such without substantial alteration. He was as vitally concerned with the *"fullness* of faith" (*i.e.* sanctification) as with its beginnings (*i.e.* justification); as con-fident of the *goal* of the Christian life as of its *foundation*. He tried earnestly to maintain the parallelism between justification and sanctifica-tion — both by faith! — and between those good works appropriate to the reconciled sinner and to the mature Christian as well. This insistent correlation between the genesis of faith and its fullness marks off Wesley's most original contribution to Protestant theology.

He carefully records his readings in the theology of holiness: Kempis, William Law, the French and Spanish mystics, Juan de Castaniza

---

1. *Cf. Sermons* (Sugden), I, 263–79.

[Lorenzo Scupoli], "Macarius the Egyptian," Ephraem Syrus.[2] But what needs to be noticed is that these people represent at least three distinct traditions of "holiness." Kempis and the author of *The Spiritual Combat* [3] speak for a mysticism of the will that issues in a strenuous program of self-denigration aimed at total resignation.[4] In the "quietists" (Molinos, Madame Guyon, François de Sales) Wesley was first attracted to and then repelled by the antinomian mysticism to which he refers in his theological memorandum of 1738.[5] One might almost say it was his experimentation with the *voluntaristic* mysticism of Kempis, Law, and Scupoli, and with the *quietistic* mysticism of the Molinists, that drove Wesley to the pitch of futile striving which was such a vivid agony in his early years. His own mature doctrine of "perfection" is strikingly different, both in substance and form, from either of these traditions of Latin mysticism. If Wesley's writings on perfection are to be read with understanding, his affirmative notion of "holiness" *in the world* must be taken seriously — active holiness in *this* life — and it becomes intelligible only in the light of its indirect sources in early and Eastern spirituality.[6]

To represent this area of Wesley's thought, we have chosen four pieces (two sermons, two tracts) that span, between them, the sequences and stresses of Wesley's efforts to apply his notions of "perfection" to the needs and circumstances of the Revival. Taken together, they communicate, as well as he ever managed to do in writing, his vision of the rightful aspirations and expectations of Christian faith and devotion.

## Christian Perfection

*Editor's introduction.* This "sermon" was first published in 1741, together with a twenty-eight-stanza hymn of Charles Wesley's on "The Promise of Sanctification." In *A Plain Account of Christian Perfection* (*Works*, XI, 374), Wesley explains why he had done this:

2. Cf. Jean Orcibal, "Les spirituels français et espagnols chez John Wesley et ses contemporains," *Revue de l'Histoire des Religions*, CXXXIX (1951), 51–109, for a heavily documented but actually misleading interpretation of Wesley's dependence upon the French and Spanish mystics.

3. See above, p. 107 f.

4. Cf. *The Spiritual Combat*'s definition of "true Christian perfection": "the perfect hatred of ourselves and the perfect love of God."

5. See above, pp. 46–47.                     6. See above, pp. 9–10.

I think it was in the latter end of the year 1740, that I had a conversation with Dr. Gibson, then Bishop of London, at Whitehall. He asked me what I meant by perfection. I told him without any disguise or reserve. When I ceased speaking, he said, "Mr. Wesley, if this be all you mean, publish it to all the world. If any one then can confute what you say, he may have free leave." I answered, "My Lord, I will"; and accordingly wrote and published the sermon on Christian perfection.

It was subsequently reprinted in *Sermons on Several Occasions* (1750 and 1787), Vol. III, and remained his standard statement of the doctrine. In it Wesley speaks to all as he had to Bishop Gibson, "without disguise or reserve." Thus, in the early days of the Revival, and with no great effort to mitigate the confusion which was bound to attend the use of the term "perfect" when applied at any level to human experience, Wesley asserts the notion of a dynamic fulfillment in Christian life which is, like faith, a gracious gift of God. During the subsequent half-century he was hard pressed to explain it to both disciples and critics; he sought earnestly to correct its misinterpretations by the cynics, on the one side, and the fanatics on the other. But he seems never to have felt seriously moved either to abandon the doctrine or to modify it to suit his objectors.

These objectors would have been fewer and less clamant if "perfection" had been urged merely as the Christian ideal to be realized *in statu gloriae* — or if the doctrine had followed the classical Protestant line that justification and sanctification are two aspects of the same thing: God's pardoning grace. Wesley, however, was adamant on the point that if "perfection" is a human possibility at all, it must at least be possible *in the span of human life* and, consequently, correlated with the whole process of Christian maturation and hope. He firmly rejected the phrase, "sinless perfection," but promptly proceeded to deny that you can rightly argue from the residue of sin in human life to its invincibility. For Wesley, the doctrine of perfection was yet another way of celebrating the *sovereignty* of grace! The copy text here is from the edition of *Sermons on Several Occasions* (1787), Vol. III, pp. 203–33, collated with the versions published in 1741 and 1750.

❖ ❖ ❖ ❖

Not as though I had already attained, either were already "perfect"
(Phil. 3:12).

1. There is scarce any expression in Holy Writ which has given more
offence than this. The word "perfect" is what many cannot bear. The
very sound of it is an abomination to them. And whosoever "preaches
perfection" (as the phrase is) — that is, asserts that it is attainable in this
life — runs great hazard of being accounted by them worse than a
heathen man or a publican.

2. And hence some have advised wholly to lay aside the use of those
expressions "because they have given so great offence." But are they not
found in the oracles of God? If so, by what authority can any messenger
of God lay them aside, even though all men should be offended? We
have not so learned Christ; neither may we thus give place to the devil.
Whatsoever God hath spoken, that will we speak, whether men will hear
or whether they will forbear — knowing that then alone can any minister
of Christ be "pure from the blood of all men," when he hath "not shunned
to declare unto them all the counsel of God" [cf. Acts 20:26–27].

3. We may not, therefore, lay these expressions aside, seeing they are
the words of God and not of man. But we may and ought to explain the
meaning of them, that those who are sincere of heart may not err, to the
right hand or left, from the mark of the prize of their high calling [cf.
Phil. 3:14]. And this is the more needful to be done, because in the verse
already repeated the apostle speaks of himself as not perfect: "Not," saith
he, "as though I were already perfect." And yet, immediately after, in the
fifteenth verse, he speaks of himself, yea, and many others, as perfect.
"Let us," saith he, "as many as be perfect, be thus minded."

4. In order, therefore, to remove the difficulty arising from this seem-
ing contradiction, as well as to give light to them who are pressing forward to the mark — and that those who are lame be not turned out of
the way — I shall endeavour to show,

First, In what sense Christians are *not:* and,

Secondly, in what sense they *are*, "perfect."

I. 1. In the first place, I shall endeavour to show in what sense Christians are *not perfect.* And both from experience and Scripture it appears,
first, that they are not perfect in knowledge. They are not so perfect in
this life as to be free from ignorance. They know, it may be in common with other men, many things relating to the present world, and
they know with regard to the world to come the general truths which
God hath revealed. They know likewise (what "the natural man receiveth
not," for these things "are spiritually discerned" [cf. 1 Cor. 2:14]) "what

manner of love it is wherewith the Father hath loved them, that they should be called the sons of God" [1 Jn. 3:1]. They know "the mighty working of his Spirit" [cf. Eph. 1:19] in their hearts and the wisdom of his providence directing all their paths and causing all things to work together for their good [cf. Rom. 8:28]. Yea, they know in every circumstance of life what the Lord requireth of them, and how "to keep a conscience void of offence both toward God and toward man" [cf. Acts 24:16].

2. But innumerable are the things which they know not. "Touching the Almighty himself, they cannot search him out to perfection" [cf. Job 11:7]. "Lo, these are but a part of his ways; but the thunder of his power, who can understand" [cf. Job 26:14]? They cannot understand, I will not say how "there are three that bear record in heaven, the Father, the Son, and the Holy Spirit, and these three are one" [cf. 1 Jn. 5:7]; or how the eternal Son of God "took upon himself the form of a servant" [Phil. 2:7], but not any one attribute, not any one circumstance of the divine nature. Neither is it for them "to know the times and seasons" when God will work his great works upon the earth; no, not even those which he hath in part revealed by his servants and prophets since the world began. Much less do they know when God, having "accomplished the number of his elect, will hasten his kingdom" [cf. Mk. 13:20], when "the heavens shall pass away with a great noise, and the elements shall melt with fervent heat" [2 Pet. 3:10].

3. They know not the reasons even of many of his present dispensations with the sons of men, but are constrained to rest here — though "clouds and darkness are round about him, righteousness and judgment are the habitation of his seat" [Ps. 97:2, B.C.P.]. Yea, often with regard to his dealings with themselves doth their Lord say unto them, "What I do thou knowest not now, but thou shalt know hereafter" [Jn. 13:7]. And how little do they know of what is ever before them, of even the visible works of his hands? How "he spreadeth the north over the empty place and hangeth the earth upon nothing" [Job 26:7]; how he unites all the parts of this vast machine by a secret chain which cannot be broken? So great is the ignorance, so very little the knowledge, of even the best of men!

4. No one, then, is so perfect in this life as to be free from ignorance. Nor, secondly, from mistake, which indeed is almost an unavoidable consequence of it, seeing those who "know but in part" [cf. 1 Cor. 13:12] are ever liable to err touching the things which they know not. It is true, the children of God do not mistake as to the things essential to salvation.

They do not "put darkness for light or light for darkness" [Is. 5:20], neither "seek death in the error of their life" [*cf.* Prov. 21:6]; for they are "taught of God" [Jn. 6:45], and the way which he teaches them, the way of holiness, is so plain that "the wayfaring man, though a fool, need not err therein" [*cf.* Is. 35:8]. But in things unessential to salvation, they do err, and that frequently. The best and wisest of men are frequently mistaken even with regard to facts, believing those things not to have been [done] which really were or those to have been done which were not. Or, suppose they are not mistaken as to the fact itself, they may be with regard to its circumstances: believing them, or many of them to have been quite different from what in truth they were. And hence cannot but arise many farther mistakes. Hence they may believe either past or present actions which were, or are evil, to be good; and such as were, or are, good, to be evil. Hence, also, they may judge not according to truth with regard to the characters of men; and that not only by supposing good men to be better, or wicked men to be worse than they are, but by believing them to have been or to be good men who were, or are, very wicked, or perhaps those to have been or to be wicked men who were, or are, holy and unreprovable.

5. Nay, with regard to the Holy Scriptures themselves, as careful as they are to avoid it, the best of men are liable to mistake, and do mistake, day by day, especially with respect to those parts thereof which less immediately relate to practice. Hence, even the children of God are not agreed as to the interpretation of many places in Holy Writ. Nor is their difference of opinion any proof that they are not the children of God, on either side. But it is a proof that we are no more to expect any living man to be *infallible* than to be *omniscient*.

6. If it be objected to what has been observed under this and the preceding head, that St. John, speaking to his brethren in the faith, says, "Ye have an unction from the Holy One and know all things" [1] the answer is plain: "Ye know all things that are needful for your souls' health." That the apostle never designed to extend this farther, that he could not speak it in an absolute sense, is clear first from hence: that otherwise he would describe the disciple as "above his Master" [Mt. 10:24], seeing Christ himself, as man, knew not all things. "Of that hour," saith he, "knoweth no man; no, not the Son, but the Father only" [*cf.* Mt. 24:36, Mk. 13:32]. It is clear, secondly, from the apostle's own words that follow, "these things have I written unto you concerning them that deceive

1. [Au.] 1 Jn. 2:20.

you" [*cf.* 1 Jn. 2:26], as well as from his frequently repeated caution, "Let no man deceive you" [1 Jn. 3:7], which had been altogether need-less had not those very persons who had that unction from the Holy One been liable not to ignorance only but to mistake also.

7. Even Christians, therefore, are not so perfect as to be free either from ignorance or error. We may, thirdly, add: nor from infirmities. Only let us take care to understand this word aright. Only let us not give that soft title to known sins, as the manner of some is. So, one man tells us, "every man has his infirmity, and mine is drunkenness." Another has the "infirmity" of uncleanness; another, of taking God's holy Name in vain; and yet another has the "infirmity" of calling his brother, "thou fool" [*cf.* Mt. 5:22], or returning "railing for railing." It is plain that all you who thus speak, if ye repent not, shall, with your infirmities, go quick into hell. But I mean hereby, not only those which are properly termed "bodily infirmities," but all those inward or outward imperfec-tions which are not of a moral nature. Such are weakness or slowness of understanding, dullness or confusedness of apprehension, incoherency of thought, irregular quickness or heaviness of imagination. Such (to men-tion no more of this kind) is the want of a ready or retentive memory. Such, in another kind, are those which are commonly, in some measure, consequent upon these: namely, slowness of speech, impropriety of lan-guage, ungracefulness of pronunication — to which one might add a thousand nameless defects either in conversation or behaviour. These are the infirmities which are found in the best of men, in a larger or smaller proportion. And from these none can hope to be perfectly freed till the spirit returns to God that gave it.

8. Nor can we expect, till then, to be wholly free from temptation. Such perfection belongeth not to this life. It is true, there are those who, being given up to work all uncleanness with greediness, scarce per-ceive the temptations which they resist not and so seem to be without temptation. There are also many whom the wise enemy of souls, seeing [them] to be fast asleep in the dead form of godliness, will not tempt to gross sin, lest they should awake before they drop into everlast-ing burnings [*cf.* Is. 33:14]. I know there are also children of God who, being now "justified freely" [*cf.* Rom. 3:24], having found "redemp-tion in the blood of Christ" [*cf.* Col. 1:14], for the present feel no temptation. God hath said to their enemies, "Touch not mine anointed, and do my children no harm" [*cf.* Ps. 105:15]. And for this season, it may be for weeks or months, he causeth them to "ride on high places" [*cf.*

Deut. 32:13]; he beareth them as on eagles' wings [*cf.* Ex. 19:4], above all the fiery darts of the wicked one [*cf.* Eph. 6:16]. But this state will not last always, as we may learn from that single consideration that the Son of God himself, in the days of his flesh, was tempted even to the end of his life. Therefore, so let his servant expect to be; for "it is enough that he be as his master" [*cf.* Mt. 10:25].

9. Christian perfection, therefore, does not imply (as some men seem to have imagined) an exemption either from ignorance, or mistake, or infirmities, or temptations. Indeed, it is only another term for "holiness." They are two names for the same thing. Thus, every one that is perfect is holy, and every one that is holy is, in the Scripture sense, perfect. Yet we may, lastly, observe that neither in this respect is there any absolute perfection on earth. There is no "perfection of degrees," as it is termed; none which does not admit of a continual increase. So that how much soever any man has attained, or in how high a degree soever he is perfect, he hath still need to "grow in grace" and daily to advance in the knowledge and love of God his Saviour.

II. 1. In what sense, then, are Christians perfect? This is what I shall endeavour, in the second place, to show. But it should be premised that there are several stages in Christian life, as well as in natural — some of the children of God being but new-born babes, others having attained to more maturity. And accordingly, St. John, in his First Epistle,[2] applies himself severally to those he terms little children, those he styles young men and those whom he entitles fathers. "I write unto you, little children," saith the apostle, "because your sins are forgiven you": because thus far you have attained, being "justified freely," you "have peace with God through Jesus Christ" [*cf.* Rom. 5:1]. "I write unto you, young men, because ye have overcome the wicked one": or (as he afterwards addeth), "because ye are strong and the word of God abideth in you." Ye have quenched the fiery darts of the wicked one, the doubts and fears wherewith he disturbed your first peace, and the witness of God that your sins are forgiven now abideth in your heart. "I write unto you, fathers, because ye have known him that is from the beginning." Ye have known both the Father and the Son and the Spirit of Christ in your inmost soul. Ye are "perfect men, being grown up to the measure of the stature of the fullness of Christ" [*cf.* Eph. 4:13].

2. It is of these chiefly I speak in the latter part of this discourse, for these only are perfect[3] Christians. But even babes in Christ are in such **a**

2. [Au.] 2:12, etc.          3. The first edition (1741) reads "properly."

sense perfect, or "born of God" (an expression taken also in divers senses) as, first, not to commit [deliberate] sin. If any doubt of this privilege of the sons of God, the question is not to be decided by abstract reasonings which may be drawn out into an endless length and leave the point just as it was before. Neither is it to be determined by the experience of this or that particular person. Many may suppose they do not commit sin when they do, but this proves nothing either way. "To the law and to the testimony" [cf. Is. 8:20] we appeal. "Let God be true, and every man a liar" [Rom. 3:4]. By his Word will we abide, and that alone. Hereby we ought to be judged.

3. Now, the Word of God plainly declares that even those who are justified, who are born again in the lowest sense, "do not continue in sin"; that they cannot "live any longer therein"; [4] that they are "planted together in the likeness of the death" of Christ (verse 5); that their "old man is crucified with him," the body of sin being destroyed, so that henceforth they do not serve sin; that, "being dead with Christ, they are freed from sin" (verses 6, 7); that they are "dead unto sin and alive unto God" (verse 11); that "sin hath no more dominion over them" who are "not under the law, but under grace"; but that these, "being made free from sin are become the servants of righteousness" (verses 14, 18).

4. The very least which can be implied in these words is that the persons spoken of therein, namely, all real Christians, or believers in Christ, are made free from outward sin. And the same freedom, which St. Paul here expresses in such variety of phrases, St. Peter expresses in that one: [5] "He that hath suffered in the flesh hath ceased from sin, that he no longer should live to the desires of men but to the will of God." For this "ceasing from sin," if it be interpreted in the lowest sense as regarding only the outward behaviour, must denote the ceasing from the outward act, from any outward transgression of the law.

5. But most express are the well-known words of St. John, in the third chapter of this First Epistle (verse 8 ff.): "He that committeth sin is of the devil, for the devil sinneth from the beginning. For this purpose the Son of God was manifested, that he might destroy the works of the devil. Whosoever is born of God doth not commit sin; for his seed remaineth in him. And he cannot sin, because he is born of God." And those in the fifth [chapter], verse 18: "We know that whosoever is born of God sinneth not. But he that is begotten of God keepeth himself and that wicked one toucheth him not."

4. [Au.] Rom. 6:1, 2.        5. [Au.] 1 Pet. 4:1, 2.

6. Indeed, it is said this means only, he sinneth not "wilfully," or he doth not commit sin "habitually," or, "not as other men do," or, "not as he did before." But by whom is this said? By St. John? No: there is no such word in the text nor in the whole chapter nor in all his Epistle nor in any part of his writings whatsoever. Why, then, the best way to answer a bold assertion is simply to deny it. And if any man can prove it from the Word of God, let him bring forth his strong reasons.

7. And a sort of reason there is which has been frequently brought to support these strange assertions, drawn from the examples recorded in the Word of God: "What," say they, "did not Abraham himself commit sin, prevaricating and denying his wife? Did not Moses commit sin when he provoked God 'at the waters of strife' [cf. Ps. 106:32]? Nay, to produce one for all, did not even David, 'the man after God's own heart' [cf. 1 Sam. 13:14; Acts 13:22], commit sin in the matter of Uriah the Hittite, even murder and adultery?" It is most sure he did. All this is true. But what is it you would infer from hence? It may be granted, first, that David, in the general course of his life, was one of the holiest men among the Jews; and, secondly, that the holiest men among the Jews *did sometimes commit sin*. But if you would hence infer that *all Christians do and must commit sin as long as they live*, this consequence we utterly deny. It will never follow from those premises.

8. Those who argue thus seem never to have considered that declaration of our Lord: [6] "Verily I say unto you, among them that are born of women there hath not risen a greater than John the Baptist. Notwithstanding, he that is least in the kingdom of heaven is greater than he." I fear, indeed, there are some who have imagined "the kingdom of heaven" here to mean the kingdom of glory; as if the Son of God had just discovered to us that the least glorified saint in heaven is greater than any man upon earth! To mention this is sufficiently to refute it. There can, therefore, no doubt be made, but "the kingdom of heaven," here (as in the following verse, where it is said to be "taken by force") or, "the kingdom of God," as St. Luke expresses it, is that kingdom of God on earth, whereunto all true believers in Christ, all real Christians, belong. In these words, then, our Lord declares two things. First, that before his coming in the flesh, among all the children of men there had not been one greater than John the Baptist; whence it evidently follows that neither Abraham, David, nor any Jew, was greater than John. Our Lord, secondly, declares that he which is least in the kingdom of God (in

6. [Au.] Mt. 11:11.

that kingdom which he came to set up on earth, and which "the violent" now began "to take by force"), is greater than he [cf. Lk. 7:28]. Not "a greater prophet," as some have interpreted the word, for this is palpably false in fact, but greater in the grace of God and the knowledge of our Lord Jesus Christ. Therefore, we cannot measure the privileges of real Christians by those formerly given to the Jews. Their "ministration" (or dispensation) we allow "was glorious"; but ours "exceeds in glory" [cf. 2 Cor. 3:7, 9]. So that whosoever would bring down the Christian dispensation to the Jewish standard, whosoever gleans up the examples of weakness recorded in the law and the prophets and thence infers that they who have "put on Christ" are endued with no greater strength, doth "greatly err, neither knowing the Scriptures nor the power of God" [cf. Mt. 22:29].

9. "But are there not assertions in Scripture which prove the same thing, if it cannot be inferred from those examples? Does not the Scripture say expressly, 'Even a just man sinneth seven times a day?' " I answer, No. The Scripture says no such thing. There is no such text in all the Bible. That which seems to be intended is the sixteenth verse of the twenty-fourth chapter of the Proverbs, the words of which are these: "A just man falleth seven times and riseth up again." But this is quite another thing. For, first, the words "a day" are not in the text. So that if a just man fall seven times in his life, it is as much as is affirmed here. Secondly, here is no mention of "falling into sin" at all. What is here mentioned is "falling into temporal affliction." This plainly appears from the verse before, the words of which are these: "Lay not [in] wait, O wicked man, against the dwelling of the righteous; spoil not his resting-place." It follows, "For a just man falleth seven times and riseth up again; but the wicked shall fall into mischief." As if he had said, "God will deliver him out of his trouble, but when thou fallest, there shall be none to deliver thee."

10. But, however, in other places, continue the objectors, Solomon does assert plainly, "There is no man that sinneth not"; [7] yea, "there is not a just man upon earth that doeth good and sinneth not." [8] I answer: "Without doubt, thus it was in the days of Solomon. Yea, thus it was from Adam to Moses, from Moses to Solomon, and from Solomon to Christ." There was then no man that sinned not. Even from the day that sin entered into the world, there was not a just man upon earth that did good and sinned not until the Son of God was manifested to take away

7. [Au.] 1 Kings 8:46; 2 Chron. 6:36.          8. [Au.] Eccles. 7:20.

our sins. It is unquestionably true that "the heir, as long as he is a child, differeth nothing from a servant" [Gal. 4:1], and that even so they (all the holy men of old who were under the Jewish dispensation) were, during that infant state of the Church, "in bondage under the elements of the world. But when the fulness of the time was come, God sent forth his Son, made under the law, to redeem them that were under the law that they might receive the adoption of sons" [Gal. 4:3–5] — that they might receive that "grace which is now made manifest by the appearing of our Saviour Jesus Christ who hath abolished death, and brought life and immortality to light through the Gospel." [9] Now, therefore, they "are no more servants, but sons" [cf. Gal. 4:7]. So that, whatsoever was the case of those under the law, we may safely affirm with St. John, that, since the gospel was given, "he that is born of God sinneth not" [cf. 1 Jn. 3:9].

11. It is of great importance to observe, and that more carefully than is commonly done, the wide difference there is between the Jewish and the Christian dispensation and that ground of it which the same apostle assigns in the seventh chapter of his Gospel.[10] After he had there related those words of our blessed Lord, "He that believeth on me, as the Scripture hath said, out of his belly shall flow rivers of living water" [Jn. 7:38], he immediately subjoins, "This spake he of the Spirit, οὗ ἔμελλον λαμβάνειν οἱ πιστεύσαντες εἰς αὐτόν, which they who should believe on him were afterwards to receive. For the Holy Ghost was not yet given because that Jesus was not yet glorified" [Jn. 7:39]. Now, the apostle cannot mean here (as some have taught) that the miracle-working power of the Holy Ghost was not yet given. For this was given. Our Lord had given it to all his apostles when he first sent them forth to preach the gospel. He then gave them "power over unclean spirits to cast them out," power "to heal the sick," yea, "to raise the dead." But the Holy Ghost was not yet given in his sanctifying graces, as he was after Jesus was glorified. It was then when "he ascended up on high and led captivity captive" [Eph. 4:8], that he "received those gifts for men, yea, even for the rebellious, that the Lord God might dwell among them" [Ps. 68:18]. And "when the day of Pentecost was fully come" [Acts 2:1], then first it was that they who "waited for the promise of the Father" [cf. Acts 1:4] were made more than conquerors over sin by the Holy Ghost given unto them.

12. That this great salvation from sin was not given till Jesus was

9. [Au.] 2 Tim. 1:10.        10. [Au.] verses 38 ff.

glorified, St. Peter also plainly testifies where, speaking of his brethren in the flesh, as now "receiving the end of their faith, the salvation of their souls," he adds, "of which salvation the prophets have inquired and searched diligently, who prophesied of the grace" (that is, the gracious dispensation) "that should come unto you"; searching what (or what manner of) time the Spirit of Christ which was in them did signify, when it testified beforehand the sufferings of Christ and the glory (the glorious salvation) that should follow — unto whom it was revealed that not unto themselves but unto us they did minister the things which are now reported unto you by them that have preached the gospel unto you with the Holy Ghost sent down from heaven" (viz. at the day of Pentecost and so unto all generations, into the hearts of all true believers). On this ground, even "the grace which was brought unto them by the revelation of Jesus Christ," the apostle might well build that strong exhortation, "wherefore girding up the loins of your mind, . . . as he which hath called you is holy, so be ye holy in all manner of conversation." [11]

13. Those who have duly considered these things must allow that the privileges of Christians are in no wise to be measured by what the Old Testament records concerning those who were under the Jewish dispensation, seeing the fullness of time is now come, the Holy Ghost is now given, the great salvation of God is brought unto men by the revelation of Jesus Christ. The kingdom of heaven is now set up on earth; concerning which the Spirit of God declared of old (so far is David from being the pattern or standard of Christian perfection), "he that is feeble among them at that day shall be as David; and the house of David shall be as God, as the angel of the Lord before them." [12]

14. If, therefore, you would prove that the apostle's words, "he that is born of God sinneth not," are not to be understood according to their plain, natural, obvious meaning, it is from the New Testament you are to bring your proofs, else you will fight as one that beateth the air [cf. 1 Cor. 9:26]. And the first of these which is usually brought is taken from the examples recorded in the New Testament. "The apostles themselves," it is said, "committed sin, nay, the greatest of them, Peter and Paul. St. Paul, by his sharp contention with Barnabas, and St. Peter, by his dissimulation at Antioch." Well, suppose both Peter and Paul did then commit sin, what is it you would infer from hence? That all the other apostles committed sin sometimes? There is no shadow of proof

11. [Au.] 1 Pet. 9–10 ff.     12. [Au.] Zech. 12:8.

in this. Or would you thence infer that all the other Christians of the apostolic age committed sin? Worse and worse. This is such an inference as, one would imagine, a man in his senses could never have thought of. Or will you argue thus: "If two of the apostles did once commit sin, then all other Christians, in all ages, do and will commit sin as long as they live?" Alas, my brother, a child of common understanding would be ashamed of such reasoning as this. Least of all can you with any colour of argument infer that any man must commit sin at all. No, God forbid we should thus speak! No necessity of sinning was laid upon them. The grace of God was surely sufficient for them. And it is sufficient for us at this day. With the temptation which fell on them, there was a way to escape, as there is to every soul of man in every temptation; so that whosoever is tempted to any sin, need not yield; for no man is tempted above that he is able to bear [cf. 1 Cor. 10:13].

15. "But St. Paul besought the Lord thrice, and yet he could not escape from his temptation." Let us consider his own words literally translated: "There was given to me a thorn in the flesh, an angel (or messenger) of Satan, to buffet me. Touching this I besought the Lord thrice, that it (or he) might depart from me. And he said unto me, my grace is sufficient for thee. For my strength is made perfect in weakness. Most gladly therefore will I rather glory in these my weaknesses, that the strength of Christ may rest upon me. Therefore I take pleasure in weaknesses; . . . for when I am weak, then am I strong" [cf. 2 Cor. 12:7–10].

16. As this Scripture is one of the strongholds of the patrons of sin, it may be proper to weigh it thoroughly. Let it be observed then, first, it does by no means appear that this thorn, whatsoever it was, occasioned St. Paul to commit sin, much less laid him under any necessity of doing so. Therefore, from hence it can never be proved that any Christian *must* commit sin. Secondly, the ancient Fathers inform us, it was bodily pain — "a violent headache," saith Tertullian,[13] to which both Chrysostom and St. Jerome agree. St. Cyprian [14] expresses it, a little more generally, in those terms, "[after] many and grievous torments of the flesh and of the body." [15] Thirdly, to this exactly agree the apostle's own words: "A thorn in the flesh to smite, beat, or buffet me." "My

13. [Au.] *De Pudic.* [Ed.] What Tertullian *says* is ". . . *per dolorem, ut aiunt, auriculae vel capitis*," "as 'they' say, an earache or headache." Cf. *De Pudicitia*, XIII, in *Corpus Christianorum, Series Latina* (Turnholti, 1953), II, 1305; see also Tertullian, *Treatises on Penance* in *ACW*, XXVIII, 88.

14. [Au.] *De mortalitate.* [Ed.] Cf. *PL*, IV, 613.

15. [Au.] "[*Post*] *carnis et corporis multa ac gravia tormenta.*"

strength is made perfect in weakness," which same word occurs no less than four times in these two verses only. But, fourthly, whatsoever it was, it could not be either inward or outward sin. It could no more be inward stirrings than outward expressions of pride, anger, or lust. This is manifest, beyond all possible exception, from the words that immediately follow: "Most gladly will I glory in these my weaknesses, that the strength of Christ may rest upon me." What! did he glory in pride, in anger, in lust? Was it through these "weaknesses" that the strength of Christ rested upon him? He goes on: "Therefore, I take pleasure in weaknesses; for when I am weak, then am I strong"; that is, when I am weak *in body*, then am I strong *in spirit*. But will any man dare to say, "When I am weak by pride or lust, then am I strong in spirit?" I call you all to record this day — who find the strength of Christ resting upon you — can you glory in anger, or pride, or lust? Can you take pleasure in these infirmities? Do these weaknesses make you strong? Would you not leap into hell, were it possible, to escape them? Even by yourselves, then, judge whether the apostle could glory and take pleasure in them. Let it be, lastly, observed, that this thorn was given to St. Paul above fourteen years before he wrote this Epistle [*cf.* 2 Cor. 12:2], which itself was wrote several years before he finished his course. So that he had, after this, a long course to run, many battles to fight, many victories to gain and great increase to receive in all the gifts of God and the knowledge of Jesus Christ. Therefore, from any spiritual weakness (if such had been) which he at that time felt, we could by no means infer that he was never made strong, that Paul the aged, the father in Christ, still laboured under the same weaknesses; that he was in no higher state till the day of his death. From all which it appears that this instance of St. Paul is quite foreign to the question and does in no wise clash with the assertion of St. John, "He that is born of God sinneth not."

17. "But does not St. James directly contradict this? His words are, 'In many things we offend all.' [16] And is not offending the same as committing sin?" In this place, I allow it is. I allow the persons here spoken of did commit sin; yea, that they all committed many sins. But who are the persons here spoken of? Why, those many masters or teachers whom God had not sent (probably the same vain men who taught that faith without works which is so sharply reproved in the preceding chapter) — not the apostle himself, nor any real Christian. That in the word "we" (used by a figure of speech common in all other as well as the inspired

16. [Au.] Jas. 3:2.

writings) the apostle could not possibly include himself or any other true believer appears evidently first, from the same word in the ninth verse: "Therewith," saith he, "bless we God and therewith curse we men. Out of the same mouth proceedeth blessing and cursing." True, but not out of the mouth of the apostle, nor of anyone who is, in Christ, a new creature. Secondly, from the verse immediately preceding the text and manifestly connected with it: "My brethren, be not many masters (or teachers), knowing that we shall receive the greater condemnation." "For in many things *we* offend all." "We!" Who? Not the apostles, not true believers — but they who knew they should "receive the greater condemnation" because of those many offences. But this could not be spoke of the apostle himself or of any who trod in his steps, seeing "there is no condemnation to them who walk not after the flesh but after the Spirit" [*cf.* Rom. 8:1]. Nay, thirdly, the very verse itself proves that "we offend all" cannot be spoken either of all men, or of all Christians: for in it there immediately follows the mention of a man who "offends not," as the "we" first mentioned did, from whom, therefore, he is professedly contradistinguished, and pronounced "a perfect man."

18. So clearly does St. James explain himself and fix the meaning of his own words. Yet, lest any one should still remain in doubt, St. John, writing many years after St. James, puts the matter entirely out of dispute by the express declarations above recited. But here a fresh difficulty may arise. How shall we reconcile St. John with himself? In one place he declares "Whosoever is born of God doth not commit sin," and again, "We know that he which is born of God sinneth not" [1 Jn. 5:18]; and yet in another he saith, "If we say that we have no sin, we deceive ourselves and the truth is not in us" [1 Jn. 1:8], and again, "If we say that we have not sinned, we make him a liar and his Word is not in us" [1 Jn. 1:10].

19. As great a difficulty as this may at first appear, it vanishes away if we observe, first, that the tenth verse fixes the sense of the eighth — "If we say we have no sin," in the former, being explained by, "if we say we have not sinned," in the latter verse. Secondly, that the point under present consideration is not whether we have or have not sinned heretofore, and neither of these verses asserts that we do sin or commit sin, now. Thirdly, that the ninth verse explains both the eighth and tenth: "If we confess our sins, he is faithful and just to forgive us our sins, and to cleanse us from all unrighteousness" — as if he had said, "I have before affirmed, 'The blood of Jesus Christ cleanseth us from all sin'" [1 Jn.

1:7]. But let no man say, I need it not, I have no sin to be cleansed from. If we say that we have no sin (that we have not sinned), we deceive ourselves, and make God a liar. But if we confess our sins, he is faithful and just, not only to forgive our sins, but also to cleanse us from all unrighteousness — that we may go and sin no more" [cf. 1 Jn. 1:9; Jn. 5:14].

20. St. John, therefore, is well consistent with himself, as well as with the other holy writers, as will yet more evidently appear if we place all his assertions touching this matter in one view. He declares, first, "the blood of Jesus Christ cleanseth us from all sin." Secondly, "no man can say I have not sinned, I have no sin to be cleansed from." Thirdly, "but God is ready both to forgive our past sins and to save us from them for the time to come." Fourthly, "These things write I unto you," saith the apostle, "that you may not sin. But if any man should sin" (or "have sinned," as the word might [17] be rendered), he need not continue in sin, seeing "we have an advocate with the Father, Jesus Christ the righteous" [cf. 1 Jn. 1:7–2:1]. Thus far all is clear. But lest any doubt should remain in a point of so vast importance, the apostle resumes this subject in the third chapter and largely explains his own meaning: "Little children," saith he, "let no man deceive you" (as though I had given any encouragement to those that continue in sin). "He that doeth righteousness is righteous, even as he [Jesus Christ] is righteous. He that committeth sin is of the devil, for the devil sinneth from the beginning. For this purpose the Son of God was manifested that he might destroy the works of the devil. Whosoever is born of God doth not commit sin, for his seed remaineth in him, and he cannot sin because he is born of God. In this the children of God are manifest, and the children of the devil." [18] Here the point, which till then might possibly have admitted of some doubt in weak minds, is purposely settled by the last of the inspired writers and decided in the clearest manner. In conformity, therefore, both to the doctrine of St. John, and to the whole tenor of the New Testament, we fix this conclusion: *a Christian is so far perfect as not to commit sin.*

21. This is the glorious privilege of every Christian; yea, though he be but "a babe in Christ." But it is only of those who "are strong" in the Lord, "and have overcome the wicked one" (or rather of those who "have known him that is from the beginning" [cf. 1 Jn. 2:13], that it can be affirmed they are in such a sense perfect as, secondly, to be freed from evil thoughts and evil tempers. First, from evil or sinful thoughts. But here let it be observed that thoughts concerning evil are not always evil

17. First edition (1741) reads, "should rather." 18. [Au.] Verses 7–10.

thoughts; that a thought concerning sin and a sinful thought are widely different. A man, for instance, may think of a murder which another has committed and yet this is no evil or sinful thought. So our blessed Lord himself doubtless thought of, or understood, the thing spoken by the devil, when he said, "All this will I give thee, if thou wilt fall down and worship me" [cf. Mt. 4:9]. Yet had he no evil or sinful thought, nor indeed was capable of having any. And even hence it follows, that neither have real Christians, for "every one that is perfect is as his Master." [19] Therefore, if he was free from evil or sinful thoughts, so are they likewise.

22. And, indeed, whence should evil thoughts proceed in the servant who is "as his Master"? "Out of the heart of man" (if at all) "proceed evil thoughts." [20] If, therefore, his heart be no longer evil, then evil thoughts can no longer proceed out of it. If the tree were corrupt, so would be the fruit. But the tree is good; the fruit, therefore, is good also; [21] our Lord himself bearing witness, "every good tree bringeth forth good fruit. A good tree cannot bring forth evil fruit," as "a corrupt tree cannot bring forth good fruit." [22]

23. The same happy privilege of real Christians, St. Paul asserts from his own experience. "The weapons of our warfare," saith he, "are not carnal, but mighty through God to the pulling down of strongholds, casting down imaginations" (or *reasonings* rather, for so the word λογισμούς signifies: all the reasonings of pride and unbelief against the declarations, promises, or gifts of God), "and every high thing that exalteth itself against the knowledge of God, and bringing into captivity every thought to the obedience of Christ." [23]

24. And as Christians indeed are freed from evil thoughts, so are they, secondly, from evil tempers. This is evident from the above-mentioned declaration of our Lord himself: "The disciple is not above his Master but every one that is perfect shall be as his Master" [Lk. 6:40]. He had been delivering, just before, some of the sublimest doctrines of Christianity, and some of the most grievous to flesh and blood: "I say unto you, 'Love your enemies, do good to them which hate you; . . . and unto him that smiteth thee on the one cheek, offer also the other'" [Lk. 6:27, 29]. Now these he well knew the world would not receive and therefore immediately adds, "Can the blind lead the blind? Will they not both fall into the ditch?" [Lk. 6:39]; as if he had said, "Do not confer with flesh

19. [Au.] Lk. 6:40.          20. [Au.] Mk. 7:21.          21. [Au.] Mt. 12:33.
22. [Au.] Mt. 7:17–18.       23. [Au.] 2 Cor. 10:4 ff.

and blood touching these things [*cf.* Gal. 1:16], with men void of spiritual discernment, the eyes of whose understanding God hath not opened
[*cf.* Eph. 1:18, 4:18], lest they and you perish together." In the next
verse he removes the two grand objections with which these wise fools
meet us at every turn — "these things are too grievous to be borne,"
or, "they are too high to be attained" — saying, "the disciple is not above
his Master. Therefore, if I have suffered, be content to tread in my steps.
And doubt ye not then but I will fulfil my word, 'For every one that is
perfect shall be as his Master.'" But his Master was free from all sinful
tempers. So, therefore, is his disciple, even every real Christian.

25. Every one of these can say with St. Paul, "I am crucified with
Christ; nevertheless I live, yet not I, but Christ liveth in me" [Gal. 2:20]
— words that manifestly describe a deliverance from inward as well as
from outward sin. This is expressed both negatively, "I live not" (my evil
nature, the body of sin, is destroyed); and positively, "Christ liveth in
me," and, therefore, all that is holy and just and good. Indeed, both these
— "Christ liveth in me" and "I live not" — are inseparably connected,
for "what communion hath light with darkness, or Christ with Belial"
[*cf.* 2 Cor. 6:14–15]?

26. He, therefore, who liveth in true believers hath "purified their
hearts by faith" [*cf.* Acts 15:9], insomuch that "every one that hath
Christ in him, the hope of glory [Col. 1:27], "purifieth himself even as
he is pure." [24] He is purified from pride, for Christ was lowly of heart.
He is pure from self-will or desire, for Christ desired only to do the will
of his Father and to finish his work. And he is pure from anger, in the
common sense of the word, for Christ was meek and gentle, patient and
long-suffering. I say, "in the common sense of the word," for all anger
is not evil. We read of our Lord himself [25] that he once "looked round
with anger." But with what kind of anger? The next word shows,
συλλυπούμενος, "being," at the same time, "grieved for the hardness of
their hearts." So then he was angry at the sin and in the same moment
grieved for the sinners, angry or displeased at the offence but sorry for
the offenders. With anger, yea, hatred, he looked upon the thing; with
grief and love upon the persons. Go thou that art perfect and do likewise. "Be thus angry and thou sinnest not": feeling a displacency at every
offence against God, but only love and tender compassion to the offender.

27. Thus doth Jesus "save his people from their sins" [*cf.* Mt. 1:21],

24. [Au.] 1 Jn. 3:3.        25. [Au.] Mk. 3:5.

and not only from outward sins but also from the sins of their hearts,
from evil thoughts and from evil tempers.[26] "True," say some, "we shall
thus be saved from our sins, but not till death; not in this world." But
how are we to reconcile this with the express words of St. John? "Herein
is our love made perfect, that we may have boldness in the day of judgment. Because as he is, so are we *in this world*." The apostle here, beyond
all contradiction, speaks of himself and other living Christians, of whom
(as though he had foreseen this very evasion and set himself to overturn
it from the foundation) he flatly affirms that not only at or after death,
but *in this world*, they are as their Master.[27]

28. Exactly agreeable to this are his words in the first chapter of this
Epistle,[28] "God is light, and in him is no darkness at all. If we walk in
the light, . . . we have fellowship one with another, and the blood of
Jesus Christ his Son cleanseth us from all sin." And again: "If we confess our sins, he is faithful and just to forgive us our sins and to cleanse
us from all unrighteousness" [*cf.* 1 Jn. 1:7–9]. Now, it is evident, the
apostle here also speaks of a deliverance wrought *in this world*. For he
saith not, "The blood of Christ will cleanse" (at the hour of death or in
the day of judgment) but it "cleanseth (at the time present) us (living
Christians) from all sin." And it is equally evident that if *any sin* remain,
we are not cleansed from *all sin;* if *any* unrighteousness remain in the
soul, it is not cleansed from *all* unrighteousness. Neither let any sinner
against his own soul say that this relates to justification only or the cleansing us from the guilt of sin: first, because this is confounding together
what the apostle clearly distinguishes, who mentions first, "to forgive
us our sins" and then "to cleanse us from all unrighteousness." Secondly,
because this is asserting justification by works in the strongest sense possible. It is making all inward as well as outward holiness necessarily previous to justification. For if the cleansing here spoken of is no other than
the cleansing us from the guilt of sin, then we are not cleansed from guilt,
that is, are not justified, unless on condition of "walking in the light, as
he is in the light." It remains, then, that Christians are saved in this world
from all sin, from all unrighteousness; that they are now in such a sense
perfect as not to commit sin, and to be freed from evil thoughts and evil
tempers.

29. Thus hath the Lord fulfilled the things he spake by his holy proph-

26. But *cf. Cautions and Directions,* as a counterweight to the enthusiastic misin-
terpretation of this; see below, p. 298 ff.
27. [Au.] 1 Jn. 4:17.         28. [Au.] Verse 5 ff.

ets, which have been since the world began [29] — by Moses in particular, saying,[30] "I will circumcise thine heart, and the heart of thy seed, to love the Lord thy God with all thy heart, and with all thy soul" — by David, crying out, "Create in me a clean heart, and renew a right spirit within me" [Ps. 51:10] — and most remarkably by Ezekiel in those words, "Then will I sprinkle clean water upon you and ye shall be clean. From all your filthiness and from all your idols will I cleanse you. A new heart also will I give you and a new spirit will I put within you; . . . and cause you to walk in my statutes and ye shall keep my judgments and do them. . . . Ye shall be my people and I will be your God. I will also save you from all your uncleannesses. . . . Thus saith the Lord your God: In the day that I shall have cleansed you from all your iniquities, . . . the heathen shall know that I the Lord build the ruined places; . . . I the Lord have spoken it, and I will do it." [31]

30. "Having therefore these promises, dearly beloved," both in the law and in the prophets, and having the prophetic Word confirmed unto us in the gospel by our blessed Lord and his apostles, "let us cleanse ourselves from all filthiness of flesh and spirit, perfecting holiness in the fear of God" [2 Cor. 7:1]. "Let us fear lest" so many promises "being made us of entering into his rest" — which he that hath entered into "hath ceased from his own works — any of us should come short of it" [cf. Heb. 4:1]. "This one thing let us do: forgetting those things which are behind, and reaching forth unto those things which are before, let us press toward the mark for the prize of the high calling of God in Christ Jesus" [cf. Phil. 3:13–14], crying unto him day and night, till we also are "delivered from the bondage of corruption, into the glorious liberty of the sons of God" [Rom. 8:21]!

## The Scripture Way of Salvation

*Editor's introduction.* If the Wesleyan theology had to be judged by a single essay, this one would do as well as any and better than most. First published in 1765, it has the same Biblical text and theme as the much earlier sermon, "Salvation by Faith," which Wesley preached in St. Mary's, Oxford, shortly after "Aldersgate" (cf. *Journal*, I, 483; see also

29. Cf. the Benedictus, in the Order of Morning Prayer, B.C.P.
30. [Au.] Deut. 30:6.        31. [Au.] Ezek. 36:25 ff.

*Sermons* (Sugden), I, 35–52). The doctrinal core of the two sermons is identical, but the experiences of the intervening quarter-century had greatly matured Wesley's powers of interpreting the balance between faith and holiness against one-sided emphases on either side. In this respect, it is a much more definitive formulation of his message than the preceding sermon on "Christian Perfection." Like the other, however, it was occasioned by a controversy — this one aroused by the antinomian teachings of John and Robert Sandeman, two Scottish ministers who had gained the following of two of Wesley's most gifted preachers, Thomas Maxfield and George Bell. (*Cf.* John Wesley, *A Sufficient Answer to Letters to the Author of Theron and Aspasio* [1758].) These people set perfection above all threat of fault or lapse: they boldly asserted that the sanctified are sinless and secure. In his response, Wesley gives minimum attention to the controversy itself. Instead, he undertakes to expound, as winsomely as possible, his most characteristic conception: the integrity of grace *and* goodness in the life of faith. The copy text used here is in *Works* (Pine), III, 252–70, collated with the first edition.

❖   ❖   ❖

"Ye are saved through faith" (Eph. 2:8).

1. Nothing can be more intricate, complex and hard to be understood than religion as it has been often described. And this is not only true concerning the religion of the heathens (even many of the wisest of them), but concerning the religion of those also who were, in some sense, Christians, yea, and men of great name in the Christian world — men "who seemed to be pillars" thereof. Yet how easy to be understood, how plain and simple a thing, is the genuine religion of Jesus Christ, provided only that we take it in its native form, just as it is described in the oracles of God! It is exactly suited by the wise Creator and Governor of the world to the weak understanding and narrow capacity of man in his present state. How observable is this, both with regard to the end it proposes and the means to attain that end. The end is, in one word, "salvation"; the means to attain it, "faith."

2. It is easily discerned that these two little words — I mean "faith" and "salvation" — include the substance of all the Bible: the marrow, as it were, of the whole Scripture. So much the more should we take all possible care to avoid all mistake concerning them and to form a true and accurate judgment concerning both the one and the other.

3. Let us then seriously inquire,
    I. What is salvation?
    II. What is that faith whereby we are saved? And,
    III. How are we saved by it?

I. 1. And, first, let us inquire what is *salvation?* The salvation which is here spoken of is not what is frequently understood by that word: the going to heaven, eternal happiness. It is not the soul's going to paradise, termed by our Lord, "Abraham's bosom" [Lk. 16:22]. It is not a blessing which lies on the other side of death or (as we usually speak) "in the other world." The very words of the text itself put this beyond all question, "Ye *are* saved." It is not something at a distance. It is a present thing, a blessing which through the free mercy of God ye are now in possession of. Nay, the words may be rendered, and that with equal propriety, "Ye *have been* saved." So that the salvation which is here spoken of might be extended to the entire work of God, from the first dawning of grace in the soul till it is consummated in glory.

2. If we take this in its utmost extent, it will include all that is wrought in the soul by what is frequently termed "natural conscience," but more properly "preventing grace"; [1] all the "drawings of the Father"; the desires after God which, if we yield to them, increase more and more; all that "light" wherewith the Son of God "enlighteneth every one that cometh into the world" [*cf.* Jn. 1:9], showing every man "to do justly, to love mercy, and to walk humbly with his God" [*cf.* Mic. 6:8]; all the "convictions" which his Spirit, from time to time, works in every child of man — although, it is true, the generality of men stifle them as soon as possible, and after a while forget, or at least deny, that ever they had them at all.

3. But we are at present concerned only with that salvation which the apostle is directly speaking of. And this consists of two general parts: justification and sanctification.

Justification is another word for pardon. It is the forgiveness of all our sins and, what is necessarily implied therein, our acceptance with God. The price whereby this hath been procured for us (commonly termed the "meritorious cause" of our justification) is the blood and righteousness of Christ; or, to express it a little more clearly, all that Christ hath done

1. *Cf.* "On Working Out Our Own Salvation," Pt. III, par. 3–4 (*Works*, VI, 511–12), and compare this with Joseph Butler's notion of "natural conscience" in his Sermons II and III, *Fifteen Sermons, preached at the Rolls Chapel* (1726). It is Wesley's most compact statement of God's initiative in every significant human experience.

and suffered for us, till "he poured out his soul for the transgressors" [*cf.* Is. 53:12]. The immediate effects of justification are *the peace of God*, a "peace that passeth all understanding" [*cf.* Phil. 4:7], and a "rejoicing in *hope* of the glory of God" [*cf.* Rom. 5:2] "with joy unspeakable and full of glory" [*cf.* 1 Pet. 1:8].

4. And at the same time that we are justified — yea, in that very moment — *sanctification* begins. In that instant we are "born again, born from above, born of the Spirit." There is a *real* as well as a *relative* change. We are inwardly renewed by the power of God. We feel "the love of God shed abroad in our heart by the Holy Ghost which is given unto us" [*cf.* Rom. 5:5], producing love to all mankind, and more especially to the children of God, expelling the love of the world, the love of pleasure, of ease, of honour, of money, together with pride, anger, self-will and every other evil temper; in a word, changing the "earthly, sensual, devilish mind" into "the mind which was in Christ Jesus" [*cf.* Phil. 2:5].

5. How naturally do those who experience such a change imagine that all sin is gone, that it is utterly rooted out of their heart and has no more any place therein! How easily do they draw that inference, "I *feel* no sin; therefore, I *have* none. It does not *stir;* therefore, it does not *exist.* It has no *motion;* therefore, it has no *being!*"

6. But it is seldom long before they are undeceived, finding sin was only suspended, not destroyed. Temptations return and sin revives; showing it was but stunned before, not dead. They now feel two principles in themselves, plainly contrary to each other, "the flesh lusting against the Spirit" [Gal. 5:17], nature opposing the grace of God. They cannot deny that although they still feel power to believe in Christ and to love God, and although his Spirit still "witnesses with" their "spirits that" they "are children of God" [*cf.* Rom. 8:16], yet they feel in themselves sometimes pride or self-will, sometimes anger or unbelief. They find one or more of these frequently *stirring* in their heart, though not *conquering;* yea, perhaps, "thrusting sore at them that they" may "fall, but the Lord is" their "help" [*cf.* Ps. 118:13, B.C.P.].

7. How exactly did Macarius,[2] fourteen hundred years ago, describe the present experience of the children of God: . . . "The unskilful" (or unexperienced), "when . . . grace operates, presently imagine they have no more sin. Whereas they that have discretion cannot deny that even we who have the grace of God may be molested again. . . . For we have

2. See note above, p. 9.

often had instances of some among the brethren who have experienced such . . . grace as to affirm that . . . they had no sin in them, and yet, after all, when they thought themselves entirely freed . . . from it, the corruption that lurked within was stirred up anew and they were well nigh burnt up." [3]

8. From the time of our being "born again," the gradual work of sanctification takes place. We are enabled "by the Spirit" to "mortify the deeds of the body" [Rom. 8:11, 13], of our evil nature, and as we are more and more dead to sin, we are more and more alive to God. We go on from grace to grace, while we are careful to "abstain from all appearance of evil" [1 Thess. 5:22] and are "zealous of good works [Tit. 2:14] as we have opportunity, doing good to all men" while we walk in all his ordinances blameless, therein worshipping him in spirit and in truth [cf. Jn. 4:23], while we take up our cross [cf. Mt. 16:24] and deny ourselves every pleasure that does not lead us to God.

9. It is thus that we wait for entire sanctification, for a full salvation from all our sins — from pride, self-will, anger, unbelief — or, as the apostle expresses it, "go on unto perfection" [Heb. 6:1]. But what is perfection? The word has various senses: here it means perfect love. It is love excluding sin, love filling the heart, taking up the whole capacity of the soul. It is love "rejoicing ever more, praying without ceasing, in everything giving thanks" [cf. 1 Thess. 5:16–18].

II. But what is that "faith" through "which we are saved"? This is the second point to be considered.

1. Faith, in general, is defined by the apostle, ἔλεγχος πραγμάτων οὐ βλεπομένων, "an evidence," a divine "evidence and conviction" (the word means both) "of things not seen" [4] (not visible, not perceivable either by sight or by any other of the external senses). [5] It implies both a supernatural "evidence" of God and of the things of God, a kind of spiritual "light" exhibited to the soul, and a supernatural "sight" or perception thereof. Accordingly, the Scripture speaks of God's giving sometimes light, sometimes a power of discerning it. So St. Paul: "God, who commanded light to shine out of darkness, hath shined in our hearts to give us the light of the knowledge of the glory of God in the face of Jesus Christ" [2 Cor. 4:6]. And elsewhere the same apostle speaks of "the eyes"

---

3. Wesley's abridgment of Homily IX, par. 4, in *The Homilies of Macarius*, in *The Christian Library* (Bristol, 1749–55), I, 97. Ellipses indicate Wesley's omissions.

4. Heb. 11:1; all standard texts read πραγμάτων ἔλεγχος.

5. See below, pp. 386–88.

of our "understanding being opened" [Eph. 1:18]. By this twofold operation of the Holy Spirit, having the eyes of our soul "opened" and "enlightened," we see the things which the natural "eye hath not seen, neither
the ear heard" [1 Cor. 2:9]. We have a prospect of the invisible things of
God; we see the "spiritual world," which is all round about us and yet
no more discerned by our natural faculties than if it had no being. And
we see the "eternal world," piercing through the veil which hangs between time and eternity. Clouds and darkness then rest upon it no more,
but we already see the glory which shall be revealed.

2. Taking the word in a more particular sense, faith is a divine evidence
and conviction not only that "God was in Christ, reconciling the world
unto himself" [2 Cor. 5:19], but also that "Christ loved *me* and gave himself for *me*." It is by this faith (whether we term it the "essence," or
rather a "property" thereof) that we "receive" Christ, that we receive
him in all his offices as our Prophet, Priest and King. It is by this that he is
"made of God unto us wisdom, and righteousness, and sanctification, and
redemption" [*cf.* 1 Cor. 1:30].

3. "But is this the 'faith of assurance,' or '[the] faith or adherence'?"
The Scripture mentions no such distinction. The apostle says, "There is
one faith and one hope of our calling" — one Christian, saving faith —
as "there is one Lord" in whom we believe and "one God and Father
of us all" [*cf.* Eph. 4:4–6]. And it is certain, this faith necessarily implies
an "assurance" (which is here only another word for "evidence," it being
hard to tell the difference between them) that "Christ loved *me*, and gave
himself for *me*." For "he that believeth" with the true living faith "hath
the witness in himself" [*cf.* 1 Jn. 5:10]. "The Spirit witnesseth with his
spirit that he is a child of God" [*cf.* Rom. 8:16]. "Because he is a son,
God hath sent forth the Spirit of his Son into his heart, crying, Abba,
Father" [*cf.* Gal. 4:6], giving him an assurance that he is so and a childlike confidence in him. But let it be observed that, in the very nature of
the thing, the assurance goes before the confidence. For a man cannot
have a childlike confidence in God till he knows he is a child of God.
Therefore, confidence, trust, reliance, adherence, or whatever else it be
called is not the first as some have supposed, but the second branch or
act of faith.

4. It is by this faith we *are saved*, justified and sanctified, taking that
word in its highest sense. But how are we justified and sanctified by faith?
This is our third head of inquiry. And this being the main point in ques-

tion, and a point of no ordinary importance, it will not be improper to give it a more distinct and particular consideration.

III. 1. And, first, how are we justified by faith? In what sense is this to be understood? I answer, faith is the condition, and the only condition, of justification. It is the condition. None is justified but he that believes; without faith no man is justified. And it is the only condition: this alone is sufficient for justification. Every one that believes is justified, whatever else he has or has not. In other words, no man is justified till he believes; every man, when he believes, is justified.

2. "But does not God command us to *repent* also — yea, and to 'bring forth fruits meet for repentance' [*cf.* Lk. 3:8] — to 'cease,' for instance, 'from doing evil,' and 'learn to do well'? And is not both the one and the other of the utmost necessity, insomuch that if we willingly neglect either, we cannot reasonably expect to be justified at all? But if this be so, how can it be said that faith is the only condition of justification?"

God does undoubtedly command us both to repent and to bring forth fruits meet for repentance, which if we willingly neglect, we cannot reasonably expect to be justified at all. Therefore, both repentance and fruits meet for repentance are, in some sense, necessary to justification. But they are not necessary in the *same sense* with faith, nor in the *same degree*. Not in the *same degree*, for those fruits are only necessary *conditionally* if there be time and opportunity for them. Otherwise a man may be justified without them, as was the "thief" [*cf.* Mt. 27:38] upon the cross (if we may call him so, for a late writer has discovered that he was no thief, but a very honest and respectable person!).[6] But he cannot be justified without faith. This is impossible. Likewise, let a man have ever so much repentance, or ever so many of the fruits meet for repentance, yet all this does not at all avail. He is not justified till he believes. But the moment he believes, with or without those fruits, yea, with more or less repentance, he is justified. Not in the *same sense*, for repentance and its fruits are only *remotely* necessary — necessary in order to faith — whereas faith is *immediately* and *directly* necessary to justification. It remains that faith is the only condition which is *immediately* and *proximately* necessary to justification.

3. "But do you believe we are sanctified by faith? We know you be-

6. A sardonic comment on the interpretation of λῃσταί (Mt. 27:38 and Mk. 15:27), which identified them as Jewish patriots caught in open and violent rebellion against the hated Roman yoke and who had been called "thieves" only by the conquerors.

lieve that we are justified by faith, but do not you believe and accordingly teach that we are sanctified by our works?"

So it has been roundly and vehemently affirmed for these five-and-twenty years. But I have constantly declared just the contrary, and that in all manner of ways. I have continually testified in private and in public that we are sanctified as well as justified by faith. And, indeed, the one of those great truths does exceedingly illustrate the other. Exactly as we are justified by faith, so are we sanctified by faith. Faith is the condition, and the only condition of sanctification, exactly as it is of justification. It is the condition: none is sanctified but he that believes; without faith no man is sanctified. And it is the only condition: this alone is sufficient for sanctification. Every one that believes is sanctified, whatever else he has or has not. In other words, no man is sanctified till he believes. Every man, when he believes, is sanctified.

4. "But is there not a repentance consequent upon, as well as a repentance previous to, justification? And is it not incumbent on all that are justified to be 'zealous of good works'? Yea, are not these so necessary that if a man willingly neglect them, he cannot reasonably expect that he shall ever be sanctified in the full sense, that is, 'perfected in love'? Nay, can he 'grow' at all 'in grace, in the' loving 'knowledge of our Lord Jesus Christ'? Yea, can he retain the grace which God has already given him? Can he continue in the faith which he has received, or in the favour of God? Do not you yourself allow all this, and continually assert it? But, if this be so, how can it be said that faith is the only condition of sanctification?"

5. I do allow all this and continually maintain it as the truth of God. I allow there is a repentance consequent upon, as well as a repentance previous to, justification. It is incumbent on all that are justified to be zealous of good works. And these are so necessary that if a man willingly neglect them, he cannot reasonably expect that he shall ever be sanctified. He cannot "grow in grace," in the image of God, [in] the mind which was in Christ Jesus. Nay, he cannot retain the grace he has received; he cannot continue in faith or in the favour of God.

What is the inference we must draw herefrom? Why, that both repentance, rightly understood, and the practice of all good works — works of piety, as well as works of mercy (now properly so called, since they spring from faith) — are, in some sense, necessary to sanctification.

6. I say, "repentance rightly understood," for this must not be confounded with the former repentance. The repentance consequent upon

justification is widely different from that which is antecedent to it. This implies no guilt, no sense of condemnation, no consciousness of the wrath of God. It does not suppose any doubt of the favour of God, or any "fear that hath torment"[*cf.* 1 Jn. 4:18]. It is properly a conviction, wrought by the Holy Ghost, of the "sin" which still "remains" in our heart, of the φρόνημα σαρκός, "the carnal mind," which "does still *remain*" (as our Church speaks) [7] "even in them that are regenerate"; although it does no longer *reign*. It has not now dominion over them. It is a conviction of our proneness to evil, of an heart bent to backsliding, of the still continuing tendency of the flesh to lust against the spirit. Sometimes, unless we continually watch and pray, it lusteth to pride, sometimes to anger, sometimes to love of the world, love of ease, love of honour, or love of pleasure more than of God. It is a conviction of the tendency of our heart to self-will, to atheism, or idolatry and, above all, to unbelief, whereby, in a thousand ways and under a thousand pretences, we are ever "departing," more or less, "from the living God" [*cf.* Heb. 3:12].

7. With this conviction of the sin *remaining* in our hearts, there is joined a clear conviction of the sin remaining in our lives; still *cleaving* to all our words and actions. In the best of these we now discern a mixture of evil, either in the spirit, the matter, or the manner of them; something that could not endure the righteous judgment of God, were he "extreme to mark what is done amiss" [*cf.* Ps. 130:3, B.C.P.]. Where we least suspected it, we find a taint of pride or self-will, of unbelief or idolatry, so that we are now more ashamed of our best duties than formerly of our worst sins. And hence we cannot but feel that these are so far from having anything meritorious in them, yea, so far from being able to stand in the sight of the divine justice, that for those also we should be guilty before God, were it not for the blood of the covenant.

8. Experience shows that — together with this conviction of sin *remaining* in our hearts, and *cleaving* to all our words and actions, as well as the guilt which on account thereof we should incur were we not continually sprinkled with the atoning blood — one thing more is implied in this repentance: namely, a conviction of our helplessness, of our utter inability to think one good thought or to form one good desire and, much more, to speak one word aright, or to perform one good action, but through his free, almighty grace, first preventing us and then accompanying us every moment.

9. "But what good works are those, the practice of which you affirm to

7. *Cf.* Articles of Religion, IX, "Of Original or Birth Sin" (B.C.P.).

be necessary to sanctification?" First, all works of piety such as public prayer, family prayer and praying in our closet, receiving the Supper of the Lord, searching the Scriptures, by hearing, reading, meditating, and using such a measure of fasting or abstinence as our bodily health allows.

10. Secondly, all works of mercy, whether they relate to the bodies or souls of men, such as feeding the hungry, clothing the naked, entertaining the stranger, visiting those that are in prison, or sick, or variously afflicted, such as the endeavouring to instruct the ignorant, to awaken the stupid sinner, to quicken the lukewarm, to confirm the wavering, to comfort the feeble-minded, to succour the tempted, or contribute in any manner to the saving of souls from death. This is the repentance and these the fruits meet for repentance which are necessary to full sanctification. This is the way wherein God hath appointed his children to wait for complete salvation.

11. Hence may appear the extreme mischievousness of that seemingly innocent opinion that there is no sin in a believer, that all sin is destroyed, root and branch, the moment a man is justified. By totally preventing that repentance [which follows justification],[8] it quite blocks up the way to sanctification. There is no place for repentance in him who believes there is no sin either in his life or heart. Consequently, there is no place for his being "perfected in love," to which that repentance is indispensably necessary.

12. Hence it may likewise appear that there is no possible danger in *thus* expecting full salvation. For suppose we were mistaken, suppose no such blessing ever was or can be attained, yet we lose nothing. Nay, that very expectation quickens us in using all the talents which God has given us; yea, in improving them all, so that when our Lord cometh, he will receive his "own with increase" [*cf.* Mt. 25:27].

13. But to return. Though it be allowed that both this repentance and its fruits are necessary to full salvation, yet they are not necessary either in the *same sense* with faith, or in the *same degree*. Not in the *same degree*, for these fruits are only necessary *conditionally*, if there be time and opportunity for them. Otherwise, a man may be sanctified without them. But he cannot be sanctified without faith. Likewise, let a man have ever so much of this repentance, or ever so many good works, yet all this does not at all avail. He is not sanctified till he believes. But the moment he believes, with or without those fruits — yea, with more or less of this repentance — he is sanctified. Not in the *same sense*, for this repentance

8. *Cf.* "The Repentance of Believers," *Sermons* (Sugden), II, 379–97.

and these fruits are only *remotely* necessary — necessary in order to the continuance of his faith, as well as the increase of it — whereas faith is *immediately* and *directly* necessary to sanctification. It remains, that faith is the only condition which is *immediately* and *proximately* necessary to sanctification.

14. "But what is that faith whereby we are sanctified, saved from sin, and perfected in love?" It is a divine evidence and conviction, first, that God hath promised it in the Holy Scripture. Till we are thoroughly satisfied of this, there is no moving one step further. And one would imagine there needed not one word more to satisfy a reasonable man of this than the ancient promise, "Then will I circumcise thy heart, and the heart of thy seed, to love the Lord thy God with all thy heart, and with all thy soul" [*cf.* Deut. 30:6]. How clearly does this express the being perfected in love? — how strongly imply the being saved from all sin? For as long as love takes up the whole heart, what room is there for sin therein?

15. It is a divine evidence and conviction, secondly, that what God hath promised, he is *able* to perform. Admitting, therefore, that "with men it is impossible" to "bring a clean thing out of an unclean" [*cf.* Job 14:4] — to purify the heart from all sin and to fill it with all holiness — yet this creates no difficulty in the case, seeing [that] "with God all things are possible" [*cf.* Mt. 19:26]. And surely no one ever imagined it was possible to any power less than that of the Almighty! But if God speaks, it shall be done. God saith, "Let there be light; and there is light" [*cf.* Gen. 1:3]!

16. It is, thirdly, a divine evidence and conviction that he is able and willing to do it now. And why not? Is not a moment to him the same as a thousand years? He cannot want more time to accomplish whatever is his will. And he cannot want or stay for any more "worthiness" or "fitness" in the persons he is pleased to honour. We may therefore boldly say, at any point of time, "Now is the day of salvation" [2 Cor. 6:2]! "*Today*, if ye will hear his voice, harden not your hearts" [*cf.* Heb. 3:7, 8]! "Behold, all things are now ready [*cf.* Lk. 14:17]; come unto the marriage" [*cf.* Mt. 22:4]!

17. To this confidence, that God is both able and willing to sanctify us *now*, there needs to be added one thing more — a divine evidence and conviction that *he doth it*. In that hour it is done. God says to the inmost soul, "According to thy faith be it unto thee" [Mt. 9:29]! Then the soul is pure from every spot of sin; "it is clean from all unrighteousness" [*cf.* 1 Jn. 1:9]. The believer then experiences the deep meaning of those solemn words, "If we walk in the light as he is in the light, we have fellow-

ship one with another, and the blood of Jesus Christ his Son cleanseth us from all sin" [1 Jn. 1:7].

18. "But does God work this great work in the soul *gradually* or *instantaneously?*" Perhaps it may be gradually wrought in some — I mean in this sense, that they do not advert to the particular moment wherein sin ceases to be. But it is infinitely desirable, were it the will of God, that it should be done instantaneously, that the Lord should destroy sin "by the breath of his mouth" [*cf.* Job 15:30], in a moment, in the twinkling of an eye. And so he generally does; a plain fact of which there is evidence enough to satisfy any unprejudiced person. *Thou,* therefore look for it every moment! Look for it in the way above described, in all those "good works" whereunto thou art "created anew in Christ Jesus" [*cf.* Eph. 2:10]. There is then no danger: you can be no worse, if you are no better, for that expectation. For were you to be disappointed of your hope, still you lose nothing. But you shall not be disappointed of your hope. It will come, and will not tarry. Look for it then every day, every hour, every moment! Why not this hour, this moment? Certainly you may look for it *now,* if you believe it is by faith. And by this token you may surely know whether you seek it by faith or by works. If by works, you want something to be done *first, before* you are sanctified. You think, "I must first *be* or *do* thus or thus." Then you are seeking it by works unto this day. If you seek it by faith, you may expect it *as you are,* and if as you are, then expect it *now.* It is of importance to observe that there is an inseparable connexion between these three points — expect it *by faith;* expect it *as you are;* and expect it *now.* To deny one of them is to deny them all. To allow one is to allow them all. Do *you* believe we are sanctified by faith? Be true then to your principle and look for this blessing just as you are, neither better nor worse; as a poor sinner that has still nothing to pay, nothing to plead but "Christ died." And if you look for it as you are, then expect it *now.* Stay for nothing! Why should you? Christ is ready and he is all you want. He is waiting for you! He is at the door! Let your inmost soul cry out,

> Come in, come in, thou heavenly Guest!
> Nor hence again remove;
> But sup with me and let the feast
> Be everlasting love.[9]

9. *Cf.* Charles Wesley, *Hymns on God's Everlasting Love* (1741); in G. Osborn, ed., *Poetical Works of John and Charles Wesley* (1872), III, 66.

## Thoughts on Christian Perfection

*Editor's introduction.* Wesley often complained against both the Romanists and Calvinists that they "set Christian perfection *too high*," *i.e.* "in the state of glory only." From their side, the Calvinists retorted that *he* set it "too low" — and then added a battery of further charges: that he was inconsistent in his claims and concessions in respect of "perfection"; that he encouraged his people to self-delusions and self-righteousness, etc. These recriminations and confusions were heightened by the rather sudden increase of "professors" of "perfect love" in the Methodist societies during the closing years of the sixth decade of the century. In 1758 the Bristol Conference raised the question rather urgently; the preachers were warned not to speak of perfection "too minutely or circumstantially but rather in general and scriptural terms" (*cf.* Tyerman, *Life*, II, 306–07). During the ensuing year, however, Wesley's critics continued to pound him with loaded questions designed to force an admission that he had modified his earlier teaching. Instead, and quite characteristically, he grouped all these "objections" into a series of questions for discussion at the London Conference of 1759 — "and soon after I published *Thoughts on Christian Perfection . . .*" (*A Plain Account of Christian Perfection* [1766], par. 19). Actually, it appeared in Vol. IV of *Sermons on Several Occasions* (1760), pp. 207–68. Later, it was included, severely abridged, in *A Plain Account, Works*, Vol. XI, pp. 395–406. It appeared in subsequent editions of the *Sermons* (*e.g.* 1777 and 1787). Since it remains Wesley's clearest answer to many of the dubieties about the doctrine which have continued to dog it to this day, and also because it is generally inaccessible, it is here reprinted from the first edition corrected by Wesley's final revision of 1787 (IV, 241–74). For what meager contextual references there are to it, see *Journal*, Vol. IV, pp. 281; *Works*, Vol. XI, pp. 394–406; and *The Arminian Magazine* (1780), p. 223 f.

✣ ✣ ✣ ✣

### To the Christian Reader

*The following tract is by no means designed to gratify the curiosity of any man. It is not intended to prove the doctrine at large in opposition*

*to those who explode and ridicule it; no, nor to answer the numerous ob-*
*jections against it which may be raised even by serious men. All I intend*
*here is simply to declare what my sentiments are on this head; what Chris-*
*tian Perfection does (according to my apprehension) include, and what*
*it does not; and to add a few practical observations and directions relative*
*to the subject.*

*As these thoughts were at first thrown together by way of question*
*and answer, I let them continue in the same form, being as plain and*
*familiar as any other. They are just the same that I have entertained for*
*above twenty years, though extremely different from what have been*
*imputed to me; and probably will be so still. For there are many who*
*think they do God service by slandering their neighbour. "Lord, lay not*
*this sin to their charge" [Acts 7:60]! "Open their eyes, that they sleep not*
*in death" [cf. Ps. 13:3, B.C.P.]!*

> *Bristol,*
> *October 16, 1759*

Q. 1. What is Christian Perfection?

A. The loving God with all our heart, mind, soul and strength. This
implies that no wrong temper, none contrary to love, remains in the soul
and that all the thoughts, words and actions are governed by pure love.

Q. 2. But do you affirm that this perfection excludes all infirmities,
ignorance and mistake?

A. I continually affirm quite the contrary, and always have done so.
The sermon on "Christian Perfection" was published above eighteen years
ago. And therein I expressly declare "Christians are not so perfect in
*this life* as to be free from ignorance. . . . [Here follows an abridgment
of "Christian Perfection," Pt. I, par. 1–8; see above, pp. 254–58.]

Q. 3. "But is not this scheme contradictory to itself? How can every
thought, word and work be governed by pure love and the man be subject at the same time to ignorance and mistake? This we think is not
Christian perfection but imperfection, and is not a pin different from Calvinism."

A. So one of my correspondents writes. But I see no argument therein.
I see nothing contradictory here. "A man may be filled with pure love
and still be liable to mistake." Indeed, I expect not to be free from actual
mistakes till this mortal puts on immortality [cf. 1 Cor. 15:54]. I believe
this to be a natural consequence of the soul's dwelling in flesh and blood.
For we cannot now think at all but by the mediation of those organs

which have suffered equally with the rest of our frame. And hence we cannot avoid sometimes thinking wrong till "this corruptible shall have put on incorruption."

But we may carry this thought farther. A mistake in judgment may possibly occasion a mistake in practice. For instance: the mistake arising from prejudice of education in M. De Renty concerning the nature of mortification occasioned that practical mistake, his wearing an iron girdle.[1] And a thousand such instances there may be, even in those who are in the highest state of grace. Yet where every word and action springs from love, such a mistake is not properly a sin. However, it cannot bear the rigour of God's justice, but needs the atoning blood.

Q. 4. What was the judgment of all our brethren who met at Bristol in August, 1758, on this head?

A. It was expressed in these words:

1. Every one may mistake as long as he lives;
2. A mistake in opinion may occasion a mistake in practice;
3. Every such mistake is a transgression of the perfect law;
4. Therefore every such mistake, were it not for the blood of atonement, would expose to eternal damnation.
5. It follows that the most perfect have continual need of the merits of Christ, even for their actual transgressions, and may well say for themselves, as well as their brethren, "forgive us our trespasses" [cf. Mt. 6:12].

This easily accounts for what otherwise might seem to be utterly unaccountable: namely, that they who are not offended when we speak of the highest degree of love, yet will not hear of "living without sin." The reason is, they know all men are liable to mistake, and that in practice as well as in judgment. But they do not know, or [do] not observe, that this is not sin if love is the sole principle of action.

Q. 5. But still, if they live without sin, does not this exclude the necessity of a mediator? At least, is it not plain that they stand no longer in need of Christ in his priestly office?

A. Far from it. None feel their need of Christ like these; none so entirely depend upon him. For Christ does not give life to the soul separate from, but in and with, himself. Hence his words are equally true of all men, in whatever state of grace they are: "As the branch cannot bear fruit of itself, except it abide in the vine, no more can ye except ye abide

1. Cf. Wesley's abridgment of Jean Baptiste Saint-Jure, *The Holy Life of Monsieur de Renty*, in *A Christian Library* (1749–55), XXIX, 213–75; see above, p. 162.

in me. . . . Without," or separate from, "me, ye can do nothing" [cf. Jn. 15:4–5].

In every state, we need Christ in the following respects:

1. Whatever grace we receive, it is a free gift from him.
2. We receive it as his purchase merely in consideration of the price he paid.
3. We have this grace not from Christ but in him. For our perfection is not like that of a tree, which flourishes by the sap derived from its own root, but (as was said before) like that of a branch, which, united to the vine, bears fruit, but severed from it, is "dried up and withered" [cf. Jn. 15:6].
4. All our blessings, temporal, spiritual and eternal, depend on his intercession for us; which is one great branch of his priestly office, of which, therefore, we have always equal need.
5. The best of men still need Christ in his priestly office to atone for their omissions, their shortcomings (as some, not improperly, speak), their mistakes in judgment and practice, and their defects of various kinds. For these are all deviations from the perfect law and consequently need an atonement. Yet that they are not properly sins, we apprehend, may appear from the words of St. Paul, "He that loveth hath fulfilled the law; for love is the fulfilling of the law." [2] Now mistakes and whatever infirmities necessarily flow from the corruptible state of the body are no way contrary to love nor therefore, in the Scripture sense, "sins."

The truth is, in a state of perfection every desire is in subjection to the obedience of Christ. The will is entirely subject to the will of God and the affections wholly fixed on him. Now what motive can remain sufficient to induce such a person to a transgression of the law? Surely none that can induce him to do any that is formally evil, although he may, through human infirmity, speak or do what is materially so and, as such, condemned by the perfect law.[3] And the soul that any way deviates from this would, without an atonement, be lost for ever. Yet these deviations are not properly sins. But if any will call them so, they may.

Q. 6. I am not yet clear on this head. Will you answer me a few questions?

2. [Au.] Rom. 13:10, 12 [cf. Rom. 13:8, 10].

3. Another version of Wesley's distinction between deliberate and indeliberate sins; one who is "perfect" does not sin *deliberately*. See above, p. 34; see also Colin Williams, *Wesley's Theology Today* (New York, 1960), 126–28; 184–88.

1. Is there any thing besides sin that would expose to eternal damnation?

2. Is there any thing besides sin that needs the atoning blood?

3. Is there no such perfection in this life as absolutely excludes all sin?

4. If we do not allow this, do we not contradict ourselves in talking of sinless perfection?

5. Can a person be filled with the love of God and yet be liable to sin, to transgress the perfect law?

6. How can we call such a transgression of the perfect law, as without the blood of atonement would expose us to eternal damnation, any other than sin?

A. The objection is here set in the strongest light. Let it be remembered, I do "not intend in this tract to prove the doctrine at large but simply to declare what my sentiments are." This premised, I answer:

1. and 2. Not only sin properly so called (that is, a voluntary transgression of a known law) but sin improperly so called (that is, an involuntary transgression of a divine law, known or unknown) needs the atoning blood, and without this would expose to eternal damnation.

3. I believe there is no such perfection in this life as excludes these involuntary transgressions, which I apprehend to be naturally consequent on the ignorance and mistakes inseparable from mortality.

4. Therefore "sinless perfection" is a phrase I never use lest it should *seem* to contradict myself.

5. I believe a person filled with the love of God is still liable to these involuntary transgressions.

6. Such transgressions you may call sins if you please. I do not for the reason above mentioned.[4]

I would only add that man, in his original state, was not liable to these transgressions. He knew every law of God in every possible case, and was able to obey it. Therefore any transgression must have exposed him to eternal damnation: and so would it every one of his posterity, but that the law of love, by virtue of the atoning blood, now stands in the room of the law of fire.

Q. 7. What advice would you give to those that do and those that do not call them so?

4. *I.e.* in par. 1 and 2.

A. Let those who do not call them sins never think that themselves or any other persons are in such a state as that they can stand before infinite justice without a mediator. This must argue either the deepest ignorance or the highest arrogance and presumption. Let those who do call them so beware how they confound these defects with sins, properly so called. But how will they avoid it? How will these be distinguished from those, if they are all promiscuously called sins? I am much afraid if we should allow any sins to be consistent with perfection, few would confine the idea to those "defects" concerning which only the assertion could be true.

To sum up this point. "He that has no sin, you say, can need no atonement." If under the term sin you comprise the above-mentioned defects, the assertion is true. But we maintain no such perfection. But if by sin you mean a transgression of the law of love, the assertion is not true. For one who has no sin, in this sense, yet has many defects which stand in need of an atonement, on which account also the blood of Christ is unspeakably precious to such a soul.

Q. 8. "I am not clear yet how a liableness to mistake can consist with perfect love. Is not a person who is perfected in love every moment under its powerful influences? And can any mistake flow from pure love?

A. I answer: 1. Many mistakes *may consist* with pure love.

2. Some may accidentally *flow from* it: — I mean, love itself may incline us to mistake. The pure love of our neighbour, springing from the love of God, "thinketh no evil, believeth and hopeth all things" [*cf.* 1 Cor. 13:5, 7]. Now this very temper — unsuspicious, ready to believe and hope the best of all men — may occasion our thinking some men better than they really are.[5]

Q. 9. I am sure [that] to set perfection too high is to make nothing of it. But is it not worse to set it too low?

A. It cannot be worse than "to make nothing of it," but it is bad enough. Therefore, let you and me steer between the two extremes and set it just as high as the Scripture does. It is nothing higher and nothing lower than this: the pure love of God and man — the loving God with all our heart and soul and our neighbour as ourselves. It is love governing the heart and life, running through all our tempers, words and actions.

Q. 10. But if we must be saved from all our sins on earth because no sin can enter into heaven, does it not follow we must be saved from these defects on earth because these cannot enter into heaven?

A. It will not; for the case is by no means parallel. These defects are the

5. *Cf. A Plain Account of Christian Perfection* (*Works*), XI, 397.

mere natural result of the present imperfect and corruptible state of the body. Consequently they must all drop off with the body; and so cannot affect the soul in its separate state or hinder its access to God. But the case is not so with respect to *sin*. Pride and anger (for instance) or vile affections tincture and defile the very essence of the soul and make it incapable of that access. Nor can its separation from the body have any such effect as to separate these from the soul. . . .

[Questions 11–16 (and their answers) are a slight revision of Q. 1–12 in the Minutes of the Fourth Annual Conference (Wednesday, June 17, 1747), and are therefore not reprinted here. See above, pp. 167–70.]

Q. 17. Suppose, then, one had attained to this. Would you advise him to speak of it?

A. At first, perhaps, he would scarce be able to refrain, the fire would be so hot within him; his desire to declare the loving kindness of the Lord carrying him away like a torrent. But afterwards he might; and then it would be advisable not to speak of it to them who know not God. It is most likely it would only provoke them to contradict and blaspheme. Nor to others without some particular reason, without some particular good in view. And then he should have especial care to avoid all appearance of boasting, to speak with the deepest humility and reverence, giving all the glory to God. Meantime, let him speak more convincingly by his life than he can do by his tongue.

Q. 18. But would it not be better to be entirely silent? Ought he to speak of it at all?

A. By silence he might avoid many crosses which will naturally and necessarily ensue, if he simply declare, even among believers, what God has wrought in his soul. If, therefore, such an one were to confer with flesh and blood, he would be entirely silent. But this could not be done with a clear conscience; for undoubtedly he ought to speak. Men do not light a candle to put it under a bushel [*cf.* Mt. 5:15]: much less does the all-wise God. He does not raise such a monument of his power and love to hide it from all mankind. Rather he intends it as a general blessing to those that are simple of heart. He designs thereby not barely the happiness of that individual person, but the animating and encouraging others to follow after the same blessing. His will is that many should see it and rejoice and put their trust in the Lord. Nor does any thing under heaven more quicken the desires of those who "are saved by faith" [*cf.* Eph. 2:8], than to converse with those whom they believe to have experienced a still higher salvation. This places that salvation full in their view and increases their hunger and thirst after it: an advantage which must have been entirely lost had the person so saved buried himself in silence.

Q. 19. But is there no way to prevent those crosses which usually fall on those who speak of being thus saved?

A. It seems they cannot be prevented altogether while so much of nature remains even in believers. But something might be done if the preacher in every place would:

1. Candidly and closely examine, and that again and again, those who speak thus;

2. Speak against none till they have thus examined them;

3. Declare more or less openly as the case requires that such and such are not what they supposed; and

4. Labour to prevent the unjust or unkind treatment of those in favour of whom there is reasonable proof.

Q. 20. What is reasonable proof? How can we certainly know one that is saved from all sin?

A. We cannot infallibly know one that is so saved (no, nor even one that is justified) unless it should please God to endow us with the miraculous discernment of spirits [cf. 1 Cor. 12:10]. But we apprehend these would be sufficient rational proofs to any reasonable man and such as would leave little room to doubt, either of the truth or depth of the work:

1. If we had sufficient evidence of his exemplary behaviour for some time before this supposed change. This would give us reason to believe he would not lie for God but speak neither more nor less than he felt;

2. If he gave a distinct account of the time and manner wherein the change was wrought, with sound speech which could not be reproved; and

3. If it appeared that all of his subsequent words and actions were holy and unblameable.

The short of the matter is this: (1) I have abundant reason to believe this person will not lie; and (2) he testifies before God, "I feel no sin, but all love. I pray, rejoice, give thanks without ceasing. And I have as clear an inward witness that I am fully renewed as that I am justified." Now if I have nothing to oppose to this plain testimony, I ought in reason to believe it.

It avails nothing to object, "But I know several things wherein he is quite mistaken." For it has been allowed that all who are in the body are liable to mistake: and that a mistake in judgment may sometimes occasion a mistake in practice (though great care is to be taken that no ill use be made of this concession). For instance, even one that is "perfected in love" may mistake with regard to another person and may think him, in a particular case, to be more or less faulty than he really is. And hence he may speak to him with more or less severity than the truth required. And in this sense (though that be not the primary meaning of St. James), "in many things we offend all" [Jas. 3:2]. This therefore is no proof at all that the person so speaking is not perfect.[6]

Q. 21. But is it not a proof if he is surprised or fluttered by a noise, a fall, or some sudden danger?

A. It is not. For one may start, tremble, change colour or be otherwise disordered in body while the soul is calmly staid on God and remains in perfect peace. Nay, the mind itself may be deeply distressed, may be exceeding sorrowful, may be perplexed and prest down by heaviness and anguish even to agony, while the heart cleaves to God by perfect love and the will is wholly resigned to him. Was it not so with the Son of God himself? Does any child of man endure the distress, the anguish, the agony which he sustained? And yet he "knew no sin" [2 Cor. 5:21].

Q. 22. But can any one that has a pure heart prefer pleasing to unpleasing food, or use any pleasure of sense which is not strictly necessary? If so, how do they differ from others?

A. The difference between these and others in taking pleasant food is:

1. They need none of those things to make them happy, for they have a spring of happiness within. They see and love God: hence they rejoice evermore and in every thing give thanks.

2. They may use them but they do not seek them.

3. They use them sparingly and not for the sake of the thing itself.

This being premised, we answer directly: Such an one may use pleasing food without the danger which attends those who are not saved from sin. He may prefer it to unpleasing, though equally wholesome [food] as a means of increasing thankfulness with a single eye to God, "who giveth us all things richly to enjoy" [cf. 1 Tim. 6:17]. On the same principle, he may smell to a flower [sic], or eat a bunch of grapes, or take any other pleasure which does not lessen but increase his delight in God. Therefore neither can we say that one perfected in love would be in-

6. Cf. *Christian Perfection*, Pt. II, par. 17-18, above, pp. 265-66, for a similar exegesis of Jas. 3:2.

capable of marriage and of worldly business if he were called thereto. He would be more capable than ever, as being able to do all things without hurry or carefulness, without any distraction of spirit.

Q. 23. But if two perfect Christians had children, how could they be born in sin, since there was none in the parents?

A. It is a possible, but not a probable, case. I doubt whether it ever was or ever will be. But waiving this, I answer: Sin is entailed upon me not by my immediate but by my first parent. "In, Adam all died; by the disobedience of one, all men were constituted sinners" [cf. Rom. 5:14, 19]. And this constitution involves all without exception who were in his loins when he ate the forbidden fruit.

We have a remarkable illustration of this in gardening. Grafts on a crabstock bear excellent fruit. But sow the kernels of this fruit and what will be the event? They produce as mere crabs as ever were eaten.

Q. 24. But what does this perfect one more than others, more than common believers?

A. Perhaps nothing, so may the providence of God have hedged him in by outward circumstances. Perhaps not so much (though he desires and longs "to spend and be spent for God" [cf. 2 Cor. 12:15]), at least not externally. He neither speaks so many words nor does so many works (as neither did our Lord himself speak so many words or do so many, no, nor so great works, as some of his apostles).[7] But what then? This is no proof that he has not more grace: and by this God measures the outward work. Hear ye him! "Verily I say unto you, this poor widow hath cast in more than them all" [cf. Mk. 12:43]. Verily this poor man with his few broken words hath spoke more than them all. O cease to judge according to appearance and learn to judge righteous judgment!

Q. 25. But is not this a proof against him: I feel no power either in his words or prayer?

A. It is not, for perhaps that is your own fault. You are not likely to feel any power therein if any of these hindrances lie in their way:

1. Your own deadness of soul (the dead Pharisees felt no power even in his words who "spake as never man spake" [cf. Jn. 7:46]);
2. The guilt of some unrepented sin lying upon your conscience;
3. Your not believing that state to be attainable wherein he professes to be;
4. Prejudice toward him of any kind;
5. Unwillingness to think or own what he has attained;

7. [Au.] Jn. 14:12.

6. Overvaluing or idolizing him;

7. Overvaluing yourself and your own judgment.

If any of these is the case, what wonder is it that you feel no power in any thing he says? But do not others feel it? If they do, your argument falls to the ground. And if they do not, do none of these hindrances lie in their way too? You must be certain of this before you can build any argument thereon. And even then, your argument will prove no more than that grace and gifts do not always go together.

"But he does not come up to my idea of a perfect Christian." And perhaps no one ever did, or ever will. For your idea may go beyond, or at least beside, the scriptural account. It may include more than the Bible includes therein or, however, something which that does not include. Scriptural perfection is pure love filling the heart and governing all the words and actions. If your idea includes any thing more, or any thing else, it is not scriptural: and then no wonder that a scripturally perfect Christian does not come up to it. I fear many stumble on this stumbling block. They include as many ingredients as they please — not according to Scripture, but their own imagination — in their idea of one that is perfect, and then readily deny any one to be such who does not answer that imaginary idea. The more care should we take to keep the simple, scriptural account continually in our eye: pure love reigning alone in our heart and life. This is the whole of scriptural perfection.

Q. 26. When may a person judge himself to have attained this?

A. When, after having been fully convinced of inbred sin by a far deeper and clearer conviction than that he experienced before justification and after having experienced a gradual mortification of it, he experiences a total death to sin and an entire renewal in the love and image of God, so as to rejoice evermore, to pray without ceasing and in every thing to give thanks [cf. 1 Thess. 5:17-18]. Not that the feeling all love and no sin is a sufficient proof. Several have experienced this for a considerable time and yet were afterwards convinced that their souls were not entirely renewed and that sin was only laid asleep, not destroyed. None, therefore, ought to believe that the work is done till there is added the testimony of the Spirit, witnessing his entire sanctification as clearly as his justification.

Q. 27. But whence is it that some imagine they are thus sanctified when in reality they are not?

A. It is hence: They do not judge by all the preceding marks but either by part of them or by others that are inconclusive. But I know no instance of any person duly attending to them all and yet [being] deceived in this matter. I believe there can be none in the world. If a man be deeply and fully convinced after justification of inbred sin; if he then experiences a gradual mortification of it and afterward an entire renewal in the image of God; if to this change, immensely greater than that wrought when he was justified, there be added a clear, direct witness of that renewal — I judge it is [as] impossible this man should be deceived herein as that God should lie. And if one whom I know to be a man of veracity testify these things to me, without some very sufficient reason I ought not to reject his testimony.

Q. 28. Is this death to sin and renewal in love gradual or instantaneous?

A. A man may be "dying" for some time, yet he does not, properly speaking, "die" till the instant the soul is separated from the body. And in that instant he lives the life of eternity. In like manner he may be "dying to sin" for some time; yet he is not "dead to sin" till sin is separated from the soul. And in that instant he lives the full life of love. And as the change undergone when the body dies is of a different kind and infinitely greater than any we had known before, yea, such as till then it is impossible to conceive, so the change wrought when the soul dies to sin is of a different kind and infinitely greater than any before, and than any one can conceive till he experiences it. Yet he still "grows in grace and in the knowledge of Christ" [cf. 2 Pet. 3:18], in the love and image of God, and will do so not only till death, but to all eternity.

Q. 29. How are we to wait for this change?

A. Not in careless indifference or indolent inactivity, but in vigorous and universal obedience; in a zealous keeping of all the commandments; in watchfulness and painfulness; in denying ourselves and taking up our cross daily; as well as in earnest prayer and fasting and a close attendance on all the ordinances of God. And if any man dream of attaining it any other way,[8] he deceiveth his own soul. It is true we receive it by simple faith; but God does not, will not, give that faith unless we seek it with all diligence in the way which he hath ordained. This consideration may satisfy those who inquire why so few have received the blessing. Inquire how many are seeking it this way and you have a sufficient answer.

Prayer especially is wanting. Who continues instant therein? Who

---

8. In his version of this in *A Plain Account*, Wesley adds, in parenthesis: ". . . (yea, or of keeping it when it is attained, when he has received it even in the largest measure)." See *Works*, XI, 403.

wrestles with God for this very thing? So "ye have not because ye ask not" or because ye ask amiss — namely, "that you may be renewed before you die." Before you die? Will that content you? Nay, but ask that it may be done now, today, while it is called today [cf. Heb. 3:13]. Do not call this "setting God a time." Certainly *today* is his time, as well as tomorrow. Make haste, man, make haste! Let

> Thy soul break out in strong desire
> Thy perfect bliss to prove!
> Thy longing heart be all on fire,
> To be dissolv'd in love! [9]

Q. 30. But may we continue in peace and joy *till* we are perfected in love?

A. Certainly we may, for the kingdom of God is not divided against itself. Therefore let not believers be discouraged from "rejoicing in the Lord always" [cf. Phil. 4:4]. Let them all their life rejoice unto God, provided it be with reverence. Neither need we be anxiously careful about perfection lest we should die before we have attained it. We ought to be "thus careful for nothing," but cheerfully to "make our request known to God" [cf. Phil. 4:6]. And yet we may be, in a sense, pained at the sinful nature which still remains in us. It is good for us to have a piercing sense of this and a vehement desire to be delivered from it. But this should only incite us the more zealously to fly every moment to our strong helper, the more earnestly to "press forward to the prize of our high calling in Christ Jesus" [cf. Phil. 3:14]. And when the sense of our sin most abounds, the sense of his love would much more abound.

Q. 31. How should we treat those who think they have attained?

A. Examine them as closely as possible and exhort them to pray fervently that God would show them all that is in their heart. The most earnest exhortations to abound in every grace and the strongest cautions to avoid all evil are given throughout the New Testament to those who are in the highest state of grace. But this should be done with the utmost tenderness, without any harshness, sternness or sourness. We should carefully avoid the very appearance of anger, unkindness or contempt. Leave it to Satan thus to tempt and to his children to cry out, "Let us examine him with despitefulness and torture, that we may know his meekness and

9. Cf. *Hymns and Sacred Poems* (1742), in G. Osborn, ed., *Poetical Works of John and Charles Wesley* (1872), II, 150 (v. 11); *see also The Methodist Hymn Book* (1933), 560, v. 3.

prove his patience." If they are faithful to the grace given, even though they mistake, they are in no danger of perishing thereby. No, not if they remain in that mistake till their spirit is returning to God.

Q. 32. But what hurt can it do to deal harshly with them?

A. Either they are mistaken or they are not. If they are, it may destroy their souls; this is nothing impossible, no, nor improbable. It may so enrage or so discourage them that they will sink and rise no more. If they are not mistaken, it may grieve those whom God has not grieved and do much hurt to our own souls. For undoubtedly he that touches them touches, as it were, the apple of God's eye [cf. Zech. 2:8]. If they are indeed full of his Spirit — his peculiar possession, the excellent ones of the earth — to behave unkindly or contemptuously to them is doing no little "despite to the Spirit of grace" [cf. Heb. 10:29]. Hereby likewise we feed and increase in ourselves evil surmising and many wrong tempers. To instance only in one: what self-sufficiency is this to set ourselves up for inquisitors-general, for peremptory judges in these deep things of God? Are we really qualified for the office? Can we pronounce in all cases how far infirmity reaches; what may, and what may not, be resolved into it; what may, in all circumstances, and what may not, consist with perfect love? Can we precisely determine how it will influence the look, the gesture, the tone of voice? If we can, doubtless, "we are the men and wisdom shall die with us" [cf. Job 12:2]!

Q. 33. Are we not apt to have a secret distaste to any who say they are saved from sin?

A. It is very possible we may, and that on several grounds: partly from a concern for the honour of God and a fear lest others should be hurt if these deceive their own souls; partly from a secret envy of those who speak of higher attainments than our own (although they who act from this principle are very rarely conscious of it); partly, from our natural slowness and unreadiness to believe the work of God. Accordingly, they who are most unready to believe them that testify entire sanctification, are likewise remarkably unready to believe the witnesses of justification; and frequently use as harsh and unkind speeches in the one case as in the other.

Q. 34. But if they are *displeased* at our not believing them, is this not full proof against them?

A. According as that displeasure is. If they are angry, it is a proof against them. If they are grieved, it is not. They ought to be grieved if we disbelieve a real word of God and thereby deprive ourselves of the advantage we might have received from it. And we may easily mistake this grief for anger, as the outward expressions of both are much alike.

Q. 35. But is it not well to find out those who fancy they have attained when they have not?

A. It is well to do it by mild, close, loving examination. But it is not well to triumph even over these. It is extremely wrong, if we find such an instance to rejoice, as if we had found great spoils. Ought we not rather to grieve, to be deeply concerned, to let our eyes run down with tears? Here is one who seemed to be a living proof of God's power to save to the uttermost. But alas, it is not as we hoped: he has been "weighed in the balance and found wanting" [cf. Dan. 5:27]. And is this a matter of joy? Ought we not to rejoice a thousand times more if we can find nothing but pure love?

"But he is deceived." What then? It is an harmless mistake while he feels nothing but love in his heart. It is a mistake which generally argues great grace, an high degree both of holiness and happiness. This then should be a matter of real joy to all that are simple of heart; not the mistake itself but that height of grace which for a time occasions it. I rejoice that this soul is always happy, always full of prayer and thanksgiving. I rejoice that he feels no unholy temper, but the pure love of God continually. And I will rejoice if sin is suspended till it is totally destroyed.

Q. 36. Is there then no danger in a man's being thus deceived?

A. Not at the time that he feels no sin. There was danger before, and there will be again, when he comes into fresh trials. But, so long as he feels nothing but love animating all his thoughts and words and actions, he is in no danger. He is not only happy, but safe, under the shadow of the Almighty. And for God's sake let him continue in that love as long as he can. Meantime you may do well to warn him of the danger that will be if his love grow cold and sin revive: even the danger of casting away hope, of being sorrowful above measure and supposing that, because he has not attained yet, therefore he never shall.

Q. 37. But what if none have attained it yet? What if all who think so are deceived?

A. Convince me of this and I will preach it no more. But understand me right. I do not build any doctrine on this or that person. This or any other may be deceived and I am not moved. But if there are none made perfect yet, God has not sent me to preach perfection.

Put a parallel case. For many years I have preached, "There is a peace of God which passeth all understanding" [cf. Phil. 4:7]. Convince me that this word has fallen to the ground, that in all these years none has attained this peace, that there is no living witness of it at this day, and I will preach it no more.

"O, but several persons have died in that peace." Perhaps so; but I want living witnesses. I cannot, indeed, without the discernment of spirits, be infallibly certain that any are such. But if I am certain that none are such, I have done with this doctrine.

So in the present case. For many years I have preached, "There is a love of God which casts out all sin." Convince me that this word has fallen to the ground, that in twenty years none has attained this love, that there is no living witness of it at this day, and I will preach it no more.

"Nay, several persons have died in this love." But these are not living witnesses. I cannot indeed be infallibly certain that this or that person is a witness. But if I were certain there were none such, I must have done with this doctrine.

"You misunderstand me. I believe some who died in this love enjoyed it long before their death. But I was not certain of this, that their former testimony was true, till some hours before they died."

You had not an *infallible* certainty then; and a *reasonable* certainty you might have had before; such a certainty as might have quickened and comforted your own soul and answered all other Christian purposes. Such a certainty as this any candid reader may have, suppose there be any living witness, by talking one hour with that person in the love and fear of God.

Q. 38. But what does it signify, whether any have attained it or no, seeing so many Scriptures witness for it?

A. If I were convinced that none in England had attained what has been so clearly and strongly preached by such a number of preachers in so many places, and for so long a time, I should be hereby convinced that we had all mistaken the meaning of those Scriptures — and, therefore, for the time to come I, too, must teach that sin will remain till death.

## Cautions and Directions Given to the Greatest Professors in The Methodist Societies

*Editor's introduction.* In the three years following the publication of *Thoughts on Christian Perfection*, the topic continued to be a bone of

contention both within the societies and between the Methodists and their
critics (*cf.* Tyerman, *Life*, II, 413–57). Moreover, just as there were
those who denounced Wesley's offer of "perfection" in this life as "enthusiasm," so also there *were* enthusiasts whose personal professions of
"entire sanctification" so disturbed Wesley that he felt compelled to
redress the balance from the other side. The year 1762 was a sort of
climax in his protracted struggle. In London George Bell and Thomas
Maxfield (*cf.* Tyerman, *Life*, II, 433–44) led a revolt that resulted in
schism — directed against Wesley's "legalism" and the compromises
they felt he had made in his teachings about perfection. In Wesley's eyes
this was enthusiasm "*properly so-called*," and a fatal misunderstanding of
his doctrine — all the worse because it displayed just that sort of spiritual
pride that the critics from the other side insisted *would* result from encouraging Christians to expect and "profess" perfection *in this life*. In
an effort then to cope with both a false doctrine (*i.e.* "*sinless* perfection")
and a false temper (*i.e.* self-righteousness) Wesley published the following short and trenchant *Cautions and Directions* (1762). Abridged, they
were then incorporated in a tract entitled *Farther Thoughts on Christian
Perfection* in 1763 (*cf.* Green, *Bibliography*, #219). This in turn, further abridged, was woven into *A Plain Account of Christian Perfection*
(*cf. Works*, XI, 427–35). But the pamphlet itself was not thereafter reprinted, and does not appear in any of the "collected" *Works*. It is,
however, arguable that the original versions of the *Thoughts* and the
*Cautions* come nearer to communicating Wesley's positive teaching in
this area than does the jumble of abridgments in *A Plain Account*. Accordingly, they are here presented and may readily be compared with
the easily accessible *Plain Account*. The copy text for this printing of
the *Cautions* is the original edition of 1762.

❖ ❖ ❖ ❖

I. What is the first advice which you would give to those who are
really renewed in love?

A. Watch and pray continually against *pride*, against every kind and
degree of it. If God has cast it out, see that it enter no more. It is full
as dangerous as desire. And you may slide back into it unawares, especially if you think you are in no danger of it. "Nay, but I ascribe all
I have to God." So you may, and be proud nevertheless. For it is pride
not only to ascribe what we have to ourselves, but to think we have

what we really have not. Mr. Law, for instance, ascribed all the light he had to God and, so far, he was humble. But then he thought he had *more light* than any man living—and this was palpable pride. So you ascribe all the knowledge you have to God, and in this respect you are humble. But if you think you have more knowledge than you really have, if you think you are so "taught of God" as no longer to need man's teaching, pride lieth at the door. Yes, you have need to be taught, not only by Mr. Maxfield, by one another, by Mr. Morgan or me, but by the weakest preacher in London — yea, by all men — for God sendeth by whom he *will* send.

Don't therefore say to any who would advise or reprove you, "You are blind; you cannot teach me; this is your 'wisdom'; this is your 'carnal reasoning'": but calmly weigh the thing before God. O let there be in you that lowly mind which was in Christ Jesus [*cf.* Phil. 2:5]. And "be ye clothed," likewise, "with humility." Let it not only *fill* but *cover you all over*. Let *modesty* and *self-diffidence* appear in all your words and actions. Let all you speak and do show that you are little and bare and mean and vile in your own eyes.

II. What is the second advice which you would give them?

A. Beware of that daughter of pride, *enthusiasm*. Sometimes likewise it is the parent of pride. O, keep at the utmost distance from it! Give no place to an heated imagination. Do not ascribe to God what is not of God. Do not easily suppose dreams, voices, impressions, visions or revelations to be from God, without sufficient evidence. They may be purely natural: they may be diabolical. Therefore remember the caution of the apostle, "Beloved, believe not every spirit but try the spirits whether they be of God" [1 Jn. 4:1]. Try all things by the written Word and let all bow down before it. You are in danger of enthusiasm every hour if you depart ever so little from Scripture — yea, or from the plain literal meaning of any text taken in connection with the context. And so you are if you despise, or lightly esteem, reason, knowledge or human learning — every one of which is an an excellent gift of God and may serve to the noblest purposes.

One general inlet to enthusiasm is the expecting the end without the means — the expecting knowledge, for instance, without searching the Scripture and consulting the children of God; the expecting spiritual strength without constant prayer; the expecting growth in grace without steady watchfulness and deep self-examination; the expecting any blessing without hearing the Word of God at every opportunity.

The very desire of "growing in grace" is sometimes an inlet to enthusiasm. As it continually leads us to seek *new grace*, it may possibly lead unawares to seek something else new, beside *new degrees of love* to God and man. So it has in fact led some to seek and imagine they had received gifts of a *new kind*, after a clean heart: as (1) the loving God with all *our mind*, (2) with all *our soul*, (3) with all *our strength*, (4) oneness with God, (5) oneness with Christ, (6) having our life hid with Christ in God, (7) being dead with Christ, (8) the rising with him, (9) the sitting with him in heavenly places, (10) the being taken up into his throne, (11) the being in the new Jerusalem, (12) the seeing the tabernacle of God come down among men, (13) the being dead to all works, (14) the not being liable to bodily death or pain, (15) or grief, (16) or temptation.[1]

One ground of many of these mistakes is the taking every fresh and strong application of any of these Scriptures to the heart, to be a gift of a *new kind*. Another is the not knowing that some of these Scriptures are not fulfilled yet. Most of the others are fulfilled when we are justified; the rest, the moment we are sanctified. It remains only that they be fulfilled in *higher degrees:* this is all we have to expect. Another ground of these and a thousand mistakes is the not considering deeply that love is the highest gift of God — humble, gentle, patient love — that all visions, revelations, manifestations whatever, are little things compared to love; and that all the gifts above mentioned are either the same with or infinitely inferior to it.

III. What is the third?

A. Beware of *antinomianism*, making void the law or any part of it through faith. Enthusiasm naturally leads to this. Indeed, they can hardly be separated. This may steal upon you in a thousand forms, so that you can never be too watchful against it. Take heed of everything, whether in principle or practice, which has any tendency thereto. Even that great truth that "Christ is the end of the law" [*cf.* Rom. 10:4] may betray us into it, if we do not consider that he has adopted every point of the moral law and grafted it into the law of love.

Beware of thinking, "Because I have faith and love, I need not have *so much* holiness; because I pray always, therefore I need no set time for private prayer; because I watch always, therefore I need no particular self-examination." Let us "magnify the law," the whole written Word, and "make it honourable" [*cf.* Is. 42:21]. Let this be our voice, "I prize thy commandments above gold or precious stones [*cf.* Ps. 119:127,

1. A collation of Scripture references: *cf.* Mk. 12:30; Col. 3:3; Rom. 6:8; Eph. 2:6; Rev. 3:1, 12; 21:2, 3.

B.C.P.]. O what love have I unto thy law! All the day long is my study in it" [*cf.* Ps. 119:97, B.C.P.]. Beware of "Moravianism" — the most refined antinomianism that ever was under the sun, and such as I think could only have sprung from the abuse of true Christian experience.[2] I cannot doubt but many of them were once exactly as you are now: feeling the living power of faith divine and experiencing Christ to be all in all. But they were not aware of Satan's devices.[3] They gave way to pride and strong imagination and then to antinomianism, into which they have fallen deeper and deeper ever since. You have unawares adopted some of their words already, if not of their sentiments. But why should we even *talk* in an exceptionable manner? Let us not call ourselves "the church," or affectedly style this or that doctrine "the thing," "the point," "the matter." Why should we pray to Christ more than to the Father? No Scripture will justify this. But these are comparatively small things. Beware of their *bigotry*. I mean bigotry to their own party. Let not your love be confined to Methodists only, much less to that very small part of them who seem to be renewed in love. Count not those your enemies who do not believe your report. Make not this your "shibboleth" [*cf.* Judg. 12:6]. Above all, beware of *Moravian stillness:* [their] "ceasing," in a wrong sense, "from their own works." To mention one instance out of many: "You had received," says one of them, "a great blessing, but you began to *talk* of it and to *do* this and that. So you lost it. You should have been 'still.'"

IV. What is the fourth?

A. Beware of *sins of omission:* lose no opportunity of doing good in any kind. Be zealous of good works. Willingly omit no work either of piety or mercy. Do all the good you possibly can, to the bodies and souls of all men. Particularly, "thou shalt in any wise reprove thy neighbour and not suffer sin upon him" [Lev. 19:17]. Be active. Give no place to indolence or sloth. Give no occasion to say, "Ye are idle, ye are idle," though they *will* say so still. Be always employed. Lose no shred of time. And what you do, do with your might. Do not talk too much, neither too long at a time. Few can converse profitably above an hour. Keep at the utmost distance from pious chit-chat and from religious gossiping.

V. What is the fifth?

A. Beware of *desiring any thing but God*. Now you desire nothing else.

2. See below, p. 353 ff.
3. *Cf.* "Satan's Devices," *Sermons* (Sugden), II, 191 f.

Every other desire is driven out. See that none enter again. "Keep thyself pure"; let your eye remain single and your whole body shall be full of light [*cf.* Lk. 11:34]. Admit no desire of pleasing food or of any other pleasure of sense; no desire of pleasing the eye or imagination by any thing grand, or new, or beautiful; no desire of money, of praise, or esteem of happiness in any creature. You *may* bring these desires back, but you *need* not. You need feel them no more. O stand fast in the liberty wherewith Christ has made you free [*cf.* Gal. 5:1].

VI. What is the sixth?

A. Above all beware of *schism*, of making a rent in the Church of Christ. Beware of everything tending thereto. Beware of a divisive spirit. Shun whatever has the least aspect that way. Therefore say not, "I am of Paul or Apollos" — the very thing which occasioned the schism at Corinth which St. Paul so sharply reproves [*cf.* 1 Cor. 1:12]. Say not, "*this* is *my* preacher, the *best* preacher in England! Give me him and take the rest." All this tends to breed or foment division, to disunite those whom God has joined. Do not extol or run down any preacher, Mr. Maxfield in particular. Do not say, "What care I for Mr. Wesley's 'Rules'? Mr. Maxfield is sufficient to teach me." Do not exalt him above all other preachers, lest you hurt both him and the cause of God. On the other hand, do not bear hard upon him for some incoherency or inaccuracy of expression; no, nor even for some mistakes in judgment, were they really such.

Suffer not one thought of separating from your brethren whether their opinions agree with yours or not. Do not dream that any man sins in not believing *you*, in not taking *your word*, or that this or that *opinion* is essential to the work, and both must stand or fall together. Beware of impatience of contradiction. Do not condemn or think hardly of those who cannot see just as you see or who judge it their duty to contradict you, whether in a great thing or a small. So I fear some of us may have condemned Silas Told, Benj[amin] Smith, John Read, Mary Anson, Sar[ah] Clay, John Jones — perhaps Sar[ah] Crosby and John Hampson, too. And why? Because they contradicted what we affirmed. All this tends to division; and by every thing of this kind we are teaching them an evil lesson against ourselves.

O beware of touchiness, or testiness, not bearing to be spoken to, starting at the least word and flying from those who do not implicitly receive mine or Mr. Maxfield's sayings.

Expect contradiction and opposition, together with sufferings of various kinds. Consider, "To you it is given not only to believe but also to suffer for Christ." [4] *It is given?* God *gives* you this opposition or reproach. It is a fresh token of his love. And will you disown the giver or spurn his gift and count it a misfortune? Will you not rather say, "Father, the hour is come that thou shouldst be glorified [*cf.* Jn. 12:16; 13:31]. Now thou givest thy child to suffer something for thee. And the cup thou givest me, shall I not drink it?" Know that these things (far from being hindrances to the work of God or to your soul, unless through your own fault) are not only unavoidable in the course of providence but profitable, yea, necessary for you. Therefore receive them from God as a peculiar mark of his favour, with willingness, with thankfulness. Receive them from men with humility, meekness, yieldingness, gentleness, sweetness. And be free and open in acknowledging what has been amiss, either in your judgment or practice; not listening to "carnal reason," which will tell you: "This would hurt the cause of God." No. It will forward the cause of God and remove a great hindrance out of the way.

And beware of tempting others to separate from *you*. Give no offence which can possibly be avoided. See that your practice be in all things suitable to your profession, adorning the doctrine of God your Saviour. Be particularly careful in speaking of yourself. You may not indeed deny the work of God; but speak of it, when you are called thereto, in the most inoffensive manner possible. Avoid all magnificent, pompous words. Indeed, you need give it no general name, neither "perfection," "sanctification," "the second blessing" nor "the having attained." Rather speak of the particulars which God has wrought. You may say, "I then felt an unspeakable change. And since that time, I have not felt pride or anger or unbelief, nor any thing but a fulness of love to God and to all mankind." And answer any other plain question that is asked with modesty and simplicity.

I would add but one word more. If any of you should at any time fall from what you now are, do not deny, do not hide, do not disguise it at all, at the peril of your soul. At all events come as soon as possible to your leader, or to Mr. Maxfield, Morgan or me, and speak just what you feel. God will then enable us to speak a word in season. It shall be health to your soul. And he will soon lift up your head and cause the bones that have been broken to rejoice [*cf.* Ps. 51:8].

Suffer me to add that the propriety and utility of the above remarks will appear to a demonstration when we consider:

4. [Au.] Phil. 1:29.

1. That we have persons among us who *believe they shall never die.*

2. That we have persons among us who go from house to house *to persuade people to believe they are perfect when God hath not persuaded them.*

3. That we have those among us who believe God has given them "the gift of discerning spirits" [*cf.* 1 Cor. 12:10], and that indiscriminately, the good as well as the bad.

4. That there are several among us who believe they cannot err.

5. That we have not a few who believe it *impossible for them to sin and fall.*

6. That the Methodist preachers who cannot subscribe the above nostrums are represented as being "in the dark" and "leading the people in the dark these twenty years past," during which time God hath taken thousands of their children in the gospel to himself — who have gone off the stage triumphantly, though they knew nothing of these extravagancies.

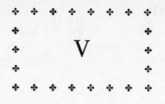

# CHURCH AND SACRAMENTS

*Editor's introduction.* Despite his own irregular position in the Church of England, Wesley seems never to have felt the need to amend the basic ecclesiology which he had developed at Epworth and Oxford, *before* the rise of the Methodist societies. He understood his own mission primarily as that of a minister extraordinary, called forth by God to help remedy the insufficiencies of the ordinary ministry of the established church. This made him something rather like the superior-general of an evangelical order within a regional division of the church catholic. His doctrines of church, ministry and sacraments have to be pieced together from scattered references throughout his writings; and here, as in the rest of his thought, we find a significant fusion of various elements in his Anglican heritage. For his understanding of the essential nature of the church, he was chiefly indebted to the sixteenth-century English reformers, notably Thomas Cranmer, John Jewel and Richard Hooker. For his sense of liturgy and worship, he owed much to the Nonjurors (*e.g.* George Hickes, John Kettlewell and Robert Nelson). For his views on ministerial order, however, he was largely dependent upon the "latitudinarians" — Edward Stillingfleet, John Tillotson, Gilbert Burnet (and the youthful *Enquiry* of Lord Peter King). Through these and other sources he was, of course, indirectly influenced by the Continental Protestant reformers; but there is very little direct influence explicitly acknowledged.

His publication in this theological domain consists of sermons and tracts, all having more to do with the practical issues of churchmanship than with its theological foundations. They include sermons on "The Means of Grace" (*Sermons* [Sugden], I, 238–60); "Of the Church";[1] "On Schism" (*Works*, VI, 401–10); "The Duty of Constant Communion";[2] "On Attending the Church Service" (*ibid.*, VII, 174–85);

1. See below, p. 308 ff.        2. See below, p. 332 ff.

"The Ministerial Office" (*ibid.*, 273–81); *On Baptism;*[3] *A Companion for the Altar* (1742)[4] and *Hymns on the Lord's Supper.*[5] To these one might add twelve collections of devotional material and fifty-two separate hymn collections by the brothers Wesley. In all this material the only distinctively Wesleyan accent is the insistence that the church is best defined *in action,* in her witness and mission, rather than by her form of polity. His stress on the church's subordination to Scripture, and her unity in Christ and the apostolic doctrine is, of course, a Protestant commonplace. His reliance on the paradigms of polity in the patristic church, his notion that the apostolic succession adheres in the continuity of apostolic teaching rather than that of apostolic persons, and his conviction that the episcopacy belongs to the good order rather than the essence of the church — all these had been clear, persistent themes in the Anglican tradition, first fully formulated by John Jewel in his sixteenth-century conflicts with the papists.[6]

Wesley's idea of the Methodist societies serving the Established Church even against the good will of her leaders was a distinctive adaptation of the pietistic patterns of the "religious societies" (*ecclesiolae in ecclesiam*) which Anthony Horneck had brought from Germany to England in 1661 and which had served as a refuge for "serious Christians," discontent with apathetic and nominal Christianity.[7] The Methodist notions of corporate Christian discipline were derived, at least in part, from Wesley's interest in the Roman Catholic religious orders — the Society of Jesus in particular. In the area of sacramental theology proper Wesley was prepared simply to borrow — from his father, his brother Charles, Daniel Brevint and others.

A limited selection from this wide and uneven mass is bound to be incomplete and arbitrary. The three texts in this section, however, are intended to serve as an introduction to the whole.

---

3. See below, p. 317.

4. An abridgment of Thomas a Kempis, *Imitation of Christ,* Bk. IV.

5. A composite volume, with a digest of Daniel Brevint, *The Christian Sacrament and Sacrifice* (1673; 3d ed., 1739), and a hundred and sixty-six eucharistic hymns by Charles Wesley and himself, published in 1745.

6. *Cf.* W. M. Southgate, *John Jewel and the Problem of Doctrinal Authority* (1962), chap. xii.

7. Horneck (1641–1697) was a German Lutheran who became preacher at the Savoy in 1670 and chaplain to William III in 1689. *Cf.* Josiah Woodward, *An Account of the Rise and Progress of the Religious Societies in the City of London,* 4th ed. (1712).

## Of the Church

*Editor's introduction.* This sermon, and its companion, "On Schism," were first published in *The Arminian Magazine* in 1786 (8–18, 71–75, and 238–44, 293–98, respectively). They then appeared in the final edition of *Sermons on Several Occasions* (1788), VI, 173–210. Both were written during the hubbub occasioned by Wesley's "ordinations" for America in 1784 and the subsequent ordinations of his British preachers, first for Scotland and Ireland and finally for England as well. These two sermons constitute his tacit apologia for these drastic breaches within Anglican polity. The first sermon defines the Church in such a way that Wesley's societies and his ordinations need not be adjudged as entailing "separation." The second defines schism in a manner plainly intended to exempt the Methodists from being taxed with it. Of especial interest in the sermon below is Wesley's explication of the Anglican Article XIX, from whence he took his title, "Of the Church." The copy text here is the 1788 edition, collated with that of 1786 and *Works*, VI, 392–401.

❖ ❖ ❖ ❖

I beseech you that ye walk worthy of the vocation wherewith ye are called, with all lowliness and meekness, with longsuffering, forbearing one another in love; endeavouring to keep the unity of the Spirit in the bond of peace. There is one body, and one Spirit, even as ye are called in one hope of your calling; one Lord, one faith, one baptism, one God and Father of all, who is above all, and through all, and in you all (Eph. 4:1–6).

1. How much do we almost continually hear about *the Church!* With many it is matter of daily conversation. And yet how few understand what they talk of! How few know what the term means! A more ambiguous word than this, the "church," is scarce to be found in the English language. It is sometimes taken for a building set apart for public worship; sometimes, for a congregation or body of people united together in the service of God. It is only in the latter sense that it is taken in the ensuing discourse.

2. It may be taken indifferently for any number of people, how small

or great soever. As, "where two or three are met together in his name" [cf. Mt. 18:20], there is Christ; so (to speak with St. Cyprian), "where two or three believers are met together, there is a church." [1] Thus it is that St. Paul, writing to Philemon, mentions "the church which is in his house" [cf. v. 2; Col. 4:15]; plainly signifying that even a Christian family may be termed a church.

3. Several of those whom God had "called out of" the world (so the original word properly signifies), uniting together in one congregation, formed a larger church: as the church at Jerusalem; that is, all those in Jerusalem whom God had so called. But considering how swiftly these were multiplied after the day of Pentecost, it cannot be supposed that they could continue to assemble in one place; especially as they had not then any large place, neither would they have been permitted to build one. In consequence, they must have divided themselves, even at Jerusalem, into several distinct congregations. In like manner, when St. Paul, several years after, wrote to the church in Rome (directing his letter "To all that are in Rome, called to be saints" [cf. Rom. 1:7]), it cannot be supposed that they had any one building capable of containing them all, but they were divided into several congregations, assembling in several parts of the city.

4. The first time that the apostle uses the word "church" is in his preface to the former Epistle to the Corinthians: "Paul, called to be an apostle of Jesus Christ, unto the Church of God which is at Corinth." The meaning of which expression is fixed by the following words: "To them that are sanctified in Christ Jesus; with all that, in every place" (not Corinth only — so it was a kind of circular letter) "call upon the name of Jesus Christ our Lord, both yours and ours." In the inscription of his second letter to the Corinthians, he speaks still more explicitly: "Unto the Church of God which is at Corinth, with all the saints that are in all Achaia." Here he plainly includes all the churches or Christian congregations which were in the whole province.

5. He frequently uses the word in the plural number. So, Gal. 1:2, "Paul an apostle, . . . unto the churches of Galatia" — that is, the Christian congregations dispersed throughout that country. In all these places (and abundantly more might be cited) the word "church" or "churches" means, not the buildings where the Christians assembled (as it frequently does in the English tongue), but the people that used to assemble there — one or more Christian congregations. But sometimes

1. Cf. St. Cyprian, *On the Unity of the Church*, chap. 12. *FC*, XXXVI, 107.

the word church is taken in Scripture in a still more extensive meaning, as including all the Christian congregations that are upon the face of the earth. And in this sense we understand it in our liturgy, when we say, "Let us pray for the whole state of Christ's Church militant here on earth." [2] In this sense it is unquestionably taken by St. Paul, in his exhortation to the elders of Ephesus: [3] "Take heed to the Church of God, which he hath purchased with his own blood." The church here, undoubtedly, means the catholic or universal Church; that is, all the Christians under heaven.

6. Who those are that are properly "the Church of God," the apostle shows at large, and that in the clearest and most decisive manner, in the passage above cited, wherein he likewise instructs all the members of the church how to "walk worthy of the vocation wherewith they are called."

7. Let us consider, first, who are properly "the Church of God"? What is the true meaning of that term? "The church at Ephesus," as the apostle himself explains it, means, "the saints," the holy persons, "that are in Ephesus" [cf. Eph. 1:1] and there assemble themselves together to worship God the Father and his Son Jesus Christ, whether they did this in one or (as we may probably suppose) in several places. But it is the church in general, the catholic or universal church, which the apostle here considers as "one body," comprehending not only the Christians "in the house of Philemon" or any one family, not only the Christians of one congregation, of one city, of one province, or nation, but all the persons upon the face of the earth who answer the character here given. The several particulars contained therein we may now more distinctly consider.

8. "There is one Spirit" who animates all these, all the living members of the Church of God. Some understand hereby the Holy Spirit himself, the fountain of all spiritual life. And it is certain, "If any man have not the Spirit of Christ, he is none of his" [Rom. 8:9]. Others understand it of those spiritual gifts and holy dispositions which are afterward mentioned.

9. "There is" (in all those that have received this Spirit) "one hope" — a hope full of immortality. They know to die is not to be lost; their prospect extends beyond the grave. They can cheerfully say, "Blessed be the God and Father of our Lord Jesus Christ, who, according to his

2. Cf. the Prayer for the Church in the Communion Office of the B.C.P. of 1662.
3. [Au.] Acts 20:28.

abundant mercy, hath begotten us again to a lively hope by the resurrection of Jesus Christ from the dead, to an inheritance incorruptible and undefiled and that fadeth not away" [1 Pet. 1:3-4].

10. "There is one Lord," who has now dominion over them; who has set up his kingdom in their hearts, and reigns over all those that are partakers of this hope [cf. 1 Cor. 9:10]. To obey him, to run the way of his commandments, is their glory and joy. And while they are doing this with a willing mind, they, as it were, "sit in heavenly places with Christ Jesus" [cf. Eph. 2:6].

11. "There is one faith," which is the free gift of God and is the ground of their hope. This is not barely the faith of a heathen: namely, a belief that "there is a God," and that he is gracious and just, and, consequently, "a rewarder of them that diligently seek him" [Heb. 11:6]. Neither is it barely the faith of a devil; though this goes much farther than the former; for the devil believes [cf. Jas. 2:19], and cannot but believe, all that is written both in the Old and New Testament[s] to be true. But it is the faith of St. Thomas, teaching him to say with holy boldness, "My Lord, and my God" [Jn. 20:28]! It is the faith which enables every true Christian believer to testify with St. Paul, "The life which I now live, I live by faith in the Son of God, who loved me, and gave himself for me" [cf. Gal. 2:20].

12. "There is one baptism," which is the outward sign our one Lord has been pleased to appoint of all that inward and spiritual grace which he is continually bestowing upon his Church. It is likewise a precious means whereby this faith and hope are given to those that diligently seek him. Some, indeed, have been inclined to interpret this in a figurative sense, as if it referred to that baptism of the Holy Ghost which the apostles received at the day of Pentecost, and which, in a lower degree, is given to all believers. But it is a stated rule in interpreting Scripture, never to depart from the plain, literal sense unless it implies an absurdity. And beside, if we thus understood it, it would be a needless repetition, as being included in, "There is one Spirit."

13. "There is one God and Father of all" that have the Spirit of adoption, which "crieth in their hearts, Abba, Father"; which "witnesseth" continually "with their spirits," that they are the children of God [cf. Rom. 8:15-16; Gal. 4:6], "who is above all" — the Most High, the Creator, the Sustainer, the Governor, of the whole universe — "and through all" — pervading all space, filling heaven and earth:

*Totam*
*Mens agitans molem, et magno se corpore miscens:* [4]

"And in you all" — in a peculiar manner living in you, that are one body, by one Spirit:

> Making your souls his loved abode,
> The temples of indwelling God.[5]

14. Here, then, is a clear, unexceptionable answer to that question, "What is the Church?" The catholic or universal Church is all the persons in the universe whom God hath so called out of the world as to entitle them to the preceding character — as to be "one body," united by "one Spirit," having "one faith, one hope, one baptism; one God and Father of all, who is above all, and through all, and in them all."

15. That part of this great body of the universal Church which inhabits any one kingdom or nation, we may properly term a "national" church, as the Church of France, the Church of England, the Church of Scotland. A smaller part of the universal Church are the Christians that inhabit one city or town, as the church of Ephesus and the rest of the seven churches mentioned in the Revelation. Two or three Christian believers united together are a church in the narrowest sense of the word. Such was the church in the house of Philemon, and that in the house of Nymphas, mentioned [in] Col. 4:15. A particular church may, therefore, consist of any number of members, whether two or three, or two or three millions. But still, whether they be larger or smaller, the same idea is to be preserved. They are one body and have one Spirit, one Lord, one hope, one faith, one baptism, one God and Father of all.

16. This account is exactly agreeable to the nineteenth Article of our Church, the Church of England (only the Article includes a little more than the apostle has expressed):

## OF THE CHURCH

The visible Church of Christ is a congregation of faithful men, in which the pure Word of God is preached, and the sacraments be duly administered.[6]

4. *Cf.* Vergil, *Aeneid*, Bk. VI, l. 726–27. Wesley has both garbled and misspelled the text, but the idea is clear: "The 'Mind' (*i.e.* the 'World-Soul') which pervades the whole, activates its mass and mingles with its mighty frame"; see also Alexander Pope, "Essay on Man," in *Works*, II (1764), p. 52, l. 265–69. See below, p. 390.

5. *Cf. Methodist Hymn Book* (1933), 280, St. 3.

6. Articles of Religion, XIX, B.C.P. Wesley omits one qualifying clause and also an entire sentence.

It may be observed that, at the same time our Thirty-nine Articles were compiled and published, a Latin translation of them was published by the same authority.[7] In this the words were *coetus credentium*, "a congregation of believers": plainly showing that by "faithful men," the compilers meant men endued with "living faith." This brings the Article to a still nearer agreement to the account given by the apostle.

But it may be doubted whether the Article speaks of a particular church, or of the Church universal. The title, "Of the Church," seems to have reference to the catholic Church, but the second clause of the Article mentions the particular churches of Jerusalem, Antioch, Alexandria, and Rome. Perhaps it was intended to take in both: so to define the universal Church as to keep in view the several particular churches of which it is composed.

17. These things being considered, it is easy to answer that question, "What is the Church of England?" It is that part (those members) of the universal Church who are inhabitants of England. The Church of England is that body of men in England in whom "there is one Spirit, one hope, one Lord, one faith"; which have "one baptism," and "one God and Father of all." This and this alone is the Church of England, according to the doctrine of the apostle.

18. But the definition of a church laid down in the Article includes not only this, but much more, by that remarkable addition: "In which the pure Word of God is preached, and the sacraments be duly administered." According to this definition, those congregations in which "the pure Word of God" (a strong expression) is not preached are no parts either of the Church of England or the Church catholic, as neither are those in which the sacraments are not duly administered.

19. I will not undertake to defend the accuracy of this definition. I dare not exclude from the Church catholic all those congregations in which any unscriptural doctrines which cannot be affirmed to be "the pure Word of God" are sometimes, yea, frequently preached; neither all those congregations in which the sacraments are not "duly administered." Certainly if these things are so, the Church of Rome is not so much as a part of the catholic Church, seeing therein neither is "the pure Word of God" preached, nor the sacraments "duly administered." Whoever they are

7. Cf. Philip Schaff, *Creeds of Christendom* (New York, 1882), III, 487–516; the original phrase is *coetus fidelium;* see also E. J. Bicknell, *A Theological Introduction to The Thirty-nine Articles of the Church of England*, 3d ed. (1955), 229. See below, p. 412 f.

that have "one Spirit, one hope, one Lord, one faith, one God and Father of all," I can easily bear with their holding wrong opinions, yea, and superstitious modes of worship. Nor would I, on these accounts, scruple still to include them within the pale of the catholic Church; neither would I have any objection to receive them, if they desired it, as members of the Church of England.

II. 20. We proceed now to the second point. What is it to "walk worthy of the vocation wherewith we are called?"

It should always be remembered that the word "walk," in the language of the apostle, is of a very extensive signification. It includes all our inward and outward motions, all our thoughts and words and actions. It takes in not only everything we do but everything we either speak or think. It is, therefore, no small thing "to walk," in this sense of the word, "worthy of the vocation wherewith we are called"; to think, speak, and act, in every instance, in a manner worthy of our Christian calling.

21. We are called to walk, first, "with all lowliness"; to have the mind in us which was also in Christ Jesus; not to think of ourselves more highly than we ought to think; to be little and poor and mean and vile in our own eyes; to know ourselves as also we are known by him to whom all hearts are open; [8] to be deeply sensible of our own unworthiness, of the universal depravity of our nature (in which dwelleth no good thing), prone to all evil, averse to all good, insomuch that we are not only sick but dead in trespasses and sins till God breathes upon the dry bones and creates life by the fruit of his lips [cf. Eph. 2:1; Ezek. 37:1-10; Is. 57:19]. And suppose this is done — suppose he has now quickened us, infusing life into our dead souls — yet how much of the carnal mind remains? How prone is our heart still to depart from the living God? What a tendency to sin remains in our heart, although we know our past sins are forgiven? And how much sin, in spite of all our endeavours, cleaves both to our words and actions! Who can be duly sensible how much remains in him of his natural enmity to God, or how far he is still alienated from God by the ignorance that is in him [cf. Eph. 4:18]?

22. Yea, suppose God has now thoroughly cleansed our heart, and scattered the last remains of sin; yet how can we be sensible enough of our own helplessness, our utter inability to all good, unless we are every hour, yea, every moment, endued with power from on high? Who is able to think one good thought, or to form one good desire, unless by that almighty power which worketh in us both to will and to do of his

8. Cf. B.C.P., "Collect for Purity," The Order for Holy Communion.

good pleasure [*cf.* Phil. 2:13]? We have need, even in this state of grace, to be thoroughly and continually penetrated with a sense of this. Otherwise we shall be in perpetual danger of robbing God of his honour, by glorying in something we have received, as though we had not received it.

23. When our inmost soul is thoroughly tinctured therewith, it remains that we be "clothed with humility" [*cf.* 1 Pet. 5:5]. The word used by St. Peter seems to imply that we be covered with it as with a surtout; that we be all humility, both within and without, tincturing all we think, speak and do. Let all our actions spring from this fountain, let all our words breathe this spirit; that all men may know we have been with Jesus and have learned of him to be lowly in heart.

24. And being taught of him who was meek as well as lowly in heart, we shall then be enabled to "walk with all meekness"; being taught of him who teacheth as never man taught, to be meek as well as lowly in heart [*cf.* Mt. 11:29]. This implies not only a power over anger, but over all violent and turbulent passions. It implies the having all our passions in due proportion, none of them either too strong or too weak, but all duly balanced with each other; all subordinate to reason, and reason directed by the Spirit of God. Let this equanimity govern your whole souls, that your thoughts may all flow in an even stream, and the uniform tenor of your words and actions be suitable thereto. In this patience you will then "possess your souls" [*cf.* Lk. 21:19], which are not our own while we are tossed by unruly passions. And by this all men may know that we are indeed followers of the meek and lowly Jesus.

25. Walk with all longsuffering. This is nearly related to meekness, but implies something more. It carries on the victory already gained over all your turbulent passions, notwithstanding all the powers of darkness, all the assaults of evil men or evil spirits. It is patiently triumphant over all opposition, and unmoved though all the waves and storms thereof go over you. Though provoked ever so often, it is still the same — quiet and unshaken — never being "overcome of evil" but overcoming evil with good [*cf.* Rom. 12:21].

26. The "forbearing one another in love" seems to mean, not only the not resenting anything and the not avenging yourselves, not only the not injuring, hurting, or grieving each other, either by word or deed; but also the bearing one another's burdens [*cf.* Gal. 6:2], yea, and lessening them by every means in our power. It implies the sympathizing with them in their sorrows, afflictions, and infirmities; the bearing them up when, without our help, they would be liable to sink under their burdens; the endeav-

ouring to lift their sinking heads and to strengthen their feeble knees [cf.
Is. 35:3; Heb. 12:12].

27. Lastly, the true members of the Church of Christ "endeavour," with
all possible diligence, with all care and pains, with unwearied patience
(and all will be little enough), "to keep the unity of the Spirit in the bond
of peace"; to preserve inviolate the same spirit of lowliness and meekness,
of long-suffering, mutual forbearance and love; and all these cemented and
knit together by that sacred tie: the peace of God filling the heart. Thus
only can we be, and continue, living members of that Church which is the
body of Christ.

28. Does it not clearly appear from this whole account why, in the
ancient creed commonly called the Apostles', we term it the universal or
catholic Church: "the holy catholic Church"? How many wonderful reasons have been found out for giving it this appellation? One learned man
informs us, "The Church is called holy, because Christ, the head of it, is
holy." Another eminent author affirms, "It is so called, because all its ordinances are designed to promote holiness"; and yet another: "because our
Lord *intended* that all the members of the Church should be holy." Nay,
the shortest and the plainest reason that can be given, and the only true
one, is: the Church is called "holy" because it is holy; because every member thereof is holy, though in different degrees, as he that called them is
holy. How clear is this! If the Church, as to the very essence of it, is a
body of believers, no man that is not a Christian believer can be a member
of it. If this whole body be animated by one Spirit and endued with one
faith and one hope of their calling, then he who has not that Spirit and
faith and hope is no member of this body. It follows that not only no
common swearer, no Sabbath-breaker, no drunkard, no whoremonger, no
thief, no liar, none that lives in any outward sin; but none that is under
the power of anger or pride, no lover of the world — in a word, none
that is dead to God — can be a member of his Church.[9]

29. Can anything then be more absurd than for men to cry out, "The
Church! The Church!" and to pretend to be very zealous for it and violent defenders of it while they themselves have neither part nor lot
therein, nor indeed know what the Church is? And yet the hand of God
is in this very thing! Even in this his wonderful wisdom appears, directing
their mistake to his own glory and causing "the earth to help the woman"
[cf. Rev. 12:16]. Imagining that they are members of it themselves, the

9. Here, as elsewhere, Wesley echoes what might be called Montanist views, without embarrassment or apology; cf. *Works*, VI, 328; X, 47–51; XI, 485.

men of the world frequently defend the Church. Otherwise the wolves that surround the little flock on every side would in a short time tear them in pieces. And for this very reason, it is not wise to provoke them more than is unavoidable. Even on this ground, let us, if it be possible, as much as lieth in us, live peaceably with all men [cf. Rom. 12:18]; especially as we know not how soon God may call them, too, out of the kingdom of Satan into the kingdom of his dear Son [cf. 1 Thess. 2:12].

30. In the meantime, let all those who are real members of the Church see that they walk holy and unblameable in all things. "Ye are the light of the world!" Ye are "a city set upon a hill, and cannot be hid." O "let your light shine before men!" Show them your faith by your works [cf. Mt. 5:14–16]. Let them see, by the whole tenor of your conversation, that your hope is all laid up above [cf. Col. 1:5]! Let all your words and actions evidence the spirit whereby you are animated! Above all things, let your love abound; let it extend to every child of man; let it overflow to every child of God. By this let all men know whose disciples ye are, because you love one another [cf. Jn. 15:12].

## On Baptism

*Editor's introduction.* Three years before John Wesley was born, a confirmation manual was published in London entitled *The Pious Communicant Rightly Prepared, or, a Discourse concerning the Blessed Sacrament, Wherein the Nature of It Is Described, Our Obligation to "Frequent Communion" Enforced, and Directions Given for Due Preparation for It, Behaviour at, and Profiting by It. With Prayers and Hymns Suited to the Several Parts of that Holy Office. To Which is Added, A Short Discourse of Baptism.* Its author was "Samuel Wesley, A.M., Chaplain to the Most Honorable Lord Marquess of Normanby and Rector of Epworth in the Diocese of Lincoln." Such importance as it had lay in its square-toed summary of what was already essentially commonplace in central Anglican sacramental theology and in its stubborn patience in dealing with any and all "objections." Otherwise, it was undistinguished and remained unnoticed. In 1756 John Wesley abridged the "short discourse on baptism" by more than half and published it as the sixth section of *A Preservative Against Unsettled Notions in Religion* (1758). He republished it in his *Works* (Pine), Vol. XIX, pp. 275–97. It appears in *Works*, Vol. X, pp. 188–201.

The obvious purpose of this "extract" was to re-enforce the wavering convictions of some of the Methodist people as to the validity of infant baptism and to re-emphasize the objectivity of divine grace in this sacrament. One ought, however, to compare this essay on baptism (with its mild allowance of the doctrine of baptismal regeneration) with the sermon on "The New Birth" (*Works*, VI, 65–76) where the stress falls heavily on conversion as a conscious adult experience of regeneration. The point is that Wesley held to both ideas.

The present text is based upon a holograph manuscript, now in the Methodist Archives in Epworth House, London — collated with the editions of 1758 and 1773. The reader who compares it with the others will notice that it differs both in its opening and concluding passages. To begin with, there is the bland claim made for "episcopal administrators" as "essential to Christian baptism" and an explicit repudiation of the "dipping of the Anabaptists." For a conclusion, Wesley adds an abridged version of his *Serious Thoughts on Godfathers and Godmothers* (1752). It is typical of Wesley that he freely rearranges and changes his material to suit the occasions in which it was to be used.

❖   ❖   ❖   ❖

Baptizing them in the name of the Father and of the Son and of the Holy Ghost (Mt. 28:19).

Before I begin to treat *of* baptism, I would just observe that three things are essential *to* Christian baptism:
1. An episcopal administrator;
2. The application of water;
3. That it be administered in the Name of the Trinity.

The two latter need no proof, and our Lord's commissioning his apostles only — and those who should derive their authority from them — to baptize, proves the former. And if so, it necessarily follows that the baptism — I ought to call it the "dipping" — of the Anabaptists, as much stress as ever they lay upon it, is no baptism at all. For they want episcopal administrators which are essential to Christian baptism. And indeed, this invalidates the baptism of all who have formally separated from our Church. But of this I need say no more to you. For there is no great danger of your employing any of them to baptize either yourselves or your children. I shall therefore immediately proceed to treat of baptism, in doing which I shall inquire:

*What* it is.

What *benefits* we receive by it.

Whether our Saviour designed it to remain *always* in his Church?

And, who are the proper subjects of it?

I. 1. What it is. It is the initiatory sacrament which enters us into covenant with God. It was instituted by Christ, who alone has power to institute a proper sacrament, a sign, seal, pledge and means of grace, perpetually obligatory on all Christians. We know not, indeed, the exact time of its institution, but we know it was long before our Lord's ascension. And it was instituted in the room of circumcision. For, as that was a sign and seal of God's covenant, so is this.

2. The "matter" of this sacrament is water, which, as it has a natural power of cleansing, is the more fit for this symbolical use. Baptism is performed by "washing," "dipping," or "sprinkling" the person, "in the Name of the Father, Son and Holy Ghost," who is thereby devoted to the ever-blessed Trinity. I say, by "washing, dipping, or sprinkling," because it is not determined in Scripture in which of these ways it shall be done, neither by any express *precept* nor by any such *example* as clearly proves it; nor by the *force* or *meaning* of the word "baptize."

3. That there is no express *precept*, all calm men allow. Neither is there any conclusive *example*. John's baptism in some things agreed with Christ's, in others differed from it. But it cannot be certainly proved from Scripture that even John's was performed by dipping. It is true, he baptized "in Enon, near Salim, where there was much water" [*cf.* Jn. 3:23]. But this might refer to breadth rather than depth, since a narrow place would not have been sufficient for so great a multitude. Nor can it be proved that the baptism of our Saviour, or that administered by his disciples, was by immersion. No, nor that of the eunuch baptized by Philip, though "they both went down to the water" [*cf.* Acts 8:38]. For that "going down" may relate to the chariot, and implies no determinate depth of water. It might be up to their knees; it might not be above their ankles.

4. And as nothing can be determined from Scripture precept or example, so neither from the force or meaning of the word. For the words baptize and baptism do not necessarily imply *dipping*, but are used in other senses in several places. Thus we read that the Jews "were all baptized in the cloud and in the sea"; [1] but they were not *plunged* in either.

1. [Au.] 1 Cor. 10:2.

They could therefore be only *sprinkled* by drops of the sea water and refreshing dews from the cloud — probably intimated in that, "Thou sentest a gracious rain upon thine inheritance and refreshedst it when it was weary." [2] Again, Christ said to his two disciples, "Ye shall be baptized with the baptism that I am baptized with." [3] But neither he nor they were *dipped* but only *sprinkled* or *washed* with their own blood. Again we read [4] of the baptisms (so it is in the original) of pots and cups, and tables or beds. Now, pots and cups are not necessarily dipped when they are washed. Nay, the Pharisees washed "the outsides" of them only [*cf.* Mt. 23:25]. And as for *tables* or *beds*, none will suppose they could be dipped. Here, then, the word "baptism" in its natural sense is not taken for dipping, but for washing or cleansing. And, that this is the true meaning of the word "baptize," is testified by the greatest scholars and most proper judges in this matter. 'Tis true, we read of being "buried with Christ in baptism" [*cf.* Rom. 6:4]. But nothing can be inferred from such a figurative expression. Nay, if it held exactly, it would make as much for "sprinkling" as for "plunging," since in burying, the body is not "plunged" through the substance of the earth, but rather earth is *poured* or *sprinkled* upon it.

5. And as there is no clear proof of *dipping* in Scripture, so there is very probable proof of the contrary. 'Tis highly probable the apostles themselves baptized great numbers, not by "dipping," but by "washing," "sprinkling" or "pouring" water. This clearly represented the cleansing from sin, which is figured by baptism. And the *quantity* of water used was not material, no more than the quantity of bread and wine in the Lord's Supper. The jailer "and all his house were baptized" in the prison, Cornelius with his friends (and so several households) at home [*cf.* Acts 16:33; 10:44–48]. Now, is it likely that all these had ponds or rivers in or near their houses sufficient to plunge them all? Every unprejudiced person must allow the contrary is far more probable. Again, three thousand at one time and five thousand at another, were converted and baptized by St. Peter at Jerusalem, where they had none but the gentle waters of Siloam; according to the observation of Mr. Fuller, "There were no water-mills in Jerusalem, because there was no stream large enough to drive them." [5]

2. [Au.] Ps. 68:9 [B.C.P.].          3. [Au.] Mk. 10:38[–39].
4. [Au.] Mk. 7:4.
5. *Cf.* Thomas Fuller, *A Pisgah-Sight of Palestine and the Confines Thereof* . . . (1650), Bk. III, chap. 6, 329, "Jerusalem was so far from boasting of any navigable river that it had no stream near, or about it, to drive any water mills."

The place, therefore, as well as the number, makes it highly probable that all these were baptized by sprinkling or pouring, and not by immersion. To sum up all, the manner of baptizing (whether by dipping or sprinkling) is not determined in Scripture. There is no *command* for one rather than the other. There is no *example* from which we can conclude for *dipping* rather than *sprinkling*. There are probable examples of both, and both are equally contained in the *natural meaning* of the word.

II. 1. What are the *benefits* we receive by baptism is the next point to be considered. And the first of these is the washing away the guilt of original sin by the application of the merits of Christ's death. That we are all born under the guilt of Adam's sin and that all sin deserves eternal misery was the unanimous sense of the ancient Church, as it is expressed in the ninth Article of our own.[6] And the Scripture plainly asserts that we were "shapen in inquity and in sin did our mother conceive us" [*cf.* Ps. 51:5, B.C.P.]; that "we were all by nature children of wrath [*cf.* Eph. 2:3] and dead in trespasses and sins"; that "in Adam all died"; that "by one man's disobedience all were made sinners" [*cf.* Rom. 5:19]; that "by one man sin entered into the world and death by sin, which came upon all men because all had sinned" [*cf.* Rom. 5:12]. This plainly includes infants, for they, too, *die*. Therefore, *they have sinned*, but not by actual sin, therefore by original — else what need have they of the death of Christ? Yea, "death reigned from Adam to Moses, even over those who had not sinned (actually) according to the similitude of Adam's transgression" [*cf.* Rom. 5:14]. This, which can relate to infants only, is a clear proof that the whole race of mankind are obnoxious both to the guilt and punishment of Adam's transgression. But "as by the offence of one, judgment came upon all men to condemnation; so by the righteousness of one, the free gift came upon all men, to justification of life" [*cf.* Rom. 5:18]. And the virtue of this free gift — the merits of Christ's life and death — are applied to us in baptism. "He gave himself for the church, that he might sanctify and cleanse it with the washing of water by the Word"[7] — namely, in baptism, the ordinary instrument of our justification. Agreeably to this, our Church prays in the baptismal office that the person to be baptized may be "washed and sanctified by the Holy Ghost, and, being delivered from God's wrath, receive remission of sins and enjoy the everlasting benediction of his heavenly washing";[8] and declares in the rubric

---

6. "Of Original or Birth Sin," B.C.P.         7. [Au.] Eph. 5:25, 26.
8. A conflation of two prayers in The Ministration of Publick Baptism . . . , B.C.P. (1662), sec. 375–76.

at the end of the office, "It is certain, by God's Word, that children who are baptized, dying before they commit actual sin, are saved" [B.C.P., 388]. And this is agreeable to the unanimous judgment of all the ancient Fathers.

2. By baptism we enter into covenant with God, into that "everlasting covenant" which "he hath commanded for ever": [9] that new covenant which he promised to make with the spiritual Israel, even to "give them a new heart and a new spirit, to sprinkle clean water upon them" [cf. Ez. 36:26, 25] (of which the baptismal is only a figure) "and to remember their sins and iniquities no more" — in a word, "to be their God," as he promised to Abraham in the evangelical covenant which he made with him and all his spiritual offspring.[10] And as circumcision was then the way of entering into this covenant, so baptism is now, which is therefore styled by the apostle (so many good interpreters render his words), "the stipulation, contract, or covenant of a good conscience with God" [cf. 1 Pet. 3:21].

3. By baptism we are admitted into the Church and consequently made members of Christ its Head. As the Jews were admitted into the Church by circumcision, so are the Christians by baptism. "For as many as are baptized into Christ," in his Name, have thereby "put on Christ" [11] — that is, are mystically "united to Christ" and made *one* with him. For "by one Spirit we are all baptized into one body" [12] — namely, "the Church, the body of Christ." [13] From which spiritual, vital union with him proceeds the influence of his grace on those that are baptized; as from our union with the Church, a share in all its privileges and in all the promises Christ has made to it.

4. By baptism, we who were "by nature children of wrath" are made the children of God. And this regeneration which our Church in so many places ascribes to baptism is more than barely being admitted into the Church, though commonly connected therewith. Being "grafted into the body of Christ's Church, we are made the children of God by adoption and grace" [B.C.P., 398–99]. This is grounded on the plain words of our Lord: [14] "Except a man be born again of water and of the Spirit, he cannot enter into the kingdom of God." By *water*, then, as a means (the water of baptism) we are regenerated or born again. Whence it is also called by the apostle, "the washing of regeneration" [cf. Tit. 3:5]. Our Church therefore ascribes no greater virtue to baptism than Christ

9. [Au.] Ps. 109:11.　　10. [Au.] Gen. 17:7, 8.　　11. [Au.] Gal. 3:27.
12. [Au.] 1 Cor. 12:13.　　13. [Au.] Eph. 4:12.　　14. [Au.] Jn. 3:5.

himself has done. Nor does she ascribe it to the *outward* washing, but to the *inward grace* which, added thereto, makes it a sacrament. Herein a principle of grace is infused which will not be wholly taken away unless we quench the Holy Spirit of God by long-continued wickedness.

5. In consequence of our being made children of God, we are heirs of the kingdom of heaven. "If children" (as the apostle observes), "then heirs, heirs with God and joint-heirs with Christ" [Rom. 8:17]. Herein we receive a title to, and an earnest of, "a kingdom which cannot be moved" [Heb. 12:28]. *Baptism doth now save us* if we live answerable thereto — if we repent, believe, and obey the gospel — supposing this, as it admits us into the Church here, so into glory hereafter.

III. 1. But did our Saviour design this should remain *always* in his Church? This is the third thing we are to consider. And this may be dispatched in a few words, since there can be no reasonable doubt but it was intended to last as long as the Church into which it is the appointed means of entering. In the *ordinary* way, there is no other means of entering into the Church or into heaven.

2. In all ages, the outward baptism is a means of the *inward*, as outward circumcision was of the circumcision of the heart. Nor would it have availed [15] to say, "I have the inward circumcision and therefore do not need the outward." Whoever had not the outward too, that soul was to be cut off from his people. He had despised, he had broken, God's everlasting covenant by despising the seal of it.[16] Now, the seal of circumcision was to last among the Jews as long as the law lasted to which it obliged them. By plain parity of reason, baptism, which came in its room, must last among Christians as long as the gospel covenant into which it admits and whereunto it obliges all nations.

3. This appears also from the original commission which our Lord gave to his apostles: "Go, disciple all nations, baptizing them in the Name of the Father, of the Son and of the Holy Ghost; teaching them. . . . And lo! I am with you always, even unto the end of the world" [Mt. 28:19-20]. Now, as long as this commission lasted, as long as Christ promised to be with them in the execution of it, so long doubtless were they to execute it, and to baptize as well as to teach. But Christ hath promised to be "with them," that is, by his Spirit in their successors — to the end of the world. So long, therefore, without dispute, it was his design that baptism should remain in the Church.

15. Both the 1758 and 1773 editions insert "a Jew" here.
16. [Au.] Gen. 17:14.

IV. 1. But the grand question is, who are the proper subjects of baptism? Grown persons only, or infants also? In order to answer this fully I shall, first, lay down the grounds of infant baptism, taken from Scripture, reason and primitive universal practice, and, secondly, answer the objections against it.

2. As to the grounds of it: if infants are guilty of original sin, then they are proper subjects of baptism, seeing [that], in the ordinary way, they cannot be saved unless this be washed away by baptism. It has been already proved that this original stain cleaves to every child of man and that hereby they are children of wrath and liable to eternal damnation. It is true, the second Adam has found a remedy for the disease which came upon all by the offence of the first. But the benefit of this is to be received through the means which he hath appointed: through baptism in particular, which is the *ordinary* means he hath appointed for that purpose and to which God hath tied *us*, though he may not have tied *himself*. Indeed, where it cannot be had, the case is different, but extraordinary cases do not make void a standing rule. This therefore is our first ground. *Infants* need to be washed from original sin; therefore they are proper subjects of baptism.

3. Secondly, if infants are capable of making a covenant, and were and still are under the evangelical covenant, then they have a right to baptism which is the entering seal thereof. But infants are capable of making a covenant, and were and still are under the evangelical covenant.

The custom of nations and common reason of mankind prove that infants may enter into a covenant and may be obliged by compacts made by others in their name and receive advantage by them. But we have stronger proof than this, even God's own word: [17] "Ye stand this day all of you before the Lord, your captains, with all the men of Israel, your little ones, your wives and the stranger — that thou shouldest enter into covenant with the Lord thy God." Now, God would never have made a covenant with "little ones" if they had not been capable of it. 'Tis not said "children" only, but "little children," the Hebrew word properly signifying infants. And these may be still, as they were of old, obliged to perform in aftertime what they are not capable of performing at the time of their entering into that obligation.

4. The infants of believers, the true children of faithful Abraham, always were under the gospel covenant. They were included in it, they had a right to it and to the seal of it, as an infant heir has a right to his estate

17. [Au.] Deut. 29:10–12.

though he cannot yet have actual possession. The covenant with Abraham was a gospel covenant — the condition being the same, namely faith, which the apostle observes was "imputed unto him for righteousness" [*cf.* Rom. 4:22]. The inseparable fruit of this faith was obedience: for by faith he left his country and offered his son. The benefits were the same, for God promised, "I will be thy God, and the God of thy seed after thee." And he can promise no more to any creature, for this includes all blessings, temporal and eternal. The Mediator is the same, for it was "in his seed" — that is, in Christ [18] — that "all nations" were to "be blessed." On which very account the apostle says, "The gospel was preached unto Abraham." [19] Now, the same promise that was made to him, the same covenant that was made with him, was made "with his children after him." [20] And upon that account it is called "an everlasting covenant." In this covenant children were also obliged to what they knew not: to the same faith and obedience with Abraham. And so they are still, as they are still equally entitled to all the benefits and promises of it.

5. Circumcision was then the seal of the covenant, which is itself therefore figuratively termed "the covenant." [21] Hereby the children of those who professed the true religion were then admitted into it and obliged to the conditions of it and, "when the law was added," to the observance of that also. And when the old seal of circumcision was taken off, this of baptism was added in its room, our Lord appointing one positive institution to succeed another. A new seal was set to Abraham's covenant. The seals differed, but the deed was the same; only that part was struck off which was political or ceremonial. That baptism came in the room of circumcision appears as well from the clear reason of the thing as from the apostle's argument, where after "circumcision," he mentions "baptism," as that wherein God had "forgiven us our trespasses" — to which he adds, the "blotting out the hand-writing of ordinances" [*cf.* Col. 2:14], plainly relating to circumcision and other Jewish rites, which as fairly implies that baptism came in the room of circumcision, as our Saviour's styling the other sacrament "the Passover" [22] shows that it was instituted in the place of it. Nor is it any proof that baptism did not succeed circumcision because it differs in some *circumstances*, any more than it proves the Lord's Supper did not succeed the Passover because in several circumstances it differs from it. This then is a second ground. Infants are capable

18. [Au.] Gen. 22:18; Gal. 3:16.          19. [Au.] Gal. 3:8.
20. [Au.] Gen. 17:7; Gal. 3:7.            21. [Au.] Acts 7:8.
22. [Au.] Col. 2:11–13; Lk. 22:15.

of entering into covenant with God. As they always were, so they still are, under the evangelical covenant. Therefore, they have a right to baptism, which is now the entering seal thereof.

6. Thirdly, if infants ought to "come to Christ," if they are capable of admission into the Church of God, and consequently of solemn, sacramental dedication to him, then they are proper subjects of baptism. But infants are capable of coming to Christ, of admission into the Church and solemn dedication to God.

That infants ought to "come to Christ" appears from his own words: "They brought little children to Christ and the disciples rebuked them. And Jesus said, 'Suffer little children to come unto me and forbid them not; for of such is the kingdom of heaven.' " [23] St. Luke expresses it still more strongly: [24] "They brought unto him even *infants* that he might touch them." These *children* were so *little* that they were *brought* to him. Yet he says, "Suffer them to *come unto me*": So little, that he "took them up in his arms"; yet he rebukes those who would have hindered their *coming* to him. And his command respected the future as well as the present. Therefore his disciples or ministers are still to *suffer* infants *to come* — that is, to be *brought* "unto Christ." But they cannot now "come to him" unless by being "brought" into the Church, which cannot be but by baptism. Yea, and "of such," says our Lord, "is the kingdom of heaven." Not of such only as were like these infants, for if they themselves were not fit to be subjects of that kingdom, how could others be so, because they were like them? Infants, therefore, are capable of being admitted into the Church and have a right thereto. Even under the Old Testament they were admitted into it by circumcision. And can we suppose they are in a worse condition under the gospel than they were under the law and that our Lord would take away any privileges which they then enjoyed? Would he not rather make additions to them? This, then, is a third ground. Infants ought to "come to Christ" and no man ought to *forbid* them. They are capable of admission into the Church of God. Therefore, they are proper subjects of baptism.

7. Fourthly, if the apostles baptized infants, then are they proper subjects of baptism. But the apostles baptized infants, as is plain from the following consideration. The Jews constantly *baptized* as well as circumcised all infant proselytes. Our Lord, therefore, commanding his apostles to *proselyte*, or "disciple," all nations by baptizing them, and to receive infants as well as others — they must needs baptize the children also.

That the Jews admitted proselytes by baptism as well as by circumcision, even whole families together, parents and children, we have the unanimous testimony of their most ancient, learned and authentic writers. The males they received by baptism and circumcision; the women by baptism only. Consequently, the apostles, unless our Lord had expressly forbidden it, would of course do the same thing.

Indeed, the consequence would hold from circumcision only. For if it was the custom of the Jews, when they gathered proselytes out of all nations, to admit children into the church by circumcision though they could not actually believe the law or obey it, then the apostles, making proselytes to Christianity by baptism, could never think of excluding children whom the Jews always admitted (the reason for their admission being the same) unless our Lord had expressly forbidden it. It follows the apostles baptized infants. Therefore, they are proper subjects of baptism.

8. If it be objected, "There is no express mention in Scripture of any infants whom the apostles baptized," I would ask, "Suppose no mention had been made in the Acts of those two women baptized by the apostles, yet might we not fairly conclude that when so many thousands, so many entire households were baptized, women were not excluded, especially since it was the known custom of the Jews to baptize them?" The same holds of children; nay, more strongly on the account of circumcision. Three thousand were baptized by the apostles in one day and five thousand in another. And can it be reasonably supposed that there were no children among such vast numbers? Again, the apostles baptized many families; nay, we hardly read of one master of a family who was converted and baptized but his whole family (as was before the custom among the Jews) were baptized with him. Thus the "jailer's household, he and all his: the household of Gaius, of Stephanus, of Crispus" [cf. Acts 16:33; 1 Cor. 1:14–16]. And can we suppose that in all these households — which we read were, without exception, baptized — there should not be so much as one child or infant? But to go one step further, St. Peter says to the multitude,[25] "Repent and be baptized, every one of you, for the remission of sins — for the promise is to you and to your children." Indeed, the answer is made directly to those who asked, "What shall we do?" But it reaches farther than to those who asked the question. And though children could not actually *repent*, yet they might be baptized. And that they are included appears (1) because the apostle addresses to *every one* of them, and in every one, children must be contained; (2) they are expressly mentioned, The "promise is to you and to your children."

9. Lastly, if to baptize infants has been the general practice of the

25. [Au.] Acts 2:38, 39.

Christian Church in all places and in all ages, then this must have been the practice of the apostles, and consequently, the mind of Christ. But to baptize infants has been the general practice of the Christian Church in all places and in all ages. Of this we have unexceptionable witnesses: St. Austin for the Latin Church (who flourished before the year 400) and Origen for the Greek (born in the second century), both declaring not only that the whole Church of Christ did then baptize infants, but likewise that they received this practice from the apostles themselves.[26] St. Cyprian likewise is express for it, and a whole council with him.[27] If need were, we might cite likewise Athanasius, Chrysostom and a cloud of witnesses. Nor is there *one instance* to be found in all antiquity of any orthodox Christian who denied baptism to children when brought to be baptized, nor any one of the fathers or ancient writers for the first eight hundred years at least, who held it unlawful. And that it has been the practice of all regular churches ever since is clear and manifest. Not only our own ancestors when first converted to Christianity, not only all the European churches, but the African, too, and the Asiatic, even those of St. Thomas in the Indies, do and ever did baptize their children. The fact being thus cleared that infant baptism has been the general practice of the Christian Church in all places and in all ages, that it has continued without interruption in the Church of God for above seventeen hundred years, we may safely conclude, it was handed down from the apostles, who best knew the mind of Christ.

10. To sum up the evidence. If outward baptism be generally, in an *ordinary* way, necessary to salvation; and infants may be saved as well as adults, nor ought we to neglect any means of saving them, if our Lord commands such to *come*, to be *brought* unto him, and declares, "of such is the kingdom of heaven"; if infants are capable of making a covenant or having a covenant made for them by others, being included in Abraham's covenant (which was a covenant of faith, an evangelical covenant), and never excluded by Christ; if they have a right to be members of the church and were accordingly members of the Jewish; if, suppose, our Lord had designed to exclude them from baptism, he must have expressly

26. [Au.] Augustin, *De Genesi ad Litteram* I, x, 23. [Ed.] But *cf. PL*, XXXIV, Bk. X, sec. xi, #18 (415–16).

[Au.] Origen, *In Rom.* vi. [Ed.] But *cf. In Epist. ad Roman.*, chap. V, 8–9, in *PG*, XIV (1038–45).

27. [Au.] Epist. ad Fidum. [Ed.] *Cf.* St. Cyprian, Epistle LVIII, "To Fidus," in *ANF*, V, 353–54; see also Epistles LXX–LXXII, pp. 377–86, for references to the Councils of Carthage, A.D. 255, 256.

forbidden his apostles to baptize them (which none dares to affirm he did), since otherwise they would do it of course, according to the universal practice of their nation; if it is highly probable they did so, even from the letter of Scripture, because they frequently baptized whole households, and it would be strange if there were no children among them; if the whole Church of Christ, for seventeen hundred years together, baptized infants and were never opposed till the last century but one by some not very holy men in Germany;[28] lastly, if there are such inestimable benefits conferred in baptism — the washing away the guilt of original sin,[29] the engrafting us into Christ by making us members of his Church and thereby giving us a right to all the blessings of the gospel — it follows that infants may, yea, ought to be baptized and that none ought to hinder them.

[V.] I am, in the last place, to answer those objections which are commonly brought against infant baptism.

1. The chief of these is, "Our Lord said to his apostles,[30] 'Go and teach all nations, baptizing them in the name of the Father, the Son, and the Holy Ghost.' Here Christ himself put *teaching* before *baptizing*. Therefore infants, being incapable of being *taught*, are incapable of being *baptized*."

I answer: (1) The order of *words* in Scripture is no certain rule for the order of *things*. We read in St. Mark 1:4, "John baptized in the wilderness and preached the baptism of repentance"; and verse 5, "They were baptized of him in Jordan, confessing their sins." Now, either the order of words in Scripture does not always imply the same order of things or it follows that John baptized before his hearers either "confessed" or "repented." But, (2) the words are manifestly mistranslated. For if we read, "Go and teach all nations, baptizing them — teaching them to observe all things," it makes plain tautology: vain and senseless repetition. It ought to be translated (which is the literal meaning of the words), "Go and make disciples of all nations, by baptizing them." That infants are capable of being made proselytes or disciples has been already proved. Therefore this text, rightly translated, is no valid objection against infant baptism.

2. Their next objection is, "The Scripture says, 'Repent and be baptized; believe and be baptized.' Therefore, repentance and faith ought to

28. *The Pious Communicant* adds: "far from being of the best characters."
29. *The Pious Communicant* adds: "and weakening the power of it."
30. [Au.] Mt. 28:19.

go before baptism. But infants are incapable of these; therefore, they are incapable of baptism."

I answer: Repentance and faith were to go before circumcision as well as before baptism. Therefore, if this argument held, it would prove just as well that infants were incapable of circumcision. But we know God himself determined the contrary, commanding them to be circumcised at eight days old. Now, if infants were capable of being circumcised, notwithstanding that repentance and faith were to go before circumcision in grown persons, they are just as capable of being baptized, nothwithstanding that repentance and faith are, in grown persons, to go before baptism. This objection, therefore, is of no force, for it is as strong against circumcision of infants as infant baptism.

3. It is objected, thirdly, "There is no command for it in Scripture. Now God was angry with his own people because they did that which, he said, 'I commanded them not.' [31] One plain text would end all the dispute."

I answer, (1) We have reason to fear it would not. It is as positively *commanded* in a very *plain text* of Scripture that we should "teach and admonish one another with psalms and hymns and spiritual songs, singing to the Lord with grace in our hearts," [32] as it is to honour our father and mother. But does this put an end to all dispute? Do not these very persons absolutely refuse to do it, notwithstanding a plain text, an express command? [33]

I answer, (2) They themselves practice what there is neither *express command* nor clear example for in Scripture. They have no *express command* for baptizing women. They say, indeed, "Women are implied in 'all nations.' " They are, and so are infants, too; but the command is not *express* for either. And for admitting women to the Lord's Supper, they have neither express command nor clear example. Yet they do it continually, without either one or the other. And they are justified therein by the plain reason of the thing. This also justifies us in baptizing infants, though without *express command* or clear example.

If it be said, "But there is a *command*,[34] 'Let a man, ἄνθρωπος, examine himself, and so let him eat of that bread' — the word 'man' in the original signifying indifferently either men or women": I grant it does in other

---

31. [Au.] Jer. 7:31.          32. [Au.] Eph. 5:19.

33. A reference to the aversion of the radical Protestants to conventional church music.

34. [Au.] 1 Cor. 11:28.

places, but here the word "himself," immediately following, confines it to men only. "But women are implied in it, though not expressed." Certainly, and so are infants in "all nations."

"But we have Scripture *example* for it, for it is said in the Acts [1:14], 'The apostles continued in prayer and supplication with the women.'" True; in prayer and supplication, but it is not said "in communicating." Nor have we one clear example of it in the Bible.

Since, then, they admit women to the Communion without any *express command* or *example*, but only by consequence from Scripture, they can never show reason why infants should not be admitted to baptism, when there are so many Scriptures which, by fair consequence, show they have a right to it and are capable of it.

As for the texts wherein God reproves his people for doing "what he commanded them not," that phrase evidently means what he had forbidden, particularly in that passage of Jeremiah. The whole verse is, "They have built the high places of Tophet to burn their sons and their daughters in the fire, which I commanded them not." Now, God had expressly forbidden them to do this, and that on pain of death. But surely there is a difference between the Jews offering theirs sons and daughters to devils and Christians offering theirs to God [*cf.* Jer. 7:31].

On the whole, therefore, it is not only lawful and innocent, but meet, right and our bounden duty, in conformity to the uninterrupted practice of the whole Church of Christ from the earliest ages, to consecrate our children to God by baptism, as the Jewish church were commanded to do by circumcision.

Having finished what I had to say with respect to baptism, I think it requisite, because you really need it, to add a few words more; and I wish all of you would give diligent heed to what shall be spoken and remember it as long as you live.

[In the holograph, this paragraph ends on a page in the manuscript which is also the title page to Bengel's *Disputatio Philosophico-Theologico,* . . . copied out in longhand. This is followed by six pages of Bengel's "Prologue." Then, without any title or heading, the discussion of baptism is resumed:]

In the ancient Church, when baptism was administered, there were usually two or more *sponsors* (so Tertullian calls them, an hundred years after the death of St. John) for every person to be baptized. As these were *witnesses,* before God and the Church, of the solemn engagement those persons then entered into, so they *undertook* (as the very word implies) to watch over those souls in a peculiar manner, to instruct, admonish, exhort and build them up in "the faith once for all delivered to the saints" [Jude 3]. These were considered as a kind of spiritual parents to the baptized, whether they were infants or at man's estate, and were expected to supply whatever spiritual helps were wanting, either through the death or neglect of natural parents.[35]


## The Duty of Constant Communion


*Editor's introduction.* It goes with Wesley's role in the Revival that he had scant interest in the speculative issues of sacramental doctrine and that he produced nothing distinctive in this domain of doctrine. This was not because of any indifference on his part or the lack of a stable perspective. On the contrary, it is just here that we may see yet once again Wesley's unique conception of his movement as an evangelical order within a catholic Church. It was his plain intention that his followers should depend on the Church, not only for the sacraments themselves but also for their doctrinal interpretation. He deliberately designed the Methodist preaching services so that they would not be taken as substitutes for Holy Communion in the parish church, and he expressly forbade their being scheduled in direct competition with stated church hours. He gives no evidence of strain in maintaining throughout his subsequent ministry the view of Holy Communion which he had formed at Oxford in the Holy Club. Moreover, since he was never challenged on this particular point, he felt no compulsion to do more than verify the central Anglican tradition with respect to "the means of grace."

As in the case of baptism (see above, pp. 317–32), so also for the Holy Communion, he was content to borrow and abridge the works of others, and was uncommonly fortunate in his choice of sources. In 1745 he published *Hymns on the Lord's Supper*, which contained, as preface, a digest of Daniel Brevint, *The Christian Sacrament and Sacrifice* (1673; 3d ed., 1739), together with an incomparable collection of a hundred and sixty-six of his and his brother's hymns (*cf.* the latest critical edition by J.

35. Cf. *Serious Thoughts on Godfathers and Godmothers* in *Works* (Pine), XIX, 335–40, and *Works*, X, 506–09, for the remainder of this peroration to the treatise *On Baptism*. In the manuscript the text of the *Serious Thoughts* is reduced by a third and there are the usual variations in phrasing and punctuation.

Ernest Rattenbury, *Eucharistic Hymns of John and Charles Wesley* [1948]).

This composite volume reflects the Anglican middle way between an extreme eucharistic realism (denounced in Articles XXVIII and XXIX, B.C.P.; *cf.* Edmund Gibson, *Codex Iuris Ecclesiastici Anglicani* [1713], I, 477, 464), and its allegoristic opposite. Like Richard Hooker and Jeremy Taylor and Daniel Brevint before them, the Wesleys conceived of sacramental grace as God's love in action in the lives of faithful men at worship. The Lord's Supper is the paradigm of *all* "the means of grace" — the chief actual means of actual grace and, as such, literally indispensable in the Christian life.

It is both interesting and puzzling to note that, whereas Wesley abridged and used his father's *A Short Discourse of Baptism*, in *The Pious Communicant Rightly Prepared* (see above, p. 317 f.), he seems to have ignored his long *Discourse concerning the Blessed Sacrament, Wherein the Nature of It Is Described, Our Obligation to "Frequent Communion" Enforced, and Directions Given for Due Preparation for It, Behaviour at, and Profiting by It.* This "discourse" was clearly the main item in *The Pious Communicant* (184 pages) and, as far as doctrinal substance is concerned (or even motifs and accents), might have served Wesley as well as Brevint did. This present sermon is indebted to the elder Wesley's *Discourse* (*e.g.* chap. 2: "Of the perpetual obligation that lies on adult Christians to communicate and even to frequent Communion, and to the pattern of dealing with various 'objections' "). The son replaces the father's conventional phrase "*frequent* Communion" with *constant*, and speaks sharply against the older usage. One might surmise that, since there is very little in the *Discourse* that is original and since there was no agitation amongst the Methodists concerning eucharistic grace, John Wesley felt that Brevint would suffice for the doctrinal guidance of his people.

But, on the side of the *practical* implications of his sacramental doctrine, Wesley found both opposition and misunderstanding. There were those who denied the necessity of any *means* of grace, on the ground of the all-sufficiency of *faith*. There were those who much preferred the vitality of the Methodist preaching services to formal liturgy in the churches. Still others pleaded the awesome danger of communicating unworthily and stressed the need for adequate preparation before receiving Communion. To these, Wesley replied in a trio of sermons. The first published was "The Means of Grace" (*Sermons* [Sugden], I, 237–62) in which he stressed the positive value of "an outward sign of inward grace and a means whereby we receive the same." In Sermon CIV, "On Attending the Church Service" (*Works*, VII, 174–85) he explains the different roles of the Societies and the Church. In the text here printed, he expounds the theme of Christian discipline in worship as well as in the rest of one's life.

In the *Works* (VII, 147–57) this essay appears as Sermon CI, having been first published in *The Arminian Magazine* for 1787 (229–36; 290–95), with an annotation that it had been written in Oxford, February 19, 1732 (*i.e.* when he was a tutor in Lincoln College). It also appears in Wesley's last edition of *Sermons on Several Occasions* (1788), Vol. VIII, pp. 133–52 — which has been taken here as the basic copy text.

As he explains in his prefatory note, this sermon had been prepared originally for his students at Lincoln College, and evidently had served as a discussion-piece in their tutorial sessions. The fact that in 1787 Wesley would reach back into his files and publish a fifty-five-year-old sermon is significant. Among other things, it was his way of reasserting his original relationship with the Church of England, despite the drastic alterations in that relationship in the interim. Many Methodists were adopting the Puritan notions of infrequent celebration. Excuses for nonattendance at parish Communions were gaining the force of conscientious objection. This was the situation in which Wesley returned to the arguments and exhortations that he had developed, in another age and setting, to bestir the wills of the Oxford undergraduates to Eucharistic obedience.

There is something vividly characteristic in the aged revivalist's concern that his people should redress the imbalance between their fervor for "the Word rightly preached" and their lessened zeal for "the sacraments duly administered." In his understanding of the nature of grace and the means of grace, Word and sacraments are dynamically integrated. This sermon is, therefore, yet another instance of the continuity and balance of Wesley's evangelical catholicism.

❖   ❖   ❖   ❖

"Do this in remembrance of me" (Luke 22:19).

*The following discourse was written above five-and-fifty years ago, for the use of my pupils at Oxford. I have added very little, but retrenched much; as I then used more words than I do now. But, I thank God, I have not yet seen cause to alter my sentiments in any point which is therein delivered.* [Wesley's Preface to the Reader.]

It is no wonder that men who have no fear of God should never think of doing this — but it is strange that it should be neglected by any that do fear God and desire to save their souls. And yet nothing is more common. One reason why many neglect it is, they are so much afraid of "eating and drinking unworthily" [1 Cor. 11:29], that they never think how much greater the danger is when they do not eat or drink it at all.[1] That I may do what I can to bring these well-meaning men to a more just way of thinking, I shall,

First, show that it is the duty of every Christian to receive the Lord's Supper as often as he can; and, secondly, answer some objections.

I. I am to show that it is the duty of every Christian to receive the Lord's Supper as often as he can.

1. The first reason why it is the duty of every Christian so to do is because it is a plain command of Christ. That this is his command appears from the words of the text — "Do this in remembrance of me" — by which, as the apostles were obliged to bless, break, and give the bread to all that joined with them in these holy things, so were all Christians obliged to receive those signs of Christ's body and blood. Here, therefore, the bread and wine are commanded to be received in remembrance of his death, to the end of the world. Observe, too, that this command was given by our Lord when he was just laying down his life for our sakes. They are, therefore, as it were, his dying words to all his followers.

2. A second reason why every Christian should do this as often as he can is because the benefits of doing it are so great to all that do it in obedience to him — namely, the forgiveness of our past sins, the present strengthening and refreshing of our souls. In this world we are never free from temptations. Whatever way of life we are in, whatever our condition be, whether we are sick or well, in trouble or at ease, the enemies of our souls are watching to lead us into sin. And too often they prevail over us. Now, when we are convinced of having sinned against God, what surer way have we of procuring pardon from him than the "showing forth the Lord's death" [cf. 1 Cor. 11:26], and beseeching him, for the sake of his Son's sufferings, to blot out all our sins?

3. The grace of God given herein confirms to us the pardon of our sins, and enables us [2] to leave them. As our bodies are strengthened by bread

1. Cf. the "Minister's Warning," in B.C.P. (1662), sec. 344. Wesley and his students obviously had before them the Order for the Administration of the Lord's Supper, or Holy Communion, for examination and comment.

2. Edition of 1787 reads "by enabling us."

and wine, so are our souls by these tokens of the body and the blood of Christ. This is the food of our souls: this gives strength to perform our duty and leads us on to perfection. If, therefore, we have any regard for the plain command of Christ, if we desire the pardon of our sins, if we wish for strength to believe, to love and obey God, then we should neglect no opportunity of receiving the Lord's Supper. Then we must never turn our backs on the feast which our Lord has prepared for us. We must neglect no occasion which the good providence of God affords us for this purpose. This is the true rule: so often are we to receive as God gives us opportunity. Whoever, therefore, does not receive, but goes from the holy table when all things are prepared, either does not understand his duty or does not care for the dying command of his Saviour, the forgiveness of his sins, the strengthening of his soul, and the refreshing it with the hope of glory.

4. Let every one, therefore, who has either any desire to please God, or any love of his own soul, obey God, and consult the good of his own soul, by communicating every time he can — like the first Christians, with whom the Christian sacrifice was a constant part of the Lord's-day service. And for several centuries they received it almost every day: four times a week always, and every saint's day beside. Accordingly, those that joined in the prayers of the faithful never failed to partake of the blessed sacrament. What opinion they had of any who turned his back upon it, we may learn from that ancient canon: "If any believer join in the prayers of the faithful, and go away without receiving the Lord's Supper, let him be excommunicated, as bringing confusion into the Church of God." [3]

5. In order to understand the nature of the Lord's Supper, it would be useful carefully to read over those passages in the Gospel [cf. Mt. 26:26–29; Mk. 14:22–25; Lk. 22:15–20] and in the first epistle to the Corinthians [11:17–34], which speak of the institution of it. Hence we learn that the design of this sacrament is the continual remembrance of the death of Christ, by eating bread and drinking wine, which are the outward signs of the inward grace — the body and blood of Christ.

3. Cf. Canon II of the Dedication Council of Antioch (in Encaeniis): "All who enter the Church of God and hear the Holy Scriptures but do not communicate with the people in prayers, or who turn away, by reason of some disorder, from partaking of the Holy Supper, are to be cast out of the Church . . . as those who bring confusion into the order of the Church." This is a reformulation of the eight and ninth of the so-called "Apostolic Canons." Cf. Karl Joseph von Hefele, Histoire des conciles d'après les documents originaux (Paris, 1907), I, Pt. 2, 702–36; see also H. R. Percival, The Seven Ecumenical Councils (NPNF², XIV), 103–09.

6. It is highly expedient for those who purpose to receive this, whenever their time will permit, to prepare themselves for this solemn ordinance by self-examination and prayer. But this is not absolutely necessary. And when we have not time for it, we should see that we have the habitual preparation which is absolutely necessary, and can never be dispensed with on any account or any occasion whatever. This is, first, a full *purpose* of heart to keep all the commandments of God; and, secondly, a sincere *desire* to receive all his promises.

II. I am, in the second place, to answer the common objections against constantly receiving the Lord's Supper.

1. I say *constantly* receiving, for as to the phrase of "frequent Communion," it is absurd to the last degree.[4] If it means anything less than constant, it means more than can be proved to be the duty of any man. For if we are not obliged to communicate "constantly," by what argument can it be proved that we are obliged to communicate "frequently"? Yea, more than once a year? Or once in seven years? Or once before we die? Every argument brought for this either proves that we ought to do it *constantly*, or proves nothing at all. Therefore, that indeterminate, unmeaning way of speaking ought to be laid aside by all men of understanding.

2. In order to prove that it is our duty to communicate constantly, we may observe that the Holy Communion is to be considered either (1) as a command of God; or (2) as a mercy to man.

First, as a command of God. God our Mediator and Governor, from whom we have received our life and all things, on whose will it depends whether we shall be perfectly happy or perfectly miserable from this moment to eternity, declares to us that all who obey his commands shall be eternally happy; all who do not shall be eternally miserable. Now one of these commands is, "Do this in remembrance of me." I ask, then, "Why do you not do this, when you can do it if you will? When you have an opportunity before you, why do not you obey the command of God?"

3. Perhaps you will say, "God does not command me to do this *as often*

---

4. It was a bone of contention between the High-churchmen (who advocated "frequency"), the Latitudinarians, who tended to rest content with the canonical requirements of 1549 (three times a year), and the Puritans, who stressed the point about adequate self-examination above all else. *Cf.* Isaac Barrow, *A Brief Exposition of the Lord's Prayer and Decalogue; to which is added The Doctrine of the Sacraments* (1681), in Barrow, *Theological Works*, A. Napier, ed. (Cambridge, Eng., 1859), VII, 524-27.

*as I can"* — that is, the words, "as often as you can" are not added in this particular place. What then? Are we not to obey every command of God as often as we can? Are not all the promises of God made to those, and those only, who "give all diligence" [*cf.* 2 Pet. 1:5, 10] — that is, to those who do all they can to obey his commandments? Our power is the one rule of our duty. Whatever we can do, that we ought. With respect either to this or any other command, he that when he may obey it if he will, does not, will have no place in the kingdom of heaven.

4. And this great truth, that we are obliged to keep every command as far as we can, is clearly proved from the absurdity of the contrary opinion; for were we to allow that we are not obliged to obey every commandment of God as often as we can, we have no argument left to prove that any man is bound to obey any command at any time. For instance, should I ask a man why he does not obey one of the plainest commands of God — why, for instance, he does not help his parents? — he might answer, "I will not do it now, but I will at another time." When that time comes, put him in mind of God's command again and he will say, "I will obey it some time or other." Nor is it possible ever to prove that he ought to do it now, unless by proving that he ought to do it as often as he can — and, therefore, he ought to do it now because he can if he will.

5. Consider the Lord's Supper, secondly, as a mercy from God to man; as God, whose mercy is over all his works [*cf.* Ps. 145:9],[5] and particularly over the children of men, knew there was but one way for man to be happy like himself, namely, by being like him in holiness. As he knew we could do nothing toward this of ourselves, he has given us certain means of obtaining his help. One of these is the Lord's Supper, which, of his infinite mercy, he hath given for this every end: that through this means we may be assisted to attain those blessings which he hath prepared for us; that we may obtain holiness on earth and everlasting glory in heaven.

I ask, then, why do you not accept of his mercy as often as ever you can? God now offers you his blessing — why do you refuse it? You have now an opportunity of receiving his mercy — why do you not receive it? You are weak — why do you not seize upon every opportunity of increasing your strength? In a word — considering this as a command of God, he that does not communicate as often as he can has no piety; considering it as a mercy, he that does not communicate as often as he can has no wisdom.

5. See also B.C.P. (1662), chap. 26: Collects of Thanksgiving, in Forms of Prayer to be Used at Sea.

6. These two considerations will yield a full answer to all the common objections which have been made against constant Communion; indeed, to all that ever were or can be made. In truth, nothing can be objected against it but upon supposition that, this particular time, either the Communion would be no mercy, or I am not commanded to receive it. Nay, should we grant it would be no mercy, that is not enough — for still the other reason would hold: whether it does you any good or none, you are to obey the command of God.

7. However, let us see the particular excuses which men commonly make for not obeying it. The most common is: "I am 'unworthy'; and 'he that eateth and drinketh unworthily, eateth and drinketh damnation to himself' [*cf.* 1 Cor. 11:27-29]. Therefore, I dare not communicate, lest I should eat and drink my own damnation." [6]

The case is this. God offers you one of the greatest mercies on this side heaven, and commands you to accept it. Why do you not accept this mercy in obedience to his command? You say, "I am unworthy to receive it." And what then? You are unworthy to receive any mercy from God. But is that a reason for refusing all mercy? God offers you a pardon for all your sins. You are unworthy of it, it is sure, and he knows it. But since he is pleased to offer it nevertheless, will not you accept of it? He offers to deliver your soul from death. You are unworthy to live. But will you therefore refuse life? He offers to endue your soul with new strength. Because you are unworthy of it, will you deny to take it? What can God himself do for us farther, if we refuse his mercy because we are unworthy of it?

8. But suppose this were no mercy to us (to suppose which is indeed giving God the lie, saying, that is not good for man which he purposely ordered for his good), still I ask, Why do not you obey God's command? He says, "Do this." Why do you not? You answer, "I am unworthy to do it." What? Unworthy to obey God? Unworthy to do what God bids you do? Unworthy to obey God's command? What do you mean by this? That those who are unworthy to obey God ought not to obey him? Who told you so? If he were even "an angel from heaven, let him be accursed" [*cf.* Gal. 1:8]. If you think God himself has told you by St. Paul, let us hear his words. They are these: "He that eateth and drinketh unworthily, eateth and drinketh damnation to himself."

Why, this is quite another thing. Here is not a word said of *being unworthy* to eat and drink. Indeed, he does speak of eating and drinking *unworthily;* but that is quite a different thing — so he has told us him-

6. *Cf.* B.C.P. (1662), par. 344.

self. In this very chapter we are told that by eating and drinking unworthily is meant taking the holy sacrament in such a rude and disorderly
way that one was "hungry and another drunken" [1 Cor. 11:21]. But
what is that to *you*? Is there any danger of *your* doing so — of your eating and drinking *thus unworthily*? However unworthy you are to communicate, there is no fear of your communicating thus. Therefore, whatever the punishment is of doing it thus unworthily, it does not concern
*you*. You have no more reason from this text to disobey God than if
there was no such text in the Bible. If you speak of "eating and drinking
unworthily" in the sense St. Paul uses the words, you may as well say,
"I dare not communicate *for fear the church should fall*, as for fear I
should eat and drink unworthily."

9. If then you fear bringing "damnation" on yourself by this, you fear
where no fear is. Fear it not for eating and drinking unworthily; for
that, in St. Paul's sense, ye cannot do. But I will tell you for what you
shall fear damnation: for not eating and drinking at all; for not obeying
your Maker and Redeemer; for disobeying his plain command; for thus
setting at nought both his mercy and authority. Fear ye this; for hear
what his apostle saith: "Whosoever shall keep the whole law, and yet
offend in one point, is guilty of all." [7]

10. We see then how weak the objection is, "I dare not receive [8] because I am unworthy." Nor is it any stronger, though the reason why you
think yourself unworthy is that you have lately fallen into sin. It is true,
our Church forbids those "who have done any grievous crime" [9] to receive without repentance. But all that follows from this is that we should
repent before we come — not that we should neglect to come at all.

To say, therefore, that "a man may turn his back upon the altar because he has lately fallen into sin; that he may impose this penance upon
himself," is talking without any warrant from Scripture. For where does
the Bible teach to atone for breaking one commandment of God by
breaking another? What advice is this: "Commit a new act of disobedience and God will more easily forgive the past?"

11. Others there are who, to excuse their disobedience, plead that they
are unworthy in another sense, that they "cannot live up to it: they cannot pretend to lead so holy a life as constantly communicating would
oblige them to do." Put this into plain words. I ask: Why do you not
accept the mercy which God commands you to accept? You answer,
"Because I cannot live up to the profession I must make when I receive

7. [Au.] Jas. 2:10.          8. [Au.] "The Lord's Supper."
9. *Cf.* Canons XXVI and CIX in Gibson, *Codex Iuris,* I, 468.

it." Then it is plain you ought never to receive it at all. For it is no more lawful to promise once what you know you cannot perform than to promise it a thousand times. You know, too, that it is one and the same promise, whether you make it every year or every day. You promise to do just as much, whether you promise ever so often or ever so seldom.

If, therefore, you cannot live up to the profession they make who communicate once a week, neither can you come up to the profession you make who communicate once a year. But cannot you, indeed? Then it had been good for you that you had never been born. For all that you profess at the Lord's table, you must both profess and keep, or you cannot be saved. For you profess nothing there but this, that you will diligently keep his commandments. And cannot you keep up to this profession? Then you cannot enter into life.

12. Think, then, what you say before you say you cannot live up to what is required of constant communicants. This is no more than is required of any communicant, yea, of every one that has a soul to be saved — so that to say you cannot live up to this is neither better nor worse than renouncing Christianity. It is, in effect, renouncing your baptism, wherein you solemnly promised to keep all his commandments. You now fly from that profession. You wilfully break one of his commandments and, to excuse yourself, say you cannot keep his commandments. Then you cannot expect to receive the promises, which are made only to those that keep them.

13. What has been said on this pretence against constant Communion is applicable to those who say the same thing in other words: "We dare not do it, because it requires so perfect an obedience afterwards as we cannot promise to perform." Nay, it requires neither more nor less perfect obedience than you promised in your baptism. You then undertook to keep the commandments of God, by his help, and you promise no more when you communicate.[10]

14. A second objection which is often made against constant Communion is the having so much business as will not allow time for such a preparation as is necessary thereto.[11] I answer: all the preparation that is absolutely necessary is contained in those words: "Repent you truly of your sins past; have faith in Christ our Saviour" (and observe, that

10. The original version has the following paragraph, which was then omitted from the edition of 1788 (perhaps as repetitive?): "But observe upon the whole, this is not so properly an objection against constantly communicating as against communicating at all. For if we are not to receive the Lord's Supper till we are worthy of it, it is certain we ought never to receive it."

11. Cf. B.C.P. (1662), par. 345.

word is not here taken in its highest sense!), "amend your lives, and be in charity with all men; so shall ye be meet partakers of these holy mysteries." [12] All who are thus prepared may draw near without fear and receive the sacrament to their comfort. Now, what business can hinder you from being thus prepared, from repenting of your past sins, from believing that Christ died to save sinners, from amending your lives and being in charity with all men? No business can hinder you from this, unless it be such as hinders you from being in a state of salvation. If you resolve and design to follow Christ,[13] you are fit to approach the Lord's table. If you do not design this, you are only fit for the table and company of devils.

15. No business, therefore, can hinder any man from having that preparation which alone is necessary, unless it be such as unprepares him for heaven, as puts him out of a state of salvation. Indeed every prudent man will, when he has time, examine himself before he receives the Lord's Supper: whether he repents him truly of his former sins; whether he believes the promises of God; whether he fully designs to walk in his ways, and be in charity with all men? In this, and in private prayer, he will doubtless spend all the time he conveniently can. But what is this to *you* who have not time? What excuse is this for not obeying God? He commands you to come and prepare yourself by prayer if you have time; if you have not, however, come. Make not reverence to God's command a pretence for breaking it. Do not rebel against him for fear of offending him. Whatever you do or leave undone besides, be sure to do what God bids you do. Examining yourself and using private prayer, especially before the Lord's Supper, is good; but, behold! "to obey is better than" self-examination, "and to hearken," than the prayer of an angel [*cf.* 1 Sam. 15:22].

16. A third objection against constant Communion is that it abates our reverence for the sacrament. Suppose it did; what then? Will you thence conclude that you are not to receive it constantly? This does not follow. God commands you: "Do this." You may do it now, but will not; and to excuse yourself, say: "If I do it so often, it will abate the reverence with which I do it now." Suppose it did. Has God ever told you that when the obeying his command abates your reverence to it, then you may disobey it? If he has, you are guiltless; if not, what you say is just nothing to the purpose. The law is clear. Either show that the lawgiver makes this exception, or you are guilty before him.

12. Cf. *ibid.*, par. 346.          13. Cf. *ibid.*, par. 347.

17. Reverence for the sacrament may be of two sorts: either such as is owing purely to the newness of the thing, such as men naturally have for anything they are not used to; or, such as is owing to our faith or to the love or fear of God. Now, the former of these is not properly a religious reverence, but purely natural. And this sort of reverence for the Lord's Supper, the constantly receiving of it must lessen. But it will not lessen the true religious reverence, but rather confirm and increase it.

18. A fourth objection is, "I have communicated constantly so long, but I have not found the benefit I expected." This has been the case with many well-meaning persons, and therefore deserves to be particularly considered. And consider this first: whatever God commands us to do, we are to do because he commands, whether we feel any benefit thereby or no. Now, God commands, "Do this in remembrance of me." This, therefore, we are to do because he commands, whether we find present benefit thereby or not. But undoubtedly we shall find benefit sooner or later, though perhaps insensibly. We shall be insensibly strengthened, made more fit for the service of God, and more constant in it. At least we are kept from falling back, and preserved from many sins and temptations. And surely this should be enough to make us receive this food as often as we can; though we do not presently feel the happy effects of it, as some have done — and we ourselves may, when God sees best.

19. But suppose a man has often been at the sacrament, and yet received no benefit. Was it not his own fault? Either he was not rightly prepared, willing to obey all the commands and to receive all the promises of God, or he did not receive it aright, trusting in God. Only see that you are duly prepared for it, and the oftener you come to the Lord's table, the greater benefit you will find there.

20. A fifth objection which some have made against constant Communion is that "the Church enjoins it only three times a year." The words of the Church are, "Note, that every parishioner shall communicate at the least three times in the year." [14] To this I answer, first: what if the Church had not enjoined it at all? Is it not enough that God enjoins it? We obey the Church only for God's sake. And shall we not obey God himself? If, then, you receive three times a year because the Church commands it, receive every time you can because God commands it. Else your doing the one will be so far from excusing you for not doing

14. The rubric (next to the last in the Order for Holy Communion) adds, "of which Easter [is] to be one." Cf. B.C.P. (1662), rubrics after par. 373.

the other, that your own practice will prove your folly and sin, and leave you without excuse.

But, secondly, we cannot conclude from these words that the Church excuses him who receives only thrice a year. The plain sense of them is that he who does not receive thrice at least shall be cast out of the Church. But they by no means excuse him who communicates no oftener. This never was the judgment of our Church. On the contrary, she takes all possible care that the sacrament be duly administered, wherever the Common Prayer is read, every Sunday and holiday in the year.

The Church gives a particular direction with regard to those that are in Holy Orders: "In all cathedral and collegiate churches and colleges, where there are many priests and deacons, they shall all receive the Communion with the priest, every Sunday at the least." [15]

21. It has been shown: first, that if we consider the Lord's Supper as a command of Christ, no man can have any pretence to Christian piety who does not receive it (not once a month, but) as often as he can; secondly, that if we consider the institution of it as a mercy to ourselves, no man who does not receive it as often as he can has any pretence to Christian prudence; thirdly, that none of the objections usually made can be any excuse for that man who does not, at every opportunity, obey this command and accept this mercy.

22. It has been particularly shown: first, that unworthiness is no excuse, because, though in one sense we are all unworthy, yet none of us need be afraid of being unworthy, in St. Paul's sense, of "eating and drinking unworthily"; secondly, that the not having time enough for preparation can be no excuse, since the only preparation which is absolutely necessary is that which no business can hinder — nor, indeed, anything on earth — unless so far as it hinders our being in a state of salvation; thirdly, that its abating our reverence is no excuse, since he who gave the command, "Do this," nowhere adds, ". . . unless it abates your reverence"; fourthly, that our not profiting by it is no excuse, since it is our own fault in neglecting that necessary preparation which is in our own power; lastly, that the judgment of our own Church is quite in favour of constant Communion. If those who have hitherto neglected it on any of these pretences will lay these things to heart, they will, by the grace of God, come to a better mind, and never more forsake their own mercies.

15. Cf. the concluding rubrics in the Order for Holy Communion, B.C.P. (1662), following par. 373.

# PART THREE

✤

*Theologies in Conflict*

# Introduction to Part Three

WESLEY often protested that he had no taste for controversy.[1] Nonetheless, he was continuously engaged in it, from the first taunting cry of "Methodist" at Oxford until his last blast at the Calvinists in *The Arminian Magazine* of 1791. What is more, his troubles arose almost invariably with those who were — or had been — his colleagues and allies. For example, his association with the Moravians and his obvious debt to them for his own experience of the assurance of faith at Aldersgate is freely acknowledged in the first three *Extracts of the Journal*, covering his journeys to Georgia and Germany and the successful first chapter of the history of the Revival.[2] The fourth *Extract*, however, recounts the tragic rupture in their relations which had begun shortly after Aldersgate and had developed into enmity and actual schism. Its preface (*cf. Journal*, II, 309–11) makes it painfully clear that Wesley proposed now to justify his revulsion from "the German stillness" and, in opposition, to show how decisively his conception of the Christian life stood over against the quietist views of the Moravians. The gist of this wide-ranging and protracted quarrel is contained in the first selection in this part.

At the heart of the conflict lay Wesley's genuine abhorrence of antinomianism — and, with it, of *any* notion of Christian ethics that allows in the believer a passive attitude toward either the means of grace or to the demand of the gospel for *actual righteousness*. If, in the faith that justifies and pardons, righteousness is *imputed* (as Wesley taught and be-

1. *Cf. Journal*, IV, 3 (for November 19, 1751): "I began writing a letter to the 'Comparer' of the Papists and the Methodists [George Lavington, bishop of Exeter, whose *The Enthusiasm of Methodists and Papists Compared* (1749) had appeared in three 'parts,' 1749–51]. Heavy work, such as I should never choose, but sometimes it must be done. Well might the ancient say: 'God made practical divinity necessary, the devil, controversial.' But it *is* necessary. We must 'resist the devil' or he will not 'flee from us.'" See also *Journal*, IV, 247 (January 9, 1758).

2. No. 1: From October 14, 1735, to February 1, 1738 (*Journal*, I, 106–426); No. 2: From February 1, 1738, to his return from Germany, September 16, 1738 (*Journal*, I, 427–II, 63); No. 3: From September 17, 1738, to November 1, 1739 (*Journal*, II, 65–311).

lieved), then the ultimate aim of such justification is that righteousness shall also be *imparted*.

His warfare with antinomianism, however, was waged on other fronts as well — some of them within the Methodist societies and with some of his own associates in the Revival. The second selection in this part is such an example — for, in the same climactic year (1762) that saw his attack on the "greatest professors" of "perfection," [3] he also found himself embroiled with those who, from their prideful heights of "perfect love," drew the comfortable conclusion that if Christ's righteousness is "imputed to us, we need none of our own, . . ." Of these, Thomas Maxfield and James Relly were the most outspoken.[4] It was, therefore, as a counterattack against this baneful notion that Wesley wrote and published *A Blow at the Root*.

The tensions between the Methodists and the hierarchy of the Church of England were, for the most part, less violent but no less basic. Wesley thought of himself as a loyal son of the Church and at least occasionally he seems to have hoped for support — or at least basic approval — from her leaders. It was a vain hope. There were clashes of personalities and vested interests from the start. Deeper than these, however, were the churchmen's apprehensions of Wesley's "irregularity" — which they regarded as the first steps toward inevitable dissent and "separation" — and of his emphasis upon "assurance" — which they regularly took as evidence of his "enthusiasm."

His first brush with the authorities came in the early months of the Revival (August 1739).[5] Called into conference with Joseph Butler, bishop of Bristol — another genius but of a different order — the point of contention was quickly defined: justification by faith and the assurance of God's gift of pardon. "Sir," said the bishop (in Wesley's report of the conversation), "our faith itself is a good work; it is a virtuous temper of mind." To this Wesley replied: "My lord, whatever faith is, our Church asserts we are justified by faith alone. But how it can be called a good work, I see not. It is the gift of God, and a gift that presupposes nothing in us but sin and misery." There followed a lively exchange in which Wesley appealed to The Homilies as his authority, only to have the bishop

3. See above, p. 298 ff.

4. The latter had written a fulsome tract entitled *Union: or a Treatise of the Consanguinity and Affinity Between Christ and His Church* (1759); cf. Tyerman, *Life*, II, 400–01.

5. *Cf*. Whitehead, *Life*, II, 118–21. Notice that Whitehead seems not to have known the bishop's name.

interpret them quite differently. From this, he then passed to a blunt verdict of episcopal disapproval: "Mr. Wesley, I will deal plainly with you. I once thought you and Mr. Whitefield well-meaning men, but I cannot think so now. . . . Sir, the pretending to extraordinary revelations and gifts of the Holy Ghost is a horrid thing, a very horrid thing." Wesley replied that he pretended to no *extra*ordinary revelations but only "what every Christian may receive and ought to expect and pray for." Taxed with irregularity in preaching in the diocese of Bristol without license, Wesley retorted: ". . . I am a priest of the Church universal, and being ordained as a Fellow of a College, I was not limited to any particular cure, but have an indeterminate commission to preach the Word of God in any part of the Church of England."

This conversation foreshadowed the continuing ambivalence of Wesley's position and the anomalous situation of the Methodists in the national church. With a main concern to clarify the issues for his own people, but also to persuade other churchmen to a more favorable view of the Revival, Wesley undertook a series of *Appeals*, designed to explain, commend and justify his movement as a providential service both to the church and to her mission to the nation.[6] The *Appeals* are apologiae; they have Joseph Butler's famous *Analogy of Religion* in mind and at least some of his antideistic aims in view. The essence of Methodism's "defense" is based upon its essential reasonableness, to which is joined the demand that religious profession be matched by performance. Wesley's jaundiced comments on the Church and its leaders were not intended to aid historians of a later age to a balanced and just estimate of the situation; instead, he is preoccupied with his bid for appropriate recognition from the leaders of the Church of the legitimacy of his own ministry and that of the Methodist movement. His chief success, as it turned out, was to bolster the Methodist people in their dignity and self-understanding in their relationship to the Church. The first of the *Appeals* is given here, as a sample of Wesley's way with his fellow Anglicans.

Wesley's most obdurate quarrel was with the Calvinists. It began with the Revival itself, when George Whitefield began "preaching up the decrees" (*i.e.* predestination) in England after his first Georgia mission. Wesley reacted by preaching a doctrine of universal atonement and then

6. *An Earnest Appeal to Men of Reason and Religion* (1743); *A Farther Appeal to Men of Reason and Religion*, Pt. I, in 1745, and Pts. II and III later in the same year. In 1796 all the *Appeals* were printed in a single volume. For a half-century they were among the most popular and most widely read of Wesley's writings.

cast lots to decide whether or not to publish against Whitefield. The result was *Free Grace: A Sermon Preached at Bristol* (1739) — in which he denounced the predestinarian doctrines as "blasphemy."[7] This opened the floodgates of controversy, which were never thereafter closed.[8]

For more than half a century Wesley waged doctrinal war with any and all who taught "predestination" as an essential article of faith. He occasionally deplored it even as an "opinion." From their side, the "Calvinists" (an imprecise label for the motley of predestinarians in eighteenth-century England) fought back with equal vigor against Wesley's "Arminianism" (an even less precise label for all notions of divine-human synergism).[9] The enemy in the Calvinist system that haunted Wesley was the old ghost of antinomianism. For their part, the Calvinists were fully persuaded that, despite his talk about faith, Wesley was finally committed to a scheme of works-righteousness. Actually, some of Wesley's best work went into this controversy — and of this, the two pieces included below are properly representative.

Like the vast majority of Englishmen in the seventeenth and eighteenth centuries, Wesley was stoutly antipapist and never omitted an opportunity to denounce Romish errors and "superstitions." To the charge that Rome is heretical, he added another ground for their segregation in the body politic — namely, that no Protestant could trust any Roman in any matter contractual because of the unrepealed "maxim" of the Council of Constance, that "no faith is to be kept with heretics."[10] In the same breath,

7. *Cf. Works*, VII, 383.

8. In addition to *Free Grace*, there were: an extract from Robert Barclay, *Serious Considerations on Absolute Predestination* (1741), and *A Dialogue between a Predestinarian and His Friend* (1741); extracts from *The Scripture Doctrine Concerning Predestination, Election and Reprobation* (1741); *Hymns on God's Everlasting Love*, which includes the weird "Cry of the Reprobate" and "The Horrible Decree" (1741); *Serious Thoughts upon the Perseverance of the Saints* (1751); an abridgment of Richard Lucas, *An Inquiry after Happiness*, in *A Christian Library* (Bristol, 1753), XXIV; *The Question, What Is an Arminian? Answered by a Lover of Free Grace* (1770); a travesty on Augustus Toplady entitled, *The Doctrine of Absolute Predestination Stated and Asserted* (1770); *The Consequence Proved* (1771); *Some Remarks on Mr. Hill's Review* (1772); *Some Remarks on Mr. Hill's Farrago Double-Distilled* (1773); *Thoughts Upon God's Sovereignty* (1777); *An Answer to Mr. Rowland Hill's Tract Entitled "Imposture Detected"* (1777); and finally, beginning in 1778, his own antipredestinarian "house organ," *The Arminian Magazine*.

9. *Cf. The Question, What Is an Arminian? Answered by a Lover of Free Grace* (1770), in which Wesley shows how misleading badges of this kind were in theological debate.

10. *Cf.* his letter to *The Public Advertiser, Works*, X, 160–61.

however, he repudiates the notion of any persecution of the Catholics, so long as they kept the public peace.

There was, however, another side to Wesley's position. He never approved of the typical Dissenter's conviction that Rome was apostate and no true church, and he freely exhibited his lifelong interest in Catholic piety and devotion. Moreover, as he made plain in his sermon "Of the Church," he was fully persuaded that the living substance of the Church, a residue of the authentic gospel, had been preserved in the Roman Communion, despite its anti-evangelical errors.[11] He records, with evident gratification, the presence of Catholics in his audiences, especially in Ireland, and he seems to have supposed that the religious grounds of alienation between Romans and Protestants were still negotiable. *A Letter to a Roman Catholic* is a rather sketchy sample of the sort of negotiation he thought might be useful. Perhaps the most unusual thing in the "letter" is Wesley's attempted summary of the doctrines common to all Christians, a sort of rough and ready *regula fidei*. Nothing quite like this appears anywhere else in his writings.

11. See above, p. 313 f.

# THE RIFT WITH THE MORAVIANS [1]

*Journal, November 1, 1739—September 3, 1741*

*Editor's introduction.* The Moravian Brethren, when Wesley first came to know them, were in a rather disturbed chapter of their checkered history (cf. Edward Langton, *History of the Moravian Church* [1956]; J. E. Hutton, *A History of the Moravian Church*, 2d ed. [1909], 255–303; W. G. Addison, *The Renewed Church of the United Brethren, 1722–1930* [1932], 47–66). "Renewed" in 1722 under the leadership of Count Zinzendorf, the Moravians had become a strongly pietistic and missionary group, with headquarters in Germany and outposts in England and America. Their influence on Wesley's spiritual development (in Georgia, at "Aldersgate" and in Germany) is a familiar theme in his early *Journals* and letters. His visit with them in Germany in the summer after "Aldersgate" had left him with a deep admiration of their piety, yet also a growing uneasiness about their "quietism," their tendencies toward spiritual complacency and the personality cult which had grown up around Count Zinzendorf. Yet, in the early days of the Revival he seems to have expected to graft his own movement onto such Anglican-Moravian groups as the Fetter Lane Society, which he and Peter Böhler had organized *before* Aldersgate (cf. *Journal*, May 1, 1738). Tensions began to develop, however, especially with Philip Molther, an *émigré* from Herrnhut. Molther's vigorous advocacy of "stillness" offended Wesley; in turn, he was offended by Wesley's insistence upon faith *and* good works *together*. The controversy was all the more painful because of Wesley's acknowledged debt of gratitude. Its

1. From *Extract of the Journal, No. 4*, covering the period from November 1, 1739, to September 3, 1741 (*Journal*, II, 307–500). Because of its length and repetitiousness, the original text has been somewhat abridged. The omissions are indicated by ellipses. The text is based on the first edition (1744), collated with those of 1774 and 1797.

immediate upshot was Wesley's withdrawal from the Fetter Lane Society and the establishment of his own United Society (see above, pp. 16–18). The rift thus opened was never healed, and gave rise to a protracted exchange of pamphlet polemics over a span of two decades. Besides the *Journal* passage presented here, one should consult *A Short View of the Difference between the Moravian Brethren Lately in England and the Rev. Mr. John and Charles Wesley, A Dialogue between an Antinomian and His Friend* and *A Second Dialogue . . .* (all three in 1745); *Hymns Composed for the Use of the* [Moravian] *Brethren* (1749; an almost malicious collection of the most sentimental of the then current Moravian hymns, all long since expunged from the Moravian hymnbook); *Queries Humbly Proposed to the Rt. Rev. and Rt. Hon. Count Zinzendorf* (1755); *Thoughts on the Imputed Righteousness of Christ* (1762).

❖   ❖   ❖   ❖

*1739, Nov. 1, Thur.* I left Bristol, and on Saturday came to London. The first person I met with there was one [Mrs. Turner] whom I had left strong in faith and zealous of good works. But she now told me, "Mr. Molther [2] had fully convinced her *she never had any faith at all;* and had advised her, till she received faith, 'to be still,' 'ceasing from outward works,' which she had accordingly done and did not doubt but in a short time she should find the advantage of it."

In the evening Mr. Bray also was highly commending the "being *still* before the Lord." He likewise spoke largely of "the great danger that attended the doing of outward works" and of "the folly of people that keep running about to church and sacrament" — "as I," said he, "did till very lately."

*Sun.* 4. Our society met at seven in the morning and continued *silent* till eight. One [Spangenberg] then spoke of "looking unto Jesus," and exhorted us all "to lie *still* in his hand."

In the evening I met the women of our society at Fetter Lane, where some of our brethren strongly intimated that none of them had any true faith, and then asserted in plain terms: (1) that "till they had true faith, they ought to be *still*"; that is (as they explained themselves), "to abstain

2. An Alsatian who had served Zinzendorf as tutor to his son and missionary to Pennsylvania. He came to London in October 1738, and began almost immediately to press, in the Fetter Lane Society and elsewhere, for an extreme version of "stillness" as the necessary prelude to the faith of "assurance."

from 'the means of grace,' as they are called, the Lord's Supper *in particular*" — (2) that "the ordinances are not means of grace, *there being no other means than Christ.*"

*Wed.* 7. Being greatly desirous to understand the ground. of this matter, I had a long conference with Mr. Spangenberg. I agreed with all he said of the power of faith. I agreed that "whosoever is *by faith* born of God doth not commit sin" [1 Jn. 3:9]. But I could not agree either that "none has any faith so long as he is liable to any doubt or fear," or that, "till we have it [faith], we ought to abstain from the Lord's Supper or the other ordinances of God."

At eight our society met at Fetter Lane. We sat an hour without speaking. The rest of the time was spent in dispute, one having proposed a question concerning the Lord's Supper, which many warmly affirmed, "none ought to receive till he had the full assurance of faith."

I observed every day more and more the advantage Satan had gained over us. Many of those who once "knew in whom they had believed" [*cf.* 2 Tim. 1:12] were thrown into idle reasonings and thereby filled with doubts and fears, from which they now found no way to escape. Many were induced to deny the gift of God and affirm they never had any faith at all, especially those who had fallen again into sin and, of consequence, into darkness. And almost all these had "left off the means of grace," saying they must now "cease from their own works"; they must now "trust in Christ alone"; they were "poor sinners," and had "nothing to do but to lie at his feet."

Till Saturday the tenth, I think I did not meet with one woman of the society who had not been upon the point of casting away her confidence in God. I then indeed found one who, when many (according to their custom) laboured to persuade her she had no faith, replied with a spirit they were not able to resist, "I know that the life which I now live, I live by faith in the Son of God, who loved *me*, and gave himself for *me* [*cf.* Gal. 2:20]. And he has never left me one moment, since the hour he was made known to me 'in the breaking of bread'" [*cf.* Lk. 24:35].

What is to be inferred from this undeniable matter of fact — [*i.e.*] one that had not faith, received it in the Lord's Supper? Why, (1) that there are "means of grace" — that is, outward ordinances — whereby the inward grace of God is ordinarily conveyed to man, whereby the faith that brings salvation is conveyed to them who before had it not; (2) that one of these means is the Lord's Supper; and (3) that he who has not this faith ought to "wait" for it in the use both of this and of the other means which God hath ordained.

*Fri.* 9. I showed how we are to "examine" ourselves "whether we be in the faith," and afterwards recommended it to all, though especially to them that believed — true stillness: that is, "a patient waiting upon God, by lowliness, meekness, and resignation, in all the ways of his holy law and the works of his commandments." . . .

*Mon.* [Dec.] 31. I had a long and particular conversation with Mr. Molther himself. I weighed all his words with the utmost care, desired him to explain what I did not understand, asked him again and again, "Do I not mistake what you say? Is this your meaning, or is it not?" So that I think, if God has given me any measure of understanding, I could not mistake him much.

As soon as I came home I besought God to assist me, and not suffer "the blind to go out of the way" [*cf.* Lk. 6:39]. I then wrote down what I conceived to be the difference between us in the following words:

As to "faith," *you* believe:

1. There are no "degrees of faith," and that no man has *any* degree of it before all things in him are become new, before he has the full assurance of faith, the abiding witness of the Spirit, or the clear perception that Christ dwelleth in him.

2. Accordingly, you believe there is *no justifying faith*, or state of justification, short of this.

3. Therefore, you believe our Brother Hutton, Edmonds and others had *no justifying faith* before they saw you.

4. And, in general, that that gift of God which many received since Peter Böhler came into England — viz. "a sure confidence of the love of God to *them*" — was *not* justifying faith.

5. And that the "joy and love" attending it were from "animal spirits," from "nature," or "imagination" not "joy in the Holy Ghost" [*cf.* Rom. 14:17], and the real "love of God shed abroad in their hearts" [*cf.* Rom. 5:5].

Whereas I believe:

1. There are *degrees in faith* and that a man may have *some degree* of it before all things in him are become new — before he has the full assurance of faith, the abiding witness of the Spirit, or the clear perception that Christ dwelleth in him.

2. Accordingly, I believe there is *a degree of justifying faith* (and, consequently, a state of justification) short of, and commonly antecedent to, this.

3. And I believe our Brother Hutton, with many others, had "justifying faith" long before they saw you.

4. And, in general, that that gift of God which many received since Peter Böhler came into England — viz. "a sure confidence of the love of God to *them*" — was "justifying faith."

5. And that the "joy and love" attending it were *not* from "animal spirits," from "nature," or "imagination," but a measure of "joy in the Holy Ghost" and of "the love of God shed abroad in their hearts."

As to "the way of faith," you believe:

That the way to attain it is to "wait" for Christ, and be "still," *i.e.*:

Not to use what *we* [Anglicans] term the "means of grace";

Not to go to church;

Not to communicate;

Not to fast;

Not to use *so much* private prayer;

Not to read the Scripture — because you believe these are *not* "means of grace" — *i.e.* do not ordinarily convey God's grace to unbelievers — and that it is impossible for a man to *use* them without *trusting* in them;

Not to do temporal good;

Nor to attempt doing spiritual good — because, you believe, no fruit of the Spirit is given by those who have it not themselves, and that those who have not faith are utterly blind, and therefore unable to guide other souls.

Whereas I believe:

The way to attain it is to "wait" for Christ and be "still" — in *using all the means of grace*.

Therefore, I believe it right for him who knows he has not faith (*i.e.* that conquering faith):

To go to church;

To communicate;

To fast;

To use as much private prayer as he can, and

To read the Scripture — because I believe these are "means of grace," *i.e.* do ordinarily convey God's grace to unbelievers, and

that it *is* possible for a man to *use* them, without *trusting* in them.
To do all the temporal good he can;

And to endeavour after doing spiritual good — because I know
many fruits of the Spirit are given by those who have them not
themselves; and that those who have not faith, or but in the lowest degree, may have more light from God, more wisdom for the
guiding of other souls, than many that are strong in faith.[3]

As to "the manner of propagating the faith," you believe — as I have
also heard others affirm:

That we may, on some accounts, "use guile" — by saying what we
know will *deceive* the hearers, or lead them to think the thing which is
not; by describing things "a little beyond the truth," in order to their
"coming up to it"; by speaking *as if* we meant what we do not.

But I believe:

That we may not "use guile" on any account whatsoever;

That we may not, on any account, say what we know will, and
design should, *deceive* the hearers;

That we may not describe things one jot "beyond the truth,"
whether they "come up to it" or no; and,

That we may not speak, on any pretence, *as if* we meant what indeed we do not.

Lastly, as to the fruits of your thus propagating the faith in England,
you believe:

Much good has been done by it;

Many unsettled from a false foundation;

Many brought into "true stillness," in order to their coming to the
true foundation; and

Some grounded thereon who were wrong before, but are right
now.

On the contrary, I believe:

That very little good, but much hurt, has been done by it:

Many who were beginning to build holiness and good works on the true
foundation of faith in Jesus, being now wholly unsettled and lost in vain
reasonings and doubtful disputations.

Many others being brought into a *false*, unscriptural "stillness"; so that
they are not likely to come to any true foundation;

And many being grounded on a faith which is without works, so that
they who were right before are wrong now. . . .

3. There is an autobiographical reference here; see above, p. 17, and also p. 80 f.

*Sat.* 19 [April 1740]. I received a letter from Mr. Simpson, and another from William Oxlee, informing me that our poor brethren in Fetter Lane were again in great confusion, and earnestly desiring that, if it were possible, I would come to London without delay.

*Wed.* 23. I went to Mr. Simpson. He told me all the confusion was owing to my brother, who *would preach up* the ordinances: "Whereas believers," said he, "are not *subject to ordinances* and unbelievers *have nothing to do with them*. They ought to be 'still'; otherwise, they will be unbelievers all the days of their life."

After a fruitless dispute of about two hours, I returned home with a heavy heart. Mr. Molther was taken ill this day. I believe it was the hand of God that was upon him. In the evening our society met — but cold, weary, heartless, dead. I found nothing of brotherly love among them now, but a harsh, dry, heavy, stupid spirit. For two hours they looked one at another, when they looked up at all, as if one-half of them was afraid of the other, yea, as if a voice was sounding in their ears, "Take ye heed every one of his neighbour; trust ye not in any brother, for every brother will utterly supplant and every neighbor will walk with slanders" [cf. Jer. 9:4].

I think not so few as thirty persons spoke to me in these two days who had been strongly solicited:

1. To deny what God had done for their souls — to own they never had living faith.

2. To "be still" till they had it; to leave off all the means of grace: not to go to church; not to communicate, not to search the Scripture, not to use private prayer — at least, not *so much*, or not *vocally*, or not at any *stated times*.

*Fri.* 25. My brother and I went to Mr. Molther again and spent two hours in conversation with him. He now also explicitly affirmed:

1. That there are *no degrees* in faith; that none has any faith who has ever any doubt or fear, and that none is justified till he has a clean heart with the perpetual indwelling of Christ and of the Holy Ghost; and

2. That every one who has not this ought, till he has it, to "be still — that is, as he explained it, not to use the ordinances, or "means of grace," so called.

He also expressly asserted (1) that to those who have a clean heart the ordinances are not "matter of duty" — they are not "commanded" to use them; they are "free"; they *may* use them, or they *may not*; (2) that those who have not a clean heart *ought not* to use them (particularly not to communicate) because God neither *commands* nor *designs* they should (commanding them to none, designing them only for believers) and because they are not "means of grace," there being no such thing as means of grace but Christ only.

Ten or twelve persons spoke to me this day also, and many more the day following, who had been greatly troubled by this new gospel and thrown into the utmost heaviness. And, indeed, wherever I went, I found more and more proofs of the grievous confusion it had occasioned, many coming to me day by day who were once full of peace and love, but were now again plunged into doubts and fears and driven even to their wit's end.

I was now utterly at a loss what course to take, finding no rest for the sole of my foot [*cf*. Gen. 8:9]. These vain janglings [1 Tim. 1:6] pursued me wherever I went and were always sounding in my ears.

*Wed.* 30. I went to my friend (that was!) Mr. St[onehouse] at Islington. But he also immediately entered upon the subject, telling me now he was fully assured that no one has any degree of faith till he is "perfect as God is perfect." I asked, "Have *you*, then, *no degree* of faith?" He said, "No, for I have not a clean heart." I turned and asked his servant, "Esther, have you a clean heart?" She said, "No, my heart is desperately wicked, but I have no doubt or fear. I know my Saviour loves *me* and I love him; I feel it every moment." I then plainly told her master, "Here is an end of your reasoning. This is the state the existence of which you deny." . . .

*Sun.* 22 [June 1740]. Finding there was no time to delay without utterly destroying the cause of God, I began to execute what I had long designed — to strike at the root of the grand delusion. Accordingly, from those words of Jeremiah, "Stand ye in the way, ask for the old paths" [Jer. 6:16], I took occasion to give a plain account both of the work which God had begun among us and of the manner wherein the enemy had sown his tares among the good seed [*cf*. Mt. 13:25-36], to this effect:

After we had wandered many years in the *new path* of *salvation by faith and works*, about two years ago it pleased God to show us the *old way* of *salvation by faith only*. And many soon tasted of this salvation, "being justified *freely*, having peace with God, rejoicing in hope of the glory of God" [*cf*. Rom. 5:1-2], and having his "love shed abroad in their hearts." These now ran the way of his *commandments:* they performed all their *duty* to God and man. They walked in all the *ordinances* of the Lord, and through these *means* which he had appointed for that end received daily *grace* to help in time of need [*cf.* Heb. 4:16], and went on "from faith to faith."

But eight or nine months ago certain men arose, speaking contrary to the doctrines we had received. They had affirmed that we were all in a wrong way still; that we had "no faith at all"; that faith admits of *no degrees* and, consequently, *weak faith is no faith;* that none is justified till he has a clean heart and is incapable of any doubt or fear.

They affirmed also that there is *no commandment* in the New Testament but *to believe;* that no other *duty* lies upon us; and that when a man does believe, he is not *bound* or *obliged* to do anything which is commanded there; in particular, that he is not *subject to ordinances*, that is (as they explained it) is not *bound* or *obliged* to pray, to communicate, to read or hear the Scriptures; but may or may not use any of these things (being in no bondage) according as he finds "his heart free to it." [4]

They farther affirmed that a believer cannot use any of these as "a means of grace"; that indeed there is no such thing as any "means of grace," this expression having no foundation in Scripture; and that an unbeliever, or one who has not a clean heart, ought not to use them at all, ought not to pray, or search the Scriptures, or communicate, but to "be still" — *i.e.* leave off these "works of the law" — and then he will surely receive faith, which, till he is "still," he cannot have.

All these assertions I propose to consider. The first was that *weak faith is no faith.*

By "weak faith" I understand: (1) That which is mixed with fear, particularly of not enduring to the end. (2) That which is mixed with doubt, whether we have not deceived ourselves and whether our sins be *indeed* forgiven. (3) That which has not yet *purified the heart* fully, at least not from all its idols. And thus "weak" I find the "faith" of almost all believers to be within a short time after they have first "peace with God."

Yet that weak faith *is* faith appears: (1) from St. Paul: "Him that is weak in the faith, receive" [*cf.* Rom. 14:1]; (2) from St. John, speaking of believers who were "little children," as well as of "young men" and "fathers" [*cf.* 1 Jn. 2:1, 12–13]; (3) from our Lord's own words, "Why are ye fearful, O ye of little faith? O thou of little faith, where-

4. *Cf.* Wesley's reference to this notion as "that enthusiastic doctrine of devils" in the Rules of the Societies; above, p. 179.

fore didst thou doubt? I have prayed for thee (Peter), that thy faith fail thee not" [*cf.* Mt. 8:26; Lk. 22:32]. Therefore he then had faith. Yet so *weak* was that *faith* that not only *doubt* and *fear*, but gross *sin* in the same night, prevailed over him.

Nevertheless he was "clean, by the word Christ had spoken to him" [*cf.* Jn. 15:3] — *i.e. justified* — though 'tis plain he had not "a clean heart."

Therefore, there are *degrees in faith;* and *weak faith* may yet be *true faith.*

*Mon.* 23. I considered the second assertion, that there is but *one commandment* in the New Testament, viz., "to believe"; that no other *duty* lies upon us, and that a believer is not obliged to do anything *as commanded:*

How gross, palpable a contradiction is this to the whole tenor of the New Testament, every part of which is full of commandments, from St. Matthew to the Revelation! But it is enough to observe:

1. That this bold affirmation is shamelessly contrary to our Lord's own words, "Whosoever shall break one of the least of *these commandments* shall be called the least in the kingdom of heaven" [*cf.* Mt. 5:19]. For nothing can be more evident than that he here speaks of more than one, of several commandments, which every soul, believer or not, is *obliged* to keep *as commanded;*

2. That this whole scheme is overturned from top to bottom by that other sentence of our Lord's, "When ye have done *all that is commanded you,* say, 'We . . . have done no more than it was *our duty* to do'" [*cf.* Lk. 17:10].

3. That although to do what God commands is a believer's *privilege,* that does not affect the question. He does it nevertheless as his "bounden duty," and "as a command of God."

4. That this is the surest evidence of his believing, according to our Lord's own words, "If ye love me" (which cannot be unless ye believe), "keep my commandments" [*cf.* Jn. 14:15].

5. That to desire to do what God commands, but not as a command, is to affect not freedom but independency; such independency as St. Paul had not, for though "the Son had made him free," yet was he not without law to God, but "under the law to Christ"; such as the holy angels have not, for they "fulfil his commandments," and hearken to the voice of his word [*cf.* Ps. 103:20, B.C.P.]; yea, such as Christ

himself had not, for "as the Father had given him commandment, so he spake" [*cf.* Jn. 12:49, 50].

*Tues.* 24. The substance of my exposition in the morning, on "Why yet are ye subject to ordinances" [*cf.* Col. 2:20]? was:

From hence it has been inferred that Christians are not subject to the ordinances of Christ; that believers *need not* and unbelievers *may not* use them; that these are not *obliged* and those are not *permitted* so to do; that these *do not sin* when they abstain from them, but those *do sin* when they do not abstain.

But with how little reason this has been inferred will sufficiently appear to all who consider:

1. That the "ordinances" here spoken of by St. Paul are evidently *Jewish* "ordinances," such as "Touch not, taste not, handle not" [Col. 2:21], and those mentioned a few verses before concerning "meats and drinks, and new moons and sabbaths" [*cf.* Col. 2:16].

2. That, consequently, this has no reference to the "ordinances of Christ," such as prayer, communicating, and searching the Scriptures.

3. That Christ himself spake that "men *ought* always to pray," and *commands* "not to forsake the assembling ourselves together" [*cf.* Heb. 10:25], to "search the Scriptures" [*cf.* Jn. 5:39], and to eat bread and drink wine "in remembrance of him" [*cf.* 1 Cor. 11:24, 25].

4. That the *commands* of Christ *oblige* all who are called by his name, whether (in strictness) believers or unbelievers, seeing "whosoever breaketh the least of these commandments shall be called least in the kingdom of heaven" [*cf.* Mt. 5:19].

In the evening I preached on, "Cast not away your confidence, which hath great recompence of reward" [Heb. 10:35].

Ye who have known and felt your sins forgiven, cast not away your confidence;

1. Though your joy should die away, your love wax cold and your peace itself be roughly assaulted; though

2. You should find doubt or fear, or strong and uninterrupted temptation; yea, though

3. You should find a body of sin still in you, and thrusting sore at you that you might fall [*cf.* Ps. 118:13].

The first case may be only a fulfilling of your Lord's words, "yet a little while, and ye shall not see me" [*cf.* Jn. 16:16, 17, 19]. But he "will come unto you again, and your hearts shall rejoice, and your joy no man taketh from you" [*cf*. Jn. 16:22].

Your being in strong temptation, yea, though it should rise so high as to throw you into an agony, or to make you fear that God had forgotten you, is no more a proof that you are not a believer than our Lord's agony — and his crying, "my God, my God, why has thou forsaken me" [Mk. 15:34]? — was a proof that he was not the Son of God.

Your finding sin remaining in you still is no proof that you are not a believer. Sin does remain in one that is justified, though "it has not dominion" over him [*cf*. Rom. 6:14]. For he has not "a clean heart" at first, neither are "all things" as yet "become new" [*cf*. 2 Cor. 5:17]. But fear not, though you have an evil heart. Yet a little while, and you shall be endued with power from on high, whereby you may "purify yourselves, even as he is pure" [*cf*. 1 Jn. 3:3]; and be "holy, as he which hath called you is holy" [*cf*. 1 Pet. 1:15].

*Wed.* 25. From those words, "All Scripture is given by inspiration of God" [2 Tim. 3:16], I took occasion to speak of the ordinances of God as they are "means of grace":

Although this expression of our church, "means of grace," be not found in the Scripture, yet, if the sense of it undeniably is, to cavil at the term is a mere strife of words [1 Tim. 6:4]. But the sense of it is undeniably found in Scripture. For God hath in Scripture ordained prayer, reading or hearing and the receiving the Lord's Supper as the ordinary means of conveying his grace to man.

And first, prayer. For thus saith the Lord, "Ask, and it shall be given you [*cf*. Mt. 7:7]. If any man lack wisdom, let him ask of God" [*cf*. Jas. 1:5]. Here God plainly ordains *prayer* as the *means* of receiving whatsoever *grace* we want; particularly that wisdom from above which is the chief fruit of the *grace* of God.

Here, likewise, God *commands* all to pray who desire to receive any *grace* from him. Here is no restriction as to *believers* or *unbelievers*, but least of all as to unbelievers; for such, doubtless, were most of those to whom he said, "Ask, and it shall be given you."

We know, indeed, that the prayer of an unbeliever is full of sin. Yet let him remember that which is written of one who could not then believe, for he had not so much as heard the gospel: "Cornelius, thy prayers and thine alms are come up for a memorial before God" [Acts 10:4].

*Thur.* 26. I showed, concerning the Holy Scriptures:

1. That to *search* (that is, read and hear them) is a *command* of God.
2. That this *command* is given *to all*, *believers* or *unbelievers*.
3. That this is commanded or ordained as "a means of grace," a means of conveying the grace of God to all, whether *unbelievers* — such as those to whom he first gave this command and those to whom "faith cometh by hearing" — or *believers* — who by experience know that "all Scripture is profitable" — or a means to this end — "that the man of God may be perfect, thoroughly furnished to all good works" [2 Tim. 3:16–17].

*Fri.* 27. I preached on, "Do this in remembrance of me" [*cf.* Lk. 22:19; 1 Cor. 11:24–25]:

In the ancient Church, every one who was baptized communicated daily. So in the Acts we read: "they all continued daily in the breaking of bread and in prayer" [*cf.* Acts 2:46].

But in latter times many have affirmed that the Lord's Supper is not a "converting" but a "confirming" ordinance.

And among us it has been diligently taught that none but those who are "converted," who "have received the Holy Ghost," who are believers in the full sense, ought to communicate.

But experience shows the gross falsehood of that assertion, that the Lord's Supper is not a "converting" ordinance. Ye are the witnesses. For many now present know, the very beginning of your "conversion" to God (perhaps, in some, the first deep "conviction") was wrought at the Lord's Supper. Now, one single instance of this kind overthrows the whole assertion.

The falsehood of the other assertion appears both from Scripture precept and example. Our Lord commanded those very men who were then *unconverted*, who had not yet "received the Holy Ghost," who (in the full sense of the word) were not *believers*, to "do this in remembrance of him." Here the precept is clear. And to these he delivered the elements with his own hands. Here is example equally indisputable.

*Sat.* 28. I showed at large:

1. That the Lord's Supper was ordained by God to be "a means" of *conveying* to men either *preventing* or *justifying* or *sanctifying grace*, according to their several necessities.

2. That the persons for whom it was ordained are all those who know and feel that they *want* the *grace* of God, either to *restrain* them from sin or to "show their sins forgiven" or to "renew their souls" in the image of God.

3. That inasmuch as we come to his table, not to *give* him anything, but to *receive* whatsoever he sees best for us, there is *no previous preparation* indispensably necessary, but *a desire* to receive whatsoever he pleases to give. And,

4. That no *fitness* is required at the time of communicating but *a sense of our state*, of our utter sinfulness and helplessness — every one who knows he is "fit for hell" being just "fit to come to Christ" in this as well as all other ways of his appointment. . . .

*Mond.* 15 [June 1741]. I set out for London, and read over in the way that celebrated book, Martin Luther's *Comment on the Epistle to the Galatians*.[5] I was utterly ashamed. How have I esteemed this book only because I heard it so commended by others, or at best, because I had read some excellent sentences occasionally quoted from it! But what shall I say, now I judge for myself, now I see with my own eyes? Why, not only that the author makes nothing out, clears up not one considerable difficulty, that he is quite shallow in his remarks on many passages, and muddy and confused almost on all — but that he is deeply tinctured with mysticism throughout, and hence often dangerously [6] wrong. To instance only in one or two points: How does he (almost in the words of Tauler) decry "reason" (right or wrong) as an irreconcilable enemy to the gospel of Christ; whereas what is "reason" (the faculty so-called) but the power of apprehending, judging and discoursing? Which power is no more to be condemned in the gross than seeing, hearing, or feeling. Again, how blasphemously does he speak of good works and of the law of God — constantly coupling the law with sin, death, hell, or the devil and teaching that Christ "delivers us from" them all alike. Whereas it can no more be proved by Scripture that Christ "delivers us from the law of God" than that he delivers us *from holiness* or *from heaven*. Here (I apprehend) is the real spring of the grand error of the Moravians. They follow Luther, for better, for worse. Hence their "no works; no law; no commandments." But who art thou that "speakest evil of the law, and judgest the law" [*cf*. Jas. 4:11]?

5. For an account of the English versions of this available to Wesley, see Martin Luther, *A Commentary on St. Paul's Epistle to the Galatians, based on lectures delivered by Martin Luther*, Philip Watson, ed. (1953), 1–14.

6. The first edition here reads, "fundamentally."

*Tues.* 16. In the evening I came to London, and preached on those words: [7] "In Christ Jesus neither circumcision availeth anything, nor uncircumcision, but faith which worketh by love." After reading Luther's miserable comment upon the text, I thought it my bounden duty openly to warn the congregation against that dangerous treatise, and to retract whatever recommendation I might ignorantly have given of it. . . .

*Thurs.* 3 [September 1741]. James Hutton having sent me word that Count Zinzendorf would meet me at three in the afternoon, I went at that time to Gray's Inn Walks. The most material part of our conversation (which I dare not conceal) was as follows:

z. Cur religionem tuam mutasti? [8]

w. Nescio me religionem meam mutasse. Cur id sentis? Quis hoc tibi retulit?

z. Plane tu. Id ex epistola tua ad nos video. Ibi, religione, quam apud nos professus es, relicta, novam profiteris.

w. Qui sic? Non intelligo.

z. Imo, istic dicis, "Vere Christianos non esse miseros peccatores." Falsissimum. Optimi hominum ad mortem usque miserabilissimi sunt peccatores. Siqui aliud dicunt, vel penitus impostores sunt, vel diabolice seducti. Nostros fratres meliora docentes impugnasti. Et pacem volentibus, eam denegasti.

---

z. Why have you changed your religion?

w. I am unaware of any change in my religion. What makes you think so? What gave you any such idea?

z. It came from you. I recognized it in your "epistle" to us. [See below, pp. 373–76.] In it, you abandon the religion we have been professing together in favor of a new one.

w. Really? I don't understand.

z. Yes, indeed. In the letter you say: "True Christians are not miserable sinners." This is entirely wrong. The best of men are miserable sinners till death. Those who speak otherwise are either deluded inwardly or else seduced by the devil. Moreover, you have opposed our brethren in their efforts to teach a better way. And when they sought amity, you spurned it.

7. [Au.] Gal. 5:6.
8. The present translation is supplied by the editor. *Cf.* the snatches of this conversation supplied by Wesley in his *Dialogue Between an Antinomian and His Friend* (1745), *Works,* X, 266–76; see also Henry Moore's translation in his *Life,* I, 281–83.

w. Nondum intelligo quid velis.

z. Ego, cum ex Georgia ad me scripsisti, te dilexi plurimum. Tum [*sic*] corde simplicem, te agnovi. Iterum scripsisti. Agnovi corde simplicem, sed turbatis ideis. Ad nos venisti. Ideae tuae tum magis turbatae erant et confusae. In Angliam rediisti. Aliquandiu post, audivi fratres nostros tecum pugnare. Spangenbergium misi ad pacem inter vos conciliandam. Scripsit mihi, "Fratres tibi injuriam intulisse." Rescripsi, ne pergerent, sed et veniam a te peterent. Spangenberg scripsit iterum, "Eos petiisse; sed te gloriari de iis, pacem nolle." Jam adveniens, idem audio.

w. Res in eo cardine minime vertitur. Fratres tui (verum hoc) me male tractarunt. Postea veniam petierunt. Respondi, "Id supervacaneum; me nunquam iis succensuisse: sed vereri, (1) ne falsa docerent; (2) ne prave viverent." Ista unica est, et fuit, inter nos quaestio.

z. Apertius loquaris.

w. Veritus sum, ne falsa docerent (1) de fine fidei nostrae (in hac vita), scil. Christiana perfectione; (2) de mediis gratiae, sic ab ecclesia nostra dictis.

---

w. I still don't understand what you are driving at.

z. When you first wrote me, from Georgia, I loved you very much. I recognized your guileless heart. Then you wrote again. I could still recognize your guileless heart, but also now your confused ideas. Afterwards, you visited us [at Marienborn]. By that time your notions were more confused and mixed up than ever. Then you returned to England. Shortly afterwards, I heard that you and our brethren were in conflict. I sent Spangenberg to make peace and reconcile you to each other. He reported that "the brethren had done you wrong." Thereupon, I ordered them to stop quarreling and to seek reconciliation with you. Spangenberg wrote that they had tried this, but that you preferred fame to peace. Since my arrival in London, I hear the same story.

w. Such an affair does not hinge on a single point. Your brethren did treat me badly and they did seek reconciliation. My response was that reconciliation was beside the point. What mattered was that they should be concerned (1) not to teach error and (2) not to live carelessly. This was, and still is, the only issue between us.

z. Speak more clearly.

w. I am concerned over their false teaching in respect of (1) the goal of our faith in this life — *i.e.* Christian perfection — and (2) "the means of grace," as our church expresses it.

z. Nullam inhaerentem perfectionem in hac vita agnosco. Est hic error errorum. Eum per totum orbem igne et gladio persequor, conculco, ad internecionem do. Christus est sola perfectio nostra. Qui perfectionem inhaerentem sequitur, Christum denegat.

w. Ego vero credo, Spiritum Christi operari perfectionem in vere Christianis.

z. Nullimode. Omnis nostra perfectio est in Christo. Omnis Christiana perfectio est, fides in sanguine Christi. Est tota Christiana perfectio, imputata, non inhaerens. Perfecti sumus in Christo, in nobismet nunquam perfecti.

w. Pugnamus, opinor, de verbis. Nonne omnis vere credens sanctus est?

z. Maxime. Sed sanctus in Christo, non in se.

w. Sed, nonne sancte vivit?

z. Imo, sancte in omnibus vivit.

w. Nonne, et cor sanctum habet?

z. Certissime.

w. Nonne, ex consequenti, sanctus est *in se?*

z. Non, non. In Christo tantum. Non sanctus *in se*. Nullam omnino habet sanctitatem *in se*.

---

z. I know of no such thing as inherent perfection in this life. This is the error of errors. I pursue it everywhere with fire and sword! I stamp it under foot! I give it over to destruction! Christ is our only perfection. Whoever affirms inherent perfection denies Christ.

w. But I truly believe that it is Christ's own Spirit that works in true Christians to achieve their perfection.

z. By no means! All our perfection is in Christ. All Christian perfection is simply faith in Christ's blood. Christian perfection is entirely imputed, not inherent. We are perfect in Christ; never perfect in ourselves.

w. It seems to me that we are fighting over terms. Isn't every true believer holy?

z. Indeed. But holy in Christ, not *in himself.*

w. But doesn't he live a holy life?

z. Of course. His whole life is holy.

w. Well, then, does he have a holy heart?

z. Certainly.

w. It follows, then, that he is holy *in se*, doesn't it?

z. No, no! Only in Christ! Not holy *in se*. No one has any holiness *in se.*

w. Nonne habet in corde suo amorem Dei et proximi, quin et totam imaginem Dei?

z. Habet. Sed haec sunt sanctitas legalis, non evangelica. Sanctitas evangelica est fides.

w. Omnino lis est de verbis. Concedis, credentis cor totum esse sanctum et vitam totam: eum amare Deum toto corde, eique servire totis viribus. Nihil ultra peto. Nil aliud volo per perfectio vel sanctitas Christiana.

z. Sed haec non est sanctitas ejus. Non magis sanctus est, si magis amat, neque minus sanctus, si minus amat.

w. Quid? Nonne credens, dum crescit in amore, crescit pariter in sanctitate?

z. Nequaquam. Eo momento quo justificatur, sanctificatur penitus. Exin, neque magis sanctus est, neque minus sanctus, ad mortem usque.

w. Nonne igitur pater in Christo sanctior est infante recens nato?

z. Non. Sanctificatio totalis ac justificatio in eodem sunt instanti; et neutra recipit magis aut minus.

w. Nonne vero credens crescit indies amore Dei? Num perfectus est amore simulac justificatur?

---

w. The believer has the love of God and neighbor in his heart, doesn't he? — and with this, the full *imago Dei?*

z. He has. But this is mere legal, not evangelical holiness. Evangelical holiness is faith.

w. Apparently, this is a squabble about words. You concede that the believer is holy in his heart and life, that he loves God with his whole heart and serves him with his whole strength. I ask no more. I'm interested in no other sort of perfection or holiness.

z. But this holiness doesn't belong to the believer. He is not more holy if more loving, or less holy if less loving.

w. What? You believe that while he is growing in love, he is also growing in holiness, don't you?

z. Not at all. From the moment one is justified, he is entirely sanctified. Thereafter till death he is neither more holy nor less holy.

w. This, then, would mean that a father in Christ is not a whit more holy than a newborn babe?

z. No, he is not. The event of sanctification and justification is completed in an instant. Thereafter, it neither increases nor decreases.

w. The true believer grows daily in his love of God, doesn't he? Is he, then, entirely perfected in love when he is justified?

z. Est. Non unquam crescit in amore Dei. Totaliter amat eo momento, sicut totaliter sanctificatur.

w. Quid itaque vult Apostolus Paulus, per, "Renovamur de die in diem?"

z. Dicam. Plumbum si in aurum mutetur, est aurum primo die et secundo et tertio. Et sic renovatur de die in diem. Sed numquam est magis aurum, quam primo die.

w. Putavi, crescendum esse in gratia!

z. Certe. Sed non in sanctitate. Simulac justificatur quis, Pater, Filius, et Spiritus Sanctus habitant in ipsius corde. Et cor ejus eo momento aeque purum est ac unquam erit. Infans in Christo tam purus corde est quam pater in Christo. Nulla est discrepantia.

w. Nonne justificati erant apostoli ante Christi mortem?

z. Erant.

w. Nonne vero sanctiores erant post diem Pentecostes, quam ante Christi mortem?

z. Neutiquam.

w. Nonne eo die impleti sunt Spiritu Sancto?

---

z. He is. One does not grow in God's love. From the moment of justification he loves as entirely as he is also entirely sanctified.

w. What then did the Apostle Paul mean by his statement, "We are renewed day by day" [2 Cor. 4:16]?

z. Let me put it this way. When a piece of lead is changed into gold, it is a piece of gold — the first day, the second and the third. It is thus "renewed day by day." But it never becomes "more gold" than it was the first day.

w. I had thought that we ought to grow in grace!

z. Of course. [In grace] but not in holiness. When a man is justified, the Father, Son and Holy Spirit make his heart their dwelling place. And from then on, his heart is as pure as it will ever be. A babe-in-Christ is as pure in heart as any father-in-Christ. There is no difference.

w. The apostles were justified before Christ's death, weren't they?

z. They were.

w. They were also more holy after the day of Pentecost than before Christ's death, weren't they?

z. Not at all.

w. But, on that day, they were "filled with the Holy Spirit," weren't they [cf. Acts 2:4]?

z. Erant. Sed istud donum Spiritus, sanctitatem ipsorum non respexit. Fuit donum miraculorum tantum.

w. Fortasse te non capio. Nonne nos ipsos abnegantes, magis magisque mundo morimur, ac Deo vivimus?

z. Abnegationem omnem respuimus, conculcamus. Facimus credentes omne quod volumus et nihil ultra. Mortificationem omnem ridemus. Nulla purificatio praecedit perfectum amorem.

w. Quae dixisti, Deo adjuvante, perpendam.

---

z. They were. But that particular gift of the Spirit had nothing to do with their holiness. It was merely the gift of miracles.

w. Perhaps I don't grasp your thought. Through self-denial, we die to the world more and more and so live more to God, don't we?

z. We reject all "denials"; we despise them. As believers, we do as we please and nothing else. We heap scorn on all "mortifications." No "purification" is prerequisite to love's perfection.

w. With God's help, I will consider what you have said. . . .

The letter referred to by the count [see above, p. 368] was written the preceding August 8. Except for two or three paragraphs, which I have omitted as less material, it was as follows:

JOHN WESLEY,
A PRESBYTER OF THE CHURCH OF GOD IN ENGLAND:
TO THE CHURCH OF GOD AT HERRNHUT IN UPPER LUSATIA

1. It may seem strange that such a one as I am should take upon me to write to you. You, I believe to be "dear children of God through faith which is in Jesus." Me, you believe (as some of you have declared) to be "a child of the devil, a servant of corruption." Yet whatsoever I am or whatsoever you are, I beseech you to weigh the following words if haply God, who "sendeth by whom he will send," may give *you* light thereby — although "the mist of darkness" (as one of you affirms) should be reserved for *me* for ever.

2. My design is freely and plainly to speak whatsoever I have seen or heard among you, in any part of your church, which seems not agreeable to the gospel of Christ. And my hope is that the God whom you serve will give you thoroughly to weigh what is spoken; and if in anything "ye have been otherwise minded" than the truth is, [he] "will reveal even this unto you" [*cf.* Phil. 3:15].

3. And first, with regard to Christian salvation, even the present salvation which is through faith, I have heard some of you affirm:

1. That it does not imply the proper "taking away" our sins, the cleansing our souls "from all sin," but only the "tearing the system of sin" in pieces.

2. That it does not imply liberty from sinful thoughts.

4. I have heard some of you affirm, on the other hand:

1. That it does imply liberty from the commandments of God, so that one who is saved through faith is not *obliged* or *bound* to obey them, does not do anything as a *commandment*, or as a *duty*. To support which they have affirmed that there is [9] *no command* in the New Testament but to believe; that there is *no duty* required therein but that of believing; and that to a believer there is *no commandment* at all.

2. That it does imply liberty to conform to the world, by talking on useless, if not trifling subjects; by joining in worldly diversions in order to do good; by putting on of gold and costly apparel, or by continuing in those professions, the gain of which depends on ministering hereto.

3. That it does imply liberty to avoid persecution, by *not reproving* even those who sin in your sight; by *not letting* your light shine before those men who love darkness rather than light; by *not using* plainness of speech and a *frank, open carriage* to all men — nay, by a close, dark, reserved conversation and behaviour, especially toward strangers. And in many of you I have more than once found (what you called "being wise as serpents" — *cf.* Mt. 10:16) much, subtlety, much evasion and disguise, much guile and dissimulation. You appeared to be what you were not, or not to be what you were. You so studied "to become all things to all men" [*cf.* 1 Cor. 9:12; 10:33] as to take the colour and shape of any that were near you. So that your practice was indeed no proof of your judgment; but only an indication of your design *nulli laedere os*,[10] and of your conformity to that (not scriptural) maxim, *sinere mundum vadere ut vult; nam vult vadere.*[11]

5. Secondly, with regard to that faith through which we are saved, I have heard many of you say, "A man may have justifying faith and not

9. At this point, Wesley begins to add a number of footnotes, consisting of excerpts from the replies he had received from Herrnhut, with additional reactions of his own; see *Journal*, II, 491–92.

10. "To affront no one." Cf. Terence, *The Brothers* (Adelphi), Act VI, Sc. V, par. iv (Loeb ed., [Cambridge, Mass., 1947], II, 308, l. 864).

11. Let the world go, as it will, for so it is bound, whatever.

know it." Others of you who are now in England (particularly Mr. Molther) I have heard affirm that there is no such thing as "weak faith"; [12] that there are "*no* degrees in faith"; that there is "no justifying faith" where there is ever any *doubt;* and there is no justifying faith without "the plerophory of faith" (the clear, abiding witness of the Spirit); that there is no justifying faith where there is not, in the full, proper sense, a new or clean heart; and that those who have not these two gifts are only "awakened," not "justified."

6. Thirdly, as to the way to faith, here are many among us whom your brethren have advised (what it is not to be supposed they would as yet speak to me or in their public preaching) [13] "not to use those ordinances" which our church terms "means of grace" till they have such a faith as implies a clean heart and excludes all possibility of doubting. They have advised them, till then, "not to search the Scriptures, not to pray, not to communicate"; and have often affirmed that to do these things is seeking salvation by works; and that till these works are laid aside, no man can receive faith; for, "No man," say they, "can do these things without trusting in them: if he does not trust in them, why does he do them?"

7. To those who answered, "It is *our duty* to use the ordinances of God," they replied, "There are *no ordinances* of Christ, the use of which is now *bound* upon Christians as a *duty*, or which we are *commanded* to use. As to those you mention in particular (viz. prayer, communicating, and searching the Scripture), if a man have faith, he *need* not; if he have not, he *must* not use them. A believer may use them, though not as *enjoined;* but an unbeliever (as before defined) *may not*."

8. To those who answered, "I hope God will through these 'means' convey his grace to my soul," they replied, "There is *no* such thing as 'means of grace.' Christ has not ordained any such in his Church. But if there were, they are nothing to you, for you are dead. You have no faith, and you cannot 'work' while you are 'dead.' Therefore, let these things alone *till* you have faith."

9. And some of our English brethren who are joined with yours have said openly, "You will never have faith till you leave running about to church and sacrament and societies." Another of them has said (in his public expounding), "As many go to hell by praying as by thieving." Another, "I knew one who, leaning over the back of a chair, received a

12. [Au.] "In the Preface to the *Second Journal,* the Moravian church is cleared of this mistake."

13. *Cf. Letters,* I, 347.

great gift. But he must kneel down to give God thanks: so he lost it immediately. And I know not whether he will ever have it again." And yet another, "You have lost your first joy; therefore you pray: that is the devil. You read the Bible: that is the devil. You communicate: that is the devil."

10. Let not any of you, my brethren, say, "*We* are not chargeable with what *they* speak." Indeed you are; for you *can* hinder it if you will. Therefore, if you do not, it must be charged upon *you*. If you do not use the power which is in your hands and thereby prevent their speaking thus, you do in effect speak thus yourselves. You make *their* words *your own;* and are, accordingly, chargeable with every ill consequence which may flow therefrom.

11. Fourthly, with regard to your *church,* you greatly, yea, above measure, exalt yourselves and despise others. I have scarce heard one Moravian brother in my life own *his* church to be wrong in anything.

I have scarce heard any of you (I think not one in England) own *himself* to be wrong in anything.

Many of you I have heard speak of your church as if it were infallible, or so led by the Spirit that it was not possible for it to err in anything.

Some of you have set it up (as indeed you ought to do if it be infallible) as the judge of all the earth, of all persons (as well as doctrines) therein; and you have accordingly passed sentence upon them at once, by their agreement or disagreement with your church.

Some of you have said that there is "no *true* church" on earth *but yours;* yea, that there are "no true Christians out of it." And your own members you require to have *implicit faith* in her decisions and to pay *implicit obedience* to her directions.

12. Fifthly, you receive not the ancients [*i.e.* the early "fathers of the Church"], but the modern mystics [14] as the best interpreters of Scripture; and in conformity to these, you mix much of man's wisdom with the wisdom of God; you greatly refine the plain religion taught by the letter of Holy Writ and philosophize on almost every part of it, to accommodate it to the mystic theory. Hence you talk much, in a manner wholly unsupported by Scripture, against "mixing nature with grace," against "imagination," and concerning the "animal spirits" mimicking the power of the Holy Ghost. Hence your brethren zealously caution us against "animal joy," against "natural love" of one another, and against "selfish

14. See above, pp. 45-47.

love" of God; against which (or any of them) there is no one caution in
all the Bible. And they have, in truth, greatly lessened and had well-nigh
destroyed brotherly love from among us.

13. In conformity to the mystics, you likewise greatly check joy in
the Holy Ghost by such cautions against "sensible comforts" as have no
tittle of Scripture to support them. Hence also your brethren here damp
the zeal of babes in Christ, talking much of false zeal, forbidding them to
declare what God hath done for their souls, even when their hearts burn
within them to declare it, and comparing those to "uncorked bottles" who
simply and artlessly speak of the ability which God giveth.

14. Hence, lastly, it is that you undervalue good works (especially
works of outward mercy), never publicly insisting on the necessity of
them, nor declaring their weight and excellency. Hence, when some of
your brethren have spoken of them, they put them on a wrong foot;
viz. "if you find yourself moved, if your heart is free to it, then reprove,
exhort, relieve." By this means you wholly avoid the taking up your cross
in order to do good; and also substitute an uncertain, precarious inward
motion in the place of the plain written word. Nay, one of your members
has said of good works in general (whether works of piety or of charity):
"A believer is no more *obliged* to do *these* works of the law than a subject of the king of England is obliged to obey the laws of the king of
France."

15. My brethren, whether ye will hear or whether ye will forbear, I
have now delivered my own soul. And this I have chosen to do in an
artless manner, that, if anything should come home to your hearts, the
effect might evidently flow not from the wisdom of man but from the
power of God.[15]

15. See the remainder of this *Extract from the Journal* for Wesley's defense of
himself against the charge of inconsistency in thus turning against his erstwhile allies;
cf. *Journal*, II, 495–500.

# II

## THE MENACE OF ANTINOMIANISM

*A Blow at the Root, or*
*Christ Stabb'd in the House of His Friends* [1]

*Editor's introduction.* First published as a twelve-page duodecimo pamphlet in 1762, this little salvo bespeaks a bitter struggle within the ranks of the Revival — between Wesley and some of his erstwhile colleagues who had pushed the consequences of "justification by *faith alone*" to extravagant limits, to which they had added a bitter contempt for "ordinary" Christians. The last entry in the *Journal* for the year 1762 reflects Wesley's difficulties with these extremists: "I now stood and looked back on the past year; a year of uncommon trials and uncommon blessings. Abundance have been convinced of sin; very many have found peace with God; and in London only, I believe, full two hundred have been brought into glorious liberty. And yet I have had more care and trouble in six months than in several years preceding" (*Journal*, IV, 542). Wesley's chief antagonists in this particular situation were Thomas Maxfield and George Bell. The latter brought the Methodists into particular disrepute by his rousing prophecy of the end of the world, scheduled for February 28, 1763 (*cf.* Tyerman, *Life*, II, 431). At the heart of it all was, yet again, the "poison" of antinomianism, and it was as an antidote that Wesley produced the following short polemic (see also *Works*, VIII, 349–51).

✥ ✥ ✥ ✥

1. The present text is based on the edition of 1773 (*Works* [Pine], XX, 265–75), collated with the first edition (1762) and the third (1780).

"Judas, betrayest thou the Son of Man with a kiss?" (Lk. 22:48)

1. "Without holiness no man shall see the Lord" [*cf.* Heb. 12:14] — *i.e.* shall see the face of God in glory. Nothing under heaven can be more sure than this, "for the mouth of the Lord hath spoken it" [Is. 1:20]. "And though heaven and earth pass away, yet his word shall not pass away" [Mk. 13:31]. As well therefore might God fall from heaven as this word fall to the ground. No, it cannot be. None shall live with God but he that now *lives to* God; none shall enjoy the glory of God in heaven but he that bears the image of God on earth. None that is not saved from sin here can be saved from hell hereafter. None can see the kingdom of God above unless the kingdom of God be in him below. Whosoever will reign with Christ in heaven must have Christ reigning in him on earth. He must have "that mind in him which was in Christ" [*cf.* Phil. 2:5], enabling him to "walk as Christ also walked."

2. And yet as sure as this is and as clearly as it is taught in every part of the Holy Scripture, there is scarce one among all the truths of God which is less received by men. It was indeed acknowledged in some degree, even among the wiser heathens. Some among them allowed that nothing would please God but the *sancti recessus mentis, et incoctum generoso pectus honesto*,[2] "a virtuous, holy mind, and an heart deep-dyed with generous honesty." But though they could not deny, yet how easily and effectually did they evade this. They fancied something else would do as well, that some rites or ceremonies, some external forms, or glorious actions would supply the place of inward holiness. So the famous Roman entitles to future happiness, not only the good and virtuous, but all

> *Ob patriam pugnando vulnera passos*
> *Quique pii vates, et Phoebo digna locuti;*
> *Inventas aut qui vitam excoluere per artes.*[3]

So, to fight for their country, to write good verses or to invent useful arts was abundantly sufficient, in the judgment of the wisest heathens, to give men a place in heaven!

3. But this would not pass with modern Romans. They despised such

2. *Cf.* Perseus Flaccus, *Satires*, II, l. 73–74; see also John Conington's translation and commentary (Oxford, 1893), 48–49.

3. *Cf.* Vergil, *Aeneid*, Bk. VI, l. 660–64. This is, as usual, a garbled quotation, the actual text of which comes into English somewhat as follows:

"... those who suffered wounds fighting for the fatherland; those who in their lifetime were pure priests; plus the good poets whose verses were worthy of Phoebus; and those as well, who enriched human existence by their arts."

gross imaginations. But though they did not allow these, they found out another way to get to heaven without holiness. In the room of them they substituted penances, pilgrimages, praying to saints and angels and, above all these, masses for the dead, absolution by a priest and extreme unction. And these satisfy the Romanists full as well as lustrations did the heathens. Thousands of them make no manner of doubt but, by a diligent use of these, without any holiness at all, they shall "see the Lord" in glory.

4. However, Protestants will not be satisfied thus. They know this hope is no better than a spider's web. They are convinced that whoever leans on this, leans on the staff of a broken reed. What then can they do? How shall they hope to see God without holiness? Why, by doing no harm, doing good, going to the church and sacrament.[4] And many thousands sit down content with this, believing they are in the high road to heaven.

5. Yet many cannot rest here. They look upon this as the very "popery of Protestantism." They well know that although none can be a real Christian without carefully abstaining from all evil, using every means of grace at every opportunity and doing all possible good to all men, yet a man may go thus far, may do all this, and be but an heathen still. They know this religion is too superficial. It is but, as it were, skin deep. Therefore, it is not Christianity. For that lies in the heart: it is worshipping God "in spirit and in truth" [Jn. 4:23]; it is no other than "the kingdom of God within us" [cf. Lk. 17:21]; it is "the life of God in the soul of man";[5] it is the mind which was in Christ Jesus; it is "righteousness and peace and joy in the Holy Ghost" [Rom. 14:17].

6. Besides, they see that, be this religion shallower or deeper, it does not stand on the right foundation, since "other foundation" for true religion "can no man lay than that which is laid, even Christ Jesus" [cf. 1 Cor. 3:11], since no one can have the mind which was in Christ till he is justified by his blood, till he is forgiven and reconciled to God through the redemption that is in Jesus Christ. And none can be justified, they are well assured, but by faith, even faith alone, seeing "to him" only "that believeth on God who justifieth the ungodly, his faith is counted to him for righteousness" [Rom. 4:5].

7. What evasion now? What way could Satan take to make all this light of none effect? What could be done when that grand truth, "By grace ye are saved through faith" [Eph. 2:8], was more and more gen-

4. I.e. the General Rules of the Methodist Societies, above, p. 177 ff.
5. The title of a then famous devotional classic by Henry Scougal (1677), which had been a long-time favorite of Wesley's.

erally received? What, indeed, but to persuade the very men who had received it to "turn the grace of God into lasciviousness" [*cf.* Jude 4]? To this end Simon Magus appeared again, and taught "that Christ had *done*, as well as suffered *all; that his righteousness* being imputed to *us*, we need none of *our own;* that seeing there was so much righteousness and holiness *in him*, there needs none more *in us;* that to think we have any, or to desire or seek any, is to renounce Christ; that from the beginning to the end of salvation, all is *in Christ*, nothing *in man;* and that those who teach otherwise are 'legal preachers' and know nothing of the gospel." [6]

8. This is indeed "a blow at the root" [*cf.* Hos. 9:16] — the root of all holiness, all true religion. Hereby Christ is "stabbed in the house of his friends" [*cf.* Zech. 13:6], of those who make the largest professions of loving and honouring him, the whole design of his death — namely "to destroy the works of the devil" [1 Jn. 3:8] — being overthrown at a stroke. For wherever this doctrine is cordially received, it leaves no place for holiness. It demolishes it from top to bottom; it destroys both root and branch [*cf.* Mal. 4:1]. It effectually tears up all desire of it, all endeavour after it. It forbids all such exhortations as might excite those desires or awaken those endeavours. Nay, it makes men afraid of personal holiness, afraid of cherishing any thought of it or motion toward it, lest they should deny the faith and reject Christ and his righteousness. So that, instead of being "zealous of good works" [Tit. 2:14], they [good works] are a stink in their nostrils. And they are infinitely more afraid of "the works of God" [*cf.* Jn. 6:28] than of "the works of the devil."

9. Here is wisdom, though not the wisdom of the saints, but wisdom from beneath! Here is the masterpiece of Satan. Farther than this he cannot go! Men are holy without a grain of holiness in them — holy in Christ, however unholy in themselves. They are in Christ, without one jot of the mind that was in Christ — in Christ, though their [fallen] nature is whole in them. They are "complete in him" [*cf.* Col. 2:10], though they are "in themselves" as proud, as vain, as covetous, as passionate as ever. It is enough. They may be unrighteous still, seeing Christ has "fulfilled all righteousness" [*cf.* Mt. 3:15].

10. O ye simple ones, "how long will ye love simplicity" [*cf.* Prov. 1:22]? How long will ye "seek death in the error of your life"? "Know ye not," whoever teacheth you otherwise, "that the unrighteous shall not inherit the kingdom of God" [*cf.* 1 Cor. 6:9]? "Be not deceived," although

6. A paraphrased summary of the teachings of Thomas Maxfield.

there are many lie in wait to deceive, and that under the fair pretence of "exalting" Christ — a pretence which the more easily steals upon *you*, because "to you he is precious" [*cf.* 1 Pet. 2:7]. But as the Lord liveth, "neither fornicators, nor idolators, nor adulterers, nor effeminate, nor sodomites, nor thieves, nor covetous, nor drunkards, nor revilers, nor extortioners, shall inherit the kingdom of God." "Such, indeed, were some of you. But ye are washed, but ye are sanctified," as well as "justified in the name of the Lord Jesus and by the Spirit of our God" [*cf.* 1 Cor. 6:9–11]. You are really changed; you are not only *accounted*, but actually *made, righteous*. "The law" — the inward power — "of the Spirit of life in Christ Jesus hath made *you* free" — really, actually free — "from the law" (or power) "of sin and death" [Rom. 8:2]. This is liberty, true gospel liberty, experienced by every believer: not freedom from the law of God or the works of God, but from the law of sin and the works of the devil. See that ye "stand fast in" this real, not imaginary, "liberty wherewith Christ hath made you free." And take heed ye "be not entangled again," by means of these vain boasters, "in the yoke of" that vile "bondage to sin," from which ye are now clean escaped [*cf.* Gal. 5:1]. I testify unto you that if you still continue in sin, Christ shall profit you nothing; that Christ is no Saviour to *you* unless he saves you *from your sins;* and that unless it purify your heart, faith shall profit you nothing. O when will ye understand, that to oppose either inward or outward holiness, under colour of exalting Christ, is directly to act the part of Judas, to "betray the Son of man with a kiss"?

Repent, repent! lest he cut you in sunder with the two-edged sword that cometh out of his mouth [*cf.* Rev. 1:16]! It is *you yourselves* that, by opposing the very end of his coming into the world, are crucifying the Son of God afresh and putting him to an open shame [*cf.* Heb. 6:6]. It is *you* that, by expecting to "see the Lord without holiness" [*cf.* Heb. 12:14], through the righteousness of Christ, "make the blood of the covenant an unholy thing" [*cf.* Heb. 10:29], keeping those unholy that so trust in it. O beware! for evil is before you. If those who name not the Name of Christ and die in their sins shall be punished sevenfold, surely you who thus make Christ "a minister of sin" [*cf.* Gal. 2:17] shall be punished seventy-and-seven-fold. What? Make Christ destroy his own kingdom? Make Christ a factor for Satan? Set Christ against holiness? Talk of Christ as "saving his people *in* their sins"? It is no better than to say, "He saves them from the guilt and not from the power of sin." Will you make the righteousness of Christ *such* a cover for the unrighteousness of man — so that by this means, "the unrighteous" of every kind "shall inherit the kingdom of God?"

Stop! Consider! What are you doing? You did run well. Who hath bewitched you? Who hath corrupted you from the simplicity of Christ, from the purity of the gospel? You *did* know, "he that believeth is born of God" and "whosoever is born of God sinneth not"; but while "he keepeth himself, that wicked one toucheth him not" [*cf.* 1 Jn. 5:1, 18]. O come back to the true, the pure, the old gospel — that which ye received in the beginning! Come back to Christ, who died to make you an holy people, "zealous of good works." "Remember from whence you are fallen and repent and do the first works" [*cf.* Rev. 2:5]. Your "Father worketh hitherto" [*cf.* Jn. 5:17]. Do ye work; else your faith is vain. For "wilt thou know, O vain," O empty "man, that faith without works is dead" [*cf.* Jas. 2:20]? Wilt thou know that "though I have all faith so as to remove mountains and have not love, I am nothing" [*cf.* 1 Cor. 13:2]? Wilt thou know that all the blood and righteousness of Christ — unless that "mind be in thee which was in" him and thou likewise "walk as Christ walked" — will only increase thy damnation? "If any man teach otherwise, and consent not to wholesome words, and to the doctrine which is according to godliness, he is proud, knowing nothing, but doting about strife of words, whereof come railings, evil surmisings, perverse disputings of men of corrupt minds and destitute of the truth" [1 Tim. 6:3–5]. Be no longer afraid of the strongest exhortations either to inward or outward holiness. Hereby God the Father is glorified and God the Son truly exalted. Do not stupidly and senselessly call this "legal" — a silly, unmeaning word. Be not afraid of being "under the law of God," but of being "under the law of sin." Love the strictest preaching best, that which most searches the heart and shows you wherein you are unlike Christ, and that which presses you most to love him with all your heart and serve him with all your strength.

11. Suffer me to warn you of another silly, unmeaning word. Do not say, "I can do nothing." If so, then you know nothing of Christ; then you have no faith. For if you have [faith], if you believe, then you "can do all things through Christ who strengtheneth you" [*cf.* Phil. 4:13]. You can love him and keep his commandments, and to you "his commandments are not grievous" [*cf.* 1 Jn. 5:3]. Grievous to them that believe? Far from it. They are the joy of your heart. Show then your love to Christ by keeping his commandments, by walking in all his ordinances blameless [*cf.* Lk. 1:6]. Honour Christ by obeying him with all your

might, by serving him with all your strength. Glorify Christ by imitating Christ in all things, by walking as he walked. Keep to Christ by keeping in all his ways. Trust in Christ to live and reign in your heart. Have confidence in Christ that he will fulfil in you all his great and precious promises, that he will work in you all the good pleasure of his goodness, and all the work of faith with power. Cleave to Christ till his blood have cleansed you from all pride, all anger, all evil desire. Let Christ do all! Let him that has done all *for* you do all *in* you. Exalt Christ as a Prince to give repentance, a Saviour both to give remission of sins and to create in you a new heart, to renew a right spirit within you [*cf.* Ps. 51:10]. This is the gospel, the pure, genuine gospel: glad tidings of great salvation. Not the new, but the old, the everlasting gospel, the gospel not of Simon Magus but of Jesus Christ. The God and Father of our Lord Jesus Christ give you, "according to the riches of his glory, to be strengthened with might by his Spirit in the inner man, that Christ may dwell in your hearts by faith: that, being rooted and grounded in love, ye may be able to comprehend with all saints, what is the length, and breadth, and depth, and height; and to know that love of Christ which passeth knowledge, that ye may be filled with all the fulness of God" [*cf.* Eph. 3:16–19]!

# III

## TENSIONS WITHIN THE CHURCH OF ENGLAND

### An Earnest Appeal to Men of Reason and Religion [1]

*Editor's introduction.* This essay was first published as a fifty-nine-page pamphlet in 1743, and often reprinted thereafter. Revised, it appeared in *Works* (Pine), Vol. XIV, pp. 104–72, and the Jackson edition (1830), Vol. VIII, pp. 1–45; the latter differs from the texts of 1772 or 1786. This first *Appeal* was followed in rapid succession by *A Farther Appeal*, Pts. I–III (published separately but all in the course of the year 1745). Taken together, these *Appeals* constitute Wesley's most important apologia for his own doctrine and for his movement as an evangelical order within the national church — beset as it was by the apathy of nominal Christianity and by the rising tides of rationalism and unbelief.

The first of the four *Appeals*, presented here, is easily the most important. In it Wesley offers (sec. 6–11) what he calls "a rude sketch of the doctrines we teach" — actually one of his clearest statements of his distinctive notion of faith as a spiritual "sense," truly analogous to sensory perception. He then takes up the challenge as to the "reasonableness" of a doctrinal position based on any such epistemological foundation, and argues that it is a reasonable view; far more reasonable than any of its alternatives. From section 38 on he accosts the deists with the threat of final meaninglessness which hangs over their presumption of the powers of unaided human reason. Finally (sec. 52 ff.), he comes to grips with the "men of religion" mentioned in the title — his fellow churchmen who are presumably devout but who have refused to recognize the Methodist contribution to the religious and moral welfare of the nation.

1. The text here is based on the first edition, revised against the editions of 1772 and 1786, the last published in Wesley's lifetime.

In the *Farther Appeal* he repeats these motifs with extensive variations — often in direct dialogue with the anti-Methodist writings of the period. His main point is that, both in its doctrine and discipline, the Revival is firmly rooted in the Anglican tradition, and because of its services to true religion, it deserves at least the sufferance if not the active support of all truly earnest Christians.

The *Appeals* were addressed rather more consciously to non-Methodists than most of Wesley's writings, and there are numerous testimonies in the *Journal* to their effect upon various readers (*cf. Journal*, III, 226, 232, 327, 378; IV, 158, 430; V, 296). Their literary style reminds us even more forcibly than, say, do his sermons that he was still a Fellow of Lincoln: the tags of his Oxford education are both more frequent and self-conscious.

❖   ❖   ❖   ❖

"Doth our law judge any man before it hear him and know what he doeth?" (Jn. 7:51)

1. Although it is with us a "very small thing to be judged of you or of man's judgment" [*cf.* 1 Cor. 4:3], seeing we know God will "make our innocency as clear as the light, and our just dealing as the noon-day" [*cf.* Ps. 37:6, B.C.P.]; yet are we ready to give any that are willing to hear, a plain account, both of our principles and actions: as having "renounced the hidden things of shame" and desiring nothing more "than by manifestation of the truth to commend ourselves to every man's conscience in the sight of God" [*cf.* 2 Cor. 4:2].

2. We see — and who does not? — the numberless follies and miseries of our fellow creatures. We see on every side either men of no religion at all or men of a lifeless, formal religion. We are grieved at the sight, and should greatly rejoice if, by any means, we might convince some that there is a better religion to be attained, a religion worthy of God that gave it. And this we conceive to be no other than love: the love of God and of all mankind; the loving God with all our heart and soul and strength, as having first loved *us*, as the fountain of all the good we have received and of all we ever hope to enjoy; and the loving every soul which God hath made, every man on earth, as our own soul.

3. This love we believe to be the medicine of life, the never-failing remedy for all the evils of a disordered world, for all the miseries and vices of men. Wherever this is, there are virtue and happiness going hand

in hand. There is humbleness of mind, gentleness, long-suffering, the whole image of God, and, at the same time, a peace that passeth all understanding and joy unspeakable and full of glory [cf. Col. 3:12; Phil. 4:7; 1 Pet. 1:8].

> Eternal sunshine of the spotless mind;
> Each prayer accepted, and each wish resign'd;
>
> . . . Desires composed, affections ever even,
> Tears that delight and sighs that waft to heaven.[2]

4. This religion we long to see established in the world: a religon of love and joy and peace, having its seat in the inmost soul, but ever showing itself by its fruits, continually springing forth not only in all innocence — for love worketh no ill to his neighbour — but likewise in every kind of beneficence, spreading virtue and happiness all around it.

5. This religion have we been following after for many years, as many know, if they would testify. But all this time seeking wisdom, we found it not; we were spending our strength in vain. And being now under full conviction of this, we declare it to all mankind; for we desire not that others should wander out of the way as we have done before them, but rather that they may profit by our loss, that they may go (though we did not, having then no man to guide us) the straight way to the religion of love, even by faith.

6. Now, faith (supposing the Scripture to be of God) is πραγμάτων ἐλεγχος οὐ βλεπομένων, the demonstrative evidence of things unseen [cf. Heb. 11:1], the supernatural evidence of things invisible, not perceivable by eyes of flesh, or by any of our natural senses or faculties. Faith is that divine evidence whereby the spiritual man discerneth God and the things of God. It is with regard to the spiritual world what sense is with regard to the natural. It is the spiritual sensation of every soul that is born of God.

7. Perhaps you have not considered it in this view. I will then explain it a little further.

Faith, according to the scriptural account, is the eye of the new-born soul. Hereby every true believer in God "seeth him who is invisible" [Heb. 11:27]. Hereby (in a more particular manner, since life and immortality have been brought to light by the gospel [2 Tim. 1:10]) he "seeth the light of the glory of God in the face of Jesus Christ" [2 Cor. 4:6] and "beholdeth what manner of love it is which the Father hath

2. Alexander Pope, "Eloisa to Abelard," in *Works* (1766), I, 171, l. 209–10, 213–14.

bestowed upon us, that we (who are born of the Spirit) should be called the sons of God" [1 Jn. 3:1].

It is the ear of the soul whereby a sinner "hears the voice of the Son of God and lives" [*cf.* Jn. 5:25], even that voice which alone wakes the dead, saying, "Son, thy sins are forgiven thee" [*cf.* Mk. 2:5].

It is (if I may be allowed the expression) the palate of the soul: for hereby a believer "tastes the good word, and the powers of the world to come" [*cf.* Heb. 6:5], and "hereby he both tastes and sees that God is gracious" [*cf.* Ps. 34:8; 1 Pet. 2:3], yea, "and merciful to him, a sinner" [*cf.* Lk. 18:13].

It is the feeling of the soul whereby a believer perceives, through the "power of the highest overshadowing him" [*cf.* Lk. 1:35], both the existence and the presence of him in whom "he lives, moves and has his being" [Acts 17:28], and indeed the whole invisible world, the entire system of things eternal. And hereby, in particular, he feels "the love of God shed abroad in his heart" [*cf.* Rom. 5:5].

8. "By this faith we are saved" from all uneasiness of mind, from the anguish of a wounded spirit, from discontent, from fear and sorrow of heart, and from that inexpressible listlessness and weariness, both of the world and of ourselves, which we had so helplessly laboured under for many years, especially when we were out of the hurry of the world and sunk into calm reflection. In this we find that love of God and of all mankind, which we had elsewhere sought in vain. This — we know and feel and, therefore, cannot but declare — saves every one that partakes of it both from sin and misery, from every unhappy and every unholy temper.

> Soft peace she brings, wherever she arrives
> She builds our quiet as she forms our lives;
> Lays the rough paths of peevish nature even,
> And opens in each breast a little heaven.[3]

9. If you ask, "Why then have not all men this faith; all, at least, who conceive it to be so happy a thing; why do they not believe immediately?" — we answer (on the Scripture hypothesis), "It is the gift of God" [Eph. 2:8]. No man is able to work it, in himself. It is a work of omnipotence. It requires no less power thus to quicken a dead soul than to raise a body that lies in the grave. It is a new creation, and none can create a soul anew but he who at first created the heavens and the earth.

---

3. St. 2 of Matthew Prior's "Charity" in *Literary Works,* H. B. Wright and M. K. Spears, eds. [Oxford, 1959], I, 208.

10. May not your own experience teach you this? Can you give yourself this faith? Is it now in your power to see, or hear, or taste, or feel God? Have you already, or can you raise in yourself, any perception of God or of an invisible world? I suppose you do not deny that there is an invisible world. You will not charge it, in poor old Hesiod, to Christian prejudice of education when he says, in those well-known words,

> Millions of spiritual creatures walk the earth
> Unseen, whether we wake, or if we sleep.[4]

Now, is there any power in your soul whereby you discern either these or him that created them? Or, can all your wisdom and strength open an intercourse between yourself and the world of spirits? Is it in your power to burst the veil that is on your heart and let in the light of eternity? You know it is not. You not only do not but cannot (by your own strength) thus believe. The more you labour so to do, the more you will be convinced, "it is the gift of God."

11. It is the "free gift of God," which he bestows, not on those who are "worthy" of his favour, not on such as are "previously holy" and so "fit" to be crowned with all the blessings of his goodness, but on the ungodly and unholy, on those who 'till that hour were "fit" only for everlasting destruction, those in whom was no good thing and whose only plea was, "God be merciful to me, a sinner." No merit, no goodness in man, precedes the forgiving love of God. His pardoning mercy supposes nothing in us but a sense of mere sin and misery; and to all who see and feel and own their wants and their utter inability to remove them, God freely gives faith, for the sake of him "in whom he is always well pleased" [cf. Mt. 3:17; 12:18; 17:5; 2 Pet. 1:17].

12. This is a short, rude sketch of the doctrine we teach. These are our fundamental principles; and we spend our lives in confirming others herein, and in a behaviour suitable to them.

Now, if you are a reasonable man, although you do not believe the Christian system to be of God, lay your hand upon your breast and calmly consider what it is that you can here condemn? What evil have we done to *you*, that *you* should join the common cry against us? Why should *you* say, "Away with such fellows from the earth; it is not fit that they should live" [cf. Acts 22:22]?

13. 'Tis true, your judgment does not fall in with ours. We believe the Scripture to be of God. This you do not believe. And how do you de-

---

4. John Milton, *Paradise Lost*, Bk. IV, l. 677-78.

fend yourselves against them who urge you with the guilt of unbelief? Do you not say, "Every man *must* judge according to the light he has," and that "if he be true to this, he ought not to be condemned"? Keep then to this, and turn the tables. *Must* not *we* also judge according to the light we have? You can in nowise condemn *us* without involving *yourselves* in the same condemnation. According to the light *we* have, we cannot but believe the Scripture is of God; and while we believe this, we dare not turn aside from it to the right hand or to the left.

14. Let us consider this point a little farther. You yourself believe there is a God. You have the witness of this in your own breast. Perhaps sometimes you tremble before him. You believe there is such a thing as right and wrong, that there is a difference between moral good and evil. Of consequence you must allow there is such a thing as conscience: I mean that every person capable of reflection is conscious to himself when he looks back on any thing he has done whether it be good or evil. You must likewise allow that every man is to be guided by his own conscience, not another's. Thus far, doubtless, you may go, without any danger of being a "volunteer" in faith.[5]

15. Now then, be consistent with yourself. If there be a God who, being just and good (attributes inseparable from the very idea of God), is "a rewarder of them that diligently seek him" [Heb. 11:6], ought we not to do whatever we believe will be acceptable to so good a master? Observe: if we *believe*, if we are fully persuaded of this in our own mind, ought we not thus to seek him, and that with all diligence? Else, how should we expect any reward at his hands?

16. Again: ought we not to do what we believe is morally good and to abstain from what we judge is evil? By good I mean, conducive to the good of mankind, tending to advance peace and good will among men, promotive of the happiness of our fellow creatures — and by evil, what is contrary thereto. Then surely you cannot condemn our endeavouring, after our power, to make mankind happy (I now speak only with regard to the present world); our striving as we can to lessen their sorrows and to teach them, in whatsoever state they are, therewith to be content.

17. Yet again. Are we to be guided by *our own* conscience, or by that of *other* men? *You* surely will not say that any man's conscience can preclude *mine*. You, at least, will not plead for robbing us of what you so strongly claim for yourselves; I mean the right of private judgment, which is indeed unalienable from reasonable creatures. *You* well know

5. *I.e.* credulous; *cf. Works*, XI, 5, for the same phrase in similar usage.

that, unless we faithfully follow the dictates of *our own* mind, we cannot have a conscience void of offence toward God and toward man [*cf.* Acts 24:16].

18. Upon your own principles, therefore, you must allow us to be, at least, innocent. Do you find any difficulty in this? You speak much of prepossession and prejudice; beware you are not entangled therein yourselves. Are you not prejudiced against *us* because we believe and strenuously defend that system of doctrines which you oppose? Are you not enemies to *us* because you take it for granted we are so to *you?* Nay, God forbid! I once saw one who, from a plentiful fortune, was reduced to the lowest extremity. He was lying on a sick bed, in violent pain, without even convenient food or one friend to comfort him: so that when his merciful landlord, to complete all, sent one to take his bed from under him, I was not surprised at his attempt to put an end to so miserable a life. Now, when I saw that poor man weltering in his blood, could I be angry at him? Surely, no. No more can I at *you.* I can no more hate than I can envy you. I can only lift up my heart to God for you (as I did then for him) and, with silent tears, beseech the father of mercies that he would look on you in your blood and say unto you: "Live!"

19. "Sir," said that unhappy man, at my first interview with him, "I scorn to deceive you or any man. You must not tell me of your Bible, for I do not believe one word of it. I know there is a God, and believe he is all in all, the *anima mundi* [world soul], the

> . . . *vastam totam*
> *Mens agitans molem et magno se corpore miscens.*[6]

But farther than this I believe not. All is dark. My thought is lost. But I hear," added he, "you preach to a great number of people every night and morning. Pray, what would you do with them? Whither would you lead them? What religion do you preach? What is it good for?" I replied, "I *do* preach to as many as desire to hear, every night and morning. You ask, what I would do with them? I would make them virtuous and happy, easy in themselves and useful to others. Whither would I lead them? To heaven: to God the Judge, the lover of all, and to Jesus the Mediator of the new covenant. What religion do I preach? The religion of love: the law of kindness brought to light by the gospel. What is this good for? To make all who receive it enjoy God and themselves: to make

---

6. "The 'Mind' which pervades the whole, activates its mass and mingles with its mighty frame." *Cf.* Vergil, *Aeneid,* Bk. VI, l. 726-27; see above, p. 312.

them like God, lovers of all, contented in their lives and crying out at their death, in calm assurance, 'O grave, where is thy victory? Thanks be unto God, who giveth *me* the victory, through *my* Lord Jesus Christ' " [*cf.* 1 Cor. 15:55, 57].

20. Will you object to such a religion as this that it is not reasonable? Is it not reasonable then to love God? Hath he not given you life and breath and all things? Does he not still continue his love to you, filling your heart with food and gladness? What have you which you have not received of him? And does not love demand a return of love? Whether, therefore, you do love God or no, you cannot but own it is reasonable so to do; nay, seeing he is the parent of all good,[7] to love him with all your heart.

21. Is it not reasonable also to love our neighbour: every man whom God hath made? Are we not brethren, the children of one Father? Ought we not then to love one another? And should we only love them that love us? Is that acting like our Father which is in heaven? He causeth his sun to shine on the evil and on the good and sendeth rain on the just and on the unjust" [Mt. 5:45]. And can there be a more equitable rule of our love than "Thou shalt love thy neighbour as thyself?" You will plead for the reasonableness of this; as also for that Golden Rule (the only adequate measure of brotherly love in all our words and actions): "Whatsoever ye would that men should do unto you, even so do unto them" [Mt. 7:12].

22. Is it not reasonable then, that, as we have opportunity, we should do good unto all men, not only friends but enemies, not only to the deserving but likewise to the evil and unthankful? Is it not right that all our life should be one continued labour of love? If a day passes without doing good, may one not well say with Titus: *Amici, diem perdidi.*[8] And is it enough to feed the hungry, to clothe the naked, to visit those who are sick or in prison? Should we have no pity for those

> Who sigh beneath guilt's horrid stain,
> The worst confinement, and the heaviest chain?[9]

Should we shut up our compassion toward those who are of all men most miserable because they are miserable by their own fault? If we have found a medicine to heal even that sickness, should we not, as we have

7. See above, pp. 184 and 186.
8. [Au.] "My friends, I have lost a day." *Cf.* Suetonius, *The Lives of the Caesars*, Loeb ed., trans. by J. C. Rolfe (Cambridge, Mass., 1914), Bk. VIII, Sec. viii, l. 3.
9. Samuel Wesley, Jr, "On the death of Mr William Morgan," in his *Poems on Several Occasions* (1736), *cf.* Journal, I, 104, l. 18–19.

freely received it, freely give [*cf*. Mt. 10:8]? Should we not pluck them as brands out of the fire: the fire of lust, anger, malice, revenge? Your inmost soul answers, "It should be done; it is reasonable in the highest degree." Well, this is the sum of our preaching and of our lives, our enemies themselves being the judges. If therefore you allow that it is reasonable to love God, to love mankind and to do good to all men, you cannot but allow that religion which we preach and live to be agreeable to the highest reason.

23. Perhaps all this you can bear. It is tolerable enough, and if we spoke only of being "saved by love," you should have no great objection. But you do not comprehend what we say of being "saved by *faith*." I know you do not. You do not in any degree comprehend what we mean by that expression. Have patience, then, and I will tell you yet again. By those words, "We are saved by *faith*," we mean that the moment a man receives that faith which is above described, he is saved from doubt and fear and sorrow of heart, by a peace that passes all understanding; from the heaviness of a wounded spirit by joy unspeakable; and from his sins of whatsoever kind they were, from his vicious desires as well as words and actions — by the love of God and of all mankind then shed abroad in his heart.

24. We grant, nothing is more unreasonable than to imagine that such mighty effects as these can be wrought by that poor, empty, insignificant thing which the world *calls* "faith," and you among them. But supposing there be such a faith on the earth as that which the apostle speaks of, such an intercourse between God and the soul, what is too hard for such a faith? You yourselves may conceive that "all things are possible to him that thus believeth" [*cf*. Mk. 9:23], to him that thus "walks with God" [*cf*. Gen. 5:22, 24], that is now a citizen of heaven, an inhabitant of eternity. If therefore you will contend with *us*, you must change the ground of your attack. You must flatly deny there is any faith upon earth. But perhaps this you might think too large a step. You cannot do this without a secret condemnation in your own breast. O that you would at length cry to God for that heavenly gift whereby alone this truly reasonable religion, this beneficent love of God and man, can be planted in your heart.

25. If you say, "But those that profess this faith are the most unreasonable of all men," I ask, "Who are those that profess this faith?" Perhaps you do not personally know such a man in the world. Who are they that so much as profess to have *this* "evidence of things not seen," that profess

to "see him that is invisible," to "hear the voice of God" [Jn. 5:25], and to have "his Spirit *ever* witnessing with their spirits, that they are the children of God" [Rom. 8:16]? I fear you will find few that even profess *this faith* among the large numbers of those who are called believers.

26. "However, there are enough that profess themselves Christians." Yea, too many, God knoweth, too many that confute their vain professions by the whole tenor of their lives. I will allow all you can say on this head, and perhaps more than all. 'Tis now some years since I was engaged unawares in a conversation with a strong reasoner who at first urged the wickedness of the American Indians as a bar to our hope of converting them to Christianity. But when I mentioned their temperance, justice, and veracity (according to the accounts I had then received), it was asked, "Why, if those heathens are such men as these, what will they gain by being made Christians? What would they gain by being *such Christians* as we see every where round about us?" I could not deny they would lose, not gain, by such a Christianity as this. Upon which she added, "Why, what else do you mean by Christianity?" My plain answer was, "What do you apprehend to be more valuable than good sense, good nature and good manners? All these are contained, and that in the highest degree, in what I mean by Christianity. Good sense (so called) is but a poor, dim shadow of what Christians call faith. Good nature is only a faint, distant resemblance of Christian charity. And good manners, of the most finished kind that nature assisted by art can attain to, is but a dead picture of that holiness of conversation which is the image of God visibly expressed. All these, put together by the art of God,[10] I call Christianity." "Sir, if this be Christianity," said my opponent in amaze, "I never saw a Christian in my life."

27. Perhaps it is the same case with *you*. If so, I am grieved for you and can only wish, till you do see a living proof of this, that you would not say you see a Christian. For this is scriptural Christianity, and this alone. Whenever, therefore, you see an unreasonable man, you see one who perhaps *calls* himself by that name but *is* no more a "Christian" than he is an "angel." So far as he departs from true, genuine reason, so far he departs from Christianity. Do not say, "This is only asserted, not proved." It is undeniably proved by the original charter of Christianity. We appeal to this, to the written word [of Scripture]. If any man's temper, or words, or actions, are contradictory to right reason, it is evident to a demonstration they are contradictory to this. Produce any possible or conceivable

10. *Cf.* Thomas Browne, *Religio Medici* (Oxford, 1909), I, 16.

instance and you will find the fact is so. The lives, therefore, of those who are *called* Christians is no just objection to Christianity.

28. We join with you, then, in desiring a religion founded on reason and every way agreeable thereto. But one question still remains to be asked, "What do you mean by 'reason'?" I suppose you mean the eternal reason, or the nature of things: the nature of God and the nature of man, with the relations necessarily subsisting between them. Why, this is the very religion *we* preach: a religion evidently founded on, and every way agreeable to, eternal reason, to the essential nature of things. Its foundation stands on the nature of God and the nature of man, together with their mutual relations. And it is every way suitable thereto: to the nature of God, for it begins in knowing him (and where but in the true knowledge of God can you conceive true religion to begin?). It goes on in loving him and all mankind (for you cannot but imitate whom you love). It ends in serving him, in doing his will, in obeying him whom we know and love.

29. It is every way suited to the nature of man, for it begins in a man's knowing himself, knowing himself to be what he really is — foolish, vicious, miserable. It goes on to point out the remedy for this, to make him truly wise, virtuous, and happy, as every thinking mind (perhaps from some implicit remembrance of what it originally was) longs to be. It finishes all by restoring the due relations between God and man, by uniting for ever the tender Father and the grateful, obedient son, the great Lord of all and the faithful servant, doing not his own will, but the will of him that sent him.

30. But perhaps by reason you mean the faculty of reasoning, of inferring one thing from another.

There are many, it is confessed (particularly those who are styled "mystic divines"),[11] that utterly decry the use of reason, thus understood, in religion; nay, that condemn all reasoning concerning the things of God as utterly destructive of true religion.

But we can in nowise agree with this. We find no authority for it in Holy Writ. So far from it that we find there both our Lord and his apostles continually reasoning with their opposers. Neither do we know, in all the productions of ancient and modern times, such a chain of reasoning or argumentation so close, so solid, so regularly connected as the Epistle to the Hebrews. And the strongest reasoner whom we have ever observed (excepting only Jesus of Nazareth ) was that Paul of Tarsus — the

11. See above, p. 375 and 45 f. :

same who has left that plain direction for all Christians: "In malice (or wickedness) be ye children, but in understanding (or reason) be ye men" [*cf.* 1 Cor. 14:20].

31. We therefore not only allow but earnestly exhort all who seek after true religion to use all the reason which God hath given them in searching out the things of God. But your reasoning justly, not only on this but on any subject whatsoever, presupposes true judgments already formed whereon to ground your argumentation. Else, you know, you will stumble at every step because *ex falso non sequitur verum* — "it is impossible, if your premises are false, to infer from them true conclusions." [12]

32. You know, likewise, that before it is possible for you to form a true judgment of them, it is absolutely necessary that you have a clear apprehension of the things of God and that your ideas thereof be all fixed, distinct and determinate. And seeing our ideas are not innate, but must all originally come from our senses, it is certainly necessary that you have senses capable of discerning objects of this kind — not those only which are called natural senses, which in this respect profit nothing, as being altogether incapable of discerning objects of a spiritual kind, but spiritual senses, exercised to discern spiritual good and evil. It is necessary that you have the *hearing ear* and the *seeing eye*, emphatically so called, that you have a new class of senses opened in your soul, not depending on organs of flesh and blood to be *the evidence* of things not seen as your bodily senses are of visible things, to be the avenues to the invisible world, to discern spiritual objects and to furnish you with ideas of what the outward "eye hath not seen, neither the ear heard" [1 Cor. 2:9].

33. And till you have these "internal senses," till the eyes of your understanding are opened, you can have no *apprehension* of divine things, no idea of them at all. Nor, consequently, 'till then, can you either *judge truly*, or *reason justly* concerning them, seeing your reason has no ground whereon to stand, no materials to work upon.

34. To use the trite instance: as you cannot reason concerning colours if you have no natural *sight* — because all the ideas received by your other senses are of a different kind, so that neither your hearing, nor any other sense, can supply your want of sight or furnish your reason in this respect with matter to work upon — so you cannot reason concerning spiritual things if you have no "spiritual sight," because all your ideas received by your "outward senses" are of a different kind; yea, far more different from those received by faith or "internal sensation" than the

12. *Cf.* "A Compendium of Logic," *Works*, XIV, 165–68.

idea of colour from that of sound. These are only different species of one genus, namely, sensible ideas, received by external sensation, whereas the ideas of faith differ *toto genere* from those of external sensation. So that it is not conceivable that external sensation should supply the want of internal senses or furnish your reason in this respect with matter to work upon.

35. What then will your reason do here? How will it pass from things natural to spiritual? From the things that are seen to those that are not seen? From the visible to the invisible world? What a gulf is here? By what art will reason get over the immense chasm? This cannot be, 'till the Almighty come in to your succour and give you that faith you have hitherto despised. Then, upborne, as it were, on eagles' wings, you shall soar away into the regions of eternity and your enlightened reason shall explore even "the deep things of God," God himself "revealing them to you by his Spirit" [1 Cor. 2:10].

36. I expected to have received much light on this head from a treatise lately published and earnestly recommended to me; I mean, *Christianity Not Founded on Argument*.[13] But on a careful perusal of that piece, notwithstanding my prejudice in its favour, I could not but perceive that the great design uniformly pursued throughout the work was to render the whole of the Christian institution both odious and contemptible. In order to [do] this, the author gleans up with great care and diligence the most plausible of those many objections that have been raised against it by late writers and proposes them with the utmost strength of which he was capable. To do this with the more effect, he *personates* a Christian. He makes a show of defending an avowed doctrine of Christianity, namely, the supernatural influence of the Spirit of God; and often, for several sentences together (indeed, in the beginning of almost every paragraph) speaks so *like* a Christian that not a few have received him according to his wish. Meanwhile, with all possible art and show of reason, and in the most laboured language, he pursues his point throughout, which is to prove "that Christianity is contrary to reason" — or, "that no man acting according to the principles of reason can possibly be a Christian."

37. It is a wonderful proof of the power that smooth words may have even on serious minds that so many have mistook such a writer as this

13. By Henry Dodwell ("the Younger"), whose essay (1741) purported to be a plea for nonrational faith, but was actually a subtle cancellation of the entire theological enterprise. Dodwell's caricature was intended to make Christianity appear obscurantist in the eyes of thoughtful men.

for a friend of Christianity, since almost every page of his tract is filled with gross falsehood and broad blasphemy, and these supported by such exploded fallacies and commonplace sophistry that a person of two or three years' standing in the university might give them a sufficient answer and make the author appear as irrational and contemptible as he labours to make Christ and his apostles.

38. I have hitherto spoken to those chiefly who do not receive the Christian system as of God. I would add a few words to another sort of men — though not so much with regard to *our* principles or practice as with regard to *their own* — to you who *do* receive it, who believe the Scripture but yet do not take upon you the character of *religious men*. I am therefore obliged to address myself to you likewise under the character of *men of reason*.

39. I would only ask, are you such indeed? Do you answer the character under which you appear? If so, you are consistent with yourselves; your principles and practice agree together.

Let us try whether this is so or not. Do you not take the name of God in vain? Do you remember the Sabbath day to keep it holy? Do you not speak evil of the ruler of your people? Are you not a drunkard, or a glutton, faring as sumptuously as you can every day, making a god of your belly? Do you not avenge yourself? Are you not a whoremonger or adulterer? Answer plainly to your own heart, before God the Judge of all.

Why then do you say you truly believe the Scripture? If the Scripture is true, you are lost. You are in the broad way that leadeth to destruction [*cf.* Mt. 7:13]. Your "damnation slumbereth not" [2 Pet. 2:3]. You are "heaping up to yourself wrath against the day of wrath and revelation of the righteous judgment of God" [Rom. 2:5]. Doubtless, if the Scripture is true (and you remain thus), it had been good for you if you had never been born.

40. How is it that you call yourselves men of reason? Is reason inconsistent with itself? You are the farthest of all men under the sun from any pretence to that character. A common swearer, a Sabbath-breaker, a whoremonger, a drunkard, who says he believes the Scripture is of God, is a monster upon earth, the greatest contradiction to his own as well as to the reason of all mankind. In the name of God (that worthy name whereby you are *called* and which you daily cause to be blasphemed) turn either to the right hand or to the left. Either profess you are an infidel, or be a Christian. Halt no longer thus between two opinions.

Either cast off the Bible or your sins. And, in the meantime, if you have any spark of your boasted reason left, do not count us your enemies — as I fear you have done hitherto and as thousands do wherever we have declared, "they who do such things shall not inherit eternal life" [cf. Gal. 5:21] — because we tell you the truth; seeing these are not our words but the words of him that sent us; yea, though in doing this, we use "great plainness of speech," as becomes the ministry we have received. "For we are not as many who corrupt" (cauponize, soften and thereby adulterate) "the word of God. But as of sincerity, but as of God, in the sight of God, speak we in Christ." [14]

41. But, it may be, you are none of these. You abstain from all such things. You have an unspotted reputation. You are a man of honour or a woman of virtue. You scorn to do an unhandsome thing and are of an unblamable life and conversation. You are harmless, if I understand you right — and useless, from morning to night. You do no hurt and no good to any one, no more than a straw floating upon the water. Your life glides smoothly on from year to year and from one season to another; having no occasion to work,

> You waste away
> In gentle inactivity the day.[15]

42. I will not now shock the easiness of your temper by talking about a future state. But suffer me to ask you a question about present things: are you now happy?

I have seen a large company of "reasonable creatures," called Indians, sitting in a row on the side of a river, looking sometimes at one another, sometimes at the sky, and sometimes at the bubbles on the water. And so they sat (unless in the time of war) for a great part of the year, from morning to night. These were doubtless much at ease. But can you think they were happy? And how little happier are you than they?

43. You eat and drink and sleep and dress and dance, and sit down to play. You are carried abroad. You are at the masquerade, the theatre, the opera house, the park, the levee, the drawing room. What do you do there? Why, sometimes you talk, sometimes you look at one another.

---

14. See above, p. 223.

15. Cf. the farce comedy of James Miller, *The Humours of Oxford*, which Wesley read while still at Christ Church, cited in V. H. H. Green, *The Young Mr. Wesley* (1961), 19. See also Wesley's sermon, "Spiritual Idolatry," in *Works*, VI, 437, with its uncited quotation of Horace, *Satires*, Bk. II, sec. vi, l. 61–62: *Somno et inertibus horis. . . .*

And what are you to do tomorrow, the next day, the next week, the next year? You are to eat and drink and sleep and dance and dress and play again. And you are to be carried abroad again, that you may again look at one another! And is this all? Alas, how little more happiness have you in this than the Indians in looking at the sky or water? [16]

Ah, poor, dull round! I do not wonder that Colonel M—— (or any man of reflection) should prefer death itself, even in the midst of his years, to such a life as this, and should frankly declare that he chose to go out of the world because he found nothing in it worth living for.

44. Yet it is certain there is business to be done, and many we find in all places (not to speak of the vulgar, the drudges of the earth) who are continually employed therein. Are you of that number? Are you engaged in trade or some other reputable employment? I suppose, profitable, too, for you would not spend your time and labour and thought for nothing. You are then making your fortune, you are getting money. True, but money is not your ultimate end. The treasuring up gold and silver for its own sake, all men own, is as foolish and absurd, as grossly unreasonable, as the treasuring up spiders or the wings of butterflies. You consider this but as a means to some farther end. And what is that? Why, the enjoying yourself, the being at ease, the taking your pleasure, the living like a gentleman: that is, plainly, either the whole or some part of the happiness above described. Supposing then your end to be actually attained, suppose you have your wish before you drop into eternity: go and sit down with Thleeanowhee and his companions on the river side. After you have toiled for fifty years, you are just as happy as they.

45. Are you, can you or any reasonable man be *satisfied* with this? You are not. It is not possible you should [be]. But what else can you do? You *would* have something better to employ your time, but you know not where to find it upon earth. And, indeed, it is obvious that the earth, as it is now constituted even with the help of all European arts, does not afford sufficient employment to take up half the waking hours of half its inhabitants.

What then can you do? How can you employ the time that lies so heavy upon your hands? This very thing which you seek, declare we unto you. The thing *you* want, is the religion *we* preach. That alone leaves no time upon our hands. It fills up all the blank spaces of life. It exactly

16. *Cf.* John Pomfret's poem "The Choice" (1699), in which the rector of Malden (Bedfordshire) extols as *ideal* the life of sybaritic ease and comfort; in Samuel Johnson, ed., *The Works of the English Poets* (1810), VIII, 307–08.

takes up all the time we have to spare, be it more or less, so that "he that hath much, hath nothing over, and he that has little, has no lack" [*cf.* Ex. 16:18; 2 Cor. 8:15].

46. Once more: can you (or any man of reason) think you was made for the life you now lead? You cannot possibly think so, at least, not 'till you tread the Bible under foot. The oracles of God bear thee witness in every page (and thine own heart agreeth thereto) that thou wast made in the image of God, an incorruptible picture of the God of glory. And what art thou even in thy present state? An everlasting spirit, going to God. For what end, then, did he create thee, but to dwell with him above this perishable world, to know him, to love him, to do his will, to enjoy him for ever and ever? O look more deeply into thyself and into that Scripture which thou professest to receive as the "word of God," as "right concerning all things." There thou wilt find a nobler, happier state described than it ever yet entered into thy heart to conceive. But God hath now revealed it to all those who "rejoice evermore" and "pray without ceasing" and "in everything give thanks" [*cf.* 1 Thess. 5:16–18], and "do his will on earth as it is done in heaven" [*cf.* Mt. 6:10]. For this thou wast made. Hereunto also thou art called. O be not disobedient to the heavenly calling! At least, be not angry with those who would fain bring thee to be a living witness of that religion, "whose ways are" indeed "ways of pleasantness and all her paths peace" [*cf.* Prov. 3:17].

47. Do you say in your heart: "I know all this already. I am not barely a man of reason. I am a religious man, for I not only avoid evil and do good, but use all the means of grace. I am constantly at church, and at the sacrament, too. I say my prayers every day. I read many good books. I fast — every *thirtieth of January and Good Friday*." [17] Do you indeed? Do you do all this? This you may do, you may go thus far and yet have no religion at all; no such religion as avails before God. Nay, much farther than this, than you have ever gone yet, or so much as thought of going. For you may "give all your goods to feed the poor," yea, "your body to be burned," and yet very possibly, if St. Paul be a judge, "have no charity" [*cf.* 1 Cor. 13:3], no true religion.

48. This religion, which alone is of value before God, is the very thing you want. You want (and in wanting this, you want all) the re-

17. A jibe at the Jacobites, who observed January 30 as the anniversary of the death of Charles I (1649). Note the bracketing of the execution of "the royal martyr" with Jesus's crucifixion. *Cf.* A Form of Common Prayer to be Used on the 30th Day of January, being the Day of the Martyrdom of K. Charles First, in B.C.P. (1662), sec. 588–602.

ligion of love. You do not love your neighbour as yourself, no more than you love God with all your heart. Ask your own heart now if it be not so? 'Tis plain you do not love God. If you did, you would be happy in him. But you know you are not happy. Your *formal* religion no more makes you happy than your neighbour's *gay* religion does him. O how much have you suffered for want of plain dealing? Can you now bear to hear the naked truth? You have "the form of godliness," but not "the power" [*cf.* 2 Tim. 3:5]. You are a mere whited wall [*cf.* Acts 23:3; Mt. 23:27]. Before the Lord your God, I ask you, are you not? Too sure. For your "inward parts are very wickedness" [*cf.* Ps. 5:9, B.C.P.]. You love "the creature more than the Creator." You are "a lover of pleasure more than a lover of God." A lover of God? You do not love God at all, no more than you love a stone.[18] You love the world; therefore, the love of the Father is not in you [*cf.* 1 Jn. 2:15].

49. You are on the brink of the pit, ready to be plunged into everlasting perdition. Indeed you have a zeal for God, but not according to knowledge [*cf.* Rom. 10:2]. O how terribly have you been deceived, posting to hell and fancying it was heaven! See, at length, that outward religion without inward is nothing; is far worse than nothing, being, indeed, no other than a solemn mockery of God. And *inward religion you have not*. You have not "the faith that worketh by love" [Gal. 5:6]. Your *faith* (so called) is no living, saving principle. It is not the apostle's faith, "the substance (or subsistence) of things hoped for, the evidence of things not seen" [Heb. 11:1]. So far from it that *this* faith is the very thing which you call "enthusiasm." You are not content with being without it unless you blaspheme it too. You even revile that "life which is hid with Christ in God" [*cf.* Col. 3:3], all seeing, tasting, hearing, feeling God. These things are foolishness unto you. No marvel, "for they are spiritually discerned" [*cf.* 1 Cor. 2:14].

50. O no longer shut your eyes against the light! Know you have a name, that you live, but are dead [*cf.* Rev. 3:1]. Your soul is utterly dead in sin, dead in pride, in vanity, in self-will, in sensuality, in love of the world. You are utterly dead to God. There is no intercourse between your soul and God. "You have neither seen him (by faith, as our Lord witnessed against them of old time) nor heard his voice at any time." You have no spiritual "senses exercised to discern spiritual good and evil." You are angry at infidels and are all the while as mere an infidel before

18. The first edition has an extra sentence here, omitted in the revision of 1772 (*Works*, [Pine]): "You cannot love God, for you love praise."

God as they. You have "eyes that see not and ears that hear not" [cf. Is. 6:10]. You have a "callous, unfeeling heart."

51. Bear with me a little longer. My soul is distressed for you. "The god of this world hath blinded your eyes" [cf. 2 Cor. 4:4], and you are "seeking death in the error of your life." Because you do not commit gross sin, because you give alms and go to the church and sacrament, you imagine that you are serving God. Yet, in very deed, you are serving the devil. For you are doing still your own will, not the will of God your Saviour. You are pleasing yourself in all you do. Pride, vanity, and self-will (the genuine fruits of an earthly, sensual, devilish heart) pollute all your words and actions. You are in darkness, in the shadow of death. O that God would say to you in thunder: "Awake, thou that sleepest, and arise from the dead, and Christ shall give thee light" [Eph. 5:14]!

52. But, blessed be God, he hath not yet left himself without witness!

> All are not lost! There be, who faith prefer,
> Tho' few, and piety to God,[19]

who know the power of faith and are no strangers to that inward, vital religion: "the mind that was in Christ, righteousness, and peace and joy in the Holy Ghost" [cf. Phil. 2:5; Rom. 14:17]. Of you who "have tasted the good word of God, and the powers of the world to come" [cf. Heb. 6:5], I would be glad to learn if we have "erred from the faith" [cf. 1 Tim. 6:10], or walked contrary to "the truth as it is in Jesus" [cf. Eph. 4:21]. "Let the righteous smite me friendly, and reprove me" [Ps. 141:5, B.C.P.], if haply that which is amiss may be done away and what is wanting supplied, till "we all come to the measure of the stature of the fulness of Christ" [cf. Eph. 4:13].

53. Perhaps the first thing that now occurs to your mind relates to the doctrine which we teach. You have heard that we say, "Men may live without sin." And have you not heard that the Scripture says the same (we mean, without committing sin)? Does not St. Paul say plainly, that those who believe "do not continue in sin" — that they cannot "live any longer therein"?[20] Does not St. Peter say, "He that hath suffered in the flesh, hath ceased from sin . . . that he no longer should live . . . to the desires of men but to the will of God?"[21] And does not St. John say expressly, "He that committeth sin is of the devil? . . . For this purpose the Son of God was manifested, that he might destroy the

19. Cf. John Milton, *Paradise Lost*, Bk. VI, l. 142–47.    20. [Au.] Rom. 6:1-2.
21. [Au.] 1 Pet. 4:1-2.

works of the devil. Whosoever is born of God doth not commit sin, for his seed remaineth in him and he cannot sin, because he is born of God." [22] And again, "we know that whosoever is born of God sinneth not." [23]

54. You see, then, it is not *we* that say this, but the Lord. These are not *our* words, but *his*. And who is he that replieth against God? Who is able to make God a liar? Surely he will be "justified in his saying, and clear when he is judged" [cf. Rom. 3:4]! Can you deny it? Have you not often felt a secret check when you was contradicting this great truth? And how often have you wished for what you was taught to deny? Nay, can you help wishing for it at this moment? Do you not now earnestly desire to cease from sin, to commit it no more? Does not your soul pant after this glorious liberty of the sons of God [cf. Rom. 8:21]? And what strong reason have you to expect it? Have you not had a foretaste of it already? Do you not remember the time when God first lifted up the light of his countenance upon you? Can it ever be forgotten, the day when the candle of the Lord first shone upon your head [cf. Job 29:3]?

> Butter and honey did you eat,
> And, lifted up on high,
> You saw the clouds beneath your feet,
> And rode upon the sky.
> Far, far above all earthly things,
> Triumphantly you rode;
> You soar'd to heaven on eagles' wings,
> And found, and talk'd with God. [24]

You then had power not to commit sin. You found the apostle's words strictly true, "He that is begotten of God keepeth himself and that wicked one toucheth him not" [1 Jn. 5:18]. But those whom you took to be experienced Christians — telling you, "this was only the time of your espousals, this could not last always, you must come down from the mount," and the like — shook your faith. You looked at men more than God, and so became weak and like another man. Whereas, had you then had any to guide you according to the truth of God, had you then heard the doctrine which now you blame, you had never fallen from your stedfastness but had found that in this sense also "the gifts and calling of God are without repentance" [cf. Rom. 11:29].

22. [Au.] 1 Jn. 3:8.    23. [Au.] 1 Jn. 5:18.
24. Charles Wesley, in *Hymns and Sacred Poems* (1742); also in G. Osborn, ed., *Poetical Works of John and Charles Wesley*, II, 120–21, st. 3, 4.

55. Have you not another objection nearly allied to this, namely, that we preach perfection? True, but what perfection? The term you cannot object to, because it is scriptural. All the difficulty is to fix the meaning of it according to the Word of God. And this we have done again and again, declaring to all the world that Christian perfection does not imply an exemption from ignorance, or mistake, or infirmities, or temptations, but that it does imply the being so crucified with Christ as to be able to testify, "I live not, but Christ liveth in me," [25] and "hath purified my heart by faith." [26] It does imply "the casting down every high thing that exalteth itself against the knowledge of God and bringing into captivity every thought to the obedience of Christ" [cf. 2 Cor. 10:5]. It does imply "the being holy as he that hath called us is holy, in all manner of conversation" [1 Pet. 1:15], and, in a word, "the loving the Lord our God with all our heart and serving him with all our strength" [cf. Mk. 12:33].

56. Now, is it possible for any who believe the Scripture to deny one tittle of this? You cannot. You dare not. You would not for the world. You know it is the pure Word of God. And this is the whole of what we preach. This is the height and depth of what we (with St. Paul) call perfection: a state of soul devoutly to be wished by all who have tasted of the love of God. O pray for it without ceasing! It is the one thing you want. Come with boldness to the throne of grace [cf. Heb. 4:16], and be assured that when you ask this of God, you shall have the petition you ask of him. We know, indeed, that to man, to the natural man, this is impossible. But we know also, that as no work is impossible with God, so "all things are possible to him that believeth" [Mk. 9:23].

57. For "we are saved by faith" [cf. Eph. 2:8]. But have you not heard this urged as another objection against us, that we preach salvation by faith alone? And does not St. Paul do the same thing? "By grace," saith he, "ye are saved through faith." Can any words be more express? And elsewhere, "Believe in the Lord Jesus and thou shalt be saved." [27]

What we mean by this (if it has not been sufficiently explained already) is that we are saved from our sins only by a confidence in the love of God. As soon as we "behold what manner of love it is which the Father hath bestowed upon us [1 Jn. 3:1], we love him" (as the apostle observes) "because he first loved us" [1 Jn. 4:19]. And then is that commandment written in our heart, that "he who loveth God love his brother also [cf. 1 Jn. 4:21], from which love of God and man, meekness, humbleness of mind, and all holy tempers spring. Now these are the very essence

25. [Au.] Gal. 2:20.          26. [Au.] Acts 15:9.          27. [Au.] Acts 16:31.

of salvation, of Christian salvation, salvation from sin. And from these, outward salvation flows; that is, holiness of life and conversation. Well, and are not these things so? If you know in whom you have believed, you need no further witnesses.

58. But perhaps you doubt whether that faith whereby we are thus saved implies such a trust and confidence in God as we describe. You cannot think faith implies assurance, an assurance of the love of God to our souls, of his being now reconciled to us and having forgiven all our sins. And this we freely confess, that if [the] number of voices is to decide the question, we must give it up at once, for you have on your side not only some who desire to be Christians indeed, but all nominal Christians in every place and the Romish Church, one and all. Nay, these last are so vehement in your defence, that, in the famed Council of Trent they have decreed, "If any man hold *fiduciam* (trust, confidence, or assurance of pardon) to be essential to faith, let him be accursed." [28]

59. If we consider the time when this decree was passed — namely, just after the publication of our Homilies — it will appear more than probable that the very design of the Council was to anathematize the Church of England, as being now convicted by her own confession, of "that damnable and heretical doctrine." [29] For the very words in the homily on salvation are:

. . . Even the devils . . . believe that Christ was born of a virgin, . . . that he wrought all kind of miracles, declaring himself very God, . . . that for our sakes he suffered a most painful death, to redeem us from death everlasting. . . . These articles of our faith the devils believe and so they believe all that is written in the Old and New Testament. . . . And yet, for all this faith, they be but devils. [They remain] still in their damnable estate, lacking the very true Christian faith.

. . . The right and true Christian faith is not only to believe the holy Scriptures and the articles of our faith are true, but also to have a sure trust and confidence to be saved from everlasting damnation by Christ. Or (as it is expressed a little after), a sure trust and confidence [in God] that by the merits of Christ his sins are forgiven and he reconciled to the favour of God. . . . [30]

28. *Cf.* Sixth Session, Canon XII: . . . *vel eam fiduciam solam esse, qua justificamur, anathema sit. . . .*" See also Canon XIII; Philip Schaff, *Creeds of Christendom, with a History and Critical Notes* (New York, 1881), II, 113.

29. This sentence was severely abridged in the editions of 1771 and 1786.

30. [Au.] "The Third Part of the Sermon of Salvation"; see above, p. 28.

60. Indeed, the Bishop of Rome saith, "If any man hold this, let him be 'anathema maranatha.' " But 'tis to be hoped papal anathemas do not move *you*. *You* are a member of the Church of England. Are you? Then the controversy is at an end. Then hear the Church: "Faith is a sure trust which a man hath in God that . . . his sins are forgiven." Or if you are not, whether you hear our church or no, at least hear the Scriptures. Hear believing Job declaring his faith, "I know that my Redeemer liveth" [*cf*. Job 19:25]. Hear Thomas (when, having seen, he believed) crying out, "My Lord and my God" [Jn. 20:28]! Hear St. Paul clearly describing the nature of *his* faith, "The life I now live, I live by faith in the Son of God, who loved me and gave himself for me" [Gal. 2:20]. Hear (to mention no more) all the believers who were with Paul when he wrote to the Colossians, bearing witness: "We give thanks unto the Father, who *hath delivered* us from the power of darkness and *hath translated* us into the kingdom of his dear Son in whom we have redemption through his blood, even the forgiveness of sins." [31]

61. But what need have we of distant witnesses? You have a witness in your own breast. For am I not speaking to one that loves God? How came you then to love him at first? Was it not because you knew that he loved *you?* Did you, could you, love God at all till you "tasted and saw that he was gracious" [*cf*. Ps. 34:8], that he was merciful to *you*, a sinner [*cf*. Lk. 18:13]? What avails then controversy or strife of words? Out of thy own mouth you own you had no love to God till you was sensible of his love to you. And whatever expressions any sinner who loves God uses to denote God's love to him, you will always, upon examination, find that they directly or indirectly imply forgiveness. Pardoning love is still at the root of all. He who was offended is now reconciled. The new song which God puts in every mouth is always to that effect: "O Lord, I will praise thee: though thou wast angry with me, thine anger is turned away. . . . Behold, God is my salvation. I will trust and not be afraid; for the Lord Jehovah is my strength and my song: he is also become my salvation." [32]

62. A confidence then in a pardoning God is essential to saving faith. The forgiveness of sins is one of the first of those unseen things whereof faith is the evidence. And if you are sensible of this, will you quarrel with us concerning an indifferent circumstance of it? Will you think it an important objection that we assert that this faith is usually given "in a moment"? First, let me entreat you to read over that authentic account

31. [Au.] Col. 1:12–14.          32. [Au.] Is. 12:1, 2.

of God's dealings with men, the Acts of the Apostles. In this treatise you will find how he wrought from the beginning on those who received remission of sins by faith. And can you find one of these (except, perhaps, St. Paul) who did not receive it "in a moment"? But abundance you find of those who did, besides Cornelius and the three thousand. And to this also agrees the experience of those who now receive the heavenly gift. Three or four exceptions only have I found in the course of several years (perhaps you yourself may be added to that number and one or two more whom you have never known). But all the rest of those who from time to time among us have believed in the Lord Jesus were in a moment brought "from darkness to light and from the power of Satan unto God" [cf. Acts 26:18].

63. And why should it seem a thing incredible to you, who have known "the power of God unto salvation" [cf. Rom. 1:16] — whether he hath wrought thus in *your* soul or no, "for there are diversities of operations, but the same Spirit" [cf. 1 Cor. 12:6] — that "the dead should hear the voice of the Son of God," and in that moment "live" [cf. Jn. 5:25]? Thus he useth to act, to show that when he willeth, to do is present with him. "Let there be light," said God, "and there was light [cf. Gen. 1:3]. He spoke the word, and it was done [cf. Ps. 33:9]. Thus the heavens and the earth were created and all the hosts of them" [cf. Gen. 2:1]. And this manner of acting in the present case highly suits both his power and love. There is therefore no hindrance on God's part, since "as his majesty is, so is his mercy" [Ecclus. 2:18]. And whatever hindrance there is on the part of man, when God speaketh, it is not. Only *ask* then, O sinner, "and it shall be given thee" [cf. Mt. 7:7], even the faith that brings salvation; and that without any merit or good work of thine, for "it is not of works, lest any man should boast" [Eph. 2:9]. No; it is of grace, of grace alone. For "unto him that worketh not, but believeth on him that justifieth the ungodly, his faith is counted to him for righteousness" [cf. Rom. 4:5].

64. "But by talking thus, you encourage sinners." I do encourage them — to repent. And do not *you?* Do not *you* know how many heap sin upon sin, purely for want of such encouragement, because they think they can never be forgiven, there is no place for repentance left? Does not *your* heart also bleed for them? What would *you* think too dear to part with? What would you not do, what would you not suffer, to bring one such sinner to repentance? Could not your love "endure all things" for them? Yes — if you *believed* it would do them good, if you

had any *hope* they would ever be better. Why do you not *believe* it would do them good? Why have you not a *hope* that they will be better? Plainly, because you do not *love* them enough, because you have not that charity which not only endureth but at the same time believeth and hopeth all things [*cf.* 1 Cor. 13:7].

65. But that you may see the whole strength of this objection, I will show you, without any disguise or reserve, how I encourage the very chief of sinners. My usual language to them runs thus:

O ye that deny the Lord that bought you, yet hear the Word of the Lord! Ye seek rest but find none. Even in laughter your heart is in heaviness. How long spend ye your labour for that which is not bread and your strength for that which satisfieth not [*cf.* Is. 55:2]? You know your soul is not satisfied. It is still an aching void. Sometimes you find (in spite of your principles) a sense of guilt, an awakened conscience. That grisly phantom, religion (so you describe her) will now and then haunt you still. "Righteousness looking down from heaven" is indeed to *us* no unpleasing sight [*cf.* Ps. 85:11]. But how does it appeal to *you?*

> *Horribili super aspectu mortalibus astans.*[33]

How often are you in fear of the very things you deny? How often in racking suspense? "What if there be an hereafter, a judgment to come, an unhappy eternity?" Do you not start at the thought? Can you be content to be always thus? Shall it be said of *you* also?

> Here lies a dicer, long in doubt
> If death could kill the soul, or not?
> Here ends his doubtfulness, at last
> Convinced—but, O, the die is cast! [34]

Or, are you already convinced there is no hereafter? What a poor state then are you in now, taking a few more dull turns upon earth, and then dropping into nothing? What kind of spirit must you be of if you can sustain yourself under the thought, under the expectation of being in a few moments swept away by the stream of time and then for ever

33. "Threatening mortals from on high with its horrible visage." *Cf.* Lucretius, *De Rerum Natura*, Bk. I, l. 65, where the text reads *instans*, in place of the unintelligible *astans*.

34. *Cf.* Samuel Wesley, *Poems on Several Occasions* (1736), 92, "Epitaph on a Gamester and Free Thinker" — where, for *dicer*, the original reads *Sceptick*.

> . . . swallow'd up, and lost,
> In the wide womb of uncreated night! [35]

But neither indeed are you *certain* of this, nor of anything else. It may be so, or it may not. A vast scene is behind, but clouds and darkness rest upon it. All is doubt and uncertainty. You are continually tossed to and fro and have no firm ground for the sole of your foot. O let not the poor wisdom of man any longer exalt itself against the wisdom of God. You have fled from him long enough: at length, suffer your eyes to be opened by him that made them. You want rest to your soul. Ask it of him who giveth to all men liberally, and upbraideth not. You are now a mere riddle to yourself and your condition full of darkness and perplexity.[36] You are one among many restless inhabitants of a miserable, disordered world, "walking in a vain shadow, and disquieting yourself in vain" [*cf*. Ps. 39:6]. But the light of God will speedily disperse the anxiety of your vain conjectures. By adding heaven to earth, and eternity to time, it will open such a glorious view of things as will lead you, even in the present world, to a peace which passeth all understanding.

66. O ye gross, vile, scandalous sinners, hear ye the Word of the Lord. "Turn ye, turn ye, from your evil ways; so iniquity shall not be your ruin" [*cf*. Zech. 1:4; Ezek. 18:30]. "As I live, saith the Lord, I have no pleasure in the death of a sinner, but rather that he should turn and live" [*cf*. Ezek. 33:11]. O make haste: delay not the time! "Come, and let us reason together. Though your sins be as scarlet, they shall be white as snow; though they be red as crimson, they shall be as wool [Is. 1:18]. . . . Who is this that cometh from Edom, with dyed garments, red in his apparel" [*cf*. Is. 63:1, 2]? It is he on whom the Lord "hath laid the iniquities of us all" [*cf*. Is. 53:6]! Behold, behold the Lamb of God, that taketh away thy sins [*cf*. Jn. 1:29, 36]! See the only begotten Son of the Father, "full of grace and truth" [*cf*. Jn. 1:14]! He loveth *thee*. He gave himself for thee. Now his bowels of compassion yearn over thee! O believe in the Lord Jesus, and *thou* shalt be saved! "Go in peace, sin no more" [*cf*. Jn. 8:11]!

67. Now cannot *you* join in all this? Is it not the very language of your heart? O when will you take knowledge that *our* whole concern, our constant labour, is to bring all the world to the religion which you feel, to

---

35. Milton, *Paradise Lost*, II, l. 149–50.
36. *Cf*. St. Augustine, *Confessions*, Bk. II, chap. ix–x.

solid, inward, vital religion! What *power* is it, then, that keeps us asunder? "Is thine heart right, as my heart is with thy heart? If it be, give me thy hand." [37] "Come with me and see," and rejoice in "my zeal for the Lord" [2 Kings 10:16]. No difference between us (if thou art a child of God) can be so considerable as our agreement is. If we differ in smaller things, we agree in that which is greatest of all. How is it possible, then, that *you* should be induced to think or speak evil of us? How could it ever come into *your* mind to oppose us, or weaken our hands? How long shall we complain of the wounds which we receive in the house of our friends? [38] Surely the children of this world are still "wiser in their generation than the children of light" [*cf.* Lk. 16:8]. Satan is not divided against himself! Why are they who are on the Lord's side? How is it that "wisdom is *not* justified of her own children" [*cf.* Lk. 7:35]?

68. Is it because you have heard that we only make religion a cloak for covetousness and because you have heard abundance of particulars alleged in support of that general charge? 'Tis probable you may also have heard how much we have gained by preaching already and, to crown all, that we are only papists in disguise, who are undermining and destroying the church.

69. You have heard this. Well, and can you believe it? Have you then never heard the fifth chapter of St. Matthew? I would to God you could believe this. What is written there? How readest thou [*cf.* Lk. 10:26]? "Blessed are ye when men shall revile you and persecute you and say all manner of evil against you falsely, for my name's sake. Rejoice, and be exceeding glad; for great is your reward in heaven, for so persecuted they the prophets that were before you" [Mt. 5:11–12], namely, by reviling them and saying all manner of evil of them falsely. Do not you know that this (as well as all other Scriptures) must needs be fulfilled? If so, take knowledge that this day also it is fulfilled in your ears [*cf.* Lk. 4:21]. For our Lord's sake, and for the sake of his gospel which we preach, men do revile us and persecute us and (blessed be God, who giveth us to rejoice therein) say all manner of evil of us falsely. And how can it be otherwise? "The disciple is not above his master. It is enough for the disciple that he be as his master and the servant as his Lord. If they have called the master of the house Beelzebub, how much more shall they call them of his household" [Mt. 10:24–25]?

70. This only we confess: that we preach *inward* salvation *now* attainable by faith. And for preaching *this* (for no other crime was then so

37. See above, p. 91 ff.                              38. See above, p. 377 ff.

much as pretended), we were forbid to preach any more in any of those churches where, till then, we were gladly received. This is a notorious fact. Being thus hindered from preaching in the places we should first have chosen, we now declare the "grace of God which bringeth salvation [cf. Tit. 2:11] . . . in all places of his dominion" [Ps. 103:22, B.C.P.]; as well knowing that God "dwelleth not" only "in temples made with hands" [Acts 17:24]. This is the real, and it is the only real, ground of complaint against us. And this we avow before all mankind: we *do* preach *this* salvation by *faith*. And not being suffered to preach it in the usual places, we declare it wherever a door is opened, either on a mountain or a plain or by a river side (for all which we conceive we have sufficient precedent) or in prison, or, as it were, in the house of Justus or the school of one Tyrannus [cf. Acts 18:7; 19:9]. Nor dare we refrain. "A dispensation of the gospel is committed to me; and woe is me, if I preach not the gospel" [cf. 1 Cor. 9:16, 17].

71. Here we allow the fact but deny the guilt. But in every other point alleged, we deny the fact, and call upon all the world to prove it, if they can. More especially, we call upon those who for many years saw our manner of life at Oxford. These well know that "after the most straitest sect of our religion we lived Pharisees" [cf. Acts 26:5], and that the grand objection to us for all those years was the being "righteous over-much" [cf. Eccles. 7:16]: the reading, fasting, praying, denying ourselves, the going to church and to the Lord's Table, the relieving the poor, visiting those that were sick and in prison, instructing the ignorant and labouring to reclaim the wicked — "more than was necessary" for salvation. These were our open, flagrant crimes, from the year 1729 to the year 1737, touching which our Lord shall judge "in that day" [cf. Jn. 12:48].

72. But, waiving the things that are past, "which of you *now* convinceth us of sin" [cf. Jn. 8:46]? Which of you (I here more especially appeal to my brethren of the clergy) can personally convict us of any ungodliness or unholiness of conversation? Ye know in your own hearts (all that are candid men, all that are not utterly blinded with prejudice) that we "labour to have a conscience void of offence both toward God and toward man" [Acts 24:16]. Brethren, I would to God that in this ye were even as we. But indeed (with grief I speak it) ye are not. There are among yourselves ungodly and unholy men, openly, undeniably such — drunkards, gluttons, returners of evil for evil, liars, swearers, profaners of the day of the Lord. Proof hereof is not wanting if

ye require it. Where, then, is your zeal against these? A clergyman so drunk he can scarce stand or speak, may, in the presence of a thousand people,[39] set upon another clergyman of the same church both with abusive words and open violence. And what follows? Why, the one is still allowed to dispense the sacred signs of the body and blood of Christ, but the other is not allowed to receive them — because he is a field-preacher.

73. O ye pillars and fathers of the church, are these things well-pleasing to him who hath made you overseers over that flock which he hath purchased with his own blood [cf. Acts 20:28]? O that ye would suffer me to boast myself a little. Is there not a cause? Have ye not compelled me? Which of your clergy are more unspotted in their lives, which more unwearied in their labours, than those whose "names ye cast out as evil," whom ye count "as the filth and offscouring of the world" [cf. 1 Cor. 4:13]? Which of them is more zealous "to spend and be spent" [cf. 2 Cor. 12:15] for the lost sheep of the house of Israel? Or who among them is more ready to be offered up for their flock "upon the sacrifice and service of their faith" [Phil. 2:17]?

74. Will ye say, as the historian of Catiline: *Si sic pro patria* ["If only this were done *for* the fatherland"]? [40] If this were done in defence of the Church and not in order to undermine and destroy it! That is the very proposition I undertake to prove — that we are now defending the Church, even the Church of England, in opposition to all those who either secretly undermine or more openly attempt to destroy it.

75. That we are papists (we, who are daily and hourly preaching that very doctrine which is so solemnly anathematized by the whole Church of Rome) is such a charge that I dare not waste my time in industriously confuting it. Let any man of common sense only look on the title pages of the sermons we have lately preached at Oxford and he will need nothing more to show him the weight of this senseless, shameless accusation — unless he can suppose the governors both of Christ Church and Lincoln College, nay, and all the university, to be papists too.

76. You yourself can easily acquit us of this, but not of the other part of the charge. You still think we are secretly undermining, if not openly destroying, the Church.

What do you mean by the Church? A visible church (as our Article

39. [Au. note] "At Epworth in Lincolnshire."
40. *Cf.* L. Annaeus Florus, *Epitome of Roman History*, trans. by J. C. Rolfe, Loeb ed. (Cambridge, Mass., 1929), Bk. II, chap. xii, l. 12: "*pulcherrima morte, si pro patria sic concidissent.*"

defines it) is "a company of faithful (or believing) people: *coetus credentium*." [41] This is the essence of a church, and the properties thereof are (as they are described in the words that follow) "among whom the pure Word of God is preached, and the sacraments duly administered." Now, then (according to this authentic account), what is the Church of England? What is it, indeed, but the "faithful people, the true believers, of England"? It is true, if these are scattered abroad, they come under another consideration. But when they are visibly joined by assembling together to hear "the pure Word of God preached" and to eat of one bread and drink of one cup, they are then properly the visible Church of England.

77. It were well if this were a little more considered by those who so vehemently cry out, "The church, the church!" (as those of old, "The temple of the Lord, the temple of the Lord!" [*cf.* Jer. 7:4]) not knowing what they speak, nor whereof they affirm. A provincial or national church, according to our Article, is the true believers of that province or nation. If these are dispersed up and down, they are only a part of the invisible Church of Christ. But if they are visibly joined by assembling together to hear his Word and partake of his Supper, they are then a visible church, such as the Church of England, of France, or any other.

78. This being premised, I ask, how do we undermine or destroy *the church:* the provincial, visible Church of England? The Article mentions three things as essential to a visible church: first, living faith, without which, indeed, there can be no church at all, neither visible nor invisible; secondly, preaching (and consequently hearing) the pure Word of God, else that faith would languish and die; and, thirdly, a due administration of the sacraments, the ordinary means whereby God increaseth faith. Now come close to the question: in which of these points do we undermine or destroy the Church?

Do we shut the door of faith? Do we lessen the number of "believing people" in England? Only remember what faith is, according to our Homilies (viz. "a sure trust and confidence . . . in God that through the merits of Christ my sins are forgiven and I reconciled to the favour of God").[42] And we appeal to all mankind, do we destroy this faith which is the life and soul of the Church? Is there, in fact, less of this faith in England than there was before we went forth? I think this is an assertion which the father of lies himself will scarce dare to utter or maintain.

With regard then to this first point, it is undeniable we neither undermine nor destroy the Church. The second thing is the preaching and hearing the pure Word of God. And do we hinder this? Do we hinder any minister from *preaching* the pure Word of God? If any preach not at all, or not the pure Word of God, is the hindrance in us or in themselves? Or do we lessen the number of those that *hear* the pure Word of God? Are then the hearers thereof (whether read or preached) fewer than they were in times past? Are the usual places of public worship less frequented by means of our preaching? Wheresoever our lot has been cast for any time, are the churches emptier than they were before? Surely, none that has any regard left either for truth or modesty will say that, in this point, we are enemies to, or destroyers of, the Church.

The third thing requisite if not to the *being*, at least to the *well-being* of a church, is the due administration of the sacraments, particularly that of the Lord's Supper. And are we, in *this* respect, underminers or destroyers of the Church? Do we, either by our example or advice, draw men away from the Lord's Table? Where we have laboured most, are there the fewest communicants? How does the fact stand in London, Bristol, Newcastle? O that you would no longer shut your eyes against the broad light which encompasses you on every side!

79. I believe you are sensible by this time not only how weak this objection is, but, likewise, how easy it would be, terribly to retort every branch of it upon most of those that make it, whether we speak of *true* living faith, of preaching the *pure* Word of God, or of the *due* administration of the sacraments, both of baptism and the Lord's Supper. But I spare you. It sufficeth that our God knoweth and will manifest in that day whether it be by reason of *us* or *you* that "men abhor the offering of the Lord" [*cf.* 1 Sam. 2:17].

80. Others object that we do not observe the *laws* of the Church, and thereby undermine it. What laws? The rubrics or canons? In every parish where I have been curate yet, I have observed the rubrics with a scrupulous exactness, not for wrath, but for conscience' sake. And this, so far as belongs to an unbeneficed minister or to a private member of the Church, I do now. I will just mention a few of them, and leave you to consider which of us has observed or does observe them most:

1. Days of fasting or abstinence to be observed:
   The forty days of Lent.
   The Ember days at the four seasons . . .
   The three Rogation days . . .
   All Fridays in the year, except Christmas Day.[43]

43. Tables and Rules for the Movable and Immovable Feasts, B.C.P. (1662).

2. So many as intend to be partakers of the Holy Communion shall signify their names to the curate at least sometime the day before. And if any of these [those] be an open and notorious evil liver . . . the curate . . . shall . . . advertise him, that in any wise he presume not to come to the Lord's Table until he hath openly declared himself to have truly repented. . . .[44]

3. Then (after the Nicene Creed) the curate shall declare unto the people what holidays or fasting days are in the week following to be observed.[45]

4. The minister shall [then shall the minister] first receive the Communion in both kinds himself and then proceed to deliver the same to the bishops, priests, and deacons, in like manner, if any be present, and *after that*, to the people. . . .[46]

5. [And] in cathedral and collegiate churches and colleges, where there are many priests and deacons, they shall *all receive the Communion with the priest every Sunday at the least* [except they have a reasonable cause to the contrary]. . . .[47]

6. [The] . . . children to be baptized . . . must be ready at the font *immediately after the last Lesson*. . . .[48]

7. The curates of every . . . parish shall warn the people that without great . . . necessity they procure not their children to be baptized *at home in their houses*. . . .

8. The curate of every parish shall diligently upon Sundays and holidays, after the Second Lesson at Evening Prayer, *openly in the Church*, instruct and examine so many children . . . as he shall think convenient in some part of the [this] Catechism.[49]

9. . . . Whensoever the bishop shall give notice [knowledge] for children to be brought unto him for their confirmation, the curate of every parish shall either bring or *send in writing, with his hand subscribed thereunto, the names of all such persons* within his parish as he shall think fit to be presented to the bishop. . . .[50]

81. Now, the question is not whether these rubrics ought to be observed (you take this for granted in making the objection), but whether

44. Rubric for The Order for the Administration of the Lord's Supper, or Holy Communion, *ibid.*, chap. 16.
45. *Ibid.*, sec. 341.        46. *Ibid.*, sec. 361.
47. The Order for . . . Holy Communion, *ibid.*, sec. 362.
48. Rubric for The Ministration of Publick Baptism of Infants, *ibid.*, chap. 17.
49. A Catechism . . . , *ibid.*, sec. 423.
50. Rubric for The Order of Confirmation, *ibid.*, chap. 19.

in fact they *have been* observed, by *you* or *me*, most? Many can witness I have observed them punctually, yea, sometimes at the hazard of my life; and as many, I fear, that *you* have not observed them at all and that several of them you never pretended to observe. And is it *you* that are accusing *me* for not observing the rubrics of the Church? What grimace is this! "O tell it not in Gath! Publish it not in the streets of Askelon" [*cf.* 2 Sam. 1:20]!

82. With regard to the canons, I would in the first place desire you to consider two or three plain questions:

> *First.* Have you read them over?
>
> *Secondly.* How can these be called "The Canons of the Church of England," seeing they were never legally established by the Church, never regularly confirmed in any full Convocation? [51]
>
> *Thirdly.* By what right am I required to observe such canons as were never legally established?

And then I will join issue with you on one question more, viz. whether you or I have observed them most? To instance only in a few:

Canon 29.[52] No person shall be admitted godfather or godmother to any child . . . before the said person hath received the Holy Communion.

Canon 59. Every parson, vicar, or curate, upon *every Sunday and holiday, before Evening Prayer, shall, for half an hour, or more,* examine and instruct the youth and ignorant persons of his parish.

Canon 64. Every parson, vicar, or curate, shall declare to the people every Sunday whether there be any holidays or *fasting days* the week following.

Canon 68. No minister shall *refuse* or *delay* to christen any child that is brought to the Church to him upon Sundays or holidays to be christened, or to bury any corpse that is brought to the church or church yard. (*N.B.* Inability to pay fees does not alter the case.) [53]

---

51. A mooted point. The canons here mentioned were codified in 1603 by Richard Bancroft (then Bishop of London), confirmed by the Convocation of Canterbury in 1604 (but with the Archbishopric vacant), then by the Convocation of York in 1606. In that same year, however, an Act of Parliament partially nullified their authority, especially in cases relating to laymen. *Cf.* George Hanford, ed., *A Prayer Book Dictionary* (n.d.), 144–45. See above, p. 75.

52. This citation of these canons is typical: the references are accurate; the texts, abridged and incomplete. *Cf.* Edmund Gibson, *Codex Iuris Ecclesiastici Anglicani* (1713). The full text of Canon 29 is in Gibson, *Codex Iuris,* I, 439; of Canon 59, *ibid.,* 453; of Canon 64, *ibid.,* 369; of Canon 68, *ibid.,* 435; of Canon 75, *ibid.,* 184.

53. Wesley's *nota bene.*

Canon 75. No ecclesiastical persons shall spend their time idly, by day or by night, playing at *dice, cards* or *tables*.

Now let the clergyman who has observed only these five canons for one year last past and who has read over all the canons in his congregation (as the king's ratification straitly enjoins him to do once every year), let him, I say, cast the first stone at us for not observing the canons (so called) of the Church of England.

83. However, we cannot be (it is said) friends to the Church, because we do not obey the governors of it and submit ourselves (as at our ordination we promised to do) to all their godly admonitions and injunctions.[54] I answer: in every individual point of an indifferent nature, we do and will (by the grace of God) obey the governors of the Church. But the "testifying the gospel of the grace of God" [*cf*. Acts 20:24] is not a point of an indifferent nature. "The ministry which we have received of the Lord Jesus" we are at all hazards to fulfil. It is "the burden of the Lord" [Jer. 23:33] which is laid upon us here; and we are "to obey God rather than man" [*cf*. Acts 5:29]. Nor yet do we in any ways violate the promise which each of us made when it was said unto him, "Take thou authority to preach the Word of God, in the name of the Father, and of the Son, and of the Holy Ghost." [55] We then promised to "submit" (mark the words) "to the *godly* admonitions and injunctions of our ordinary." But we did not, could not, promise to obey such injunctions as we know are *contrary to the Word of God*.

84. "But why then" (say some) "do you leave the Church?" "Leave the Church!" What can you mean? Do we leave so much as the *church walls?* Your own eyes tell you we do not. Do we leave the *ordinances* of the Church? You daily see and know the contrary. Do we leave the *fundamental doctrine* of the Church, namely, salvation by faith? It is our constant theme, in public, in private, in writing, in conversation. Do we leave the *practice* of the Church (the standard whereof are the Ten Commandments), which are so essentially inwrought in her constitution

---

54. [Au.] The author of a tract just published at Newcastle (entitled *The Notions of the Methodists Fully Disproved . . . in a Letter to the Rev. Mr. John Wesley*) much insists upon this objection. I have read, and believe it quite needless to take any further notice of, this performance; the writer being so utterly unacquainted with the merits of the cause, and showing himself so perfectly a stranger both to my life, preaching and writing — and to the Word of God, and to the Articles and Homilies of the Church of England. [Ed.] *cf*. Richard Green, *Anti-Methodist Publications Issued During the Eighteenth Century* (1902), #162, 163.

55. The Ordering of Priests, B.C.P.

(as little as you may apprehend it) that whosoever breaks one of the least of these is no member of the Church of England? I believe you do not care to put the cause on this issue. Neither do you mean this by "leaving the Church." In truth, I cannot conceive what you mean. I doubt, you cannot conceive [it] yourself. You have retailed a sentence from somebody else, which you no more understand than he. And no marvel, for it is a true observation, "Nonsense is never to be understood."

85. Nearly related to this is that other objection that we "divide the Church." Remember, the Church is "the faithful people," or true believers. Now, how do we *divide* these? Why, by our societies. Very good. Now the case is plain. We "divide them" (you say) by *uniting them together*. Truly, a very uncommon way of *dividing*. "O, but you divide those who are thus united with each other from the rest of the Church." By no means. Many of them were before joined to all their brethren of the Church of England (and many were not, until they knew us) by "assembling themselves together" to hear the Word of God, and to eat of one bread and drink of one cup. And do they now *forsake* that assembling themselves together? You cannot, you dare not say it. You know they are more diligent therein than ever; it being one of the fixed rules of our societies, "that every member attend the ordinances of God," *i.e.* that he *do not divide from the Church*. And if any member of the Church does thus divide from or leave it, he hath no more place among us.

86. I have considered this objection the more at large because it is of most weight with sincere minds. And to all these, if they have fairly and impartially weighed the answer as well as the objection, I believe it clearly appears that we are neither *undermining* nor *destroying*, neither *dividing* nor *leaving* the Church. So far from it that we have great heaviness on her account, yea, continual sorrow in our hearts [*cf.* Rom. 9:2]. And our prayer to God is that he would "repair the breaches of Zion, and build the walls of Jerusalem" [*cf.* Ps. 51:18], that this our desolate church may flourish again and "be the praise of the whole earth" [*cf.* Is. 62:7].

87. But perhaps you have heard that we in truth regard no church at all, that *gain* is the true spring of all our actions; that I, in particular, am well paid for my work, having thirteen hundred pounds a year (as a reverend author accurately computes it) at the Foundery alone, over and above what I receive from Bristol, Kingswood, Newcastle and other places; and that whoever survives me will see I have made good use of my time, for I shall not die a beggar.

88. I freely own this is one of the best-devised objections which has ever yet been made, because it not only puts me upon proving a negative (which is seldom an easy task), but also one of such a kind as scarce admits of any demonstrative proof at all. But for such proof as the nature of the thing allows, I appeal to my manner of life which hath been from the beginning. Ye who have seen it (and not with a friendly eye) for these twelve or fourteen years last past, or for any part of that time, have ye ever seen any thing like the love of gain therein? Did I not continually remember the words of the Lord Jesus, "It is more blessed to give than to receive" [cf. Acts 20:35]? Ye of Oxford, do ye not know these things are so? What gain did I seek among you? Of whom did I take anything? From whom did I covet silver or gold or apparel? To whom did I deny anything which I had even to the hour that I departed from you? Ye of Epworth and Wroot, among whom I ministered for (nearly) the space of three years, what gain did I seek among you? Or of whom did I take or covet anything? Ye of Savannah and Frederica, among whom God afterwards proved me and showed me what was in my heart, what gain did I seek among you? Of whom did I take anything? Or whose food or apparel did I covet (for silver or gold had ye none, no more than I myself for many months), even when I was in hunger and nakedness? Ye yourselves, and the God and Father of our Lord Jesus Christ, know that I lie not.

89. "But" (it is said) "things are fairly altered now. Now I cannot complain of wanting any thing, having the yearly income of a bishop of London, over and above what I gain at other places." At what other places, my friend? Inform yourself a little better, and you will find that both at Newcastle, Bristol and Kingswood (the only places, beside London, where any collection at all is made) [56] the money collected is both received and expended by the stewards of those several societies and never comes into my hands at all, neither first nor last. And you, or any who desire it, shall read over the accounts kept by any of those stewards and see with your own eyes that by all these societies I gain just as much as you do.

90. The case in London stands thus. In November 1739 two gentlemen, then unknown to me (Mr. Ball and Mr. Watkins) came and desired

---

56. The text for this parenthesis in the edition of 1772 reads: ("and all other places where any collection is made"). At the time of the first edition, however (1744), the text above corresponded to the facts. By 1770, the situation had changed and the text was altered accordingly. The edition of 1786 reverts to the first reading.

me once and again to preach in a place called the Foundery, near Moorfields. With much reluctance I at length complied. I was soon after
pressed to take that place into my own hands. Those who were most
earnest therein lent me the purchase money, which was one hundred and
fifteen pounds. Mr. Watkins and Mr. Ball then delivered me the names of
several subscribers who offered to pay, some four or six, some ten shillings
a year towards the repayment of the purchase money and the putting the
buildings into repair. This amounted one year to near two hundred
pounds, the second to about one hundred and forty pounds, and so to the
last.

91. The United Society began a little after, whose weekly contribution (chiefly for the poor) is received and expended by the stewards and
comes not into my hands at all. But there is also a quarterly subscription
of many of the society, which is nearly equal to that above mentioned.

92. The uses to which these subscriptions have been hitherto applied, are: first, the payment of that one hundred and fifteen pounds;
secondly, the repairing (I might almost say rebuilding) that vast, uncouth heap of ruins at the Foundery; thirdly, the building galleries both
for men and women; fourthly, the enlarging the society room to near
thrice its first bigness. All taxes and occasional expenses are likewise de-
frayed out of this fund. And it has been hitherto so far from yielding any
overplus, that it has never sufficed for these purposes yet. So far from it,
that I am still in debt on these accounts near three hundred pounds. So
much have I hitherto gained by preaching the gospel, besides a debt of
one hundred and fifty pounds still remaining on account of the schools
built at Bristol and another of above two hundred pounds on account
of that now building at Newcastle! I desire any reasonable man would
now sit down and lay these things together and let him see whether,
allowing me a grain of common sense (if not of common honesty), he
can possibly conceive that a view of *gain* would induce me to act in
this manner.

93. You can never reconcile it with any degree of common sense that
a man who wants nothing, who has already all the necessaries, all the
conveniences, nay, and many of the superfluities of life, and these not
only independent on any one, but less liable to contingencies than even
a gentleman's freehold estate,[57] that such an one should calmly and deliberately throw up his ease, most of his friends, his reputation and that
way of life which of all others is most agreeable both to his natural tem-

57. Such was the financial security of his Lincoln fellowship. See above, p. 8.

per and education; that he should toil day and night, spend all his time and strength, knowingly destroy a firm constitution, and hasten into weakness, pain, diseases, death — to gain a debt of six or seven hundred pounds!

94. But supposing the balance on the other side, let me ask you one plain question, "For what gain (setting conscience aside) will you be obliged to act thus, to live exactly as I do? For what price will you preach — and that with all your might; not in an easy, indolent, fashionable way — eighteen or nineteen times every week, and this throughout the year? What shall I give you to travel seven or eight hundred miles, in all weathers, every two or three months? For what salary will you abstain from all other diversions than the doing good and the praising God? I am mistaken if you would not prefer strangling to such a life, even with thousands of gold and silver.

95. And what is the comfort you have found out for me in these circumstances? Why, that "I shall not die a beggar." So now I am supposed to be heaping up riches, that I may leave them behind me. Leave them behind me? For whom? My wife and children? Who are they? They are yet unborn, unless thou meanest the children of faith whom God hath given me. But my heavenly father feedeth them [cf. Mt. 6:26]. Indeed, if I lay up riches at all, it must be "to leave behind me" (seeing my fellowship is a provision for life). But I cannot understand this. What comfort would it be to my soul, now launched into eternity, that I had left behind me gold as the dust and silver as the sand of the sea? Will it follow me over the great gulf? Or can I go back to it? Thou that liftest up thy eyes in hell, what do thy riches profit thee now? Will all thou once hadst under the sun gain thee a drop of water to cool thy tongue [cf. Lk. 16:19-24]? O the comfort of riches left behind to one who is tormented in that flame! You put me in mind of those celebrated lines (which I once exceedingly admired), addressed by way of consolation to the soul of a poor self-murderer:

> Yet shall thy grave with rising flowers be dress'd,
> And the green turf lie lightly upon thy breast!
> Here shall the year its earliest beauties show:
> Here the first roses of the spring shall blow:
> While angels, with their silver wings o'ershade
> The place, now sacred by thy relics made.[58]

58. Cf. Alexander Pope, "Elegy to the Memory of an Unfortunate Lady" (1717); in Pope, Works (1764), I, 142, l. 63-68.

96. I will now simply tell you my sense of these matters, whether you will hear or whether you will forbear. Food and raiment I have, such food as I choose to eat and such raiment as I choose to put on. I have a place where to lay my head. I have what is needful for life and godliness. And I apprehend this is all the world can afford. The kings of the earth can give me no more. For as to gold and silver, I count it dung and dross; I trample it under my feet. I (yet not I, but the grace of God that is in me) esteem it just as the mire in the streets. I desire it not, I seek it not, I only fear lest any of it should cleave to me and I should not be able to shake it off before my spirit returns to God. It must indeed pass through my hands, but I will take care (God being my helper) that the mammon of unrighteousness shall only pass through; it shall not rest there. None of the accursed thing shall be found in my tents [cf. Josh. 6:18; 7:1] when the Lord calleth me hence. And hear ye this, all you who have discovered the treasures which I am to leave behind me. If I leave behind me ten pounds (above my debts and the little arrears of my fellowship [59]), you and all mankind bear witness against me that I lived and died a thief and a robber.

97. Before I conclude, I cannot but entreat you who know God to review the whole matter from the foundation. Call to mind what the state of religion was in our nation a few years since. In whom did you find the holy tempers that were in Christ: bowels of mercies, lowliness, meekness, gentleness, contempt of the world, patience, temperance, long-suffering [cf. Col. 3:12], a burning love to God rejoicing evermore and in everything giving thanks [1 Thess. 5:16–18], and a tender love to all mankind, covering, believing, hoping, enduring all things [cf. 1 Cor. 13:7]? Perhaps you did not know one such man in the world. But how many that had all unholy tempers? What vanity and pride, what stubbornness and self-will, what anger, fretfulness, discontent, what suspicion and resentment, what inordinate affections, what irregular passions, what foolish and hurtful desires, might you find in those who were called the *best* of men, in those who made the strictest profession of religion? And how few did you know who went so far as the *profession* of religion, who had even "the form of godliness" [2 Tim. 3:5]? Did you not frequently bewail, wherever your lot was cast, the general want of even *outward religion?* How few

---

59. Thus the text of 1744. But when Wesley revised it in 1772, he had resigned his fellowship and his financial situation had changed. The 1772 revision: "above my debts and my books, or what may happen to be due on account of them." Cf. *Journal*, VIII, 342–44, for text of Wesley's "Last Will and Testament."

were seen at the public worship of God? How much fewer at the Lord's Table? And was even this little flock zealous of good works, careful, as they had time, to do good to all men? On the other hand, did you not with grief observe *outward irreligion* in every place? Where could you be for one week without being an eye or an ear witness of cursing, swearing, or profaneness, of Sabbath-breaking or drunkenness, of quarrelling or brawling, of revenge or obscenity? Were these things done in a corner? Did not gross iniquity of all kinds overspread our land as a flood — yea, and daily increase, in spite of all the opposition which the children of God did or could make against it?

98. If you had then been told that the jealous God would soon arise and maintain his own cause; that he would pour down his Spirit from on high and renew the face of the earth; that he would shed abroad his love in the hearts of the outcasts of men, producing all holy and heavenly tempers, expelling anger and pride and evil desire and all unholy and earthly tempers, causing outward religion — the work of faith, the patience of hope, the labour of love — to flourish and abound; and, wherever it spread, abolishing outward irreligion, destroying all the works of the devil: if you had been told that this living knowledge of the Lord would in a short space overspread our land, yea, and daily increase, in spite of all the opposition which the devil and his children did or could make against it, would you not have vehemently desired to see that day, that you might bless God and rejoice therein?

99. Behold, the day of the Lord is come. He is again visiting and redeeming his people. Having eyes, see ye not? Having ears, do ye not hear, neither understand with your hearts? At this hour the Lord is rolling away our reproach. Already his standard is set up. His Spirit is poured forth on the outcasts of men and his love shed abroad in their hearts. Love of all mankind, meekness, gentleness, humbleness of mind, holy and heavenly affections, do take place of hate, anger, pride, revenge, and vile or vain affections. Hence, wherever the power of the Lord spreads, springs outward religion in all its forms. The houses of God are filled; the Table of the Lord is thronged on every side. And those who thus show their love of God show they love their neighbour also, by being careful to maintain good works, by doing all manner of good (as they have time) to all men. They are likewise careful to abstain from all evil. Cursing, Sabbath-breaking, drunkenness, with all other (however fashionable) works of the devil are not once named among them. All this is plain, demonstrable fact. For this also is not done in a corner. Now, do you acknowledge the

day of your visitation? Do you bless God and rejoice therein [*cf.* 1 Pet. 2:12]?

100. What hinders? Is it this, that men say all manner of evil of those whom God is pleased to use as instruments in his work? O ye fools, did ye suppose the devil was dead? Or that he would not fight for his kingdom? And what weapons shall he fight with, if not with lies? Is he not a liar and the father of it? Suffer ye then thus far. Let the devil and his children say all manner of evil of us. And let them go on deceiving each other, and being deceived. But ye need not be deceived also — or if you are, if you will believe all they say, be it so: that we are weak, silly, wicked men without sense, without learning, without even a desire or design of doing good — yet I insist upon the fact: Christ is preached and sinners are converted to God. This none but a madman can deny. We are ready to prove it by a cloud of witnesses. Neither therefore can the inference be denied that God is now visiting his people. O that all men may know, in this their day, the things that make for their peace!

101. Upon the whole, to men of the world I would still recommend the known advice of Gamaliel: "Refrain from these men, and let them alone; for if this work be of men, it will come to nought, but if it be of God, ye cannot overthrow it, lest haply ye be found even to fight against God" [Acts 5:38–39]. But unto you whom God hath chosen out of the world, I say, ye are our brethren and of our father's house. It behoveth you, in whatsoever manner ye are able, "to strengthen our hands in God" [*cf.* Ezra 6:22]. And this ye are all able to do: to wish us good luck in the name of the Lord, and to pray continually that none of these things may move us and that we may not count our lives dear unto ourselves, so that we may finish our course with joy, and the ministry which we have received of the Lord Jesus! 60

60. The 1772 text adds, "Written in the year 1744." This is an evident mistake, for both first and second editions are dated 1743.

# IV

## THE STRUGGLE WITH THE CALVINISTS

*Editor's introduction.* This essay, containing the sum of Wesley's rejection of the predestinarian position, was written and published in 1752. It gathers up the threads of his earlier polemics and establishes the main lines along which the controversy would thereafter proceed, somewhat spasmodically, until his death. In 1770, under pressure from his preachers, Wesley published a carelessly drafted "minute" of a discussion in the annual conference that ended what little hope there might have been for a reconciliation between the "Calvinists" and the "Arminians" (*cf.* Tyerman, *Life*, III, 71–80). At this point Wesley was joined by the only nearly comparable theological talent he ever had in a colleague, John William Fletcher, the Swiss-born rector of Madeley (*cf. The Works of the Rev. John Fletcher* [1802]). In a somewhat sprawling but clearly organized series of essays he called "Checks" (*First Check to Antinomianism; or, A Vindication of the Rev. Mr. Wesley's Last Minutes; A Second Check,* etc., in his *Works* [1802], II–III), Fletcher laid out the arguments against predestinarianism and antinomianism, from a perspective quite similar to Wesley's, with equal emphasis on the fusion and balance of God's sovereign grace and man's moral responsibility.

The Calvinists counterattacked with a barrage of pamphlets and journals (*The Christian Magazine, The Spiritual Magazine, The Gospel Magazine*). In 1778 Wesley launched his own partisan review, which he called *The Arminian Magazine* — thus turning the epithet "Arminian" into a crusader's badge, much as he had done earlier with the label Methodist. "Our design," he informs "the readers" of the first issue, "is to publish some of the most remarkable tracts on the universal love of God and his willingness to *save all men from all sin,* which have been written in this and the last century. . . . To these will be added original pieces, wrote either directly upon this subject, or on those which are equally opposed by the patrons of 'particular redemption.' " Editing this magazine constituted the chief literary enterprise of Wesley's closing years.

The basic difficulty in this tenacious and unruly struggle lay less in the affirmations made from either side than with their denials. The first affirmative premise of the predestinarians was God's sovereign freedom — and this the Wesleyans had no disposition to deny. But a second predestinarian premise was a conclusion drawn from the fact that a clear majority of God's human creatures seemed not to have responded in faith to God's provision of salvation. The conclusion taken from these premises — strictly implied, as the Calvinists insisted — is that the fact of reprobation, too, was also a part of God's *original intention* — *i.e.* his *pre*destination of human affairs.

To support this logic, they had then to deny both human *merit* and also human *agency* in the business of grace and salvation. It was this *denial* which seemed to Wesley to disfigure the gospel and to image God in caricature. On the other hand, however, Wesley's denial of God's "right" to damn as well as to save — and both unconditionally — blocked him from even understanding the Calvinists' contention that predestination is a "*comfortable* doctrine" (*i.e.* a source of *strength*), important chiefly *to the believer*, reminding him that his destiny (and that of all men) is secure in God's hands, withdrawn from the random mercies of human contingency. Both parties professed a common belief in the authority of Scripture; both were equally agreed on the doctrine of justification by faith alone. The Calvinists preferred to measure God's sovereignty by his freedom *from* the world; the "Arminians," by his victorious involvement *in* it. One side saw salvation threatened by "free will," the other saw God's character defamed by "reprobation." *Predestination Calmly Considered* reflects these two rigid ideas in collision, under the pretense of dialogue. The reader who compares this text with others (especially *Works* [Pine], XX, 154–250) will notice certain discrepancies in the number of the paragraphs. This is due to the omission from the latter of section XLI, with its quotation from Isaac Watts. The sections in the present version follow those in the first edition (with the Watts quotation included). The principal copy text, however, is that of 1773, collated with the first edition and those of 1779 and 1786.

❖   ❖   ❖   ❖

## Predestination Calmly Considered

> That to the height of this great argument,
> I may assert eternal providence,
> And justify the ways of God to men.
>
> JOHN MILTON, *Paradise Lost*, Bk. I, l. 24-27

I. I am inclined to believe that many of those who enjoy the faith which worketh by love may remember some time when the power of the Highest wrought upon them in an eminent manner, when the voice of the Lord laid the mountains low, brake all the rocks in pieces [*cf.* 1 Kings 19:11] and mightily shed abroad his love in their hearts by the Holy Ghost given unto them [*cf.* Rom. 5:5]. And at that time, it is certain they had no power to "resist" the grace of God. They were then no more able to stop the course of that torrent which carried all before it than to stem the waves of the sea with their hand or to stay the sun in the midst of heaven.

II. And the children of God may continually observe how his love leads them on from faith to faith, with what tenderness he watches over their souls, with what care he brings them back if they go astray, and then upholds their going in his path, that their footsteps may not slide. They cannot but observe how unwilling he is to let them go from serving him, and how, notwithstanding the stubbornness of their wills and the wildness of their passions, he goes on in his work, "conquering and to conquer" [Rev. 6:2], till he "hath put all his enemies under his feet" [1 Cor. 15:25].

III. The farther this work is carried on in their hearts, the more earnestly do they cry out: "Not unto us, O Lord, but unto thy Name give the praise, for thy mercy and for thy truth's sake" [Ps. 115:1], the more deeply are they convinced that "by grace we are saved, not of works, lest any man should boast" [*cf.* Eph. 2:8-9], that we are not pardoned and accepted with God for the sake of anything we have done, but wholly and solely for the sake of Christ — of what he hath done and suffered for us — the more assuredly likewise do they know that the condition of this acceptance is faith alone, before which gift of God no good work can be done, none which hath not in it the nature of sin.

IV. How *easily*, then, may a believer infer from what he hath experienced in his own soul that the true grace of God *always* works *irresistibly*

428 THEOLOGIES IN CONFLICT

in every believer — that God will finish wherever he has begun this work, so that it is "impossible" for any believer to "fall from grace"; and lastly, that the reason why God gives this to some only and not to others, is because (of his own will, without any previous regard either to their faith or works) he hath "absolutely, unconditionally predestinated" them to life, before the foundation of the world.

V. Agreeably hereto, in "The Protestant Confession of Faith," drawn up at Paris, in the year 1559, we have these words (Article 12): [1]

> We believe that out of the general corruption and condemnation in which all men are plunged, God draws those whom, in his eternal and unalterable counsel, he has elected by his own goodness and mercy, though our Lord Jesus Christ, without considering their works, leaving the others in the same corruption and condemnation.

VI. To the same effect speak the Dutch divines, assembled at Dort, in the year 1618.[2] Their words are (Art. 6, *et seq.*): [3]

> Whereas, in [the] process of time, God bestowed faith on some and not on others, this proceeds from his eternal decree, according to which he softens the hearts of the elect and leaveth them that are not elect in their wickedness and hardness.
> And herein is discovered the difference put between men equally lost, that is to say, the decree of election and reprobation.
> Election is the unchangeable decree of God by which, before the foundation of the world, he hath chosen in Christ unto salvation a set number of men. This election is one and the same of all which are to be saved.
> Not all men are elected; but some not elected, whom God, in his unchangeable good pleasure, hath decreed to leave in the common

1. An abridgment of Article XII of the *Confession du Foi* . . . , prepared by Calvin and Antoine de la Roche Chandieu, then revised and adopted by the Synod of Paris, 1559. It is also cited as "The Confession of La Rochelle" (*cf.* Philip Schaff, *Creeds of Christendom, with a History and Critical Notes* [New York, 1881], III, 356 ff.). The full text of the article (in John Quick, *Synodicon in Gallia Reformata* [1692], Wesley's probable source) is as follows:
XII. We believe that from this general corruption and condemnation in which all men are plunged, God draws those whom, in his eternal and unalterable counsel, he has elected by his sole goodness and mercy in our Lord Jesus Christ, without considering their works, leaving the others in this same corruption and condemnation; *to show forth in the latter his justice, as in the former to make plain the riches of his mercy.* [Italics added to show what Wesley omitted.]
2. Convened, November 13, 1618; adjourned, May 9, 1619.
3. It is worth comparing Wesley's severe abridgment here (which amounts to garbling) with the full text in Schaff, *Creeds of Christendom*, III, 582-84, Articles VI, VII, and XV under "The First Head of Doctrine: Concerning Divine Predestination" (*cf.* also the Latin text, *ibid.*, 552-55).

misery and not to bestow saving faith upon them; but leaving them in their own ways, at last to condemn and punish them everlastingly for their unbelief and also for their other sins. And this is the decree of reprobation.

VII. Likewise, in the "Confession of Faith" set forth by the Assembly of English and Scotch divines, in the year 1646, are these words (chap. 3): [4]

God from all eternity did unchangeably ordain whatsoever comes to pass.

By the decree of God, for the manifestation of his glory, some men and angels are predestinated unto everlasting life and others fore-ordained to everlasting death.

These angels and men thus predestinated and fore-ordained are particularly and unchangeably designed, and their number so certain and definite, that it cannot be either increased or diminished.

Those of mankind that are predestinated unto life, God, before the foundation of the world, hath chosen in Christ unto everlasting glory, without any foresight of faith or good works. The rest of mankind God was pleased, for the glory of his sovereign power over his creatures, to pass by and to ordain them to dishonour and wrath.

No less express are Mr. Calvin's words, in his *Christian Institutions* (chap. xxi, 1): [5]

All men are not created for the same end, but some are fore-ordained to eternal life, others to eternal damnation. So according as every man was created for the one end or the other, we say he was *elected* (*i.e.* predestinated to life) or *reprobated* (*i.e.* predestinated to damnation).

VIII. Indeed, there are some who assert the decree of election, and not the decree of reprobation. They assert that God hath, by a positive, unconditional decree, chosen some to life and salvation, but not that he hath by any such decree devoted the rest of mankind to destruction. These are they to whom I would address myself first. And let me beseech you, brethren, by the mercies of God, to lift up your hearts to him, and to beg of him to free you from all prepossession, from the prejudices even of your tender years and from whatsoever might hinder the light of

4. The Westminster Assembly, 1646–47. Wesley was right about this date for the *writing* of the Westminster Confession, although it was not published until 1647. Cf. Wesley's abridgment with the full text, in Schaff, *Creeds of Christendom*, III, 608–10, and note that Wesley omits chap. V, VI and VIII.

5. Cf. John Calvin, *The Institutes of the Christian Religion*, Bk. III, chap. xxi, 5; in *LCC*, J. T. McNeill, ed., XXI, 926.

God from shining in upon your souls. Let us calmly and fairly weigh these things in the balance of the sanctuary [cf. Lev. 5:15]. And let all be done in love and meekness of wisdom, as becomes those who are fighting under one Captain, and who humbly hope they are joint heirs through him of the glory which shall be revealed.

I am verily persuaded that, in the uprightness of your hearts, you defend the decree of unconditional election, even in the same uprightness wherein you reject and abhor that of unconditional reprobation. But consider, I entreat you, whether you are consistent with yourselves; consider whether this election can be separate from reprobation, whether one of them does not imply the other; so that, in holding one, you must hold both.

IX. That this was the judgment of those who had the most deeply considered the nature of these decrees, of the Assembly of English and Scotch divines, of the Reformed Churches both in France and the Low Countries, and of Mr. Calvin himself, appears from their own words, beyond all possibility of contradiction. "Out of the general corruption," saith the French Church, "he draws those whom he hath elected, leaving the others in the same corruption, according to his immovable decree." "By the decree of God," says the Assembly of English and Scotch divines, "some are predestinated unto everlasting life, others fore-ordained to everlasting death." "God hath once for all," saith Mr. Calvin, "appointed, by an eternal and unchangeable decree, to whom he would give salvation, and whom he would devote to destruction" (*Instit.*, III, [xxi], 7).[6] Nay, it is observable, Mr. Calvin speaks with utter contempt and disdain of all who endeavour to separate one from the other, who assert election without reprobation. "Many," says he, "as it were to excuse God, own election and deny reprobation. But this is quite silly and childish. For election cannot stand without reprobation. Whom God passes by, those he reprobates. It is one and the same thing" (*Instit.*, III, [xxiii], 1).[7]

X. Perhaps upon deeper consideration you will find yourself of the same judgment. It may be, you also hold reprobation, though you know it not. Do not you believe that God, who made "one vessel unto honour," hath made "another unto" eternal "dishonour" [cf. Rom. 9:21]? Do not you believe that the men who "turn the grace of our God into lasciativious-

6. *Institutes*, Bk. III, chap. xxi, par. 7. *Cf.* the full text of this in *LCC*, XXI, 931. What Wesley *omits* is revealing.

7. Bk. III, chap. xxiii, par. 1. But *cf.* the context: *LCC*, XXI, 947–49.

ness were before ordained of God unto this condemnation" [Jude 4]? Do
not you think that "for this same purpose God raised Pharaoh up," that
he might show his sovereign power in his destruction [*cf.* Rom. 9:17 ff.]
— and that "Jacob have I loved, but Esau have I hated" [*cf.* Rom. 9:13;
Mal. 1:1–2], refers to their eternal state? Why, then, you hold absolute
reprobation and you think Esau and Pharaoh were instances of it, as well
as all those "vessels made unto dishonour," those men "before ordained
unto condemnation."

XI.[8] To set this matter in a still clearer light, you need only answer one
question: Is any man saved who is not elected? Is it possible that any not
elected should be saved? If you say, "No," you put an end to the doubt.
You espouse election and reprobation together. You confirm Mr. Calvin's
words that "without reprobation, election itself cannot stand." You allow
(though you was not sensible of it before) that "whom God elects not,
them he reprobates."

Try whether it be possible, in any particular case, to separate election
from reprobation. Take one of these who are supposed not to be elected,
one whom God hath not chosen unto life and salvation. Can this man be
saved from sin and hell? You answer, "No." Why not? "Because he is
not elected. Because God hath unchangeably decreed to save so many
souls and no more, and he is not of that number. Him God hath decreed
to pass by, to leave him to everlasting destruction, in consequence of
which irresistible decree, the man perishes everlastingly." Oh, my brethren, how small is the difference between this, and broad, barefaced reprobation?

XII. Let me entreat you to make this case your own. In the midst of
life, you are in death;[9] your soul is dead while you live, if you live in
sin; if you do not live to God. And who can deliver you from the body
of this death? Only the grace of God in Jesus Christ our Lord [*cf.* Rom.
7:24–25]. But God hath decreed to give this grace to others only, and
not to you; to leave you in unbelief and spiritual death, and for that unbelief, to punish you with death everlasting. Well then mayest thou cry,
even till thy throat is dry, "O wretched man that I am" [Rom. 7:24]! For
an unchangeable, irresistible decree standeth between thee and the very
possibility of salvation. Go now and find out how to split the hair be-

8. *Cf.* this section with the sermon on "Free Grace," par. 8 f. (*Works*, VII, 375–
77). The language is similar; the argument, identical.
9. *Cf.* The Order for the Burial of the Dead, B.C.P., (1662), sec. 477.

tween thy being reprobated and not elected; how to separate reprobation, in its most effectual sense, from unconditional election!

XIII. Acknowledge then that you hold reprobation. Avow it in the face of the sun. To be consistent with yourself, you must openly assert that "without reprobation this election cannot stand." You know it cannot. You know if God hath fixed a decree that *these men only* shall be saved, in such a decree it is manifestly implied that *all other men* shall be damned. If God hath decreed that *this part* of mankind, and no more, shall live eternally, you cannot but see, it is therein decreed, that *the other part* shall never see life. O, let us deal ingenuously with each other. What we really hold, let us openly profess. And if reprobation be the truth, it will bear the light, for "the word of our God shall stand for ever" [Is. 40:8).

XIV. Now then, without any extenuation on the one hand or exaggeration on the other, let us look upon this doctrine, call it what you please, naked and in its native colour. Before the foundations of the world were laid, God, of his own mere will and pleasure, fixed a decree concerning all the children of men who should be born unto the end of the world. This decree was unchangeable with regard to God and irresistible with regard to man. And herein it was ordained that one part of mankind should be saved from sin and hell and all the rest left to perish for ever and ever, without hope. That none of these should have that grace which alone could prevent their dwelling with everlasting burnings, God decreed for this cause alone, "because it was his good pleasure," and for this end, "to show forth his glorious power and his sovereignty over all the earth."

XV. Now can you, upon reflection, believe this? Perhaps you will say, "I do not think about it." That will never do. You not only think about it (though it may be confusedly), but speak about it, too, whenever you speak of unconditional election. You do not think about it? What do you mean? Do you never think about Esau or Pharaoh? or, in general, about a *certain number* of souls whom alone God hath decreed to save? Why, in that very thought reprobation lurks: it entered your heart the moment that entered. It stays as long as that stays, and you cannot speak that thought without speaking of reprobation. True, it is covered with fig leaves, so that a heedless eye may not observe it to be there. But, if you narrowly observe, unconditional election cannot appear without the cloven foot of reprobation.

XVI. "But do not the Scriptures speak of 'election'? They say, St. Paul was an elected, or chosen, vessel; nay, and speak of great numbers of men as 'elect' according to the foreknowledge of God? You cannot, therefore, deny there is such a thing as 'election.' And, if there is, what do you mean by it?"

I will tell you, in all plainness and simplicity. I believe it commonly means one of these two things. First, a divine appointment of some particular men to do some particular work in the world. And this election I believe to be not only personal but absolute and unconditional. Thus Cyrus was "elected" to rebuild the temple, and St. Paul, with the Twelve, to preach the gospel. But I do not find this to have any necessary connexion with eternal happiness. Nay, it is plain it has not; for one who is "elected" in this sense may yet be lost eternally. "Have I not chosen" (elected) "you twelve?" saith our Lord, "yet one of you hath a devil" [cf. Jn. 6:70]? Judas, you see, was "elected" as well as the rest, yet is his lot with the devil and his angels.

XVII. I believe "election" means, secondly, a divine appointment of some men to eternal happiness. But I believe this election to be conditional, as well as the reprobation opposite thereto. I believe the eternal decree concerning both is expressed in those words: "He that believeth shall be saved; he that believeth not shall be damned" [Mk. 16:16]. And this decree, without doubt, God will not change and man cannot resist. According to this, all true *believers* are in Scripture termed "elect," as all who continue in *unbelief* are so long properly "reprobates," that is, *unapproved* of God and "without discernment" touching the things of the Spirit.

XVIII. Now, God, to whom all things are present at once, who sees all eternity at one view, "calleth the things that are not as though they were" [Rom. 4:17], the things that are not yet as though they were now subsisting. Thus he calls Abraham the "father of many nations" before even Isaac was born. And thus Christ is called "the Lamb slain from the foundation of the world" [Rev. 13:8]; though he was not slain, in fact, till some thousand years after. In like manner, God calleth true believers "elect from the foundation of the world," although they were not actually elect, or believers, till many ages after, in their several generations. Then only it was that they were actually elected, when they were made the "sons of God by faith" [cf. Gal. 3:26]. Then were they, in fact, "chosen and taken out of the world, elect" (saith St. Paul) "through belief of the truth" [*cf.* 2 Thess. 2:13]; or (as St. Peter expresses it) "elect according to the foreknowledge of God, through sanctification of the Spirit" [1 Pet. 1:2].

XIX. This election I as firmly believe as I believe the Scripture to be of God. But unconditional election I cannot believe; not only because I cannot find it in Scripture, but also (to waive all other considerations) because it necessarily implies unconditional reprobation. Find out any election which does not imply reprobation and I will gladly agree to it.[10] But reprobation I can never agree to while I believe the Scripture to be of God; as being utterly irreconcilable to the whole scope and tenor both of the Old and New Testament.

O that God would give me the desire of my heart! That he would grant the thing which I long for! Even that your mind might now be free and calm and open to the light of his Spirit! That you would impartially consider how it is possible to reconcile reprobation with the following scriptures . . . [In the original, the following catena of Scripture passages is quoted extensively, with occasional interspersed comments: Gen. 3:17; 4:7; Deut. 7:9, 12; 11:26–28; 30:15–19; 2 Chron. 15:1, 2; Ezra 9:13, 14; Job 36:5; Ps. 145:9; Prov. 1:23–29; Is. 65:2–15; Ezek. 18:20–23; Mt. 7:26; 11:20–24; 12:41; 13:11–12; 22:8]. The whole twenty-fifth chapter [of Matthew] requires, and will reward, your most serious consideration. If you can reconcile unconditional reprobation with this, you may reconcile it with the eighteenth of Ezekiel . . . [Jn. 3:18–19; 5:44; Acts 8:20 ff.; Rom. 1:20 ff.; 2 Thess. 2:10 ff.].

XX. How will you reconcile reprobation with the following Scriptures, which declare God's willingness that all should be saved? . . . [Mt. 22:9; Mk. 16:15; Lk. 19:41; Jn. 5:34; Acts 17:24 ff.; Rom. 5:18; 10:12; 1 Tim. 2:3, 4; 4:10; Jas. 1:5; 2 Pet. 3:9; 1 Jn. 4:14].

XXI. How will you reconcile reprobation with the following Scriptures which declare that Christ came to save all men, that he died for all, that he atoned for all, even for those that finally perish? . . . [Mt. 18:11; Jn. 1:29; 3:17; 12:47; Rom. 14:15; 1 Cor. 8:11; 2 Cor. 5:14 f.; 1 Tim. 2:6; Heb. 2:9; 2 Pet. 2:1; 1 Jn. 2:1, 2].

You are sensible, these are but a very small part of the Scriptures which might be brought on each of these heads. But they are enough; and they require no comment. Taken in their plain, easy and obvious sense, they

---

10. This is the nub of Wesley's protest. He belabors the point, for he regarded the arbitrary damnation of any man with such horror that he ignores all else in the opposing argument.

abundantly prove that there is not, cannot be, any such thing as unconditional reprobation.

XXII. But to be a little more particular. How can you possibly reconcile reprobation with those Scriptures that declare the justice of God? To cite one for all . . . [Ezek. 18:2–31 is quoted *in extenso*]. .

Through this whole passage God is pleased to appeal to man himself, touching the *justice* of his proceedings. And well might he appeal to our own conscience, according to the account of them which is here given. But it is an account which all the art of man will never reconcile with unconditional reprobation.

XXIII. Do you think it will cut the knot to say, "Why, if God might justly have passed by all men" (speak out, if God might *justly* have *reprobated* all men, for it comes to the same point), "then he may justly pass by some? But God might *justly* have passed by all men." Are you sure he might? Where is it written? I cannot find it in the Word of God. Therefore I reject it as a bold, precarious assertion, utterly unsupported by Holy Scripture.

If you say, "But you know in your own conscience, God might justly have passed by *you*," I deny it. That God might *justly*, for my unfaithfulness to his grace, have "given me up" long ago, I grant. But this concession supposes me to have had that grace which you say a reprobate never had.

But besides, in making this supposition of what God might have justly done, you suppose his justice might have been separate from his other attributes, from his mercy in particular. But this never was, nor ever will be; nor, indeed, is it possible it should. All his attributes are inseparably joined; they cannot be divided; no, not for a moment. Therefore, his whole argument stands not only on an unscriptural, but on an absurd, impossible supposition.

XXIV. Do you say, "Nay, but it is just for God to pass by whom he will, because of his sovereignty; for he saith himself, 'May not I do what I will with my own?' and, 'Hath not the potter power over his own clay' " [*cf.* Rom. 9:21]? I answer: the former of these sentences stands in the conclusion of that parable [11] wherein our Lord reproves the Jews for murmuring at God's giving the same reward to the Gentiles as to them. To one of these murmurers it is that God says, "Friend, I do thee no wrong. Take that thine is and go thy way. I will give unto this last even as unto thee" [*cf.* Mt. 20:13–15]. Then follows: "Is it not lawful for me to do what I will with mine own? Is thine eye evil, because I am good?" As if

11. [Au.] Mt. 20.

he had said, "May I not give my own kingdom to whom I please? Art thou angry because I am merciful?" It is then undeniably clear that God does not here assert a right of reprobating any man. Here is nothing spoken of reprobation, bad or good. Here is no kind of reference thereto. This text therefore has nothing to do with the conclusion it was brought to prove.

XXV. But you add, "Hath not the potter power over his own clay" [Rom. 9:21]? Let us consider the context of these words also. They are found in the ninth chapter of the Epistle to the Romans, an epistle, the general scope and intent of which is to publish the eternal, unchangeable πρόθεσις, purpose or decree, of God. "He that believeth shall be saved; he that believeth not shall be damned" [Mk. 16:16]. The justice of God in condemning those that believed not, and the necessity of believing in order to salvation, the apostle proves at large in the three first chapters, which he confirms in the fourth by the example of Abraham. In the former part of the fifth and in the sixth chapter, he describes the happiness and holiness of true believers. (The latter part of the fifth is a digression, concerning the extent of the benefits flowing from the death of Christ.) In the seventh he shows in what sense believers in Christ are delivered from the law, and describes the miserable bondage of those who are still under the law, i.e. who are truly convinced of sin but not able to conquer it. In the eighth, he again describes the happy liberty of those who truly believe in Christ, and encourages them to suffer for the faith, as by other considerations, so by this in particular, "We know that all things work together for good to them that love God, to them that are called" (by the preaching of his Word) "according to his purpose" (or decree) unalterably fixed from eternity. "He that believeth shall be saved. For whom he did foreknow" (as believing), "he also did predestinate to be conformed to the image of his Son. Moreover, whom he did predestinate, them he also called" (by his Word: so that term is usually taken in St. Paul's epistles), "and whom he called, them he also justified" (the word is here taken in its widest sense, as including sanctification also), "and whom he justified, them he glorified" [cf. Rom. 8:29-30]. Thence to the end of the chapter, he strongly encourages all those who had the love of God shed abroad in their hearts to have a good hope that no sufferings should ever "be able to separate them from the love of God which is in Christ Jesus" [Rom. 8:39].

XXVI. But as the apostle was aware how deeply the Jews were offended at the whole tenor of his doctrine, and more especially at his asserting:

1) That the Jews themselves could not be saved without believing in Jesus and

2) That the heathens, by believing in him, might partake of the same salvation.

He spends the whole ninth chapter upon them, wherein

1) he declares the tender love he had for them (1–3); [12]

2) allows the great national privileges they enjoyed above any people under heaven (4, 5);

3) answers their grand objection to his doctrine taken from the justice of God to their fathers (6–13);

4) removes another objection, taken from the justice of God, interweaving all along strong reproofs to the Jews for priding themselves on those privileges which were owing merely to the good pleasure of God, not to their fathers' goodness, any more than their own (14–23);

5) resumes and proves by Scripture his former assertion that many Jews would be lost and many heathens saved (24–29); and lastly

6) sums up the general drift of this chapter, and indeed of the whole epistle.

"What shall we say then?" What is the conclusion from the whole; the sum of all which has been spoken? Why, that many Gentiles already partake of the great salvation, and many Jews fall short of it. Wherefore? Because they would not receive it by faith. And whosoever believeth not, cannot be saved; whereas, "whosoever believeth in Christ," whether Jew or Gentile, "shall not be ashamed." [13]

XXVII. Those words — "Hath not the potter power over his own clay?" — are part of St. Paul's answer to that objection that it was unjust for God to show that mercy to the Gentiles which he withheld from his own people. This he first simply denies — saying, "God forbid!" — and then observes that, according to his own words to Moses, God has a right to fix the terms on which he will show mercy, which neither the will nor the power of man can alter (v.15, 16), and to withdraw his mercy from them who, like Pharaoh, will not comply with those terms (v.17). And that accordingly, "he hath mercy on whom he will have mercy" (namely, those that truly believe, "and whom he will" (namely, obstinate unbelievers), he suffers to be "hardened."

XXVIII. But "why then," say the objectors, "doth he find fault" with those that are hardened, "for who hath resisted his will" (v.19)? To this insolent misconstruction of what he had said, the apostle first gives a

12. The citations of verses in the following sections are Wesley's.
13. [Au.] Rom. 9:30–33.

severe rebuke, and then adds, "Shall the thing formed say unto him that formed it, Why hast thou made me thus?" Why hast thou made me capable of salvation only on those terms? None indeed "hath resisted *this* will" of God. "He that believeth not shall be damned." But is this any ground for arraigning his justice? "Hath not," the great "potter power over his own clay to make" (or appoint) one sort of "vessels" (namely, believers) "to honour" and the others to "dishonour"? Hath he not a right to distribute eternal honour and dishonour, on whatever terms he pleases — especially considering the goodness and patience he shows, even towards them that believe not — considering that when they have provoked him "to show his wrath, and to make the power" of his vengeance "known, yet" he "endures, with much longsuffering," even those "vessels of wrath" who had before "fitted" themselves "to destruction"? There is then no more room to reply against God for making his vengeance known on those vessels of wrath than for making known his glorious love "on the vessels of mercy whom he had before" by faith "prepared for glory: even us, whom he hath called, not of the Jews only, but also of the Gentiles" [*cf.* Rom. 9:22–24].

XXIX. I have spoken more largely than I designed in order to show that neither our Lord in the above-mentioned parable nor St. Paul in these words had any view to God's sovereign power as the ground of unconditional reprobation. And beware that you go no further therein than you are authorized by them. Take care, when you speak of these high things, to "speak as the oracles of God" [1 Pet. 4:11]. And if so, you will never speak of the sovereignty of God but in conjunction with his other attributes. For the Scripture nowhere speaks of this single attribute as separate from the rest. Much less does it anywhere speak of the sovereignty of God as singly disposing the eternal states of men. No, no: in this awful work, God proceeds according to the known rules of his justice and mercy,[14] but never assigns his sovereignty as the cause why any man is punished with everlasting destruction.[15]

XXX. Now then, are you not quite out of your way? You are not in the way which God hath revealed. You are putting eternal happiness and misery on an unscriptural and a very dreadful footing. Make the

14. In most editions, Section XXX begins here, and reads: "But never assign his sovereignty as the cause. . . ." In the edition of 1773, Wesley revises the order as given here and confirms the reading "assigns" in his Errata.

15. *Cf.* Wesley's striking little tract, *Thoughts Upon God's Sovereignty* (1777; *Works*, X, 361–63), where he distinguishes between God's sheer freedom as *Creator* and his self-dedication to justice as *Governor* of the creation.

case your own. Here are you, a sinner, convinced that you deserve the damnation of hell. Sorrow, therefore, and fear have filled your heart. And how shall you be comforted? By the promises of God? But perhaps you have no part therein, for they belong only to the elect. By the consideration of his love and tender mercy? But what are they to *you*, if you are a reprobate? God does not love *you* at all: *you*, like Esau, he hath hated even from eternity. What ground then can you have for the least shadow of hope? Why, it is *possible* (that is all) that God's sovereign will may be on your side. *Possibly*, God may save you, because he will! O poor encouragement to despairing sinners! I fear "faith" rarely "cometh by hearing" *this!*

XXXI. The sovereignty of God is then never to be brought to supersede his justice. And this is the present objection against unconditional reprobation (the plain consequence of unconditional election). It flatly contradicts, indeed utterly overthrows, the Scripture account of the justice of God. This has been proved in general already; let us now weigh a few particulars. And, first, the Scripture describes God as the Judge of the earth. But how shall God in justice judge the world? O consider this, as in the presence of God, with reverence and godly fear [*cf*. Heb. 12:28]! How shall God in justice judge the world, if there be any decree of reprobation? On this supposition, what should those on the left hand be condemned for? For their having done evil? They could not help it. There never was a time when they could have helped it. God, you say, "of old ordained them to this condemnation" [Jude 4]. And "who hath resisted his will?" He "sold" them, you say, "to work wickedness," even from their mother's womb. He "gave them up to a reprobate mind" [*cf*. Rom. 1:28] or ever they "hung upon their mother's breast." Shall he then condemn them for what they could not help? Shall the Just, the Holy One of Israel, adjudge millions of men to everlasting pain because their blood moved in their veins? Nay, this they might have helped, by putting an end to their own lives. But could they even thus have escaped from sin? Not without that grace which you suppose God had absolutely determined never to give them. And yet you suppose him to send them into eternal fire, for not escaping from sin! That is, in plain terms, for not having that grace which God had decreed they should never have! O strange justice! What a picture do you draw of the Judge of all the earth?

XXXII. Are they not rather condemned for not doing good, according to those solemn words of the great Judge, "Depart, ye cursed; for

I was an hungered, and ye gave me no meat; I was thirsty, and ye gave me no drink; a stranger, and yet took me not in; I was naked, and ye clothed me not; sick, and in prison, and ye visited me not. Then shall they answer . . ." [*cf.* Mt. 25:41–44]. But how much better an answer do you put into their mouths? Upon *your* supposition might they not say (O consider it well, in meekness and fear!): "Lord, we might have done the outward work; but thou knowest it would have but increased our damnation. We might have fed the hungry, given drink to the thirsty, and covered the naked with a garment. But all these works, without thy special grace, which we never had, nor possibly could have (seeing thou hast eternally decreed to withhold it from us) would only have been 'splendid sins.' [16] They would only have heated the furnace of hell seven times hotter than before." Upon *your* supposition, might they not say, "Righteous art thou, O Lord; yet let us plead with thee. O why dost thou condemn us for not doing good? Was it possible for us to do any-thing well? Did we ever abuse the power of doing good? We never re-ceived it, and that thou knowest. Wilt thou, the Holy One, the Just, condemn us for not doing what we never had the power to do? Wilt thou condemn us for not casting down the stars from heaven [*cf.* Dan. 8:10], for not holding the winds in our fist [*cf.* Prov. 30:4]? Why, it was as possible for us to do this as to do any work acceptable in thy sight! O Lord, correct us, but with judgment! And, before thou plungest us into everlasting fire, let us know how it was ever possible for us to escape the damnation of hell."

XXXIII. Or how could they have escaped — suppose you assign that as the cause of their condemnation — from inward sin, from evil desires, from unholy tempers and vile affections? Were they ever able to deliver their own souls, to rescue themselves from this inward hell? If so, their not doing it might justly be laid to their charge, and would leave them without excuse. But it was so. They never were able to deliver their own souls; they never had power to rescue themselves from the hands of those bosom enemies. This talent was never put into their hands. How then can they be condemned for hiding it in the earth, for nonimprovement of what they never had? Who is able to purify a corrupt heart, to "bring a clean thing out of an unclean" [Job 14:4]? Is man, mere man, sufficient for this? No, certainly. God alone. To him only can the polluted of heart say, "Lord, if thou wilt, thou canst make me clean" [Mt. 8:2]. But what if he answer, "I will not because I will not; be thou unclean still"? Will

16. See above, p. 150.

God doom that man to the bottomless pit because of that uncleanness which he could not save himself from, and which God could have saved him from but would not? Verily, were an earthly king to execute such justice as this upon his helpless subjects, it might well be expected that the vengeance of the Lord would soon sweep him from the face of the earth.

XXXIV. Perhaps you will say, "They are not condemned for actual but for original sin." What do you mean by this term? The inward corruption of our nature? If so, it has been spoken of before. Or do you mean the sin which Adam committed in paradise? That this is imputed to all men, I allow; yea, that by reason hereof, "the whole creation groaneth and travaileth in pain together until now" [Rom. 8:22]. But that any will be damned for this alone, I allow not, till you show me where it is written. Bring me plain proof from Scripture, and I submit; but till then, I utterly deny it.

XXXV. Should you not rather say that unbelief is the damning sin and that those who are condemned in that day will be, therefore, condemned "because they believed not on the name of the only-begotten Son of God" [cf. Jn. 3:18]? But *could* they believe? Was not this faith both the gift and the work of God in the soul? And was it not a gift which he had eternally decreed never to give them? Was it not a work which he was of old unchangeably determined never to work in their souls? Shall these men then be condemned because God would not work, because they did not receive what God would not give? Could they "ungrasp the hold of his right hand, or force omnipotence?" [17]

XXXVI. There is, over and above, a peculiar difficulty here. You say, "Christ did not die for those men." But if so, there was an impossibility, in the very nature of the thing, that they should ever savingly believe. For what is saving faith but "a confidence in God through Christ that loved *me*, and gave himself for *me*?" [18] Loved *thee*, thou reprobate? Gave himself for *thee*? Away! thou hast neither part nor lot herein. Thou believe in Christ, thou accursed spirit, damned or ever thou wert born? There never was any object for thy faith; there never was any thing for

17. Cf. *Hymns for the Use of the People Called Methodists* (1780), 138, st. 6.
18. An interesting conflation of the Homily, "Of Salvation" (Pt. III), with Gal. 2:20. Cf. *Journal*, I, 424, where, at the dead end of the Georgia mission, Wesley defines "saving faith" in the same terms he uses here; and repeatedly elsewhere through his works. In *Sermons* (Sugden), cf. "The Almost Christian" (I, 63–65, par. 5, 6); "The Circumcision of the Heart" (I, 269–71, par. 7); and "The Marks of a New Birth" (I, 284–86, par. 3, 4).

thee to believe. God himself (thus must you speak, to be consistent with yourself), with all his omnipotence, could not make thee believe Christ atoned for thy sins, unless he had made thee believe a lie.

XXXVII. If, then, God be just, there cannot, on *your* scheme, be any judgment to come. We may add, nor any future state, either of reward or punishment. If there be such a state, God will therein "render to every man according to his works" [*cf.* Rom. 2:6]. "To them who, by patient continuance in well-doing, seek for glory and honour and immortality: eternal life; but to them that do not obey the truth but obey unrighteousness, indignation and wrath: tribulation and anguish upon every soul of man that doeth evil." [19]

But how is this reconcilable with *your* scheme? You say, "The reprobates cannot but do evil, and the elect, from the day of God's power, cannot but continue in well-doing." You suppose all this is unchangeably decreed; in consequence whereof, God acts irresistibly on the one and Satan on the other. Then, it is impossible for either one or the other to help acting as they do; or rather, to help being acted upon, in the manner wherein they are. For if we speak properly, neither the one nor the other can be said to act at all. Can a stone be said to act when it is thrown out of a sling, or a ball when it is projected from a cannon? No more can a man be said to act, if he be only moved by a force he cannot resist. But if the case be thus, you leave no room either for reward or punishment. Shall the stone be rewarded for rising from the sling, or punished for falling down? Shall the cannon ball be rewarded for flying towards the sun, or punished for receding from it? As incapable of either punishment or reward is the man who is supposed to be impelled by a force he cannot resist. Justice can have no place in rewarding or punishing mere machines, driven to and fro by an external force. So that your supposition of God's ordaining from eternity whatsoever should be done to the end of the world, as well as that of God's acting irresistibly in the elect and Satan's acting irresistibly in the reprobates, utterly overthrows the Scripture doctrine of rewards and punishments, as well as of a judgment to come.

XXXVIII. Thus ill does that election which implies reprobation agree with the Scripture account of God's justice. And does it agree any better with his truth? How will you reconcile it with those plain assertions? . . . [Here again Wesley quotes Ezek. 18:23–32; 33:11 *in extenso*.]

XXXIX. But perhaps you will say, "These ought to be limited and

---

19. An abridged and slightly altered quotation of Rom. 2:6–9. *Cf.* Wesley's "note" on this passage in *Explanatory Notes upon the New Testament* (1755), 386 f,

explained by other passages of Scripture wherein this doctrine is as clearly affirmed as it is denied in these." I must answer very plain: if this were true, we must give up all the Scriptures together; nor would the infidels allow the Bible so honorable a title as that of a "cunningly devised fable" [2 Pet. 1:16]. But it is not true. It has no colour of truth. It is absolutely, notoriously false. To tear up the very roots of reprobation, and of all doctrines that have a necessary connexion therewith, God declares in his Word these three things, and that explicitly, in so many terms:

1. "Christ died for all," [20] namely, all that "were dead" in sin, as the words immediately following fix the sense. Here is the fact affirmed.

2. "He is the propitiation for the sins of the whole world," [21] even of all those for whom he died. Here is the consequence of his dying for all. And,

3. "He died for all, that they should not live unto themselves, but unto him which died for them," [22] that they might be saved from their sins. Here is the design, the end, of his dying for them. Now, show me the Scriptures wherein God declares in equally express terms (1) Christ did not die *for all*, but for some only; (2) Christ is not "the propitiation for the sins of the whole world." And (3) he did not die for all, at least, not with that intent "that they should live unto him who died for them." Show me, I say, the Scriptures that affirm these three things in equally express terms. You know there are none. Nor is it possible to evade the force of those above recited but by supplying in number what is wanting in weight, by heaping abundance of texts together whereby (though none of them speak home to the point) the patrons of that opinion dazzle the eyes of the unwary and quite overlay the understanding both of themselves and those that hear them.

XL. To proceed: what an account does this doctrine give of the sincerity of God in a thousand declarations, such as those . . . [Deut. 5:29; Ps. 81:11–14].

And all this time, you suppose God had unchangeably ordained that there never should be "such an heart in them," that it never should be possible for the people whom he thus *seemed* to lament over to "hearken unto him" [Mk. 7:14] or to "walk in his ways" [1 Kings 2:3; Ps. 119:3]!

XLI. How clear and strong is the reasoning of Dr. Watts on this head: [23]

---

20. [Au.] 2 Cor. 5:14.     21. [Au.] 1 Jn. 2:2.     22. [Au.] 2 Cor. 5:15.

23. Isaac Watts, *The Ruin and Recovery of Mankind; or, An Attempt to Vindicate the Scriptural Account of these Great Events upon the Plain Principles of Reason*, in *Works* (1753), VI, 283.

It is very hard, indeed, to vindicate the sincerity of the blessed God or his Son, in their universal offers of grace and salvation to men and their sending ministers with such messages and invitations to accept of mercy, if there be not at least a conditional pardon and salvation provided for them.

His ministers, indeed, as they know not the events of things, may be sincere in offering salvation to all persons, according to their general commission, "Go ye into all the world and preach the gospel to every creature." But how can God or Christ be sincere in sending them with this commission, to offer his grace to all men, if God has not provided such grace for *all men* — no, not so much as conditionally?

'Tis hard to suppose that the great God, who is truth itself, and . . . faithful in all his dealings, should call upon dying men to trust in a Saviour for eternal life, when this Saviour has not eternal life entrusted with him to give them if they do as he requires.[24] 'Tis hard to conceive how the great Governor of the world can be sincere in inviting [25] sinners, who are on the brink of hell, to cast themselves upon an empty word of invitation, a mere shadow and appearance of support, if there be nothing real to bear them up from those deeps of destruction, nothing but mere words and empty invitations. Can we think that the righteous and holy God would encourage his ministers to call them to lean and rest the weight of their immortal concerns [26] upon a gospel, a covenant of grace, a mediator and his merit and righteousness, all which are a mere nothing with regard to them, a heap of empty names, an unsupporting void which cannot uphold them?

XLII. Our blessed Lord does indisputably command and invite "all men everywhere to repent" [Acts 17:30]. He calleth all. He sends his ambassadors, in his name, "to preach the gospel to every creature" [Mk. 16:15]. He himself "preached deliverance to the captives" [Lk. 4:18], without any hint of restriction or limitation. But now, in what manner do you represent him while he is employed in this work? You suppose him to be standing at the prison doors, having the keys thereof in his hands, and to be continually inviting the prisoners to come forth, commanding them to accept of that invitation, urging every motive which can possibly induce them to comply with that command; adding the most precious promises, if they obey; the most dreadful threatenings, if they obey not. And all this time you suppose him to be unalterably determined in himself never to open the doors for them, even while he is crying, "Come

24. Watts: "if they do repent."          25. Watts: "in requiring."
26. Here Wesley deletes "and happiness" from Watts's text.

ye, come ye, from that evil place. For why will ye die, O house of Israel" [cf. Ezek. 18:31]? "Why" (might one of them reply), "because we cannot help it. We *cannot* help ourselves, and thou *wilt* not help us. It is not in our power to break the gates of brass [cf. Ps. 107:16], and it is not thy pleasure to open them. Why *will* we die? We *must* die, because it is not thy *will* to save us." Alas, my brethren, what kind of sincerity is this which you ascribe to God our Saviour?

XLIII. So ill do election and reprobation agree with the truth and sincerity of God! But do they not agree least of all with the scriptural account of his love and goodness: that attribute which God peculiarly claims wherein he glories above all the rest? It is not written, "God is justice," or "God is truth" (although he is just and true in all his ways). But it is written, "God is love" [1 Jn. 4:8] (love in the abstract, without bounds), and "there is no end of his goodness" [cf. Ps. 52:1]. His love extends even to those who neither love nor fear him. He is good, even to the evil and the unthankful; yea, without any exception or limitation, to all the children of men. For "the Lord is loving" (or good) "unto every man, and his mercy is over all his works" [Ps. 145:9, B.C.P.].

But how is God good or loving to a "reprobate," or one that is not "elected"? You may choose either term, for if none but the unconditionally elect are saved, it comes precisely to the same thing. You cannot say, he is an object of the love or goodness of God, with regard to his external state, whom he created (says Mr. Calvin plainly and fairly) *in vitae contumeliam et mortis exitium*, "to live a reproach and die everlastingly." [27] Surely, no one can dream that the goodness of God is at all concerned with this man's eternal state. "However, God is good to him in this world." What? When by reason of God's unchangeable decree, it had been good for this man never to have been born, when his very birth was a curse, not a blessing? "Well, but he now enjoys many of the gifts of God, both gifts of nature and of providence. He has food and raiment, and comforts of various kinds. And are not all these great blessings?" No, not to him. At the price he is to pay for them, every one of these also is a curse. Every one of these comforts is, by an eternal decree, to cost him a thousand pangs in hell. For every moment's pleasure which he now

27. Cf. *Corpus Reformatorum*, XXX: *Ioannis Calvini Opera quae Supersunt Omnia*, II, 722: *Institutio Christianae Religionis*, Bk. III, chap. XXIV, par. 12. Calvin's full sentence is actually a rhetorical question: "What of those, then, whom he created for dishonor in life and destruction in death, to become the instruments of his wrath and examples of his severity?" Cf. Calvin, *Institutes of the Christian Religion* (LCC), XXI, 978.

enjoys, he is to suffer the torment of more than a thousand years; for the smoke of that pit which is preparing for him ascendeth up for ever and ever. God knew this would be the fruit of whatever he should enjoy, before the vapour of life fled away. He designed it should. It was his very purpose, in giving him those enjoyments. So that, by all these (according to *your* account) he is, in truth and reality, only fatting the ox for the slaughter. "Nay, but God gives him grace, too." Yes, but what kind of grace? "Saving grace," you own, he has none; none of a saving nature. And the "common grace" he has was not given with any design to save his soul, nor with any design to do him any good at all; but only to restrain him from hurting the elect. So far from doing him good, this grace also necessarily increases his damnation. "And God knows this," you say, "and designed it should; it was one great end for which he gave it!" Then I desire to know, how is God good or loving to this man, either with regard to time or eternity?

XLIV. Let us suppose a particular instance. Here stands a man who is reprobated from all eternity; or, if you would express it more smoothly, one who is not elected, whom God eternally decreed to pass by. "Thou hast nothing therefore to expect from God after death but to be cast into the lake of fire burning with brimstone; God having consigned thy unborn soul to hell, by a decree which cannot pass away. And from the time thou wast born under the irrevocable curse of God, thou canst have no peace. For there is no peace to the wicked, and such thou art doomed to continue, even from thy mother's womb. Accordingly, God giveth thee of this world's goods on purpose to enhance thy damnation. He giveth thee now substance or friends in order hereafter to heap the more coals of fire upon thy head [*cf*. Rom. 12:20]. He filleth thee with food, he maketh thee fat and well-liking [*cf*. Ps. 92:13, B.C.P.], to make thee a more specious sacrifice to his vengeance. Good nature, generosity, a good understanding, various knowledge, it may be, or eloquence, are the flowers wherewith he adorneth thee, thou poor victim, before thou art brought to the slaughter. Thou hast grace, too! But what grace? Not saving grace. That is not for thee, but for the elect only. Thine may properly be termed 'damning' grace, since it is not only such in the event but in the intention. Thou receivedst it of God for that very end, that thou mightest receive the greater damnation. It was given, not to convert thee, but only to convince; not to make thee without sin, but without excuse; not to destroy, but to arm the worm that never dieth and to blow up the fire that never shall be quenched" [*cf*. Mk. 9:44, 48].

XLV. Now, I beseech you to consider calmly, how is God good or loving to this man? Is not this such love as makes your blood run cold, as causes the ears of him that heareth to tingle? And can you believe there is that man on earth or in hell who can truly tell God, "Thus hast thou done?" Can you think that the loving, the merciful God ever dealt thus with any soul which he had made? But you must and do believe this if you believe unconditional election. For it holds reprobation in its bosom. They never were, never can be, divided. Take then your choice. If, for the sake of election, you will swallow reprobation, well. But if you cannot digest this, you must necessarily give up unconditional election.

XLVI. But you cannot do this, for then you should be called a "Pelagian," an "Arminian" and what not! And are you afraid of hard names? Then you have not begun to be a disciple of Jesus Christ. "No, that is not the case." But you are afraid, if you do not hold election, you must hold free-will, and so rob God of his glory in man's salvation.

I answer: (1) Many of the greatest maintainers of election utterly deny the consequence and do not allow that even "natural" free-will in man is repugnant to God's glory. These accordingly assert that every man living has a measure of natural free-will. So the Assembly of Divines (and therein the body of Calvinists both in England and Scotland): "God hath endued the will of man with that *natural liberty*,[28] that is neither forced, nor, by an absolute necessity of nature, determined to do good or evil." (IX, 1.)[29] And this they assert of man in his fallen state even before he receives the grace of God.

But I do not carry free-will so far (I mean, not in moral things). "Natural free-will," in the present state of mankind, I do not understand. I only assert that there is a measure of free-will *supernaturally* restored to every man, together with that *supernatural* light which "enlightens every man that cometh into the world" [cf. Jn. 1:9]. But indeed, whether this be natural or no, as to your objection, it matters not. For that equally lies against both, against any free-will of any kind — your assertion being thus: "If man has any free-will, God cannot have the whole glory of his salvation," or, "It is not so much for the glory of God to save man as a free agent — put into a capacity of concurring with his grace on the one hand and of resisting it on the other — as to save him in the way of a necessary agent, by a power which he cannot possibly resist."

XLVII. With regard to the former of these assertions, "If man has any free-will, then God cannot have the whole glory of his salvation," is your

28. Wesley's italics; *cf. Works*, VI, 270; VII, 228.     29. See above, pp. 428–30.

meaning this: "If man has any power to 'work out his own salvation,' then God cannot have the whole glory"? If it be, I must ask again, what do you mean by God's "having the whole glory"? Do you mean, "his doing the whole work, without any concurrence on man's part"? If so, your assertion is, "If man do at all 'work together with' God in 'working out his own salvation,' then God does not do the whole work without man's 'working together with him.'" Most true, most sure. But cannot you see how God nevertheless may have all the glory? Why, the very power to "work together with him" was from God. Therefore to him is all the glory. Has not even experience taught you this? Have you not often felt, in a particular temptation, power either to resist or yield to the grace of God? And when you have yielded to work together with him, did you not find it very possible, notwithstanding, to give him all the glory? So that both experience and Scripture are against you here and make it clear to every impartial inquirer that though man has "freedom" to work or not "work together with God," yet may God have the whole glory of his salvation.

XLVIII. If then you say, "We ascribe to God alone the whole glory of our salvation," I answer, "So do we, too." If you add, "Nay, but we affirm that God alone does the whole work without man's working at all," in one sense, we allow this also. We allow it is the work of God alone to justify, to sanctify, and to glorify, which three comprehend the whole of salvation. Yet we cannot allow that man can only resist and not in any wise "work together with God," or that God is so the whole worker of our salvation as to exclude man's working at all. This I dare not say, for I cannot prove it by Scripture. Nay, it is flatly contrary thereto; for the Scripture is express that (having received power from God) we are to "work out our own salvation" [Phil. 2:12], and that (after the work of God is begun in our souls) we are "workers together with him" [2 Cor. 6:1].

XLIX. Your objection, proposed in another form, is this: "It is not so much for the glory of God to save man as a free agent — put into a capacity of either concurring with, or resisting, his grace — as to save him in the way of a necessary agent, by a power which he cannot possibly resist."

O that the Lord would answer for himself! That he would arise and maintain his own cause, that he would no longer suffer his servants, few as they are, to weaken one another's hands and to be wearied not only with "the contradiction of sinners" [cf. Heb. 12:3] but even of those who are in a measure saved from sin! "Woe is me, that I am constrained to dwell with Meshech, among them that are enemies to peace! I labour for peace, but when I speak thereof," they still "make themselves ready for battle" [*cf*. Ps. 120:4–6, B.C.P.].

L. If it must be, then, let us look one another in the face. How is it more for the glory of God to save man irresistibly than to save him as a free agent, by such grace as he may either concur with or resist? I fear you have a confused, unscriptural notion of "the glory of God." What do you mean by that expression? The glory of God, strictly speaking, is his glorious essence and his attributes, which have been ever of old. And this glory admits of no increase, being the same yesterday, today, and for ever. But the Scripture frequently speaks of the glory of God in a sense something different from this, meaning thereby the manifestation of his essential glory, of his eternal power and godhead, and of his glorious attributes — more especially his justice, mercy and truth. And it is in this sense alone that the glory of God is said to be advanced by man. Now then, this is the point which it lies on you to prove: "that it does more eminently manifest the glorious attributes of God, more especially his justice, mercy, and truth, to save man irresistibly, than to save him by such grace as it is in his power either to concur with or to resist."

LI. But you must not imagine I will be so unwise as to engage you here on this single point. I shall not now dispute (which yet might be done) whether salvation by irresistible grace (which indeed makes man a mere machine and consequently no more rewardable than punishable), whether, I say, salvation by irresistible grace, considered apart from its consequences, manifests the glory of God more or less than salvation by grace, which may be resisted. Not so; but (by the assistance of God) I shall take your whole scheme together: irresistible grace for the elect, implying the denial of saving grace to all others; or unconditional election with its inseparable companion, unconditional reprobation.

The case is clearly this. You may drive me, on the one hand, unless I will contradict myself or retract my principles, to own a measure of free-will in every man (though not "by nature," as the Assembly of Divines). And on the other hand, I can drive you and every assertor of unconditional election, unless you will contradict yourself or retract your principles, to own unconditional reprobation.

Stand forth, then — free-will, on the one side, and reprobation on the other — and let us see whether the one scheme, attended with the absurdity (as you think it) of free-will, or the other scheme, attended with the absurdity of reprobation, be the more defensible. Let us see — if it please the Father of lights [*cf.* Jas. 1:17] to open the eyes of our understanding [*cf.* Eph. 1:18] — which of these is more for the glory of God, for the display of his glorious attributes, for the manifestation of his wisdom, justice, and mercy to the sons of men.

LII. First, his wisdom. If man be in some measure free; if, by that light which "lighteth every man that comes into the world," there be "set before him life and death, good and evil" [*cf.* Deut. 30:15, 19], then how gloriously does the manifold wisdom of God appear in the whole economy of man's salvation? Being willing that all men should be saved, yet not willing to force them thereto; willing that men should be saved, yet not as trees or stones but as men, as reasonable creatures, endued with understanding to discern what is good, and liberty either to accept or refuse it; how does he suit the whole scheme of his dispensations to this his πρόθεσις, his plan, "the counsel of his will" [Eph. 1:11]? His first step is to enlighten the understanding by that general knowledge of good and evil. To this he adds many secret reproofs if they act contrary to this light; many inward convictions, which there is not a man on earth who has not often felt. At other times he gently moves their wills, he draws and woos them, as it were, to walk in the light. He instils into their hearts good desires, though perhaps they know not from whence they come. Thus far he proceeds with all the children of men, yea, even with those who have not the knowledge of his written word. But in this, what a field of wisdom is displayed, supposing man to be in some degree a free agent? How is every part of it suited to this end, to save man as man: to set life and death before him, and then persuade (not force) him to choose life! According to this grand purpose of God, a perfect rule is first set before him, to serve as a "lantern to his feet, and a light in all his paths" [*cf.* Ps. 119:105]. This is offered to him in form of a law, enforced with the strongest sanctions, the most glorious rewards for them that obey, the severest penalties on them that break it. To reclaim these, God uses all manner of ways, he tries every avenue of their souls. He applies sometimes to their understanding, showing them the folly of their sins; sometimes to their affections, tenderly expostulating with them for their ingratitude, and even condescending to ask, "What could I have done for" you (consistent with my eternal purpose not to force you) "which I have not done" [*cf.* Is. 5:4]? He intermixes sometimes threats, "Except ye repent, ye shall all likewise perish" [Lk. 13:3]; sometimes promises,

"Your sins and your iniquities will I remember no more" [cf. Heb. 10:17]. Now, what wisdom is seen in all this, if man may indeed choose life or death? But if every man be unalterably consigned to heaven or hell before he comes from his mother's womb, where is the wisdom of this: of dealing with him, in every respect, *as if* he were *free*, when he is no such thing? What avails, what can this whole dispensation of God avail a reprobate? What are promises or threats, expostulations or reproofs to thee, thou firebrand of hell? What, indeed — O my brethren, suffer me to speak, for "I am full of matter" [cf. Job 32:18] — but empty farce, but mere grimace, sounding words, that mean just nothing? O where — to waive all other considerations now — is the wisdom of this proceeding? To what end does all this apparatus serve? If you say, "To insure his damnation," alas, what needed that, seeing this was insured before the foundation of the world? Let all mankind then judge which of these accounts is more for the glory of God's wisdom!

LIII. We come next to his justice. Now, if man be capable of choosing good or evil, then is he a proper object of the justice of God, acquitting or condemning, rewarding or punishing. But otherwise he is not. A mere machine is not capable of being either acquitted or condemned.[30] Justice cannot punish a stone for falling to the ground; nor (on *your* scheme) a man for falling into sin. For he can no more help it than the stone, if he be (in *your* sense) "foreordained to this condemnation." Why does this man sin? "He cannot cease from sin." Why can't he cease from sin? "Because he has no saving grace." Why has he no saving grace? "Because God, of his own good pleasure, hath eternally decreed not to give it him." Is he then under an unavoidable necessity of sinning? "Yes, as much as a stone is of falling. He never had any more power to cease from evil than a stone has to hang in the air." And shall this man, for not doing what he never could do, and for doing what he never could avoid, be sentenced to depart into everlasting fire, prepared for the devil and his angels [cf. Mt. 25:41]? "Yes, because it is the sovereign will of God." Then you have either found a new God, or *made* one! This is not the God of the Christians. Our God is just in all his ways; he reapeth not where he hath not strewed. He requireth only according to what he hath given; and where he hath given little, little is required. The glory of his justice is this, to "reward every man according to his works" [cf. 2 Tim. 4:14]. Hereby is that glorious attribute shown, evidently set forth before

30. See below, p. 481 f.

men and angels, in that it is accepted of every man according to that he hath, and not according to that he hath not. This is that just decree which cannot pass, either in time or in eternity.

Thus one scheme gives the justice of God its full scope, leaves room for it to be largely displayed in all its branches, whereas the other makes it a mere shadow; yea, brings it absolutely to nothing.

LIV. Just as gloriously does it display his love, supposing it to be fixed on one in ten of his creatures (might I not rather say, one in a hundred?), and to have no regard to the rest. Let the ninety-and-nine reprobates perish without mercy. It is enough for him to love and save the one elect. But why will he have mercy on these alone and leave all those to inevitable destruction? "He will — because he will!" O that God would give unto you who thus speak meekness of wisdom [cf. Jas. 3:13]! Then would I ask, "What would the universal voice of mankind pronounce of the man that should act thus: that being able to deliver millions of men from death with a single breath of his mouth, should refuse to save any more than one in an hundred and say, 'I will not, because I will not'? How then do you exalt the mercy of God when you ascribe such a proceeding to him?" What a strange comment is this on his own word that "his mercy is over all his works!"

Do you think to evade this by saying, "His mercy is more displayed in irresistibly saving the elect than it would be in giving the choice of salvation to all men and actual salvation to those that accepted it"? How so? Make this appear if you can. What proof do you bring of this assertion? I appeal to every impartial mind, whether the reverse be not obviously true: whether the mercy of God would not be far less gloriously displayed in saving a few by his irresistible power, and leaving all the rest without help, without hope, to perish everlastingly, than in offering salvation to every creature, actually saving all that consent thereto and doing for the rest all that infinite wisdom, almighty power and boundless love can do without *forcing* them to be saved — which would be to destroy the very nature that he had given them? I appeal, I say, to every impartial mind, and to your own, if not quite blinded with a prejudice, which of these accounts places the mercy of God in the most advantageous light?

LV. Perhaps you will say, "But there are other attributes of God, namely, his sovereignty, unchangeableness, and faithfulness. I hope you do not deny these." I answer, "No; by no means." The sovereignty of God appears:

1. In fixing from eternity that decree touching the sons of men, "He that believeth shall be saved: he that believeth not shall be damned";

2. In all the general circumstances of creation: in the time, the place, the manner of creating all things, in appointing the number and kinds of creatures, visible and invisible;

3. In allotting the natural endowments of men, these to one, and those to another;

4. In disposing the time, place and other outward circumstances (as parents, relations) attending the birth of every one;

5. In dispensing the various gifts of his Spirit, for the edification of his church;

6. In ordering all temporal things (as health, fortune, friends) — every thing short of eternity.

But in disposing the eternal states of men (allowing only what was observed under the first article), it is clear that not sovereignty alone, but justice, mercy and truth hold the reins. The Governor of heaven and earth, the I AM over all, God blessed for ever, takes no step here but as these direct, and prepare the way before his face. This is his eternal and irresistible will, as he hath revealed [it] unto us by his Spirit; declaring in the strongest terms, adding his oath to his word, and, because he could swear by no greater, swearing by himself: " 'As I live, saith the Lord God, I have no pleasure in the death of him that dieth' [Ezek. 18:32]. The death of him that dieth can never be resolved into my pleasure or sovereign will." No, it is impossible. We challenge all mankind to bring one clear scriptural proof to the contrary. You can bring no Scripture proof that God ever did, or assertion that he ever will, act as mere sovereign in eternally condemning any soul that ever was or will be born into the world.

LVI. Now you are probably thinking of Esau and Pharaoh. Do you then set it down as an unquestionable truth that these were eternally condemned by the mere sovereign will of God? Are you sure that they were eternally condemned? Even that point is not altogether certain. It is nowhere asserted in Holy Writ, and it would cost you some pains to prove it. It is true, Pharaoh's death was a punishment from God, but it does not follow that he was punished everlastingly. And if he was, it was not by the *mere sovereign will of God,* but because of his own stubbornness and impenitence.

Of this Moses has given us a particular account. Accordingly we read,

"When Pharaoh saw that there was respite" (after he was delivered from the plague of frogs) "he hardened his heart, and hearkened not unto them." [31] So after the plague of flies, "Pharaoh hardened his heart at this time also, neither would he let the people go." [32] Again, "When Pharaoh saw that the rain and the hail were ceased, he sinned yet more, and hardened his heart, he and his servants." [33] After God had given him all this space to repent and had expostulated with him for his obstinate impenitence, in those solemn words, "How long wilt thou refuse to humble thyself before me?" [34] What wonder is it if God then "hardened his heart" — that is, permitted Satan to harden it — if he at length wholly withdrew his softening grace and "gave him up to a reprobate mind?"

LVII. The case of Esau is widely different from this, although his conduct also is blameable in many points. The first was the selling his birthright to Jacob; [35] the next, his marrying against his father's consent (26:34–35).[36] But it is highly probable he was sensible of his fault, because Isaac appears to have been fully reconciled to him when he said, "My son, make me savoury meat, that my soul may bless thee before I die" (27:4).[37]

In the following verses we have an account of the manner wherein he was supplanted by his brother Jacob. Upon Isaac's relation of this, "Esau cried with a great and exceeding bitter cry, and said unto his father, Bless me, even me also, O my father!" But "he found no place," says the apostle, "for repentance" (for recovering the blessing), "though he sought it carefully with tears" [cf. Heb. 12:17]. "Thy brother," said Isaac, "hath taken away thy blessing; I have blessed him, yea, and he shall be blessed." So that all Esau's sorrow and tears could not recover his birthright, and the blessing annexed thereto.

And yet there is great reason to hope that Esau (as well as Jacob) is now in Abraham's bosom. For although for a time "he hated Jacob" [Gen. 27:41], and afterward came against him "with four hundred men," very probably designing to take revenge for the injuries he had sustained, yet we find when they met, "Esau ran and embraced him, and fell on his neck and kissed him." So thoroughly had God changed his heart. And why should we doubt but that happy change continued?

LVIII. You can ground no solid objection to this on St. Paul's words in the Epistle to the Romans: "It was said unto her, The elder shall serve the younger. As it is written, Jacob have I loved, but Esau have I

---

31. [Au.] Ex. 8:13.          32. [Au.] Ex. 8:32.          33. [Au.] Ex. 9:34.
34. [Au.] Ex. 10:3.          35. [Au.] Gen. 25:31–39.
36. [Au.] Gen. 26:34–35.          37. [Au.] Gen. 27:4.

hated." [38] For it is undeniably plain that both these Scriptures relate, not to the persons of Jacob and Esau, but to their descendants: the Israelites sprung from Jacob, and the Edomites sprung from Esau. In this sense only did "the elder" (Esau) "serve the younger": not in his person (for Esau never served Jacob), but in his posterity. The posterity of the elder brother served the posterity of the younger.

The other text referred to by the apostle runs thus: "I loved Jacob and I hated Esau and laid his mountains and his heritage waste for the dragons of the wilderness." [39] Whose heritage was it that God laid waste? Not that which Esau personally enjoyed, but that of his posterity (the Edomites) for their enormous sins, largely described by several of the prophets. So neither here is there any instance of any man being finally condemned by the "mere sovereign will" of God.

LIX. The unchangeableness of God we allow likewise. "In him is no variableness, neither shadow of turning" [cf. Jas. 1:17]. But you seem to lie under a mistake concerning this also, for want of observing the Scripture account of it. The Scripture teaches, first, that God is unchangeable with regard to his decrees. But what decrees? The same that he has commanded to be "preached to every creature" [cf. Mt. 28:19; Mk. 16:15]: "He that believeth shall be saved; he that believeth not shall be damned." The Scripture teaches, secondly, that God is unchangeable with regard to his love and hatred. But how? Observe this well, for it is your grand mistake and the root of almost all the rest. God unchangeably loveth righteousness and hateth iniquity. Unchangeably he loveth faith and unchangeably hateth unbelief. In consequence hereof he unchangeably loves the righteous and hateth the workers of iniquity. He unchangeably loves them that believe, and hates wilful, obstinate unbelievers. So that the Scripture account of God's unchangeableness with regard to his decrees is this: he has unchangeably decreed to save holy believers and to condemn obstinate, impenitent unbelievers. And according to Scripture, his unchangeableness of *affection* properly and primarily regards tempers and not persons, and persons (as Enoch, Noah, Abraham) only as those tempers are found in them. Let then the unchangeableness of God be put upon the right foot — let the Scripture be allowed to fix the objects of it — and it will full as soon prove transubstantiation as unconditional election.

LX. The *faithfulness* of God may be termed a branch of his truth. He *will perform* what he *hath promised*. But then let us inquire of the oracles

38. [Au.] Rom. 9:12–13.        39. [Au.] Mal. 1:2–3.

of God, "To whom are the promises made, the promises of life and immortality?" The answer is, "To Abraham and his seed"; that is, to those who "walk in the steps of the faith of their father Abraham" [cf. Rom. 4: 12]. To those who believe, as believers, are the gospel promises made. To these hath the faithful God engaged that he will do what he hath spoken. "He will fulfil his covenant and promise which he hath made to a thousand generations." The sum of which is (as we find it expressly declared by the Spirit of God): "The Lord will give grace" (more grace) "and glory; and no good thing will he withhold from them that live a godly life" [cf. Ps. 84: 12, B.C.P.].

LXI. This covenant of God I understand.[40] But I have heard of another which I understand not. I have heard "that God the Father made a covenant with his Son, before the world began, wherein the Son agreed to suffer such and such things, and the Father to give him such and such souls for a recompense; that in consequence of this, those souls *must* be saved, and those only, so that all others *must* be damned." [41] I beseech you, where is this written? In what part of Scripture is this covenant to be found? We may well expect a thing of this moment to be revealed very expressly, with the utmost clearness and solemnity. But where is this done? And if it is not done, if there is no such account in all the Bible, which shall we wonder at most: that any serious man should advance or that thousands should believe so strange an assertion, without one plain text of Scripture to support it, from Genesis to the Revelation?

LXII. I suppose you do not imagine that the bare word "covenant," if it occurred ever so often in Holy Writ, is a proof of any such covenant as this. The grand covenant which we allow to be mentioned therein is a covenant between God and man, established in the hands of a Mediator, "who tasted death for every man" [Heb. 2:9], and thereby purchased it for all the children of men. The tenor of it (so often mentioned already) is this: "Whosoever believeth unto the end — so as to show his faith by his works — I, the Lord, will reward that soul eternally. But whosoever will not believe — and consequently dieth in his sins — I will punish him with everlasting destruction."

LXIII. To examine thoroughly whether this covenant between God and man be unconditional or conditional, it may be needful to go back

40. Cf. John Wesley, *An Extract of Mr. Richard Baxter's Aphorisms of Justification* (1745), 1–36, as the chief source of "covenant theology," to which Wesley refers here and elsewhere.
41. Wesley's caricature of the conventional "covenant theology" in the Puritan tradition. But *cf.* the *Westminster Confession*, chap. VII, *et seq.*

as far as Abraham, the father of the faithful [*cf.* Gal. 3:9], to inquire what manner of covenant it was which God made with him and whether any reason be assigned of God's peculiarly blessing Abraham, and all the nations of the earth in him?

The first mention of the covenant between God and him occurs in Genesis 15:18: "The same day the Lord made a covenant with Abram, saying, 'Unto thy seed will I give this land.'" But this is much more explicitly related in the seventeenth chapter. . . . [Here follows an abridgment of Gen. 17:1–14.]

So we see, this original covenant, though *everlasting*, was conditional, and man's failing in the condition cleared God.

LXIV. We have St. Paul's account of this covenant of God with Abraham, in the fourth chapter of his Epistle to the Romans (3 ff.): "Abraham," saith he, "believed God and it was counted to him for righteousness." This was a little before God established his covenant with him, and is related in Genesis 15:6 . . . [Rom. 4:11–12].

Now, if these words do not express a conditional covenant, certainly none can.

LXV. The nature and ground of this covenant of God with Abraham is farther explained in . . . [Gen. 18:17–19].

Does God say here, "*I will* do it, because I will?" Nothing less. The reason is explicitly assigned: "All nations shall be blessed in him; for he will command his children, and they shall keep the way of the Lord."

1. The reason is yet more (clearly it cannot, but more) fully set down in the twenty-second chapter, . . .[42]

This is yet again declared in . . . [Gen. 26:2–5].

LXVI. This covenant, made to Abraham and his seed, is mentioned again in . . . [Ex. 19:3–5].

In the following chapter, God declares the terms of the covenant they were to keep, in ten commandments. And these themselves are sometimes termed "the covenant," sometimes "the book of the covenant." So, after God had made an end of speaking to the people, it is said, . . . [Ex. 24:4–8].

After the people had broken this covenant by worshipping the golden calf, God renews it (Chap. 34) where we read (verse 27, 28), "And the Lord said unto Moses, 'Write thou these words, for after the tenor of these words I have made a covenant with thee and with Israel' . . .

42. Here follows Gen. 22:16–18. Author's added comment: "That is, the Messiah shall spring from thee BECAUSE thou hast obeyed my voice."

and he wrote upon the tables the words of the covenant, the Ten Commandments."

LXVII. According to the tenor of this covenant, made to Abraham and his seed, God afterward declares . . . [Lev. 26:3–42, abridged].

Consequently the covenant with Abraham, Isaac and Jacob was conditional, as well as that with their posterity.

LXVIII. "But is not the faithfulness of God engaged to keep all that now believe from falling away?" I cannot say that. Whatever assurance God may give to particular souls, I find no general promise in Holy Writ "that none who once believes shall finally fall." Yet, to say the truth, this is so pleasing an opinion, so agreeable to flesh and blood, so suitable to whatever of nature remains in those who have tasted the grace of God, that I see nothing but the mighty power of God which can restrain any who hears it from closing with it. But still it wants one thing to recommend it: plain, cogent Scripture proof.

Arguments from experience alone will never determine this point. They can only prove thus much, on the one hand: that our Lord is exceeding patient; that he is peculiarly unwilling any believer should perish; that he bears long, very long, with all their follies, waiting to be gracious, and to heal their back-sliding; and that he does actually bring back many lost sheep who, to man's apprehensions, were irrecoverable. But all this does not amount to a convincing proof that no believer can or does fall from grace. So that this argument, from experience, will weigh little with those who believe the possibility of falling.

And [on the other hand] it will weigh full as little with those who do not. For if you produce ever so many examples of those who were once strong in faith and are now more abandoned than ever, they will evade it by saying, "O, but they will be brought back; they will not die in their sins." And if they do die in their sins, we come no nearer; we have not gained one point still. For it is easy to say, "They were only hypocrites; they never had true faith." Therefore, Scripture alone can determine this question. And Scripture does so fully determine it that there needs only to set down a very few texts, with some short reflections upon them.

LXIX. That one who is a true believer, or, in other words, one who is holy or righteous in the judgment of God himself, may nevertheless finally fall from grace, appears, (1) from the word of God by Ezekiel, 18:24: "When the righteous turneth away from his righteousness and committeth iniquity, in his trespass that he hath trespassed, and in his sin that he hath sinned, in them shall he die."

Do you object,[43] "This chapter relates wholly and solely to the Jewish church and nation?" I answer, "Prove this." Till then, I shall believe that many parts of it concern all mankind.

If you say, (2) "The righteousness spoken of in this chapter was merely an outward righteousness, without any inward principle of grace or holiness," I ask: How is this consistent with the thirty-first verse, "Cast away from you all your transgressions whereby ye have transgressed, and make you a new heart and a new spirit"? Is this a "merely outward righteousness, without any inward principle of grace or holiness"?

Will you add, "But admitting the person here spoken of to be a truly righteous man, what is here said is only a supposition"? That I flatly deny. Read over the chapter again, and you will see the facts there laid down to be not barely *supposed* but expressly *asserted*.

That the death here mentioned is eternal death appears from the twenty-sixth verse. "When a righteous man turneth away from his righteousness, and committeth iniquity, and dieth in them" (here is temporal death) "for his iniquity that he hath done, he shall die." Here is death eternal.

If you assert, "Both these expressions signify the same thing, and not two different deaths," you put a palpable force upon the text in order to make the Holy Ghost speak nonsense.

" 'Dying *in* his iniquity' " (you say) "is the same thing as 'dying *for* his iniquity.' " Then the text means thus: "When he dieth in them, he shall die in them." A very deep discovery!

But you say, "It cannot be understood of eternal death because they might be delivered from it by repentance and reformation." And why might they not by such repentance as is mentioned in the thirty-first verse be delivered from eternal death?

"But the whole chapter" (you think) "has nothing to do with the spiritual and eternal affairs of men." I believe every impartial man will think quite the contrary if he reads calmly either the beginning of it — "all souls are mine, saith the Lord God; the soul that sinneth, it shall die" (where I can by no means allow that by the death of the soul is

43. [Au.] See a pamphlet entitled, *The Doctrine of the Saint's Final Perseverance, Asserted and Vindicated.* [Ed.] The author, John Gill (1697–1771) was an eminent Hebrew scholar and ardent Calvinist; he was a Baptist preacher in Southwark from 1719 to 1771. The "pamphlet" here cited had been published in 1752.

meant only a temporal affliction) — or the conclusion: "repent and turn yourselves from all your transgressions; so iniquity shall not be your ruin. Cast away from you all your transgressions, whereby ye have transgressed, and make you a new heart, and a new spirit: for why will ye die, O house of Israel?"

It remains, then: one who is righteous in the judgment of God himself, may finally fall from grace.

LXX. Secondly, that one who is endued with the faith which produces a good conscience may nevertheless finally fall, appears from the words of St. Paul to Timothy (1 Tim. 1:18–19): "War a good warfare, holding faith and a good conscience; which some, having put away concerning faith, have made shipwreck."

Observe (1) these men had once the faith that produces "a good conscience"; which they once had, or they could not have "put it away."

Observe (2) they "made shipwreck" of the faith, which necessarily implies the total and final loss of it.

You object, "Nay, the 'putting away' a good conscience does not suppose they had it, but rather that they had it not." This is really surprising. But how do you prove it? "Why, by Acts 13:46, where St. Paul says to the Jews, 'It was necessary that the word of God should first have been spoken to you. But seeing ye put it from you . . . lo, we turn to the Gentiles.' Here you see the Jews, who never had the gospel, are said to 'put it away.'"

How? Are you sure they "never had what they are here said 'to put away'"? Not so. What they put away, it is undeniable, they had, till they "put it away" — namely, "the word of God spoken" by Paul and Barnabas. This instance, therefore, makes full against you. It proves just the reverse of what you cited it for.

But you object further, "Men may have 'a good conscience,' in some sense, without true faith."

I grant it in a restrained, limited sense; but not "a good conscience," simply and absolutely speaking. But such is that of which the apostle here speaks and which he exhorts Timothy to "hold fast," unless you apprehend that "the holding it fast" likewise rather supposes he never had it.

"But the faith here mentioned means only the doctrine of faith." I want better proof of this.

It remains, then: one who has the faith which produces a good conscience may yet finally fall.

LXXI. Thirdly, those who are grafted into the good olive tree, the spiritual, invisible Church, may, nevertheless, finally fall.

For thus saith the apostle:

> Some of the branches are broken off and thou art grafted in among them, and with them partakest of the root and fatness of the olive tree. . . . Be not high-minded, but fear: If God spared not the natural branches, take heed lest he . . . spare not thee. Behold the goodness and severity of God: on them which fell, severity; but toward thee, goodness, if thou continue in his goodness; otherwise thou shalt be cut off.[44]

We may observe here,

1. The persons spoken to were actually ingrafted into the olive tree:
2. This olive tree is not barely the outward, visible church but the invisible, consisting of holy believers. So the text, "if the first fruit be holy, the lump is holy; and if the root be holy, so are the branches." And "because of unbelief they were broken off, and thou standest by faith."
3. These holy believers were still liable to be cut off from the invisible Church, into which they were then grafted.
4. Here is not the least intimation of their being ever grafted in again.

To this you object, (1) "This olive tree is not the invisible Church, but only the outward gospel church-state." You affirm this, and I prove the contrary: namely, that it is the invisible Church, for it "consists of holy believers," which none but the invisible Church does.

You object, (2) "The Jews who were broken off were never true believers in Christ." I am not speaking of the Jews, but of those Gentiles who are mentioned in the twenty-second verse, whom St. Paul exhorts to "continue in his goodness"; "otherwise," saith he, "thou shalt be cut off." Now, I presume these were true believers in Christ. Yet they were still liable to be cut off.

You assert, (3) "This is only a cutting off from the outward church-state." But how is this proved? So forced and unnatural a construction requires some argument to support it.

You say, (4) "There is a strong intimation that they shall be grafted in again." No, not that those Gentiles "who did not continue in his goodness" should be grafted in after they were once cut off! I cannot find the

---

44. Cf. Rom. 11:16–22; see also Wesley's comments on this passage in his *Explanatory Notes upon the New Testament* (1755). Notice that he changes a conditional clause into a declarative one. But see below, sec. LXXIV, where he taxes Dr. Gill with the error of changing a declarative clause into a conditional one.

least intimation of this. "But all Israel shall be saved." I believe they will; but this does not imply the re-ingrafting of these Gentiles.

It remains then, that those who are grafted into the spiritual, invisible Church may nevertheless finally fall.

LXXII. Fourthly, those who are branches of Christ, the true vine, may yet finally fall from grace.

For thus saith our blessed Lord himself . . . [Jn. 15:1–6, abridged]. Here we may observe:

1. The persons spoken of were *in Christ*, "branches of the true vine."

2. Some of these branches "abide not" in Christ, but "the Father taketh them away."

3. The branches which "abide not" are "cast forth," cast out from Christ and his Church.

4. They are not only "cast forth" but "withered"; consequently, never grafted in again.

5. They are not only "cast forth and withered," but also "cast into the fire." And,

6. "They are burned." It is not possible for words more strongly to declare that those who are branches of the true vine may finally fall.

"But this," you say, "furnishes an argument for, not against, the persevering of the saints." Yes, just such an argument for final perseverance as the above cited words of St. Paul to Timothy.

But how do you make it out? "Why thus: 'There are two sorts of branches in Christ the vine; the one fruitful, the other unfruitful. The one are eternally chosen; and these abide in him and can never wither [45] away.'" Nay, this is the very point to be proved. So that you now immediately and directly beg the question. "The other sort of branches are such as are in Christ only by profession, who get into churches, and so are reckoned in Christ; and these in time wither away. These never had any life, grace, or fruitfulness from him." Surely you do not offer this by way of argument! You are again taking for granted the very point to be proved.

But you will prove that "those are 'branches in Christ' who never had any life or grace from him, because the churches of Judea and Thessalonica are said to be in Christ, though every individual member was not savingly in him." I deny the consequence, which can never be made good, unless you can prove that those very Jews or Thessalonians who never

---

45. First edition reads "wither"; changed to "withdraw" in the fourth (1769); *cf.* Jn. 15:6.

had any life or grace from him are nevertheless said by our Lord to be "branches in him."

It remains: that true believers, who are branches of the true vine, may nevertheless finally fall.

LXXIII. Fifthly, those who so effectually know Christ, as by that knowledge to have escaped the pollutions of the world, may yet fall back into those pollutions and perish everlastingly.

For thus saith the Apostle Peter (2 Peter 2:20), "If, after they have escaped the pollutions of the world, through the knowledge of the Lord and Saviour Jesus Christ" (the only possible way of escaping them), "they are entangled again therein and overcome, the latter end is worse with them than the beginning."

But you say, (1) "Their knowledge was not an experimental knowledge." And how do you prove this? "Because had it been such, they could not have lost it." You are begging the question again.

You say, (2) " 'Escaping the pollutions of the world' signifies no more than an outward reformation." How prove you that? You aim at no proof at all. But he that will grant it, may.

You say, (3) "These persons never had any change wrought upon them. They were no other than dogs and swine, not only before and after, but even while they outwardly abstained from gross enormities." I grant that *before* and after that time, during which they "escaped the pollutions of the world" (or, as St. Peter words it in his former [*sic*] epistle, "the corruption that is in the world" [*cf.* 2 Pet. 1:4]), they might well be termed either "dogs" or "swine," for their gross enormities. But that they deserved such an appellation during that time, I cannot grant without some proof.

It remains: that those who, by the inward knowledge of Christ, have escaped the pollutions of the world, may yet fall back into those pollutions and perish everlastingly.

LXXIV. Sixthly, those who see the light of the glory of God in the face of Jesus Christ [*cf.* 2 Cor. 4:6] and who have been made partakers of the Holy Ghost [*cf.* Heb. 6:4], of the witness and the fruits of the Spirit [*cf.* Rom. 8:16; Gal. 5:22], may nevertheless so fall from God as to perish everlastingly. For thus saith the writer to the Hebrews . . . [6: 4-6]. Must not every unprejudiced person see, the expressions here used are so strong and clear that they cannot, without gross and palpable wresting, be understood of any but true believers?

"But the apostle makes only a supposition, 'If they shall fall away.' "

The apostle makes no supposition at all. There is no *if* in the original. The words are Ἀδύνατον [γὰρ] τούς ἄπαξ φωτισθέντας . . . , καὶ παραπεσόντας . . . , *i.e.* in plain English: "It is impossible to renew again unto repentance those who were once enlightened and have fallen away."

"No. The words in the original lie literally thus: 'It is impossible for those who were once enlightened' (and they falling away) 'to renew them again unto repentance.' That is, should they fall away, which is, in plain English, *if* they fall away."

Excuse me for speaking plain English here. "Shall a man lie for God?" Either you or I do; for I flatly aver (and let all that understand Greek judge between us) that the words in the original do not lie literally thus, "and they falling away" (if so, they must be καὶ παραπιπτόντας, in the present tense, not καὶ παραπεσόντας, in the indefinite), but that they are translated, "and have fallen away," as literally as the English tongue will bear.

Therefore, here is no *if* in the case, no supposition at all, but a plain declaration of matter of fact.

LXXV. "But why do you imagine these persons were true believers?" Because all the expressions, in their easy, natural sense, imply it. They "were once enlightened," an expression familiar with the apostle, and never by him applied to any but believers. So "the God of our Lord Jesus Christ give unto you the Spirit of wisdom and revelation. . . . The eyes of your understanding being enlightened, that ye may know what is the hope of his calling . . . and what is the exceeding greatness of his glory [A.V., "power"] to us-ward that believe." [46] So again, "God who commanded the light to shine out of darkness, hath *shined* in our hearts, to give the light of the knowledge of the glory of God in the face of Jesus Christ.[47]

"Nay, 'they were enlightened' means only they were baptized, or knew the doctrines of the gospel." I cannot believe this till you bring me a few passages from St. Paul's writings, wherein that expression is evidently taken in either of these senses.

Again, they "had tasted of the heavenly gift" (emphatically so called) "and were made partakers of the Holy Ghost." So St. Peter likewise couples them together (Acts 2:38), "Be baptized for the remission of sins, and ye shall receive the gift of the Holy Ghost," whereby the love of God was shed abroad in their hearts, with all the other fruits of the Spirit.

46. [Au.] Eph. 1:17-19.        47. [Au.] 2 Cor. 4:6.

The expression, "They had *tasted* of the heavenly gift," is taken from the Psalmist, "Taste and see that the Lord is good" [Ps. 34:8]. As if he had said, "Be ye as assured of his love as of any thing you see with your eyes. And let the assurance thereof be sweet to your soul, as honey is to your tongue."

"But this means only they had some notions of remission of sins and heaven, and some desires after them, and they had received the extraordinary gifts of the Holy Ghost." This you affirm, but without any colour of proof.

It remains that those who see the light of the glory of God in the face of Jesus Christ, and who have been made partakers of the Holy Ghost, of the witness and the fruits of the Spirit, may nevertheless so fall from God as to perish everlastingly.

LXXVI. Seventhly, those who live by faith may yet fall from God and perish everlastingly.

For thus saith the apostle, "The just shall live by faith: but if any man draw back, my soul shall have no pleasure in him" (Heb. 10:38). "The just" (the justified person, of whom only this can be said) "shall live by faith" — even now shall live the life which is hid with Christ in God, and if he endure unto the end, shall live with God for ever. "But if any man draw back," saith the Lord, "my soul shall have no pleasure in him"; that is, I will utterly cast him off. And, accordingly, the drawing back here spoken of is termed in the verse immediately following, "drawing back to perdition."

"But the person supposed to draw back is not the same with him that is said to live by faith." I answer, (1) Who is it then? Can any man draw back from faith who never came to it? But, (2) had the text been fairly translated, there had been no pretence for this objection. For the original runs thus: ὁ [δὲ] δίκαιός μου ἐκ πίστεως ζήσεται, καὶ ἐὰν ὑποστείληται . . . If ὁ [δὲ] δίκαιός — "the just man that lives by faith" (so the expression necessarily implies, there being no other *nominative* to the *verb*) — "draws back, my soul shall have no pleasure in him."

"But your translation, too, is inaccurate." Be pleased to show me wherein.

"I grant he may draw back, and yet not draw back to perdition." But then it is not the drawing back which is here spoken of.

"However, here is only a supposition, which proves no fact." I observe, you take that as a general rule, "suppositions prove no facts." But this is not true. They do not always; but many times they do. And whether they do or no in a particular text must be judged from the nature of the supposition and from the preceding and following words.

"But the inserting 'any man' into the text is agreeable to the grammatical construction of the words." This I totally deny. There is no need of any such insertion. The preceding *nominative* suffices.

"But one that lives by faith cannot draw back. For 'whom he justified, them he also glorified.'" This proves no more than that all who are glorified are pardoned and sanctified first.

"Nay, but St. Paul says, 'Ye are dead; and your life is hid with Christ in God. When Christ, who is our life, shall appear, then shall ye also appear with him in glory'" [Col. 3:3–4]. Most sure, if you endure to the end. "Whosoever believeth in him *to the end*" shall never die.

LXXVII. "But, to come more home to the point: I say, this text is so far from militating against perseverance that it greatly establishes it." You are very unhappy in your choice of texts to establish this doctrine. Two of these which establish it, just as this does, we have already seen. Now, pray let us hear how you prove perseverance from this text.

"Very easily. Here are two sorts of persons mentioned: he that lives by faith, and he that draws back to perdition." Nay, this is the very question. I do not allow that two persons are mentioned in the text.[48] I have shown it is one and the same person, who once lived by faith and afterwards draws back.

Yet thus much I allow: two sorts of believers are in the next verse mentioned; some that draw back and some that persevere. And I allow, the apostle adds, "We are not of them who draw back unto perdition." But what will you infer from thence? This is so far from contradicting what has been observed before, that it manifestly confirms it. It is a farther proof that there are those who draw back unto perdition, although these were not of that number.

"I must still aver that the text is rightly translated, which I prove thus: The original text runs thus (Hab. 2:4), 'Behold, his soul who is lifted up is not upright in him, but the just shall live by his faith.' This the Seventy [*i.e.* the Septuagint] render Ἐὰν ὑποστείληται, οὐκ εὐδοκεῖ ἡ ψυχή μου ἐν αὐτῷ — ὁ δὲ δίκαιος ἐκ πίστεώς μου ζήσεται, 'If a man draw back, my soul hath no pleasure in him. But the just shall live by my faith,' *i.e.* faith in me. Now

---

48. It is interesting to note that here and also in his comments on this passage, Wesley quietly ignores Bengel (whom he follows otherwise at his convenience), who treats verses 38–39 as a chiasmus, just as Gill had done.

here the man in the former clause, who 'draws back,' is distinguished from him, in the following clause, who 'lives by faith.' But the apostle quotes the text from this translation."

True, but he does not "distinguish the man in the former clause who 'draws back' from him in the latter who 'lives by faith.'" So far from it that he quite inverts the order of the sentence, placing the latter clause of it first. And by this means it comes to pass that although in translating this text from the Septuagint, we must insert "a man" (because there is no *nominative* preceding), yet in translating it from the apostle, there is no need or pretence for inserting it, seeing ὁ δὲ δίκαιος stands just before. Therefore, such an insertion is a palpable violence to the text, which, consequently, is not rightly translated.

It remains: that those who live by faith may yet fall from God, and perish everlastingly.

LXXVIII. Eighthly, those who are sanctified by the blood of the covenant may so fall as to perish everlastingly.

For thus again saith the apostle . . . [Heb. 10:26–29].

It is undeniably plain (1) that the person mentioned here was once sanctified by the blood of the covenant; (2) that he afterward, by known, wilful sin, trod under foot the Son of God; and (3) that he hereby incurred a sorer punishment than death, namely, death everlasting.

"Nay, the immediate antecedent to the relative 'he' is 'the Son of God.' Therefore it was he, not the apostate, who was sanctified (set apart for his priestly office) by the blood of the covenant."

Either you forgot to look at the original, or your memory fails. "The Son of God" is not the immediate antecedent to the relative "he." The words run thus: "Of how much sorer punishment shall he be thought worthy, who hath trodden under foot the Son of God: καὶ τὸ αἷμα τῆς διαθήκης κοινὸν ἡγησάμενος ἐν ᾧ ἡγιάσθη. . . ." You see, ἡγησάμενος, not υἱός, is the immediate antecedent to the relative *he*. Consequently, it is the apostate, not the Son of God, who is here said to be sanctified.

"If he was sanctified, yet this cannot be understood of inward sanctification. Therefore it must mean, either that he said he was sanctified, or that he made an outward profession of religion." Why cannot the word be understood in its proper, natural sense of inward sanctification?

"Because that is by the Spirit of God." From this very consideration it appears that this must be understood of inward sanctification; for the words immediately following are, "and hath done despite to the Spirit of grace," even that grace whereby "he was *once* sanctified."

It remains: that those who are sanctified by the blood of the covenant may yet perish everlastingly.

LXXIX. If you imagine these texts are not sufficient to prove that a true believer may finally fall, I will offer a few more to your consideration, which I would beg you to weigh farther at your leisure . . . [here Wesley prints the following catena of New Testament verses: Mt. 5:13; 12:43–45; 24:10–13, 45–51; Lk. 21:34; Jn. 5:14; 8:31, 32; 1 Cor. 9:27; 10:3–12; 2 Cor. 6:1; Gal. 5:4; 6:9; Heb. 3:14; 2 Pet. 3:17; 2 Jn. 8; Rev. 3:11; Mt. 18:35, with occasional comments].

LXXX. "Why, then you make salvation conditional." I *make* it neither conditional nor unconditional, but I *declare* just what I find in the Bible, neither more nor less; namely, that it is bought for every child of man, and actually given to every one that believeth. If you call this conditional salvation, God *made* it so from the beginning of the world; and he hath *declared* it so to be, at sundry times and in divers manners: of old by Moses and the prophets and in later times by Christ and his apostles.

"Then I never can be saved, for I can perform no conditions — for I can do nothing." No, nor I, nor any man under heaven — without the grace of God. But, "I can do all things through Christ strengthening me" [*cf.* Phil. 4:13]. So can you. So can every believer. And he has strengthened and will strengthen you more and more, if you do not wilfully resist, till you quench his Spirit.

LXXXI. "Nay, but God must work *irresistibly* in me, or I shall never be saved." Hold! Consider that word. You are again advancing a doctrine which has not one plain, clear text to support it. I allow, God *may* possibly, at *some times*, work irresistibly in *some souls*. I believe he *does*. But can you infer from hence that he *always* works thus in all that are saved? Alas, my brother, what kind of conclusion is this? And by what Scripture will you prove it? Where, I pray, is it written that none are saved but by irresistible grace? By almighty grace, I grant; by that power alone, to which all things are possible. But show me any one plain Scripture for this, that "all saving grace is irresistible."

LXXXII. But this doctrine is not only unsupported by Scripture. It is flatly contrary thereto. How will you reconcile it (to instance in a very few) with the following texts? . . . [Mt. 22:3; Mk. 6:5–6; Lk. 5:17; 7:30; 13:34; Jn. 6:63–64; Acts 7:51; 13:46; Heb. 3:7–8; 3:12; 12:25.]

LXXXIII. I do but just give you a specimen of the innumerable Scriptures which might be produced on this head. And why will you adhere to an opinion not only unsupported by but utterly contrary both to reason and Scripture? Be pleased to observe here also that you are not to consider the doctrine of irresistible grace by itself, any more than that of unconditional election or final perseverance, but as it stands in connexion with unconditional reprobation — that millstone which hangs about the neck of your whole hypothesis.

Will you say, "I adhere to it because of its usefulness"? Wherein does that usefulness lie? "It exalts God and debases man." In what sense does it exalt God? God in himself is exalted above all praise. Your meaning, therefore, I suppose is this: it displays to others how highly he is exalted in justice, mercy and truth. But the direct contrary of this has been shown at large. It has been shown by various considerations that God is not exalted, but rather dishonoured, and that in the highest degree, by supposing him to despise the work of his own hands, the far greater part of the souls which he hath made. And as to the debasing man, if you mean, "This opinion truly humbles the men that hold it," I fear it does not. I have not perceived — and I have had large occasion to make the trial — that all, or even the generality of them that hold it, are more humble than other men. Neither, I think, will you say, that none are humble who hold it not. So that it is neither a *necessary* nor a *certain* means of humility. And if it be so sometimes, this only proves that God can bring good out of evil.

LXXXIV. The truth is, neither this opinion nor that, but the love of God humbles man, and that only. Let but this be shed abroad in his heart and he abhors himself in dust and ashes [*cf.* Job 42:6]. As soon as this enters into his soul, lowly shame covers his face. That thought, "What is God? What hath he done for *me?*" is immediately followed by, "What am I?" And then he knoweth not what to do or where to hide or how to abase himself enough before the great God of love, of whom he now knoweth, that "as his majesty is, so is his mercy" [*cf.* Ecclus. 2:18]. Let him who has *felt* this (whatever be his opinion) say whether he could then take glory to himself, whether he could ascribe to himself any part of his salvation, or the glory of any good word or thought? Lean then, who will, on that broken reed for humility, but let the love of God humble my soul!

LXXXV. "Why, this is the very thing which recommends it. This doctrine makes men love God." I answer as before. Accidentally it may, because God can draw good out of evil. But you will not say, all who hold it love God; so, it is no *certain* means to that end. Nor will you say that none love him who hold it not. Neither, therefore, is it a *necessary* means.

But, indeed, when you talk at all of its "making men love God," you know not what you do. You lead men into more danger than you are aware of. You almost unavoidably lead them into *resting* on that opinion; you cut them off from a true dependence on the fountain of living waters, and strengthen them in hewing to themselves broken cisterns which can hold no water [*cf.* Jer. 2:13].

LXXXVI. This is my grand objection to the doctrine of reprobation or (which is the same) unconditional election. That it is an error, I know, because if this were true, the whole Scripture must be false. But it is not only for this (because it is an error) that I so earnestly oppose it, but because it is an error of so pernicious consequence to the souls of men; because it directly and naturally tends to hinder the inward work of God in every stage of it.

LXXXVII. For instance. Is a man careless and unconcerned, utterly dead in trespasses and sins? Exhort him, then (suppose he is of your own opinion), to take some care of his immortal soul. "I take care!" says he. "What signifies *my* care? Why, what must be, must be. If I am elect, I must be saved; and if I am not, I must be damned." And the reasoning is as just and strong as it is obvious and natural. It avails not to say, "Men may *abuse* any doctrine." So they may. But this is not *abusing* yours. It is the plain, natural *use* of it. The premises cannot be denied (on your scheme), and the consequence is equally clear and undeniable. Is he a little serious and thoughtful now and then, though generally cold and lukewarm? Press him then to stir up the gift that is in him, to work out his own salvation with fear and trembling [*cf.* Phil. 2:12]. "Alas," says he, "what can I do? You know, man can do nothing." If you reply, "But you do not desire salvation, you are not willing to be saved." "It may be so," says he, "but God shall make me willing in the day of his power." So, waiting for irresistible grace, he falls faster asleep than ever. See him again, when he thoroughly awakes out of sleep; when, in spite of his principles, fearfulness and trembling are come upon him and an horrible dread hath overwhelmed him. How then will you comfort him that is well nigh swallowed up of over-much sorrow? If at all, by applying the promises of God. But against these he is fenced on every side. "These, indeed," says he, "are great and precious promises. But they belong to the elect only. Therefore, they are nothing to me. I am not of that number. And I never can be, for his decree is unchangeable." Has he already tasted of the good word, and the powers of the world to come [*cf.* Heb. 6:5]? Being justified by faith, hath he peace with God? Then sin hath no dominion over him [cf. Rom. 6:14]. But by and by, considering he may fall *foully* indeed, but cannot fall *finally*, he is not so jealous over himself as he was at first. He grows a little and a little slacker, till ere long he falls again into the sin from which he was clean escaped. As soon as you perceive he is entangled again and overcome, you apply the Scriptures relating to that state. You conjure him not to harden his heart any more, lest his last state be worse than the first [cf. Mt. 12:45]. "How can that be?" says he. "Once in grace, always in grace; and I am sure I was in grace once. You shall never tear away my shield." So he sins on, and sleeps on till he awakes in hell.

LXXXVIII. The observing these melancholy examples day by day, this dreadful havoc which the devil makes of souls (especially of those who had begun to run well) by means of this antiscriptural doctrine, constrains me to oppose it from the same principle whereon I labour to save souls from destruction. Nor is it sufficient to ask, "Are there not also many who wrest the opposite doctrine to their own destruction?" If there are, that is nothing to the point in question; for that is not the case here. Here is no *wresting* at all. The doctrine of absolute predestination naturally leads to the chambers of death.

Let an instance in each kind be proposed and the difference is so broad, he that runneth may read it [cf. Hab. 2:2]. I say, "Christ died for all. He tasted death for every man, and he willeth all men to be saved." "Oh," says an hearer, "then I can be saved *when* I will; so I may safely sin a little longer." No; this is no consequence from what I said. The words are *wrested* to infer what does not follow. You say, "Christ died only for the elect, and all these must and shall be saved." "Oh," says an hearer, "then if I am one of the elect, I must and shall be saved. Therefore, I may safely sin a little longer; for my salvation cannot fail." Now, this is a fair consequence from what you said, the words are not *wrested* at all. No more is inferred than what plainly and undeniably follows from the premises. And the very same observation may be made on every article of that doctrine. Every branch of it, as well as this (however the wisdom of God many sometimes draw good out of it) has a natural, genuine tendency, without any wresting, either to prevent or obstruct holiness.

LXXXIX. Brethren, would ye lie for the cause of God? I am persuaded ye would not. Think, then, that as ye are, so am I. I speak the truth before God my judge, not of those who were trained up therein but of those who were lately brought over to your opinion. Many of these have I known, but I have not known one in ten of all that number in whom it did not speedily work some of the above-named effects, according to the state of soul they were then in. And one only have I known among them all, after the closest and most impartial observation, who did not evidently show within one year that his heart was changed, not for the better, but for the worse.

XC. I know indeed ye cannot easily believe this. But whether ye believe it or no, you believe as well as I that "without holiness no man shall see the Lord" [cf. Heb. 12:14]. May we not then, at least, join in this — in declaring the nature of inward holiness and testifying to all the necessity of it? May we not all thus far join in tearing away the broken reeds wherein so many rest without either inward or outward holiness and which they idly trust will supply its place? As far as is possible, let us join in destroying the works of the devil and in setting up the Kingdom of God upon earth, in promoting righteousness, peace, and joy in the Holy Ghost [cf. Rom. 14:17].

Of whatever opinion or denomination we are, we must serve either God or the devil. If we serve God, our agreement is far greater than our difference. Therefore, as far as may be, setting aside that difference, let us unite in destroying the works of the devil, in bringing all we can from the power of darkness into the Kingdom of God's dear Son [cf. Col. 1:13]. And let us assist each other to value more and more the glorious grace whereby we stand, and daily to grow in that grace and in the knowledge of our Lord Jesus Christ [cf. 2 Pet. 3:18].


## Thoughts upon Necessity

*Editor's introduction.* This essay carried Wesley as far into the arcanum of speculative theology as he ever got. It cannot be said to have made much of an impression either on his disciples or his critics. It is, however, yet another example of the Wesleyan method and manner in theologizing. Its occasion (1774) was the predestinarian furor, as this had been further complicated by a vigorous debate which had broken out among several British philosophers, such as David Hume, Richard Price, Thomas Reid and Joseph Priestley. (Cf. Frederick Coplestone, *A History of Philosophy* [1959], V, 361–74.) One should note that Wesley's essay was written in Glasgow but published in London. It is obvious that he had only scant interest in the intricacies of the arguments involved, but he recognized in them a grave threat to his cherished notions of moral responsibility from what he took to be the passivist conclusions of the determinists. In 1749 David Hartley had published his two-volume treatise, *Observations on Man: His Frame, His Duty, and His Expectations*. This was an elaborate study of the body-mind problem, which attempted to explain sensation in terms of nerve-vibrations and their patterned "associations" (a sort of primitive reflex psychology). In 1754 Jonathan Edwards's *Freedom of the Will* had set forth with stringent logic the deterministic implications of his earlier *Treatise Concerning Religious Affections* (1746). Wesley had abridged and published the latter in Vol. XXIII (pp. 178–279) of his own collected *Works* (Pine), with an interesting comment "to the reader": "Out of this dangerous heap, wherein much wholesome food is mixed with much deadly poison, I have selected many remarks and admonitions which may be of great use to the children of God."

The fresh outbreak of hostilities with the Calvinists in 1770 had brought John Fletcher and Walter Sellon into the fray on the Wesleyan side with effective polemics against the doctrine of predestination and the antinomianism often linked with it in evangelical circles in England. This left Wesley free to concentrate on the correlative question of human "free will." While he was writing a first draft of these *Thoughts*, he discovered a balder statement of the deterministic theory than those of Hartley or Hume in Lord Kames's "Essay on Liberty and Necessity," in *Essays on the Principles of Morality and Natural Religion* (Edinburgh, 1751). Publication of this volume had brought its author under church discipline in Scotland. Kames's conclusion — that man's sense of freedom is a delusion — was taken by Wesley to imply that "the noblest creature in the visible world is only a fine piece of clockwork." This was intolerable; and it scarcely mattered that the other determinists denied that this was the intended or necessary implication of *their* arguments. Wesley published what must be considered two drafts of the same essay: *Thoughts upon Necessity* and *A Thought on Necessity* (both in 1774). (A further "digest" of them both appeared in *The Arminian Magazine* for 1780.)

It cannot be claimed that Wesley's efforts here come even close to matching the scope and learning of his opponents. They do succeed, however, in exhibiting the folk-theologian in reaction to a theoretical menace to the Christian message. His presupposition is that if the conclusion of an argument cancels either the premises or the consequences of the gospel, something is wrong with the argument. This Wesley manages to demonstrate, even if his own constructive alternative is only sketchy and assertoric. There are obvious affinities between Wesley's counter-attack and the refutation of Hume by the Scottish "common-sense real-ists." (Cf. Coplestone, *History of Philosophy*, V, 361–69.) This is not accidental. In the *Journal* for May 5, 1772 (close to the time when Wesley decided to write on the subject), he records that, on his journey from Aberdeen to Arbroath, he "read . . . Dr. Beattie's ingenious *Inquiry After Truth* (James Beattie, *An Essay on the Nature and Immutability of Truth in Opposition to Sophistry and Superstition* [Edinburgh, 1771]). He is a writer equal to his subject and far above the match of all the 'minute philosophers' [a phrase of Berkeley's], David Hume in particular — the most insolent despiser of truth and virtue that ever appeared in the world" (*Journal*, V, 458).

The copy text here is the second (and last) edition, 1775.

❖    ❖    ❖    ❖


## To the Reader

*I had finished what I designed to say on this subject when the "Essay on Liberty and Necessity" fell into my hands, a most elaborate piece, touched and retouched with all possible care. This has occasioned a considerable enlargement of the following tract. I would fain place mankind in a fairer point of view than that writer has done, as I cannot believe the noblest creature in the visible world to be only a fine piece of clockwork.*

*Is man a "free agent," or is he not? Are his actions "free" or "necessary"? Is he self-determined in acting or is he determined by some other being? Is the principle which determines him to act in himself or in another? This is the question which I want to consider. And is it not an important one? Surely there is not one of greater importance in the whole nature of things. For what is there that more nearly concerns all that are born of women? What can be conceived which more deeply affects, not some only, but every child of man?*


I. 1. That man is not self-determined, that the principle of action is lodged not in himself but in some other being, has been an exceeding ancient opinion, yea, near as old as the foundation of the world. It seems none that admit of revelation can have any doubt of this. For it was unquestionably the sentiment of Adam, soon after he had eaten of the forbidden fruit. He imputes what he had done, not to himself but another: "The woman whom thou gavest me" [cf. Gen. 3:12]. It was also the sentiment of Eve: "The serpent, he beguiled me and I did eat" [cf. Gen. 3:13]. "It is true, *I* did eat, but the cause of my eating, the spring of my action, was in *another*."

2. The same opinion that man is not self-determined took root very early and spread wide, particularly in the Eastern world, many ages before Manes was born. Afterwards indeed, he and his followers, commonly called Manichees, formed it into a regular system.[1] They not only maintained that all the actions of man were necessarily determined by a power exterior to himself, but likewise accounted for it by ascribing the good to Oromasdes, the parent of all good; the evil to the other independent being, Arimanius, the parent of all evil.

3. From the Eastern world, "when arts and empire learned to travel west," this opinion travelled with them into Europe, and soon found its way into Greece. Here it was earnestly espoused and vehemently maintained by the Stoic philosophers, men of great renown among persons of literature and some of the ablest disputants in the world. These affirmed with one mouth that from the beginning of the world, if not rather from all eternity, there was an indissoluble chain of causes and effects which included all human actions, and that these were by fate so connected together that not one link of the chain could be broken.

4. A fine writer of our own country, who was a few years since gathered to his fathers,[2] has with admirable skill drawn the same conclusion from different premises. He lays it down as a principle (and a principle it is which cannot reasonably be denied) that as long as the soul is vitally united to the body, all its operations depend on the body; that, in particular, all our thoughts depend upon the vibrations of the fibres of the brain, and, of consequence, vary more or less as those vibrations vary. In that expression "our thoughts," he comprises all our sensations, all our reflections and passions, yea, and all our volitions and consequently our

1. *Cf.* Wesley's two letters to his father (Dec. 19, 1729, and Jan. 1731), in which the problem of evil is discussed and the "monstrous scheme of the Manichees" denounced as "next door to contradiction," since it involves "two absolute infinites" (*Letters*, I, 44–46, 68–72).

2. David Hartley (1705–57), *Observations on Man.*

actions, which, he supposes, unavoidably follow those vibrations. He premises, "But you will say, this scheme infers the universal necessity of human action"; and frankly adds, "Certainly it does. I am sorry for it, but I cannot help it."

5. And this is the scheme which is now adopted by not a few of the most sensible men in our nation. One of these, fairly confessing that "he did not think himself a sinner," was asked, "Do you never feel any wrong tempers? And do you never speak or act in such a manner as your own reason condemns?" He candidly answered:

"Indeed I do. I frequently feel tempers and speak many words and do many actions which I do not approve of. But I cannot avoid it. They result, whether I will or no, from the vibrations of my brain, together with the motion of my blood and the flow of my animal spirits. But these are not in my own power. I cannot help them. They are independent on my choice. And therefore I cannot apprehend myself to be a sinner on this account."

6. Very lately another gentleman, in free conversation, was carrying this matter a little farther. Being asked, "Do you believe God is almighty?" he answered, "I do, or he could not have made the world." "Do you believe he is wise?" "I cannot tell. Much may be said on both sides." "Do you believe he is good?" "No, I cannot believe it; I believe just the contrary. For all the evil in the world is owing to him. I can ascribe it to no other cause. I cannot blame that cur for barking or biting. It is his nature and he did not make himself. I feel wrong tempers in myself, but that is not *my* fault, for I cannot help it. It is my nature, and I could not prevent my having this nature, neither can I change it."

7. The Assembly of Divines who met at Westminster in the last century express very nearly the same sentiment, though placed in a different light. They speak to this effect: [3]

Whatever happens in time, was unchangeably determined from all eternity. God ordained or ever the world was made, all the things that should come to pass therein. The greatest and the smallest events were equally predetermined; in particular, all the thoughts, all the words, all the actions of every child of man; all that every man thinks, or speaks, or does, from his birth till his spirit returns to God that gave it. It follows that no man can do either more or less good, or more or less evil, than he does. None can think, speak, or act any otherwise than he does, not in any, [even] the smallest circumstance.

3. A garbled version of the Westminster Confession, III, "Of God's Eternal Decree," and V, "Of Providence."

In all he is bound by an invisible, but more than adamantine, chain. No man can move his head or foot, open or shut his eyes, lift his hand, or stir a finger, any otherwise than as God determined he should, from all eternity.

8. That this chain is *invisible*, they allow. Man himself perceives nothing of it. He suspects nothing less. He imagines himself to be free in all his actions; he *seems* to move hither and thither, to go this way or that, to choose doing evil or doing good, just at his own discretion. But all this is an entire mistake; it is no more than a pleasing dream. For all his ways are fixed as the pillars of heaven, all unalterably determined. So that notwithstanding these gay, flattering appearances,

> In spite of all the labour we create,
> We only *row;* but we are *steer'd* by Fate! [4]

9. A late writer [Jonathan Edwards], in his celebrated book upon free-will, explains the matter thus:

> The soul is now connected with a material vehicle and placed in the material world. Various objects here continually strike upon one or other of the bodily organs. These communicate the impression to the brain; consequent on which, such and such sensations follow. These are the materials on which the understanding works in forming all its simple and complex ideas, according to which our judgments are formed. And according to our judgments are our passions: our love and hate, joy and sorrow, desire and fear, with their innumerable combinations. Now, all these passions together are the will, variously modified, and all actions flowing from the will are voluntary actions. Consequently, they are good or evil, which otherwise they could not be. And yet it is not in man to direct his own way while he is in the body and in the world.[5]

10. The author of an "Essay on Liberty and Necessity," [6] published some years since at Edinburgh, speaks still more explicitly, and endeavours to trace the matter to the foundation:

---

4. *Cf.* Samuel Butler, *Hudibras*, Bk. I, can. 1, l. 877–80:
> Success, the mark no mortal wit,
> Or surest hand, can always hit:
> For whatso'er we perpetrate,
> We do but row, w'are steer'd by Fate, . . .

5. This seems to be Wesley's "digest" of Edwards's *Freedom of the Will*, Pt. I, sec. 1–2. It is clearly not a quotation.

6. Henry Home, Lord Kames; this "quotation" is also a rough digest of his essay, p. 152 ff.

The impressions, says he, which man receives in the natural world do not correspond to the truth of things. Thus the qualities called secondary which we by natural instinct attribute to matter, belong not to matter, nor exist without us; but all the beauty of colours with which heaven and earth *appear* clothed is a sort of romance or illusion. For in external objects there is really no other distinction but that of the size and arrangement of their constituent parts, whereby the rays of light are variously reflected and refracted.[7]

In the moral world whatever is a cause with regard to its proper effect is an effect with regard to some prior cause, and so backward without end. Events, therefore, being a train of causes and effects, are necessary and fixed. Every one *must be* and cannot be otherwise than it is.[8]

And yet a feeling of an opposite kind is deeply rooted in our nature. Many things *appear* to us as not predetermined by an invariable law. We naturally make a distinction between things that *must be* and things that *may be* or *may not*.

So with regard to the actions of men. We see that connection between an action and its motive to be so strong that we reason with full confidence concerning the future actions of others. But if actions necessarily arise from their proper motives, then all human actions are necessary and fixed. Yet they do not *appear* so to us. Indeed, before any particular action, we always judge that the action will be the necessary result of some motive. But afterwards the feeling instantly varies. We accuse and condemn a man for doing what is wrong. We conceive he had a power of acting otherwise, and the whole train of our feelings suppose[s] him to have been entirely a free agent.

But what does this liberty amount to? In all cases our choice is determined by some motive. It *must be* determined by that motive which appears the best upon the whole. But motives are not under our power or direction. When two motives offer, we have not the power of choosing as we please. We are necessarily determined.

Man is passive in receiving impressions of things, according to which the judgment is necessarily formed. This the will necessarily obeys, and the outward action necessarily follows the will.

Hence it appears that God decrees all future events. He who gave such a nature to his creatures and placed them in such circumstances that a certain train of actions must necessarily follow — he who did so, and who must have foreseen the consequences — did certainly decree that those events should fall out and that men should act just as they do.

The Deity is the first cause of all things. He formed the plan on which all things were to be governed, and put it in execution by establishing, both in the natural and moral world, certain laws that

7. [Au.] p. 152, etc.        8. [Au.] p. 157, etc.

are fixed and immutable. By virtue of these, all things proceed in a regular train of causes and effects, bringing about the events contained in the original plan, and admitting the possibility of no other. This universe is a vast machine, winded up and set agoing. The several springs and wheels act unerringly one upon another. The hand advances and the clock strikes, precisely as the artist has determined. In this plan, man, a rational creature, was to fulfil certain ends. He was to *appear* as an *actor*, and to act with consciousness and spontaneity. Consequently, it was necessary he should have some idea of liberty, some feeling of things possible and contingent, things depending on himself, that he might be led to exercise that activity for which he was designed. To have seen himself a part of that great machine would have been altogether incongruous to the ends he was to fulfil. Had he seen that nothing was contingent, there would have been no room for forethought nor for any sort of industry or care. Reason could not have been exercised in the way it is now; that is, man could not have been man. But now, the moment he comes into the world, he acts as a free agent. And contingency, tho' it has no real existence in things, is made to appear as really existing. Thus is our natural feeling directly opposite to truth and matter of fact, seeing it is certainly impossible that any man should act any otherwise than he does.

See necessity drawn at full length and painted in the most lively colours!

II. 1. It is easy to observe that every one of these schemes implies the universal necessity of human actions. In this they all agree, that man is not a "free" but a "necessary" agent, being absolutely determined in all his actions by a principle exterior to himself. But they do not agree what that principle is. The most ancient of them, the Manichaean, maintained that men are determined to evil by the evil god, Arimanius; that Oromasdes, the good god, would have prevented or removed that evil, but could not; the power of the evil god being so great that he is not able to control it.

2. The Stoics, on the other hand, did not impute the evil that is in this world to any intelligent principle, but either to the original stubbornness of matter which even divine power was not capable of removing, to the concatenation of causes and effects which no power whatever could alter, or to unconquerable Fate, to which they supposed all the gods, the supreme not excepted, to be subject.

3. The author of two volumes entitled *Man* [9] rationally rejects all the preceding schemes, while he deduces all human actions from those passions and judgments which, during the present union of the soul and

9. David Hartley, *Observations on Man*. Cf. above, p. 473.

body, necessarily result from such and such vibrations of the fibres of the brain. Herein he indirectly ascribes the necessity of all human actions to God; who, having fixed the laws of this vital union according to his own good pleasure, having so constituted man that the motions of the soul thus depend on the fibres of the body, has thereby laid him under an invincible necessity of acting thus, and in no other manner. So do those likewise, who suppose all the judgments and passions necessarily to flow from the motion of the blood and spirits. For this is indirectly to impute all our passions and actions to him who alone determined the manner wherein our blood and spirits should move.

4. The gentleman next mentioned does this directly without any softening or circumlocution at all. He flatly and roundly affirms [that] the Creator is the proper author of everything which man does; that by creating him thus, he has absolutely determined the manner wherein he shall act; and that, therefore, man can no more help sinning than a stone can help falling. The Assembly of Divines do as directly ascribe the necessity of human actions to God, in affirming that God has eternally determined whatsoever shall be done in time. So likewise does Mr. Edwards of New England, in proving by abundance of deep, metaphysical reasoning, that we *must* see, hear, taste, feel, the objects that surround us, and *must* have such judgments, passions, actions, and no other.[10] He flatly ascribes the necessity of all our actions to him who united our souls to these bodies, placed us in the midst of these objects and ordered that these sensations, judgments, passions and actions should spring therefrom.

5. The author last cited connects together and confirms all the preceding schemes, particularly those of the ancient Stoics and the modern Calvinists.

III. 1. It is not easy for a man of common understanding, especially if unassisted by education, to unravel these finely woven schemes, or show distinctly where the fallacy lies. But he knows, he feels, he is certain, they cannot be true; that the holy God cannot be the author of sin. The horrid consequences of supposing this may appear to the meanest understanding from a few plain, obvious considerations, of which every man that has common sense may judge.

If all the passions, the tempers, the actions, of men are wholly independent on their own choice, are governed by a principle exterior to

10. Cf. *Freedom of the Will*, Pt. I, sec. 4; "Of the Distinction of Natural and Moral Necessity, and Inability."

themselves, then there can be no moral good or evil.[11] There can be neither virtue nor vice, neither good nor bad actions, neither good nor bad passions or tempers. The sun does much good — but it is no virtue — but he is not capable of moral goodness. Why is he not? For this plain reason: because he does not act from choice. The sea does much harm; it swallows up thousands of men, but it is not capable of moral badness, because it does not act by choice, but from a necessity of nature — if, indeed, one or the other can be said to *act* at all. Properly speaking, it does not. It is purely passive; it is only acted upon by the Creator, and *must* move in this manner and no other, seeing it cannot resist his will. In like manner, St. Paul did much good: but it was no virtue if he did not act from choice. And if he was in all things necessitated to think and act, he was not capable of moral goodness. Nero does much evil, murders thousands of men and sets fire to the city, but it is no fault; he is not capable of moral badness if he does not act from choice but necessity. Nay, properly, the man does not act at all; he is only acted upon by the Creator and *must* move thus, being irresistibly impelled. For who can resist his will [*cf.* Rom. 9:19]?

2. Again, if all the actions and passions and tempers of men are quite independent on their own choice, are governed by a principle exterior to themselves, then none of them is either rewardable or punishable, is either praise- or blame-worthy. The consequence is undeniable. I cannot praise the sun for warming nor blame the stone for wounding me, because neither the sun nor the stone acts from choice but from necessity. Therefore, neither does the latter deserve blame, nor the former deserve praise. Neither is the one capable of reward, nor the other of punishment. And if a man does good as necessarily as the sun, he is no more praiseworthy than that. If he does evil as necessarily as the stone, he is no more blameworthy. The dying to save your country is no way rewardable if you are compelled thereto; and the betraying your country is no way punishable if you are necessitated to do it.

3. It follows, if there be no such thing as virtue or vice, as moral good or evil, if there be nothing rewardable or punishable in the actions or passions of men, then there can be no judgment to come, and no future

11. But *cf.* Edwards's "Remarks on the Essay on the Principles of Morality and Religion" (1757), in which he reviews Kames's "Essay" and denies that he himself has ever held the position here ascribed to him by Wesley. *Cf. Freedom of the Will*, in *The Works of Jonathan Edwards*, Paul Ramsey, ed. (New Haven, 1957), I, 443–65.

rewards and punishments. For might not God as well judge the trees of the wood or the stones of the field as man, if man was as totally passive as they, as irresistibly determined to act thus or thus? What should he be commended or rewarded for, who never did any good but when he could not help it, being impelled thereto by a force which he could not withstand? What should he be blamed or punished for, who never did any evil to which he was not determined by a power he could no more resist than he could shake the pillars of heaven?

This objection the author of the "Essay" gives in its full strength:

> The advocates for liberty reason thus: If actions be necessary and not in our own power, what ground is there for blame, self-condemnation, or remorse? If a clock were sensible of its own motions and knew that they proceeded according to necessary laws, could it find fault with itself for striking wrong? Would it not blame the artist who had so ill adjusted the wheels? So that, upon this scheme, all the moral constitution of our nature is overturned, there is an end to all the operations of conscience, about right and wrong. Man is no longer a moral agent, nor the subject of praise or blame for what he does.

He strangely answers:

> Certainly the pain, the remorse, which is felt by any man who had been guilty of a bad action, springs from the notion that he has a power over his own actions, that he might have forborne to do it. It is on this account that he is angry at himself and confesses himself to be blameable. That uneasiness proceeds on the supposition that he is free and might have acted a better part. And one under the dominion of bad passions is condemned upon this ground, that it was in his power to be free from them. Were not this the case, brutes might be the objects of moral blame as well as man. But we do not blame them because they have not freedom, a power of directing their own actions. We must therefore admit that the idea of freedom is essential to the moral feeling. On the system of universal necessity there could be no place for blame or remorse. And we struggle in vain to reconcile to this system the testimony which conscience clearly gives to freedom.

Is this an answer to the objection? Is it not fairly giving up the whole cause?

He adds:

> A feeling of liberty, which I now scruple not to call deceitful, is interwoven with our nature. Man must be so constituted in order to attain virtue.

To attain virtue! Nay, you have yourself allowed that, on this supposition, virtue and vice can have no being. You go on:

> If he saw himself as he really is (Sir, do not *you* see yourself so?), if he conceived himself and all his actions necessarily linked into the great chain which renders the whole order both of the natural and moral world unalterably determined in every article, what would follow?

Why, just nothing at all. The great chain must remain as it was before, since whatever you see or conceive, that is "unalterably determined in every article."

To confute himself still more fully, he says:

> If we knew good and evil to be necessary and unavoidable (contradiction in terms, but let it pass), there would be no place for praise or blame, no indignation at those who had abused their rational powers (no accountableness for the use of those powers); no sense of just punishment annexed to crimes, or of any reward deserved by good actions. All these feelings vanish at once with the feeling of liberty. And the sense of *duty* must be quite extinguished, for we cannot conceive any "moral obligation" without supposing a power in the agent over his own actions.

If so, what is he who publishes a book to show mankind that they have no power over their own actions?

To the objection that this scheme "makes God the author of sin," the essayist feebly answers, "Sin, or moral turpitude, lies in the evil intention of him that commits it, or in some wrong affection. Now, there is no wrong intention in God." What then? Whatever wrong intention or affection is in man, you make God the direct author of it. For you flatly affirm, "Moral evil cannot exist without being permitted of God. And with regard to a first cause, *permitting* is the same thing as *causing*." That I totally deny: but if it be, God is the proper cause of all the sin in the universe.

4. Suppose, now, the Judge of all the earth, having just pronounced the awful sentence, "Depart, ye cursed, into everlasting fire, prepared for the devil and his angels," should say to one on the left hand, "What canst thou offer in thy own behalf?" Might he not, on this scheme, answer,

> Lord, why am I doomed to dwell with everlasting burnings? For not doing good? Was it ever in my power to do any good action? Could I ever do any but by that grace which thou hadst determined not to give me? For doing evil? Lord, did I ever do any which I was

not bound to do by thy own decree? Was there ever a moment when it was in my power, either to do good or to cease from evil? Didst not thou fix whatever I should do, or not do, or ever I came into the world? And was there ever one hour, from my cradle to my grave, wherein I could act otherwise than I did?

Now, let any man say whose mouth would be stopped, that of the criminal or the judge?

5. But if, upon this supposition, there can be no judgment to come and no future rewards or punishments, it likewise follows that the Scriptures, which assert both, cannot be of divine original. If there be not "a day wherein God will judge the world, by that man whom he hath appointed" [*cf.* Acts 17:31], if the wicked "shall *not* go into eternal punishment," neither the righteous into "life eternal" [*cf.* Mt. 25:46], what can we think of that book which so frequently and solemnly affirms all these things? We can no longer maintain that "all Scripture was given by inspiration of God" [*cf.* 2 Tim. 3:16], since it is impossible that the God of truth should be the author of palpable falsehoods. So that, whoever asserts the predetermination of all human actions (a doctrine totally inconsistent with the Scriptural doctrines of a future judgment, heaven and hell), strikes hereby at the very foundation of Scripture, which must necessarily stand or fall with them.

6. Such absurdities will naturally and necessarily follow from the scheme of necessity. But Mr. Edwards has found out a most ingenious way of evading this consequence:

> I grant (says that good and sensible man), if the actions of men were *involuntary*, the consequence would inevitably follow: they could not be either good or evil; nor, therefore, could they be the proper object either of reward or punishment. But here lies the very ground of your mistake: their actions are not *involuntary*. The actions of men are quite *voluntary*, the fruit of their own *will*. They love, they desire, evil things; therefore, they commit them. But love and hate, desire and aversion, are only several modes of *willing*. Now, if men voluntarily commit theft, adultery, or murder, certainly the actions are evil, and therefore punishable. And if they voluntarily serve God, and help their neighbours, the actions are good, and therefore rewardable.[12]

7. I cannot possibly allow the consequence, upon Mr. Edwards's supposition. Still I say: if they are *necessitated* to commit robbery or murder,

12. Evidently intended to be a précis of Edwards's position, but nowhere in Edwards in this form. *Cf. Freedom of the Will*, Pt. III, sec. 1, 4, 7.

they are not punishable for committing it. But you answer, "Nay, their actions are voluntary, the fruit of their own will." If they are, yet that is not enough to make them either good or evil. For their will, on *your* supposition, is irresistibly impelled, so that they cannot help willing thus or thus. If so, they are no more blameable for *that will* than for the actions which follow it. There is no blame if they are under a *necessity* of willing. There can be no moral good or evil unless they have *liberty* as well as *will*, which is entirely a different thing. And the not adverting to this seems to be the direct occasion of Mr. Edwards's whole mistake.

8. God created man an *intelligent* being and endued him with *will* as well as *understanding*. Indeed, it seems without this his understanding would have been given to no purpose. Neither would either his will or understanding have answered any valuable purpose if *liberty* had not been added to them, a power distinct from both, a power of choosing for himself, a self-determining principle. It may be doubted whether God ever made an intelligent creature without all these three faculties; whether any spirit ever existed without them; yea, whether they are not implied in the very nature of a spirit. Certain it is, that no being can be accountable for its actions which has not liberty, as well as will and understanding.

How admirably is this painted by Milton, supposing God to speak concerning his new-made creature:

> . . . I made him just and right
> Sufficient to have stood, though free to fall.
> Such I created all the ethereal powers . . .
> Freely they stood who stood, and fell who fell.
> Not free, what proof could they have given sincere
> Of true allegiance, constant faith, and love
> Where only what they *needs must do* appear'd,
> Not what they *would?* What praise could they receive,
> What pleasure I, from such obedience paid,
> When will and reason (reason also is choice),
> Useless and vain, of freedom both despoiled
> Made passive both, had served *necessity*,
> Not *me*. They therefore, as to right belonged
> So were created, . . .
> So without least impulse or shadow of fate,
> Or aught by me immutably foreseen,
> They trespass, authors to themselves in all
> Both what they judge and what they choose; for so
> I formed them free: and free they must remain,

Till they enthrall themselves. I else must change
Their nature, and reverse the high decree,
Unchangeable, eternal, which ordained
Their freedom; they themselves ordained their fall.[13]

9. It seems, they who divide the faculties of the human soul into the understanding, will and affections — unless they make the will and affections the same thing (and then how inaccurate is the division?) — must mean by affections the will, properly speaking, and by the term "will," neither more nor less than "liberty," the power of choosing, either to do or not to do (commonly called "liberty of contradiction"), or to do this or the contrary, good or evil (commonly called "liberty of contrariety"). Without the former at least, there can be nothing good or evil, rewardable or punishable. But it is plain, the doctrine of necessity as taught either by ancient heathens or by the moderns (whether deists or Christians), destroys both, leaves not a shadow of either in any soul of man. Consequently, it destroys all the morality of human actions, making man a mere machine, and leaves no room for any judgment to come, or for either rewards or punishments.

IV. 1. But whatever be the consequences deducible from this, that all human actions are necessary, how will you answer the arguments which are brought in defence of this position? Let us try whether something of this kind may not be done in a few words.

Indeed, as to the first scheme, that of the Manichees, the maintainers of a good and an evil god, though it was formerly espoused by men of renown (St. Augustine in particular), yet it is now so utterly out of date that it would be lost labour to confute it. A little more plausible is this scheme of the Stoics, building necessity upon fate, upon the insuperable stubbornness of matter, or the indissoluble chain of causes and effects. Perhaps they invented this scheme to exculpate God, to avoid laying the blame upon him, by allowing he would have done better if he could, that he was *willing* to cure the evil but was not *able*. But we may answer them short: there is no fate above the Most High. That is an idle, irrational fiction. Neither is there any thing in the nature of matter which is not obedient to his Word. The Almighty is able in the twinkling of an eye to reduce any matter into any form he pleases or to speak it into nothing; in a moment to expunge it out of his creation.

2. The still more plausible scheme of Dr. Hartley (and I might add,

13. *Paradise Lost*, Bk. III, l. 98–128; note Wesley's alterations of Milton's text; omissions are here indicated by the elipses.

those of the two gentlemen above-mentioned, which nearly coincide with it), now adopted by almost all who doubt of the Christian system, requires a more particular consideration, were it only because it has so many admirers. And it certainly contains a great deal of truth, as will appear to any that considers it calmly. For who can deny that not only the memory but all the operations of the soul are now dependent on the bodily organs, the brain in particular, insomuch that a blow on the back part of the head (as frequent experience shows) may take away the understanding and destroy at once both sensation and reflection; and an irregular flow of spirits may quickly turn the deepest philosopher into a madman. We must allow likewise that while the very power of thinking depends so much upon the brain, our judgments must needs depend thereon and in the same proportion. It must be farther allowed that, as our sensations, our reflections and our judgments, so our will and passions also, which naturally follow from our judgments, ultimately depend on the fibres of the brain. But does all this infer the total necessity of all human actions? "I am sorry for it," says the doctor, "but I cannot help it." I verily think I can. I think I can not only *cut* the knot, by showing (as above) the intolerable absurdities which this scheme implies, but fairly *untie* it, by pointing out just where the fallacy lies.

3. But first permit me to say a word to the author of the "Essay." His grand reason for supposing all mankind in a dream is drawn from analogy, "We are in a continual delusion as to the natural world; why not as to the moral?" Well, how does he prove that we are in a continual delusion as to the natural world? Thus: "All the qualities which are termed secondary qualities we, by a natural instinct, ascribe to matter. But it is a mere deceit. They do not belong to matter, neither exist without us." As commonly as this is asserted, it is absolutely false, as will appear quickly.[14] You instance in colours, and confidently say, "All this beauty of colours with which heaven and earth appear to be clothed, is a sort of romance or illusion. In external objects there is no other distinction but that of the size and arrangement of their constituent parts, whereby the rays of light are variously reflected or refracted."

But are those "rays of light" real? And do they exist without us? Cer-

14. Here follows Wesley's version of Berkeley's refutation of John Locke and others on the distinction between primary and secondary qualities of matter. *Cf.* George Berkeley, *Of the Principles of Human Knowledge*, sec. 87–117, in *Works*, Alexander Campbell Fraser, ed. (Oxford, 1871), I, 200–217; and his *Siris*, sec. 231–69, in *ibid.*, II, 449–67. See also H. Høffding, *History of Modern Philosophy* (1900), I, 384 f., 420 f.

tainly, as much as the sun does. And are the *constituent parts* of those objects real? Nobody questions it. But are they really of such a *size* and *arranged* in such a manner? They are; and what will you infer from that? I infer that colour is just as real as size or figure, and that all colours do as really exist without us as trees, or corn, or heaven, or earth.

"But what do you mean by colour?" When I say, "That cloth is of a red colour," I mean its surface is so disposed as to reflect the red (that is, the largest) rays of light. When I say, "The sky is blue," I mean it is so disposed as to reflect the blue (that is, the smallest) rays of light. And where is the delusion here? Does not that disposition, do not those rays, as really exist, as either the cloth or the sky? And are they not as really reflected as the ball in a tennis court? It is true that, when they strike upon my eye, a particular sensation follows in my soul. But that sensation is not colour; I know no one that calls it so. Colour therefore is a real, material thing. There is no illusion in the case, unless you confound the perception with the thing perceived. And all other secondary qualities are just as real as figure or any other primary one. So you have no illusion in the natural world to countenance that you imagine to be in the moral. Wherever, therefore, this argument occurs (and it occurs ten times over), "The natural world is all illusion; therefore, so is the moral," it is just good for nothing.

But, take it all together, and what a supposition is this! Is it not enough to make one's blood run cold? "The great God, the Creator of heaven and earth, the Father of the spirits of all flesh, the God of truth, has encompassed with falsehood every soul that he has made, has given up all mankind 'to a strong delusion,' to believe a lie: yea, all his creation is a lie, all the natural and all the moral world." If so, you make God himself, rather than the devil (horrid thought!) "the father of lies" [*cf.* Jn. 8:44]! Such you doubtless represent him when you say not only that he has surrounded us with illusion on every side, but that the feelings which he has interwoven with our inmost nature are equally illusive!

> That all these shadows, for things we take,
> Are but the empty dreams which in death's sleep we make! [15]

And yet, after this, you make a feint of disputing in defence of a material world! Inconsistency all over! What proof have we of this, what

15. *Cf.* Abraham Cowley, *Pindarique Odes*, II, "To the New Year," in *Works* (1707), I, 250.

possible proof can we have, if we cannot trust our own eyes, or ears, or any or all of our senses? But it is certain, I can trust none of my senses if I am a mere machine. For I have the testimony of all my outward and all my inward senses that I am a free agent. If therefore I cannot trust them in this, I can trust them in nothing. Do not tell me there are sun, moon, and stars, or that there are men, beasts or birds in the world. I cannot believe one tittle of it if I cannot believe what I feel in myself; namely, that it depends on *me*, and no other being, whether I shall now open or shut my eyes, move my head hither and thither, or stretch my hand or my foot. If I am *necessitated* to do all this, contrary to the whole both of my inward and outward senses, I can believe nothing else, but must necessarily sink into universal scepticism.

Let us now weigh the main argument on which this author builds the melancholy hypothesis of necessity: "Actions necessarily arise from their several motives: therefore all human actions are necessary." Again: "In all cases the choice must be determined by that motive which appears the best upon the whole. But motives are not under our power. Man is passive in receiving impressions of things, according to which the last judgment is necessarily formed. This the will necessarily obeys, and the outward action necessarily follows the will."

Let us take this boasted argument in pieces and survey it part by part:

1. "Motives are not under our power." This is not universally true. Some are, some are not. That man has a strong motive to run his neighbour through — namely, violent anger — and yet the action does not *necessarily* follow. Often it does not follow at all, and where it does, not necessarily. He *might* have resisted that motive.

2. "In all cases the choice *must be* determined by that motive which appears the best upon the whole." This is absolutely false. It is flatly contrary to the experience of all mankind. Who may not say on many occasions — *video meliora?* [16] — "I know what I do is not best upon the whole."

3. "Man is passive in receiving the impressions of things." Not altogether. Even here much depends on his own choice. In many cases he may or may not receive the impression; in most he may vary it greatly.

4. "According to these his last judgment is necessarily formed."

16. Cf. Ovid, *Metamorphoses*, Bk. VII, l. 20: *Video meliora, proboque; deteriora sequor* ("I see and approve the better; I follow the worse").

Nay, this too depends much upon his choice. Sometimes his first, sometimes his last, judgment is according to the impressions which he has
received; and frequently it is not.

   5. "This the will necessarily obeys." Indeed it does not. The mind
has an intrinsic power of cutting off the connexion between the judgment and the will.

   6. "And the outward action necessarily follows the will." Not so.
The thing I would, I do not; and the thing I would not, that I do [cf.
Rom. 7:19]. Whatever then becomes of the chain of events, this chain
of argument has not one good link belonging to it.

   4. But allowing all he contends for — that upon such vibrations of the
brain such sensations directly follow, and indirectly (as the various com-
binations and results of them), all our judgments and passions, and consequently words and actions — yet this infers no necessity at all, if there
be a God in the world. Upon this the whole matter turns. And this circumstance the doctor had forgot.

   And so indeed have almost the whole tribe of modern philosophers.
They do not at all take God into their account; they can do their
whole business without him. But in truth this, their "wisdom," is their
folly; for no system, either of morality or philosophy, can be complete,
unless God be kept in view, from the very beginning to the end. Every
true philosopher will surely go at least as far as the poor heathen poet: [17]

> Ἐκ Διός ἀρχώμεθα, καὶ ἐν Διὶ λήγετε Μμσαί.
> Muses, begin and end with God supreme!

Now, if there be a God, he cannot but have all power over every creature
that he has made. He must have equal power over matter and spirits, over
our souls and bodies. What are then all the vibrations of the brain to him,
or all the *natural* consequences of them? Suppose there be *naturally* the
strongest concatenation of vibrations, sensations, reflections, judgments,
passions, actions. Cannot he, in a moment, whenever and however he
pleases, destroy that concatenation? Cannot he cut off, or suspend in any
degree, the connexion between vibrations and sensations, between sensations and reflections, between reflections and judgments, and between
judgments and passions or actions? We cannot have any idea of God's
omnipotence without seeing he can do this if he will.

   5. "If he will," you may say, "we know he *can*. But have we any reason to think he *will?*" Yes, the strongest reason in the world, supposing

17. *Cf.* Hesiod, *Theogony*, l. 36–49.

that "God is love" [*cf.* 1 Jn. 4:8]. More especially, suppose "he is loving to every man" and that "his mercy is over all his works" [*cf.* Ps. 145:9]. If so, it cannot be that he should see the noblest of his creatures under heaven necessitated to do evil and incapable of any relief but from himself, without affording that relief. It is undeniable that he has fixed in man, in every man, his umpire, conscience, an inward judge which passes sentence both on his passions and actions, either approving or condemning them. Indeed, it has not power to remove what it condemns. It *shows* the evil which it cannot *cure*. But the God of power *can* cure it and the God of love *will* — if we choose he should. But he will no more necessitate us to be happy than he will permit anything beneath the sun to lay us under a necessity of being miserable. I am not careful, therefore, about the flowing of my blood and spirits, or the vibrations of my brain — being well assured that, however my spirits may flow or my nerves and fibres vibrate, the Almighty God of love can control them all, and will (unless I obstinately choose vice and misery) afford me such help as, in spite of all these, will put it into my power to be virtuous and happy for ever.

*Glasgow, May 14, 1774.*

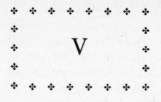
# AN OLIVE BRANCH TO THE ROMANS

*Editor's introduction.* Wesley's first visit to Ireland was in August of 1747, at the behest of a few zealous Methodists who had migrated there from England and had formed a small society in Dublin. (*Cf. Journal*, III, 310–16.) He returned the following year for two months of preaching and organization (*ibid.*, 337–53). In 1749 he spent from mid-April to mid-July in eventful labor in this overseas mission field (*cf. ibid.*, 395–414). It was on the eve of his departure after this third visit that he wrote this open "letter." It was published as a tract in Dublin that same year, and reprinted in 1750. A second edition then appeared in London in 1755. It was included in Vol. XIX of the *Works* (Pine), pp. 3–14, and in *Works*, Vol. X, pp. 80–86. It is "an earnest appeal" to an unidentified but interesting small group of Irish Catholics!

Though often called a "papist" himself by those who could not identify his peculiar brand of Protestantism, Wesley shared the typical Englishman's fear and mistrust of Roman Catholicism, and of popery most especially. He regarded Rome as a foreign power intent on the resubjugation of England and the violation of English liberties. Yet he often reports, with evident satisfaction, that Catholics frequently attended the Methodist preaching services and, generally speaking, were not inhospitable to his ministry. Thus, his "letter" to a presumably friendly Irish Catholic is an amicable appeal to the potential community of faith and love between the Roman Catholics and those "commonly *called* Protestants." As usual, Wesley assumes that the residual difficulties could be more fruitfully discussed *within* such a community than in the actual situation of estrangement and conflict. This is why such unusual interest attaches to his summary statement of the beliefs of a "true Protestant" in par. 8–10. Nothing quite like this little essay in ecumenical theology appears anywhere else in his writings, but it is consistent with his familiar distinction between essential beliefs and heterogeneous opinions; it is also a fair sample of what he actually meant by "catholic *spirit*." (See above, p. 91 ff.) The letter is obviously addressed to Catholic laymen rather than clergy. It would be interesting to know if Wesley actually had seen an earlier attempt along the same general lines in Archbishop Edward Synge, *Charitable Address to All Who Are in the Communion of the Church of Rome*, which had caused such a stir in 1727 and had been republished in Synge's *Works* (1744). There is no positive evidence of actual dependence, but the similarities between them are suggestive.

The copy text here is the Pine edition of 1773, collated with the second edition (1750).

❖  ❖  ❖  ❖

## A Letter to a Roman Catholic

1. You have heard ten thousand stories of us who are commonly called Protestants, of which, if you believe only one in a thousand, you must think very hardly of us. But this is quite contrary to our Lord's rule, "judge not, that ye be not judged" [Mt. 7:1], and has many ill consequences, particularly this: it inclines us to think as hardly of you. Hence, we are on both sides less willing to help one another and more ready to hurt each other. Hence brotherly love is utterly destroyed and each side, looking on the other as monsters, gives way to anger, hatred, malice, to every unkind affection — which have frequently broke out in such inhuman barbarities as are scarce named even among the heathens.

2. Now can nothing be done, even allowing us on both sides to retain our own opinions, for the softening our hearts towards each other, the giving a check to this flood of unkindness and restoring at least some small degree of love among our neighbours and countrymen? Do not you wish for this? Are you not fully convinced that malice, hatred, revenge, bitterness (whether in us or in you, in our hearts or yours) are an abomination to the Lord [*cf.* Prov. 15:26; 16:5]? Be our opinions right or be they wrong, these tempers are undeniably wrong. They are the broad road that leads to destruction, to the nethermost hell.

3. I do not suppose all the bitterness is on your side. I know there is too much on our side also. So much that I fear many Protestants (so-called) will be angry at me, too, for writing to you in this manner, and

494 THEOLOGIES IN CONFLICT

will say, " 'Tis showing you too much favour; you deserve no such treatment at our hands."

4. But I think you do. I think you deserve the tenderest regard I can show, were it only because the same God hath raised you and me from the dust of the earth and has made us both capable of loving and enjoying him to eternity; were it only because the Son of God has bought you and me with his own blood. How much more, if you are a person fearing God (as without question many of you are) and studying to have a conscience void of offence towards God and towards man?

5. I shall therefore endeavour, as mildly and inoffensively as I can, to remove in some measure the ground of your unkindness by plainly declaring what our belief and what our practice is: that you may see we are not altogether such monsters as perhaps you imagined us to be.

A true Protestant may express his belief in these or the like words:

6. As I am assured that there is an infinite and independent Being and that it is impossible there should be more than one, so I believe that this one God is the Father of all things, especially of angels and men; that he is in a peculiar manner the Father of those whom he regenerates by his Spirit, whom he adopts in his Son as co-heirs with him and crowns with an eternal inheritance; but in a still higher sense, the Father of his only Son, whom he hath begotten from eternity.

I believe this Father of all not only to be able to do whatsoever pleaseth him but also to have an eternal right of making what and when and how he pleaseth; and of possessing and disposing of all that he has made; and that he of his own goodness created heaven and earth, and all that is therein.

7. I believe that Jesus of Nazareth was the Saviour of the world, the Messiah so long foretold; that, being anointed with the Holy Ghost, he was a *prophet*, revealing to us the whole will of God; that he was a *priest*, who gave himself a sacrifice for sin, and still makes intercession for transgressors; that he is a *king*, who has all power in heaven and in earth, and will reign till he has subdued all things to himself [*cf.* 1 Cor. 15:27–28].

I believe he is the proper, natural Son of God, God of God, very God of very God; and that he is the Lord of all, having absolute, supreme universal dominion over all things; but more peculiarly *our* Lord (who believe in him), both by conquest, purchase, and voluntary obligation.

I believe that he was made man, joining the human nature with the divine in one person, being conceived by the singular operation of the

Holy Ghost and born of the Blessed Virgin Mary, who, as well after as she brought him forth, continued a pure and unspotted virgin.

I believe he suffered inexpressible pains both of body and soul and at last death, even the death of the cross [cf. Phil. 2:8], at the time that Pontius Pilate governed Judea under the Roman Emperor; that his body was then laid in the grave and his soul went to the place of separate spirits; [1] that the third day he rose again from the dead; that he ascended into heaven, where he remains in the midst of the throne of God in the highest power and glory as Mediator till the end of the world, as God to all eternity; that, in the end, he will come down from heaven to judge every man according to his works, both those who shall be then alive and all who have died before that day.

8. I believe the infinite and eternal Spirit of God, equal with the Father and the Son, to be not only perfectly holy in himself, but the immediate cause of all holiness in us: enlightening our understandings, rectifying our wills and affections, renewing our natures, uniting our persons to Christ, assuring us of the adoption of sons, leading us in our actions, purifying and sanctifying our souls and bodies to a full and eternal enjoyment of God.

9. I believe that Christ and his Apostles gathered unto himself a church to which he has continually added such as shall be saved; that this catholic (that is, universal) Church, extending to all nations and all ages, is holy in all its members, who have fellowship with God the Father, Son and Holy Ghost; that they have fellowship with the holy angels who constantly minister to these heirs of salvation, and with all the living members of Christ on earth, as well as all who are departed [this life] in his faith and fear.[2]

10. I believe God forgives all the sins of them that truly repent and unfeignedly believe his holy gospel; and that, at the last day, all men shall arise again, every one with his own body.

1. Wesley is everywhere unemphatic about the addition to the Apostles' Creed of the phrase, "he descended into Hell," possibly because of its consistent absence from the early texts. In at least one version of his "Sunday Service" it was simply dropped out; it was then omitted in subsequent usage in the American Methodist Church. Cf. Wesley's pallid comment on 1 Pet. 3:18-19 in his *Explanatory Notes Upon the New Testament* (1755); see also J. N. D. Kelly, *Early Christian Creeds* (1950), 378-83.

2. Cf. The prayer "for the whole state of Christ's Church," in the Order for Holy Communion, B.C.P.

I believe that, as the unjust shall after their resurrection be tormented in hell for ever, so the just shall enjoy inconceivable happiness in the presence of God to all eternity.

11. Now, is there anything wrong in this? Is there any one point which you do not believe as well as we?

But you think we ought to believe more? We will not now enter into the dispute. Only let me ask: "If a man sincerely believes thus much and practices accordingly, can any one possibly persuade you to think that such a man shall perish everlastingly?"

12. "But does he practice accordingly?" If he does not, we grant all his faith will not save him. And this leads me to show you, in few and plain words, what the practice of a true Protestant is. I say "a true Protestant," for I disclaim all common swearers, Sabbath-breakers, drunkards, all whoremongers, liars, cheats, extortioners — in a word, all that live in open sin. These are no Protestants; they are no Christians at all. Give them their own name: they are open heathens. They are the curse of the nation, the bane of society, the shame of mankind, the scum of the earth.

13. A true Protestant believes in God, has a full confidence in his mercy, fears him with a filial fear, and loves him with all his soul. He worships God in spirit and in truth, in every thing gives him thanks, calls upon him with his heart as well as his lips, at all times and in all places, honours his holy Name and his Word and serves him truly all the days of his life.

Now, do not you yourself approve of this? Is there any one point you can condemn? Do not you practice as well as approve of it? Can you ever be happy if you do not? Can you ever expect true peace in this, or glory in the world to come, if you do not believe in God through Christ, if you do not thus fear and love God? My dear friend, consider: I am not persuading you to leave or change your religion, but to follow after that fear and love of God without which all religion is vain. I say not a word to you about your opinions or outward manner of worship. But I say, all worship is an abomination to the Lord unless you worship him in spirit and in truth, with your heart as well as your lips, with your spirit and with your understanding also [cf. 1 Cor. 14:15]. Be your form of worship what it will, but in every thing give him thanks; else it is all but lost labour. Use whatever outward observances you please, but put your whole trust in him, but honour his holy Name and his Word, and serve him truly all the days of your life.

14. Again: a true Protestant loves his neighbour (that is, every man, friend or enemy, good or bad) as himself, as he loves his own soul, as Christ loved us. And as Christ laid down his life for us, so is he ready to lay down his life for his brethren. He shows this love by doing to all men in all points as he would they should do unto him. He loves, honours, and obeys his father and mother and helps them to the uttermost of his power. He honours and obeys the king and all that are put in authority under him. He cheerfully submits to all his governors, teachers, spiritual pastors and masters. He behaves lowly and reverently to all his betters. He hurts nobody, by word or deed. He is true and just in all his dealings. He bears no malice or hatred in his heart. He abstains from all evil-speaking, lying and slandering, neither is guile found in his mouth. Knowing his body to be the temple of the Holy Ghost [cf. 1 Cor. 3:16], he keeps it in sobriety, temperance and chastity. He does not desire other men's goods, but is content with that he hath, labours to get his own living and to do the whole will of God in that state of life unto which it has pleased God to call him.

15. Have you any thing to reprove in this? Are you not herein even as he? If not (tell the truth), are you not condemned both by God and your own conscience? Can you fall short of any one point hereof without falling short of being a Christian?

Come, my brother, and let us reason together. Are you right if you only love your friend and hate your enemy? Do not even the heathens and publicans so [cf. Mt. 5:43–46]? You are called to love your enemies, to bless them that curse you and to pray for them that despitefully use you and persecute you. But are you not disobedient to the heavenly calling [cf. Acts 26:19]? Does your tender love to all men, not only the good but also the evil and unthankful, approve you the child of your Father which is in heaven? Otherwise, whatever you believe and whatever you practice, you are of your father the devil. Are you ready to lay down your life for your brethren? And do you do unto all as you would they should do unto you? If not, do not deceive your own soul: you are but a heathen still. Do you love, honour and obey your father and mother, and help them to the utmost of your power? Do you honour and obey all in authority, all your governors, spiritual pastors and masters? Do you behave lowly and reverently to all your betters? Do you hurt nobody, by word or deed? Are you true and just in all your dealings? Do you take care to pay whatever you owe? Do you feel no malice, or envy or revenge, no hatred or bitterness to any man? If you do, it is plain you are not of God, for all these are the tempers of the devil. Do you speak the truth from your heart to all men, and that in tenderness and love? Are you an Israelite indeed, in whom is no guile [*cf*. Jn. 1:47]? Do you keep your body in sobriety, temperance and chastity, as knowing it is the temple of the Holy Ghost and that, if any man defile the temple of God, him will God destroy [*cf*. 1 Cor. 3:17]? Have you learned in every state wherein you are, therewith to be content? Do you labour to get your own living, abhorring idleness as you abhor hell-fire? The devil tempts other men, but an idle man tempts the devil. An idle man's brain is the devil's shop, where he is continually working mischief. Are you not slothful in business? Whatever your hand finds to do, do you do it with your might? And do you do all as unto the Lord, as a sacrifice unto God, acceptable in Christ Jesus?

This, and this alone, is the old religion. This is true, primitive Christianity. O when shall it spread over all the earth? When shall it be found both in us and you? Without waiting for others, let each of us, by the grace of God, amend one['s own self].

16. Are we not thus far agreed? Let us thank God for this, and receive it as a fresh token of his love. But if God still loveth us, we ought also to love one another. We ought, without this endless jangling about opinions, to provoke one another to love and to good works. Let the points wherein we differ stand aside: here are enough wherein we agree, enough to be the ground of every Christian temper and of every Christian action.

O brethren, let us not still fall out by the way. I hope to see *you* in heaven. And if I practice the religion above described, you dare not say I shall go to hell. You cannot think so. None can persuade you to it. Your own conscience tells you the contrary. Then if we cannot as yet *think alike* in all things, at least we may *love alike*. Herein we cannot possibly do amiss. For of one point none can doubt a moment: God is love; and he that dwelleth in love, dwelleth in God, and God in him [1 Jn. 4:16].

17. In the name, then, and in the strength of God, let us resolve, first, not to hurt one another, to do nothing unkind or unfriendly to each other, nothing which we would not have done to ourselves. Rather let us endeavour after every instance of a kind, friendly and Christian behaviour towards each other.

Let us resolve, secondly, God being our helper, to speak nothing harsh or unkind of each other. The sure way to avoid this is to say all the good we can, both of and to one another; in all our conversation, either with or concerning each other, to use only the language of love; to speak with all softness and tenderness, with the most endearing expression which is consistent with truth and sincerity.

Let us, thirdly, resolve to harbour no unkind thought, no unfriendly temper towards each other. Let us lay the axe to the root of the tree [cf. Mt. 3:10], let us examine all that rises in our heart and suffer no disposition there which is contrary to tender affection. Then shall we easily refrain from unkind actions and words, when the very root of bitterness is cut up [cf. Heb. 12:15].

Let us, fourthly, endeavour to help each other on in whatever we are agreed leads to the Kingdom. So far as we can, let us always rejoice to strengthen each other's hands in God. Above all, let us each take heed unto himself (since each must give an account of himself to God) that he fall not short of the religion of love; that he be not condemned in that he himself approveth. O let you and me (whatever others do) press on to the prize of our high calling — that, being justified by faith, we may have peace with God through our Lord Jesus Christ; that we may rejoice in God through Jesus Christ, by whom we have received the atonement [cf. Rom. 5:1–2]; that the love of God may be shed abroad in our hearts by the Holy Ghost which is given unto us [cf. Rom. 5:5]. Let us count all things but loss for the excellency of the knowledge of Jesus Christ our Lord, being ready for him to suffer the loss of all things and counting them but dung, that we may win Christ [cf. Phil. 3:8].

Dublin,

*July 18, 1749*

# Selected Bibliography

The following titles have been chosen from an immense and highly uneven literature, with special reference to the interests and needs of the reader of this particular volume.

ABBEY, C. J., *The English Church and Its Bishops, 1700–1800* (1887).

———, and OVERTON, J. H., *The English Church in the Eighteenth Century*, (1878). 2 vols.

*Ante-Nicene Fathers. Translations of the Writings of the Fathers Down to A.D. 325*, A. C. Coxe, ed. (Buffalo, N.Y., 1885–97); Vol. IX, Allan Menzies, ed. (New York, 1897).

*Arminian Magazine, The.* Consisting of Extracts and Original Treatises on Universal Redemption (1778–91).

ASBURY, FRANCIS, *Journal and Letters*, Elmer T. Clark, ed. (1958). 3 vols.

BAKER, FRANK, *Charles Wesley* (1948).

BARCLAY, ROBERT, *Apology for the True Christian Religion as the Same Is Set Forth and Preached by the People Called in Scorn "Quakers"* (1678).

BAXTER, RICHARD, *Aphorisms of Justification With Their Explication Annexed* (1649).

BEATTIE, JAMES, *An Essay on the Nature and Immutability of Truth in Opposition to Sophistry and Superstition* (Edinburgh, 1771).

BEDFORD, ARTHUR, *The Doctrine of Assurance; or, The Case of a Weak and Doubting Conscience* (1738).

BELOFF, MAX, *Public Order and Popular Disturbances, 1660–1714* (1938).

BENEZET, ANTHONY, *Some Historical Account of Guinea . . .* (Philadelphia, 1771).

BENGEL, JOHN ALBERT, *Gnomon of the New Testament . . .* according to the edition brought out by his son, M. Ernest Bengel; and subsequently completed by J. C. F. Steudel, 7th ed. (Edinburgh, 1877). 2 vols.

BENHAM, DANIEL, *Memoirs of James Hutton; Comprising the Annals of His Life and Connection with the United Brethren* (1856).

BEVERIDGE, WILLIAM, Συνόδικον, *sive Pandectae Canonum SS. Apostolorum et Conciliorum ab Ecclesiae Graecae receptorum . . . totum opus in duos tomos divisum* (1672). 2 vols.

———, *Sermons* (Oxford, 1842–48). (Vols. 1–6 of *The Theological Works of William Beveridge, D.D.*)

BICKNELL, E. J., *A Theological Introduction to the Thirty-nine Articles of the Church of England*, 3d ed. (1955).

Book of Common Prayer as Revised and Settled at the Savoy Conference Anno 1662. 14 Charles II. Reprinted from the Sealed Book in the Tower of London (1844).

BOWMER, JOHN C., *The Sacrament of the Lord's Supper in Early Methodism* (1951).

BRAY, THOMAS, *Bibliotheca Parochialis, &c., or a Scheme of such Theological and Other Heads, as Seem Requisite to be Perus'd, or Occasionally Consulted, by the Reverend Clergy*, 2d ed. (1707).

BURTNER, R. W., and CHILES, R. E., eds., *A Compend of Wesley's Theology* (New York, 1954).

CALVIN, JOHN, *The Institutes of the Christian Religion*, J. T. McNeill, ed. Trans. and ind. by F. L. Battles (1961). (Vol. XX and XXI in Library of Christian Classics [Philadelphia, 1953–      ]).

CANNON, WILLIAM, *The Theology of John Wesley* (New York, 1946).

CASTANIZA, JUAN DE, *The Spiritual Combat; or, The Christian Pilgrim in His Spiritual Conflict and Conquest*, trans. by Richard Lucas (1698). (Also attributed to Scupoli, Lorenzo. See *The Spiritual Combat* [Springfield, Ill., 1960].)

*Catechismus Romanus. The Catechism of the Council of Trent*, trans. into English; with notes by Theodore Alois Buckley (1852).

CELL, G. C., *The Rediscovery of John Wesley* (New York, 1935).

*Certain Sermons or Homilies, Appointed to Be Read in Churches*, . . . (Oxford, 1683; 1864).

CLARK, GEORGE, *The Later Stuarts, 1660–1714*, 2d ed. (Oxford, 1955). (Vol. X of *The Oxford History of England.*)

COPLESTONE, FREDERICK, *A History of Philosophy* (1959). (Vol. V of the Bellarmine Series, XVI.)

*Corpus Christianorum, Series Latina* (Turnholti, 1953–      ). (Vol. I, II: *Tertullianus.*)

*Corpus Scriptorum Ecclesiasticorum Latinoum* (Vienna, 1866–      ). (Vol. XLI; *Sancti Aureli Augustini*, 1900.)

COULTER, E. MERTON, and SAYE, ALBERT B., *A List of the Early Settlers of Georgia* (Athens, Ga., 1949).

DAVIES, SIR JOHN, *Poems*. Reproduced in facsimile from first edition in the Henry E. Huntington Library and Art Gallery with an Introduction and Notes by Clare Howard (New York, 1941).

DONNE, JOHN, *Poems*, ed. from old editions and numerous manuscripts by Herbert J. C. Grierson (Oxford, 1912). 2 vols.

ECHARD, LAURENCE, *A General Ecclesiastical History from the Nativity of our*

*Blessed Saviour to the First Establishment of Christianity by Human Laws, Under the Emperor Constantine the Great,* 5th ed. (1719).

EDWARDS, JONATHAN, *A Careful and Strict Enquiry into the modern prevailing Notions of that Freedom of the Will, which is supposed to be essential to Moral Agency, Vertue and Vice, Reward and Punishment, Praise and Blame* (Boston, 1754). (Ed. by Paul Ramsey as Vol. I in *The Works of Jonathan Edwards* [New Haven, 1957].)

————, *The Distinguishing Marks of the Work of the Spirit of God, Applied to That Uncommon Operation That Has Lately Appeared on the Minds of Many of the People in New England.* (Boston, 1741; London, 1742).

————, *A Faithful Narrative of the Surprising Work of God in the Conversion of Many Hundred Souls in Northampton . . . in New England.* In a letter to the Rev. Dr. Benjamin Colman of Boston (1737).

————, *Some Thoughts Concerning the Present Revival of Religion in New England, and the Way in Which It Ought to Be Acknowledged and Promoted* (Boston, 1742).

————, *A Treatise Concerning the Religious Affections* (Boston, 1746).

FLETCHER, JOHN WILLIAM, *Works* (1802–09). 8 vols.

FLORUS, LUCIUS ANNAEUS, *Epitome of Roman History,* Loeb ed. (Cambridge, Mass., 1929).

*A Form of Discipline for the Ministers, Preachers and Members of the Methodist Episcopal Church in America, Considered and Approved at a Conference Held at Baltimore . . . 27th of December, 1784* (Elizabeth-Town, N.J., 1788).

FRANCKE, AUGUST HERMANN, *Pietas Hallensis; or, An Abstract of the Marvellous Footsteps of Divine Providence . . . to Which is Added a Short History of Pietism,* 2d ed. (1707).

GIBSON, EDMUND, *Codex Iuris Ecclesiastici Anglicani; or, The Statutes, Constitutions, Canons, Rubrics and Articles of the Church of England* (1713). 2 vols.

GODLEY, A. D., *Oxford in the Eighteenth Century* (1908).

GREEN, RICHARD, *The Works of John and Charles Wesley. A Bibliography* (1896).

GREEN, V. H. H., *The Young Mr. Wesley* (1961).

GREGORIUS, SAINT, *Gregorii Nysseni Opera Auxilio Aliorum Virorum Doctorum,* edenda curavit Wernerus Jaeger (Leiden, 1960–    ).

HARRISON, G. ELSIE, *Son to Susanna* (Nashville, Tenn., 1938).

HEFELE, KARL JOSEPH VON, *Histoire des Conciles d'après les Documents Originaux* (Paris, 1907–    ).

HERBERT, T. W., *John Wesley as Editor and Author* (Princeton, 1940).

HEYLYN, PETER, "*Historia Quinquarticularis*" (1681). (Pt. 3 in *Historical and Miscellaneous Tracts.*)

HOOKER, RICHARD, *Of the Lawes of Ecclesiasticall Politie. Eyght [five] Bookes* (1594–97).

HORACE, *Satires, Epistles and Ars Poetica*, trans. by H. Rushton Fairclough, Loeb ed. (Cambridge, Mass., 1926).

JAEGER, WERNER, *Two Rediscovered Works of Ancient Christian Literature: Gregory of Nyssa and Macarius* (Leiden, 1954).

JANVIER, AMBROSE, *Rabbi Davidis Kimchi Commentarii in Psalmos Davidis . . . ex Hebraeo Latiné Redditi* (1702).

KAMES, HENRY HUME, LORD, *"Essay on Liberty and Necessity"* (Edinburgh, 1751). (Chap. 3 in *Essays on the Principles of Morality and Natural Religion.*)

KELLY, J. N. D., *Early Christian Creeds* (1950).

KNOX, R. A., *Enthusiasm; A Chapter in the History of Religion with Special Reference to the XVII and XVIII Centuries* (Oxford, 1950).

LECKY, WILLIAM EDWARD HARTPOLE, *A History of England in the Eighteenth Century* (1892), Vol. III.

LEE, UMPHREY, *John Wesley and Modern Religion* (Nashville, Tenn., 1936).

LINDSTRÖM, HARALD, *Wesley and Sanctification* (Stockholm, 1946).

LUCRETIUS, *De Rerum Natura*, trans. by W. H. D. Rouse, Loeb ed. (Cambridge, Mass, 1924).

LUTHER, MARTIN, *Commentary on the Epistle to the Galatians*, Philip Watson, ed. (1953).

———, *Works* . . . with Introductions and Notes (Philadelphia, 1915–32). 6 vols.

McADOO, H. R., *The Structures of Caroline Moral Theology* (1949).

McNEILL, J. T., "Luther at Aldersgate," in *London Quarterly and Holborn Review*, Vol. 164 (1939), 200–217.

MAKOWER, FELIX, *The Constitutional History and Constitution of the Church of England* (1895).

*Methodist Hymn Book, The* (1933).

*Methodist Hymnal, The* (New York, 1932).

MIDDLETON, CONYERS, *A Free Inquiry into the Miraculous Powers Which Are Supposed to Have Subsisted in the Christian Church* (1749).

*Minutes of Several Conversations Between Thomas Coke, Francis Asbury and Others at a Conference Begun in Baltimore . . . the 27th of December, in the Year 1784. Composing a Form of Discipline* (Philadelphia, 1785).

*Minutes of the Methodist Conferences, From the First, Held in London, by the Late Rev. John Wesley, A.M., in the Year 1744* (1862).

MOORE, HENRY, *Life of the Rev. J. Wesley* (1826). 2 vols.

ORCIBAL, JEAN, "Les Spirituels français et espagnols chez John Wesley et ses contemporains," in *Revue de l'Histoire des Religions*, Vol. 139 (1951), 50–109.

OVID, *Metamorphoses*, trans. by Frank Justus Miller, Loeb ed. (Cambridge, Mass., 1946). 2 vols.

*Oxford Dictionary of the Christian Church*, F. L. Cross, ed. (1957).

*Patrologiae Cursus Completus. Series Graeca*, J. P. Migne, ed. (Paris, 1857–66). Vols. XIV, XXXIV, XXXIX.

*Patrologiae Cursus Completus. Series Latina*, J. P. Migne, ed. (Paris, 1878–90). Vols. XXXIV, XL.

PERCEVAL, SIR JOHN, *Diary of Viscount Perceval, Afterwards First Earl of Egmont*, R. A. Roberts, ed. (1920–23). 3 vols.

PERSIUS, *The Satires of A. Persius Flaccus*, trans. and com. by John Conington, 3d. ed., rev. (Oxford, 1893).

PETERS, J. L., *Christian Perfection and American Methodism* (New York, 1956).

PIETTE, MAXIMIN, *John Wesley in the Evolution of Protestantism* (New York, 1937).

PRIOR, MATTHEW, *Literary Works of Matthew Prior*, H. Bunker Wright and Monroe K. Spears, eds. (Oxford, 1959), Vol. 1.

QUASTEN, JOHANNES, *Patrology* (Utrecht, 1950–   ).

RASHDALL, HASTINGS, *The Universities of Europe in the Middle Ages*, F. M. Powicke and A. B. Emden, eds. (Oxford, 1936). 3 vols.

SCHAFF, PHILIP, *Creeds of Christendom, with a History and Critical Notes* (New York, 1881–82). 3 vols.

SCHMIDT, MARTIN, *John Wesley* (Frankfurt, 1953).

SCOUGAL, HENRY, *The Life of God in the Soul of Man*, Winthrop S. Hudson, ed. (Philadelphia, 1948).

SHERMAN, DAVID, *History of the Revisions of the Discipline of the Methodist Episcopal Church* (New York, 1874).

SIMON, J. S., *John Wesley and the Religious Societies* (1921).

——, *John Wesley and the Methodist Societies* (1923).

——, *John Wesley and the Advance of Methodism* (1925).

——, *John Wesley, The Master Builder* (1927).

——, *John Wesley, the Last Phase* (1934).

SOUTHEY, ROBERT, *The Life of Wesley and the Rise of Methodism* (1925). 2 vols.

SOUTHGATE, W. M., *John Jewel and the Problem of Doctrinal Authority* (Cambridge, Mass., 1962).

SYKES, NORMAN, *From Sheldon to Secker* (Cambridge, 1959).

TERENCE, trans. by John Sargeaunt, Loeb ed. (Cambridge, Mass., 1912).

TERTULLIAN, *Treatises on Penance: on Penitence and on Purity*, trans. and annotated by William P. Le Saint (Westminster, Md., 1959). (Vol. XXVIII of *Ancient Christian Writers.*)

TOMLINSON, JOHN, *The Prayer Book, Articles and Homilies* (1897).

TREVELYAN, G. M., *History of England*, 3d ed. (New York, 1945). (Vol. III, *From Utrecht to Modern Times.*)

TYERMAN, LUKE, *Life and Times of Rev. John Wesley, M.A.* (1870). 3 vols.

URLIN, R. D., *John Wesley's Place in Church History Determined with the Aid of Facts and Documents Unknown to or Unnoticed by his Biographers* (Edinburgh, 1870).

VIRGIL, trans. by H. Rushton Fairclough, Loeb ed., rev. (Cambridge, Mass., 1934).

WAKEFIELD, G. S., *Puritan Devotion; Its Place in the Development of Christian Piety* (1957).

WARNICK, MRS. JOHN, "Four Unpublished Letters of John Wesley," in *The Perkins School of Theology Journal*, XIII (1960), No. 2, 28–32.

WATERLAND, DANIEL, *Regeneration Stated and Explained, According to Scripture and Antiquity* (1740).

WATTS, ISAAC, *The Ruin and Recovery of Mankind; or, An Attempt to Vindicate the Scriptural Account of These Great Events Upon the Plain Principles of Reason* (1753). (Vol. VI of *Works*.)

WESLEY, CHARLES, *Journal*, John Telford, ed. (1909).

WESLEY, JOHN, *A Christian Library. Consisting of Extracts from and Abridgments of the Choicest Pieces of Practical Divinity, Which Have Been Publish'd in the English Tongue* (Bristol, 1749–55). 50 vols.

——, *Christian Perfection as Believed and Taught by John Wesley*, Thomas S. Kepler, ed. (Cleveland, 1954).

——, *A Collection of Hymns for the Use of the People Called Methodists* (1780).

——, *Explanatory Notes Upon the New Testament* (1755).

——, *An Extract of Mr. Richard Baxter's Aphorisms of Justification* (Newcastle upon Tyne, 1745).

——, *An Extract of the . . . Journal from his Embarking for Georgia to his Return to London* (Bristol, 1739).

——, *Journal*, standard ed., Nehemiah Curnock, ed. (1909–16), 8 vols.

——, *Letters*, John Telford, ed. (1931). 8 vols.

——, *Poetical Works of John and Charles Wesley*. Collected and arranged by G. Osborn (1868–72). 13 vols.

——, *Sermons on Several Occasions*, 1st ed., in 4 vols. (1746–60); 4th ed., in 8 vols. (1787–88); Vol. IX (1800).

——, *Standard Sermons*, 4th annotated ed., Edward H. Sugden, ed. (1955–56), 2 vols.

——, *The Works of the Rev. John Wesley, M.A.* (printed by William Pine, Bristol, 1771–74), 32 vols.

——, *The Works of the Rev. John Wesley, A.M.*, 3d ed., with last corrections of the author; Thomas Jackson, ed. (1829–31); (see also *Works* [Grand Rapids, Mich., 1958–59], a reprint of the Jackson ed.). 14 vols.
(N.B. For items in the Wesley bibliography cited in the text but not listed in the entries above, *cf.* Green, *Bibliography*.)

WESLEY, SAMUEL, *A Letter from a Country Divine to His Friend in London, Concerning the Education of Dissenters in Their Private Academies in Several Parts of this Nation; Humbly Offered to the Consideration of the Grand Committee of Parliament for Religion, Now Sitting* (1703).

————, *The Pious Communicant Rightly Prepared. . . . To Which Is Added a Short Discourse on Baptism* (1698).

WESLEY HISTORICAL SOCIETY, *Publications* and *Proceedings* (Burnley, England, 1896–   ).

WHITEFIELD, GEORGE, *Journals* (1960).

WHITEHEAD, JOHN, *The Life of the Rev. John Wesley, M.A.* (1793–96). 2 vols.

WILLIAMS, BASIL, *The Whig Supremacy, 1714–60* (Oxford, 1952). (Vol. IX of *The Oxford History of England.*)

WILLIAMS, COLIN, *John Wesley's Theology Today* (New York, 1960).

WOODWARD, JOSIAH, *An Account of the Rise and Progress of the Religious Societies in the City of London . . . and of Their Endeavours for the Reformation of Manners,* 3d ed. (1712).

*Works of the English Poets, from Chaucer to Cowper,* Samuel Johnson, ed. (1810). (Vol. VII, Cowley and others; Vol. VIII, Butler and others.)

# Index

Abiram, 236
Aldersgate experience, 14, 15, 17, 29, 38,
41, 51–69, 121, 347, 353
Aldrich, Henry, 6
Ambrose, St., 126
American Indians. *See* Indians, American.
American Revolution, 24. *See also* Methodism, American; Methodists, American.
Anabaptists, 318, 329 f.
Anaxagoras, 192
Annesley, Samuel, 4, 6
Anson, Mary, 303
Antinomianism, 119, 139, 236, 301 f., 347,
350, 354, 377 ff., 425
"that enthusiastic doctrine of devils,"
179
virtues of, 152
Apostles' Creed, 494 ff.
Apostolic succession, 323
Aquinas, Thomas, 31
Arimanius, 479
Arminian, 23, 31, 447
Arminianism, 23, 350, 426
*Arminian Magazine, The,* 23, 84, 104, 231,
283, 308, 334, 347, 425 f., 473
Arndt, Johann, 147
*Ars moriendi,* 32
*Articulus mortis,* 32. *See also* Death,
article (moment) of.
Asbury, Francis, 24, 25, 82, 83
Assurance, notion of, 29, 50, 52, 58, 65, 68,
149, 159 f., 165 ff., 188 f., 211, 215, 220,
262, 363 f., 405
Athanasius, 85, 328
Atonement, 226, 273 f., 286 f., 288, 383
and incarnation, 200, 494 f.
reconciliation, 205
universal, 23, 443 ff.
Atterbury, Francis, 6
Augustine, St., vii, 53, 124, 126, 131, 132,
328, 409, 486

## B

Baker, Frank, xii, 18, 70
Bancroft, Richard, 75, 416
Baptism, 33, 318 ff.
as a covenant, 324 ff.
godparents in, 332
infant, 124, 324–31, 415
mode of, 97, 319 f.
in place of circumcision, 119, 319 f.,
322 ff., 330
regeneration through, 321 ff.
*Baptism, On,* 307, 317 f.
Barclay, Robert, 4
Barrow, Isaac, 337
Basil, St., 126
Bateman, Richard, 165
Baxter, Richard, 148, 456
Beattie, James, 474
Beckett, Mrs. Thomas A., xii
Bedford, Arthur, 52
Belial, 247
Bell, George, 272, 299, 377
Benezet, Anthony, 86
Bengel, J. A., 223, 331, 466
Bennet, John, 135, 136, 164, 235
Berkeley, George, 210, 474, 487
Berridge, John, 18
Beveridge, William, ix, 12, 45, 62, 162
Bigotry, 79, 302
Bilson, Thomas, 75, 173
Blackwell, Ebenezer, 231
Böhler, Peter, 14, 17, 41, 52, 53, 54, 56 ff.,
65, 68, 353, 356 f.
Boehm, Anthony William, 147, 162
Brackenbury, Robert Carr, 10
Bray, Thomas, 12
Brevint, Daniel, 307, 332, 333
Bristol, 17, 71, 91, 110, 111, 155, 235, 284,
285, 418, 419
Browne, Thomas, 393
Buchanan, George, 146